to H.O. Bawden S.C.
with kind respects
H. O. Clemens

COMERFORD AND FOGARTY
ENVIRONMENTAL LAW:
A GLOSSARY AND HANDBOOK
(First Edition)

ERRATA

p. 15, col. 2:
for "(4) Submissions ..." read "(a) Submissions ..."

p. 15, col. 2:
for "(5) Submissions ..." read "(b) Submissions ..."

p. 16, col. 1:
for "(6) Powers ..." read "(c) Powers ..."

p. 16, col. 2:
for "(7) Withdrawal ..." read "(d) Withdrawal ..."

p. 16, col. 2:
for "(8) Reference ..." read "(e) Reference ..."

p. 17, col. 1:
for "(9) Reports ..." read "(f) Reports ..."

p. 17, col. 1:
for "10 Matters ..." read "(g) Matters ..."

p. 17, col. 1:
for "(11) Licensing ..." read "(h) Licensing ..."

p. 17, col. 2:
for "(12) Appeal ..." read "(i) Appeal ..."

p. 160, col. 2:
read as bold type **162***, **163***

p. 161, col. 1:
read as bold type **183***, **156***, **157***, **182****

p. 312, col. 1:
for "(7) PROTECTION ..." read "(8) PROTECTION ..."

Environmental Law

A Glossary and Handbook

UNITED KINGDOM
Sweet & Maxwell
London

AUSTRALIA
LBC Information Services
Sydney

Canada and the USA
Carswell
Toronto

NEW ZEALAND
Brooker's
Auckland

SINGAPORE and MALAYSIA
Thomson Information (S.E. Asia)
Singapore

Environmental Law

A Glossary and Handbook

ROUND HALL SWEET & MAXWELL
DUBLIN
2000

Published in 2000 by
Round Hall Ltd
43, Fitzwilliam Place
Dublin 2

Typeset by
AME Design & Marketing
Drogheda
Ireland

Printed by
MPG Books
Cornwall

Environmental Law

A Glossary and Handbook

Henry Comerford
Aengus R.M. Fogarty

ISBN 1-899738-96-7

A catalogue record for this book
is available from the British Library

TABLE OF CONTENTS

INTRODUCTION

In 1661 when John Evelyn suggested some practical remedies for the appalling pollution of the City of London caused by the burning of sea coal in "Fumifugium, or the Inconvenience of the Air and Smoke of London dissipated" he was not to know that, apart from the Great Fire of 1666 which destroyed the greater part of the nuisance, in fact legislation dealing with the problem would not be passed until 1956. That was the year the Clean Air Act became law in England. In Ireland we did not have corresponding legislation until the Air Pollution Act of 1987 and, even now, regulations regarding the use of carboniferous fuels apply only in certain cities across the country.

The first real environmental statute passed in Ireland was the Local Government (Water Pollution) Act 1977. The Fisheries (Consolidation) Act 1959 did contain a section, section 171, which was frequently used by the then boards of conservators and their successors - the regional fisheries boards - to combat water pollution involving damage to fish life. Section 171 is still widely used.

Why? Why did we all come so late to the serious business of protecting our environment? There were of course difficulties; nothing in the world of lawyers is ever easy or simple. There was one almost insurmountable and extremely basic problem. In so far as the common law is concerned the environment was and is a nonentity. It has no legal rights and no legal identity as does the individual in personam in respect of his personal rights and in rem in relation to his property rights.

There were, therefore, great difficulties in protecting public interests in the "unowned" environment. As there was no basic common law legal principle on which a system of protection could be based or from which it which might have naturally evolved, the difficulty was overcome simply by legislation. As the environment had no inherent legal right to its own protection, that protection was afforded for it by a series of statutes.

One other great problem in relation to the enforcement of environmental protection is the difficulty in fitting it into any existing branch of law and deciding who was to enforce it. For better or for worse, environmental protection legislation ended up in Ireland under the Local Government code, meaning it was implemented by local authorities. It became attached at an early stage to the planning process and the evolution of the development plan as enunciated in the Local Government (Planning and Development) Acts for which local authorities were primarily responsible.

The use of the Environmental Impact Statement as a means of assessing the impact of development on the environment began in 1989 with the European Communities (Environmental Impact Assessment) Regulations, 1889 (S.I. No.349 of 1989) giving effect to Council Directive 85/337/EEC (O.J. No. L175/40, July 5th, 1985) on the assessment of the effects of certain public and private projects on the environment. This reinforced the connection between Local Government and environmental law and that connection has evolved through various amending regulations right up to 1999.

At a later stage, when it became necessary to introduce legislation dealing with new European refuges for wildlife, under the Birds Directive and the protection of natural habitats, under the Natural Habitats Directive, protection at the core of the development and planning process was afforded by amending the Third Schedule to the Planning Acts which sets out the objectives of development plans.

As local authorities are planning authorities it was an obvious step to off load both the Local Government (Water Pollution) Act 1977 and the Air Pollution Act 1987 onto them and make them responsible for licensing, policing and enforcement. This was a retrograde step. The record of local authorities in Ireland in the protection of the environment has been a dismal failure. In the 19 years which passed from the operative date of the Local Government (Water Pollution) Act 1997 (on October 1st 1978 for licensing) and the date when the Environmental Protection Agency (EPA) took over the functions of the local authority in relation to water pollution under the Environmental Protection Agency (Extension of Powers) Order 1996 (S.I. No. 126 of 1996) (May 26th, 1996), virtually no prosecutions were brought by local authorities for water pollution under the 1977 Act.

All local authorities had, of course, the added problem in that period as they were, through no fault of their own, the main polluters of watercourses because of the inadequacy of public funds available to upgrade and improve sewage treatment plants throughout their functional areas. This was one of their main responsibilities as sanitary authorities.

The regional fisheries boards took up the slack in this period and prosecuted wholesale for water pollution. Local authorities allowed this to colour their whole approach to the subject. They were frequently publicly embarrassed by reports in local newspapers of District Court hearings when as defendants they had to pay hefty fines for dereliction of their duties as sanitary authorities.

The inactivity on the part of local authorities in this area must have contributed substantially to the build up of phosphates in groundwater and the dreadfully polluted water bodies we now have in this country. The local authorities had no excuse. In the Local Government (Water Pollution) (Amendment) 1990, under section 21, a system of bye-laws to deal with pollution by farmers was proffered to local authorities to solve whatever problems they had experienced in enforcing the 1977 Act and give them more teeth in dealing with water pollution in sensitive areas adjoining water bodies. Not one authority made the bye-laws, nor indeed did successive Ministers for the Environment direct them to do so as they were entitled to do under the Act.

A great deal of this is in the past. The various statutes which set out to tackle the pollution of the environment are now working. These Acts, the Local Government (Water Pollution) 1977 and its Amendment Act of 1990, the Air Pollution Act of 1987 and Mary Harney's great consolidating Act, the Environmental Protection Agency Act of 1992, establishing the Environmental Protection Agency which effectively carries out all but the most minor licensing and control functions of the local authorities under the Acts of 1977 and 1987 and, lastly, the Waste Management Act of 1996, which deals with the prevention, management and control of waste, completes the hand-over to the Agency of all of the anti-pollution functions of Irish law. The Environmental Protection Agency also polices local authorities in the performance of such functions as are left to it to perform. Taken as a unit, these statutes should now be wholly effective. The Agency has shown itself to be not only reliable but consistent in granting Integrated Pollution Control (IPC) licences and has also performed admirably in its role as a powerful enforcer and fearless prosecutor.

All of the foregoing "pollution" statutes deal with the protection of what the Environmental Protection Agency Act of 1992 calls the "environmental medium" and which is defined in the Act as comprising "the atmosphere, land,. soil and waters". The other half of the environment, the life which inhabits the environment, those organisms that are called "wildlife", are also dealt with extensively in this book and for the first time in Ireland.

"Wildlife" is defined in the Wildlife Act of 1976 as meaning "fauna and flora". The same Act defines "fauna" as meaning all wild animals (both aquatic and terrestrial) although the same definition also excepts certain categories of fish. It was always intended that the Wildlife Act 1976 would deal with flora and fauna and the Fisheries Acts with fish but the increasingly sophisticated approaches to the protection of rare and endangered species of fish under European Directives make it necessary to treat certain such species of fish as wildlife for protection purposes. This has become more common since the Habitats Directive of 1992 and the Wildlife Bill of 1999 is designed to make it even more so. An Annex to this book deals with the main points of the Bill which had not been passed into law at the date of publication.

Apart from dealing with the Wildlife Act 1976 this book is intended to deal with the many orders made under that Act and the large numbers of Directives and orders on wildlife implementing the two Directives on Wildlife, the Birds Directive and the Habitats Directive. The book lists areas protected in Ireland under these Directives and under the Wildlife Act itself. There are also definitive lists of all flora and fauna protected to date under Irish legislation.

All of the Acts dealing with inland fisheries are dealt with in this book. This has involved consideration and organisation of many anachronistic provisions as the structure of fisheries has been neglected for years and now spans over 17 statutes from 1953 to 1999. The Department of the Marine has consistently failed to amend existing legislation, as a result of which the great Fisheries (Consolidation) Act of 1959 has become a shapeless mass of statutory provisions which, at times, are almost dangerous to implement. The government agencies involved in enacting fisheries legislation appear to act on the principle that it is easier to pile new legislation on top of the old rather than amend it in a logical fashion.

In dealing with fisheries, and particularly the new aquaculture licensing system introduced by the Fisheries (Amendment) Act 1997, it has been necessary to devote a great deal of space to the law relating to the foreshore but the authors believed this was necessary and that the material has now been usefully presented in context for the first time.

As the authors believe that a knowledge of the control structure of inland fisheries is crucial to the understanding of the system, there is detailed treatment of the formation and functions of the Central Fisheries Board and the regional fisheries boards and election to the latter boards. The same treatment has been afforded to the Environmental Protection Agency and the Heritage Council.

The main object of bringing together what might at first appear to be two disparate branches of environmental law, the "pollution" statutes and the "wildlife" statutes, in one book is an attempt to show the commonality of their functions - for example, under licensing, review of licences, duration of licences, regulations, appointment and powers of authorised officers and probably, most significantly, enforcement.

The book's title - *Environmental Law: A Glossary and Handbook* - reflects the two main functions it is intended to perform. The book is a "glossary" in the sense that the material is presented alphabetically and contains numerous statutory definitions of terms and phrases used in Irish environmental laws. The book is a "handbook" in that it is designed to allow the user readily to access relevant statutory material organised in a consolidated, updated manner - including full references to all regulations made under various statutory provisions covered in the book. It also contains useful practical guidance on matters related to the application and enforcement of environmental law in Ireland, particularly as regards fishery law.

The complex interaction between Irish legislation (primary and subordinate) and European Directives is explored in detail in this book. The disparate sources of law relating to the protection of the environment in Ireland is one of the reasons why newcomers find the subject difficult to understand. It is hoped that the presentation of material in this work will assist the user in coming to that understanding.

The book is intended to be used not only by lawyers and other legal professionals but by environmental scientists, local government officials, park rangers, fishery protection officers, architects, civil engineers, planners and others involved in environmental protection in Ireland. To assist the non-professional user, extensive complete quotation is made of important legislation under various major headings (for example, enforcement, licensing, prohibition and waste management) over and above the definitions covered in the book.

It is becoming increasingly obvious that the agencies which share responsibility for the protection of the environment must work closer to one another and it is not too farfetched to look to a day when there might be a common enforcement agency dealing with fisheries, wildlife, pollution prevention and environmental protection. The authors sincerely hope that this book will prove to be helpful to the many people involved in the regulation and enforcement of environmental protection in Ireland.

The law is stated as at January 31st, 2000.

Henry Comerford
Aengus R.M. Fogarty

April 2000

Galway, Ireland.

Table of Statutory Instruments

References in this table are to page numbers. Where the page number for an entry appears in **bold type** it indicates that the statutory instrument in question is reproduced in whole (or in part) on that page. Where different provisions of a statutory instrument are reproduced on a number of pages, the entries are listed in normal type. Please note that no references to material in Schedules to various enactments (reproduced in the Appendices) and the summary of the provisions of the Wildlife Amendment Bill of 1999 (set out in the Annex) have been included in this table.

Please note that references to material appearing in the Appendix and the Wildlife Amendment Bill of 1999 (Annex) is not included in this table.

	6	**207**
1998	Fisheries (Amendment) Act, 1997 (Section 23) Regulations (S.I. No. 84)	21
1998	European Communities (Natural Habitats) (Amendment) Regulations (S.I. No 94)	204
1998	Air Pollution Act, 1987 (Marketing, Sale and Distribution of Fuels) Regulations (S.I. No. 118)	341
1998	European Communities Act, 1972 (Access to Information on the Environment) Regulations (S.I. No. 125)	2
1998	Waste Management (Amendment of Waste Management Act, 1996) Regulations (S.I. No. 146)	345, 408
1998	Waste Management (Movement of Hazardous Waste) Regulations (S.I. No. 147)	207, 345
	Reg 2	207
	(3)	410
	3-11	410-411
	4	**207**, 260
	13A	**207**
	14	54
1998	Waste Management (Use of Sewage Sludge in Agriculture) Regulations (S.I. No. 148)	77, 345, 410
	Art 8(2)	335
1998	Waste Management (Transfrontier Shipment of Hazardous Waste) Regulations (S.I. No. 149)	
	Art 10	54, 260, 345
1998	European Communities (Conservation of Wild Birds) (Amendment) Regulations (S.I. No. 154)	36
1998	Waste Management (Licensing) (Amendment) Regulations (S.I. No. 162)	242, 345
1998	Waste Management (Hazardous Waste) Regulations (S.I. No 163)	206-207, 236, 345
	Reg 3	**206-207**
	23A	**207**
1998	Waste Management (Miscellaneous Provisions) Regulations (S.I. No 164)	345, 403
	Art 4	315, 316, 401, 404
	5	**209-210**, 401
	6	401
	7	401
	8	401
	9	401

Table of Statutes

References in this table are to page numbers. Where the page number for an entry appears in **bold type** it indicates that the statutory provision in question is reproduced in whole (or in part) on that page. Where different parts of a statutory provision are reproduced on a number of pages, the entries are listed in normal type. Please note that no references to material in Schedules to various enactments (reproduced in the Appendices) and the summary of the provisions of the Wildlife Amendment Bill of 1999 (set out in the Annex) have been included in this table.

	s 69	247
	126	247
1964	Fisheries (Amendment) Act	
	(Act No. 23)	169
	s 2	176
1965	Protection of Animals (Amendment) Act	
	(Act No. 10)	
	s 7	384
1966	Diseases of Animals Act	
	(Act No. 6)	33, 156
1968	Firearms (Proofing) Act	
	(Act No. 20)	169
1968	Road Traffic Act	
	(Act No. 25)	
	s 63	390
1970	Health Act	
	(Act No. 1)	327
1972	European Communities Act	
	(Act No. 27)	148, 208, 235
	s 3	336, 392, 415
1974	Local Government (Roads and Motorways) Act	
	(Act No. 6)	
	s 4(3), (3A)	141, 142
1974	Fisheries (Amendment) Act	
	(Act No. 25)	169
1976	Gas Act	
	(Act No. 30)	139, 140
1976	Local Government (Planning & Development) Act	
	(Act No. 20)	122, 349
	s 2	41
	20	139
	40(a)	370
	(b)	72, 323
	43(1)(f)	90
	45	72
1976	Wildlife Act	
	(Act No. 39)	23
	s 1(2)	285
	2(1)	9, 32, 60, 70, 152, 154, 165, 182, 204 210, 219-220, 253, 285, 316, 345, 377, 379, 380, 415
	6	203
	7	346, 347

Abbreviations

APA 1987	Air Pollution Act, 1987
EPAA 1992	Environmental Protection Agency Act, 1992
FA's	Fisheries Acts
F(C)A 1959	Fisheries (Consolidation) Act, 1959
FA 1980	Fisheries Act, 1980
F(A)A...	Fisheries (Amendment) Act ... followed by the year.
LG(WP)A 1977	Local Government (Water Pollution) Act, 1977
LG(WP)(A)A 1990	Local Government (Water Pollution) (Amendment) Act, 1990
LG(P&D)A 1963	Local Government (Planning and Development) Act, 1963
LPA 1997	Litter Pollution Act, 1997
NH 97	European Communities (Natural Habitats) Regulations, 1997
RTA 1961	Road Traffic Act, 1961
WLA 1976	Wildlife Act, 1976
EC	European Community
EU	European Union
BATNEEC	best available technology not entailing excessive cost
BPM	best practicable means
ELV	emission limit value
EPA	Environmental Protection Agency
WMP	Waste Management Plan

A

ABANDONED VEHICLE
(WMA 1996, s. 71)

Section 71 of the WMA 1996 gives local authorities powers to deal with abandoned vehicles. *See:* VEHICLES, ABANDONED.

ACCESS TO AND ENTRY ON LAND
(WLA 1976/EPAA 1992)

Access to or *(qv)* entry onto land arises in environmental law under two main headings: Access by (qv) authorised persons and others and Access by the public.

ACCESS BY AUTHORISED PERSONS

In all environmental statutes there are classes of persons, usually called "*(qv)* authorised persons", who are involved in the protection of the environment and the enforcement of environmental law. They are formally appointed under a statute which gives them specific functions. Some of those functions involve an entry onto land and the right of entry is strictly limited to such entry as is required and necessary to be effected in the performance of those functions. Members of an Garda Síochána who have extensive powers by virtue of their office as members of the Gardaí are specifically appointed under certain sections of the Fisheries Acts and the WLA 1976 and exercise the same powers under those sections as do the non-Gardaí personnel authorised for the same purpose. *See:* ENTRY AND SEARCH.

ACCESS BY THE PUBLIC

(1) FA 1980

Section 39 of the FA 1980 entitles the Minister to make an order, on the application of the *(qv)* Central Board or a *(qv)* regional board, where he is satisfied that a right of way is required either to enable the applicant to perform its functions under the Act or to enable fishermen to gain access to fishing waters for the purpose of lawfully fishing and that in either case it would be reasonable to make an order under the section creating a right of way. There is a right of appeal against the Ministers order under the section either creating the right of way or refusing the application. *See:* ACQUISITION OF LAND.

(2) WLA 1976

Section 59 of the WLA 1976 provides:

"(1) Subject to subsections (3), (4) and (7) of this section, the Minister may make regulations permitting the public generally or any particular class or section of the public or the members of any body of persons which is of a particular class or description or the members of a particular body of persons, to have access to and use in accordance with the regulations —
(a) foreshore which is the property of the State,
(b) land (in this section subsequently referred to as a *(qv)* refuge) to which a *(qv)* designation order applies,
(c) any land (including land covered by inland waters) to which an *(qv)* establishment order applies and which is land owned by the State but in which the Minister has not a joint or several interest (which land is so referred to as a State land nature reserve),
(d) land other than foreshore mentioned in paragraph (a) of this subsection, which forms the seabed under part of the *(qv)* territorial seas of the State and to which an *(qv)* establishment order applies (which land is so referred to as a seabed nature reserve)
(2) Regulations under this section may apply to all foreshore which is the property of the State, every *(qv)* refuge, State land *(qv)* nature reserve and seabed nature reserve, or to any such foreshore or any refuge, State land nature reserve or seabed nature reserve which is of a particular class or description, or to a particular such foreshore or a particular refuge, State land nature reserve or seabed nature reserve."

Subsection (3) provides that access to the foreshore shall be limited to access necessary for the conservation of *(qv)* wildlife and regulations will only be made after consultation with the Minister for Transport and Power and, where the foreshore is not held by the Minister, after consultation with the body who does hold it, either the (*qv*) Commissioners or the Minister of State by whom the foreshore is held.

Subsection (4) provides that regulations which apply to a refuge shall regulate access to or use of the refuge to such extent as is necessary to enable the relevant designation order to have effect.

Subsection (5) provides that in the case of a (*qv*) recognition order or where there is a section 18 agreement in force (*See:* MANAGEMENT AGREEMENT), the Minister may by regulation permit and regulate access to and use by the public generally with, in the case of a recognition order, on the request of and with the consent of the owner of the land, and in the case of a section 18 agreement, with the consent of all the parties to the agreement other than the Minister if he is a party.

Subsection (6) provides for the Minister making regulations permitting access at the request of various bodies appointed under section 14 - none of these were ever appointed.

As section 4 of the Heritage Act 1995 repealed section 13 of the WLA 1976 which provided for the Appointment of a Wildlife Advisory Council and as section 6 the same Act gave the Council's functions to the Heritage Council it is unlikely any board will ever be established under section 14.

Subsection (7) provides that the Minister must consult with the appropriate (*qv*)planning authority when making regulations under subsection (5) or where the regulations regulate access to the foreshore or a refuge (not being a refuge held by the Minister) to which, immediately before the commencement of this section, the public generally had access.

Subsection (8) provides that regulations under the section shall cease to have effect when the State ceases to own the land or where the designation or recognition orders are revoked.

Subsection (9) provides that copies of regulations made under this section must be sent to the (*qv*) Board and the appropriate (*qv*) planning authority where they affect the foreshore or where a refuge is situate on the land.

Subsection (10) provides for the giving by the Minister of particulars to the Board or the appropriate planning authority of the making, variation or revocation of any bye-law, rule, regulation or otherwise permitting the public generally to have access, subject to specified conditions, to land held by him for educational or leisure purposes.

offence
Subsection (11) creates the offence of failing to comply with specified conditions of access to land held by the Minister for educational or recreational purposes.

Section 60 of the WLA 1976 provides for the creation by the Minister of rights-of-way when he then had joint functions as Minister with responsibility for Lands and as Minister with responsibility for Forestry. This is no longer the case and the section now has limited application. *See:* RIGHTS-OF-WAY.

ACCESS TO INFORMATION ON THE ENVIRONMENT
(EPAA 1992, ss. 67 and 100)

Section 67 deals with records to be kept by the Agency under the EPAA 1992 of the result of monitoring it carried out or arranged to have carried out. The section also requires the Agency to make such records available for inspection by the public subject to the requirements as to confidentiality specified under section 39 of the 1992 Act.

Section 110 is concerned with the making by the Minister of regulations for availability by specified public authorities of information relating to the environment to any person upon request and to give full effect to Council Directive 90/313/EEC of June 7, 1990 on the freedom of access to the environment (O.J. L158 (June 23 1990) p. 56). Subsection (2) deals with information which may be required under regulations and subsection (3) defines "information relating to the environment" for the purposes of section 110. The current regulations implementing this directive are the European Communities Act, 1972 (Access to Information on the Environment) Regulations, 1998 (S.I. No. 125 of 1998) which revoked and replace corresponding 1996 Regulations (S.I. No. 185 of 1996) with effect as from 1st May 1998.

ACCIDENT
(GMO Regs, Art. 3(1))

"means any incident involving a significant and unintended release of genetically modified organisms in the course of their *(qv)* contained use which could present an immediate or delayed hazard to human health or the environment."

ACCIDENTAL DISCHARGE/ ACCIDENTAL EMISSION
(LG(WP)A 1977, s.14)

Section 14 of the LG(WP)A 1977, as amended by Article 9 of, and the First Schedule to, the Environmental Protection Agency (Extension of

Powers) Order 1996 (S.I. No. 126 of 1996) provides:

"(1) As soon as practicable after the occurrence of an accidental discharge, spillage or deposit of any (qv)polluting matter which enters or is likely to enter any *(qv)* waters or a *(qv)* sewer, the person responsible shall notify -

(a) the local authority in whose functional area the discharge, spillage or deposit occurs or, in the case of a sewer, the sanitary authority in which the sewer is vested or by which it is controlled, [and

(b) in the case of an *(qv)* activity in respect of which a licence or a revised licence under Part IV of the Environmental Protection Agency Act, 1992, is in force, the Environmental Protection Agency].

Offence

(2) A person who fails to comply with sub section (1) shall be guilty of an offence and shall be liable on summary conviction to a fine not exceeding [£1000].

(3) [A prosecution for an offence under this section may be taken by a local authority, a sanitary authority or the Environmental Protection Agency]."

Subsection (2) of this section was amended by s 24(3) of the LG(WP)(A)A 1990, subsection (3) was amended by s. 30 of the LG(WP)(A)A 1990 and the same subsection was amended as was subsection (1) by the insertion of the words in square brackets by the First Schedule Environmental Protection Agency (Extension of Powers) Order 1996 (S.I. No. 126 of 1996) *See:* EXTENSION OF POWERS.

(APA 1987, s. 29)

Section 29 of the APA 1987:

"(1) The *(qv)*occupier of any *(qv)*premises, other than a *(qv)*private dwelling, shall as soon as practicable after the occurrence of any incident which may cause *(qv)*air pollution notify the relevant local authority of the incident.

(2) In this section "incident" includes an accidental emission."

See: The County Council of the County of Cork, Complainant v. Angus Fine Chemicals Limited, Defendant [1990] 2 I.R. 369 where section 29 of the APA 1987 was the basis for prosecution and where the question of the Defendant being exempted from prosecution because of an application for a licence was pending under section 30(3) of the APA 1987 was considered.

ACCOUNTS, AUDITS/ ANNUAL REPORTS

(EPAA 1992, ss. 50 and 51)

Section 50 of the EPAA 1992 provides for the keeping by the Agency, in such form as may be approved by the Minister with the consent of the Minister for Finance, all proper and usual accounts of all monies received or expended by it and subsection (2) provides that the accounts are to be submitted annually to the Comptroller and Auditor General for audit and when audited are presented to the Minister with a report and then laid before each house of the Oireachtas.

Section 51 of the EPAA 1992 provides that not later than six months after the end of the financial year the Agency will present the annual report of its functions to the Minister and will supply him with such information relating to the performance of its functions as he shall from time to time request.

ACCREDITATION SCHEME, LABORATORIES, ESTABLISHMENT OF

(EPAA 1992, s.66)

This section deals with the recognition by the Agency of laboratories and services other than their own which are of a standard acceptable to them and which they can use.

It also deals with the establishment by the Agency of an analytical quality control programme using these laboratories and services and their own.

Section 66 of the EPAA 1992:

"(1) (a) The Agency may, for the purposes of assessing analytical performance and ensuring the validity and comparability of *(qv)* environmental data, establish, or arrange for the establishment of, an analytical quality control programme involving its own laboratories, laboratories provided and operated by local authorities, and such other laboratories as it deems appropriate from which data are submitted to the Agency in connection with the performance of any of its functions.

(b) The Agency may require any such laboratory to furnish it with such data as it may request for the purposes of any such programme.

(c) Without prejudice to the generality of paragraph (a), the Agency may establish different analytical quality control programmes for different laboratories or for different tests.

(2) The Agency may require any laboratory which supplies environmental data to the Agency or in connection with any function under this Act to be accredited in accordance with Irish Standard I.S./EN 45001: 1989-General Criteria for the Operation of Testing Laboratories - or equivalent and with such other or further standards as may be set, from time to time, by the National Standards Authority of Ireland or equivalent standards.

(3) The Agency may provide for the imposition of charges and the payment of fees in connection with the provision of services or any procedural matters under this section.

(4) The Agency shall maintain a register of laboratories which comply with the requirements of subsection (1) or which are required to be accredited under sub section (2).

(5) The register shall include a list of tests to which such compliance or accreditation relates and shall be available for inspection by any person free of charge at the Agency's headquarters during office hours."

ACQUISITION OF LAND

(FA 1980/WLA 1976)

This section deals with the acquisition by various Ministers of land or interests in land or over land or other property or property rights such as *profits a prendre* (including (*qv*) several fisheries) or rights of way.

(1) UNDER THE FISHERIES ACTS

Part III of the FA 1980 sets out the powers of acquisition and transfer of fisheries by the State and the Fifth Schedule to the Act contains details of the procedures to be adopted. The part of the 1959 Act dealing with the transfer of fisheries to the Minister "transferable fisheries" Chapters 1 to VI of Part XII, sections 184 to 218, excepting only section 217, were repealed by section 6, First Schedule, of the FA 1980. For section 217 *See:* POWERS (1)(A) RESTRICTIONS ON MINISTER'S POWERS.

ACQUISITION OF A FISHERY

Section 37 of the FA 1980 provides that on the application of the (*qv*) Central Board the Minister after satisfying himself:

(a) that it is necessary to acquire a particular fishery to carry out a development programme, or

(b) that it is expedient to acquire any fishery for the purpose of its management, operation, protection, conservation or development in accordance with such a programme,

with the consent of the Minister for Finance may authorise such acquisition.

Subsection (2)(a) provides that the acquisition may be by agreement or by order under section 37.

Subsection (2)(b) provides that it addition to the fishery the Central Board may acquire:

(i) the bed and soil of waters where they form part of a fishery (by its definition ownership of a "several fishery" does not necessarily include the bed and soil), and

(ii) any estate or interest in land, or any way-leave, right of access or easement or other right over, in or under land required in connection with the preservation, conservation, operation, development or improvement of the fishery being acquired.

The Minister is obliged under the section before he gives the authorisation to consult in the first instance with the Minister for Finance and then with such other Ministers as may be concerned.

Subsection (5) provides that where there is a public right to fish in the fishery, the fishery will only be acquired if the Minister is satisfied that it is in the public interest to do so.

There is a right of objection under subsection (6) both to an authorisation and to an acquisition order to an (*qv*) arbitrator appointed under section 44.

Section 17 of the (F)(A)A 1999 makes a number of amendments to section 37 mainly by substituting "board" for the "Central Board". This follows the downgrading of the *(qv)* regional boards on an equal footing with the Central

Board in the acquisition and transfer of fisheries. The Fisheries (Amendment) Act, 1999 (save for section 23) came into force on 20 December 1999 by virtue of the Fisheries (Amendment) Act, 1999 (Commencement) Order, 1999 (S.I. No. 419 of 1999).

(qv) Compensation is dealt with under section 43. *See:* COMPENSATION.

ACQUISITION OF CONTIGUOUS RIVERS AND LAKES

Section 38 of the FA 1980 gives the Minister power to make an order acquiring parts of rivers and lakes contiguous to a fishery owned by the State or acquired under section 37 which is quite separate and distinct from his powers under section 37.

Section 18 of the F(A)A 1999 amends this section by substituting "a board" for "the Central Board" placing the *(qv)* regional boards on an equal footing with the *(qv)* Central Board in such acquisitions which had been the function of the Central Board only in the original section 38.

ACQUISITION OF A RIGHT-OF-WAY

Section 39 of the FA 1980 gives the Minister power to acquire compulsorily under the section, on the application of the *(qv)* Central Board or a *(qv)* regional fisheries board, a right-of-way by a particular route over any land which must be shown on the plan sent with the application.

The Minister must be satisfied that the acquisition would be reasonable and that the right of way is required either to enable the applicants to perform a function assigned to it under the Act or that it is necessary to enable fishermen to gain access to fishing waters for the purposes of lawfully fishing.

Both the owner of the servient tenement, if the order is made, and the applicants, if the order is refused, have a right of appeal. The appeal lies to an *(qv)* Arbitrator appointed under section 44.

INTERNAL TRANSFERS

Section 40 of the FA 1980 deals with the transfer of fisheries to the Minister/Central Board by the *(qv)* Commissioners and section 41 deals with like transfers by the Irish Land Commission.

Section 42 of the FA 1980 as amended by section 19 of the F(A)A 1999 deals with transfers of fisheries by the Minister to a Board. *See:* TRANSFER OF FISHERIES.

In each of the above instances the order made under the section operates to vest the fishery in the transferee without further or any conveyance.

POWER TO AMEND OR REVOKE ORDERS

Section 5(2) of the FA 1980 gives the Minister extensive powers to revoke or amend, *inter alia*, orders made under sections 37, 38, 39 or 42 and there is provision, in sections 37(6)(a) and (b), 38(3) and 39(3)(b) for an appeal to an Arbitrator by any person aggrieved by such amendment or revocation.

The other sections affected by section 5 are given at subsection (1), sections 8(3)(b), 10, 11, 15, 24(6), 54, 55, 56 or 57 of the FA 1980 and sections 81(3) or 159(6) of the F(C)A 1959.

In so far as these latter sections refer to ordinary licence duties those which relate to a duty on fishing for trout are affected by section 3 of the F(A)A 1991. *See:* DUTIES ON ORDINARY FISHING LICENCES.

SALE

Section 45 of the FA 1980 gives the Minister the right, with the consent of the Minister for Finance, to sell (other than to the Central Board) any fishery or fishery right vested in him.

Section 21 of the F(A)A 1999 substitutes "a board" for "the Central Board" placing the *(qv)* regional boards on an equal footing with the *(qv)* Central Board in respect of such sales.

(1A) UNDER THE IRISH LAND COMMISSION (DISSOLUTION) ACT 1992

Section 5 of the Irish Land Commission (Dissolution) Act 1992:

"(1) All land and other property which, immediately before the commencement of this Act, stood vested in or reserved to the Commission shall on such commencement, without any conveyance, assignment or transfer –

(a) as to land and other property (except fishing rights and fisheries) stand vested in the Minister, and

(b) as to fishing rights and fisheries, stand vested in or reserved to the *(qv)* Central Fisheries Board - for all the estate or interest of the

Commission subject, as far as not modified by virtue of this Act, to all trusts and equities, covenants, conditions and restrictions affecting the property.

(2) Any fishing rights and fisheries which but for this Act would on a sale to the Commission under the Land Purchase Acts have required to be vested in or reserved to the Commission shall be vested in the Central Fisheries Board and any other sporting rights shall be vested in the Minister."

By virtue of section 1(1) of the 1992 Act "the Commission" means the Irish Land Commission and "the Minister" means the Minister for Agriculture and Food. By virtue of Article 2 of the Irish Land Commission (Dissolution) Act, 1992 (Commencement) Order 1999 (S.I. No. 75 of 1999) the 31st day of March 1999 is the day on which the 1992 Act comes into operation.

(2) UNDER THE WLA 1976

ACQUISITION BY THE MINISTER UNDER SECTION 55

Section 55 of the WLA 1976 provides that the Minister can only acquire land if it is registered under the Registration of Title Acts. The land must be acquired either for a purpose under the WLA 1976 or the Forestry Acts (the Minister responsible for Wildlife, the Minister for Arts, Heritage, the Gaeltacht and the Islands is not concerned with Forestry any longer) and can only be acquired by agreement.

ACQUISITION OF COMMONAGE

Section 55(2)(e) of the WLA 1976 provides that if the land to be acquired forms part of a commonage and one or more of the commoners do not agree to the acquisition of his or her share then the agreement for the sale by the person who is agreeable to sell can proceed if the person or persons unwilling to sell agree to exchange for his or their share of the entire commonage an undivided share in common with the remaining owners in the remaining land in shares proportionate to the portion of their former shares.

COMPENSATION – LATE CLAIMANTS

Section 55(7) of the WLA 1976 provides for the payment of (*qv*) compensation to a person who had an interest in lands being acquired under the section but who failed to bring a claim in respect of that interest to the notice of the Minister prior to the making of the purchase order. There is a time limit on the bringing of such a claim, six years or, where there is a disability, six years from the date the disability ends or the person dies but not more than thirty years in any event.

Subsection (8) provides that in default of agreement as to the amount, compensation is fixed by the Land Commission under section 31 of the Forestry Act 1946.

The Irish Land Commission was dissolved by the Irish Land Commission (Dissolution) Act 1992 *See:* LAY COMMISSIONERS.

The Wildlife Act 1976 (Acquisition of Lands) Regulations, 1978 (S.I. No. 29 of 1978) gives precedents of forms required under this section.

EXTENSION OF MINISTER'S POWERS TO ACQUIRE LAND

Section 63 of the WLA 1976 extends to the Minister and enlarges for the purposes of the Act powers to acquire land which he enjoyed under sections 9 and 22 of the Forestry Act 1946.

Sections 60 and 61 of the WLA 1976 also extended the Minister's powers, in these cases, his powers to acquire or extinguish rights and easements over land.

ORDERS WHICH AFFECT THE USE OF LAND UNDER THE WLA 1976

Chapter III of the WLA 1976 gives the Minister power to make orders in relation to land which do not constitute acquisition but which affect and inhibit the use of the land.
These are dealt with under separate headings.
They are:

(1) An (*qv*) Establishment order under section 15,
(2) A (*qv*) Recognition Order under section 16,
(3) A (*qv*) Designation Order under section 17.
(4) (*qv*) Management agreements relating to land under section 18.

See: (1) RESERVES AND REFUGES: (2) MANAGEMENT AGREEMENTS.

(3) ACQUISITION OF FORESHORE UNDER SECTION 5 FORESHORE ACT 1933

See: FORESHORE.

ACTIVITY
(EPAA 1992/LG(WP)A 1977)

The word "activity" is an important word in the EPAA 1992 as it defines, by reference to the Third Schedule to the Act, all of the "activities" that require *(qv)* Integrated Pollution Control Licences under the Act.

In the LG(WP)A 1977 the word could have

been extremely significant if local authorities in environmentally sensitive areas, particularly beside waters, had made the bye-laws under section 21 of the LG(WP)(A)A 1990 for whose implementation the definition of the word was designed and intended but this was not done. (*See:* AGRICULTURAL ACTIVITIES)

Section 21A, which was inserted by section 66(3) of the WMA 1996, introduces a new but similar concept for dealing with pollution of waters from agricultural waste and nutrients. Under section the local authority had a discretion and were under no obligation to make a bye-law. Section 21 does not require the making of a bye-law and the local authority's powers under the section take effect from the operative date of the WMA 1996. However, it is still a discretionary remedy in so far as the local authorities are concerned. The Agency have powers in relation to the performance by local authorities of their functions. Under the EPAA 1992, section 63, the Agency can request a report, issue recommendations, give a direction and ultimately, in default, carry out the function themselves. *See:* PERFORMANCE OF STATUTORY FUNCTIONS BY LOCAL AUTHORITIES. They can also have the Minister transfer such functions to them under section 54 of the same Act. *See:* TRANSFER OF FUNCTIONS FROM LOCAL AUTHORITIES TO AGENCY. *See:* NUTRIENT MANAGEMENT PLANS.

(LG(WP)(A)A 1990, s. 21(1)):

"means any one or more of the following:
(a) the collection, storage, treatment and disposal of any (*qv*) polluting matter used in connection with, or arising from any operation, activity, practice or use of land or other premises carried on for the purposes of agriculture, horticulture or forestry;
(b) any activity that involves the application to land or to growing crops, or the injection into land, of any silage effluent, animal slurry, manure, fertilizer, pesticide or other polluting matter;
(c) any other operation, activity, practice or use of land or other premises for the purposes of agriculture, horticulture or forestry."

(EPAA 1992, s.3(1)):

"means any process, development or operation specified in the First Schedule."

See: (1) SCHEDULES HERETO, FIRST SCHEDULE EPAA; (2) SPECIAL CASES.

(NH 97, REG.17)

See: OPERATION OR ACTIVITY

ADVISORY COMMITTEE TO EPAA
(EPAA 1992, s.27)

Section 27 of the EPAA 1992 provides for the appointment of an Advisory Committee of twelve including the Director General or his designate who is an *ex–officio* member. Of the remaining eleven members, four are appointed by the Minister and seven from persons nominated by bodies prescribed by Ministerial regulation under subsection (5) from bodies concerned with environmental protection, the promotion of economic or other development and the promotion of social, economic or general interests in relation to the community.

FUNCTIONS OF THE ADVISORY COMMITTEE

Section 28 of the EPAA 1992 sets out the functions of the Advisory Committee as follows:

"(1)(a) It shall be the duty of the Advisory Committee to make recommendations to the Agency or to the Minister relating to the functions of the Agency.
(b) The Agency or the Minister, as may be appropriate, shall have regard to any recommendations made by the Advisory Committee."

Recommendations that are suggested are specified at subsection (2) of section 28.

Subsection (3) provides that the Minister may consult the Agency on his environmental protection functions.

Subsection (4) provides that the Advisory Committee is entitled at its meetings to be informed in broad terms about the work of the Agency but not (*qv*) confidential information, as in section 39, and taking into account the accessibility of information under section 110.

Subsection (5) spells out quite clearly the limitations of the Advisory Committee, in that:
(a) They are not entitled to specific information on any individual licence in process under Part IV, and
(b) They are not entitled to have their rec-

ommendations regarding such a licence taken into account.

ADVISORY FUNCTIONS OF AGENCY
(EPAA 1992, ss. 55 and 56)

The Agency has advisory function under the EPAA, to Ministers of Government under section 55, and to local authorities under section 56. *See:* FUNCTIONS OF THE ENVIRONMENTAL PROTECTION AGENCY.

AFTERCARE
(WMA 1996, s.5(1))

"means, in relation to a (*qv*) facility, which has been used for the purpose of waste (*qv*) recovery or (*qv*) disposal, any measures that are necessary to be taken in relation to the facility for the purpose of preventing (*qv*) environmental pollution following the cessation of the activity in question at the facility."

AGENTS FOR FISHERY OWNERS
(F(C)A 1959, s.328)

Section 328 of the F(C)A 1959 entitles a fishery owner by power of attorney under his hand to appoint an agent to act for him in carrying into execution the provisions of the Fisheries Acts and the agent has power to deal and be dealt with in all matters as his principal would have done or had done to him.

By virtue of section 309 of the F(C)A 1959 any person can prosecute but section 328 intends that the agent can also be prosecuted.

AGENCY, THE
(EPAA 1992, s.19)

By virtue of section 19 of the EPAA 1992 "the Agency" is the Environmental Protection Agency which was established by that section. *See:* ESTABLISHMENT OF ENVIRONMENTAL PROTECTION AGENCY.

AGREEMENTS BETWEEN AGENCY AND OTHER PUBLIC BODIES AS TO PERFORMANCE OF FUNCTIONS
(EPAA 1992, s.45)

Section 45 of the EPAA 1992 provides:

"(1) Subject to section 25(6), where –
(a) the Agency is of the opinion that any function or any service which may be exercised or performed by it should be exercised or performed on its behalf, whether generally or in a particular case, by a public authority, and
(b) the public authority is able and willing so to exercise or perform the function or service,

the Agency and the public authority may enter into an agreement that the function or service shall be so exercised and performed on behalf of the Agency by the public authority, and it shall thereupon become so exercisable or performable by the public authority.

(2) Where –
(a) consequent upon an agreement under subsection (1) a function or service becomes exercisable or per formable by a public authority, and
(b) the Agency would, if it exercised or performed the function or service, be authorised by law to do any act or thing in relation to such exercise or performance,

the public authority shall be authorised to do that act or thing in relation to the exercise or performance by it of the function or service as if it were the Agency.

(3) The Agency shall furnish the Minister with a copy of an agreement to which this section applies.

(4) Any agreement under this section may include such terms and conditions (including terms as to payment or other wise) as may be decided between the parties to the agreement.

(5) Entry into an agreement under this section by a local authority shall be a reserved function.

(6) In this section –
"local authority" has the meaning assigned to it by the Local Government Act, 1941 "reserved function" means -
(a) with respect to the council of a county (or an elective body for the purposes of the County Management Acts, 1940 to 1991) a reserved function for the purposes of the County Management Acts, 1940 to 1991,
(b) with respect to a corporation of a county borough, a reserved function for the purposes of the Acts relating to the management of the county borough."

AGRICULTURE
(LG(WP)A 1977, s. 1(1))

"includes the breeding, keeping and sale of livestock (including pigs, poultry and any creature kept for the production of food, wool, skins or fur) and the making and storing of silage."

AGRICULTURAL ACTIVITIES
(LG(WP)(A)A 1990, s. 21)

REGULATION AND PROHIBITION OF CERTAIN AGRICULTURAL ACTIVITIES

Section 21(2) of the LG(WP)(A)A 1990 –

"(2) (a) Whenever a local authority considers that, for the purpose of preventing or eliminating the entry of *(qv)* polluting matter to *(qv)* waters, it is necessary to do so, it may make *(qv)* bye-laws prohibiting the carrying on of a specified activity in the whole or a specified part of its functional area or providing for the regulation of the carrying on of a specified activity in the whole or a specified part of its functional area."

(b) Whenever the Minister considers that, for the purpose of preventing or eliminating the entry of *(qv)* polluting matter to waters, it is necessary to do so, the Minister may direct a local authority to make bye-laws prohibiting the carrying on of a specified activity in the functional area of the authority or in a specified part of that area or providing for the regulation in such manner as the Minister shall specify of the carrying on of a specified activity in the functional area of the authority or in a specified part of that functional area and the local authority shall comply with the direction."

Section 21(2)*(c)* and *(d)* describe the matters which may be contained in bye-laws and (e) provides that bye-laws under the subsection shall be subject to the approval of the Minister.

Offence
Section 21(3)*(a)* creates the offence of contravention of or failure to comply with bye-laws under the subsection.

Section 21(4) sets out the steps which must be taken by a local authority in making a bye-law under the subsection and section 21(5) provides that in applying section 28 of the LG(WP)A 1977 (*See:* ENTRY AND SEARCH), the reference in subsection (1)(c) of that section to regulations under the LG(WP)A 1977 shall be construed as including a reference to bye-laws under this section.
See: (1) ACTIVITY; (2) NUTRIENT MANAGEMENT PLANS.

Standards in relation to phosphates in water, which has long been identified as one of the main *(qv)* pollutants in *(qv)* waters, were not regulated for until late 1998. (*See:* The Local Government (Water Pollution) Act, 1977 (Water Quality Standard for Phosphorus) Regulations, 1998 (S.I. No. 258 of 1998)).

AIRGUN
(WLA 1976, s.2(1))

"means any weapon, including an air-rifle or air-pistol, incorporating a barrel from which metal or other slugs can be discharged."

The definition of "*(qv)* firearm" under the WLA 1976 includes an airgun and therefore an airgun used for hunting must be licensed under section 29 of that Act.

AIR POLLUTION
(APA 1987, s. 4)

"means a condition of the atmosphere in which a pollutant is present in such quantity as to be liable to –

(i) be injurious to public health, or
(ii) have a deleterious effect on *(qv)* flora and *(qv)* fauna or damage property, or
(iii) impair or interfere with amenities or with the environment."

AIR QUALITY MANAGEMENT (AQM) PLAN
(APA 1987, s. 6(1))

"has the meaning specified in section 46."

Section 46 of the APA 1987:

"(1) A local authority may, and shall if the Minister so directs, make, in relation to all or any part of its functional area, a plan (in this Act referred to as an "air quality management plan") for the preservation or the improvement of the air quality in the area to which such plan relates."

Subsection (2) provides that the plan must be reviewed at least once every five years with any variations (whether by way of alteration, addition or deletion) which the local authority consider proper or they can replace it with a new plan.

Subsection (3) provides for two or more local authorities making joint air quality management (AQM) plans.

Subsection (4) provides that an AQM plan shall contain such objectives as seem reasonable and necessary for the prevention or limitation of (*qv*) air pollution or the preservation or improvement of air quality but such objectives cannot be inconsistent with regulations under sections 50 or 51 (*See:* (1) AIR QUALITY STANDARDS (2) EMISSION LIMIT VALUES) or with any (*qv*) special control area order in operation in the area.

Subsection (5) provides that the making, review, variation or replacement of an AQM plan is a reserved function.

POWER OF MINISTER IN RELATION TO AQM PLANS

Section 47 of the APA 1987:

"The Minister may –

(a) direct a local authority, or two or more local authorities jointly, to make an air quality management plan;
(b) require a local authority or, as the case may be, two or more local authorities, to vary (whether by alteration, addition or deletion) an air quality management plan made or jointly made by them in such manner as the Minister may specify or to replace the plan by a new plan;
(c) require that an air quality management plan made or to be made by two or more local authorities be co-ordinated in such manner and in relation to such matters as the Minister may specify;

and a local authority shall comply with every such direction or requisition of the Minister."

Section 48(1) and (2) of the APA 1987 provide for publication of notice of the proposal to make, vary or replace an AQM plan in at least one newspaper circulating in their functional area stating where and when the plan may be inspected and that representations may be made within a stated period and will be taken into consideration before making or varying the plan.

Subsection (3) provides that the local authority may vary or replace the AQM plan after they have considered the representations, with or without amendment.

Subsection (4) provides that:

(a) Any person may obtain from the local authority a copy of or extract from a plan,
(b) A copy or extract of the plan certified by an officer of the local authority to be a true copy is prima facie evidence that it is a true copy without further proof,
(c) Production of such a copy duly certified is evidence of the plan.
(d) Where a copy is furnished under (a) above the fee for so doing will not exceed the reasonable cost of making the copy.

Section 49 of the APA 1987 provides that as soon as may be after the plan has been varied or replaced the local authority shall transmit a copy to the Minister and such other persons as may be prescribed.

AIR QUALITY STANDARD
(APA 1987, s.7(1))

"means a standard prescribed for the purposes of this Act by the Minister pursuant to section 50."

Section 50(1) of the APA 1987 provides for the Minister by regulation specifying air quality standards (AQS), for the purposes of the APA 1987, and different AQSs may be specified for different areas or classes of areas, different circumstances or classes of circumstances or for different periods of time.

See: Air Pollution Act 1987 (Commencement (No. 2) Order 1987 (S.I. No. 243 of 1987) which provided that sections 50 and 52 of the Act should come into operation on the 1st day of October 1987.

Section 50(2) and (3) provide:

"(2) Without prejudice to the provisions of subsection (1), regulations under this section may make provision for all or any of the following matters -

(a) relate an air quality standard to a particular (qv)pollutant or to a combination of pollutants;
(b) express an air quality standard as a concentration in the air, or as a mass depositing on a specified area, of the particular pollutant or combination of pollutants which is not to be exceeded for specified periods and under specified conditions,
(c) provide that the Minister may suspend, relax or modify an air quality standard for such period and in such

circumstances as may be specified either generally or in relation to a particular area.

(3) Where it appears as a result of monitoring carried out under section 54 or otherwise, that an air quality standard is being, or is likely to be, exceeded in any part of their functional area, a local authority shall -

(a) include in any air quality management plan prepared by them such objectives as the local authority consider appropriate for the improvement of the quality of the air and for the prevention or limitation of air pollution in the affected area so that within such period as the local authority consider reasonable, or such period as the Minister may direct, the air quality standard will not be exceeded, and

(b) take such other steps as may be appropriate in discharge of their functions under this Act to secure compli ance with the air quality standard."

See: (1) EXTENSION OF POWERS; (2) EMISSION LIMIT VALUES.

Air Pollution Act 1987 (Air Quality Standards) Regulations 1987 (S.I. No. 244 of 1987) provides air quality standards by reference to the Parts of the Schedule to the Regulations as follows: Part I Sulphur Dioxide, Part II Suspended Particulates, Part III Lead and Part IV Nitrogen Dioxide.

These regulations implement Council Directive 80/779/EEC of July, 15 1980 on air quality limit value for sulphur dioxide with suspended articulates as amended (O.J. L229/30, August, 30 1980, Council Directive 82/884/EEC of December, 3 1982 on a limit value for lead in air (O.J. L378 31 December 82) and Council Directive 85/203/EEC on a limit value for nitrogen dioxide (O.J. L87/1, March, 27 1985).

Article 2 defines, for the purpose of the Regulations:

""air quality standards" means a concentration in the air of a pollutant, in the quantity specified in the Schedule, which is not exceeded for the period and under the conditions specified in the schedule in relation to that pollutant.

"suspended particulates" includes smoke."

ALL REASONABLE CARE, DEFENCE OF
(LG(WP)A 1977, s.3(3))

Section 3(3) of the LG(WP)A 1977, as amended by substitution by section 3(1) of the LG(WP)(A)A 1990, provides that it shall be a defence to a prosecution under section 3(1) of the LG(WP)A 1977 for the accused to prove that he took all reasonable care to prevent the entry to (*qv*)waters by providing, maintaining, using, operating and supervising facilities or by employing practices or methods of operation, that were suitable for the purpose of such prevention.

ALTERATION OF ACTIVITY
(EPAA 1992, s.92)

Section 92 of the EPAA 1992:

"(1) The person in charge of -

(a) an (*qv*) activity in respect of which a licence or revised licence is in force or required under this Part, or

(b) an (*qv*) established activity which for the time being is not required to be licensed under this Act,

shall give notice in writing to the Agency if he proposes to effect any (*qv*) alteration to, or reconstruction in respect of, the activity and such alteration or reconstruction would, or is likely to, materially change or increase (qv) emissions from the activity or cause new emissions there from."

Subsections (2) and (3) provide for the various ways in which the Agency can react to such a notice depending on whether or not there is a licence or a revised licence in force in relation to the activity.

ALTERATION OF PREMISES BY AN OCCUPIER
(APA 1987, s.38(1))

Section 38(1) of the APA 1987 requires the (*qv*) occupier of (*qv*) industrial plant, either licensed under the APA or (*qv*) existing industrial plant, to give notice in writing to the appropriate local authority if he proposes to:

(i) effect any alteration or reconstruction of plant, or

(ii) effect any alteration in the processes being carried out therein

and such alteration would, or is likely to, materially increase emissions or cause new emissions.

Section 38(2) provides that a local authority receiving such a notice can, where there is a licence in force, review that licence, or direct an application for a new licence and where there is no licence in force direct an application for a new licence and the alteration cannot be effected until the completion of the review or grant of the new licence.

ALTERATION OF PREMISES AT THE REQUEST OF LOCAL AUTHORITY
(APA 1987, s.44)

Section 44 of the APA 1987 provides that where a (*qv*) special control area is or will be coming into operation within an area when confirmed by the Minister the local authority may by notice in writing served on the owner/occupier –

(a) specify the works necessary to comply with the order,
(b) direct the carrying out of the specified works,
(c) specify the period, being not less than 28 days from the date of service of the notice to the date the special area order comes into operation, within which the works must be completed, and
(d) specifying that representations in writing in relation to the terms of the notice may be made by the recipient within the same period.

Subsection (3) requires the local authority to consider the representations and to amend or revoke the order if they consider it reasonable to do so.

Subsection (4) obliges the person on whom the notice is served to comply with the requirements within the time specified.

Subsection (5) provides that on failure to comply the local authority may take such steps as are reasonably necessary to secure compliance, and under subsection (6) recover the expenses of doing so as a simple contract debt in any court of competent jurisdiction.

AMENDMENT OF AN AQUACULTURE LICENCE
(F(A)A 1997, s.18)

Section 18 of the F(A)A 1997 entitles the (*qv*) licensing authority to amend an aquaculture licence so as to give effect to any undertaking or agreement which, after the date of the licence, may have been given or entered into by or on behalf of a licensee or any other person.

Section 68 of the F(A)A 1997 provides for notices to be served by the Minister before revoking or amending an aquaculture licence and other matters. *See:* REVOCATION AND AMENDMENT OF AN AQUACULTURE LICENCE.

ANGLING WITH ROD AND LINE
(F(C)A 1959, s.3(1))

References to angling for salmon and trout as references to angling for salmon or trout with rod and line was amended by section 2 of the F(A)(No. 2)A, 1987, which reads:

"references to angling for salmon, trout and coarse fish or references to angling for any such fish, shall be construed as references to angling with rod and line."

This amendment was sought in the overall context of the 1987 Act which sought to impose a rod licence duty on angling for trout and coarse fish which was intended to be in addition to the existing licence duty in respect of salmon rod ordinary licences. This additional licence duty proved so unpopular that it was necessary to revoke its imposition in its entirety and this was achieved, after a fashion, by the provisions of the F(A)A 1991 which provided at section 3 that a licence under the Principal, 1959 Act,

"shall not be required for angling for trout or coarse fish".

The amendment of the definition was left unchanged. It should have been restored to its original meaning. *See:* DUTIES ON ORDINARY FISHING LICENCES.

ANNEX I,II,III AND IV
(NH 97)

The (*qv*) Natural Habitats Directive refers to four Annexes as follows:

ANNEX I
Natural habitat types of community interest whose conservation requires the designation of (*qv*) special areas of conservation.
These are broken down in the Annex into the following general habitat designations:
Coastal and Halophytic Habitats
Coastal Sand Dunes and Continental Dunes
Freshwater Habitats
Temperate Heath and Scrub
Sclerophyllous Scrub (Matorral)
Natural and Semi-natural Grassland Formations
Raised Bogs and Mires and Fens

Rocky Habitats and Caves
Forests

ANNEX II
Animal and plant species of community interest whose conservation requires the designation of special areas of conservation.
These are broken down in the Annex into the following species designations:
(A) Animals, Mammals, Amphibians, Arthropods and Molluscs
(B) Plants

ANNEX III
Criteria for selecting sites eligible for identification as sites of community importance and designation as special areas of conservation.
There are two stages:
(1) Assessment at national level of the relative importance of sites for each natural habitat type in Annex I and each species in Annexes II (including (*qv*) priority natural habitat types and ((*qv*) priority species)
(2) Assessment of the community importance of the sites included on the national lists.

ANNEX IV
Animal and plant species of community interest in need of strict protection.

See: CONSERVATION, SPECIAL AREAS OF.

ANNUAL CLOSE SEASON
(F(C)A 1959)

See: CLOSE SEASON.

ANNUAL REPORT BY THE MINISTER
(F(C)A 1959, s. 18)

Section 18 of the F(C)A 1959:

"The Minister shall as soon as may be after the expiration of each year lay before each House of the Oireachtas a report containing for such year
(a) particulars of his proceedings under this Act, and
(b) so far as practicable, a statistical account of the fisheries in the State, arranged and classified under such different heads as appears to the Minister to be most suited for the purpose."

ANNUAL REPORT TO THE MINISTER
(EPAA 1992, s. 51)

Section 51 of the EPAA 1992:

"(1) As soon as may be after the end of each financial year, but not later than six months thereafter, the Agency shall cause a report on the performance of its functions during that year to be laid before each house of the Oireachtas.

(2) The Agency shall supply the Minister with such information relating to the performance of its functions as he shall from time to time request."

APPEALS
(F(C)A 1959/WLA 1976/LG(WP)A 1977/ APA 1987/WMA 1996/LG(P&D)A 1963)

Appeals may be taken under each of the enactments relating to the environment in Ireland. The following headings have been chosen for this entry:

UNDER THE FISHERIES ACTS 1959–1997

(1) Appeal to the circuit court from a dismiss in a district court prosecution
(2) Appeals under sections 37, 39 or 54 of the FA 1980 – acquisitions
(3) Appeals under Part III of Chapter II of the F(A)A 1997 – aquaculture
 (a) Submissions and observation by other parties to appeal
 (b) Submissions and observations by persons other than parties
 (c) Powers of the board in relation to appeals
 (d) Withdrawal of appeal by appellant
 (e) Reference to high court on questions of law
 (f) Reports of inspections and oral hearings
 (g) Matters other than those raised by parties or other persons may be taken into account in determining appeals from the fisheries acts
 (h) Licensing authority, matters to which it shall have regard in determining aquaculture licence applications and appeals
 (i) Appeal against conditions only
(4) Appeal to High Court against making an instrument under section 11 of the F(C)A 1959

UNDER THE WLA 1976

(1) Appeal against seizure and detention
(2) Appeal against a refusal to grant or renew a section 29 hunting licence

UNDER THE LG(WP)A 1977

(1) Appeals in relation to sections 4 and 7 – section 8
(2) Appeals in relation to sections 16 and 17 – section 20

UNDER THE APA 1987

Appeals in relation to a decision under sections 32 and 34

UNDER THE NH 97

Appeals against decisions under regulation 16

UNDER WMA 1996

Revocation of waste collection permit

APPEALS TO THE MINISTER UNDER LG(P&D)A 1963

Environmental issues arising under LG(P&D)A 1963

UNDER THE FISHERIES ACTS 1959–1997

(1) Appeal to the circuit court from a dismiss in a district court prosecution

By virtue of **section 310 of the F(C)A 1959**, prosecutors under the Fisheries Acts have a unique right of appeal from a dismiss of a prosecution brought by them in the District Court. The appeal lies to the Circuit Court, whether the dismiss be on the merits or without prejudice.

Section 310:

"(1) Where any proceedings in the District Court for an offence under any provision of this Act are dismissed, whether on the merits or without prejudice, the prosecutor may appeal against the order of dismissal to the Judge of the Circuit Court within whose Circuit the Courthouse in which such order was made is situate.

(2) Where by virtue of subsection (1) of this section a right of appeal against an order of the District Court in any proceedings under this Act lies to the Judge of the Circuit Court, such Judge on such appeal may vary, confirm or reverse such order, and the decision of such Judge on such appeal shall be final and conclusive and not appealable."

By virtue of section 309 of the F(C)A 1959, amended by substitution by section 49 of the FA 1980, an offence under any provision of the Fisheries Acts 1959 to 1980, other than a section specified in Table I to section 2 of the F(A)A 1987, may be heard and determined in a summary way by a District Justice upon the complaint, verbal or otherwise, of a member of the Gardaí Síochána, the Central Board, a regional board, an officer or servant of a board, a private water-keeper within the meaning of Part XVIII of this Act or any other person. *See:* TRIAL OF ACTION.

There is a recent exception to the above under **section 65(3) of the F(A)A 1997** which provides that, notwithstanding section 309 of the Principal Act, a summary offence under the F(A)A 1997, shall be prosecuted only:
(a) by the Minister; or
(b) at the suit of the Director of Public Prosecutions.

The F(C)A 1959 was the first Statute to open prosecuting to the general public which became common under other Statutes affecting the environment passed after 1959. For this reason section 65(3) of the F(A)A 1997 is a retrograde step in the democratisation of the enforcement of environmental legislation.

(2) Appeals under sections 37, 39 or 54 of the FA 1980 – acquisitions

For sections 37 and 39, *See:* ACQUISITIONS. Section 54 was repealed by section 4 F(A)A 1997.

(3) Appeals under Part III of Chapter II of F(A)A 1997 – aquaculture

Section 40(1) of the F(A)A 1997 provides that a person aggrieved by a decision of the Minister on:
(1) an application for an aquaculture licence (s. 14 (2))
(2) a revocation (s. 68(1)) or amendment (s. 68(2)) of an aquaculture licence,
may appeal to (*qv*) the Board against the decision, revocation or amendment, before the expiration of one month beginning on the date of publication of the decision or notification of the revocation or amendment, by serving on the Board a notice of appeal.

(It is confusing that there are now two appeal bodies, an (*qv*) Bord Pleanála and the (*qv*) Aquaculture Licence Appeals Board, both known as "the Board". In this case the Aquaculture Licence Appeals Board is the appropriate body.)

The Aquaculture Licences Appeal Board was established pursuant to the Aquaculture Licences Appeal Board (Establishment) Order, 1998 (S.I. No. 204 of 1998).

Subsection (2) provides for the methods of service of a notice of appeal which may be sent by registered post, be left at the office of the board with an employee or by such other method as may be prescribed.

Subsection (3) provides the Board cannot consider an appeal received later than the time prescribed in subsection (1). Section 55 extends that time where the office of the Board is closed to the day next following the day when the offices are open.

Subsection (4) provides that where an appeal is brought under the section and is not withdrawn, the Board shall, subject to subsection (5), determine the appeal by:

(a) confirming the decision or action of the Minister,
(b) determining the application for the licence as if the application had been made to the Board in the first instance, or
(c) in relation to the revocation or amendment of a licence, by substituting its decision on the matter for that of the Minister.

Subsection (5) provides that the Board shall not determine an appeal as provided in subsection (4)(a) except in circumstances referred to in section 48 (Power to summarily determine an appeal after service of notices under sections 46 or 47), 51 (Power to dismiss vexatious appeal) or 52 (Appeal against conditions). Subsection (5) appears to intend that the Board will only determine the appeal when it is confirming a decision or action of the Minister in the circumstances referred to in Section 48, in dismissing an appeal after serving notices under Sections 46 and 47, in dismissing a vexatious appeal under Section 51 and when the appeal is against conditions only under 52.

For Sections 46, 47, 48, 51 and 52 see below.

Subsection (6) provides that the determination under subsection (4)(b) or (c) of an appeal shall annul the decision or action of the Minister immediately the determination is made.

"(7) Section 7, with the necessary modifications, shall apply to and in relation to the determination under subsection (4) (b) of an application or so far as it relates to an amendment of a licence referred to in subsection (4) (c), as applies to and in relation to the determination by the Minister of such an application or the amendment of such a licence, as the case may be."

Section 41 of the F(A)A 1997 sets out the detailed provisions as to the making of appeals.

Section 42 gives the Board power to treat two appeals as one.

Section 43 deals with intercommunication between the Minister and the Board as the Board takes over from the Minister his file on the application for consideration by them in the appeal.

(4) Submissions and observations by other parties to appeal

Section 44(1) provides that the Board shall, as soon as practicable, after receiving a notice of appeal, give a copy (of that notice) to each other party to the appeal.

Subsection (2) provides that the Minister and each other party, other than the appellant, then have one month within which to make submissions or observations and any such received by the Board after the month has expired shall not be considered by it.

Subsection (3) provides that where there are no submissions or observations from a party within the month the Board may, without further notice to that party, determine the appeal.

Subsection (4) provides that without prejudice to section 46 (below), a party shall not be entitled to elaborate in writing on submissions or observations or make further submissions and observations in relation to the appeal, and any such elaborations or further submissions or observations shall not be considered by the Board.

(5) Submissions and observations by a person other than parties

Section 45(1) provides that a person who is not a party to an appeal may make submissions or observations in writing to the Board in relation to an appeal.

Subsection (2) places a time limit of one month on such submissions or observations, without prejudice to subsection (3), and submissions or observations after that date shall not be considered by the Board.

Subsection (3) excludes from the limits placed by subsection (2) submissions or observations by Member States of the EU arising from consultation in accordance with Council

Directive 85/337/EEC of 27 June 1985 on the assessment of certain private and public projects on the environment (O.J. L175, 5.7.1985, p. 40 as amended by O.J.L073, 14.3.1997, p. 5).

(6) Powers of the board in relation to appeals

POWER TO REQUEST SUBMISSIONS AND OBSERVATIONS

Section 46(1) of the F(A)A 1997 provides that where the Board is of the opinion that, in the particular circumstance of an appeal, it is appropriate in the interests of justice to request a party or other person, who has made submissions or observations, to make submissions or observations in relation to the matter it may, at its discretion, serve on the party or person a notice requesting submissions or observations within a period of not less than 14 or more than 28 days, notwithstanding sections 41(3), 44(4), 45(4) or 50(4), and stating that in default of receiving such submissions or observations the Board will proceed to determine the appeal.

Subsection (2) precludes elaboration by further submissions and observations as in section 44(4), *above.*

POWER TO REQUEST DOCUMENTS

Section 47(1)(a) of the F(A)A 1997 confers a similar power by notice to require the submission of documents within the same period with a similar threat to determine the appeal under section 48 in default of compliance.

Offence
Section 47(2) creates the offence of failing to comply with a requirement under subsection (1)(a).

POWER TO DETERMINE THE APPEAL AFTER NOTICE

Section 49 of the F(A)A 1997 provides that where a notice is served under section 46 or 47, the Board, at any time after the expiration of the period specified in the notice, may, having considered all submissions or observations or documents, particulars or other information, as the case may be, submitted by the person on whom the notice has been served, without further notice to that person, determine the appeal.

POWER TO DISMISS VEXATIOUS APPEALS

Section 51(1) of the F(A)A 1997 gives the Board an absolute discretion in dismissing appeals which in their opinion are vexatious, frivolous or without substance or foundation.

Subsection (2) provides that in so doing the Board may have regard to the matters to which, under section 61, it is required to have regard in determining an appeal. *See:* section 61, *above.*

POWER TO DECLARE APPEALS AND APPLICATIONS WITHDRAWN

Section 54(1) of the F(A)A 1997 provides that where the Board is of the opinion that an appeal, or an application for a licence to which the appeal relates, has been abandoned it may serve a notice stating that it is of that opinion and specifying a period of not less than 14 or more than 28 days, and requiring, within the period specified, a submission in writing as to why the appeal or application should not be regarded as having been withdrawn.

Subsection (2) provides that at any time after the expiration of the period specified and after considering any submissions the Board may declare:
(a) in a case where the notice refers to an application for an (*qv*) aquaculture licence, that the application shall be regarded as being withdrawn,
(b) in a case where the notice refers to an appeal, that the appeal has been withdrawn.

Subsection (3) provides that on such a declaration under subsection (2)(a):
(a) any appeal in relation to an application shall be regarded as having been withdrawn and shall not be considered by the Board, and
(b) notwithstanding any previous decision relating to the application, no aquaculture licence shall be granted as a result of the application.

(7) Withdrawal of appeal by appellant

Section 53 of the F(A)A 1997 provides for the withdrawal of an appeal by an appellant by notice in writing which may be done at any time before determination by the Board.

(8) Reference to high court on questions of law

Section 58 of the F(A)A 1997 provides that where a question of law arises on any appeal to the Board the question may be referred by the Board to the High Court for decision.

(9) Reports of inspections and oral hearings

Section 59 of the F(A)A 1997 provides that where, in connection with the performance by the Board of its functions, an inspection is carried out or an oral hearing is conducted the person carrying out the inspection or conducting the hearing shall make to the Board a written report on the inspection or hearing which, in the case of an appeal, shall include a recommendation in relation to the appeal and the Board must consider the report and recommendations before determining the appeal.

(10) Matters other than those raised by parties or other persons may be taken into account in determining appeals

Section 50(1) of the F(A)A 1997 provides that the Board, in determining an appeal, may take into account matters other than those raised by the parties or by any person who has made submissions or observations to the Board in accordance with section 45 (see *above*), if the matters are matters to which, under section 61 (see *below*), it may have regard.

Subsection (2) provides that the Board shall give notice in writing to each of the parties to the appeal and to persons who made submissions or observations, of the matters it proposes to take into account under subsection (1) and shall indicate in the notice:

(a) where it proposes to hold an oral hearing or to reopen an oral hearing, that written submissions may be made to the person conducting the hearing, or
(b) where there is to be no oral hearing that submissions in writing may be made to the Board within not less than 14 and not more than 28 days beginning on the date of service of the notice.

Subsection (3) provides that submissions received after the period specified will not be considered by the Board and subsection (4) precludes elaboration of submissions as in section 46(2).

(11) Licensing authority, matters to which it shall have regard in determining aquaculture licence applications and appeals

This important section, 61, is oddly located in Part IV of the F(A)A 1997 under the heading "miscellaneous". It is directed to the "(*qv*) licensing authority" and sets out the matters to which the licensing authority shall have regard in determining (*qv*) aquaculture licence applications and appeals.

Section 61 of the F(A)A 1997:

"The (*qv*) licensing authority, in considering an application for an (*qv*) aquaculture licence or an appeal against a decision on an application for a licence or a revocation or amendment of a licence, shall take account, as may be appropriate in the circumstances of the particular case, of –

(a) the suitability of the place or waters at or in which the (*qv*) aquaculture is or is proposed to be carried on for the activity in question,
(b) other beneficial uses, existing or potential, of the place or waters concerned,
(c) the particular statutory status, if any, (including the provisions of any development plan, within the meaning of the Local Government (Planning and Development) Act, 1963, as amended) of the place or waters,
(d) the likely effects of the proposed aquaculture [licence?], revocation or amendment on the economy of the area in which the aquaculture is or is proposed to be carried on,
(e) the likely ecological effects of the aquaculture or proposed aquaculture on wild fisheries, (*qv*) natural habitats and (*qv*) flora and (*qv*) fauna, and
(f) the effect or likely effect on the environment generally in the vicinity of the place or water on or in which that aquaculture is or is proposed to be carried on –
    (i) on the (*qv*) foreshore, or
    (ii) at any other place, if there is or would be no discharge of trade or sewage effluent within the meaning of, and requiring a licence under section 4 of the Local Government (Water Pollution) Act, 1977, and
(g) the effect or likely effect on the man-made environment of heritage value in the vicinity of the place or waters."

This section creates further confusion in relation to section 7 and 14. Section 7 provides for the granting of licences by the licensing authority (which includes the Minister) and section 14 provides for the granting of licences by the Minister only.

(12) Appeal against conditions only

Section 52 of the F(A)A 1997:

"(1) Where –
- (a) an appeal is brought against a decision to grant or amend an aquaculture licence,
- (b) the appeal relates only to a condition or conditions to which the decision provides the aquaculture licence shall be subject, and
- (c) the Board is satisfied, having regard to the nature of the condition or conditions, that the determination by the Board of the relevant application as if the application had been made to the Board in the first instance would not be warranted.

then, subject to compliance by the Board with subsection (2), it may, in its absolute discretion, deal with the appeal by reference only to the condition or conditions to which the appeal relates, and such other conditions, if any, as the Board considers relevant.

(2) In exercising its powers under subsection (1), apart from considering the condition or conditions to which the relevant appeal relates and other conditions, if any, which, in accordance with that subsection it considers relevant, the Board shall be restricted to considering the matters which under section 61 it would be restricted to considering were it determining the relevant application as if it had been made to it in the first instance."

(13) Appeal to High Court against making an instrument under section 11 of the F(C)A 1959

See: BYE-LAWS, PUBLICATION, DEPOSIT.

UNDER THE WLA 1976

(1) Appeal against seizure and detention

Section 77 of the WLA 1976:

"Any person who is aggrieved by a (*qv*)seizure and detention under the Act may appeal to a Justice of the District Court and in determining the appeal the Justice may -
- (a) if he is satisfied that the document or other thing was properly seized, confirm the seizure and detention, and
- (b) if he is not so satisfied, order the person who made the seizure to return to the person the document or other thing seized and order the Minister to pay to the person such compensation (if any), costs (if any) and expenses (if any) as he considers reasonable having regard to any loss, costs and expenses incurred by the person by reason of the seizure and detention."

See: Order 89, 7(1) to (5) District Court Rules, 1997.

(2) Appeal against a refusal to grant or renew a section 29 hunting licence

Section 29(7) of the WLA 1976:
"A person aggrieved by a refusal by the Minister to grant a licence under subsection (1) or (2) of this section or to renew a licence under subsection (6) of this section may appeal to a Justice of the District Court against the refusal, and in determining the appeal the Justice may:
- (a) confirm the refusal, or
- (b) allow the appeal, inform the Minister of his decision and direct the Minister as soon as may be to grant to the applicant or renew, as may be appropriate, a licence under this section."

See: Order 89, 2(1) and (2) District Court Rules 1997.

UNDER THE LG(WP)A 1977

(1) Appeals in relation to sections 4 and 7 under section 8

Section 8 of the LG(WP)A 1977, substituted by section 6 of the LG(WP)(A)A 1990:

"(1) (a) a person may, before the expiration of such period as may be prescribed, appeal to An (*qv*) Bord Pleanála in relation to:
- (i) the grant, refusal to grant or revocation of a licence under section 4,
- (ii) the attachment of conditions or additional conditions to such a licence, or
- (iii) the amendment or deletion of any condition attached to such a licence by a local authority."

Section 8(1)(b) sets out the events which determine the effective date the licence comes into operation.

Section 8(2) outlines the powers of An Bord Pleanála in relation to the appeal. It may allow or refuse the appeal and may give any direction consequent on its decision (including a direction that a specified condition be attached to the licence concerned or be amended or deleted) and a local authority shall comply with such direction.

(2) Appeals in relation to sections 16 and 17 – section 20

Section 20 of the LG(WP)A 1977, as substituted by section 15 of the LG(WP)(A)A 1990:

"(1) (a) The occupier of a premises from which a discharge to which a licence under section 16 relates is made may, before the expiration of such period as may be prescribed, appeal to An Bord Pleanála in relation to
(i) the revocation of the licence,
(ii) the attachment of conditions or additional conditions to the licence, or
(iii) the amendment or deletion of any conditions attached to the licence,
by a sanitary authority.
(b) A person whose application for a licence under section 16 has been refused by a sanitary authority may, before the expiration of such period as may be prescribed, appeal to An Bord Pleanála in relation to the refusal.
(c) An act of a sanitary authority referred to in paragraph (a) or (b) shall have effect -
(i) in case an appeal is not brought against it, upon the expiration of the period referred to in paragraph (a) or (b), as the case may be,
(ii) in case an appeal is brought against it and the final determination of the appeal does not set the act aside, upon and in accordance with such final determination,
(iii) in case an appeal is brought against it and the appeal is withdrawn, upon the withdrawal of the appeal.

(2) An Bord Pleanála, after consideration of an appeal under this section, shall, as it thinks proper, allow or refuse the appeal and may give any direction consequent on its decision that it considers appropriate to the sanitary authority concerned (including a direction that a specified condition be attached to the licence concerned or be amended or deleted) and a sanitary authority shall comply with such direction."

REGULATIONS: Local Government (Water Pollution) Regulations, 1978 (S.I. No. 108 of 1978) Part IV and Local Government (Water Pollution) Regulations, 1992 (S.I. No. 271 of 1992) Part IV. In the case of both paragraphs (a) and (b) above the prescribed period is one month.

These procedures will be extremely rare now that the Agency is fully operational in granting Integrated Pollution Control licences for "activities" under Part IV of the EPAA 1992. There is no provision in the EPAA 1992 for an appeal against a decision in relation to the granting or refusal to grant an Integrated Pollution Control licence under section 83 but section 85(5) which deals with the actual processing of applications for licences or reviews of licences allows an *(qv)* objection against the proposed determination by the Agency. Section 85(6) gives the Agency a discretion in deciding whether or not to have an oral hearing and the Agency alone decides on the objection.

An objection to the granting of waste licences under Part V of the Waste Management Act 1996 is dealt with in the same manner as in the case of an objection in respect of an IPC licence above.

UNDER THE APA 1987

Appeals in relation to a decision under sections 32 and 34

Section 34 of the APA 1987:

"(1) Any person may, at any time before the expiration of the prescribed period, appeal to *(qv)* An Bord Pleanála in relation to the granting or refusing of a licence under section 32, or to the granting of a revised licence under section 33."

Subsection (2) gives the Bord the same powers to determine the appeal as in the case of appeals under the LG(WP)A 1977, above.

Subsection (3) gives the Minister power to make regulations regarding matters of procedure in relation to an appeal under this section.

See: Air Pollution, 1987 (Licensing of Industrial Plant) Regulations, 1988 (S.I. No. 266 of 1988), Articles 19 to 36.

Subsection (4) describes the scope of these regulations and the Minister may, in drafting the regulations, modify or apply any provisions of the LG(P&D)A 1963 as he deems necessary.

Article 28 of the 1988 Licensing Regulations referred to above contains a modification to section 82(4), (5), (6) and (7) of the LG(P&D)A 1963 as set out in the Table to the Article.

The same comments apply in relation to these appeals with reference to Part IV of the EPAA 1992 as they do to LG(WP)A 1977 appeals.

UNDER NH 97 REGULATIONS

Appeals against decisions under regulation 16

See: DECISIONS BY THE MINISTER UNDER REG. 16.

UNDER WMA 1996

Revocation of waste collection permit

Section 34(9) of the WMA 1996 provides for an appeal to the District Court against the revocation of a waste collection permit.
See: WASTE COLLECTION PERMIT.

APPEALS TO THE MINISTER UNDER LG(P&D)A 1963

Environmental issues arising under LG(P&D)A 1963
This heading only relates to appeals where there is a direct environmental issue and does not attempt to deal with planning appeals overall.

(A) Appeals against the making of a conservation order under section 46 LG(P&D)A 1963 as amended. *See:* CONSERVATION ORDERS.

(B) Appeals against a notice requiring the removal or alteration of a hedge under section 44 LG(P&D)A 1963. *See:* HEDGES.

(C) Appeals against a tree preservation order under section 45. *See:* TREE PRESERVATION ORDER.

APPLICATION OF APA 1987 TO PREMISES BELONGING TO THE STATE
(APA 1987, s. 8)

Section 8 of the APA 1987:

"This Act shall apply to premises belonging to or in the occupation of the State."

APPROVAL, ENVIRONMENTAL
(EPAA 1992, s. 73)

Section 73 of the EPAA 1992, as amended by section 80 of the F(A)A 1997 deals with the approval by the Agency of aquaculture licences and leases, licences, permits and other authorisation.

Subsections (1) and (2) permit the Minister to make, with the consent of the Minister for the Marine, regulations relating to the grant or renewal of leases, licences, permits or other authorisations which the Minister for the Marine or the Aquaculture Appeals Board is authorised to grant specifying that such authorisations shall, for the purposes of *(qv)* environmental protection, be subject to the approval of the Agency with or without conditions. These conditions will be attached to the grant of authorisation by the Minister for the Marine.

Subsection (3) provides that the Minister and the Minister for the Marine are to consult regarding regulations specifying procedures.

Subsection (4), (5) and (6) provide that where there is any class of case not provided for in the regulations and the Minister for the Marine is of the opinion that it is in the public interest to do so he may, with the consent of the Minister, by order provide that the class of case, including such matters as may be prescribed under subsection (3), should, for the purposes of environmental protection, be subject to the approval of the Agency and with like consent he may by order revoke or amend such an order.

APPROVED BODY
(WMA 1996, s. 29)

"Approved body" is defined in the Waste Management (Packaging) Regulations 1997 (S.I. No. 242 of 1997) referred to in section 29 of the WMA 1996, as meaning a body corporate approved by the Minister in accordance with Article 15.

AQUACULTURE
(F(A)A 1997, s.3(1))

"means the culture or farming of any species of fish, aquatic invertebrate animal of whatever habitat or aquatic plant, or any aquatic form of food suitable for the nutrition of fish."

AQUACULTURE LICENCE
(F(A)A 1997, s.3(1)):

"means a licence granted under section 14 to engage in aquaculture or operations in relation to aquaculture, not being a (*qv*) trial licence."

AQUACULTURE LICENCE, INTERFERING WITH LICENSEE'S RIGHTS
(F(A)A 1997, s.20)

Offence
Section 20 of the F(A)A 1997:

"Except as permitted by or under this Act, if a person, by trespass, fishing or otherwise interferes with anything done or being done pursuant to a (*qv*) licence, and the interference is carried on without the permission of the licensee, then, notwithstanding the existence of any public right to fish, the person so interfering will be guilty of an offence."

AQUACULTURE LICENCES APPEALS BOARD
(F(A)A 1997, s.22(1))

Section 22(1) of the F(A)A 1997 established the Aquaculture Licences Appeals Board, 'the Board', to perform the functions assigned to it under the Act.

The 17th of June 1998 was appointed as the established day by virtue of Aquaculture Licences Appeals Board (Establishment) Order 1998 (S.I. No. 204 of 1998).

Chapter I of Part III of the F(A)A 1997 contains provisions dealing with the composition, appointment and remuneration of the Board. These provisions correspond to similar sections dealing with the Environmental Protection Agency contained in Part III of the EPAA 1992.

Note that the Minister for the Marine and Natural Resources now has power under the Fisheries Acts, 1959-198 and the Foreshore Acts, 1933-1998 insofar as these relate to aquaculture. *See:* Marine and Natural resources (Delegation of Ministerial Functions) Order, 2000 (S.I. No. 14 of 2000).

Section 23(3) of the F(A)A 1997 allows the Minister to prescribe organisations representative of certain classes of organisations named at section 23(3)*(a)*, *(b)*, *(c)*, *(d)*, *(e)* and *(f)* and the Fisheries (Amendment) Act, 1997 (Section 23) Regulations, 1998 (S.I. No. 84 of 1998) which came into operation on 31st March 1998 and contain a list of prescribed organisations for the purposes of the section.

The Fisheries (Amendment) Act 1997 (Section 33) Regulations 1998 (S.I. No. 269 of 1998) provide for declarations of interests by a wide range of people including the chairperson and officers of the Aquaculture Licences Appeals Board and others having an interest.

FUNCTIONS OF THE BOARD

Section 40(1) of the F(A)A 1997 provides for appeals to the Board against the decision in relation to an application for an *(qv)* aquaculture licence or the revocation or amendment of an aquaculture licence by the Minister.
Subsection (5) provides for the determination by the Board of such appeals.

Section 22(2) of the F(A)A 1997 provides that the provisions of the Schedule to the Act shall have effect in relation to the Board.

DUTY AND OBJECTIVES OF BOARD

Section 56 of the F(A)A 1997:

"(1)The Board shall, as far as practicable, ensure that appeals are dealt with and determined expeditiously and that all steps are taken to avoid unnecessary delays.

(2) Without limiting the generality of subsection (1) but subject to subsections (3) and (4), the Board shall endeavour to ensure that every appeal is determined within –
(a) a period of four months beginning on the date of the receipt by the Board of the notice of appeal, or
(b) such other period as the Minister may prescribe, either generally or in respect of a particular class or classes of appeals.

(3) Where it appears to the Board that it would not be possible or appropriate, because of the particular circumstances of an appeal, to determine an appeal within the period required by subsection (2) it shall, by notice in writing served on the parties to the appeal and all persons who made submissions or observations to the Board in accordance with section 45 before the expiration of that period, inform those parties and persons of the reasons why the appeal would not be determined within that period and shall specify the date before which, or the period within which, the Board intends

that the appeal shall be determined.

(4) Where a notice has been served under subsection (3), the Board shall endeavour to ensure that the appeal is determined before the date, or within the period, specified in the notice.

(5) The Minister may make regulations –
(a) providing that subsection (2) shall not have effect for such period as is specified in the regulations, or
(b) varying a period mentioned in that subsection either generally or in respect of a particular class or classes of appeals,
where it appears to the Minister to be necessary, because of exceptional circumstances, to do so and, for so long as such regulations are in force, this section shall be construed and have effect accordingly.

(6) The Board shall, at such intervals as it thinks fit or the Minister may direct, conduct reviews of its organisation and of the systems and procedures used by it in relation to appeals.

(7) Where the Minister gives a direction under subsection (6), the Board shall report to the Minister the results of the review and shall comply with any direction which the Minister may, after consultation with the Board on those results, give in relation to all or any of the matters which are the subject of the review.

(8) The Board may, on its own initiative or at the request of the Minister, make submissions or recommendations to the Minister on any matter relating to its functions or to licensing (including trial licensing) policy.

(9) The Minister may consult with the Board on any matter relating to the performance of –
(a) the functions of the Board, or
(b) the functions in relation to aquaculture assigned to the Minister by or under the Fisheries Acts, 1959 to 1995 as amended by this Act, or by any order, regulation or other instrument under those Acts or this Act."

Part III of Chapter III of the F(A)A 1997 concerns the hearing of appeals by the Board.

AQUACULTURE POLICY
(F(A)A 1997, s. 62(1))

Section 62(1) of the F(A)A 1997 entitles the Minister from time to time to issue such general policy directives in relation to aquaculture as he or she considers necessary and the (*qv*) licensing authority shall have regard to these directives when performing its functions.

Subsection (2) prohibits the Minister from exercising any power or control under the section in a particular case which is being dealt with by the (*qv*) Board or its officer to whom functions have been delegated under section 21(1).

Subsection (3) deals with the procedures which must be adopted by the Minister in giving a directive and subsection (4) empowers the Minister to amend or revoke a directive.

AQUIFER
(LG(WP)A 1977, s.1(1))

"means any stratum or combination of strata that stores or transmits ground water."

This definition was substituted by section 2 of the LG(QP)(A)A 1990.

ARBITRATOR
(FA 1980, s.44)

Under FA 1980

An arbitrator (who must be a barrister of not less than 7 years standing) appointed pursuant to **section 44(1) of the FA 1980** has two functions.

Firstly, under section 44(2), he may hear and determine appeals under sections 37 and 39 of the FA 1980 or an appeal by virtue of section 38(3) of that Act. These sections deal with the (*qv*) acquisition of various interests in land by the Minister.

Secondly, under section 44(3), he is empowered to perform functions assigned to the arbitrator by section 5(2)(b) of the FA 1980 which entitles the Minister to amend orders under sections 37, 38 or 39 of the said Act which relate to acquisitions of land as aforesaid.

Under NH 97 Regulations

Under Regulations 16(4)(b) of the European Communities (Natural Habitats) Regulations 1997 (S.I. No. 94 of 1997) the Minister may appoint an arbitrator (being a barrister or solicitor of not less than 7 years standing) to determine an appeal brought against a refusal to give consent to an (*qv*) operation or activity under the Regulation.

ARTS, HERITAGE, GAELTACHT AND THE ISLANDS, MINISTER AND DEPARTMENT OF
(Heritage Act 1995)

This Department was originally known as Arts, Culture and the Gaeltacht. Section 24 of the Heritage Act, 1995 clearly defines its environmental relationship with the (*qv*) Commissioners of Public Works in Ireland.

By virtue of section 24, this Department is now the Government Department primarily responsible for the conservation of (*qv*) wildlife under the WLA 1976.
See: COMMISSIONERS, THE; COMMISSIONERS OF PUBLIC WORKS IN IRELAND.

ASSAULT
(F(C)A 1959/F(A)A 1994)

The Fisheries Acts are unique in environmental law in providing specific offences of assault on the persons of the (*qv*) authorised persons/authorised officers/water keepers appointed under those Acts. This means that these protection officers are not dependent on the Garda Síochána to prosecute but can initiate their own prosecutions. It is also indicative of the hazardous nature of their duties.

(F(C)A 1959, s.308)

Offence
Section 308 of the F(C)A 1959:

"If any person assaults or (*qv*) obstructs any person exercising any power conferred on him by this Part, such first mentioned person shall be guilty of an offence under this section."

(Note that the maximum penalty prescribed under this section has been increased. *See:* FINES AND IMPRISONMENT (IMPOSITION OF)).

The Part referred to supra is Part XVIII of the F(C)A 1959 which deals with powers of enforcement of the Act by these persons. *See:* (1) AUTHORISED PERSONS; (2) ENTRY AND SEARCH.

(F(A)A 1994, s.15)

Offence
Section 15 of the F(A)A 1994:

"(1) In this section 'officer to whom this section applies' means an officer of the Minister, a sea fisheries protection officer, an (*qv*) authorised person or an authorised officer as defined for the purposes of any section of the Principal Act.

(2) Any person who assaults an officer to whom this section applies in the exercise of any power conferred on that officer by any provisions of the Principal Act shall be guilty of an offence."

As to the penalty imposed under this provision, *see:* FINES AND PENALTIES.

ASSESSMENT OF IMPLICATIONS FOR CONSERVATION OBJECTIVES OF CERTAIN PUBLIC BODIES
(NH 97)

The main objectives of the (*qv*) Habitats Directive (92/435/EEC of May 21, 1992 on the conservation of natural habitats and of wild fauna and flora (O.J. L206, July 22, 92 p. 7) and the NH 97 Regulations (S.I. No. 94 of 1997), which implement the Directive in Ireland, is the identification, conservation, protection and management of (*qv*) European sites.

Regulations 27 to 32 of the NH 97 Regulations protect by ensuring that development which, although not directly connected with a European site or necessary to its management, could not, either individually or in combination with other development, have a significant adverse effect on the site.

To achieve some degree of control over development under this heading the Regulations require that the body having obligations in relation to the carrying out of the development, or approving or directing it in some way, as part of their functions, carry out an assessment of the implications of the site in view of its conservation objectives. If they receive a negative assessment, that there will be no significant adverse effect, then the development can be permitted to proceed. If the assessment is positive then the development cannot proceed unless there are imperative reasons of overriding public interest.

The assessment is carried out by means of an (*qv*) environmental impact assessment (EIS).

Regulations 27–32 of the NH 97 Regulations (S.I. No. 94 of 1997) deal with the obligations of local authorities, an Bord Pleanála, the Minister for the Environment, the (*qv*) Environmental Protection Agency and certain Government Departments to undertake assessments in relation to their functions.

Regulation 27, which concerns the obligations of local authorities when granting planning permission and an Bord Pleanála when considering an appeal on an application for planning permission, provides:

"(1) A local authority when duly considering an application for planning permission, or the (*qv*) Board when duly considering an appeal on an application for planning permission, in respect of a proposed (*qv*) development that is not directly connected with, or necessary to the management of, a (*qv*) European site but likely to have a significant effect thereon either individually or in combination with other developments, shall ensure that an appropriate assessment of the implications for the site in view of the site's conservation objectives is undertaken.

(2) An environmental impact assessment in respect of a proposed development prepared in accordance with a requirement of or under the Local Government (Planning and Development) Regulations, 1994 (S.I. No. 86 of 1994), shall be an appropriate assessment for the purposes of paragraph (1).

(3) Notwithstanding section 26 of the Local Government (Planning and Development) Act, 1963, and subject to paragraphs (4),(5) and (6) a local authority or the Board, as the case may be, shall, having regard to the conclusions of the assessment to which paragraph (1) relates, decide to grant permission for the proposed development only after having ascertained that it will not adversely affect the integrity of the European site concerned.

(4) In considering whether a development will adversely affect the integrity of the European site concerned, the local authority or the Board, as the case may be, shall have regard to the manner in which it is proposed to be carried out or to any conditions or restrictions subject to which they propose that the permission should be given.

(5) A local authority or the Board, as the case may be, may, notwithstanding a negative assessment and in the absence of alternative solutions, decide to grant planning permission for a proposed development where such development has to be carried out for imperative reasons of overriding public interest.

(6) (a) Subject to sub paragraph (b), imperative reasons of overriding public interest shall include reasons of a social or economic nature;
(b) if the site concerned hosts a (*qv*) priority natural habitat type or a *(qv)* priority species the only considerations of overriding public interest shall be:
(i) those relating to human health or public safety, or
(ii) the beneficial consequences of primary importance for the environment, or
(iii) further to an opinion from the Commission to other imperative reasons of overriding public interest."

Paragraph (7) provides that a request for an opinion under (6)(a)(iii) as to whether reasons are to be considered imperative reasons of overriding public interest, should be referred to the Minister for the Environment who will communicate with the Commission and by notice convey the Commission's opinion to the local authority or the Board.

Paragraph (8) provides that a decision to proceed will not be taken by the local authority or the Board until the Commissions's opinion has been communicated to them.

Paragraphs (9) and (10) provide that as section 2(2) of the LG (P&D)A 1992, and section 26(4) of the LG(P&D)A 1963, place constraints on the time allowed the Board to consider an appeal, in assessing the appropriate period under either section, the period beginning on the day the matter is referred by the Board to the Minister for the Environment (under Regulation 27(7)) and ending on the day the Board receive notice of the opinion of the Commission shall not be included which means that the time constraints are suspended during that period.

"(11) Where immediately before the making of these Regulations a planning authority or the Board, as the case may be, have granted permission in respect of a development within a (*qv*) European site and such development is considered by the Minister to have a significant adverse effect on the ecological features of the site that Minister may request the local authority or the Board to review the permission in accordance with the provisions of this Regulation and the local authority or the Board shall affirm, modify or revoke such permission depending on the results of the review."

Regulation 28, which deals with the obligation of the Minister for the Environment in relation to local authority development where an EIS is required, provides:

"(1) Where a proposed development in respect of which an application for the certification of the Minister for the Environment has been made in accordance with Article 123 of the Local Government (Planning and Development) Regulations, 1994 is neither directly connected with nor necessary to the management of a (*qv*) European site but likely to have a significant effect thereon either individually or in combination with other developments, the Minister for the Environment shall ensure that an appropriate assessment of the implications for the site in view of the sites conservation objectives is undertaken.

(2) An environmental impact assessment in respect of the proposed development referred to in paragraph (1) shall be an appropriate assessment for the purposes of this Regulation.

(3) The Minister for the Environment shall, having regard to the conclusions of the assessment undertaken under paragraph (1), agree to the proposed development only after having ascertained that it will not adversely affect the integrity of the European site concerned.

(4) In considering whether the proposed development will the adversely affect the integrity of the European site concerned, the Minister for the Environment shall have regard to the manner in which the proposed development is to be carried out or to any conditions or restrictions subject to which the proposed development is being carried out."

Paragraphs (5) and (6) provide that notwithstanding a negative assessment and where he is satisfied there are no alternative solutions, the Minister may decide to agree to the development for imperative reasons of overriding public interest which shall include reasons of a social or economic nature but if the site concerned hosts a (*qv*) priority natural habitat type or a (*qv*) priority species the only consideration of overriding public interest shall be:

(i) those relating to public health or safety,
(ii) beneficial consequences of primary importance for the environment, or
(iii) further to an opinion from the Commission to other imperative reasons of overriding public interest.

Regulation 29, which deals with the obligations of local authorities in carrying out development covered by Part X of the Local Government (Planning and Development) Regulations 1994, provides:

"(1) Subject to paragraphs (3) and (4) where a proposed development to which Part X of the Local Government (Planning and Development) Regulations, 1994, applies is neither directly connected with nor necessary to the management of a European site but likely to have a significant effect thereon, either individually or in combination with other developments, the local authority shall ensure that an appropriate assessment of the implications for the site in view of the site's conservation objectives is undertaken.

(2) The local authority, having regard to the conclusions of the assessment undertaken under paragraph (1), shall undertake the proposed development only after having ascertained that it will not adversely affect the integrity of the European site concerned.

(3) In considering whether the proposed development will adversely affect the European site concerned, the local authority, shall have regard to the manner in which it is proposed to carry out the proposed development or to any conditions or restrictions subject to which the proposed development is being carried out."

Paragraphs (4) and (5) provide that notwithstanding a negative assessment and where they are satisfied that there are no alternative solutions, the local authority may decide to agree to the development for imperative reasons of overriding public interest which shall include reasons of a social or economic nature but if the site concerned hosts a (*qv*) priority natural habitat type or a (*qv*) priority species the only considerations of overriding public interest shall be:

(i) those relating to public health or safety,
(ii) beneficial consequences of primary importance for the environment, or
(iii) further to an opinion from the (*qv*) Commission to other imperative reasons of overriding public interest.

"(6) Where a local authority decides to seek

an opinion from the Commission under paragraph (5) the provisions of paragraphs (7) and (8) of Regulation 27 will apply."

Regulation 30, which deals with the obligations of the Minister for the Environment in relation to road development by a road authority, provides:

"(1) Where a proposed road development in respect of which an application for the approval of the Minister for the Environment has been made in accordance with section 51 of the Roads Act, 1993, is neither directly connected with nor necessary to the management of a (*qv*) European site but likely to have a significant effect thereon either individually or in combination with other developments, the Minister for the Environment shall ensure that an appropriate assessment of the implications for the site in view of the site's conservation projectives is undertaken.

(2) An environmental impact assessment as required under section 51(2) of the Roads Act, 1993, in respect of a proposed road development referred to at paragraph (1) shall be an appropriate assessment for the purposes of this Regulation.

(3) The Minister for the Environment shall, having regard to the conclusions of the assessment undertaken under paragraph (1), agree to the proposed road development only after having ascertained that it will not adversely affect the integrity of the European site concerned.

(4) In considering whether the proposed road development will adversely affect the European site concerned, the Minister for the Environment shall have regard to the manner in which the proposed development is being carried out or to any conditions or restrictions subject to which the approval is given."

Paragraphs (5) and (6) provide that notwithstanding a negative assessment and where he is satisfied there are no alternative solutions, the Minister may decide to agree to the development for imperative reasons of overriding public interest which shall include reasons of a social and economic nature but if the site concerned hosts a (*qv*) priority natural habitat type or a (*qv*) priority species the only consideration of overriding public interest shall be:

(i) those relating to public health or safety,
(ii) beneficial consequences of primary importance for the environment, or
(iii) further to an opinion from the (*qv*) Commission to other imperative reasons of overriding public interest.

Regulation 31, which deals with requirements in relation to the discharge by certain Ministers of Government of their functions under certain enactments, provides:

"(1) Where an (*qv*) operation or activity to which any of the enactments set out in Part I of the Second Schedule applies is neither directly connected with nor necessary to the management of a (*qv*) European site but likely to have a significant effect thereon, either individually or in combination with other operations or activities, and such operation or activity is to be undertaken by or requires the concurrence, consent or approval (however expressed in the enactment) of any Minister of the Government, then that Minister shall ensure that an appropriate assessment of the implications for the site in view of the site's conservation objectives is undertaken."

(2) An environmental impact assessment in respect of an operation or activity referred to in paragraph (1), shall be an appropriate assessment for the purposes of this Regulation.

(3) A Minister of the Government in carrying out powers and functions under any of the enactments set out in Part I of the Second Schedule shall undertake, concur, consent or approve of the operation or activity, having regard to the conclusions of the assessment undertaken under paragraph (1), only after having ascertained that the operation or activity will not adversely affect the integrity of the site concerned.

(4) In considering whether an operation or activity will adversely affect the integrity of the site, a Minister of the Government shall have regard to the manner in which it is proposed to be carried out or to any conditions or restrictions subject to which that Minister proposes that the operation or activity is to be carried out."

Paragraphs (5) and (6) provide that notwithstanding a negative assessment and where he is satisfied there is no alternative solution, the Minister may undertake, or so concur, consent or approve of, an operation or activity where it has to be carried out for imperative reasons of overriding public interest which shall include reasons of a social or economic nature but if the site concerned hosts a (*qv*) priority natural habitat type or a (*qv*) priority species the only considerations of overriding public interest shall be:

(i) those relating to public health or safety,
(ii) beneficial consequences of primary importance for the environment, or
(iii) further to an opinion from the (*qv*) Commission to other imperative reasons of overriding public interest.

"(7) Before exercising any function to which this Regulation relates under any of the enactments set out in Part I of the Second Schedule, the Minister of the Government concerned shall consult the Minister."

Regulations 32, which deals with the obligations of local authorities, an Bord Pleanála or the Environmental Protection Agency in the discharge of their powers and functions under certain enactments, provides:

"(1) where an (*qv*) operation or activity or an (*qv*) established activity to which an application for a licence or a revised licence or the review of a licence or revised licence, as appropriate, under any of the enactments set out in Part II of the Second Schedule applies is neither directly connected with nor necessary to the management of a (*qv*) European site but likely to have a significant effect thereon either individually or in combination with other operations or activities or established activities a local authority, the (*qv*) Board or the (*qv*) Environmental Protection Agency shall ensure that an appropriate assessment of the environmental implications for the site in view of the site's conservation objectives is undertaken."

Note that although the definition of "operation or activity" appears in the NH 97 Regulations, the definition of "established activity" is peculiar to the EPAA 1992 and the phrase is only defined in that Act.

Regulations 31(2), (3), (4) (5) and (6) correspond to Regulation 30(2), (3), (4), (5) and (6) by substituting "local authority, the Board or the EPA" for "the Minister for the Environment", "decide to grant a licence" for "decide to agree" and by omitting the reference to the Roads Act 1933 in paragraph (2).

"(7) Where a local authority or the Environmental Protection Agency decide to seek an opinion from the Commission under paragraph (6), the provisions of paragraphs (7) and (8) of Regulation 27 shall apply as if the reference to the Board were a reference to the Environmental Protection Agency.

(8) Notwithstanding subsection 910) of section 85 of the Environmental Protection Agency Act, 1992 the appropriate period referred to in that subsection shall not, in a case in which a request is made to the Minister for the Environment under paragraph (6), include the period beginning on the day the matter is referred by the Environmental Protection Agency to the Minister for the Environment under that paragraph and ending on the day of receipt by the Environmental Protection Agency of notice by the Minister for the Environment of an opinion by the Commission on the matter."

(Section 85(10) of the EPAA 1992 gives and "appropriate period" of 28 days or 21 days for notification under subsection (2) of the manner of determination of an application. *See:* LICENCES (5) PROCESSING OF APPLICATIONS).

COMPENSATORY MEASURES

Regulation 33 deals with compensatory measures to be taken to ensure that the overall coherence of (*qv*) Natura 2000 is protected where an (*qv*) operation or activity is permitted despite a negative assessment. The Regulations are silent as to what these compensatory measures might be. The Regulation is taken directly from Article 6 of the (*qv*) Habitats Directive omitting only the last sentence which reads: "It shall inform the Commission of the compensatory measures adopted.".

Regulation 33 of the NH 97 Regulations:

"Where in accordance with Regulations 27(5), 28(5), 29(4), 30(5), 31(5) or 32(5) an (*qv*) operation or activity is agreed to, notwithstanding a negative assessment of the implications for a (*qv*) European site, the Minister shall ensure that the necessary compensatory measures are taken to ensure that the overall coherence of (*qv*) Natura 2000 is protected."

The compensation referred to in this Regulation is not necessarily financial compensation. It is not the land owner carrying out the "operation or activity" who needs to be compensated as he has got the green light to proceed. It is the imbalance of Natura 2000, the "coherent European ecological network of special areas of conservation", which requires to be compensated.

ASSESSMENT,
REG. 15 AND EFFECT ON
SUBSISTING LICENCES
(NH 97)

Regulation 15 of the NH 97 Regulations:

"(1) Where it appears to the Minister that an application for consent under paragraph (2)(a) of Regulation 14 relates to an (*qv*) operation or activity which:
(a) is neither directly connected with nor necessary to the management of the site, but
(b) is likely to have a significant effect on the site, either alone or in combination with other operations or activities,
The Minister shall cause an assessment to be made of the implication-cation for the site in view of that site's conservation objectives.

(2) (a) Where immediately before the making of these Regulations there is any subsisting licence, approval, consent or other authorisation granted or issued pursuant to any of the enactments set out in the Second Schedule to these Regulations pursuant to which licence, approval, consent or other authorisation an operation or activity has been under taken or is proposed to be undertaken and which is considered by the Minister to be having or likely to have a significant adverse effect on the ecological features of the site proposed for designation as a (*qv*) special area of conservation, then the Minister may request the relevant Minister of the Government responsible for granting or issuing the licence, approval, consent or other authorisation or for supervising the person to whom it was granted or issued, to have an assessment made of the implications for that site in view of the site's conservation objectives and having regard to such assessment to affirm, modify or revoke such licence, approval, consent or other authorisation.
(b) Without prejudice to the generality of sub paragraph (a), where the Minister for the Marine is requested by the Minister, pursuant to sub paragraph (a), to have an assessment made of the implications for a site proposed for designation as a special area of conservation of an operation or activity authorised by a lease under section 2, or a licence under section 3, of the Foreshore Act, 1933, the Minister for the Marine may, having regard to such assessment and notwithstanding any provision of the Foreshore Acts, 1933 to 1992, affirm, modify or revoke such lease or licence."

The outcome of an assessment under this heading leads to a decision by the Minister on whether or not he will give his consent to the operation or activity.

See: (1) DECISIONS; (2) SCHEDULES HERETO, NH 97 SCHEDULES.

ASSISTANCE BY AGENCY
TO LOCAL AUTHORITIES
(EPAA 1992, s.57)

Section 57 of the EPAA 1992 provides for the provision of support and assistance by the Agency to local authorities for the purpose of (*qv*) environmental protection in the performance of any of its functions.

ATTEMPTS, MISC. OFFENCES
UNDER WLA 1976
(WLA 1976, s.69)

Section 69 of the WLA 1976 provides in this section for certain offences which affect wildlife as follows:

Offences
(1) that a person who attempts to commit, or who aids, abets, counsels or procures the commission or who solicits or incites any other person to commit an offence under the Act is guilty of an offence under the section.

(2) that any person who, whether by act or omission, contravenes or fails to comply with regulations under this Act shall be guilty of an offence.

(3) that any person who –
   (a) refuses or fails to give correct name and address on demand under sections 72 or 73 of the Wildlife Act 1976 is guilty of an offence,
   (b) without reasonable excuse fails to comply with a requirement by a member of an Garda Síochána or an authorised person made under sections 72 or 73 of the Act or by act or omission impedes or obstructs such a member or person shall be guilty of an offence and if, in the case of a continuing offence, the impediment or obstruction is continued after conviction, shall be guilty of a further offence.

(4) that a person who, in purported compliance with any obligation to give information to which he is subject under this Act, gives any information which he knows to be false in a material particular or recklessly gives information which is so false shall be guilty of an offence.

(5) that any person who conceals from a person lawfully exercising a power under section 72 or 73 of this Act any specimen of flora or fauna or any part or product of such specimen or any part or product of such specimen or any thing which is a thing mentioned in section 73(1) of this Act shall be guilty of an offence.

(6) Any person who contravenes a condition attached to a licence granted by the Minister under this Act shall be guilty of an offence.

(7) Any person who, for the purpose of obtaining, whether for himself or another, the grant or renewal of a licence or permission under this Act –
   (a) makes any statement or gives information which he knows to be false in a material particular or recklessly gives information which is so false, or
   (b) produces or otherwise makes use of any book, record or other document which to his knowledge contains any statement or information which he knows to be false in a material particular, shall be guilty of an offence."

As to the penalty imposed under this provision, *see:* FINES AND PENALTIES.

AUDIT, ENVIRONMENTAL
(EPAA 1992, s.74)

Section 74 of the EPAA 1992:

"(1) In this section "environmental audit" means in relation to any process, development or operation, a systematic, documented and objective periodic assessment of the organisational structure, management systems, processes and equipment pertaining to, or incidental to, that process, development or operation, for the purposes of environmental protection and, in particular for the purposes of –
   (a) facilitating management control of practices which may have an impact on environmental protection,
   (b) assessing compliance with enactments related to environmental protection and with such environmental conditions as may be attached to any licence or permit granted or issued in connection with the aforesaid process, development or operation, and
   (c) minimising the impact of the process, development or operation on the environment.

(2) (a) The Agency may promote the carrying out of environmental audits.
   (b) The Agency may, and shall at the request of the Minister, prepare and publish guidelines on the carrying out of environmental audits, and such guidelines may relate to all processes, developments or operations or to any particular class of process, development or operation or to processes, developments or operations in particular areas or classes of areas.

(3) Without prejudice to the generality of subsection (1), guidelines may relate to -
   (a) the aims of an environmental audit,
   (b) the expertise to be included in an environmental audit team,
   (c) the criteria to be considered and procedures to be followed in carrying out an environmental audit.

(4) For the purposes of promoting the carrying out of environmental audits, the Agency may, in relation to any process, development or operation or classes of processes, developments or operations –

(a) provide such assistance and support, on such terms and conditions as may be agreed with any person or body, for the purposes of developing and carrying out environmental audits or pilot or demonstration projects, and
(b) organise and promote, or assist in organising and promoting, conferences, seminars, lectures, demonstrations, training courses or publications."

AUTHORISED FIREPLACE
(APA 1987, s. 7(1))

"means a fireplace declared to be an authorised fireplace by the Minister in regulations under section 40(2)."
See: Air Pollution Act 1987 (Authorised Fireplace) Regulations 1988, (S.I. No. 297 of 1988) which were revoked by Air Pollution Act 1987 (Authorised Fireplace) (Revocation) Regulations 1989 (S.I. No. 293 of 1989) which approved a solid fuel appliance specified in the Special Control Area (Ballyfermot) Order 1989.

AUTHORISED FUEL
(APA 1987, s.7(1))

"means a fuel declared to be an authorised fuel by the Minister in regulations under section 40 (3)."

See: Air Pollution Act 1987 (Authorised Fuel) Regulations 1988, (S.I. No. 298 of 1988).

AUTHORISED PERSONS/AUTHORISED OFFICERS AND WATERKEEPERS
(F(C)A 1959/LG(WP)A 1977/APA 1987/ EPAA 1992/WMA 1996/WLA 1976/NH 97)

The titles of the persons who enforce environmental legislation given in this title vary from Statute to Statute.

As to their powers, *see:* ENTRY AND SEARCH.

Their appointment and status arise under the following legislation:

Under the F(C)A 1959

The three categories of persons who may enforce powers under the F(C)A 1959, as amended, are a private water keeper, an authorised person and an authorised officer.

(1) A PRIVATE WATER KEEPER

Section 294(1) of the F(C)A 1959 allows certain persons, being persons interested in the preservation of fish of any river or lake, persons who have united into a society for the preservation of any fishery in any river or lake, and the owners of any such fishery or a salmon fishery on the sea coast to appoint in writing a private water keeper.

Section 294(2A) (inserted by section 17 F(A)A 1991) provides for the issue by the appropriate regional board of a certificate of suitability of appointment prior to confirmation by the District Court and that the appointment shall be a for a period of not more than 5 years. (The new subsection is silent on criteria for "suitability" so regional boards are compelled to issue certificates whether or not they regard the applicant as suitable for appointment).

The original appointment, under section 294 (1), is confirmed by the District Court under subsection (3).

Section 293 of the F(C)A 1959 provides:

"(1) The powers conferred by this Part on a private water keeper shall be exercisable only for the protection of the fisheries specified in his instrument of appointment."

The limitation of powers of private waterkeepers under subsection (1) means their powers are not as extensive as the powers of members or officers of a regional board or other persons appointed under Part XVIII by such a board as under section 293(2)*(a)*, substituted by section 11(5) of the FA 1980, the powers of those members or officers cover the protection of the entire fishery district of the board who makes the appointment or of which the person is a member.

Subsection (2) was further amended by section 11(5) of the FA 1980. The amended subsections, (2)*(b)* and *(c)*, deal with two or more boards agreeing to appoint officers to exercise powers in each of their regions and formal proof of such an agreement.

By virtue of section 282 of the F(C)A 1959, substituted by section 11(5) of the FA 1980, a water keeper with others, enjoys the status of an "authorised person" for the purposes of Part XVIII of the F(C)A 1959 as described hereunder.

(2) AN AUTHORISED PERSON

Section 292 of the F(C)A 1959, as amended by section 11(5) of the FA 1980, provides:

"In this Part: 'authorised person' means, except where the context otherwise requires, any person being:
(a) an officer of the Minister or other per-

son appointed in writing by the Minister to be an authorised person for the purposes of this Part,
(b) an officer of the (*qv*) Central Board appointed in writing by that Board to be an authorised person for the said purposes,
(c) an officer of a (*qv*) regional Board or other person appointed in writing by that board to be an authorised person for the said purposes, and
(d) a private water keeper;
'private water keeper' means a water keeper appointed under section 294."

(3) AN AUTHORISED OFFICER

The following are "authorised officers" under section 301(1) of the F(C)A 1959 (as amended):
(a) a member of the Garda Síochána,
(b) any person, whether or not he is a member of the regional board, appointed in writing by a regional board to be an authorised officer for the purposes of the section,
(c) an officer of the Minister, authorised in writing by the Minister to be an authorised officer for the purposes of the section, and
(d) an officer or servant of the Electricity Supply Board authorised in writing by the Minister to be an authorised officer for the purposes of the section.

Section 301 was amended by section 25 of the F(A)A 1962, sections 50 and 53 of the FA 1980 and section 11(5) FA 1980.

Section 301 (2) to (5) inclusive give the powers and statutory responsibilities of an authorised officer.

Section 301(6) exonerates an authorised officer from liability for loss or damage occasioned by him in the course of the exercise of his powers under the section unless caused wantonly or maliciously.

Offences
Section 301(7) creates the offences of obstructing or impeding an authorised officer in the exercise of his powers or refusing to give his own name and address or the name and address of any other person (so far as known to him) when lawfully demanded under the section.
(Note that the maximum penalty prescribed under this section has been increased. *See:* FINES AND IMPRISONMENT (IMPOSITION OF)).

AUTHORISED OFFICERS UNDER F(A)A 1999
Section 24 of the F(A)A 1999 creates, by way of definition, another species of "authorised officer" quite separate from that created by section 301 of the F(C)A 1959 for the purposes of the 1999 Act appointed either by the Minister or by a *(qv)*regional board under the section to be an authorised officer for the purposes of the section. The Fisheries 9Amendment Act, 1999 (save for section 23) came into force on 20 December 1999 by virtue of the Fisheries (Amendment) Act, 1999 (Commencement) Order, 1999 (S.I. No. 419 of 1999).

It is difficult to understand why there should be a need for a new species of authorised officer. This means fishery officers will have to carry an extra warrant. The innovatory measure in the 1999 Act requiring extra policing is the Minister's new power to make regulations under section 24 in relation to the new wild salmon and sea trout tagging scheme.
See: SALMON, WILD SALMON AND SEA TROUT TAGGING SCHEME.

Under the LG(WP)A 1977

Section 28(9) of the LG(WP)A 1977 provides that in this section:
"'authorised person' means a person appointed by a local authority, a sanitary authority, the Minister, the Minister for Fisheries or a (*qv*) board of conservators to be an authorised person for the purposes of this Act."
"board of conservators" is now "any regional fisheries board" by virtue of the FA 1980, but this amendment does not appear to have been made.

Section 28 (1) to (7) inclusive give the powers and statutory obligations of an authorised officer appointed under the section.

Subsection (8) was repealed by section 30 of the LG(WP)(A)A 1990.

This function to appoint authorised persons under section 28 of the LG(WP)A 1977 applies to the Agency by virtue of Article 4 of the Environmental Protection Agency (Extension of Powers) Order 1996 (S.I. No. 126 of 1996). *See:* EXTENSION OF POWERS.

Under the APA 1987

Section 7(1) of the APA 1987 provides that for the purposes of that Act:
"'authorised person' means a person who is:
(a) appointed in writing by a local authority to be an authorised person for the purposes of this Act, or
(b) appointed in writing to be an autho-

rised person pursuant to regulations under this Act by a person specified in those regulations."

This function, for the purpose of the appointment of "authorised person" applies to the Agency by virtue of Article 10 of the Environmental Protection Agency (Extension of Powers) Order 1996 (S.I. No. 126 of 1996). *See:* EXTENSION OF POWERS.

Section 14(1) to (4) inclusive give the powers and statutory obligations of an authorised person appointed under this section.

Under the EPAA 1992

Section 3(1) of the EPAA 1992 provides that for the purposes of that Act, unless the context otherwise requires:

"'authorised person' means a person who is –

(a) appointed in writing by a Minister, a local authority or the Agency or such other person or body as may be prescribed, as the case may be, to be an authorised person for the purposes of this Act or any Part or section thereof, or
(b) appointed in writing to be an authorised person pursuant to regulations under this Act by a person specified in those regulations."

Section 13 (1) to (4) inclusive give the powers and statutory obligations of an authorised person appointed under this section.

Article 60 of the (*qv*) Genetically Modified Organisms Regulations 1994 (S.I. No. 345 of 1994) provides that the Agency may appoint such of its officers to be authorised persons as it considers necessary for the purposes of the Regulations.

Under the WMA 1996

Section 5(1) of the WMA 1996 provides that for the purposes of that Act, save where the context otherwise requires:

"'authorised person' means a person who is appointed in writing by the Minister, a local authority, the Agency or such other person as may be prescribed to be an authorised person for the purposes of this Act or any Part or section thereof."

Section 14 (1) to (5) inclusive give the powers and statutory obligations of an authorised person appointed under the section.

Under the WLA 1976

(A) SECTION 72 AUTHORISED PERSON

"Authorised person" is defined in the WLA 1976, section 2(1), as meaning a person who is appointed under section 72 by the Minister to be an authorised person for the purposes of the Act.

Section 72(1) confers the power of appointment in writing on the Minister.

Subsections (2) to (4) inclusive describe the powers and statutory obligations in relation to the exercise of the powers of authorised officers and members of the Garda Síochána who have the same powers as authorised officers under the section.

Subsection (5) provides for the issue to a person exercising a power under this Act of a certificate of his authorisation which must be produced on demand.

(B) SECTION 68 AUTHORISED OFFICERS

Section 68 deals with persons appointed by the Minister under section 11 of the Forestry Act 1946 who are called authorised officers under the section.

AUTHORISED OFFICERS UNDER REGULATION 7 – EU NATURAL HABITAT REGULATIONS, 1997 (S.I. No. 94 of 1997)

Regulation 1(2) of the NH 97 Regulations provides:

"The Wildlife Act, 1976, and these Regulations (other than Part IV) shall be construed together as one."

Regulation 2 (1) defines an "authorised officer" as meaning a person appointed as an authorised officer under Regulation 7.

Regulation 7 (2)(a):

"For the purposes of undertaking (*qv*) surveillance of the conservation status of the (*qv*)natural habitats and species under paragraph (1), and generally for the purposes of giving effect to the (qv) Habitats Directive, (92/43/EEC of May 21, 1992 O.J. L206 July 22, 1992, p.7) the Minister and the Minister for the Marine may, in respect of the fish species specified in Part II of the First Schedule (Lampern, Pollan, Allis shard, Twaite shard and Salmon) and to the extent (if any) specified therein, each appoint in writing, one or more than one person to be an authorised officer for those purposes."

Regulation 7 (2)(b) describes the circumstances in which the appointment may be terminated and the duration of the appointment in any event.

Regulation 7(3) provides for the issue to and production by the appointed officer of his certificate of appointment.

Regulation 7(4) provides for the reappointment of an authorised officer after termination of his appointment.

AUTHORISED OFFICERS UNDER EUROPEAN COMMUNITIES (WILDLIFE ACT 1976) (AMENDMENT) REGULATIONS, 1986

The European Communities (Wildlife Act, 1976) (Amendment) Regulations 1986 (S.I. No 254 of 1986), regulation 5(1) authorises the Minister to appoint in writing a person "to be an authorised person for the purposes of these regulations."

Regulation (2) provides for the furnishing of a certificate of appointment and its production on request.

Regulation 6(1) sets out the main powers which are (a) entry and inspection and (b) requests for information when he reasonably believes that the killing or capturing of wild birds has taken place.

See: DAMAGE TO PROTECTED WILD BIRDS.

AUTHORISED OFFICERS UNDER MAMMALIAN ANIMAL WASTE REGULATIONS (S.I. No. 2 of 1998 and No. 62 of 1998)

Regulation 7(1) of the European Communities (Mammalian Animal Waste) Regulations 1998 (S.I. No. 2 of 1998) and Regulation 8(1) of the European Communities (Processing of Mammalian Waste) Regulations 1998 (S.I. No. 62 of 1998) permit the Minister for Agriculture and Food to appoint such persons as he thinks fit to be authorised officers for the purpose of the Regulations. Regulations 7(2) and 8(2) each require the production of evidence in writing of that appointment as an authorised officer or inspector if so requested by any person affected when the authorised officer is exercising any powers conferred on him by the Regulations.

"inspector" above by virtue of Regulation 2(1) in both Regulations means an Inspector within the meaning of the Diseases of Animals Act 1966 (No. 6 of 1966).

AUTHORISED WASTE COLLECTOR
(WMA 1996, s.5(1))

"means the holder of a (*qv*) waste collection permit that is in force."

B

BAG NET

F(C)A 1959, s. 3(1))

"includes a (*qv*) fixed engine of similar construction to a bag net."

(BATNEEC) BEST AVAILABLE TECHNOLOGY NOT ENTAILING EXCESSIVE COST

(EPAA 1992/WMA 1996)

In the evolution of the language of environmental law the phrase Best Available Technology Not Entailing Excessive Cost (or "BATNEEC") comes at the end of a succession of principles variously enunciated as "vorsorgeprinzip" or "action through foresight", "Best Practicable Means" (or "BPM") and "Best Practicable Environmental Option" (or "BPEO").

The principle contained at section 5 is intended to act as a guideline for a prospective industrialist, chemist or manufacturer in deciding what plant, technology and equipment it would be permissible for him to use in his business to ensure that when the plant is in operation it will be competent to prevent a discharge or emission constituting *(qv)* environmental pollution and as a corollary be inconsistent with or in breach of the conditions likely to be attached to his licence. The appropriate licence is known as as an *(qv)* Integrated Pollution Control (IPC) licence and is granted by the *(qv)* Environmental Protection Agency (the EPA) under Part IV of the EPAA 1992. *See:* LICENCES (5).

As it is the policy of the Agency to have a detailed consultative process before granting an IPC licence, section 5 is designed to advance that process in order to arrive at a system which is satisfactory to the Agency, available on the market and within the projected budget for setting up the operation.

BATNEEC is one of the matters on which the Agency must be satisfied as a statutory requirement under section 83(3)*(f)* before they grant an IPC licence.

Section 5 of the EPAA 1992:

"(1) Subject to subsection (3), a reference in this Act to the use of the best available technology not entailing excessive costs to prevent or eliminate, or where that is not practicable, to limit, abate or reduce an (*qv*) emission from an (*qv*) activity, shall be construed as meaning the provision and proper maintenance, use, operation and supervision of facilities which, having regard to all the circumstances, are the most suitable for the purposes.

(2) (a) For the purposes of subsection (1), regard shall be had to –
(a) in the case of an activity other than an (*qv*) established activity –
(i) the current state of technical knowledge,
(ii) the requirements of environmental protection, and
(iii) the application of measures for these purposes,which do not entail excessive costs, having regard to the risk of significant (*qv*) environmental pollution which, in the opinion of the Agency, or any other licensing authority in relation to section 111, exists;
(b) In any other case, in addition to the matters specified in paragraph (a) –
(i) the nature, extent and effect of the emission concerned,
(ii) the nature and age of the existing facilities connected with the activity and the period during which the facilities are likely to be used or to continue in operation, and
(iii) the costs which would be incurred in improving or replacing the facilities referred to in sub paragraph (ii) in relation to the economic situation of activities of the class concerned.

(3) (a) The Agency may, from time to time as occasion demands, specify the best available technology not entailing excessive costs for preventing, limiting, eliminating, abating or reducing such emissions as may be specified either from an activity or activities of a particular class or description and regard shall be had, in the administration of this Act, to any such specifications.
(b) Where the Agency specifies the best available technology not entailing excessive costs in relation to an emission from an activity as provided for in paragraph (a), a direction issued under section 5(3) of the Air Pollution Act, 1987, related to such emission shall cease to have effect in relation to such emission.

(4) Whenever the Agency issues a specification under subsection (3), it shall cause, as soon as may be –
- (a) A copy of such specification to be sent to the Minister, each local authority, An Bord Pleanála and such other bodies, if any, as may be prescribed,
- (b) notice of the issue of the specification to be published in Iris Oifigiúil, and
- (c) a copy of the specification to be made available to every person who makes application for such a copy on payment of such fee (if any) as the Agency shall fix not exceeding the reasonable cost of making the copy."

(5) Amends section 5 of the APA, 1987 by inserting a new subsection (4A).

"(6) In this section –

"facilities" includes plant and premises;

"an emission from an activity" includes a release of a (*qv*) genetically modified organism as defined in section 111;

"activity" includes any process or action involving a genetically modified organism."

BATNEEC IN THE WMA 1996

Section 5(2)(a) of the WMA 1996 contains a definition of Best Available Technology Not Entailing Excessive Costs or BATNEEC which is the same as that in the section 5(1) and (2) of the EPAA 1992. Under section 40(4)*(c)*, BATNEEC is one of the matters on which the Agency must be satisfied before granting a *(qv)* waste licence under section 40(1)*(a)*.

BAY
(F(C)A 1959, s.3(1))

"includes any harbour or roadstead."

BEACH MATERIAL
(Foreshore Acts, 1933 and 1992)

See: FORESHORE.

BEST PRACTICABLE MEANS (BPM)
(APA 1987)

As the APA 1987 predates the EPAA 1992 it uses the now outdated BPM system rather than the now universally accepted and more sophisticated (*qv*) BATNEEC which is used in licensing in both the EPAA 1992 and the WMA 1996. It is to be hoped that BPM will be replaced by BATNEEC in the APA 1987 at some future time so that there might be consistency. Basically BPM is based on the same principles as BATNEEC but is not as far advanced in the evolutionary process described in the Introduction to BATNEEC.

Section 5 of the APA 1987:

"(1) Subject to subsection (3), a reference in this Act to the use of the best practicable means to prevent or limit an (*qv*) emission shall be construed as meaning the provision and proper maintenance, use, operation and supervision of facilities which, having regard to all the circumstances, are the most suitable for such prevention or limitation.

(2) In considering whether facilities are the most suitable for the prevention or limitation of an emission, regard shall be had –
- (a) In the case of (*qv*) industrial plant, other than (*qv*) existing industrial plant, to
  - (i) the current state of technical knowledge, and
  - (ii) the requirements of the environment, and
  - (iii) the costs which would be incurred in providing, maintaining, using, operating and supervising the facilities concerned, and
- (b) In any other case, in addition to the matters specified in paragraph (a) (i), (ii) and (iii), to
  - (i) the nature, extent and effect of the emission concerned, and
  - (ii) the age of the existing industrial plant or other premises, the nature of the facilities installed therein and the period during which the plant or other premises is likely to be used or continue in operation, and
  - (iii) the costs which would be incurred in renovating the plant or other premises, or of renovating or replacing the facilities therein, in relation to the economic situation of undertakings or enterprises of the class concerned.

(3) The Minister may, from time to time as occasion demands, issue directions specifying the best practicable means for preventing or limiting such emission as may be specified in the direction either generally, or from premises of a particular class or description, and regard shall be had, in the administration of this Act, to any such directions.

(4) Whenever the Minister issues a direction under subsection (3), he shall cause as soon as may be –
   (a) a copy of such direction to be sent to each local authority and to An Bord Pleanála,
   (b) notice of the issue of the direction to be published in Iris Oifigiúil, and
   (c) a copy of the direction to be made available, on payment of such fee (if any) as may be fixed by the Minister, to every person who makes application for such a copy.

(4A) Directions under subsection (3) shall not be issued in relation to an activity for the purposes of the Environmental Protection Agency Act, 1992, or in relation to any process, development or operation as regards which an order has been made, and remains in force, under section 95 of the said Act."

This subsection amends section 5 of the APA 1987 by adding a new subsection (4A) after section 4 with the intention of ensuring that "activities" or "special cases" under section 95 of the EPAA 1992 would be dealt with under the BAT-NEEC principle in the EPAA 1992 rather than the BPM principle which applies under the APA 1987. *See:* SPECIAL CASES.

"(5) In this section "facilities" mean machinery, plant, equipment, appliances, apparatus, buildings and other structures."

OBLIGATION TO PREVENT AIR POLLUTION

Section 24 of the APA 1987 places an obligation on the occupier of any *(qv)* premises, other than a *(qv)* private dwelling, to use the best practicable means to limit and, if possible, to prevent an emission from such premises.

Offence
Failure to comply with this section becomes an offence by reference to section 11(1) which provides that a person who contravenes any provision of the Act...is guilty of an offence. Section 24(2) provides that in a prosecution for an offence under the section it shall be a good defence to establish that, *inter alia*, the best practicable means have been used to prevent or limit the emission concerned.

BPM is one of the matters on which the local authority must be satisfied before they grant a licence to operate an *(qv)* industrial plant under section 32(3)*(a)* of the APA 1987.

BIRDS DIRECTIVE, THE
(WLA 1976)

"The Birds Directive" in the European Communities (Natural Habitats) Regulations, 1987 (S.I. No 94 of 1997) and by virtue of Regulation 2(1) means Council Directive No. 79/409/EEC of April 2, 1979 ([1979] O.J. L103/1) on the conservation of wild birds.

It is referred to in other regulations, *e.g.*, European Communities (Wildlife Act 1976) (Amendment) Regulations 1986 as "the Directive".

The implementation of the Birds Directive has been achieved by regulations passed in exercise of the powers conferred by Section 3 of the European Communities Act, 1972. There are eighteen to date, The European Communities (Conservation of Wild Birds) Regulations, 1985 (S.I. No. 291 of 1985) "the 1985 Regulations" and S.I. No. 48 of 1986, S.I. No. 59 of 1994, S.I. No. 349 of 1994, S.I. No. 31 of 1995, S.I. No. 284 of 1995, S.I. No. 285 of 1995, S.I. No. 286 of 1995, S.I. No. 287 of 1995, S.I. No. 269 of 1996, S.I. No. 298 of 1996, S.I. No. 305 of 1996, S.I. No. 210 of 1997, S.I. No. 154 of 1998, S.I. No. 131 of 1999 and S.I. No. 367 of 1999.

The 1985 Regulations refer to *(qv)* "special protection areas" which are set out in the Schedule to the 1985 Regulation and thereafter by reference to the schedules in subsequent regulations, with a present total of 102 sites in the classification of special protection areas.

These areas are not to be confused with *(qv)* special areas of conservation (SACs) which became current under the NH 97 Regulations, (S.I. No. 94 of 1997). The first formal creation of special protection areas arose under Article 3 of the 1985 Regulations which provided that in order to ensure the survival and reproduction of the species to which Article 4 of the Directive relates and having taken account of the matters referred to in Article 4 of the said Directive each area in the Schedule to the Regulations was thereby classified as a special protection area. (Article 4 of the Birds Directive is dealt with hereunder and all the special protection areas to date are listed hereunder).

DELETERIOUS MATTER

Article 2 of the Regulations defines deleterious matter. *See:* DELETERIOUS MATTER.

PROHIBITION IN RELATION TO DISPOSALS IN SPECIAL PROTECTED AREAS

Article 4(1) of the 1985 Regulations provides –

"A person shall not dispose of, throw down place or leave in any part of a special protection area

(a) any food remnants, orange peel, banana skin or other organic matter (whether waste or dead animal), or
(b) any rubble, old metal, glass, china, earthenware, tin, carbon, paper, rags or other rubbish, or
(c) any (*qv*) deleterious matter so as to create or tend to create pollution or deterioration of habitats or any disturbance whatsoever affecting the species to which Article 4 of the Directive relates in so far as the pollution, deterioration or disturbance would be significant having regard to the objectives of Article 4 of the Directive."

Article (2) exempts the deposit of such materials when a receptacle for the deposit of litter is used.

Offence
Article 5 provides that contravention of a provision of the Regulations constitutes an offence attracting a penalty on summary conviction of a fine not exceeding £1000.

No indictable offence is created under these regulations.

SCHEDULE

The dates and numbers in the left hand margin indicate the date and number of the appropriate statutory instrument which establishes the areas.

The following are the special protection areas created under the various European Communities (Conservation of Wild Birds) Regulations from 1985 to date.

SPECIAL PROTECTION AREAS – SPAS

1985
1. Wexford Wildfowl Reserve (the subject matter 9291) of Establishment Order under section 15 WLA S.I. No. 205 of 1981 which predated the SPA Order).
2. Saltee Islands (Great and Little) Wexford.
3. Puffin Island, Kerry.
4. Isiskea Islands, Mayo.

1986
5. Cliffs of Moher, Clare. (48)
6. North Bull Island, Dollymount, Dublin.
7. Great and Little Skellig, Kerry.
8. Inishvickillane, Inishnabro, Inishtooskert, Beginish and Teraght Islands, Kerry.
9. Lady's Island Lake, Wexford.
10. Inish and Sgarbheen (Lady's Island), Wexford.
11. Lough Gill, Kerry.
12. Hornhead, Donegal.
13. Port of Drumcliff Bay (including Lisadell Strand), Sligo.

1994
14. Ballycotton Bay, Cork (59)
15. Ballymacoda Bay, Cork.
16. Sandymount Strand and the Tolka Estuary, Dublin (note S.I. No. 367 of 1999 cited under second item 24 below).
17. Broadmeadow Estuary and Malahide Estuary, Dublin.
18. Dundalk Bay, Louth.

1994
19. Tramore Bay Back Strand, Waterford. (349)
20. Blackwater Estuary, Cork and Waterford.
21. Castlemine Harbour, Kerry.
22. Cork Harbour, Cork.
23. Inner Galway Bay, Clare and Galway.
24. Dungarvan Harbour, Waterford.

1999
24. Sandymount Strand/Tolka Estuary, Dublin. (367)
25. Bannow Bay, Wexford.

1995
26. Trawbreaga Bay, Donegal. (31)
27. Cumeen Strand, Sligo.
28. Killala Bay and River Moy Estuary, Mayo and Sligo.
29. Blacksod and Broadheaven Bay, Mayo.
30. Killarney National Park, Killarney.
31. Glenveagh National Park, Wicklow.
32. Wicklow National Park, Wicklow.

1995
33. Ballyallia Lake Wildfowl Sanctuary, Clare. (284)
34. Lough Corrib, Galway and Mayo.
35. Lough Derravaragh, Westmeath.
36. Lough Ennel, Sligo.
37. Glen Lough, Westmeath.
38. Lough Iron, Westmeath.
39. Lough Owel, Westmeath.
40. Lough Gara, Roscommon and Sligo.
41. Lough Oughter, Cavan.

1995
42. Lough Arrow, Roscommon and Sligo. (285)
43. Lough Carra, Mayo.
44. Carrowmore Lough, Mayo.
45. Lough Conn, Mayo.
46. Lough Cullin, Mayo.
47. Cross Lough, Mayo.
48. Lough Cutra, Galway.
49. Lough Derg, Donegal.
50. Lough Derg, Clare, Galway, Tipperary.

1995
51. Dunfanaghy New Lake, Donegal.
52. Lough Fern, Donegal.
53. Lough Kinale and Derragh Lough, Cavan, Longford, Westmeath.
54. Lough Mask, Galway, Mayo.
55. Poulaphouca Reservoir, Wicklow.
56. Lough Ree, Longford, Roscommon, Westmeath.
57. Lough Sheelin, Cavan, Meath, Westmeath.

1995
58. The Bull and the Cow Rocks, Cork. (287)
59. High Island, Galway.
60. Inishmurray, Sligo.
61. Lambay Island, Dublin.
62. Mutton Island, Clare.
63. Mattle Island, Clare.
64. The Stags of Broadhaven, Mayo.
65. Tory Island, Donegal.
66. Ilanmaster, Mayo.
67. Lough Swilly, Donegal.

1996
68. Akera Lough, Banna and Barrow Harbour, Kerry. (269)
69. Boyne Estuary, Louth and Meath. (Note: area covered here been added to be S.I. No. 131 of 1999).
70. Greers Island, Donegal.
71. Inishboffin, Inishdooey, Inishbeg, Donegal.
72. The Islands of Inishglora and Inishkeeragh, Mayo.
73. Lough Scannive, Galway.
74. Rahasane Turlough, Galway.
75. Sheskinmore Lough, Donegal.
76. Stabann - Braganstown, Louth.
77. Termoncarragh Lake, Mayo.

1996
78. Carlingford Lough, Louth. (298)
79. Kilcolman Bay, Cork.
80. the Owenduff River Catchment and the Nephin Beg Mountain Range, Mayo.
81. Pettigoe Plateau, Donegal.
82. Inishtrahull, Donegal.
83. Lough Forbes and the Ballykenny and Fisherstown Bog Complex, Longford, Roscommon.
84. Garriskil Bog, Westmeath.
85. All Saints Bog, Offaly.
86. Bellangare Bog, Roscommon.
87. Lough Barra Bog, Donegal.
88. Coole Park and Garryland Nature Reserve, Galway.
89. Eirk Bog, Kerry.
90. The Gearagh, Cork.
91. Loughnillan Bog, Donegal.

1996
92. Kilcoole Marshes, Wicklow. (309)
93. The River Little Brosna Callows, Offaly, Tipperary.
94. Lough Foyle, Donegal.
95. Tacumshin Lake, Wicklow.
96. The River Blackwater Callows, Cork, Waterford.
97. The River Shannon Callows, Galway, Offaly, Tipperary.
98. The River Suck Callows, Galway and Roscommon.

1997
99. Broad Lough, Wicklow. (210)
100. Inch Lough, Donegal.
101. The River Shannon and the River Fergus Estuary, Clare, Kerry, Limerick.

1998
102. Wexford Harbour, Wexford. (154)

EFFECT OF NH 97 REGULATIONS ON BIRDS DIRECTIVE

Regulations 34 of the NH 97 Regulations:

"The provisions of Regulations 4, 5, 7, 13, 14, 15 and 16 shall, where appropriate, apply with any necessary modifications to areas classified pursuant to paragraph 1 and 2 of Article 4 of the Birds Directive."

This means that the areas designated under the 1985 Regulations and the subsequent Conservation of Wildbirds Regulations as special protection areas have the same protection under the NH 97 Regulations as do the habitats designated as (*qv*)special areas of conservation by virtue of the NH 97 Regulations.

BIRDS DIRECTIVE
ARTICLE FOUR

Article Four of the Birds Directive is central to the conservation of wild birds in Europe and should be quoted in full. It provides:

"1. The species mentioned in Annex I shall be the subject of special conservation measures concerning their (*qv*) habitat in order to ensure their survival and reproduction in their area of distribution.
In this connection account shall be taken of
(A) species in danger of extinction;
(B) species vulnerable to specific changes in their habitat;
(C) species considered rare because of small populations or restricted local distribution;
(D) other species requiring particular attention because for reasons of the specific nature of their habitat.
Trends and variations in population levels shall be taken into account as a background for evaluation.
Member States shall classify in particular the most suitable territories in number and size as special protection areas for the conservation of these species, taking into account their protection requirements in the geographical sea and land area where the Directive applies."

The Annex I referred to here is not the Annex 1 featured in this book. The Annexes I and II/I referred to here are lists of some 146 birds dealt with by the Directive.

"2. Member States shall take similar measures for regularly occurring migratory species not listed in Annex I, bearing in mind their need for protection in the geographical sea and land area where this Directive applies, as regards their breeding, moulting and wintering areas and staging posts along their migration routes. To this end, Member States shall pay particular attention to the protection of wetlands and particularly to wetlands of international importance.
3. Member States shall send the (*qv*) Commission all relevant information so that it may take appropriate initiatives with a view to the coordination necessary to ensure that the areas provided for in paragraphs 1 and 2 above form a coherent whole which meets the protection requirements of these species in the geographical sea and land area where this Directive applies.
4. In respect of the protection areas referred to in paragraphs 1 and 2 above, Member States shall take appropriate steps to avoid pollution or deterioration of habitats or any disturbances affecting the birds, in so far as these would be significant having regard to the objectives of this Article. Outside these protection areas, Member States shall also strive to avoid pollution or deterioration of habitats."

BIRDS OF PREY
(WLA 1976)

"Birds of prey" are defined in the **Wildlife Act 1976 (Birds of Prey) Regulations, 1984** (S.I. No. 8 of 1984), Regulation 3 as meaning any eagle, hawk, falcon or other bird of the order Falconiformes. (*See:* FALCONRY).

BIRDS PERCHING
(WLA 1976, s. 31)

Section 31 of the WLA 1976

Offence
"(1) It shall be an offence for any person to sell, purchase or have in his possession a live perching bird to which this section applies other than a close-ringed specimen bred in captivity.
(2) This section applies to any live perching bird (order Passeriformes) of a species which occurs in a wild state in the State, Northern Ireland, Great Britain, the Channel Islands or the Isle of Man and which is not a species specified in the Third Schedule to this Act."

See: SCHEDULES HERETO, WLA SCHEDULES.

Subsection (3) provides for two statutory defences that the bird was lawfully acquired before the commencement of the section or from a person who so acquired it before that date.(June 6, 1977)

"(4) In this section 'close-ringed specimen' means a specimen of live perching bird (order Passeriformes) fitted with a continuous metal band or ring which has been slipped over its foot and on to its leg while a fledgling."

BIRDS, RINGING OF AND TRAPPING OFFENCES
(WLA 1976, s. 32)

See: RINGING OF BIRDS AND TRAPPING OFFENCES.

BOARDS OF CONSERVATORS
(F(C)A 1959)

The Boards of Conservators were established by **section 21 of the F(C)A 1959** and were dissolved by **section 34 of the FA 1980**.

Their successors were the (*qv*) Central Board which was established by section 7 of the FA 1980 and the (*qv*) regional fisheries boards which were established by three orders (*See:* REGIONAL FISHERIES ORDERS) made under section 10 of the FA 1980. After the FA 1980 the Central Board and the regional fisheries boards divided between them the functions of the old boards of conservators and the Inland Fisheries (*qv*) Trust which was also dissolved by the FA 1980.

BOARD,
(FA 1980, s. 2(1))

"except in Part II of the Second Schedule or where the context otherwise requires, means the *(qv)* Central Board or a *(qv)* regional board means the *9qv)* Central Fisheries Board or a *(qv)* regional fisheries board established under the Act of 1980."

See: COMMISSION UNDER F(A)A 1995.

BOARD, THE
(F(A)A 1997, s. 3(1))

"means the (*qv*) Aquaculture Licences Appeals Board established by section 22 and in relation to an oral hearing of an appeal in pursuance of section 49, includes a person authorised by the Board to conduct the hearing."

BOARDING AND EXAMINATION OF FISHING VESSELS
(F(C)A 1959, s. 298)

Section 298(1) of the F(C)A 1959 as amended by section 11(5), Fourth Schedule, of the FA 1980:

"(1) Any member of the Garda Síochána or officer appointed by the Minister or by a (*qv*) regional board may, subject to any directions and regulations given or made by the Revenue Commissioners, do with respect to any vessel employed in fishing, all or any of the following things:
(a) board such vessel,
(b) examine the certificate of registry and the (*qv*) fishing engines of such vessel, and ascertain whether the provisions of this Act have been complied with and whether the master and other persons on board are carrying on fishing in the manner required by this Act,
(c) seize any unlawful fishing engine or any lawful fishing engine unlawfully used.

Offence

(2) If the master of any fishing vessel refuses to produce the certificate of registry of such vessel when required to do so by a member of the Garda Síochána or officer of the Minister or an officer of a regional board, he shall be guilty of an offence under his subsection."

Section 298 would commonly be invoked in relation to sea, rather than inland, fisheries protection.

(Note that the maximum penalty prescribed under this section has been increased. *See:* FINES AND IMPRISONMENT (IMPOSITION OF)).

BOAT
(F(C)A 1959, s. 3(1))

"includes barge, cot, curragh or other vessel."

BOAT or VEHICLE USE OF TO AID THE COMMISSION OF AN OFFENCE
(F(C)A 1959, s. 285A)

Offence

Section 285A of the F(C)A 1959, inserted by section 24 of the F(A)A 1962:

"(1) If any person uses a boat or vehicle as an aid to the commission of an offence under any provision of this Act or any Act amending this Act or of an instrument made under this Act or any Act amending this Act he shall be guilty of an offence under this section...
(2) (a) Subject to paragraph (c) of this subsection, where a person is convicted of an offence under any provision of this Act or any Act amending this Act or of an instrument made under this Act or any Act amending this Act, any boat used in the commission or as an aid to the commission of the offence shall, as a statutory consequence of conviction, stand forfeited.
(b) Where a person is convicted on indictment of an offence under any provision of this Act that is triable on indictment, any vehicle used in the

commission or as an aid to the commission of the offence may be forfeited by order of the Court.

(c) Paragraph (a) of this subsection shall not apply in relation to a boat used by a person who is not the owner thereof if the owner proves that such use was without his knowledge or consent.

(3) This section does not apply to offences under Part XIII of this Act or section 35 of the Fisheries (Amendment) Act, 1962."

(Note that the maximum penalty prescribed under this section has been increased. *See:* FINES AND IMPRISONMENT (IMPOSITION OF).

Part XIII of the F(C)A 1959 deals exclusively with sea fisheries. Section 35 of the F(A)A 1962 deals with the making by the Minister, having regard to any international agreement to which the State is a party, of orders prescribing and adopting measures of conservation of fish stocks and rational exploitation of fisheries, and the contravention thereof. *See:* CONSERVATION OF FISH STOCKS.

BOAT, USE OF
TO CAPTURE SALMON OR TROUT DURING ANNUAL CLOSE SEASON
(F(C)A 1959, s. 133)

Offence
Section 133 of the F(C)A 1959 creates the offence of using a boat for the capture of salmon or trout during the annual close season for salmon and trout otherwise than such use by a person lawfully angling by rod and line.

This is a curiosity in that the original penalty of £5 is unchanged despite a complete overhaul of penalties by section 32 of the F(A)A 1962 and section 50 of the FA 1980 which would suggest that it has never been invoked.

BORD An, An BORD PLEANÁLA/ BOARD, the, the PLANNING BOARD
(LG(P&D)A 1976)

An Bord Pleanála, orse the Planning Board, was established on March 15, 1977 under section 2 of the LG(P&D)A 1976. It replaced the appeals procedure which had been established by the Principal Act, the LG(P&D)A 1963. It was intended to operate and has operated as an independent and responsible body to take over most of the functions previously exercised by the Minster for Local Government.

It had been suggested that planning appeal decisions under the old dispensation had a political dimension although in fairness this was never proven. All of the functions of the Department for Local Government in 1997 are now performed by the Department of the Environment. The Board consists of a chairman and five ordinary members and among its functions are:

(1) The hearing and determining of appeals made to it against the decision of the (*qv*) planning authority in relation to applications for planning permission for the (*qv*) development of land. This is its main function.

Regulation 27 of the NH 97 Regulations requires the Board, where there is a planning appeal in respect of development likely to have a significant effect on a (*qv*) European site, to ensure that an appropriate (*qv*) assessment is undertaken of the implications for the site in view of the site's conservation objectives.
See: ASSESSMENT OF IMPLICATIONS.

(2) It also hears and determines references to it under section 5 of the LG(P&D)A 1963 where the question arises between a developer and a planning authority as to whether a development is or is not exempted development and therefore exempted from the necessity of obtaining planning permission.
By virtue of the Local Government (Planning and Development) Regulations, 1994 (S.I. No. 86 of 1994), golf courses, which had enjoyed exempted development status, are now subject to the full rigours of the planning system.

(3) It has power to confirm or annul Purchase Notices under section 29 of the LG(P&D)A 1963.

(4) It has power to confirm or annul Notices served by a planning authority revoking or modifying a planning permission under section 30 of the LG(P&D)A 1963.

(5) It has power, if necessary, to assess contributions under section 26(7) of the LG(P&D)A 1963.

(6) It has power under section 85 of the LG(P&D)A 1963 to determine whether or not a consent has been unreasonably withheld.

(7) It has power under section 8 of the LG(WP)A 1977, as amended by section 6 of the LG(WP)(A)A 1990, to hear and determine appeals against determinations by local authorities under sections 4 and 7 of the LG(WP)A 1977.

See: APPEALS (3)(A).

(8) It has power under section 34 of the APA 1987 as in (7) above.
See: APPEALS(4).

BOUNDS
(F(C)A 1959)

Section 313 of the F(C)A 1959:

"In any action or prosecution for or in respect of any (*qv*) trespass or nuisance in respect of a fishery it shall not be necessary to set out in the declaration or indictment the bounds of the place in which the trespass or nuisance complained of was committed, but it shall be sufficient to state generally that the same was committed within the (*qv*) fishery district in which the fishery is situate."

BOX
(F(C)A 1959, s. 3(1))

"in relation to a (*qv*) fishing weir or a (*qv*) fishing mill dam, includes a crib or cruive."

BROKER
(WMA 1996, s. 5(1))

"means, in relation to (*qv*) waste, any person who on behalf of or as a service to any other person buys, sells or arranges for the purchase, sale or transfer from one person to another of waste or for the collection, (*qv*) recovery or (*qv*) disposal of waste."

BURNING OF VEGETATION
(WLA 1976, s. 39)

Section 39(1) of the WLA 1976 prohibits the burning by a person of vegetation growing within one mile of:
- (a) a wood which is not the property of such person,
- (b) land to which an (*qv*) establishment order, a (*qv*) recognition order, a (*qv*) designation order or an agreement under section 18 of the Act (*See:* MANAGEMENT AGREEMENT) relates.

The section provides for notice in writing of not less than seven and not more than 35 days before burning to the local Garda Síochána and:
- (i) in the case of a wood, the occupier of the wood,
- (ii) where there is an establishment or recognition order or an agreement under section 18, the Minister and where the Minister is not the owner of the land, the occupier,
- (iii) where there is a designation order, the Minister.

Subsection (2) provides that the Minister or other person served with such a notice has three days after receipt of the notice to serve a counter-notice of objection on the ground that it is liable to cause damage to the wood or land concerned.

Offences
Section 39 creates two separate headings for offences at subsections:

Subsection (3) provides a person shall not:
- (a) light a fire,
- (b) do any other act, which causes, or is likely to cause the burning of vegetation which is growing within one mile either of a wood which is not the property of such person or of land mentioned in subsection (1)*(b).*

Subsection (4) provides that any person who burns vegetation, lights a fire or does any other act in contravention of this section shall be guilty of an offence.

Subsection (5) provides that where the burning, lighting a fire or other act causes injury to any wood or land, it shall be deemed to have been caused by the negligent act of the person burning, and damages to the extent of that injury shall be recoverable accordingly in any court of competent jurisdiction from that person by the owner of such wood or land, as the case may be.

Subsection (6) provides that in section 39 "wood" includes a plantation.

BYE-LAWS
(F(C)A 1959/LG(WP)A 1977/WMA 1996)

A bye-law has been defined as:
"an ordinance affecting the public or some portion of the public imposed by some authority clothed with statutory powers, ordering something to be done or not to be done and accompanied by some sanction or penalty for its non-observance".

An example of this is the power conferred on local authorities and on the Minister to direct local authorities to make bye-laws for the regulation and prohibition of certain (qv)agricultural activities by section 21 of the LG(WP)(A)A 1990.

The Minister for the Marine has extensive powers to make specific bye-laws under various sections of the Fisheries Acts and there are a number of sections giving him power to make a bye-law for a specific purpose where the power is only an adjunct to the main object of the section, *e.g.* section 95(3) and (4) F(C)A 1959 which provide for the making of bye-laws permitting the use of nets in specified areas in freshwater in a section the main object of which is the prohibition of the use of nets in freshwater.

However, the Minister's main power to make bye-laws in the Fisheries Acts arises under section 9 of the F(C)A 1959 and it is under this section that he usually makes bye-laws.

There is no provision for the making of bye-laws in the WLA 1976, the APA 1987 or the EPAA 1992. All of these Acts, however, make extensive provision for the making of Ministerial regulations. Bye-laws can be made under the LG(WP)(A)A 1990, section 21 and the WMA 1996, section 35.

The making of a bye-law should be distinguished from that involved in making (*qv*) orders or (*qv*)regulations. Because bye-laws usually have a local application they are often potentially contentious so their making involves complex procedures described below in section 11 of the F(C)A 1959.

The making of orders and regulations is much simpler. They only require the tacit approval of both Houses of the Oireachtas. *See:* (1) REGULATIONS; (2) ORDERS.

Bye-laws are the appropriate regulatory instrument when made by local authorities who have no other right to legislate. It is noteworthy that in section 21 of the LG(WP)(A)A 1990 and section 35 of the WMA 1996 the power of making bye-laws is reserved exclusively to local authorities.

In the Fisheries Acts, where the Minister has extensive powers of making bye-laws, the control of fishing and the protection of fisheries still depends to a large extent on these bye laws which are peculiarly suitable to an industry which is still dependent on the vagaries of local fishing customs and the individual requirements of particular species of fish which vary from habitat to habitat over different periods of a year.

As a bye-law must derive from and be made under a statute and has no existence apart from the statute from which it derives that fact must be stated on any summons that may issue for contravention of the provisions of a bye-law. If the specific statute is not mentioned in the summons it is usual to use the phrase "contrary to the statute in that case made and provided".

FISHERIES ACTS

SECTION 9 F(C)A 1959 BYE-LAWS

Section 9 of the F(C)A 1959 as amended, shown in square brackets, by section 3*(a)*, *(b)* and *(c)* of the F(A)A 1962 provides:

"(1) In addition to the power of making bye-laws conferred on him by any other section of this Act, the Minister may, subject to the provisions of this Act, make such bye-laws as are in his opinion expedient for the more effectual government, management, protection and improvement of the fisheries of the State and, without prejudice to the generality of the foregoing, may make bye-laws in relation to all or any of the following matters

(a) the regulation of the fisheries of the State and the preservation of good order amongst the persons engaged therein,

(b) the times and seasons at which the taking of the several species of fish shall commence and cease [including bye-laws varying the weekly close time in relation to any river or the weekly close time in relation to any fishing weir which is the subject of an order under subsection (2) of section 107 (being bye-laws which do not reduce the weekly close time to less than forty-eight hours)],

(c) the times and places or the manner at and in which any fishing engine to be employed in the said fisheries may be used,

(d) the description and form of nets to be used in the said fisheries and the size of the meshes thereof,

(e) the prohibition of the use of nets,

(f) the prohibition of the use at any time of any fishing engine which is in the opinion of the Minister injurious to the fisheries,

(g) the prohibition of any practice whatsoever tending in the opinion of the Minister to impede the lawful capture of fish or be in any way detrimental to the said fisheries,

[(gg) the imposition of prohibitions or restrictions of an emergency character on the taking by any specified engine or engines of the several species of fish or of any of those species for a specified period not exceeding one year in duration where, in the opinion of the Minister, such prohibitions or restrictions are necessary],

(h) any other matter or thing relating in any manner to the government and protection of the said fisheries."

Subsection (2) provided for the fixing of a penalty of £5 where no other penalty was provided and forfeiture of all (*qv*) fishing engines as a statutory consequence of conviction. This was amended by section 3 of the F(A)A 1962 which inserted a new subsection, (4), which increased the penalty to £25 and fish illegally taken joined fishing engines as things to be forfeited as a statutory consequence. Section 3, amended by section 50(2)(a) of the FA 1980, also increased the penalty to £200 where it now stands.

Subsections (3) and (4) provide:

"(3) No bye-law shall be made under this Act which is repugnant to any law in force in the State or which would tend to injure the effective working power of any mill or factory.

[(4) Subsection (2) of this section shall not apply in relation to bye-laws made under this Act after the commencement of section 3 of the Fisheries (Amendment) Act, 1962, and if any person contravenes (whether by act or omission) any such bye-law, he shall be guilty of an offence against this Act and shall, where no other penalty is provided under this Act, be liable on summary conviction to a fine not exceeding twenty-five pounds and any fish illegally taken by him or in his possession at the time of the offence and also any fishing engine or thing by means or in respect of which the offence is committed shall, as a statutory consequence of conviction, stand forfeited.]"

PUBLICATION AND DEPOSIT, BYE-LAWS, ORDERS and APPEALS

Section 11 of the F(C)A 1959 as amended by the F(A)A 1999, s.27 –

"(1) The following provisions shall apply in relation to any instrument to which this section applies –

(a) notwithstanding any appeal which may be pending, but without prejudice to any order which may be made on such appeal, such instrument shall come into operation on the day specified in that behalf therein, or, if no such day is so specified, on the twenty-eighth day after the day on which it was made;

(b) such instrument shall, as soon as may be after it is made, be published in the Iris Oifigiúil [and a notice advising of the instrument and its contents shall be published in one or more newspapers circulating in the district affected by the instrument];

(c) a copy of such instrument shall, within one month after it comes into operation, be deposited –

(i) with the county registrar for every county or county borough which or part of which is affected thereby, and

(ii) with the District Court Clerk of every Court District which or part of which is affected thereby, and

(iii) in every station of the Garda Síochána within the area affected thereby;

(d) any person aggrieved by such instrument may, within twenty-eight days after the publication in Iris Oifigiúil, appeal against such instrument to the High Court, and the following provisions shall apply in relation to such appeal -

(i) the appeal may be heard by one or more judges of the High Court as may be convenient,

(ii) the High Court may on appeal confirm or annul such instrument, but if such instrument is annulled such annulment shall be without prejudice to the validity of anything done under or in pursuance of such instrument before such annulment,

(iii) the decision of the High Court on the appeal shall be final and conclusive,

(iv) the order made by the High Court on such appeal shall be published in like manner as such instrument is required by paragraph (b) of this subsection to be published and shall be deposited in like manner as such instrument is required by paragraph (c) of this subsection to be deposited.

(2) This section applies to any instrument being -

(a) a bye-law made under this Act, or

(b) an order made under section 10, or

(c) a licence granted under section 245 or 281, or

(d) an order made under section 251, 256, 266 or 275."

Section 27(b) of the F(A)A 1999 amended section 11(1)(b).

This section was considered at length and approved by the High Court in an unreported appeal entitled:

"No. 1994 797 AP Ct.5 In The Matter of the Fisheries Acts, 1959 - 1991 and in Particular in the Matter of the Fisheries (Consolidation) Act, 1959 and in the matter of the Galway, Connemara and Ballinakill Districts Bye-law No. 689 of 1994 and in the Matter of an Application by John Needham, Drift-net Fisherman of Old Head, Louisburgh, Co. Mayo."

(Two other Irish cases which were referred to in this judgment with approval, *Dunne v. Minister for Fisheries* [1984] I.R. 230 and *Dodd v. Minister for Fisheries* [1934] I.R. 291)

INDICTABLE BYE-LAWS

In 1980 it was discovered that the provision for the forfeiture of fishing engines, particularly nets, as a statutory consequence of conviction was creating problems. When you added the value of the net to the amount of the fine the combined figure was in excess of the notional figure for minor offences which by virtue of Art. 38(2) of the Irish Constitution were the only offences which could be tried summarily in the District Court.

This figure is now reckoned to be a fine not in excess of a figure somewhere between £500 and £1000 and a period of imprisonment of not more than six months.

For this reason and because Fisheries now wanted higher fines and longer sentences they had to create a series of indictable offences as, on indictment and trial by jury, a much higher penalty could be fixed.

At this time also the Department of the Marine were concentrating their energies on the control of salmon netting which was seen internationally as the main reason for the decline in salmon stocks.

Section 46(1) of the FA 1980:

For all of these reasons, section 46(1) of the FA 1980 provided that a whole series of sections involving netting and the seizure of fishing gear and fish may be tried on indictment. These were sections — 65, 66, 69, 73, 94, 95, 96, 97, 127, 128, 129, 130, 132, 134, 135, 137, 140, 145, 146, 156, 176, 177 or 182 of the F(C)A 1959. These are all offence sections involving salmon.
Subsection (3) provided for the same right of trial by indictment for a person charged with an offence under section 29 of the F(A)A 1962 which was an entirely new section under the 1962 Act providing for the Minister making orders prohibiting, restricting or controlling the catching of salmon at sea or the landing of salmon caught at sea.

Section 46(4) provides that a person charged with contravening a bye-law made by the Minister under section 9 of the Principal Act, being a bye-law which prohibits:

(a) the use of drift nets in fishing for salmon,
(b) having a drift net on board a boat in a specified area,
(c) the use of a monofilament net in fishing for salmon or trout,
(d) the possession of a monofilament net with a specified mesh on a quay, on or near the bank of any river or estuary or on or near any sea coast or at sea,

may be tried on indictment and on conviction on indictment under section 9 of the F(C)A 1959 for any bye-law in respect to any of the above, the penalty is a fine not exceeding £2,000 or imprisonment for not more than two years or both such fine and such imprisonment.

PENALTY UNDER NON-INDICTABLE BYE-LAWS

Section 50(2)(a) of the FA 1980 provides that a person who is convicted of an offence under subsection (4) of section 9 of the 1959 Act (inserted by section 3 of the Act of 1962) other than an offence described in section 46(4) of this Act shall, in lieu of so much of the penalty in that subsection as consists of a fine, be liable to a fine not exceeding £200, and the said subsection (4) shall be construed accordingly.

– This refers to a bye-law made after the commencement of the FA 1962.

Section 50(4) provides a penalty of £500 for conviction of an offence under a bye-law to which both subsection (4) of section 9 of the F(C)A 1959, as inserted, and subsection (4) of section 46 of the FA 1980 apply, that is, an offence under a bye-law which can be tried on indictment but which is tried summarily.

As a matter of practice once a District Court is satisfied that the offence, although one which may be tried by indictment, is minor it will accept the election of the prosecutor that the case be dealt with in a summary manner in the District Court. This practice has not been tested by higher courts.

In the case of an ordinary indictable offence if the DPP agrees and if the defendant elects for trial in the District Court then the matter can proceed in that Court.

It is assumed that the solicitor acting for the fishery board or other prosecutor could take the same decision.

Once a decision has been made that the offence must be tried on indictment before a Judge and jury in the Circuit Court the file must be referred to the appropriate state solicitor who is the only person who can prosecute in the Circuit Court. This applies in all environmental statutes where there are offences which can be tried on indictment.

BYE-LAWS UNDER SECTION 21 OF THE LG(WP)(A)A 1990

These may be made by local authorities in relation to certain agricultural activities to prevent or eliminate the entry of (*qv*) polluting matter to waters. *See:* AGRICULTURAL ACTIVITIES.

BYE-LAWS UNDER SECTION 35 OF THE WMA 1996

Section 35 of the WMA 1996 provides for the making by local authorities of bye-laws for the purpose of the proper management of waste or the prevention or control of (*qv*)environmental pollution. *See:* WMA 1996 (3), PRESENTATION OF WASTE FOR COLLECTION.

FIFTH SCHEDULE

The Fifth Schedule to the F(C)A 1959 provides for bye-laws made as follows:

1. Under section 283 which provides for (*qv*) close seasons for molluscs other than oysters,
2. For close seasons for salmon and trout (section 126), angling for salmon (section 137), angling for trout (section 138), pollen (section 148), molluscs other than oysters (section 283),
3. Under section 272 prohibiting the dredging for, or the taking, catching or destroying of oysters during a particular period,
4. Under section 284 on application or on the Minister's own motion prohibition against taking oysters during a specified period.

In every case the Minister appoints an officer of the Minister to hold an (*qv*) inquiry and makes the bye-law after considering his report.

Where the bye-law is sought by a person interested in the oyster fishery in a particular locality and where the bye-law is sought by any interested person, the Minister first seeks a deposit of a sum sufficient to defray his expenses of the enquiry before he appoints the officer to hold the inquiry.

BYE-LAWS, SPECIFIC
(F(C)A 1959)

The following sections of the F(C)A 1959 provide for the making of specific bye-laws in specific localities for specific species of fish:

(1) Section 126 annual close season for salmon and trout,
(2) Section 137 annual close season for angling for salmon,
(3) Section 138 (*qv*) annual close season for angling for trout,
(4) Section 148 annual close season for pollen (a white fish found in Lough Neagh),
(5) Section 151 annual close season for eels,
(6) Section 271 close season for oysters,
(7) Section 272 prohibition on dredging for oysters during a particular period,
(8) Section 283 close season for molluscs (other than oysters),
(9) Section 284 prohibiting the taking of molluscs (other than oysters) during a specified period.

These bye-laws, if they still exist or were ever made, vary from fishery region to fishery region. In any event, the Minister when he makes a bye-law invariably does so under section 9 to avoid holding expensive and troublesome inquiries.

In each of these sections a subsection provides that the provisions set out in the Fifth Schedule to the F(C)A 1959 shall apply in relation to the making of any bye-law under the section and the Fifth Schedule directs that in every case an inquiry shall be held.

See: CLOSE SEASON.

BYE-LAWS,
SECTION 95(3) &(4)
(F(C)A 1959, s. 95(3), (4))

Bye-laws made under **section 95(3) of the F(C)A 1959** authorising the use of nets in freshwater are one of the exceptions to section 95(1)*(a)* of the F(C)A 1959 which, with its sister section 96 of that Act, are the main enforcement sections prohibiting the use of nets in the freshwater portions of rivers and freshwater lakes.

Apart from an attempt to preserve a customary right to use draft nets in certain unspecified lakes these bye-laws under section 95(3) must also have been intended to have been used in connection with various schemes over the years to exterminate predators, such as pike, from freshwater lakes.

Section 95(3) provides that the Minister may authorise by bye-law the use of any kind or kinds of net, subject to such conditions as he considers proper, in any specified area in the freshwater portion of any river or any freshwater lake, for the capture of any fish other than salmon trout, or eels. Subsection (4)*(a)* permits the making of bye-laws, on an application to permit the use of a draft net for the capture of trout in a specified freshwater lake exceeding 30 square miles in area. The applicant must have the consent in writing of the owners of any fisheries in the lake and must establish that within 20 years before the January 1948 nets were used as of right in the lake for the capture of trout by members of the public who depended on such netting as a means of livelihood.

This provision under section 95(4)(a) is a carry over from a Fisheries Act which preceded the F(C)A 1959 and would have limited, if any, application.

Subsection 4*(b)* preserves from the terms of the F(C)A 1959 existing bye-laws for the benefit of the ESB in waters vested in them permitting the use of draft nets in those waters.

Subsection 4*(c)* gives the Minister the right to hold a public (*qv*) inquiry under an officer appointed by him under the section to enquire into the desirability of making a particular bye-law.

Subsection (4)*(d)* requires the giving of (*qv*) notice of the holding of the inquiry, in accordance with section 322.

C

CANDIDATE LIST OF EUROPEAN SITES
(NH 97, Reg. 2(1))

"has the meaning assigned to it by Regulation 3(1)."

Regulation 3(1) of the NH 97 Regulations (S.I. No. 94 of 1997)

"The Minister shall, for the purpose of identifying as sites of Community importance and based on the criteria set out in (*qv*) Annex III (Stage 1) to the (*qv*) Habitats Directive and relevant scientific information, prepare a list of sites (in these Regulations referred to as a 'candidate list of European sites') indicating in respect of each such site either or both —

(a) the (*qv*) natural habitat type or types in Annex 1 to the Habitats Directive which the site hosts, and
(b) the species in Annex II to the Habitats Directive that are native to the State which the site hosts.

(2) (a) For animal species ranging over wide areas, these sites shall correspond to the places within the natural range of such species which present the physical or biological factors essential to their life and reproductions;
(b) for aquatic species which range over wide areas the Minister shall propose such sites only where there is a clearly identifiable area representing the physical and biological factors essential to their life and reproduction.

(3) Where appropriate, the Minister may propose modification of the candidate list of European sites having regard to the surveillance carried out pursuant to Regulation 7(1) or if the Minister receives a request that a site be included in the list."

See: SURVEILLANCE OF CONSERVATION STATUS.

The acronym PCSAC is popularly used for "proposed candidate special area of conservation" but there is no basis in the NH 97 Regulations or elsewhere for the use.

See: CONSERVATION, SPECIAL AREAS OF

CENTRAL BOARD, THE
(FA 1980, s. 2(1))

"has the meaning assigned to it by section 7(1)."

Section 7(1) of the FA 1980:

"(1) On the appointed day there shall be established a body to be known as the Central Fisheries Board (which body is in this Act referred to as 'the Central Board') to perform the functions assigned to it by this Act.

(2) The provisions of Part I of the Second Schedule to this Act shall have effect with respect to the Central Board."

The Fisheries Act 1980 (Appointed Day) Order 1980 (S.I. No. 323 of 1980) fixed the October 29, 1980 as the appointed day.

CENTRAL BOARD, FUNCTIONS OF
(FA 1980, s. 8(1)*(a)*)

See: FUNCTIONS OF CENTRAL BOARD.

CERTIFICATE OF FITNESS, RESTRICTIONS ON SALE, PURCHASE AND EXPORT OF SALMON, TROUT, EELS AND MOLLUSCAN SHELLFISH
(F(C)A 1959, ss. 154 to 163)

Part X of the F(C)A 1959, sections 154 to 163, dealt with restrictions on dealing with (*qv*) salmon and (*qv*) trout. It was amended piecemeal by the FA 1980 to give effect to the new (*qv*) Central Board/(*qv*) regional fisheries boards structures introduced by that Act and section 20 of the F(A)A 1994 amended it by substituting an entirely new Part X which extended the scope of the Part to include (*qv*) eels and molluscan shellfish. Section 20 also inserted a new section 163A.

Section 154 of the F(C)A 1959:

"In this Part –
the expression 'certificate of fitness' means a certificate granted under section 158;

The word 'inspector' means any person being:
(a) a person appointed by the Minister or a

regional board to be an inspector for the purposes of this part,
(b) a member of the Garda Síochána, or
(c) in the case of the exercise by an inspector of powers under this section in the Moville area, an inspector appointed under section 55 of the Foyle Fisheries Act, 1952;

the expression 'Part X Licence' means a licence being –
(a) a salmon Dealer's licence, or
(b) an eel dealer's licence, or
(c) a molluscan dealer's licence;

the expression 'salmon dealer's licence' means a licence issued under subsection 91) of section 159 to deal in salmon and trout;

the expression 'eel dealer's licence' means a licence issued under subsection 91) of section 159 to deal in eels;

the expression 'molluscan dealer's licence' means a licence issued under subsection (1) of section 159 to deal in molluscan shellfish;

the word 'trout' includes fish commonly called or known as rainbow trout."

The word "salmon, trout, eels and molluscan shellfish" in this Article are called "Part X fish".

Section 155 of the F(C)A 1959 exempts salmon, trout, eels and molluscan shellfish preserved and sold in tins, bottles, jars and other sealed packaging holding only portions of Part X fish or products thereof from the requirements of Part X.

PROHIBITION AGAINST SELLING

Section 156(1) of the F(C)A 1959 prohibits the selling, exposing for sale or keeping for sale at any place Part X fish by a person unless:
(a) such person is the holder of the appropriate Part X fish dealer's licence as appropriate, for the time being in force, and
(b) such place is a place at which he is authorised by that licence to sell Part X fish.

Section 156 of the F(C)A 1959 creates two offences of contravention of subsection (1):
(a) sale, exposure or keeping for sale of salmon, trout, eels or molluscan shellfish without that person having the appropriate licence;
(b) sale exposure or keeping for sale of above named fish or shellfish at a place not being where he is authorised by the licence to do so.

Offences
Subsection (2) where a person sells, exposes for sale or keeps for sale not being the holder of a licence and at a place that is not authorised, and subsection (3) where a person buys from a seller who he knows or has reason to believe is selling in contravention of subsection (1).

(Note that the maximum penalty prescribed under this section has been increased. *See:* FINES AND IMPRISONMENT (IMPOSITION OF).

Subsection (4) provides that the section shall not apply to a fisherman selling Part X fish of his own lawful capture.

Section 157(1) of the F(C)A 1959 deals with restrictions on export for sale or attempt to export for sale from any place Part X fish without a licence in the same terms as section 156(1).

Offence
Subsection (2) creates in relation to a contravention of subsection (1) an offence in the same terms as subsection (2) of section 156(2) supra.

(Note that the maximum penalty prescribed under this section has been increased. See: FINES AND IMPRISONMENT (IMPOSITION OF).

Subsection (3) contains an exclusion for fishermen exporting their own lawful capture.

APPLICATION FOR A PART X LICENCE

Section 158(1) of the F(C)A 1959 provides that:

"(1) Where a person who carries on or proposes to carry on the business of selling salmon, trout, eels or molluscan shellfish, or of exporting for sale salmon, trout, eels or molluscan shellfish in a particular Court district applies to a judge of the District court for the time being assigned to that Court District for a certificate under this section, such judge shall, if satisfied that such person is a fit and proper person to hold a Part X licence, grant him a certificate in writing to that effect.

(2) A person making an application to a judge of the District Court for the grant by the District Court of a certificate under this section in relation to a salmon dealer's licence, eel dealer's licence or molluscan shellfish dealer's licence shall give notice in writing of the application to the (*qv*) regional board in whose (*qv*) fisheries region is situate any (*qv*) fisheries district in which he carries on or propos-

es to carry on the business of selling, or exporting for sale, salmon and trout, eels or molluscan shellfish, as the case may be, not less than fourteen days before the date of the hearing of the application, and each such board shall, through such of its officers as it shall nominate for the purpose, be entitled to appear in court and be heard on the hearing of the application."

It is noteworthy that although the fisheries board is entitled to be heard on the application there are no guidelines as to any possible grounds for objection.
See: Order 65, Rule 2 District Court Rules, 1997.

Section 159 of the F(C)A 1959 deals with the steps which must be taken by the applicant who must apply to the appropriate regional board within 28 days of receiving his certificate of fitness from the District Court for his licence authorising him to carry on the business of selling salmon and trout, eels or molluscan shellfish, whichever is appropriate, at any specified place within such board's (*qv*) fisheries region.

He has to apply in writing, in the prescribed form sending the certificate of fitness and £60 and section 159 (1)*(b)* provides that the regional board may issue to such person whatever licence is appropriate. Every licence shall be in the prescribed form and expires on the December 31 of the year in which it issues.

See Fisheries (Salmon, Eel and Molluscan Shellfish Dealer's Licences) Regulations 1994 (S.I. No. 462 of 94) which give the form prescribed for applications for licences and the forms of the licences, *i.e.* a salmon dealer's licence, an eel dealer's licence and a molluscan shellfish dealer's licence.

RENEWAL OF A PART X LICENCE

Section 160 of the F(C)A 1959 provides for the renewal of a Part X licence.

TERMINATION OF A PART X LICENCE

Section 161 of the F(C)A 1959 provides for the termination of a Part X licence on the death of the holder, on termination by the Minister under subsection (2)(a) on conviction of any offence under the Act (14 days notice of revocation must be given and representations may be made within that period) and on surrender by the holder.

Offence
Section 162 of the F(C)A 1959 provides for prominent display of a Part X licence and failure to do so constitutes an offence.

(Note that the maximum penalty prescribed under this section has been increased. *See:* FINES AND IMPRISONMENT (IMPOSITION OF).

PART X REGISTER

Section 163(1)*(a)* of the F(C)A 1959 provides for the keeping by every holder of a Part X licence at the place to which the licence relates a register in the prescribed form of all purchases and receipts and sales, exportations, disposals and removals of Part X fish at or from such place.

Subsection (1)*(b)* requires the holder within 3 hours of such sale, exportation, disposal or removal and within six hours of such purchase or receipt to enter in the register the prescribed particulars of the transaction and of the person with whom it was transacted or the place to which the Part X fish were removed.

Subsection (2) provides for the production of the register and all invoices, consignment notes, receipts and other documents for inspection by an inspector at any time during which the premises to which the register relates are open for the carrying on of business.

Subsection (3) provides that the register must be kept for six months after the latest entry.

Offences
Subsection (4) provides that on:
(a) failing to keep or causing to keep the register,
(b) failing to make or causing to make required entries within the time prescribed,
(c) failing to produce the register on demand for inspection as required or obstructing any inspector in making such an inspection,
(d) failing to comply with the provisions of subsection (3) of this section, or
(e) wilfully or negligently making or causing to be made in such register any entry which is false and misleading in any material particular a holder of a Part X licence shall be guilty of an offence.

Prosecutions by fishery boards under Part X have been virtually abandoned because it proved impossible to keep the Register in accordance with the strict requirements of the Part and because of difficulties experienced by regional fishery boards in proving breaches and obtaining convictions.

(Note that the maximum penalty prescribed under this section has been increased. *See:* FINES AND IMPRISONMENT (IMPOSITION OF).

Subsection (5) provides for the purpose of the section:

(a) inspection of a register shall include taking copies or extracts,
(b) a demand for inspection shall be deemed to have been duly made to a licence holder if made verbally on the premises of a licence holder to any person in the employment of the licence holder,
(c) a refusal to produce the register or document by that person shall be deemed to be a refusal by the licence holder,
(d) references to a licence shall be deemed to include references to any renewal there of.

Offence
Section 163A(1) of the F(C)A 1959, subject to subsection (2), creates the offence of purchasing Part X fish by a person who is not the holder of a Part X licence or a duly authorised agent in writing.

Subsection (2) provides that subsection (1) does not apply to:

(a) a bona fide purchase by a person for use in his own home,
(b) a purchase for catering purposes by the proprietor of a hotel, restaurant, guest house or of a business providing board and lodging or meals for reward if the purchase is made from:
  (i) the holder of a Part X licence for the time being in force,
  (ii) a licensed fisherman from whom the purchaser must obtain a statement in writing containing particulars of the transaction which the purchaser must retain for production to an inspector on request.

Offences
Subsection (3) provides that a purchasing agent who fails to produce on demand to an inspector his authorisation or refuses or fails to permit the inspector to read it is guilty of an offence.

Subsection (4) provides that a person who fails to produce his authorisation on demand is deemed to have refused or failed to produce it.

Offence
Subsection (5) provides that a vendor, selling salmon, trout, eels or molluscan shellfish to another person, who gives a statement in writing which is, to his knowledge, false or misleading is guilty of an offence.

CESSER OF AQUACULTURE LICENCES
(F(A)A 1997, s. 69)

Section 69 of the F(A)A 1997:

"(1) Where aquaculture in respect of which a licence has been granted has not commenced within two years after the date on which the licence was granted, the licence shall cease to have effect.

(2) Where aquaculture in respect of which a licence has been granted has ceased for a continuous period of two years, the Minister shall, without compensation to the licensee, revoke the licence."

The Minister has power of revocation in certain circumstances under section 68 of the F(A)A 1997. *See:* REVOCATION.

CHAIRPERSON
(F(A)A 1997, s. 3(1))

"means the Chairperson of the Board (the (*qv*) Aquaculture Licences Appeals Board) and includes the Deputy Chairperson and a member appointed under section 28(3) to preside at a meeting, while so presiding."

CHANGE OF OWNERSHIP
(APA 1987, s. 37)

Section 37 of the APA 1987:

"(1) Where a licence is granted under this Act, then, except as may be otherwise provided by the licence, the grant of the licence shall enure for the benefit of the (*qv*)industrial plant and of all persons for the time being interested therein, but without prejudice to the provisions of section 33 in relation to the *(qv)* review of the licence.

(2) Where a person to whom a licence was granted under this Act ceases to hold, or transfers to another person, his interest in the industrial plant to which the licence relates, he shall forthwith give notice to the local authority by whom the licence was granted –

(a) that he no longer holds an interest in the industrial plant concerned, and
(b) of the name of the person to whom his interest in the plant is transferred."

(EPAA 1992, s. 91)

Section 91 of the EPAA 1992:

"(1) Where a licence or revised licence is granted under this Part, the grant of the licence or revised licence shall, except as may be otherwise provided by the licence or revised licence, enure for the benefit of the (*qv*) activity and of all persons for the time being interested therein.

(2) Where a licensee ceases to hold, or transfers to another person, his interest in the activity to which the licence or the revised licence relates, he shall forthwith give notice to that effect to the Agency, specifying, in the case of the transfer of his interest, the name of the person to whom his interest in the activity is transferred."

CHARGES/FEES, FOR SERVICES
(F(A)A 1997, s. 63)

Section 63 of the F(A)A 1997:

"(1) The Minister may, with the consent of the Minister for Finance, make regulations providing for –
(a) the payment to the Minister of prescribed fees in relation to applications for licences, applications for renewals of licences or applications under section 70 for reviews of licences, and
(b) the payment to the (*qv*) Board of prescribed fees in relation to (*qv*) appeals to the Board under section 40, including (*qv*) oral hearings of such appeals,
and the regulations may provide for the payment of different fees in relation to cases of different classes or descriptions, for exemption from payment of fees in specified circumstances, for the waiver, remission or refund (in whole or in part) of fees in specified circumstances and for the manner in which fees are to be disposed of."

(LG(WP)A 1977, s. 6)

This section, which deals with Ministerial regulations for the purposes of sections 4 and 8 (4 is licensing and 8 appeals) at subsection (2)*(e)* and *(f)*, provides that the Minister may, in his regulations, specify charges for the discharge of effluents and the defraying or contributing towards the cost of investigations carried out by a local authority in relation to an application for a licence under section 4.

In the same section 6 there was inserted, by section 4 of the LG(WP)(A)A 1990, suggested extensive regulations for the Minister to include regulations dealing exclusively with the charging of fees for services and methods of calculating these fees. The subsections added to section 6 are (2A), (2B), (2C), (2D) and (2E).

(APA 1987, s. 22)

Subsection (1) permits a local authority, in accordance with regulations made by the Minister under this section, to make charges in relation to such (*qv*) emissions as may be specified in the regulations.

Subsection (2) lists the matters which the Minister may include in the regulations.

Subsection (3) provides the local authority may recover these charges as a simple contract debt in any court of competent jurisdiction.

(APA 1987, s. 35)

This section deals with Ministerial regulations providing for the charging by the local authority of fees for the granting of licences and the reviewing of licences and by an Bord Pleanála in relation to appeals under section 34.

(EPAA 1992, s. 49)

Subsection (1) provides that the Agency may determine charges or scales of charges in relation to the provision by it of services.
Subsection (2) provides the Agency may make those charges in accordance with scale.

Subsection (3) provides the Agency may recover the charges as a simple contract debt in any court of competent jurisdiction.

(EPAA 1992, s. 93)

Subsection (1) permits the Agency, in accordance with regulations made by the Minister, subject to the consent of the Minister for Finance and the Minister for Industry and Commerce, under this section, to make charges in relation to such (*qv*) emissions to the environment from such (*qv*) activities as may be specified in the regulations.

Subsection (2) lists the matters which the Minister may include in the regulations.

Subsection (3) provides that the Agency may recover the charges as a simple contract debt in any court of competent jurisdiction.

(EPAA 1992, s. 94)

"(1) The Minister may make regulations providing for the payment to the Agency, or such other public authority or body as may be specified, of fees in relation to -
(a) licences under section 83 or reviews of licences under section 88
(b) the operation of an (*qv*)accreditation scheme or an (*qv*)analytical quality control programme under section 66,
(c) the operation of a (*qv*)labelling scheme under section 78,
(d) the operation of a system of control for the prevention or limitation of (*qv*)noise under section 106, or
(e) the operation of a system of control over (*qv*)genetically modified organisms under section 111,
and the regulations may provide for different fees or for exemption from the payment of fees or for the waiver, remission or refund (in whole or in part) of fees in different circumstances or classes of circumstances or for different cases or classes of cases and for the manner in which fees are to be disposed of. Regulations have been made under this section in 1994, 1995 and 1996 (S.I.Nos. 130 of 1994, 60 of 1995 and 239 of 1996)

(2) Where under regulations under this section a fee is payable in respect of any application or matter, the application or matter shall be invalid and shall not be decided or otherwise dealt with, as may be appropriate, by the Agency or other public authority or other public body, as the case may be, until the fee is paid.

(3) Regulations under subsection 1(a) shall be subject to the consent of the Minister for Finance and the Minister for Industry and Commerce."

Regulations made under section 94 include the Environmental Protection Agency (Licensing Fees) Regulations, 1994 (S.I. No. 130 of 1994), the Environmental Protection Agency (Licensing Fees) (Amendment) Regulations, 1995 (S.I. No. 60 of 1995), the Environmental Protection Agency (Licensing Fees) (Amendment) (No. 2) regulations, 1995 (S.I. No. 76 of 1995) and the Environmental Protection Agency (Licensing Fees) (Amendment) Regulations (S.I. No. 239 of 1996).

(EPAA 1992, s. 66)

ACCREDITATION SCHEME

"(3) The Agency may provide for the imposition of charges and the payment of fees in connection with the provision of services or any procedural matters under this section."

(WMA 1996, s. 50(1))

This section deals with Ministerial regulations providing for the payment of fees to a local authority or the Agency, on
(a) the grant by a local authority of a (*qv*) waste collection permit under section 34,
(b) An application to the Agency for a (*qv*) waste licence under section 40, a (*qv*) review of a waste licence under section 46, the (*qv*) transfer of a waste licence under section 47, a (*qv*) surrender under section 48 and an extension of time for the purposes of section 49 (For section 49, *see:* LIMIT ON DURATION),
(c) an (*qv*) objection to the Agency under section 42(3) or a request for an *(qv)* oral hearing under section 42.

In each case where there is provision for payment of a fee the body receiving the fee does not have to determine the matter in respect of which the fee is chargeable until the fee is paid.

See: Part VII (Articles 41 to 46) Waste Management (Licensing) Regulations 1997 (S.I. No. 133 of 1997) for the amount of specific fees for application for a waste licence, for review or surrender of a waste licence, for making objections, for application for a transfer and for a request for an oral hearing.

See: Article 25 of the Waste Management (Permit) Regulations 1998 (S.I. No. 165 of 1998) defrayal of local authority or Agency's costs of performing their functions under the regulations

including costs of inspection and investigation and the taking and analysis of samples of waste. The Article provides for collection of these costs by notice in writing and in default of payment within three weeks the costs may be recovered as a simple contract debt. There is no provision in the Article for appealing against the costs, the imposition or the amount. *See:* PERMIT, WASTE PERMIT.
See: Article 14 of the Waste Management (Movement of Hazardous Waste) Regulations 1998 (S.I. No. 147 of 1998) which contains a similar provision in relation to the recovery by a local authority of costs.

See: Article 10 of the Waste Management (Transfrontier Shipment of Waste) Regulations, 1998 (S.I. No. 149 of 1998) which contains a similar provision in relation to the Agency and local authorities with this proviso:

"10(2) The amount of any payment under sub-article (1) shall not exceed the reasonable costs incurred by the Agency or local authority, as the case may be, in the performance of its functions in respect of the relevant shipment of waste."

Section 36(2) of the WMA 1996 which provides for regulations in respect of the movement of waste at subsection (2)(l), provides for regulations in respect of charges payable to the Agency or local authority to defray their charges. *See*: MOVEMENT OF WASTE.

CHASE, INJURE OR DISTURB SPAWNING FISH
(F(C)A 1959, s. 174)

Offence
Section 174 of the F(C)A 1959

"(1) If any person chases, injures or disturbs spawning fish or fish on the spawning beds or attempts (except by means of lawful angling with rod and line) to catch fish thereon, such person shall be guilty of an offence under this section."

(Note that the maximum penalty prescribed under this section has been increased. *See:* FINES AND IMPRISONMENT (IMPOSITION OF).

CHIEF EXECUTIVE OFFICER

The chief officers of the *(qv)* Central Board and *(qv)* regional fisheries boards named in section 25 of the FA 1980 are, by virtue of section 15 of the F(A)A 1999, to be known as Chief Executive Officer who, subject to any directions or guidelines of the boards, shall carry on, manage and control generally the administration and business of the boards and perform such other functions as the boards may require.

CITES CONVENTION

The "CITES' Convention means the Convention on International Trade in Endangered Species of Wild Flora and Fauna done at Washington on the 3rd day of March 1973 as amended.

CITES REGULATIONS

The "CITES Regulations" mean Council Regulations –

(1) EC No. 338/97 of 9 December 1986 on the protection of species of wild fauna and flora by regulating trade therein (O.J. L. No. 61, 3 March 1997, P 1).
(2) (EC) No. 939/97 of 26 May 1996 laying down detailed rules concerning the implementation of Council Regulation (EC) No. 338/97 (O.J. L. No. 140, 30 May 1997, p. 9).

CIVIL LIABILITY
(LG(WP)(A) 1990, s. 20)

Section 20 of the LG(WP)(A)A 1990:

"(1) Where (*qv*) trade effluent, (*qv*) sewage effluent or other (*qv*) polluting matter enters (*qv*) waters and causes injury, loss or damage to a person or to the property of a person, the person may, without prejudice to any other cause of action that he may have in respect of the injury, loss or damage, recover damages in any court of competent jurisdiction in respect of such injury, loss or damage -
(a) from the occupier of the premises from which the (*qv*) effluent or matter originated unless the entry to the waters was caused by act of God or an act or omission of a third party over whose conduct such occupier had no control, being an act or omission that such occupier could not reasonably have foreseen and guarded against, or
(b) if the entry to the waters was occasioned by an act or omission of any person that, in the opinion of the court, constitutes a contravention by the person of a provision of the Principal Act or this Act, from that

person.

(2) Subsection (1) does not apply to the entry of trade effluent, sewage effluent or other polluting matter to waters by virtue of anything specified in section 3(5) of the Principal Act or under and in accordance with a licence under section 4 of the Principal Act or section 171 of the Act of 1959."

For section 3(5) of the LG(WP)A 1977 *see:* PROHIBITION (2). For section 4 of the LG(WP)A 1977 and section 171 of the F(C)A 1959 *see:* LICENCES (3) and (1).

(APA 1987, s. 28B)

Section 28B of the APA 1987, inserted by the Third Schedule to the EPAA 1992:

"(1) Where an (*qv*) emission causes injury, loss or damage to a person or to the property of a person, the person may, without prejudice to any other cause of action that he may have in respect of the injury, loss or damage, recover damages in any court of competent jurisdiction in respect of such injury loss or damage -
(a) from the (*qv*) occupier of the premises from which the emission originated unless the omission was caused by an act of God or an act or omission of a third party over whose conduct such occupier had no control, being an act or omission that such occupier could not reasonably have foreseen or guarded against, or
(b) if the emission was occasioned by an act or omission of any person that, in the opinion of the court, constitutes a contravention by the person of the provision of this Act, from that person.

(2) Subsection (1) does not apply to an emission under and in accordance with a licence granted under this Act or an emission in compliance with an (*qv*) emission limit value specified under section 51 of this Act or an emission which is in accordance with directions specifying (*qv*) best practicable means issued by the Minister under subsection (3) of section 5 of this Act."

CLOSE SEASON AND WEEKLY CLOSE TIME
(F(C)A 1959)

A "close season" in fishery law is a varying period being a part of a year fixed by statute or bye-law during which it is forbidden to catch, take or destroy certain species of fish. The annual period usually corresponds with the spawning season of the species.

For an overall view of the protection of fish under the Fisheries Acts, *see:* SALMON AND OTHER FISH, PROTECTION OF.

ANNUAL CLOSE SEASON

Section 3(1) of the F(C)A 1959 contains a number of annual close seasons for various species of fish:

Salmon	section 137
Trout	section 138
Eels	section 151
Pollen	section 148
Oysters	section 271
Salmon and trout (excluding rod and line)	section 126

To which can be added species which are not dealt with in section 3(1):

Molluscs (other than oysters)	section 283
Oysters (on application of any person for a period not exceeding 3 years)	section 272
Molluscs (other than oysters for a period not exceeding 3 years)	section 284

to give the full complement of sections which deal with close seasons for different species of fish, these are fixed as follows:

In section 137 (salmon) the section only fixes the close season period, October 13 to January 31 in the next following year.

In sections 148 (pollen), 151 (eels), and 271 (oysters) there is provision both for a statutory fixed period and for the fixing of the period by the Minister by bye-law.

In section 138 (trout) there is provision for a period to be fixed by the Minister by bye-law only but it must include the (*qv*) October close season period (October 13 to 31).

In sections 126 (salmon and trout), 283 (molluscs other than oysters), 272 (3 year period) and 284 (3 year period) the close season period can only be fixed by bye-law by the Minister.

Every section provides that the Fifth Schedule to the Act shall apply to the bye-law. *See:* BYE-LAWS.

In the following cases section 137 (subsection (1)*(b)*), section 148 (section 149), section 151 (section 152), section 138 (subsection (2)*(a)*), section 126 (section 127) and section 272 (section 273) the section quoted in brackets creates the offence.

By virtue of section 46 of the FA 1980 the offence created by section 127 may be tried on indictment.

There is provision for the forfeiture of the fishing engine on conviction for an offence under section 137, 138, 127 and 149 and for forfeiture of the catch on conviction for an offence under sections, 137, 138, 127, 273, 149, 152 and 273.

Bye-laws made for the purpose of fixing close seasons are mostly of local application and are not listed in this book. Inquiries should be directed to the local regional fisheries board.

FISHING WITH DRIFT NET, DRAFT NET, SNAP NET, OTHER NET, MON0FILAMENT AND MULTISTRAND MONOFILAMENT

See: SALMON AND TROUT CONSERVATION BYE-LAW NO. 743, 1998.

AUTHORISATION TO TAKE OYSTERS DURING CLOSE SEASON

Section 274 of the F(C)A 1959:

"(1) The Minister may, for the purpose of replenishing and supplying any oyster bed the exclusive property of any person, authorise the dredging for and taking of oysters from any natural public bed lying below the level of the lowest water of spring tides during such part of the close season for oysters as the Minister thinks proper and specifies in the authorisation."

Offence
Subsection (2) provides a penalty for improper use of subsection (1) by bringing them on shore and selling or offering them for sale.

(Note that the maximum penalty prescribed under this section has been increased. *See:* FINES AND IMPRISONMENT (IMPOSITION OF).

ORDER PERMITTING FOREIGN OYSTERS

Section 275 of the F(C)A 1959 provides that the Minister may, on the application of any person interested in any oyster fishery, make an order permitting the taking or having in possession foreign oysters during such part of the close season for oysters as the Minister thinks fit.

Subsection (2) provides that where such an application is made under the section:

(a) the Minister shall cause a public inquiry into such application to be held,
(b) the Minister shall cause notice to be given of the time and place of the inquiry in accordance with section 322,
(c) the Minister shall appoint an officer to hold such inquiry,
(d) the Minister shall take no decision on the application until he has considered the report of the said officer.

See: INQUIRIES INTO FISHERIES:

MULTIPLICITY OF CLOSE SEASONS

In Galway Bay you have the situation where a large private oyster bed which was the property of the St George family was acquired by the State sometime around 1978 and, after an extensive enquiry by the Minister, was given to a local co-op, the Clarenbridge Oyster Co-operative Society Ltd.

The rules of the Clarenbridge Co-operative and the schedule to the order, the Oyster Fishery (Clarenbridge) Order 1978, made by virtue of sections 256 and 260 F(C)A 1959 (repealed by section 5(6) F(A)A 1997) provide for a close season for the area covered by the order, from December 15 in any year to the October 11 in the following year. The Minister can no longer make such orders.

The adjoining "public" beds, by virtue of Galway Bay Oysters Close Season Bye-law No. C.S. 118, 1972, have two different close seasons, February 1 to October 31 in the area to the east of a line drawn from Rinville Point to Comyn's point (West) and from January 1 to November 30 in the remainder of the "public" beds.

Fisheries officers have to police the oyster beds in Galway bay in three different areas – some of whose boundaries are the open sea – having three different "close season" periods when it is illegal to dredge for oysters.

It is noteworthy that the bye-laws quoted above, 118, 72, is made under section 9 of the F(C)A 1959 and not under section 271 quoted above. The reason being that section 9 is not required to comply with the Fifth Schedule which requires the Minister to hold an inquiry as does section 271.

WEEKLY CLOSE TIME

Offence
Section 140(1) of the F(C)A 1959 provides for the offence of fishing for or taking salmon or trout other than by rod and line during the weekly close time.

(Note that the maximum penalty prescribed under this section has been increased. *See:* FINES AND IMPRISONMENT (IMPOSITION OF).

Subsection (2) provides for the forfeiture of the (*qv*) fishing engine in respect of which the offence was committed as a statutory consequence of conviction.

"The weekly close time" by virtue of section 139(1) means the period commencing at 6 a.m. on Saturday and ending at 6 a.m. on the next following Monday and, by virtue of section 139(3), in relation to any *(qv)* fishing weir which is the subject of an order under section 107(2), the period commences at 6 a.m. on Saturday and ends at 6 a.m. on the next following Monday with the extension of a period of 24 hours as directed by the order.

This offence can also be tried on indictment by virtue of section 46 of the FA 1980.

COARSE FISH
(F(C)A 1959, s. 3(1))

"The expression 'coarse fish' means any freshwater fish or the spawn or fry thereof other than salmon, trout (including rainbow trout and char) or eels or their spawn or fry."

This definition was inserted by section 11(5) of the FA 1980 and substituted by section 2(b) of the F(A)(N. 2) A 1987.

CODES OF PRACTICE EVIDENCE OF SUCH CODES
(EPAA 1992, s. 76)

Section 76(1) of the EPAA 1992 entitles the Agency to prepare and publish its own code of practice or to adopt the code of practice of another body, to provide practical guidance to ensure compliance with legislation or otherwise for the purposes of (*qv*) environmental protection.

Subsection (2) provides that before publishing or approving a code of practice the Agency shall consult with and have regard to the views of such Government Department or other body as is thought to be appropriate.

Subsection (3) obliges the Agency to publish notice in Iris Oifigiúil of the publication or approval of a code of practice.

Subsection (4) entitles the Agency, after the consultation specified in subsection (2), to revoke, revise or withdraw its approval from a code of practice or any part and shall publish a notice to that effect in an Irish Oifigiúil.

PROOF OF A CODE OF PRACTICE

Section 77 of the EPAA 1992 provides that a document under the seal of the Agency purporting to be a code, or part of a code, of practice published or approved under section 76, shall be received in evidence without further proof.

COLLECTION
(WMA 1996, s. 5(1))

"means, in relation to waste, the gathering, sorting or mixing of waste for the purpose of its being transported, and includes the transport of waste and the acceptance of control of waste."

COLLECTION OF WASTE, OBLIGATIONS OF LOCAL AUTHORITIES
(WMA 1996, s. 33)

Section 33 of the WMA 1996:

"(1) (a) Each local authority shall collect, or arrange for the collection of, (*qv*) household waste within its functional area.

(b) The corporation of a borough (other than a county borough) or the council of an urban district may collect, or arrange for the collection of, household waste.

(2) Subsection (1)(a) shall not apply to household waste in any part of a local authority's functional area to the extent that any of the conditions mentioned in subsection (3) applies to that part or, as appropriate, to that household waste.

(3) the conditions referred to in subsection (2) are –
(a) an adequate waste collection service is available in the part concerned of the local authority's functional area,
(b) the estimated costs of the collection of the waste concerned by the local authority would, in the opinion of the authority, be unreasonably high,
(c) the local authority is satisfied that adequate arrangements for the disposal of the waste concerned can reasonably be made by the holder of the waste.

(4) A local authority may collect, or arrange for the collection of waste, other than household waste.

(5) A local authority may enter into arrangements with one or more other local authorities, or with one or more other persons, for the collection on its behalf by the said authority or authorities or, as the case may be, by the said person or persons, of waste in its functional area or in a part or parts of that area.

(6) Notwithstanding any other provision of this Act, a local authority shall be under no duty to collect or arrange for the collection of, waste from any person-
(a) if any provision of bye-laws under section 35 regarding the (*qv*) presentation of the waste for collection is not complied with, or
(b) if the waste contains any product or substance or packaging therefore in contravention of regulations under section 29.

(7) Waste collected or recovered by a local authority shall become the property of the authority.

(8) (a) A person shall not, without lawful authority, disturb, interfere with or remove -
(i) anything deposited at a (*qv*) facility provided by or on behalf of a local authority or an (*qv*) authorised waste collector for the deposit or storage of waste, or any (*qv*) plant, including any receptacles therein,
(ii) anything deposited in a receptacle for waste, whether such receptacle is for the use by members of the public or otherwise.
(b) A person shall not obstruct or interfere with the collection of waste by a local authority or an authorised waste collector.

Offence
(c) A person who contravenes paragraphs (a) or (b) shall be guilty of an offence.

(9) For the purposes of this section, other than subsection (1), 'local authority' includes the corporation of a borough of any kind and the council of an urban district."

COMBINED DRAIN
(LG(WP)A 1977, s. 1(1))

"means a drainage pipe, or a system of such pipes, that is not vested in or controlled by a sanitary authority and is used to convey (*qv*) trade effluent or other matter (other than storm water) from two or more premises to any (*qv*) waters or to a sewer."

This definition was inserted by section 2 of the LG(WP)(A)A 1990.

Section 22 of the LG(WP)(A)A 1990 –

"(1) A sanitary authority may declare by order that a specified combined drain shall become and be a sewer for the purposes of the Principal Act and this Act and, whenever it does so, the drain concerned shall, upon the commencement of the order concerned, become and be a sewer for those purposes."

Subsection (2) deals with the steps which must be taken by way of giving notice and receiving and considering representations before the order is made.

Subsection (3) provides that the order shall come into operation on such date (not being less than six months after the date of its making) as may be specified therein.

Subsection (4) provides for the depositing and making available for inspection and purchase of copies of the order and serving it on the owner of the drain concerned and any occupiers affected.

Subsection (5) provides that where an order is made by a sanitary authority under subsection (1)*(a)* the occupier of each premises discharging into the drain has six months to apply for a licence in respect of the *(qv)* discharge under section 16 of the LG(WP)A 1977. Subsection (1)*(b)* provides for the interim position of a person who has to apply under this section for a section 16 licence and his legal standing between the date of application and the date the licence is granted or refused.

COMMERCIAL WASTE
(WMA 1996, s. 5(1))

"means waste from premises used wholly or mainly for the purpose of a trade or business or for the purposes of sport, recreation, education or entertainment but does not include household, agricultural or industrial waste."

COMMISSION UNDER F(A)A 1995
(F(A)A 1995)

In 1995 when it became necessary to have a full investigation into the performance of the functions of a fisheries board it was decided that the existing legislation was inadequate.

The powers of the Minister in relation to investigation which existed in 1995 and which are still law are contained in section 50 of the F(C)A 1959 which entitles him to hold an (*qv*) inquiry into the performance by a *(qv)* board of conservators of its duties. This section was extended by section 65 of the FA 1980 to the (*qv*) Central Board and any (*qv*) regional fisheries board both of which were newly established under the 1980 Act.

In addition to the powers under section 50, section 24(1) of the FA 1980 entitles the Minister to remove from office members of the Central Board or a regional board after inquiry under section 50 as amended and under section 24(2) the Minister has power to appoint other persons to perform the functions of the board. *See:* REMOVAL OF MEMBERS.

Despite all of this armament, in response to the problems which arose in 1995 the F(A)A 1995, whose only purpose was to do so, established an entirely new procedure parallel to the existing procedures under the sections quoted above of the F(C)A 1959 and 1980.

It is difficult to see any substantial difference between the two procedures or the necessity for establishing an entirely new procedure in 1985 when judicious amendment of section 50 of the FA 1980 could have achieved exactly the same result.

REPORT BY APPOINTED OFFICER AND ESTABLISHMENT OF COMMISSION

Under the terms of the 1995 Act, the Minister has power, after a report received by him prepared by an officer appointed by him under section 2 in relation to the management and organisation of a (*qv*) board and the performance by it of its functions generally and on being satisfied that the affairs of the board are not being, or, in any period following the preparation of the report are not likely to be, managed in an efficient manner, to establish under section 3, by order, a commission to perform the functions of the board either at the request in writing of the board or on his own initiative after considering the report.

Subsections (2) and (3) of section 2 oblige the board to cooperate fully with the person appointed to report to the Minister, to make all records or documents available to that person for inspection and copying and to recoup his expenses to the Minister out of the board's revenue.

Subsection (2) of section 3 provides that for so long as the section 3 order establishing a commission remains in force such functions of the commission as are delegated to it by the order shall not be performed by the board.

Subsection (5) of section 3 provides that the order remains in force for so long as is provided in the order except where it is made other than at the request of the board when it remains in force for not longer than two years but there is provision for extensions.

Section 4 provides that the Minister shall, when he appoints a commission other than at the request of the board, give notice in writing to the board indicating the terms of the proposed order and the board have 14 days within which to make representations as to why the order should not be made and the Minister is obliged under the section to have regard to any such representations.

Section 5 (1) provides that a commission shall consist of one or more members as the Minister may determine and subsection (2) provides that the member or members shall be appointed by the Minister.

The general terms of appointment are set out at subsections (3), (4), (5), (6), (7) (8) and (9) of section 5.

Section 6 provides for co-ordination of the performance of functions where these are shared by the board and a commission and provides that the

Minister shall be the final arbiter in determining disputes and disagreements between them.

Section 7 provides that the board and all its members and employees will furnish such information as is requested by the commission for the purpose of performing any of its functions.

Section 8 provides that the Minister may remove from office any member of a board who is responsible for the failure by that board to comply with a requirement or request made under section 2(2) or (3) or section 7 without prejudice to section 25 Article 7 of Part I and Article 11 of Part II of the Second Schedule to the FA 1980.

Section 9(1) provides for the making of orders amending or revoking orders under the Act including orders under section 9 and subsection (3) extends that power to include provisions adapting any provision of the Fisheries Acts 1959 to 1994 relating to the functions of a board where necessary to remove any difficulty arising in respect of the performance of that function by the commission concerned.

FISHERIES (COMMISSION) ACT 1997

The Fisheries (Amendment) Act, 1995, was amended by the Fisheries (Commission) Act, 1997. The short title of this unusual Act reads as follows *"An Act to provide for Certain Validations, to Amend the Fisheries (Amendment) Act, 1995, to provide for the indemnification of Members of Commissions under that Act, and for related purposes"*.

The 1997 Act was specifically passed to deal with difficulties arising out of the appointment of Séan Keating as a member of the Southern Regional Fisheries Commission. The Southern Regional Fisheries Commission was established under the Fisheries (Amendment Act, 1995 (Southern Regional Fisheries Commission) Order 1996 (S.I. No. 51 of 1996). This Order was made under section 3(1) of the Fisheries (Amendment) Act, 1995.

Section 3 of the 1997 Act validates all actions done by or on behalf of Mr Séan Keating as a member of that Commission subject to constitutional limitations (section 4 of the 1997 Act).

Section 5 of the 1997 Act extends the application of the Order from 26th February 1996 to 22nd February 1998. Note that the period for which the Fisheries (Amendment) Act, 1995 (Southern Regional Fisheries Commission) Order, 1996 (S.I. No. 51 of 1996) (as extended by section 5) was further extended to the 31st day of December 1998 by the Fisheries (Amendment Act, 1995 (Soughern Regional Fisheries) (Commission) Order 1998 (S.I. No. 32 of 1998).

Section 8 of the 1997 Act provides that all prosecutions to enforce any provisions of Fisheries Acts 1959 to 1995, brought on or before the commencement of that Act, by or in the name or upon complaint of the Commission to be deemed to have been brought by, in the name of or upon the complaint of the Southern Regional Fisheries Board established under the Fisheries Act, 1980.

Section 7 amends subsection (3A) of section 5 of the Fisheries (Amendment) Act, 1995, so that now reads as follows (and applied that subsection to any prior actions of Séan Keating) –

"(3A) The Minister shall indemnify each member of a commission against all and any actions, expenses, costs, claims, demands and other liabilities in respect of any action by or omission of the commission or member in the performance or exercise (or purported performance or exercise) of the commission's or member's functions or powers under or in pursuance of this Act."

Section 9(2) provides that a draft of an order extending or further extending the period provided by a section 3 order for the duration of a commission must be laid before each House not less than 2 months before the period provided in the order expires.

COMMISSION, THE
(NH 97 Reg. 2(1))

"means the Commission of the European Communities."

COMMISSIONERS, COMMISSIONERS OF PUBLIC WORKS IN IRELAND
(Heritage Act 1995, s. 2(1))

"means the Commissioners of Public Works in Ireland."

The same interpretation appears at section 2(1) of the WLA 1976.

Section 24 of the Heritage Act 1955:

"The functions of the Commissioners in relation to the national heritage under the enactments set out in the Table to this section shall, notwithstanding anything to the contrary in the Ministers and Secretaries Act, 1924, be performed subject to the supervision of the Minister (for Arts, Culture and the Gaeltacht) and to such directions as the

Minister may give in relation thereto and the Commissioners shall provide the Minister with such information as the Minister may require for those purposes.

TABLE

The Act of the British Parliament 2 & 3 Vict., c.61 ("the Shannon Act")
Saint Stephen's Green (Dublin) Act, 1877
Phoenix Park Act, 1925
National Monuments Act, 1930
Bourn Vincent Memorial Park Act, 1932
Whale Fisheries Act, 1937
National Monuments (Amendment) Act, 1954
Holycross Abbey (County Tipperary) Act, 1969
Wildlife Act, 1976
Canals Act, 1986
National Monument (Amendment) Act, 1987
Shannon Navigation Act, 1990
National Monuments (Amendment) Act, 1994."

By virtue of section 2(1) of the Heritage Act 1995, "the Minister" means the Minister for Arts, Culture and the Gaeltacht. The title has since been changed to "Arts, Heritage, Gaeltacht and the Islands".

The Commissioners of Public Works in Ireland form part of and are under the direct control of the Department of Finance.

Subject to the provisions of section 24 of the Heritage Act it is the Commissioners who have direct responsibility "on the ground" for National Parks and Nature Reserves and the implementation of policy on the conservation of wildlife (flora and fauna). The National Parks and Wildlife Services (NPWS) (now (*qv*) Dúchas) are under the control of the Commissioners as circumscribed by section 24.

The description of all functions of the Commissioners under section 24 has recently been amalgamated under the name or title "Dúchas" meaning heritage.

COMMITTEES AND CONSULTATIVE GROUPS, CONSULTANTS AND ADVISERS IN THE AGENCY
(EPAA 1992, s. 41)

Section 41 of the EPAA 1992 permits the Agency to set up committees and consultative groups and delegate to them functions of the Agency which the Agency considers can be better or more conveniently performed by them. The section refers to their existing powers of delegation under section 25(6). The Agency reserves to itself the right to appoint a person to chair such a group but the group itself regulates its own procedure. Payment of the groups' expenses is out of the funds of the Agency as the Minister, with the consent of the Minister for Finance, may determine.

Section 42 of the EPAA 1992 entitles the Agency to engage consultants and advisers necessary for the discharge of its functions and to pay their fees out of its own monies. The Agency prepares a list of such persons from those who notify them in writing of their willingness to act as such a consultant or adviser giving their qualifications and experience and the Agency must have regard to the list of such persons when engaging a consultant or adviser. They can, however, appoint someone who is not on their list. Subsection (5) obliges the Agency to give a list of the names of such persons in its annual report.

COMMUNICATIONS, PROHIBITION OF
(EPAA 1992, s. 40(1))

Attempts to exercise improper influence.

Section 40(1) of the EPAA 1992

(1) Prohibits communications with the (*qv*) Director General, other director, an employee of the Agency, a member of the Advisory Committee or of a committee or consultative group established by the Agency, a consultant, adviser or other person engaged by the Agency, or a person whose services are availed of by, or supplied to the Agency under section 44 (*See:* SERVICES, PROVISION OF TO THE AGENCY) or who exercises or performs any function on behalf of the Agency under an agreement under section 45 (*See:* AGREEMENTS BETWEEN AGENCY AND OTHER PUBLIC BODIES AS TO PERFORMANCE OF FUNCTIONS), for the purpose of influencing improperly his consideration of any matter which falls to be considered by the Agency, committee or consultative group.

(2) Obliges the recipient of such a communication not to entertain the communication further and to forthwith inform the Agency in writing and the Agency is obliged to acknowledge the receipt of the information in writing.

COMMUNITY ACT
(WMA 1996, s. 5(1))

"means an act adopted by an institution of the European Communities."

COMMUNITY'S ACTS, POWER TO GIVE EFFECT TO
(WMA 1996)

See: REGULATIONS.

COMMUNITY ACTS GIVEN EFFECT TO BY WMA 1996
(WMA 1996, s. 2)

COMMUNITY LAW

This is the body of law arising from membership of the EU. It evolves from the treaties of the Community with annexes and protocols; conventions between member States; legislation; and judicial determination of the European Court of Justice. It takes precedence over the domestic law of Ireland in the event of conflict.

Legislation in the Community consists of:
(a) Regulations, which have a general application and are binding in their entirety and directly applicable to all member States;
(b) Directives, which state an objective which the member State must realise within a stated period; and
(c) Decisions, which are binding on those to whom they are addressed.

Section 2 of the WMA 1996:

"The purposes for which the provisions of this Act are enacted include the purpose of giving effect to the (*qv*) Community acts specified in the Table to this section.

TABLE

Council Directive 75/439/EEC of 16 June 1975 on the disposal of waste oils (O.J. No. L 194/23, 25.07.1975)
Council Directive 75/442/EEC of 15 July 1975 on waste (O.J. No. L 194/39, 25.07.1975)
Council Directive 76/403/EEC of 6 April 1976 on the disposal of polychlorinated biphenyls and polychlorinated terphenyls (O.J. No. L 108/41, 26.04.1976)
Council Directive 80/68/EEC of 17 December 1979 on the protection of groundwater against pollution caused by certain dangerous substances (O.J. No. L 20/43, 26.01.1980)
Council Directive 85/337/EEC of 27 June 1985 on the assessment of the effects of certain public and private projects on the environment (O.J. No. L 175/40 5.07.85)
Council Directive 86/278/EEC of 12 June 1986 on the protection of the environment, and in particular of the soil, when sewage sludge is used in agriculture (O.J. No. L 181/6, 4.07.1986)
Council Directive 87/101/EEC of 22 December 1986 amending Directive 75/439/EEC on the disposal of waste oils (O.J. No. L 42/43, 12.02.1987)
Council Directive 87/217/EEC of 19 March 1987 on the prevention and reduction of environmental pollution by asbestos (O.J. No.L 85/40, 28.03.1987)
Council Directive 89/369/EEC of 8 June 1989 on the prevention of air pollution from new municipal waste incineration plants (O.J. No. L 163/32, 14.06.1989)
Council Directive 91/156/EEC of 18 March 1991 amending Directive 75/442/EEC on waste (O.J. No.L 78/32, 26.03.1991)
Council Directive 91/157/EEC of 18 March 1991 on batteries and accumulators containing dangerous substances (O.J. No. L 78/38, 26.03.1991)
Council Directive 91/271/EEC of 21 May 1991 concerning urban waste water treatment (O.J. No. L 135/40, 30.05.1991)
Council Directive 91/689/EEC of 12 December 1991 on hazardous waste (O.J. No.L 377/20, 31.12.1991)
Council Directive 93/86/EEC of 4 October 1993 adapting to technical progress Council Directive 91/157/EEC on batteries and accumulators containing certain dangerous substances (O.J. No. L 264/51, 23.10.1993)
Council Regulation (EEC) No. 259/93 of 1 February 1993 on the supervision and control of shipments of waste within, into and out of the European Community (O.J. No. L 30/1, 6.02.1993)
European Parliament and Council Directive 94/62/EC of 20 December 1994 on packaging and packaging waste (O.J. No. L 365/10, 31.12.1994)"

COMPENSATION

Compensation is payable where any part of the necessary functions of a Minister involves the acquisition of land, rights over land, in the case of the F(A)A 1997, where a licence is revoked by the Minister under section 68(5) and under the NH 97 Regulations where the Minister refuses consent to (*qv*) operations and activities or modifies or revokes a lease or licence.

The Ministers concerned are Marine and Natural Resources under the Fisheries Acts and Arts, Heritage, Gaeltacht and the Islands under the WLA 1976 which includes the NH 97 Regulations.

(FA 1980, s. 43)

Section 43(1) of the FA 1980 provides that, subject to subsection (3) of the section, the exercise of any power under sections 18, 37, 38 or 39 of this Act shall be subject to payment of compensation in respect of:

(a) any estate or interest in any fishery, or any other estate or interest in land, acquired under or by virtue of this Act,

(b) any easement or other right in, over, under or in respect of land or any estate or interest in an easement or such other right, so acquired,

(c) any diminution, by reason of the exercise of the power, in the value of the easement or other right in, over, under or in respect of land, or any estate or interest in any land or in any easement or such right, and the compensation, together with any interest payable thereon by virtue of subsection (2), shall be paid:

(a) in case the power to acquire is exercised under the said section 37, by the Central Board,

(b) otherwise, by the person in whose favour the power is exercised.

Subsection (2)*(a)* provides that where compensation is payable under the section interest is payable at such rates as shall be determined from time to time by the Minister for Finance from the date on which the power is exercised until the payment of such compensation.

Subsection (2)*(b)* provides for a "lodgment" system where the person paying the compensation makes an unconditional offer in writing to the land owner and if the sum offered is not accepted and the sum awarded as compensation by the official (*qv*) arbitrator does not exceed the sum so offered no interest will be payable on such compensation.

Subsection (3) provides that a claim under section 43 for compensation shall be determined by arbitration under the Acquisition of Land (Assessment of Compensation) Act 1919.

Subsection (4) gives specific guidelines in relation to the basis for valuation of a fishery in respect of which an authorisation under section 37 is made in fixing the amount of compensation.

Subsection (5) provides that the Central Board or the official arbitrator, as the case may be, when determining the level of compensation payable, may have regard to the following:

(1) the current market value of the fishery,

(2) evidence of profitability of the fishery by reference to both -

(a) profits for a period ending prior to such authorisation, and

(b) a profit forecast regarding the fishery which is:

(i) related to a period equal in length to the period referred to in subparagraph (i) of this paragraph but beginning on a day which is subsequent to such authorisation, and

(ii) estimated both on a reasonable basis and on the assumption that the fishery continued to be used by the occupier and had not been so acquired.

Subsection (6) places a time limit of six years on the time within which a claim for compensation may be brought, or, in the case of a disability, six years from the end of the disability but, in any event, not more than thirty years.

Section 20 of the F(A)A 1999 amends this section by substituting "board" for "Central Board" placing the *(qv)* regional boards on an equal footing with the *(qv)* Central Board for the purposes of the section.

AQUACULTURE LICENCES

Section 68(5) of the F(A)A 1997 provides that where the Minister revokes or amends an (*qv*) aquaculture licence under subsection (1)*(c)* or (2) of section 65, the licensee shall be entitled to be paid compensation. *See:* REVOCATION AND AMENDMENT OF AQUACULTURE LICENCES.

(WLA 1976, ss. 17, 18 and 55)

DESIGNATION ORDERS

Section 17 of the WLA 1976 is the section under which the Minister makes (*qv*) Designation Orders, designating certain land as a refuge for (*qv*) fauna when he considers that a particular species of fauna on any land which is, or is contiguous to, a habitat of the species should be specially protected. *See:* DESIGNATION ORDERS.

Section 17(10) provides that the owner/occupier of the land is entitled to be paid compensation by the Minister in respect of any diminution of the value of his interest in or over the land consequent upon the making of the order and in default of agreement the compensation is fixed under the Acquisition of Land (Assessment of Compensation) Act 1919.

AGREEMENTS AS TO USE AND MANAGEMENT OF LAND

Section 18 of the WLA 1976 is still an important section and has been revived by its use in recent times to implement the Rural Environmental Protection Schemes (REPS).
See: MANAGEMENT AGREEMENTS, USE AND MANAGEMENT OF LAND.

By virtue of subsection (3) the agreement entered into can provide for the payment of a single or an annual sum.

This is not proper compensation as the Minister acquires no interest and cannot compel the acquisition of any interest in the lands. It can only arise under the section by agreement.

Under the REPS system of agreement the farmer continues to farm his land but he does so in a manner directed by an officer of the Forestry and Wildlife division of the Commissioners (now Dúchas) which is environmentally friendly to some species of flora or fauna *e.g.* the corncrake.

LAND PURCHASE ORDERS

Section 55 of the WLA 1976 provides that when the Minister wishes to purchase land and makes a purchase order under the section compensation is payable to the person whose interest he is acquiring by virtue of subsection (7). Subsection (8) provides that in default of agreement the amount of compensation is fixed by the Lay Commissioners of the Land Commission under section 31 of the Forestry Act 1946 as if it were compensation for an interest in vested land within the meaning of Part III of that Act. The Irish Land Commission was dissolved by the Irish Land Commission (Dissolution) Act 1992 *See:* LAY COMMISSIONERS.

(NH 97, Regs. 17 to 20)

Regulation 20 of the NH 97 Regulations:

"(1) (a) Where the Minister refuses his consent to an (*qv*) operation or activity under Chapter III of this Part, the Minister, shall save for the reasons set out in paragraphs (5) and (6), pay to the owner or occupier or user as the case may be by way of compensation an amount equal to the loss suffered by the owner, occupier or user by the depreciation of an interest in the land to which he or she is entitled.

(b) Where a Minister of the Government modifies or revokes a lease, licence, by virtue of Regulation 15(2), the Minister shall, save for the reasons set out in paragraph (6), pay to the lessee or licensee concerned by way of compensation an amount equal to the loss suffered by the lessee or licensee by the depreciation of any interest in land to which he or she would, but for the modification or revocation, be entitled."

For Regulation 15(2) *See:* ASSESSMENT, REG 15 AND EFFECT ON EXISTING LICENCES.

"(2) (a) The amount of compensation payable by the Minister under paragraph (1) shall be determined by reference to the difference between the antecedent and subsequent value of the land or of an interest in land consequent on the refusal of consent, which amount shall be offset by any amounts which the owner, occupier or user is receiving under the scheme dated 1st June 1994, and operated by the Minister for Agriculture , Food and Forestry and known as the Rural Environment Protection Scheme.

Provided that any amounts which the proposed operation or activity would have attracted by way of grant aid from any Minister of the Government or any body established or regulated by or under a statute, if consent had been given under Chapter II of this Part, shall not be taken into account in assessing the difference between the antecedent and subsequent value of the land."

Chapter II is obviously a mistake, consents to operations and activities are given under Chapter III. Regulation 14 of that Chapter provides for such consents. *See:* PROHIBITION (8)

"(b) The amount of compensation payable by the Minister under paragraph (1)(b) shall be determined by reference to the difference between the antecedent and subsequent value of the interest in the land consequent on the modification or revocation of the licence or lease concerned.

(3) Any claims for payment of compensation

under this Regulation shall, in default of agreement, be determined by arbitration under the Acquisition of Land (Assessment of Compensation) Act, 1919, and sections 69 to 83 of the Lands Clauses Consolidation Act, 1845, in all respects as if the claims arose in relation to compulsory acquisition of land.

(4) A claim for compensation under this Regulation shall be made not later than 6 months from the date of issue of the decision by the Minister under Chapter III of this Part or the modification or revocation of the lease or licence to which paragraph (1)(b) relates.

(5) Compensation under this Regulation shall not be payable for any loss arising from a refusal of consent for an operation or activity for as long as –
- (a) the Minister is in negotiation with the owner or occupier, as the case may be, for the purchase by agreement of the land, or
- (b) the Minister is in negotiation with the owner or occupier, as the case may be, to enter into a *(qv)* management agreement under section 18 of the Principal Act, or
- (c) proceedings for the compulsory acquisition of the lands are in train.

(6) Save where the refusal of consent or the modification or revocation of a lease or licence results in the discontinuance of the use to which the land has been put by the person concerned in the period of 5 years immediately preceding such refusal, modification or revocation or in the curtailment of such use of land, compensation will not be payable when the proposed operation or activity would significantly adversely affect: -
- (a) one or more specific (*qv*) natural habitat types in (*qv*) Annex 1 to the (*qv*) Habitats Directive or
- (b) one or more species or the habitats of these species in Annex II to the Habitats Directive, or
- (c) one or more species of bird or their habitat or other habitat specified in Article 4 of the (*qv*) Birds Directive.

(7) (a) Where the Minister has refused consent to an operation or activity under Chapter III of this Part, the Minister may make an order declaring that it would not be just and reasonable in the particular circumstances that payment of compensation should be prevented by the provisions of paragraph (6).
(b) Where a Minister of the Government modifies or revokes a licence or lease to which Regulation 15(2) relates the Minister may make an order declaring that it would not be just and reasonable in the particular circumstances that payment of compensation should be prevented by the provisions of paragraph (6).

(8) Any compensation payable under this Regulation may be made by the Minister either by way of a single payment or by way of payment of an annual sum to a person having, or claiming to be entitled to an interest in or over the land on which the compensation is payable."

COMPENSATION, PAYMENT OF FINES AS COMPENSATION

(FA 1980, s. 52)

Section 52 of the FA 1980 provides that in cases involving oysters where there is a prosecution under section 54 of the FA 1980 or sections 253 or 265 of the F(C)A 1959 the Court can, on the hearing of the prosecution and where there is a conviction, direct the payment to any witness for the prosecution who suffered loss or damage resulting wholly or partly from the offence, of a specified part of the fine as compensation for that loss or damage. The application must be brought before the imposition of the penalty and an application cannot be brought if there is a claim pending in any court in respect of the same loss or damage.

This section lost a great deal of its force on the repeal of section 54, which dealt with aquaculture and salmon levy, by section 4 of the F(A)A 1997 which also repealed section 54A which had been inserted by Regulation 21 (e) of the EC (EIA) Regulations, 1989.

The other two sections are still law. Section 253 deals with injuring or disturbing licensed oyster beds or oyster fisheries and section 265 deals with trespass on an oyster fishery granted under an oyster fishery order. *See:* OYSTERS.

COMPENSATORY MEASURES

(NH 97, Reg. 33)

Regulation 33 of the NH 97 Regulations provides:

"Where in accordance with Regulations 27(5), 28(5), 29(4), 30(5), 31(5) or 32(5) an (*qv*) operation or activity is agreed to, notwithstanding a negative assessment of the implications for a (*qv*) European site, the Minister shall ensure that the necessary compensatory measures are taken to ensure that the overall coherence of (*qv*) Natura 2000 is protected."

The Regulations quoted are dealt with under – ASSESSMENT OF IMPLICATIONS FOR CONSERVATION OBJECTIVES OF CERTAIN PUBLIC BODIES.

In spite of their title, these measures are not financial compensation but instead are measures which are designed to ameliorate or limit the impact or effect of operations or activities which have been approved.

CONDITIONS ATTACHING TO LICENCES ON THEIR GRANT OR REVIEW
(F(C)A 1959/LG(WP)A 1977/ APA 1987/EPAA 1992/WMA 1996)

Conditions imposed in return for the granting of licences are common in the field of environmental and planning legislation. The headings chosen under this entry are as follows:

CONDITIONS OF LICENCES ISSUED UNDER THE FISHERIES ACTS 1959–1997

(1) Section 171 licences under the F(C)A 1959
(2) Aquaculture licences under sections 7, 14 of the F(A)A 1997

CONDITIONS OF LICENCES ISSUED UNDER THE LG(WP)A 1977 AND LG(WP)(A)A 1990

(1) Licence to discharge trade and sewage effluent
(2) Review of licences under section 4
(3) Licensing of discharges to sewers

CONDITIONS OF LICENCES ISSUED UNDER APA 1987 TO OPERATE INDUSTRIAL PLANT

CONDITIONS FOR AN INTEGRATED POLLUTION CONTROL LICENCE ISSUED UNDER EPAA 1992

CONDITIONS FOR WASTE LICENCES ISSUED UNDER WMA 1996

CONDITIONS OF LICENCES ISSUED UNDER THE FISHERIES ACTS 1959–1997

(1) Section 171 licences under the F(C)A 1959

Section 171 of the F(C)A 1959, as well as dealing with an offence of pollution, deals with the issue of licences in respect of two separate operations:

(a) steeping in any (*qv*) waters flax or hemp,
(b) throwing, emptying, permitting to fall, causing to fall into any waters any (*qv*) deleterious matter.

Section 171(3) provides for the grant of such licences by the Minister for the purposes of the section, and may attach conditions to any licence, and may after like consultation revoke any licence. This applies to both (a) and (b) above. The section gives no assistance on the scope or nature of these conditions.

Note that in this, as in the case of licences under the LG(WP)A 1977 and the APA 1987, where the licence is in respect of an (*qv*) activity which comes within the meaning of "activity" in section 3(1) of the EPAA 1992, the licence will be granted under Part IV of that Act by the (*qv*) Agency and is called an "(*qv*) Integrated Pollution Control Licence" ("IPC Licences"). Under the WMA 1996 the Agency is the sole licensing authority for the granting of a (*qv*) waste licence.

(2) Aquaculture licences under sections 7, 14 of the F(A)A 1997

The F(A)A 1997 distinguishes, at section 6, between an (*qv*) aquaculture licence, a (*qv*) trial licence, an (*qv*) oyster bed licence or an (*qv*) oyster fishery order.

SECTION 7 LICENCE

Section 7(1) of the F(A)A 1997 provides:

"Subject to subsection 8, the (*qv*) licensing authority may, if satisfied that it is in the public interest to do so, licence a person, at a place or in (*qv*) waters specified in the licence, to engage in (*qv*) aquaculture or such operations in relation to aquaculture, and subject to such conditions, as it thinks fit and specifies in the licence."

SECTION 7 LICENCE CONDITIONS

Section 7(3) of the F(A)A 1997 provides:

"Without limiting the generality of subsection (1), conditions to which an (*qv*) aquaculture licence may be subject may include or relate to all or any of the following:

(a) a specification, by means of a map or otherwise, of the boundaries or limits of the place or waters in relation to which the licence is granted;
(b) the amount of feed inputs;
(c) annual or seasonal limits on stock inputs, outputs and standing stock on site;
(d) operational practices, including the fallowing of sites;
(e) the reporting of the incidences of disease and the presence of parasites;
(f) the disposal of dead fish;
(g) measures for preventing escapes of fish, and arrangements for the reporting of escapes,
(h) monitoring and inspection of the aquaculture carried on in pursuance of the licence;
(i) the keeping of records by the licensee;
(j) the protection of the environment (including the man-made environment of heritage value) and the control of discharges;
(k) appropriate environmental, water quality and biological monitoring."

SECTION 9 LICENCE CONDITIONS

Section 9(1) of the F(A)A 1997 provides for a (*qv*) trial licence. The Minister may licence a person, subject to such conditions, which may include or relate to all or any of the matters specified in section 7(3).

APPEAL AGAINST CONDITIONS ONLY

Section 52 of the F(A)A 1997 provides for the dealing by the (*qv*) Board with an appeal by reference only to the conditions. *See:* APPEAL, FA(3), APPEAL AGAINST CONDITIONS ONLY.

CONDITIONS OF LICENCES ISSUED UNDER THE LG(WP)A 1977 AND LG(WP)(A)A 1990

(1) Licence to discharge trade and sewage effluent

Section 4(3)*(a)* of the LG(WP)A 1977 provides:

"A local authority may at its discretion refuse to grant a licence under this section or may grant a licence subject to such conditions as it considers appropriate and specifies in the licence."

Section 4(5) of the LG(WP)A 1977 sets out the matters related to which conditions may be attached to licences issued under section 4.

Section 4(6) provides:

"Any conditions attached to a licence under this section shall be binding on any person discharging, or causing or permitting the discharge of, effluent to which the licence relates."

See: (1) REGULATIONS, SECTION 6 OF THE LG(WP)A 1977; (2) DISCHARGES TO AQUIFERS, CONTROL OF.

(2) Review of licences under section 4

Section 7(3) of the LG(WP)A 1977 (as substituted by section 5(a) of the LG(WP)(A)A 1990) provides:

"Upon completion of a review under this section, a local authority may amend or delete any condition of the licence or attach conditions or additional conditions to the licence or revoke the licence; and if the local authority proposes to exercise a power aforesaid, it shall do so as soon as may be after the completion of the appropriate review under this section."

See: REGULATIONS, SECTION 6 OF THE LG(WP)A 1977.

(3) Licensing of discharges to sewers

Section 16(2)*(a)* of the LG(WP)A 1977 provides:

"A sanitary authority may at its discretion refuse to grant a licence under this section or may grant such a licence subject to such conditions as it thinks appropriate and specifies in the licence."

Section 16(4) lists the matters relating to which conditions may be imposed on licences issued under section 16.

Section 16(5) provides:

"Any conditions attaching to a licence under this section shall be binding on any person discharging, or causing or permitting the discharge of, trade effluent or other matter to which the licence relates."

See: REGULATIONS, section 19 of the LG(WP)A 1977.

CONDITIONS OF LICENCES ISSUED UNDER APA 1987 TO OPERATE INDUSTRIAL PLANT

Section 32(1) of the APA 1987 provides:

"Where:
(a) an application is made to a local authority in accordance with regulations under section 31 for a licence under this Act,
(b) the requirements of, or made pursuant to such regulations have been complied with,
the local authority may, subject to section 35(2), decide to grant the licence subject to, or without, conditions or to refuse the application."

Section 32(4) lists the matters relating to which conditions may be imposed on licences issued under section 32.

Section 33 deals with review of licences.
*See:*REVIEW

Section 34 deals with appeals to an *(qv)* Bord Pleanála in relation to the granting or refusing of a licence or the granting of a revised licence. However, there is no appeal under the APA 1987 against conditions attaching to a reviewed licence.
See: LICENCES

CONDITIONS FOR AN INTEGRATED POLLUTION CONTROL LICENCE ISSUED UNDER EPPA 1992

Section 83(1) of the EPAA 1992 provides:

"Where an application is made to the Agency in the prescribed manner for a licence under this Part, it may, subject to section 94 and to compliance with any regulations under section 87, grant the licence subject to, or without, conditions or refuse the application."

Section 84(1) lists the matters relating to which conditions may be imposed on licences issued under section 83.

Sections 84(2), (3) and (4) provide:
Offence
"(2) It shall be an offence not to comply with any condition attached to a licence or revised licence.

(3) The Agency, or the sanitary authority, as the case may be, may recover the amount of any payment due to it arising from a condition attached to a licence or revised licence as a simple contract debt in any court of competent jurisdiction.

(4) Where a permission under Part IV of the Act of 1963 has been granted or an application has been made for such permission in relation to an activity, the Agency –
(a) shall consult the planning authority in whose functional area the activity is or will be situate in relation to any *(qv)* development which is necessary to give effect to any conditions to be attached to a licence or revised licence and which the Agency considers is not the subject of a permission or an application for permission under Part IV of the Act of 1963, and
(b) may attach to the licence or revised licence such conditions related to the above-mentioned development as may be specified by the planning authority for the purposes of the proper planning and development of the area or stricter conditions as the Agency may consider necessary for the prevention, limitation, elimination or abatement or reduction of pollution."

CONDITIONS FOR WASTE LICENCE ISSUED UNDER WMA 1996

Section 40 of the WMA 1996 provides:

"(1) (a) On application being made in that behalf to it, the Agency may grant to the applicant a waste licence subject to, or without, conditions or refuse to grant to the applicant such a licence.
(b) This subsection is subject to sections 42 and 50 and regulations under section 45."

Section 41 of the WMA 1996 provides:

"A waste licence may provide as respects any condition attached to it that the condition shall be complied with before or after any activity to which the licence relates has been commenced or has ceased."

Section 41(2) lists the matters relating to which conditions may be attached to a licence issued under section 49 of the WMA 1996.

Sections 41(3), (4), (5) and (6) provide:

"(3) The Minister may by regulations –
(a) require the Agency to attach as conditions to any waste licence that may be granted by it in respect of a specified class or classes of waste recovery or disposal activity, provisions requiring compliance with any specified standard, specification, procedure or other requirement, including any requirement the imposition of which is required or necessary to give effect to any *(qv)* Community act in relation to waste,
(b) require the Agency to attach as a condition to a waste licence of a specified class or classes a provision prohibiting the recovery or disposal of specified waste in a facility concerned or by means of a specified recovery or disposal activity, or
(c) require the Agency to take account of any other specified matter in attaching conditions to a waste licence.

(4) Conditions attached to a waste licence may apply in respect of any plant, or land or any part of any land, which is, or has been, used for the purpose of, or incidental to, an activity to which the licence relates and any emission from the facility concerned.

(5) The Agency may recover the amount of any payment due to it arising from a condition attached to a waste licence as a simple contract debt in any court of competent jurisdiction.

(6) Prior to the commencement of the waste recovery or disposal activity to which a waste licence relates, as the case may be, or the coming into force of a waste licence in respect of an activity to which section 39(3) applies, the Agency shall inspect the facility concerned in order to ensure that it complies with the relevant conditions attached to the waste licence."

EFFECT OF REVIEW OR SURRENDER ON CONDITIONS

Section 46(2) of the WMA 1996 provides that on completion of a review the Agency may grant to the holder thereof a waste licence ("a revised waste licence") the terms and conditions of which are, in such respects as the Agency thinks appropriate, different from the first-mentioned licence and the revised waste licence shall have effect in lieu of the first-mentioned licence.

Section 48(4), which deals with surrender of a waste licence, provides that for the purpose of subsection (3), the Agency may, by notice in writing served on the person who has applied under subsection (2) to surrender, requiring that person to carry out, or arrange to have carried out, in such manner as may be specified in the notice, such monitoring, sampling and investigations, in addition to those which may be required under a condition attached to the waste licence concerned, as the Agency considers necessary, and so specifies, and any requirements so made shall be regarded as a condition attaching to that licence and subsection (9) provides that the making of an application to surrender or the cesser of the activity to which the licence relates shall in no way affect or diminish such conditions, requirements or obligations applying to or falling on the holder as are specified in or arise under the licence. *See:* SURRENDER OF A WASTE LICENCE.

WASTE MANAGEMENT (LICENSING REGULATIONS) 1997 (S.I. No. 133 of 1997) PART VI

Licences issued under the Waste Management (Licensing Regulations) 1997 are dealt with in Articles 37–39 of those regulations. These articles provide:

"37. The Agency shall attach to any waste licence that may be granted by it such conditions as are, in the opinion of the Agency, necessary to give effect to the provisions, specified in column (1) of the Second Schedule, of the *(qv)* Community acts specified correspondingly in column (2) of the Schedule, in so far as such provisions are relevant to the waste recovery or disposal activity concerned.

38. In attaching conditions to a waste licence that may be granted by the Agency in respect of the disposal of waste at a *(qv)* landfill *(qv)* facility, the Agency shall, as far as is practicable, require the installation of systems to facilitate the collection and recovery or flaring of landfill gas.

39. For the purpose of the attachment by the Agency of conditions to a waste licence that may be granted by it in respect of the recovery or disposal of waste oils -
(a) Article 11 of Council Directive 75/439/EEC of 16 June 1975 on the disposal of waste oils (O.J. No.L

194/23, 25 July 1975) shall apply in respect of an activity disposing of more than 500 litres of waste oil per annum, and

(b) The Agency shall take such steps as are necessary for the purpose of compliance with Article 13.2 of the said Council Directive."

CONFIDENTIAL INFORMATION, DISCLOSURE OF
(EPAA 1992, s. 39)

Section 39 of the EPAA 1992:

"(1) A person shall not disclose confidential information obtained by him in his capacity as (*qv*) Director General, another director, an employee of the Agency, a member of the (*qv*) Advisory Committee or of a committee or consultative group established by the Agency, a consultant, adviser or other person engaged by the Agency, or a person whose services are availed of by, or supplied to, the Agency under section 44 or who exercises or performs any functions on behalf of the Agency under an agreement under section 45, unless he is duly authorised to do so.

(2) In this section –
'confidential information', without prejudice to the provisions of section 110, includes information that is expressed by the Agency to be confidential either as regards particular information or as regards information of a particular class or description.
'duly authorised' means authorised by the Agency or by some person authorised in that behalf by the Agency for the purposes of this section."

CONSERVATION
(WLA 1976, s. 2(1))

"includes management and regulation of the use of land in relation to the interests of wildlife and, where appropriate, development and improvement of land having regard to those interests."

(NH 97 Reg. 2(1))

"means a series of measures required to maintain or restore the natural habitats and the populations of species of wild (*qv*) fauna and (*qv*) flora at a favourable conservation status of a natural habitat and of a species."

Regulation 2(1) of the NH 97 Regulations also provides that the WLA 1976 and "these Regulations (other than Part IV)" shall be construed together as one.

ADDITIONAL DEFINITIONS IN NH 97 REGULATIONS

Apart from the definition of "conservation" and related words and phrases in the NH 97 Regulations, all of which derive from the Habitats Directive, there are a number of definitions in the Directive itself which do not appear in the Regulations but which may be helpful in bringing us closer to the European concept of "conservation" expressed in the Directive.

These are as follows:

Article 1 provides in paragraph (e) that the "conservation status of a natural habitat" means the sum of the influences acting on a natural habitat and its typical species that may affect its long-term natural distribution, structure and functions as well as the long-term survival of its typical species within the territory referred to in Article 2 and that the "conservation status of a natural habitat" will be taken as "favourable" when

– its natural range and areas it covers within that range are stable and increasing, and
– the specific structure and functions which are necessary for its long-term maintenance exist and are likely to continue to exist for the foreseeable future, and
– the conservation status of its typical species is favourable.

Article 1 provides in paragraph (i) that the "conservation status of a species" means the sum of the influences acting on the species concerned that may affect the long-term distribution and abundance of its populations within the territory referred to in Article 2 and that the "conservation status of a species" will be taken to be "favourable" when

– population dynamics data on the species concerned indicate that it is maintaining itself on a long-term basis as a viable component of its natural habitat, and
– the natural range of the species is neither being reduced nor is likely to be reduced for the foreseeable future, and
– there is, and will probably continue to be, a sufficiently large habitat to maintain its population on a long term basis.

"Species of community interest" means species which, within the territories referred to in Article 2, are:

(i) endangered, except those species whose natural range is marginal in that territory and which are not endangered or vulnerable in the western paleartic region; or
(ii) vulnerable, *i.e.* believed likely to move into the endangered category in the near future if the causal factors continue operating; or
(iii) rare, *i.e* small populations that are not at present endangered or vulnerable, but are at risk. The species are located within restricted geographical areas or are thinly scattered over a more extensive range; or
(iv) endemic and requiring particular attention by reason of the specific nature of their habitat and/or the potential impact of their exploitation on their habitat and/or the potential impact of their exploitation on their conservation status.

Such species are listed or may be listed in (*qv*) Annex II and/or Annex IV or V.

The references to the "territory in Article 4" is confusing. Article 4 sets out the requirements under EU law for the preparation of the list of sites by Member States to transmit to the Commission which will form the basis of the SAC (Special Area of Conservation) designations. *See:* CONSERVATION, SPECIAL AREAS OF.

CONSERVATION OF FISH STOCK
(F(A)A 1962, s. 35)

Offence
Section 35 of the F(A)A 1962 creates the offence of contravening an order made by the Minister which, having regard to any international agreement to which the State is a party, prescribes and adopts such measures of conservation of fish stocks and rational exploitation of fisheries as the Minister thinks proper.

A number of orders were made under this section but they and the section would appear to refer to sea fisheries which are not dealt with in this book. In any event the section does not appear as one for which the penalty was increased by section 50 of the FA 1980 which suggests that it is a dead letter in terms of enforcement.

CONSERVATION MEASURES
(NH 97, Reg. 13)

This Regulation provides for conservation measures to be undertaken by the Minister to protect (*qv*)special areas of conservation.

Regulation 13 of the NH 97 Regulations (S.I. 94 of 1997) provide:

"(1) The Minister shall establish the conservation measures which the Minister considers appropriate, in respect of (*qv*) special areas of conservation designated under Regulation 9 including, if necessary, management plans either specifically designated for the sites or integrated into appropriate plans.

(2) The Minister shall establish the administrative or contractual measures which correspond to the ecological requirements of the natural habitat types in (*qv*) Annex I to the (*qv*) Habitats Directive and the species in Annex II to that Directive present on the sites. (Article 6.1 of the Directive)

(3) The Minister shall take the appropriate steps to avoid, in the special areas of conservation designated under Regulation 9, the deterioration of natural habitats and the habitats of species as well as disturbance of the species for which the areas have been designated insofar as such disturbance could be significant in relation to the objectives of the Habitats Directive." (Article 6.2 of the Directive).

These two Regulations slavishly repeat almost verbatim the convoluted prose style of the Directive, the language of which bears no relation to the expression of any Irish legal discipline.

It was a great pity that no attempt was made to adapt the NH 97 Regulations to the WLA 1976 despite the language barrier. As it is you now have two sets of regulatory laws running side by side and often contradicting one another and expressed to be construed together as one. The much awaited Wildlife Bill, whenever it is enacted, will add a third dimension to the confusion. A consolidated Wildlife Act is called for.

Regulation 2(2) of the NH 97 Regulations provides that a word or expression that is used in the Regulations and is also used in the Habitats Directive shall, unless the contrary intention is expressed, have in the Regulations the meaning that it has in the Habitats Directive.

The Minister, having conferred upon him-self/herself the power and undertaken the obligation to provide "conservation measures" under Regulation 13 as required by the Habitats Directive must now proceed to fulfil that obligation.

CONSERVATION ORDERS UNDER LG(P&D)A 1963
(LG(P&D)A 1963, s. 46)

Section 46(1) of the LG(P&D)A 1963 as amended by substitution by section 40(b) of the LG(P&D)A 1976 provides that if it appears to a (*qv*) Planning Authority, after consultation with prescribed authorities (such as an Taisce, the National Monuments Advisory Council (now the (*qv*) Heritage Council) and Bord Fáilte) that it is expedient in the interests of amenity to make provision to preserve from extinction or otherwise protect any flora or fauna in an area, or part of an area, to which a *(qv)* Special Amenity Area Order relates, being flora or fauna which are of special amenity value or special interest, it may make an order prohibiting (subject to any exemptions for which provision may be made by the order) the taking, killing, or destroying of such flora and fauna.

Subsections (2), (7) and (10) of this section were repealed by section 45 of the LG(P&D)A 1976.

Subsection (3) provides that an order under this section may be revoked or varied by a subsequent order under this section.

Subsection (4) provides that where a planning authority make an order under this section, they shall cause a notice stating the effect of the order and stating the right of appeal under subsection (5) to be published in at least one newspaper circulating in the area to which the order relates.

Subsection (5) provides that any person may, at any time before the expiration of one month after the publication of a notice under the foregoing subsection, appeal to the Minister against the order to which the notice relates.

Subsection (6) provides that where an appeal is brought under this section against an order, the Minister may confirm the order with or without modifications or annul the order.

Offence
Subsection (8) provides that if any person contravenes the provisions of an order under this section (other than an order which has been annulled), he shall be guilty of an offence and liable on summary conviction to a fine not exceeding two hundred pounds.

Subsection (9) provides that particulars of an order under this section shall be entered in the planning register.

Subsection (11) provides that any reference in this Act to a conservation order shall be construed as a reference to an order under this section (other than an order which has been annulled).

CONSERVATION, SPECIAL AREAS OF:
(NH 97, Reg. 2(1))

"means a site of European importance designated by the Member States through a statutory, administrative or contractual act, or any combination thereof, where the necessary conservation measures are applied for the maintenance or restoration, at a favourable conservation status, of either or both the natural habitats and the populations of species for which the site is designed."

Part II of the NH Regulations under the heading "the conservation of natural habitats and the habitats of species" from Reg. 3 to Reg. 12 fulfils the Irish legislative obligation to implement the main objective of the Directive which is "the conservation of natural habitats and of wild fauna and flora" as follows:

Reg. 3. SELECTION FOR DESIGNATION

Selection of sites for identification as sites of European importance and preparing a list known as a candidate list of (*qv*) European sites

Reg. 4. NOTIFICATION

(1) Of the appropriate Irish Government and other agencies by sending them a copy of the candidate list,
(2) Of every owner and occupier of land mentioned in the *(qv)* candidate list of European sites and the holders of prospecting or exploration licences relating to such land of the proposal to list the land.

A copy of the list is also transmitted to the Commission.

Each notification shall, in respect of each site:

(a) be accompanied by an ordnance map identifying the site and its boundaries;
(b) indicate the (*qv*) operation or activity which would be likely to alter, damage, destroy or interfere with the integrity of the site;
(c) indicate the habitat type, or types, the site hosts or the species the site hosts and for which the site is proposed to be identified as a site of Community importance;
(d) indicate the procedures by which a person can object.

See: NOTICE OF NOTIFIABLE ACTIONS.

Reg. 5(1) OBJECTION
A person on whom a notice is served can (*qv*) object only on scientific grounds. That person or any other person claiming to have or to be entitled to an interest in the land has three months from the date of service of the notice to object.

Reg. 5(2) REVIEW OR MODIFICATION
The Government Departments and other agencies notified under Reg. 4(1) have a right, within the same period, to seek a review or modification of the list.

Reg. 5(4) AMENDMENT AND TRANSMISSION
The Minister, having considered the objections and requests under Reg. 5(3) amends the candidate list and transmits it to the Commission in accordance with Article 4(1) of the Habitats directive.

Reg. 6 INITIATION OF CONSULTATION
The Commission is entitled under paragraph (1) of Article 5 of the Habitats Directive to initiate consultation with respect to a site following which the Minister either agrees that the site should be added to the list or the Council of the European Communities decides that the site should be included in accordance with paragraph 3 Article 5 of the Habitats Directive.

Reg. 7 SURVEILLANCE
Deals with the obligation placed on the Minister and the Minister for the Marine, in respect of the natural habitats and species specified in Article 2 of the Habitats Directive, to undertake surveillance of the conservation status, of the fish species specified in Part II of the First Schedule. *See:* SCHEDULES HERETO, NH 97 SCHEDULES. The two Ministers have the right under the Regulations to appoint (*qv*)authorised officers for the purpose of the surveillance. *See:* AUTHORISED PERSONS UNDER WLA 1976; (2) ENTRY AND SEARCH (D).

Reg. 8 ADOPTION OR DECISION
The Commission then proceeds to adopt the candidate list in accordance with the procedures laid down in paragraph 2 of Article 4 of the Habitats Directive or they take a decision in accordance with paragraph 3 of Article 5 of the Habitats Directive.

Once the Minister has been informed of adoption or decision he must again notify the owners and occupiers of the site and persons having prospecting and exploration licences in relation to the site and the Government Departments and Agencies specified in Reg. 4 (1) and this Regulation that the site has been so adopted or a decision taken and that he intends to proceed in accordance with Regulation 9 to designate the site as a special area of conservation.

Reg. 9 DESIGNATION
(1) Not later than six years from the date the site is adopted by the Commission the Minister shall designate the site as a special area of conservation and the Minister shall publish in an Iris Oifigúil a copy of every such designation.
(2) Provides for registration of a designation in the Land Registry as a burden on the land.
(3) (a) The Minister may, in agreement with the Commission, amend or revoke a designation.
    (b) Before amending or revoking he must carry out the consultation in paragraph (1) and the notification in paragraph (2) of regulation 4 prior to obtaining the agreement of the Commission.

Reg. 10(1) PRIORITIES FOR DESIGNATION
The Minister shall establish priorities for the designation of sites having regard to:
(a) the importance of the sites for the maintenance or restoration at a (*qv*)favourable conservation status of
  (i) a (*qv*) natural habitat type or types in (*qv*) Annex I to the (*qv*) Habitats Directive, or,
  (ii)a species in (*qv*) Annex II to the Habitats Directive, or
(b) the coherence of (*qv*) Natura 2000, or
(c) the threats of degradation or destruction to which these sites are exposed.

Reg. 11(1) SITE NOTICE OF DESIGNATION
(1) The Minister will erect on the designated lands or nearby a notice of the existence of the designation and the regulations confers a right of entry onto land for this purpose.

offence
(2) Any person who destroys, alters, defaces, disfigures, marks or otherwise interferes with such a notice shall be guilty of an offence.

See: NOTICE OF DESIGNATION OF SAC.

Reg. 12(1) MANAGEMENT AGREEMENT
(1) The Minister may enter into a (*qv*) management agreement in accordance with section 18 of the WLA 1976 in relation to lands which have become a European site by virtue of these Regulations or which is near such a site

(2) Any agreement already in existence under that section shall have the same effect as if entered into under these Regulations.

PCSAC in environmental jargon has become the abbreviated manner of expressing "proposed candidate site special area of conservation".

PROTECTION OF SPECIAL AREAS OF CONSERVATION

The protection of these sites is dealt with under separate headings. *See:* (1) OPERATIONS AND ACTIVITIES; (2) PROTECTION (9) AND (10).

CONSULTATION
(LG(WP)A 1977, s. 24)

Section 24 of the LG(WP)A 1977:

"The Minister may, after consultation with the Minister for Fisheries, the Minister for Industry and Commerce, any other Minister who appears to him to be interested and the (*qv*) Water Pollution Advisory Council, make regulations requiring local authorities, sanitary authorities and (*qv*) boards of conservators to consult with such persons and in such manner in relation to the exercise of such powers and duties under this Act as may be prescribed."

This would have been extended to the Agency by virtue of section 81 of the EPAA 1992 but the section would appear to be ineffective in light of the failure to establish a Water Advisory Council and subsequent legislation which is quoted hereunder.

(LG(WP)(A)A 1990, s. 29)

Section 29 of the LG(WP)(A)A 1990:

"(1) Where the Minister considers that, having regard to any of the functions of any Minister of the Government, that Minister of the Government ought to be consulted in relation to the making of regulations under sections 4(10), 16(10), 24, 25(1), 26(1) or 27(1) of the Principal Act (the LG(WP)A 1977), he shall not make the regulations without having consulted that Minister of the Government.

(2) So much of the enactments aforesaid as provide for consultation with specified persons in relation to the making of regulations shall cease to have effect."

(APA 1987, s. 20)

Section 20 of the APA 1987:

"The Minister may make regulations requiring a local authority to consult with such bodies or persons as may be specified in relation to the performance of such of their functions under this Act as may be prescribed."

(EPAA 1992, s. 80)

Section 80 of the EPAA 1992:

"The Agency shall consult with such public authorities, persons or bodies as it considers necessary or as may be prescribed in relation to the performance of its functions under this Act or such of those functions as may be prescribed and shall have regard to any views given or recommendations made by such public authority, person or body."

Section 81 of the EPAA 1992:

"The Agency shall be consulted by such public authorities prior to the discharge of such functions related to the environment as the Minister, following consultation with any other Minister of the Government who in the opinion of the Minister is concerned, may, by regulations, specify and such public authorities shall have regard to the views of the Agency prior to carrying out the functions specified."

(WMA 1996, s. 54)

Section 54(4)*(a)* of the WMA 1996 provides for consultation, in the circumstances envisaged by the section, between the Agency and a (*qv*)planning authority. *See:* PLANNING PERMISSION, APPLICATION OF LG(P&D)A 1963 TO SECTION 54 WMA 1996.

CONTAINED USE
(EPAA 1992)

""Contained use" is defined in Article 3(1) of the Genetically Modified Organisms Regulations, 1994 (S.I. No. 345 of 1994) as meaning any operation in which organisms are genetically modified or in which such genetically modified organisms are cultured, stored, used, transported, destroyed or disposed of and for which physical barriers, or a combination of physical barriers, together with chemical and/or biological barriers, are used to limit their contact with the general population and the environment."

CONTRAVENTION, CONTINUANCE OF CONTRAVENTION
(LG(WP)A 1977, ss. 10 and 11)

See: PROHIBITION (2).

CONVICTION
(WMA 1996, s. 18)

Section 18(6) of the WMA 1996 provides that particulars of a conviction for any offence under the WMA 1996 must be given to each local authority and the Agency. *See:* INFORMATION

COSTS OF PROSECUTION, PAYMENT TO PROSECUTOR
(F(C)A 1959/LG(WP)(A)A 1990, s. 28)

Section 28 of the LG(WP)(A)A 1990:

"Where a person is convicted of an offence under the Principal Act [LG(WP)A 1977], this Act or sections 171 or 172 of the Act of 1959 committed after the commencement of this section, the court shall, unless it is satisfied that there are special and substantial grounds for not so doing, order the person to pay any local authority, sanitary authority or *(qv)* regional board concerned the costs and expenses, measured by the court, reasonably incurred by the authority or board in relation to the investigation, detection and prosecution of the offence, including costs incurred in the taking of samples, the carrying out of tests, examinations and analyses and in respect of remuneration and other expenses of employees, consultants and advisers."

The Act of 1959 is the F(C)A 1959.

(EPAA 1992, s. 12)

Section 12 of the EPAA 1992 gives an exactly similar right to the Agency to recover their costs and expenses of prosecuting under the EPAA 1992.

(WMA 1996, s. 28)

Section 28 of the WMA 1996 gives an exactly similar right to a local authority, the Agency, or a person specified under section 11(2) to recover their costs and expenses of prosecuting under the WMA1996.

COUNCIL, THE HERITAGE COUNCIL, THE
(Heritage Act 1995, s. 2(1))

means the body established under section 5.

Section 5(2) of the Heritage Act 1995:

"There shall stand established on the establishment day a body to be known as An Chomhairle Oidhreachta or, in the English language, the Heritage Council to perform the functions conferred on it by this Act."

The Council was established on July 10, 1995 by virtue of the Heritage Act 1995 (Establishment Day) Order 1995 (S.I. No. 177 of 1995).

FUNCTIONS OF THE HERITAGE COUNCIL

Section 6 of the Heritage Act 1995:

"(1) The functions of the Council shall be to propose policies and priorities for the identification, protection, preservation and enhancement of the national heritage, including monuments, archaeological objects, heritage objects, architectural heritage, *(qv)* flora, *(qv)* fauna, *(qv)* wildlife habitats, landscapes, seascapes, wrecks, *(qv)* geology, heritage gardens and parks and *(qv)* inland waterways.

(2) References to the National Monuments Advisory Council, the Historic Monuments Council, or the Wildlife Advisory Council in any enactment or instrument made thereunder shall, where appropriate, be construed as references to the Council.

(3) The Council shall in particular –
(a) promote interest, education, knowledge and pride in, and facilitate the appreciation and enjoyment of the national heritage,
(b) co-operate with public authorities, educational bodies and other organisations and persons in the promotion of the functions of the Council,
(c) promote the coordination of all activities relating to the functions of the Council."

Section 7 of the Heritage Act 1995:

"(1) The Council may make recommendations to the Minister [Arts, Heritage, Gaeltacht and the Islands] on any matter relating to the Council's functions, and may make such recommendations public.

(2) The Minister shall respond to a recommendation referred to in subsection (1)

within six months of receipt thereof."

Section 8:

"The Council shall, if the Minister so requests, furnish the Minister with advice on any matter relating to the functions of the Council and with information regarding the performance of its functions."

Section 9:

"(1) The Minister may, by order, after consultation with the Council, and after consideration by the Government, confer on the Council such additional functions relating to the national heritage as the Minister thinks appropriate.

(2) Where an order is proposed to be made under this section, a draft of the order shall be laid before each House of the Oireachtas and the order shall not be made until a resolution approving the draft has been passed by each House."

Section 11:

"(1) The Council may co-operate with and provide assistance and advice to any person or body, including a public authority, in respect of any matter which is related to the performance of its functions as it considers desirable.

(2) In this section 'assistance' includes payments of money on such terms and conditions as the Council may decide."

STANDING COMMITTEES

Article 9(2) of the Schedule, section 5, to the Heritage Act provides for the establishment of standing committees on

(a) wildlife,
(b) archaeology,
(c) architectural heritage, and
(d) inland waterways,

and the Minister may appoint three persons who are not members of the Council to each standing committee.

COUNTY COUNCILS

Section 1 Local Government (Ireland) Act 1898 established County Councils, consisting of a chairman and councillors, with responsibility for the administration of the Counties of Ireland. They took over the various functions of Grand Juries and Boards of Guardians who preceded them as administrative bodies.

The County Councillors are an elected body who elect a Chairman from amongst their numbers.

RESERVED FUNCTIONS

The functions reserved to the Council are called "reserved functions" and these functions are exercised by way of resolution of the Council.

EXECUTIVE FUNCTIONS

All other functions are called "executive functions" and are exercised by the County Manager on behalf of the Council, and he, in his turn, employs engineers, chemists, environmental advisers and all other persons necessary to assist him in the performance of those functions.

FUNCTIONS OF COUNTY COUNCILS

Among the functions of a County Council are the following:

(1) Planning
They are the planning authority for their functional area under the LG(P&D)Acts, 1963 to 1999.

(2) Housing
They are the housing authority for their functional area by virtue of the Housing Acts 1966 to 1979.

(3) Fire
They are the fire authorities for their functional area by virtue of the Fire Services Act 1981.

(3) Sanitary Authority/LG(WP)A 1977
They are sanitary authorities for their functional area for the purposes of the Local Government (Sanitary Services) Acts 1878 to 1964 and in that capacity have the powers of prosecution described at section 27 of the LG(WP)(A)A 1990 and set out in the Table to the section.

(4) Water Pollution Acts
They have other powers of prosecution as local authorities described in the same section 27 as distinct from their powers under the same section as sanitary authorities.

(5) APA 1987
They have powers of prosecution and enforcement under section 13 of the APA 1987.

(6) Water Pollution Acts
They have powers of enforcement other than prosecution under sections 10(5), 12, 13 and 23 of the LG(WP)A 1977 and sections 21 and 22 of the LG(WP)(A)A 1990.

(7) APA 1987
They have powers of enforcement other than prosecution under sections 26, 27 and 43 of the APA 1987.
(8) WMA 1996
They share with the Agency the power to prosecute conferred by section 11 of the WMA 1996.
(9) WMA 1990
They have powers of enforcement other than prosecution under sections 55 and 56 of the WMA 1996.
(10) Management Plans
They have obligations to prepare management plans:
(i) Water, section 15 LG(WP)A 1977 as amended by section 11 LG(WP)(A)A 1990.
(ii) Air, Air Quality Management Plans and Standards, of the section 26 APA 1996
(iii) Waste, section 22 of the WMA 1996.
(11) They have specific functions under Article 10 of the Waste Management (Use of Sewage Sludge in Agriculture) Regulations 1998, and Article 19 in both the Waste Management (Packaging) Regulations 1997 and the Waste Management (Farm Plastics) Regulations 1997.

County Councils also have statutory powers and obligations in respect of sewers, water supply, dangerous buildings, refuse collection, street cleaning, baths, wash-houses, offensive trades, burial grounds, temporary dwellings, building bye-laws, street lighting, markets and slaughterhouses.

County Boroughs and City Councils have the same powers and obligations.

CRAB
(F(C)A 1959, s. 285)

Offence
Section 285(1) of the F(C)A 1959 creates the offences of having in possession, selling, exposing for sale, consigning for sale or buying for sale:
(a) any edible crab by whatever name known, carrying any spawn attached to the tail or other exterior part of the crab, or
(b) any edible crab by whatever name known which has recently cast its shell.

(Note that the maximum penalty prescribed under this section has been increased. *See:* FINES AND IMPRISONMENT (IMPOSITION OF)).

Subsection (2) provides for forfeiture of any crab as a statutory consequence of conviction.

Subsection (3) provides that it shall be a good defence to a prosecution under the section to prove that the crab was intended as bait for fishing.

CROSS LINES
(F(C)A 1959, s. 167)

See: METHODS OF FISHING, PROHIBITION OF.

D

DAM

(F(C)A 1959, s. 3(1))

"means (except in section 115) dam, weir, dyke, sluice, embankment or other structure built or placed in or in connection with any river for or in connection with the sustaining of water for any purpose."

DAMMING, TEEMING OR EMPTYING A RIVER

(F(C)A 1959, s. 169)

Offence

"If any person dams, teems or empties any river or mill race for the purpose of taking or destroying any (*qv*) salmon or (*qv*) trout, such person shall be guilty of an offence under this section."

(Note that the maximum penalty prescribed under this section has been increased. *See:* FINES AND IMPRISONMENT (IMPOSITION OF).

DAMS AND NATURAL OBSTRUCTIONS

(F(C)A 1959, Chap V, Part VIII)

"Dam" is defined in the F(C)A 1959, section 115 as follows –

"(1) In this section, the word 'dam' means any dam, weir, dyke or other erection placed in or across a salmon river for sustaining the (*qv*) water of such river for mill power, navigation, irrigation or other purposes."

The object of Part VIII of the F(C)A 1959 is to ensure the free passage and migration of fish in salmon rivers at all times and at one or more places through dams built across the rivers for the purpose of sustaining the water of such river for the purposes specified in the definition in section 115(1) above.

The Minister is given extensive powers to ensure that the passage of fish is free and uninterrupted.

REQUIREMENTS FOR A DAM

Subsection (2) of section 115 deals with the requirements, for the purposes of the section, of a dam built after August 10, 1842 – there was a Fisheries Act in that year – which are that it must be so constructed as to permit or allow, in one or more parts thereof, the free run or migration of all fish at all periods of the year.

Subsection (3) deals with the requirements for a dam built before that date which involves an application to the Minister, a survey and a direction by the Minister as to what works are necessary to bring the dam into compliance with the terms of the section.

The cost of these works is borne by the person interested in the fishery of that river.

Subsection (5) allows a (*qv*) regional board, after consultation with the Minister, to contribute from its own funds towards the cost of such works on dams.

NOTICES

Section 116 and 117 of the F(C)A 1959 provide for service of notices by the Minister on an occupier specifying the works to be carried out, section 116 where the free run of fish has been obstructed, and section 117 where a dam has been abandoned and disused for over five years.

Under section 116(2) the dam owner has a complex right of appeal where he can prove that the works specified in the notice would involve a reduction of more than 5% of the working horsepower available to his mill or factory.

Offence

Section 116(5) of the F(C)A 1959 creates the offence of failing to comply with the requirements of a notice under section 116.

(Note that the maximum penalty prescribed under this subsection has been increased. *See:* FINES AND IMPRISONMENT (IMPOSITION OF)).

The Minister has power under both sections 116 and 117 to carry out the works himself where there is default and recover the cost as a simple contract debt.

ALTERING AND REMOVING NATURAL OBSTRUCTIONS

Section 118 of the F(C)A 1959 empowers the Minister to alter or remove natural obstructions such as ledges of rocks or shoals which prevent or impede free passage. The *(qv)* regional fishery board is entitled to contribute to the cost.

A FISH PASS

Section 119(1) of the F(C)A 1959 defines "fish pass", as a fish pass made under sections 62 or 63 of the 1842 Fisheries Act or sections 115 or 118 of this Act.

Offence
Section 119(2) of the F(C)A 1959 makes it an offence for a person:

(a) to take, kill or destroy any fish in a fish pass, or
(b) to hang, fix, use or set in a fish pass any fishing engine, or
(c) to place any obstruction, use any contrivance or do any act whereby fish may be scared, deterred or in any way prevented from freely passing up and down through a fish pass at all periods of the year, or
(d) to fail to preserve a fish pass free from every obstruction.

On conviction in addition to imposing a penalty the court may direct the defendant to remove the obstruction at his expense.

(Note that the maximum penalty prescribed under this subsection has been increased. *See:* FINES AND IMPRISONMENT (IMPOSITION OF)).

Subsection (2) of this section foreshadows attempts in later environmental legislation to catch the hidden "bosses" and it describes the circumstances in which the owner or occupier can be prosecuted in respect of an act done by an employee with the knowledge or connivance of the owner or where the offence occurs through "the default of reasonable precaution" on the part of the owner to prevent it.

Offence
Section 120(1) of the F(C)A 1959 creates the offence of using a (*qv*) fishing engine (other than rod and line) within two hundred yards above or below dams used for supplying water to mills and factories or for navigation.

(Note that the maximum penalty prescribed under this subsection has been increased. *See:* FINES AND IMPRISONMENT (IMPOSITION OF)).

Subsection (2) provides that the fishing engine is forfeited as a statutory consequence of conviction.

Subsection (3) provides that a person who had a (*qv*) several fishery for twenty years next before August 14, 1850 is not bound by this section.

Offence
Section 121(1) of the F(C)A 1959 creates the offence of a person, even the owner of a several fishery excused at section 120(3), using a fishing engine (other than rod and line) at or within fifty yards of a mill dam unless:

(a) there is attached to such mill dam a fish pass of such form and dimensions as may be approved by the Minister, and
(b) such fish pass has constantly running through it such flow of water as will enable salmon to pass up and down it.

(Note that the maximum penalty prescribed under this subsection has been increased. *See:* FINES AND IMPRISONMENT (IMPOSITION OF)).

MILLS, MILL SLUICES AND WHEEL SLUICES ON SALMON RIVERS

Section 122(1) of the F(C)A 1959 defines the words "mill" for the purposes of the section, as including any factory, machine, building or other work by or for which water is used for any purpose, but does not include any work for the generation, by means of hydraulic power, of electricity, for distribution and supply to the public.

Section 122(1) defines the expression "wheel sluices", in relation to a mill as meaning "the sluices which admit water to the wheels of a mill."

Subsection (2) provides that where a mill derives its water from a salmon river:

(a) where there is a free pass in the dam, the wheel sluices and the waste gates or over-falls shall be kept shut
  (i) for 24 consecutive hours in each week between the hours of 6 p.m. on Saturday and the hour of 6 a.m. on the next following Monday, and
  (ii) during any other period when the mill is not being worked,
(b) where there is no free pass and the waste gate on the upstream side of the wheel sluices is erected in a channel suitable for the passage of fish, the wheel sluices shall be kept shut and the waste gate kept open for the same periods as above.

Offence
Failure to comply with subsection 2(a) or (b) is an offence for the occupier of the mill.

(Note that the maximum penalty prescribed under this subsection has been increased. *See:* FINES AND IMPRISONMENT (IMPOSITION

OF)).

Subsection (3) provides that it is a good defence for the occupier to prove that compliance with either (a) or (b) of the section would in any way have injuriously interfered with the machinery or water power of the mill.

GRATINGS IN WATERCOURSES

Section 123(1) of the F(C)A 1959 provides for the provision of gratings in watercourses diverted from salmon rivers for the supply of towns or the irrigation of lands or as moving power for machinery or for any other purpose, to prevent entry therein of salmon and trout. This does not apply where the water is diverted for navigation or fish ponds. It is only necessary in the months of March, April and May and such other periods of the year when the brood of salmon or trout are descending the river.

Offence
Subsection (2) creates an offence of failing to comply with subsection (1).

(Note that the maximum penalty prescribed under this subsection has been increased. *See:* FINES AND IMPRISONMENT (IMPOSITION OF)).

Subsection (3) permits the Minister to grant an exemption for any period from the obligations imposed by (1) where water is used as a moving power for machinery and it is necessary for the effective working of that machinery.

Subsection (4) gives the Minister power to revoke an exemption under subsection (3) hereof or under section 4 of the Salmon Fishery (Ireland) Act 1869.

GRATINGS ON HYDRAULIC MACHINES

Section 124(1) of the F(C)A 1959 places an obligation on the owner of a turbine or similar hydraulic machines, supplied from a salmon river, which may be injurious to salmon in their descent to the sea, during the time when such descent takes place, to provide grating to prevent salmon passing into such machine.

Offence
Subsection (2) provides that failure to perform the duty imposed by subsection (1) constitutes an offence.

(Note that the maximum penalty prescribed under this subsection has been increased. *See:* FINES AND IMPRISONMENT (IMPOSITION OF)).

TAKING FISH IN WORKS OR WATERCOURSES APPURTENANT TO MILLS

Offence
Section 125(1) of the F(C)A 1959 creates the offence of using a (*qv*) fishing engine (other than rod and line) or by any means taking, destroying or obstructing salmon or other fish in any season of the year in any mill pool or mill dam or in any works appurtenant to any mill or factory or in any of the watercourses leading the water to or from any mill or factory.

(Note that the maximum penalty prescribed under this subsection has been increased. *See:* FINES AND IMPRISONMENT (IMPOSITION OF)).

Section 125(2) provides a fishing engine in respect of which the offence was committed is forfeited as a statutory consequence.

LIABILITY OF OWNER OR OCCUPIER

Offence
Section 125(3) of the F(C)A 1959 creates the offence of taking fish under section 125 by shutting down the sluice gate where the sluice gate is under the exclusive power of the occupier of a mill or factory and the perpetrator of the offence is unknown or cannot be found, then where the commission of the offence can be proved the occupier can be charged with an offence under subsection (3).

(Note that the maximum penalty prescribed under this subsection has been increased. *See:* FINES AND IMPRISONMENT (IMPOSITION OF)).

Subsection (4) sets out a complex set of circumstances designed to prove the guilt of the owner or occupier where:

(a) it can be proved that the offence was committed in such circumstances as to afford reasonable grounds for believing that the offence was committed -
   (i) by some person in the employment or under the control of the owner or occupier, or
   (ii) with the knowledge or connivance of such owner or occupier or of the person in charge,
   (iii) through the default of reasonable precaution on the part of such owner or occupier to prevent such offence, and
(b) it is alleged and proved that the offence was committed but the perpetrator is unknown and cannot be found, and
(c) the owner or occupier is charged with the

offence, such owner or occupier shall be deemed to be guilty of such offence and shall be punished accordingly.

DAMAGE BY PROTECTED WILD BIRDS AND PROTECTED WILD ANIMALS

(WLA 1976 s. 42 and 1986 Regs., Art. 3)

The strategy under the WLA 1976 for the protection of protected wild birds and protected wild animals was formulated by reference to sections 22 and 23 and the Third and Fifth Schedules, referred to in those sections.

In section 22, by reference to the Third Schedule, the birds which are not mentioned are protected, or, in the words of the section "this section applies to every wild bird other than a wild bird of a species specified in the Third Schedule". These birds which are excluded from the Schedule become protected wild birds.

Section 23, on the other hand, by reference to the Fifth Schedule, protects as protected wild animals those species which appear in that Schedule or, in other words, those that are included.

Over the years these Schedules were much amended by regulations as species of birds, particularly, came under threat.

Eventually, the orders made under section 22 resulted in the protection of all wild birds without exception. This was no help to farmers for whom a number of these wild birds had always been pests and traditionally were shot as vermin. The killing of some even attracted a bounty from the State.

To allay these fears the European Communities (Wildlife Act 1976) (Amendment) Regulations 1986 (S.I. No. 254 of 1986) were passed, which listed in the first schedule birds which, although usually regarded as vermin, had received protection as protected wild birds. Under these 1986 Regulations the Minister can now declare any of these species of wild bird as being species which may be captured or killed under the circumstances and in the manner described in the Regulations. These Regulations are dealt with in detail below.

There are now, therefore, two main provisions in respect of damage by protected wild birds or protected wild animals:

(1) UNDER THE WLA 1976

Section 42 of the WLA 1976:

"(1) Where damage is being caused by protected wild birds or by protected wild animals to –
- (a) livestock, poultry or agricultural crops (including vegetables or fruit) either on pasture or on cultivated land,
- (b) pen-reared wild birds on any land,
- (c) other fauna,
- (d) flora,
- (e) a woodland or a forest plantation, or
- (f) a fishery,

notwithstanding any other provision of this Act, the Minister may cause to be taken by a person authorised by him in that behalf (who is hereby empowered to take) such steps, including entering on any land and the capture or killing of any such wild bird or any such wild animal, as he thinks appropriate to stop the damage."

Subsection (2) gives the Minister power before he exercises his powers under (1) and where damage is being caused, to require the owner or occupier of the property being damaged to give him and any person acting on his behalf an indemnity against all claims relating to anything done by the Minister or on his behalf by virtue of subsection (1) in relation to the damage.

Subsections (3), (4) and (5) provide for an application for permission under the section to capture or kill any protected wild bird or protected wild animal where damage is being caused as is described in subsection (1) or to take such other steps (if any) to stop the damage.

The application may be brought by the owner or occupier to the Minister, to the forester in charge of any forest owned by the Minister or to any other person authorised to receive such applications.

Subsection (6) provides in relation to a permission under the section that:
- (a) the permission shall only be valid for such period as is specified therein,
- (b) particulars of the protected wild birds and protected wild animals captured or killed shall be furnished to the Minister, by the person given the permission at such times, and in such manner as is specified,
- (c) the Minister may grant the permission subject to a condition that:
  - (i) any capture pursuant to the permission is to be effected by a specified means,
  - (ii) any wild bird or wild animal captured pursuant to the permission shall be

removed to a place specified by the Minister for subsequent release or be disposed of in such other manner as may be specified.

Subsection (7) provides that these powers are in addition to the powers conferred on the Minister under sections 59 and 60 of the Forestry Act 1946.

Section 22(6) of the WLA 1976 provides the defence of urgent necessity where it is impractical to wait for permission from the Minister under section 42. *See:* PROTECTION, PROTECTED WILD BIRDS.

(2) UNDER THE 1986 REGULATIONS

Article 3(1) and (b) of the European Communities (Wildlife Act 1976) (Amendment) Regulations 1986 (S.I. No. 254 of 1986) gives the Minister power to make declarations permitting the capture and killing of a species of wild bird specified in the First Schedule to the Regulations where they are a threat to public health or safety, likely to cause serious damage to crops (spelt "corps" in the regulations), livestock, fisheries or forestry or likely to cause damage to (*qv*) flora or (*qv*) fauna.

The First Schedule lists:

Carrion crow, Hooded (Grey) Crow, Magpie, Rook, Jackdaw, Starling, Herring Gull, Greater Black-backed gull, Lesser Black-backed Gull, Sparrow, Pigeon, including Wood pigeon, but not including Carrier pigeons, Racing Homing Pigeons or Doves.

This schedule was amended by European Communities (Wildlife Act 1976) (Amendment) Regulations 1997 (S.I. No. 152 of 1997) which substituted "House Sparrow" for "Sparrow" and "Pigeon and Dove including Wood Pigeon, Feral Pigeon and Collared Dove but not including Carrier Pigeon, Fan Tailed Pigeon, Homing Pigeon or other domestic types of Rock Dove, Stock Dove, Wild Rock Dove or Turtle Dove" for "Pigeon, including Wood Pigeon but not including carrier Pigeons, Racing Homing Pigeons or Doves".

The Second Schedule specifies the means by which the species may be captured or killed which includes shooting with a rifle or shotgun, using poisoned or anaesthetic bait, cage traps with or without decoys and traps, snares or nets approved under the Wildlife Act 1976 (Approved Traps, Snares and Nets) Regulations, 1977 (S.I. No. 307 of 1977). *See:* TRAPS, SNARES, NETS, PROHIBITION OF.

A declaration is made formally each year by the Minister under Regulation 3(1)(a) of the 1986 Regulations on the basis of four regions. The administrative Counties of Cavan, Donegal and Monaghan together comprise one region and the Provinces of Munster, Leinster and Connaught each comprise one of the other three.

There are four separate declarations one for each of the four regions and each has a different Schedule. In fact there is no variation in the four Schedules for the 1998 season.

The list of species of wild birds appears in column (1) of each Schedule. In 1998 there are five separate species specified; hooded (grey) Crow, magpie, rook, jackdaw and pigeons and doves, including wood pigeon, feral pigeon and collar dove but not including carrier pigeon, fan tailed pigeon, homing pigeon or other domestic types of rock dove, stock dove, wild rock dove or turtle dove.

Column (2) is headed crops, livestock, fauna, public health and the "occasions" of damage in accordance with Article 3(1)(a) are given ranging from "threat to public health and vector in the spread of animal diseases" to "serious damage to various cereal crops, brassicas and various root crops such as potatoes and beet". Again, this is for the 1998 season.

Column (3) gives the period covered by the declaration which in all but one case is from the June 1 to the following September 30, the exception being June 1 to August 31 where the event giving rise to the need for protection is "serious damage to fauna notably the nests and young of game birds" and the likely predator would be the magpie.

Column (4) specifies the method of control which ranges from plain shooting with rifle or shotgun which is a general method of control to which is added in certain instances traps (including decoys), poisons and stupefying bait.

THREAT TO AIR SAFETY

Article 3(1)(b) of the 1986 Regulations allows the Minister to make a declaration in relation to any species of wild birds where he/she is of opinion that the species of wild bird is a threat to air safety.

The means and methods of killing specified in the Second Schedule apply.

Article 6(1) and (2) confers certain powers on (*qv*) authorised persons and creates a further offence of (*qv*) obstructing or interfering with an authorised person.

DATA
(EPAA 1992, ss. 110, 69 and 64)

(1) INSPECTION OF AGENCY DATA

Section 110 of the EPAA 1992 provides for the Agency making its records available to the public for inspection. *See:* ACCESS.

(2) HYDROMETRIC PROGRAMME/DATA

Section 64 of the EPAA 1992 obliges the Agency to prepare a national programme for the collection, analysis and publication of information on the levels, volumes and flows of water in rivers, lakes and groundwaters in the State (referred to in the Act as "hydrometric data") which must be sent to the Minister as soon as may be.

The programme must be reviewed at least every five years.

The Agency have wide responsibilities in directing local authorities on the provision and running of equipment and the furnishing of specified information to the Agency and, as in section 63, when the local authority fails to comply with its directions the Agency has the power to go in and do the work themselves and bill the local authority. For section 63 *see*: PERFORMANCE OF STATUTORY FUNCTIONS BY LOCAL AUTHORITIES.

(3) ENVIRONMENTAL QUALITY DATA STORAGE SYSTEM

Section 69 of the EPAA 1992 obliges the Agency to provide, establish and maintain a data base related to environmental quality including:

(a) ambient air quality,
(b) the quality of inland waters, estuarial and coastal waters and groundwaters,
(c) soil quality,
(d) (*qv*) noise levels,
(e) inventories of (*qv*) emissions to the environment, and
(f) such other matters as may be prescribed.

The Agency has power under the section to require any public body to supply any information on environmental quality to it and the authority cannot unreasonably withhold the information. They have power to make arrangements for such information held by any person or body to be made available to it for inclusion in the data base.

They may compile and maintain a register of sources of data related to environmental quality which must be made available to the public for inspection.

Subsection (5) obliges the Agency, subject to the confidentiality section 39, to make arrangements for public access to the information contained in a data base prepared under this section but on such terms and conditions as the Agency thinks fit.

This last proviso must relate to the mechanics of the public access rather than giving the Agency any discretion in relation to what may or may not be made available.

DAY-TIME
(F(C)A 1959, s. 3(1))

"means the period between sunrise and sunset."

DEALER
(WMA 1996, s. 5(1))

"means, in relation to waste, any person who buys or sells waste on his or her own behalf or arranges on behalf of or as a service to any other person for the purchase, sale or transfer from one person to another of waste or for the collection, recovery or disposal of waste."

DECISIONS UNDER REG. 16 CONSENT TO OPERATION OR ACTIVITY
(NH 97, Reg.16)

Regulation 16 of the NH 97 Regulations (S.I. No. 94 of 1997):

"(1) Having regard to the conclusions of the (*qv*) assessment under regulation 15(1), the Minister may decide to give consent to the (*qv*) operation or activity only after having ascertained that it will not adversely affect the integrity of the site and, if the Minister considers it to be appropriate, having obtained the opinion of the general public.

(2) Where the Minister is satisfied that –
(a) notwithstanding a negative assessment of the implications for the site of any operation or activity thereon, and
(b) in the absence of an alternative solution,

the operation or activity must be carried out for imperative reasons of overriding public interest, which interest may, subject to paragraph (5), be of a social or economic nature, the Minister may decide to give the owner, occupier or user consent to undertake the operation or activity."

Regulation 16

"(3) The Minister shall give reasons for a decision to refuse to give consent under paragraph (1).

(4) (a) The owner, occupier or user of land -
(i) to which natural habitat types and species specified in the Habitats Directive relate, other than those specified in paragraph (5),
(ii) to which the refusal to give consent relates,
may, not later then 30 days after the day on which decision to refuse is given, serve notice of appeal on the Minister against that refusal.
(b) Where in circumstances to which sub paragraph (a) relates the Minister shall appoint a person, who shall be a barrister or solicitor of not less than 7 years standing, to be an arbitrator for the purposes of hearing and determining the appeal and, where the arbitrator determines that the minister should give consent under paragraph (4), such consent shall be given.
(c) An arbitrator appointed under subparagraph (b) shall be paid such remuneration (if any) and allowances for expenses incurred by him or her as the Minister, with the consent of the Minister for Finance, may determine.

(5) Where the site concerned hosts a (*qv*) priority natural habitat type or a (*qv*) priority species, the reasons referred to in paragraph (2) shall be either -
(a) reasons relating to human health, public safety or beneficial consequences of primary importance to the environment, or
(b) other reasons which, in the opinion of the European Communities, are imperative reasons of overriding public interest.

(6) Where, in accordance with paragraph (2) an operation or activity is agreed to, notwithstanding a negative assessment of the implications for a European site, the Minister shall insure that the necessary compensatory measures are taken to ensure that the overall coherence of Natura 2000 is protected."

See: (1) ASSESSMENT UNDER REG. 15, NH 97 REGULATIONS (2) OPERATIONS OR ACTIVITIES (3) PROHIBITION AGAINST WORKS (OPERATIONS OR ACTIVITIES) ON CERTAIN PROTECTED LANDS.

DECLARATION OF INTERESTS
(EPAA 1992, s. 37 F(A)A 1997, s.33)

Section 37(1) of the EPAA 1992 provides for the duty of persons to whom the section applies to give to the Agency a declaration of interests and of any change regarding such interest or the acquisition of a new interest to which the section applies to be entered in a public (*qv*) register.

Subsection (2)(a) provides that the section applies to the (*qv*) Director General, directors, employees or other persons to be prescribed whose services are availed of by the Agency although it does not necessarily apply to the members of the (*qv*) Advisory Committee.

Subsection (2)*(b)* provides that the interests to be declared relate to any estate or interest in any land or (*qv*) activity, or any business of dealing in or developing land or in any activity in which a person to whom the section applies is engaged or employed or any such business carried on by a company or other body of which he, or any nominee of his, is a member, or membership of any profession, business or occupation in which such person is engaged, whether on his own behalf or otherwise, and which relates to dealing in or developing land or to an activity.

Subsection (3) provides that notice of the acquisition of the interest must be given to the Agency within 28 days in the circumstances described in paragraphs (a), (b) and (c) of the subsection.

Subsections (4), (5) and (6) provide that a person who either on his own behalf or through a nominee is a member of a company or other body having an estate or interest in a land or activity shall be regarded as himself having an estate or interest but not if the interest is so remote or insignificant that it cannot be reasonably regarded as being likely to influence and the subsection suggests a holding valued at not more than £1000 or 100th part of the total value of the holding.

Subsections (7), (8) and (9) deal with the keeping by the Agency of a public register of interests, the entries therein and the public's right of access thereto.

Offence
Subsection (10) of the section creates the offence of failing to comply with subsection (1) or giving particulars which are false and knowingly misleading in a material respect.

defence

"(11) In any proceedings for an offence under this section it shall be a defence for the defendant to prove that at the relevant time he believed, in good faith and upon reasonable grounds, that –
(a) the relevant particulars were true,
(b) there was no matter as regards which he was then required to make a declaration under subsection (1), or
(c) that the matter in relation to which the offence is alleged was not one as regards which he was so required to make such a declaration.

(12) in this section "land" includes land covered by water."

(F(A)A 1997, s.33)

Section 33 of the F(A)A 1997 relates to declaration of interests to be completed by the Chairperson and all other members and the Secretary of the Aquaculture Licences Appeals Board and by any consultant or adviser who may be engaged by the Board. The form of these declarations is prescribed in the Schedule to the Fisheries (Amendment) Act, 1997 (Section 33) Regulations, 1998 (S.I. No. 269 of 1998).

DECOYS
(WLA 1976 s. 35)

Section 35(1) of the WLA 1976. *See:* SCARECROWS.

DEFINITIONS OF MOUTHS OF RIVERS
(F(C)A 1959, s. 10)

Section 10(1) of the F(C)A 1959 permits the Minister by order to define by reference to a map or otherwise:
(a) what is to be the boundary of the mouth of any river,
(b) what is to be the boundary of the mouth of any tributary river at its entrance into the mouth of any other river,
(c) what is to be the boundary between the tidal and freshwater portions of any river,
(d) the points of termination of the distances referred to in sections 94 and 103 and illustrate, by map or otherwise, the said points of termination and the space within which it is prohibited by the said section to use or practice certain modes of fishing,
(e) the point or points of the mouth of any river from which distances are to be measured under the Act.

Subsection (2) provides where several streams flow into a common mouth or estuary, the Minister may declare that the outlets of such streams shall form separate mouths.

Subsection (3) provides that the Minister may by order revoke or amend any order.

For section 94, *see:* MESH OF NETS AND ENGINES
For section 103, *see:* FIXED ENGINES, RESTRICTIONS ON SITES.

DELEGATION OF FUNCTIONS BY MINISTER
(F(A)A 1997 s. 21)

Section 21 of the F(A)A 1997 entitles the Minister by instrument under seal to delegate to a named officer of the Minister who is an established civil servant for the purposes of the Civil Services Regulation Act 1956, the functions of determining applications for licences, or applications of a particular class or description.

DELETERIOUS MATTER
(F(C)A 1959, s. 3(1))

This phrase "deleterious matter" is the statutory phrase used to describe the substance entering (*qv*) waters the toxicity of which is the basis for a prosecution for water pollution under section 171 of the F(C)A 1959 and the same phrase, but with a different definition, is used in the Regulations which gave effect to (*qv*) special protection areas under the (*qv*) Birds Directive.

The wording of the Fisheries Acts definition of deleterious matter became the basis for other definitions in other statutes, *e.g.* (*qv*) polluting matter in the LG(WP)A 1977.

Section 3(1) of the F(C)A 1959 as amended by section 2(1) of the F(A)A 1962 defines "deleterious matter" as –

"means any substance (including any explosive, liquid or gas) the entry or discharge of which into any (*qv*) waters is liable to render those or any other waters poisonous or injurious to (*qv*) fish, spawning grounds or the food of any fish or to injure fish in their value as human food or to impair the usefulness of the bed and soil of any waters as spawning grounds or their capacity to produce the food of fish."

The European Communities (Conservation of Wild Birds) Regulations 1985 (S.I. No. 291 of 1985), Article 2(1) defines deleterious matter:

"means any substance (including an explosive substance) which, on entry or discharge into a (*qv*) special protection area, would be liable to cause death or injury to any species of (*qv*) fauna or to damage or destroy any species of flora or the habitat of any such species of fauna or flora and includes domestic and industrial waste, animal excrement and slurry, bilge water, oil and any other form of petroleum."

DELIBERATE RELEASE
(EPAA 1992, Art. 3(1) GMO Regs. 1994)

"Deliberate release" at Article 3(1) of the (*qv*) Genetically Modified Organisms Regulations 1994 (S.I. No. 345 of 1994) defines deliberate release as

"meaning any intentional introduction into the environment of a genetically modified organism or a combination of genetically modified organisms without provision for containment such as physical barriers or a combination of physical barriers together with chemical and/or biological barriers used to limit their contact with the general population and the environment, and cognate words and expressions shall be construed accordingly."

DEPOSIT AND REFUND SCHEME
(WMA s. 27(1))

"Deposit and refund scheme" is defined in the WMA 1996 for the purposes of Part III of the Act, section 27(1), as meaning, in relation to any product substance, component or packaging, a scheme whereby the (*qv*) producer, distributor or retailer, as the case may be, who operates the scheme requires a purchaser of a product or substance to pay to him or her a refundable deposit in relation to the product or substance or any component thereof or packaging therefor, that is to say a deposit of money the amount of which will be repaid by the producer, distributor or retailer, as the case may be, to the purchaser if the purchaser returns to him or her the product, substance, component or packaging, as the case may be.

Section 29 of the WMA 1996, which deals with regulations which the Minister is empowered to make in relation to the (*qv*) recovery of (*qv*) waste, provides as one of the matters for which he may provide at section 29(4)*(f)* a requirement that a producer, distributor or retailer operate a deposit and return scheme in relation to a product or substance made, distributed or sold by him or her.

DEROGATION
(NH 97, Reg. 25)

To derogate is to deviate from, in this case, the rules relating to the protection of flora. This occurs only where there is no satisfactory alternative and where the derogation is not detrimental to the maintenance and conservation of the species being protected.

Regulation 25 of the NH 97 Regulations (S.I. No. 94 of 1997):

"(1) Where there is no satisfactory alternative and the derogation is not detrimental to the maintenance of the populations of the species to which the (*qv*) Habitats Directive relates at a (*qv*) favourable conservation status in their natural range, the Minister may, in respect of those species, grant a licence to one or more persons permitting a derogation from complying with the requirements of the provisions of section 21 of the Principal Act and Regulations 23 and 24, where it is –

(a) in the interests of protecting wild fauna and flora and conserving natural habitats, or
(b) to prevent serious damage, in particular to crops, livestock, forests, fisheries and water and other types of property, or
(c) in the interests of public health and public safety, or for other imperative reasons of overriding public interest, including those of a social or economic nature and beneficial consequences of primary importance for the environment, or
(d) for the purpose of research and education, of repopulating and reintroducing these species and for the breeding operation necessary for these purposes, including the artificial propagation of plants,
(e) to allow, under strictly supervised conditions, on a selective basis and to a limited extent, the taking or keeping of certain specimens of the species to the extent (if any) specified therein, which are set in the First Schedule.

"The Principal Act" is the WLA 1976, For section 21 WLA 1976 *see:* PROTECTION (7) (C)
For Regulation 23 NH 97 *see:* PROTECTION FAUNA, NH 97 REGULATIONS.
For Regulation 24 NH 97 *see:* PROTECTION,

TAKING IN THE WILD, SPECIES IN PART II, FIRST SCHEDULE, REG. 24.
For First Schedule *see:* SCHEDULES HERETO, NH 97 SCHEDULES.

(2) The Minister shall forward to the Commission every two years a report, in accordance with a format established by the Commission, on the derogations to which paragraph (1) relates.
(3) The Report referred to in paragraph (2) shall specify –
   (a) the species which are subject to the derogations and the reason for the derogation, including the nature of the risk, if appropriate, a reference to alternatives rejected and scientific data used;
   (b) the means, devices or methods authorised for the capture or killing of animal species and the reasons for their use;
   (c) the circumstances of when and where such derogations are granted;
   (d) the authority empowered to declare and check that the required conditions obtain and to decide what means, devices or methods may be used, within what limits and by what agencies, and which persons are to carry out the task;
   (e) the supervisory measures used and the results obtained."

DESIGNATION ORDER
(WLA 1976, s. 17)

It is under this section that the Minister designates or sets aside for special protection (*qv*) refuges for (*qv*) fauna. No such orders have been made.

Section 17(1) of the WLA 1976:

"(1) Where the Minister considers that a particular species, or particular species, of (*qv*) fauna should be specially protected on any land which is, or is contiguous to, a habitat of the species, then, subject to subsection (5) of this section, he may publish in the Iris Oifigiúil and in at least one newspaper circulating in this locality in which the land is situate a notice of his intention to make an order (in the Act referred to as a designation order) designating the land as a refuge for such fauna."

Subsection (2) provides that before publishing the order he must consult with named Government Ministers, the (*qv*) Commissioners and the planning authority concerned and the particulars to be contained in the notice must be served on the owner or occupier of such land.

Subsection (3) provides for amendment of a designation order and publication in an Iris Oifigiúil and a newspaper circulating locally of notice of the Minister's intention to so amend.

Subsection (4) provides that a notice published pursuant to this section shall indicate any species of fauna which the Minister proposes, by the provisions of the proposed order to which the notice relates, to protect, the land to which the proposed designation order or amending order, as the case may be, will apply and the protective measures which he proposes to include in the proposed order, including any measures he proposes to take for the protection of the habitat requirements of such fauna.

Subsection (5)

"The Minister shall not include in a notice published pursuant to this section any reference to a species of fish or aquatic invertebrate animal without the prior concurrence of the Minister for Agriculture and Fisheries."

Subsections (6), (7) and (8) provide that the occupier of any land to which the notice relates, a person to whom the making of the order would be detrimental or the planning authority in whose functional area the land is situate have a right of (*qv*) objection within two months of the publication of the notice and there is provision for (*qv*) compensation to any person who has an interest in or over the land under subsections (10), (11) and (12) for the diminution in value, loss or disadvantage arising from the measures contained in the order such compensation to be determined, in default of agreement, under the Acquisition of Land (Assessment of Compensation) Act 1919.

Subsection (9) provides that the Minister, after considering any objection may, if he thinks fit, make
   (a) a designation order designating the land, or any part thereof, as, and establishing thereon, a refuge for all or any of the fauna indicated in the notice, or
   (b) an appropriate order under section 8 amending a designation order,

and the order may include such provisions as the Minister thinks fit which relate to protective measures as specified.

Subsection (11) provides for payment of compensation to persons other than those having interest who has suffered financial loss or any inconvenience or other disadvantage.

Subsection (13) provides that the Minister shall not revoke a designation order unless he considers that it is no longer practicable or is no longer desirable to maintain the refuge established by the order.

Subsection (14) provides for the furnishing of copies of the order to the (*qv*) Commissioners, the (*qv*) Board and the appropriate (*qv*) planning authority.

Offence

Subsection (15) provides that any person who contravenes a designation order shall be guilty of an offence.

Section 59(1)*(b)* of the WLA 1976 provides for the making of regulations permitting public access to land to which a designation order applies. See: ACCESS TO OR ENTRY ON LAND.

DESTRUCTION OF VEGETATION
(WLA 1976, s. 40)

Offence
Section 40(1) of the WLA 1976 creates the offence of cutting, grubbing, burning or otherwise destroying during the period from April 15 to August 31 in any year, any vegetation growing on land not then cultivated or in the course of cultivation for agriculture or forestry.

Subsection (2) excepts –

(a) in the ordinary course of agriculture or forestry destroying vegetation growing on or in any hedge or ditch,
(b) cutting or grubbing isolated clumps of gorse, furze, whin or ferns in the ordinary course of agriculture,
(c) cutting, grubbing or destroying vegetation in the course of works being carried out by a Minister of State or a body established or regulated by Statute,
(d) destroying noxious weeds to which the Noxious Weeds Act, 1936 applies,
(e) clearing of vegetation from sites for building,
(f) when required by Notice from the Minister under the Forestry Act, 1946.

But these exceptions will not apply in the case of *(qv)* burning.

DETENTION OF BOATS, VEHICLES, AND EQUIPMENT
(F(C)A 1959, s. 301)

BOATS

Section 301(2)(dA) of the F(C)A 1959, inserted by section 53(a) of the FA 1980, provides for the taking of a boat by an *(qv)* authorised officer if he believes or suspects that the boat contains fish unlawfully captured and section 301(2A) (inserted by s. 53*(b)* of the FA 1980) provides for the procedures he must follow after the taking. *See:* ENFORCEMENT(7).

VEHICLES

Section 301(2)(ff) of the F(C)A 1959, inserted by section 25(b) of the F(A)A 1962, provides for an (*qv*) authorised officer taking, removing and detaining in his custody any boat or vehicle liable or believed to be liable to forfeiture under this Act.

There is no specific provision for dealing with a vehicle after detention but before conviction. Section 301(2) of the F(C)A 1959 provides that where an authorised officer detains in his custody under the authority of the section any fish or other article he shall, as soon as may be, take such steps as may be proper to have the person guilty or believed to be guilty of the offence committed or believed to have been committed in relation to such fish or other article dealt with according to law.

As the only circumstance in which a vehicle can be forfeited under the Fisheries Acts is on conviction on indictment for use of the vehicle as an aid to the commission of an offence under section 285(a) of the F(C)A 1959 (inserted by section 24 of the F(A)A 1962) it is unlikely that an authorised officer would seize a vehicle as a prelude to such a prosecution as they are rarely brought on indictment. The section is commonly prosecuted summarily where forfeiture is not a penalty (WMA 1996, s. 61).

VEHICLES OR EQUIPMENT

Section 61 of the WMA 1996:

"(1) (a) Where proceedings are instituted for an offence under section 36, 39 or 51 and those proceedings are to be prosecuted on indictment, a Judge of the District Court for the appropriate District Court district may, on application to him or her in that behalf by the local authority in whose functional area the offence is alleged to have been committed, or by the Agency, make an order requiring the defendant in those proceedings to enter into a bond of an amount equal to the value which the Judge estimates to be the value of any vehicle or equipment owned by the defendant that is alleged by the local authority or by the Agency to have been used in the commission of the offence.

(b) In this subsection "appropriate District Court district" means the District Court district in which the offence concerned is alleged to have been committed or the defendant concerned resides or carries on business."

Subsection (2) provides that if a defendant fails to comply with an order of a judge of the District Court under subsection (1), the judge may (without prejudice to any other means of enforcing the order) make an order authorising the local authority concerned or the Agency to detain any vehicle or equipment in respect of which the first-mentioned order was made pending the determination of the proceedings for the offence concerned.

Subsection (3) provides that if a person is convicted of an offence under sections 36, 39 or 51, the court, before which the person is convicted, may order the forfeiture to the local authority in whose functional area the offence was committed, or the Agency, of any vehicle or equipment owned by the defendant that was used in the commission of the offence or the amount of any bond entered into by the defendant in compliance with an order under subsection (1).

Subsection (4) provides that an order under subsection (3) shall not take effect until the ordinary time for instituting an appeal against the conviction or order concerned has expired, or, where such an appeal is instituted, until it or any further appeal is finally decided or abandoned or the ordinary time for instituting any further appeal has expired.

Subsection (5) provides that a local authority or the Agency may deal with or dispose of as it thinks fit any vehicle or equipment forfeited to it under subsection (3).

The sections referred to in subsection (3) above deal with, section 36, regulations in relation to the supervision or control of the movement of waste, (*See:* MOVEMENT OF WASTE, REQUIREMENTS) section 39, the requirement to hold a waste licence and section 51, sludge and agricultural waste. *See:* WMA 1996(4).

DETERMINATION OF OYSTER FISHERY ORDERS
(F(C)A 1959)

Part XIV of the F(C)A 1959 deals with oysters and Chapter III of that Part deals with oyster fishery orders.

Section 5(5) of the F(A) A 1997 repeals the part of Part XIV which deals with the making of oyster fishery orders as the farming of oysters now comes within the new definition of (*qv*) "aquaculture licence" under the F(A)A 1997 and in the place of the F(C)A 1959 oyster fishery order you now have aquaculture licences governed by Part II of the F(A)A 1997.

However, there are oyster fishery orders under both the Oyster Cultivation (Ireland) Act 1884 and the F(C)A 1959 which are still in existence. These are described at length at section 244 of the F(C)A 1959 as amended by section 12 of the F(A)A 1997 to give recognition to the new procedures and definitions in that Act. *See:* OYSTERS.

Section 266 of the F(C)A 1959:

Subsection (1) provides that the Minister may determine an oyster fishery order if it appears to him that the grantee is not maintaining the oyster fishery granted therein and thereupon all the rights and privileges thereunder absolutely determine and are null and void.

Subsection (2) gives the Minister power, for the purposes of subsection (1), from time to time to make such enquiries and examination and require from the grantee such information as the Minister thinks necessary and proper and the grantee is obliged to afford all facilities and give such information accordingly.

DEVELOPMENT
(LG(P&D)A 1963, s. 3)

"(1) "Development" in the Act means, save where the context otherwise requires, the carrying out of any works on, in, or under land or the making of any material change in the use of any structures or other land.

(2) For the purposes of subsection (1) of this section and without prejudice to the generality thereof –

(a) where any structure or other land or any tree or other object on land becomes used for the exhibition of advertisements, or

(b) where land becomes used for any of the following purposes:

(i) the placing or keeping of any vans, tents or other objects, whether or not moveable and whether or not collapsible, for the purpose of caravanning, or camping or the sale of goods,
(ii) the storage of caravans or tents,
(iii) the deposit of bodies or other parts of vehicles, old metal, mining or industrial waste, builders waste, rubble or debris
the use of the land shall be taken to have materially changed.

(3) For the avoidance of doubt it is hereby declared that for the purposes of this section the use of two or more dwellings of any structure previously used as a single dwelling involves a material change in the use of the structure and each part thereof which is so used."

"Development" in the EPAA 1992, section 3(1), has the meaning assigned to it by section 3 of the LG(P&D)A 1963.

DEVELOPMENT PLAN
(LG(P&D)A 1963)

Part III of the LG(P&D)A 1963 (sections 19 to 23) as amended by section 43(1)*(f)* of the LG(P&D)A 1976 provides for development plans. It imposes upon each planning authority a duty to prepare a development plan indicating development objectives for its functional area and to revise the plan every five years.

A development plan consists of a written statement of the policy objectives of the Planning Authority together with a set of maps to illustrate the written statement, to indicate land rezoning, to show major road proposals and to identify areas of amenity.

The draft of each revision of the development plan must be put on public display and any interested person is entitled to object to the provisions of a draft development plan. The Planning Authority must hear and determine such objections before the plan is adopted.

The adoption of a development plan is a (*qv*) reserved function which is exercised by the elected representatives.

DIRECTIVE, EUROPEAN

A European Directive is a legislative act of the European community stating an objective which must be achieved by Member States within a prescribed period. A Directive is implemented in Ireland by an Act of the Oireachtas or, as is more usual by Ministerial regulation. *See:* (1) BIRDS DIRECTIVE; (2) HABITATS DIRECTIVE.

DIRECTOR GENERAL OF THE ENVIRONMENTAL PROTECTION AGENCY (EPA)
(EPAA 1992, s. 21)

Section 21 of the EPAA 1992 provides for the appointment of the Director General of the Agency by the Government from a list of candidates or the candidate selected by a committee.

The committee itself consists of the Secretary to the Government, the Secretary to the Department of the Environment, the Chairperson of the Council of an Taisce, the Managing Director of the IDA, the General Secretary of the ICTU and the Chief Executive of the Council for the Status of Women.

Subsections (3) and (4) provide for the Government filling vacancies in the committee from the same bodies where the persons chosen are unable or unwilling to act.

Subsection (12) provides that the appointment is in a whole time capacity and during his term of office the Director General cannot hold any other salaried office.

Subsection (13) provides that the appointment is for a term of seven years and the outgoing Director General can be appointed for a second or subsequent term of seven years or less.

Subsection (16) provides that the Director General can be removed from office by the Government is he is incapable from ill health of performing his duties, or for stated misbehaviour, or if his removal appears to the Government to be necessary or desirable for the effective performance by the Agency of its functions and, if removed from office under this subsection, the Government shall cause to be laid before each house of the Oireachtas a statement in writing of the reasons for the removal.

FUNCTIONS OF DIRECTOR GENERAL

Section 23 provides that it shall be the function of the Director General or, where he is not available or where the office is vacant, of the Deputy Director General:

(a) to ensure the efficient discharge of the business of the Agency,
(b) to arrange the distribution of the business of the Agency among its directors.

DEPUTY DIRECTOR GENERAL OF THE EPA
(EPAA 1992, s. 22)

This section provides for the appointment of the

Deputy Director General of the Agency by the Agency from among the directors.

DIRECTORS OF THE EPA
(EPAA 1992, s. 24)

This section provides for the appointment and removal of directors in the same manner as is provided in section 21 for the appointment or removal of the Director General. The Government must consult with the Director General and the Deputy before appointment and subsection (3)(b) provides for the matters to which the Government must have regard in making the appointment.

DISCHARGE OF BALLAST
(F(C)A 1959, s. 290)

Offence
"If any person throws out or unloads from any vessel the ballast thereof or any part of the said ballast, within any (*qv*) estuary, (*qv*) harbour or place then, unless such throwing out or unloading is allowed by the Minister or by the local regulations of such harbour or place, each of the following persons, namely, such person, the master of such vessel and the owner of such vessel, shall be guilty of an offence under this section."

(Note that the maximum penalty prescribed under this subsection has been increased. *See:* FINES AND IMPRISONMENT (IMPOSITION OF)).

DISCHARGES TO AQUIFERS, CONTROL OF
(LG(WP)A 1977)

Part VI of the Local Government (Water Pollution) Regulations 1992 (S.I. No. 271 of 1992) (hereinafter called "the 1992 Regulations") deals with the control of discharges of harmful substances to (*qv*) aquifers and implements Council Directive 80/68/EEC of December 17, 1979 on the protection of groundwater against pollution caused by certain dangerous substances (O.J. L20/43, January 26, 1980) and was amended by the substitution of an entirely new Part VI by the Local Government (Water Pollution) (Amendment) Regulations 1999 (S.I. No. 42 of 1999) (hereinafter called "the 1999 Regulations").

The 1999 Regulations extended the procedures established by Part VI of the 1992 Regulations for the grant of a new licence under section 4 of the LG(WP)A 1977 by developing the concept of "prior investigation" for the control of discharges under section 4 to aquifers and also provides for new standards in respect of harmful substances specified in the First Schedule contained in (*qv*) sewage effluent or (*qv*) trade effluent discharged to an aquifer and the special position of certain bodies in relation to those standards.

SECTION 4 OF LG(WP)A 1977 LICENCE UNDER THE REGULATIONS

The 1992 and 1999 Regulations create a hybrid licence which is derived and has evolved from a licence under section 4 of the LG(WP)A 1977 and which could be called "a section 4 – Local Government (Water Pollution) Act 1977 licence in respect of sewage effluent or trade effluent containing harmful substances which is discharged to an aquifer".

Such a licence is granted by the local authority concerned. Under the Protection of Groundwater Regulations 1999 (S.I. No. 41 of 1999), which are dealt with hereunder, a licence is granted by the Agency authorising the discharge of effluent to an aquifer by local authorities as sanitary authorities.

HARMFUL SUBSTANCES

"Harmful substances" are defined as substances or groups of substances specified in the First Schedule or Second Schedule to the 1992 Regulations. These Schedules are taken from Annexes 1 and 2 of Council Directive 80/68/EEC of December 17, 1979 on the protection of groundwater against pollution caused by certain dangerous substances (O.J. L20/43, January 26, 1980). Except for minor difference in the headings, the same Schedules are used in the Protection of Groundwater Regulations, 1999 (S.I. No. 41 of 1999). *See:* SCHEDULES HERETO; LG(WP)A 1977 SCHEDULE.

PRIOR INVESTIGATION

Article 40 of the 1999 Regulations –

Prior investigation involves assessing the environmental impact of alternative means of disposal of harmful substances and the examination of the aquifer into which it is to be discharged with a view to ascertaining the viability of that means of disposal into the particular aquifer in advance of the licence application. The results of the prior investigation accompany the application.

The examination of the aquifer involves ascertaining:

(i) the extent and estimated volume of

water therein,
(ii) the quality of water therein,
(iii) the estimated rate of recharge,
(iv) the identification of any existing or proposed uses of the water therein,
(v) the hydrogeological condition of the area in which the aquifer is located,
(vi) the nature and depth of underlying soil and subsoil and its effectiveness in preventing or reducing the entry of the harmful substance to water in the aquifer,
(vii) the risk of deterioration in the quality of the water therein due to the entry of the harmful substance,
(viii) the risk of the water therein being affected by the harmful substance so as to endanger human health or water supplies, harm living resources and the aquatic ecosystem or interfere with the use of the water for agricultural, commercial, domestic, fisheries, industrial or recreational purposes, and
(ix) such other matters as the local authority may reasonably require.

The local authority shall take into account the results of the prior investigation before deciding to grant or refuse a licence.

STANDARDS

Article 47 of the 1999 Regulations:

"(1) Article 41 shall not apply in a case where a local authority, An Bord Pleanála or the Environmental Protection Agency, as the case may be, finds that the harmful substance is present in so small a quantity and concentration as to obviate present or future danger of deterioration of the quality of water in the aquifer.
(2) A local authority, An Bord Pleanála or the Environmental Protection Agency, as the case may be, may specify a standard different from the standard specified in Article 41(1) in respect of the discharge or entry to an aquifer of a harmful substance specified in the First Schedule –
(a) where the results of a prior investigation show that the water in the aquifer is permanently unsuitable for agricultural, commercial, domestic, fisheries, industrial or recreational uses, and all practical technical precautions have been taken to prevent the entry of the harmful substance to other waters so as to avoid the risk set out in article 40(2)(b)(viii), or
(b) in respect of the re-injection into the same aquifer, following prior investigation, of water used for geothermal purposes, water pumped out of mines or quarries or water pumped out for civil engineering works."

Sewage effluent and trade effluent

Article 41(1) provides for a quality standard of zero (0) milligrams per litre for sewage effluent and trade effluent discharged to an aquifer in respect of a harmful substance specified in the First Schedule.

Water in an Aquifer

Article 41(2) provides for a quality standard of zero (0) milligrams per litre for water in an aquifer in respect of a harmful substance specified in the First Schedule which might be caused or permitted to enter the waters as a result of any disposal or tipping of the substance or any material containing the substance or any activities on or in the ground.

See: SCHEDULES HERETO; LG(WP)A SCHEDULES.

CONDITIONS

Article 42 –

"In the light of a prior investigation carried out in accordance with the requirements of Article 40, a local authority may specify conditions in a licence requiring a standard different from the quality standard prescribed in sub-article (1) of article 41 in respect of a harmful substance specified in the Second Schedule provided that all practical technical precautions are observed to prevent water in an aquifer being affected by that harmful substance in the manner set out in article 40(2)(b)(viii)."

Article 43 provides, without prejudice to the generality of section 4(5) of the LG(WP)A 1977, for the kind of conditions which may be attached to a licence, such as the location of the discharge, method of discharge, methods of treatment, maximum quantity to be discharged, monitoring of the quality of the effluent discharge and the quality of the water in the aquifer.

Article 44 provides for licence review every four years. Section 7 of the LG(WP)A 1977 provides for the review of an ordinary section 4 licence every three years. *See:* REVIEW.

Article 45 provides for monitoring by local authorities to determine compliance with licence conditions and effects of a discharge of water in an aquifer.

Article 46 provides for the taking of steps to secure compliance with the quality standards specified in Article 41, subject to Article 47, by a local authority in discharge of functions under the LG(WP)A 1977. The LG(WP)(A)A 1990, and the WMA 1996, an Bord Pleanála in discharge of its functions under the Local Government (Planning and Development) Acts 1963–1994 and the Environmental Protection Agency in discharge of its functions under the LG(WP)A 1977, LG(WP)(A)A 1990, the EPAA 1992 and the WMA 1996.

HISTORY OF REGULATIONS

The first water pollution regulations under the LG(WP)A 1977 were the Local Government (Water Pollution) Regulations 1978 (S.I. No. 108 of 1978). These regulations were expressed to deal with procedural matters in relation to licensing discharges to waters and sewers under sections 4 and 16 of the 1977 Act, (*qv*) appeals to An Bord Pleanála in relation thereto, (*qv*) registers of licences and of water abstractions, (*qv*) water quality management and other miscellaneous matters under the LG(WP)A 1977.

The Local Government (Water Pollution) Regulations 1992 (S.I. No. 271 of 1992) amended and enlarged these procedures in an unexceptional manner but Part VI of the 1992 Regulations moved into entirely new territory in dealing with discharges to aquifers of harmful substances under section 4 of the LG(WP)A 1977.

After the 1992 Regulations were made, two subjects, licensing under section 4 and licensing under section 4 of discharges of harmful substances to aquifers were separated so that the 1999 Regulations deal solely with discharges to aquifers.

GROUNDWATER REGULATIONS

There was another departure or division in 1999 with the making of the Protection of Groundwaters Regulations 1999 (S.I. No. 41 of 1999). These Regulations (hereinafter referred to as "the 1999 Groundwater Regulations") were made under sections 6, 53 and 59 of the EPAA 1992 and not under the LG(WP)A 1977. The 1999 Groundwater Regulations were intended to implement the same Directive as was implemented by the Local Government (Water Pollution) Regulations 1992 (S.I. No. 271 of 1992) and the Local Government (Water Pollution) (Amendment) Regulations 1999 (S.I. No 42 of 1999). This Directive is Council Directive 80/68/EEC of December 17, 1979 on the protection of groundwater against pollution caused by certain dangerous substances (O.J. L20/43, January 26, 1980).

The 1999 Groundwater Regulations distinguish between an (*qv*) aquifer, which defined by virtue of Article 3 of the Local Government (Water Pollution) (Amendment) Regulations 1996 (S.I. No. 184 of 1996), as having the same meaning as in the LG(WP)A 1977 and LG(WP)(A)A 1990, and "groundwater" which is defined in the 1999 Groundwater Regulations as meaning "all water which is below the surface of the ground in the saturation zone and in direct contact with the ground or subsoil."

The 1999 Groundwater Regulations make provision for the licensing, after "prior investigations" as defined in the Regulations, by the Environmental Protection Agency of a direct discharge by a (*qv*) sanitary authority to an aquifer of an effluent which contains a harmful substance. "Direct discharge" is defined as meaning the discharge to the aquifer without percolation through the ground and subsoil. The only significance attached, throughout the regulations, to the word "groundwater" is as an identifiable wording for statutory notices. It is difficult to see why the word "groundwater" is used as it creates confusion with the word "aquifer". However, the original EEC Directive uses the word "groundwater" and the word is now popularly associated with what has become a national problem.

DISCHARGES TO GROUNDWATER OF DANGEROUS SUBSTANCES
(WMA 1996)

These are dealt with by **Article 40 of the Waste Management (Licensing) Regulations 1997** (S.I. No. 133 of 1997). *See:* REVIEW(4) WASTE.

DISCHARGES TO SEWERS
(EPAA 1992, s. 97)

Section 97 of the EPAA 1992:

"(1) Where the Agency proposes to grant a licence (including a revised licence) which involves a discharge of any (*qv*) trade effluent or other matter (other than domestic sewage or storm water) to a sewer, it shall obtain the consent of the sanitary authority in which the sewer is vested or by which it is controlled.

(2) A sanitary authority may consent to a discharge under subsection (1) subject

to such conditions as it considers appropriate and the Agency shall include such conditions or stricter conditions in the licence or revised licence.

(3) Without prejudice to the generality of subsection (2), conditions to a consent by a sanitary authority under this section may –
  (a) relate to –
    (i) the nature, composition, temperature, volume, level, rate, method of treatment and location of a discharge and the period during which a discharge may, or may not, be made,
    (ii) the provision, operation, maintenance and supervision of meters, gauges, manholes, inspection chambers and other apparatus and other means for monitoring the nature, extent and effect of emissions,
    (iii) the taking and analysis of samples, the keeping of records and the furnishing of information to the sanitary authority,
  (b) provide for the payment by the licensee to the sanitary authority concerned of such amount or amounts as may be determined by the sanitary authority having regard to the expenditure incurred or to be incurred by it in monitoring, treating and disposing of discharges of trade effluent, sewage effluent and other matter to sewers in its functional area or a specified part of its functional area,
  (c) specify a date not later than which any conditions shall be complied with.

(4) A sanitary authority may request the Agency to review a licence or revised licence to which this section relates –
  (a) at intervals of not less than three years from the date of the licence or the last review of the licence,
  (b) at any time with the consent, or on the application, of the person making, causing or permitting the discharge, or
  (c) at any time if –
    (i) the sanitary authority has reasonable grounds for believing that the discharge authorised by the licence or revised licence is, or is likely to be, injurious to public health or is likely to render the waters to which the sewer concerned discharges unfit for use for domestic, commercial, industrial, fishery (including fish-farming), agricultural or recreational uses or is, or is likely to be otherwise, a serious risk to the quality of the waters,
    (ii) there has been a material change in the nature or volume of the dis charge,
    (iii) there has been a material change in relation to the waters to which the sewer concerned discharges, or
    (iv) further information has become available since the date of the grant of the licence or revised licence relating to *(qv)* polluting matter present in the discharge concerned or relating to the effects of such matter,

  and the Agency shall consider and may comply with such request and shall have regard to any submission on the matter received from the sanitary authority."

Section 85 which provides for the interaction which must take place between the Agency and the planning authority on an application for a licence under section 83 or a review of a licence or revised licence under section 88, provides, by subsection (9), that the provisions of section 85 do not apply in relation to a licence under section 97 to such extent as may be prescribed.

(WMA 1996, s. 52)

Section 52 of the WMA 1996:

"Section 97 of the Act of 1992 shall apply in relation to the grant of a *(qv)* waste licence under this Part as if a reference in that section to a licence or revised licence was a reference to a waste licence under this Part."

DISCHARGES UNDER LG(WP)A 1977

(LG(WP)A 1977, ss. 4 and 16)

Local authorities as local authorities and local authorities as sanitary authorities have important licensing functions under sections 4 and 16 of the LG(WP)A 1977.

Under section 4 of the LG(WP)A 1977 a local authority licenses the discharge of *(qv)* trade effluent and *(qv)* sewage effluent to *(qv)* waters and the section prohibits the discharge otherwise than under and in accordance with a licence under the section.

Under section 16 of the LG(WP)A 1977 a sanitary authority licences the discharge of any trade effluent or other matter (other than domestic sewage or storm water) to a sewer and prohibits the discharge other than under and in accordance with a licence under the section.

See: LICENCES (3)

DISCLOSURE OF INTERESTS
(EPAA s. 38)

Section 38 of the EPAA 1992 deals with disclosures of interests and should be read in conjunction with its sister section, 37 which deals with (*qv*) declarations of interests.

Section 38 requires certain persons who have beneficial interests in or material to matters falling to be considered under the Act to disclose that interest in advance and then withdraw from the decision-making process regarding the matter concerned.

Subsection (1) outlines the classes of persons affected by the section and the scope is much wider than in section 37 and includes the Director General, a director, an employee of the Agency, a member of the Advisory Committee or of a committee or consultative group established by the Agency, a consultant, adviser or other person engaged by the Agency or a person whose services are availed of by, or supplied to the Agency under section 44 or who exercises or performs any function on behalf of the Agency under an agreement under section 45.

A person having an interest must disclose the nature of that interest in advance, neither influence nor seek to influence a decision on the matter, take no part in any consideration of the matter, withdraw from a meeting discussing the matter and take no part in any vote on the matter.

Subsection (2) provides that without prejudice to the generality of subsection (1), a person shall be regarded as having a beneficial interest if:

(a) he or any member of his household, or any nominee of his or any member of his household, is a member of a company or any other body which has a beneficial interest in, or material to a matter referred to in that subsection (which falls to be considered by the Agency),
(b) he or any member of his household is in partnership with or is in the employment of a person who has a beneficial interest in, or material to, such a matter,
(c) he or any member of his household is a party to any arrangement or agreement (whether or not enforceable) concerning land to which such a matter relates,
(d) any member of his household has a beneficial interest in, or material to, such a matter.

Subsection (3) deals with the situation where the interest is so remote or insignificant that it may be disregarded.

There is no provision, as there is in section 37, for the specific exclusion of interests in shares worth less than £1000 or 1%.

Subsection (4) provides that it is for the Agency to determine whether or not conduct constitutes a breach of the requirements of subsection (1) and particulars of the determination must be recorded in the minutes and by virtue of subsection (5) particulars of a disclosure of interest pursuant to subsection (1) must also be recorded.

Breach of section 38 does not create an offence as does a breach of section 37, under section 37(10).

DISMANTLEMENT OF FIXED ENGINES DURING CLOSE SEASONS
(F(C)A 1959, s. 128)

Section 128 of the F(C)A 1959 as amended by sections 46 and 50 of the FA 1980:

"(1) During the annual close season for salmon and trout –
(a) every *(qv)* bag net and stake net shall be removed from the poles or fixtures to which it is attached and carried away,
(b) there shall be made and maintained in every *(qv)* fixed engine (other than a bag net or stake net) a clear opening of four feet in width in the heads, traps, eyes or gaps from the top to the bottom thereof so as to allow the free passage of all fish through them and effectually to prevent the taking of fish therein.

offence
(2) If in respect of any fixed engine the provisions of subsection (1) of this section are not complied with, the occupier thereof shall be guilty of an offence under this section."

By virtue of section 46 of the FA 1980 this offence is one that may be tried on indictment.

(Note that the maximum penalty prescribed

under this subsection has been increased. *See:* FINES AND IMPRISONMENT (IMPOSITION OF)).

Subsection (3) provides that on conviction the (*qv*) fixed engine is forfeited as a statutory consequence of conviction.

Subsection (4) excepts persons who were prevented by floods, storm or stress of weather from complying with the requirements of subsection (1).

Subsection (5) excepts persons whose predecessor in title were on August 10, 1842, lawfully entitled by charter or prescriptive right to use any fixed engine in the tideway of a river for catching white sea fish.

DISPOSAL
(EPAA 1992, s. 3(1))

"in relation to waste, includes the selection, sorting, carriage, treatment, storage and tipping above or under ground, and the transformation operations necessary for its recovery, reuse or recycling."

(WMA 1996 s. 4(3))

"in relation to waste, includes any of the activities specified in the Third Schedule, and 'waste disposal activity' shall be construed accordingly."

See: SCHEDULES HERETO, WMA 1996 SCHEDULE.

DISPOSAL OF FORFEITURES
(F(C)A 1959, ss. 317 to 319)

The Fisheries Acts provide widely for the forfeiture of both (*qv*) fishing engines and the catch on conviction or lawful seizure. The following sections deal with the disposal of these things after the Court. The Judge merely makes the order for forfeiture but it is no part of his function under these sections to direct the method of disposal. *See:* DISPOSAL OF THINGS SEIZED.

Section 317(1) and (2) of the F(C)A 1959 provide that where anything is forfeited under the Act or any instrument made thereunder, whether by forfeiture order, as a statutory consequence of conviction or by lawful seizure, the Minister may, under this section, either direct that such thing be returned to the person who appears to him to be the owner or be sold or otherwise disposed of and if sold the net proceeds of sale shall be paid into the Exchequer.

Subsection (3), however, provides that this does not apply where oysters the property of the grantee of an oyster fishery are seized and ordered by the Judge to be delivered to that grantee under section 265.

Section 318 of the F(C)A 1959 provides that where a member of the Gardaí Síochána is involved in seizure and "was the means of bringing to justice" the person committing the offence and there is a direction that the thing be sold under section 317 then the proceeds are to be paid as to two-thirds to the regional board and as to one-third to the Garda Síochána Reward Fund. Otherwise the entire proceeds are paid to the regional board.

Section 319 provides for the disposal of the proceeds of sale of fish sold pursuant to a direction under section 301(4). *See:* DISPOSAL OF THINGS SEIZED.

DISPOSAL OF THINGS SEIZED
(F(C)A 1959, ss. 301 and 302)

FISH

Section 301(4) of the F(C)A 1959 provides that where an (*qv*) authorised officer detains any fish under section 301 which is likely to become unfit for human consumption before the matter can conveniently be dealt with by any court he must produce the fish before a Peace Commissioner.

Subsection (4) provides that if the commissioner is of the opinion that the fish should be destroyed he shall direct its destruction and if not he shall direct its sale. The authorised officer must comply with the direction.

Subsection (5) provides that a direction by a Peace Commissioner under subsection (4) of this section shall –

(a) be in writing
(b) be in such form as the Minister may direct,
(c) describe such fish and any mark, peculiarities or other particulars thereof pointed out by such authorised officer,
(d) be conclusive evidence in any court of the matters of fact stated therein.

BOATS OR FISHING ENGINES

Section 302 of the F(C)A 1959 as amended by substitution by section 26 of the F(A)A 1962 provides:

"Where a person, in the exercise of the powers conferred on him by this Part, seizes any boat or fishing engine, he shall, as soon as may be, apply to the District Justice in whose district it was seized for an order for its disposal under this section and thereupon the following provisions shall have effect –

(a) if, in the case of a boat, the Justice finds that, at the time of its seizure, it had been, was being, or was about to be, used for a purpose which under this Act is unlawful, he shall order it to be forfeited;
(b) if, in the case of a fishing engine, the Justice finds it is one the use of which is prohibited by law, he shall order it to be forfeited and destroyed;
(c) if, in the case of a fishing engine, the Justice finds that it was a lawful fishing engine which at the time of its seizure had been, was being, or was about to be unlawfully used, he shall order it to be forfeited;
(d) in any other case, the Justice shall order the boat or fishing engine to be returned to the person who appears to him to be the owner thereof."

The power to "seize" a boat is not in fact conferred anywhere in the Fisheries Acts. Section 301(2)*(ff)* refers to the power "to take, remove and detain in his custody" and section 301(2)*(da)* refers to the power to "take...to port").

(WLA 1976, s. 78)

Section 78 of the WLA 1976 –

"(1) A person who, in accordance with this Act, has seized any document or other thing shall not dispose of it –
(a) without the consent in writing of the owner or the person in apparent charge or control of it, or
(b) in case of anything other than a document, unless a direction is given pursuant to this section by a Peace Commissioner for its disposal."

Subsection (2), (3) and (4) provide for notice in writing to be given to the owner or other person in apparent charge or control above of intention to apply to a Peace Commissioner for a direction and the Peace Commissioner shall, if satisfied that anything in respect of which the application is made is likely, before it can be used in evidence in proceedings for an offence under this Act, to become unfit for human consumption, or if he is satisfied for any other reason that the thing ought not to be further retained, give a direction under this section authorising its disposal (by destruction or otherwise) and notice must be given to the owner or other person of this direction as soon as may be.

Subsection (5) provides that the recipient of the notice has a right of appeal against the direction to the District Court within seven days and The Justice hearing the appeal may either confirm or annul the direction.

Subsection (6) deals with various time limits:
(a) a direction does not take effect for seven days,
(b) in the case of an appeal where the direction is confirmed it shall have effect at the time the court determines,
(c) despite (a) the Peace Commissioner can specify his direction to take effect before the expiration of seven days,
(d) where a thing has been disposed of before appeal and the direction is annulled the court may order payment by the Minister to the owner of compensation, costs and expenses as he considers reasonable.

Subsection (7) gives the details which the Peace Commissioner must insert in the certificate which he is obliged to complete.

See: Wildlife Act 1976 (Certificate of Peace Commissioner) Regulations 1977 (S.I. No. 210 of 1977)

Subsection (8) provides that moneys payable pursuant to a disposal under this section shall be paid to the Minister.

See: Order 89, 8(1) to (4) District Court Rules, 1997.

Comparison: See: ENTRY, SEARCH (2) Section 301 (3) (4) and (5) and section 302 (substituted by section 26 of the F(A)A, 1962) provide for forfeiture of both fish and fishing engines by a Peace Commissioner but do not provide for the giving of notice and no appeal lies.

DISSOLUTION OF AN FORAS FORBARTHA
(EPAA 1992, s. 32)

Section 32 of the EPAA 1992 dissolved An Foras Forbartha Teoranta (The National Institute for Physical Planning and Construction Research Ltd) and the dissolution was effective from the August 1, 1993 (S.I. No. 215 of 1993). Its functions were taken over by the Agency.

DISTRIBUTOR
(WMA 1996, s. 27(1))

"means a person who sells or supplies a product or substance by wholesale and "distribute" shall be construed accordingly."

DOMESTIC WATER
(Waterworks Clauses Act 1847 and
Public Health (Ireland) Act 1878)

Section 35 of the Waterworks Clauses Act 1847 provides for the supply of "pure and wholesome" water sufficient for the domestic use of a town or district and makes special provision for the water pressure "at such pressure as will make the water reach the top storey of the highest house..."

Section 53 of the same Act gave the owner or occupier of a dwelling house, when he has laid his/her connecting pipes and paid the appropriate water rate, to demand and receive a sufficient supply of water for domestic purposes.

Section 61 prohibited, in respect of any stream, reservoir, aqueduct or other waterworks the property of the undertaker, bathing, washing dogs, throwing rubbish, dirt, filth or other noisome thing or washing or cleaning therein any cloth, wool, leather or skin of any animal, or any clothes or other thing or do any other act whereby the water of the undertakers shall be fouled.

Section 12 of the Waterworks Clauses Act 1863 provides that the supply of water for domestic purposes shall not include watering animals, washing carriages where such horses or carriages are kept for sale or hire, or a supply for any trade, manufacture or business, or for watering gardens, or for fountains, or for any ornamental purpose.

Sections 61, 65 and 74 of the Public Health (Ireland) Act 1878 provide that sanitary authorities are empowered to supply their districts with a supply of water which is proper and sufficient for both public and private purposes and must provide and keep in their waterworks a supply of pure and wholesome water.

Offence
Section 77 of the Public Health (Ireland) Act 1878 creates the offence for a person engaged in the manufacture of gas of causing water in any stream, reservoir, aqueduct, pond or place for water to be fouled by any washing or other substance produced in making or supplying gas.

Section 78 of the Public Health (Ireland) Act 1878 permits a sanitary authority, with the sanction of the Attorney General, either in their own name or in the name of any other person, with the consent of such person, to take such proceedings by indictment, bill in chancery, action or otherwise for the purpose of protecting any watercourse from pollution arising from sewage and section 79 of the same Act gives them power, on the representation of any person, to apply summarily for an order to close any well, tank, cistern, public or private, or supplied from any public pump, or used or likely to be used by man for drinking or domestic purpose which is so polluted as to be injurious to health. *See:* DRINKING WATER.

DRAFT NET
(F(C)A 1959, s. 3(1))

"includes a seine."

For permitted use and prohibition, *see:* SALMON AND TROUT CONSERVATION BYE-LAW NO. 743, 1998.

DRIFT NET
(F(C)A 1959)

For permitted use and prohibition, *see:* SALMON AND TROUT CONSERVATION BYE-LAW NO. 743, 1998.

DRINKING WATER
(EPAA 1992, s. 58)

Section 58(1) of the EPAA 1992 provides that the Agency may require a sanitary authority to submit to it in such manner and at such time as it may direct, such information as the Agency may specify about the monitoring of the quality of the water intended for human consumption pursuant to the European Communities (Quality of Water Intended for Human Consumption) Regulations 1988 (S.I. No. 81 of 1988) which gives effect to Council Directive 80/778/EEC of July 11, 1980 (O.J. L229, August 30, 1980, p.11), or any enactment amending or replacing those regulations or any other enactment relating to drinking water as may be prescribed.

Subsection (2) provides that the Agency shall, in relation to each year, prepare and submit to the Minister a report on the monitoring and assessment of the results, referred to in subsection (1), and shall include in the report such recommendations as seems to it to be appropriate.

Subsection (3) provides that each report under subsection (2) shall be laid by the Minister before each House of the Oireachtas and shall be published by the Agency.

See: WATER, SURFACE WATER.

DÚCHAS
(Heritage Act 1995)

"Dúchas" ("heritage") is the name or title recently adopted by the Commissioners of Public

Works in Ireland to describe their heritage functions under section 24 of the Heritage Act, 1995. *See:* COUNCIL, THE, HERITAGE COUNCIL, THE.

DURATION OF LICENCES
(F(C)A 1959/LG(WP)A 1977/
APA 1987/EPAA 1992/WMA 1996)

LICENCES FOR A YEAR OR LESS

Licences which are granted or renewed from year to year or for a shorter period are granted for a fixed or finite period from the date of granting, *e.g.* a hunting licence under section 29 of the WLA 1976 expires on the next following July 31, after the date of grant.

The same would apply to all district fishing licences, other than a licence under section 171 or aquaculture licences under the F(A)A 1997, which are expressed on the face of the licence to be "valid to end of season".

LICENCES UNDER LG(WP)A 1977, APA 1987, EPAA 1992 AND WMA 1996

In the case of the more substantial licences under other environmental statutes which are intended to last indefinitely, subject to review, the following applies:

In the case of the LG(WP)A 1977 as amended, the APA 1987, the EPAA 1922 and the WMA 1996 there is no specific provision as to the duration of the licences granted under the statutes but in each case the licence terminates on review. *See:* REVIEW. There is, however, a provision in these Acts for the lapse of moribund licences which are not used or which are allowed to fall into disuse for a period of 3 years. *See:* LIMITS ON THE DURATION OF LICENCES.

AQUACULTURE LICENCES

Section 15 of the F(A)A 1997:

"(1) Where an (*qv*) aquaculture licence is granted with the consent of a person referred to in section 8 and a period is specified in that consent, the licence shall remain in force for that period only.

(2) Subject to subsection (1), an aquaculture licence shall be for such period, not exceeding 20 years, as may be specified in the licence."

For section 8 *see:* LICENCES (1), AQUACULTURE LICENCES, LIMITATION ON LICENSING TO ENGAGE IN AQUACULTURE.

Section 19 of the F(A)A 1997:

"Subject to section 15(1), an aquaculture licence granted for a period specified in the licence may, on the expiration of the period, be renewed or further renewed by the (*qv*) licensing authority for such period as may be specified by it, after consultation with such bodies, if any, as may be prescribed for that purpose."

It is noteworthy that licences under LG(WP)A 1977, APA 1987, EPAA 1992 and the WMA 1996 do not have any limit on the duration of an active licence. *See:* LIMITS ON DURATION OF LICENCES.

Any problems are obviously intended to be addressed on review whereas in the case of an aquaculture licence under the F(A)A 1997, which is intended as a whole new concept in licensing, the licence can be in force for a period of up to 20 years with no provision for review except at the request of the licensee under section 70.

The Minister does have powers of revocation in certain circumstances under section 68, on misconduct of the licence in the running of his operation or where it is in the public interest to do so but this does not give the regular protection of fixed periodic review which enables the person granting the licence to monitor the operation, whether or not there is a crisis, and this must be of particular importance in the light of continuing advances in scientific research and the need to change parameters from time to time.

DUTIES ON ORDINARY FISHING LICENCES
(F(C)A 1959/F(A)(No. 2)A 1987/F(A)A 1991)

The legislation relating to duties on ordinary fishing licences (otherwise known as "rod licences") is complex. The reason for this complexity is the inefficient tangle of legislation dating from 1959 which was amended in an unsatisfactory manner both in 1987 and again in 1991.

F(A)(No. 2)A 1987

In 1987, the Government attempted to introduce a duty on rod licences for fishing for trout or coarse fishing which had formerly been free of any such duty or charge. Salmon fishing with a rod and line had for many years been subject to a duty under the Fourth Schedule to the F(C)A 1959.

The Fourth Schedule contains two parts, the

first of which relates to engines "subject to a licence duty in respect of salmon rod ordinary licences" and the second of which deals with ordinary licence duties applicable to all other types of "scheduled engines". *See:* SCHEDULES HERETO, FISHERIES ACTS SCHEDULES.

The F(A)(No. 2)A 1987 introduced a new and additional licence duty on fishing for trout and coarse fish with a rod and line. This was attempted by means of amendments to the Fourth Schedule to the 1959 Act which included provision for duties on freshwater ordinary rod licences for trout and coarse fish and a composite licence for salmon, trout and coarse fish.

The 1987 Act also made substantial amendments to Chapter I of Part VI of the 1959 Act and amended section 66 (penalties for taking salmon by rod and line by an unlicensed person) and section 67 (issue of fishing licences) and section 68 (imposition of fishing licence duties). *See:* SCHEDULES HERETO, FISHERIES ACTS SCHEDULES.

ROD LICENCE DISPUTE

The attempt to change the rules in respect of duties on trout and coarse fishing with rod and line led to a nationwide dispute involving anglers on all the major trout fishing lakes in the country. These disputes included public protests and the attempted boycotting of fishing activities on Western lakes for a number of years. Eventually, in 1991, the Government acceded to the demands of the protesting trout fishermen and further amended the F(C)A 1959 and section 18 of the amending F(A)A 1991 was used to introduce the new Fourth Schedule Part I which now contains the classes of salmon rod ordinary licences liable to duty. *See:* SCHEDULES HERETO, FISHERIES ACTS SCHEDULES.

F(A)A 1991

Section 3 of the F(A)A 1991 provided that a licence shall not be required for *(qv)* angling for trout or coarse fish and, as we have already seen, section 18 substituted a new Part I for the existing Part I of the Fourth Schedule to the 1959 Act.

After 1991 salmon had been restored as the only species of fish appearing in this Fourth Schedule albeit the type of salmon licences were different.

Section 16 of the F(A)A 1991 provides:

"(1) A salmon rod ordinary licence (to be known as a salmon rod (annual) district licence) shall on payment of the licence duty provided therefor in Part I of the Fourth Schedule to the Principal Act (as inserted by the Schedule to this Act) be made available for use in the fishery district in respect of which application for the licence is made and which is specified in the licence and being a fishery district in the fisheries region of the regional board by which it was issued.

(2) A salmon rod (annual) district licence shall operate to authorise the person named therein, but no other person, to use, during the period and in the fishery district specified therein, a salmon rod, subject to the provisions of the Principal Act and any instrument made thereunder.

(3) Where a person applies to a regional board for the issue to him of a salmon rod (annual) ordinary licence and satisfies the board that he is for the time being under the age of 18 years and pays the licence duty provided therefor in Part I of the said Fourth Schedule, the board shall issue such licence (to be known as a salmon rod (annual) juvenile licence) to him.

(4) Each regional board shall make available a salmon rod (one-day) ordinary licence on payment of the licence duty provided therefor in Part I of the said Fourth Schedule."

Subsections (5)–(7) of section 16 deal with the adjustment and refund of duties on licences issued and paid for pursuant to the 1987 Act.

POSITION AFTER 1991

Unfortunately, the 1987 Act made no changes in the enforcement provisions contained at sections 66, 67 or 68 of the 1959 Act.

Thus, it would appear that the legal position after 1991 is that the issue of and imposition of duty on ordinary fishing licences described in Part I the Fourth Schedule to the F(C)A 1959 is still governed by sections 66, 67 and 68 of that Act as amended by various sections of the F(A)(No. 2)A 1987 and, to the extent that it is compatible with that legislation, by section 19 of the F(A)A 1991.

Offences
There are two separate sections creating offences arising out of failure to pay the licence duties, firstly, use of a scheduled engine other than by rod and line (section 65) and fishing for or taking

salmon by rod and line (section 66).

USE OF A SCHEDULED ENGINE OTHER THAN BY ROD AND LINE

Section 65 of the F(C)A 1959:

"(1) If any person uses or erects in any (*qv*) fishery district any (*qv*) scheduled engine for the taking of salmon, [coarse fish], trout or eels, in respect of which there is not for the time being in force an ordinary fishing licence authorising the use of that engine in that fishery district,
such person shall be guilty of an offence under this section."

The words "coarse fish" in square brackets were added by the F(A)(No. 2)A 1987 to give effect to the additional duties provided for in that Act and although the words are now superfluous they have not been repealed. Note that fishing for trout other than by rod and line was licensable since 1959 and was never a reason for objection.

Subsection (2) provides that on conviction the engine is forfeited as a statutory consequence.

Subsection (3) provides that the section does not apply to the use of rod and line, which offence is dealt with in the following section 66.

FISHING FOR OR TAKING SALMON BY ROD AND LINE

offences

Section 66(1) of the F(C)A 1959 (prior to the passing of the F(A) (No. 2)A 1987) read:

"(1) If –
(a) any person fishes for or takes or kills salmon with rod and line in a (*qv*) fishery district and
(b) such person is not the holder of a salmon rod ordinary licence which is for the time being in force and is available for use in that fishery district,
such person shall be guilty of an offence under this section."

Section 66(1) of the F(C)A 1959 (as substituted by F(A)(No. 2)A 1987) reads:

"(1) Subject to subsection (2) of this section, if any person fishes for or takes or kills any salmon, trout and coarse fish or any of them with rod and line in any fishery district and such person is not the holder of-
(a) in the case of such salmon, a salmon rod ordinary licence or a composite freshwater angling ordinary licence,
(b) in the case of such trout, a trout rod ordinary licence or a composite freshwater angling ordinary licence,
(c) in the case of such coarse fish, a coarse fish rod ordinary licence or a composite freshwater angling ordinary licence,
which is for the time being in force, such person shall be guilty of an offence under this section."

If one reads section 66(1) by blocking out the references to trout rod ordinary licences, coarse fish ordinary licences and, a creature which was peculiar to that Act, a composite freshwater angling ordinary licence, which have never been repealed, then it reads:

"(1) Subject to subsection (2) of this section, if any person fishes for or takes or kills any salmon.....with rod and line in any fishery district and such person is not the holder of-
(a) in the case of such salmon, a salmon rod ordinary licence or..................
which is for the time being in force, such person shall be guilty of an offence under this section."

A judge hearing a prosecution under section 66(1) would have to be persuaded that this blocking out process is acceptable. He should do so if he can be persuaded surplusage can be disregarded.

Section 66(2), as amended, provides that subsection (1) shall not apply where the person fishing is under 18 or over 66 but only in respect of fishing for trout or coarse fish so it no longer applies.

Subsection (3), as amended, repeats the penalty of £500 provided by section 50 of the FA 1980 for summary conviction under section 66 and introduces a truly nonsensical provision that a person convicted on indictment could be fined £2000 or jailed for two years. This was wholly disproportionate when it was enacted and it is disgraceful that it should still appear in the Statute Books.

Section 66 was one of the sections which could be tried on *(qv)* indictment by virtue of section 46 of the FA 1980.

Subsection (4) provides for the usual statutory forfeiture of the rod and line on conviction.

GRANT OF LICENCE

The actual grant of licence is under section 67 which provides:

"(1) Every regional board shall, in accordance with this section, issue fishing licences (in this Act referred to as (*qv*) ordinary fishing licences) in respect of (*qv*) scheduled engines."

Section 5 of the F(A) (No. 2)A 1987 deleted subsection (2) of section 67 and substituted new subsections for subsections (3) and (4) which new subsections related to the type of licences created by the 1987 Act and which, as we have seen, are no longer of any relevance. Given the changes which took place by virtue of the F(A)A 1991, subsections (3) and (4) seem to be wholly inoperable and although they have never been formally repealed one must assume some form of constructive repeal and rely on section 18 of the F(A)A 1991, which is completely incompatible with subsections (3) and (4), when it comes to the issue of licences in respect of the various classes of salmon licences.

However, the remaining subsections of section 67 are still important. They provide that:

"(5) A separate ordinary fishing licence shall be issued for each separate (*qv*) fishing engine.

(6) Every ordinary fishing licence issued by a regional board shall –
   (a) be in such form as the Minister may from time to time direct,
   (b) shall state thereon –
      (i) the name of the regional board concerned,
      (ii) the period for which it is to be valid and in force,
      (iii) where appropriate, the number or name of the (*qv*) fishery district to which it relates,
      (iv) the kind of fishing engine to which it relates."

(as substituted by section 5 of the F(A)(No. 2)A 1987).

Subsection (7) Refers to a freshwater rod ordinary licence which no longer applies.

"(8) Where an application is made to a regional board for a licence for a fishing engine (being a (*qv*) fixed engine, a box in a (*qv*) fishing weir or a (*qv*) fishing mill dam, or an eye, gap or basket for taking (*qv*) eels in or on a fishing weir or a fishing mill dam) such licence shall be issued in the (*qv*) electoral division in which such engine is situate.

(9) Every ordinary licence issued in respect of an engine for fishing (other than rod and line) shall contain on the face thereof –
   (a) in the case of an engine to be used in a (*qv*) several fishery, the name of the person (in this section referred to as "the owner") who is for the time being entitled so to use such engine for his own benefit, or
   (b) in every other case the name and address of the person paying the licence duty on such engine,

together with, if such person, or in case the licence relates to an engine so to be used, the owner, makes a request in writing in that behalf to the regional board concerned, the name of not more than one other person specified in the request, and every ordinary licence which is so issued shall operate to authorise the use of the engine to which it relates by any person named in the licence."

(as substituted by section 67 of the FA 1980).

Note that the licence is issued for the *(qv)* fishery district created by the F(C)A 1959 and not the *(qv)* fishery region created by the FA 1980. *See:* (1) FISHERY DISTRICT; (2) FISHERY REGION

"(10) Every ordinary fishing licence shall be sealed with the seal of the board by which it was issued.

(11) An ordinary fishing licence (not being a freshwater rod ordinary licence) shall be available for use in the fishery district as regards which the application for the licence was made and which is specified in the licence and being a regional district in the fisheries region of the fisheries board by which it was issued and in no other fishery district."

This was substituted by section 5 of the F(A)(No. 2)A 1987.

(12) Does not apply for the reason given in (7) above.

(13) Does not apply for the reason give in (7)

above.

"(14) Every ordinary fishing licence (other than a freshwater rod ordinary licence) shall operate to authorise the use, during the period specified therein and in the fishery district specified therein, of a fishing engine of the kind specified therein, but subject to the provisions of this Act and any instrument made thereunder."

This was substituted by section 5 of the F(A)(No. 2)A 1987.

(15) Does not apply for the reason given in (7) above.

(16) Repealed by section 5(e) of the F(A)(No. 2)A 1987.

"(17) An ordinary fishing licence shall not be construed as giving or conferring any right of fishing or of using any engine for the taking of fish by any means or in any place where the person having or using the licence would not have possessed if this Act had not been passed or as altering or affecting the rights of any other person."

Section 67 was considered at length in an application to the High Court for an order of mandamus in *Patrick Slevin, Applicant v. Shannon Regional Fisheries Board, Respondent* ([1994] J.R. 293) ([1995] 1 I.R. 460) where an application to a regional fisheries board for a draft net fishing licence in Lough Ree, that was within the powers of the regional board to grant, was refused because the applicants had failed to furnish documentary evidence of their claim to have fishing rights in the lake. The court, in granting the order of mandamus sought, held that section 67 made it mandatory upon the board to issue the licence, subject only to the provisions of that section, and that there was no statutory requirement that an applicant produce to the respondent evidence of his right to fish.

Sections 66, 67 and 68 badly need to be amended and re-enacted in a manner consistent with the current legal position as to duties on ordinary angling (rod) licences.

E

EASEMENT
(FA 1980, s. 2(1))

"includes a *profit a prendre* and any right in or over water."

EEL
(F(C)A 1959, s. 3(1))

"includes the fry and young of eels, commonly called elvers."

There are three recognised methods of fishing for eels:

(1) An eel trap, also known as an "eye, gap or basket for taking eels on eel fishing weirs or fishing mill dams";
(2) by long line with hooks; or
(3) by fyke net.

All appear in the Fourth Schedule to the F(C)A 1959 and are (*qv*) scheduled engines and are therefore liable to the annual licence duty provided for in that Schedule and payable under section 68(4)a of the F(C)A 1959.

Fyke nets were added to the Schedule by section 11(5) of the FA 1980. Long lines for eels always appeared in the Fourth Schedule to the 1959 Act but otherwise their use was unrestricted until the amendment of section 100 by section 27 of the F(A)A 1999. Section 100 is dealt with immediately hereunder. Section 100(5)(a) now requires an eel fishery authorisation in respect of a long line (whether fixed or otherwise). The Fisheries (Amendment) Act, 1999 (save for section 23) came into force on 20 December 1999 by virtue of the Fisheries (Amendment) Act, 1999 (Commencement) Order, 1999 (S.I. No. 419 of 1999).

A fyke net is both a net and a (*qv*) fixed engine and its use is restricted. *See:* EEL FISHERY AUTHORISATIONS.

EEL FISHERY AUTHORISATIONS
(F(C)A 1959, s. 100)

An eel fishery authorisation is difficult to find in the Fisheries Acts in that it is located "astride" two sections, section 95 dealing with the prohibition of the use of nets in freshwater and section 100 dealing with restrictions on the use of certain fixed engines in freshwater.

Section 95(1) of the F(C)A 1959 as amended by section 18(c) of the F(A)A 1994, contains a prohibition in respect of the use of any net for the capture of fish in the freshwater portion of any river or in any freshwater lake. The subsection then lists four exceptions to this prohibition. The exceptions at (9)(a), (b) and (c) are not relevant to this article but the exception at (9)(d), which was amended by section 18 of the F(A)A 1994, is and it provides –

"unless
"(d) such net is constructed for the capture of eels and is operated in accordance with the conditions set out in an authorisation issued under section 100 of this Act."

Section 95(2) creates the offence of using a net in contravention of this section.

(Note that the maximum penalty prescribed under this section has been increased. *See:* FINES AND IMPRISONMENT (IMPOSITION OF)).

Section 100(5) and (6) of the F(C)A 1959 (as amended by s. 27 of the F(A)A 1999) –

"(5) (a) A *(qv)* regional board may, if it thinks fit, grant to –
(i) the occupier of a *(qv)* fishing engine (being a *(qv)* fishing weir, *(qv)* fishing mill dam or a *(qv)* fixed engine) for the capture of eels, or
(ii) any person in respect of a long line (whether fixed or otherwise), an authorisation in this section called an eel fishery authorisation) to use such fishing engine or long line for the capture of eels with a regional board if it so thinks fit,
(b) A regional board may attach to an eel fishery authorisation such conditions (including a condition limiting the period during which the authorisation is to remain in force) as it thinks fit,
(c) A regional board, if it so thinks fit may amend an eel fishery authorisation within ten years from the date on which the authorisation was granted.
(d) A regional board may revoke an eel fishery authorisation –
(i) if the holder thereof is convicted of an offence under the repealed enactments or an offence under any provision of this Act, or
(ii) if the board is satisifed that there has

been a breach of any condition attached to the authorisation."

Offence

"(e) If the holder of an eel fishery authorisation fails to comply with the conditions attached to that authorisation he shall be guilty of an offence under this subsection and shall be liable on summary conviction to a fine not exceeding £1,000.

(f) Where a person is convicted of an offence under this subsection, any (*qv*) fish and any (*qv*) fixed engine in respect of which the offence was committed shall, as a statutory consequence of conviction, stand forfeited.

(6) The following provisions shall apply in relation to the amendment or revocation of an eel fishery authorisation under this section –

(a) a regional board shall not amend or revoke the authorisation unless and until it has given by post to the holder of the authorisation at least one fortnight's notice in writing stating that the board has under consideration, as the case may be, the amendment or revocation of the authorisation,

(b) the notice shall also state –

(i) in case it states that the regional board has under consideration the amendment of the authorisation – the specific amendment under consideration and the grounds on which it is so under consideration, or

(ii) in case it states that the regional board has under consideration the revocation of the authorisation – the grounds on which such revocation is so under consideration,

(c) the regional board shall consider any representations in relation to such amendment or revocation, as the case may be, made to it by the holder of the authorisation before the expiration of the notice.

(6A) A regional board shall not exercise a power under subsection (5) and (6) of this section except in relation to its own fisheries region and unless it has first consulted the Marine Institute, and in exercising the power it shall have regard to any scientific advice given to it by the Marine Institute and any policy guidelines or instructions the Minister may establish or give."

Subsection (7) provides for certain exemption from the provisions of the section which relate to the prohibitory portion of the section which is dealt with elsewhere.
See: FIXED ENGINES, FISHING WEIRS, FISHING MILL DAMS, PROHIBITION OF.

The offence provisions in sections 100(5)(e) (e) and (f) were inserted by section 19 of the F(A)A 1994. They were not replacements. No offence had been provided for in subsection (5) prior to the F(A)A 1994 which made it extremely difficult for regional boards to "police" these authorisations which were often abused.

Section 27(c) of the F(A)A 1999 substantially amended section 100(5) and (6) and added subsection (6A). This gave effect to the process of downgrading the *(qv)* Central Board and giving additional responsibilities to the regional boards undertaken by that Act. Prior to these amendments, authorisations were granted, altered or revoked, by the Minister. the Fisheries (Amendment) Act, 1999 (save for section 23) came into force on 20 December 1999 by virtue of the Fisheries (Amendment) Act, 1999 (Commencement) Order, 1999 (S.I. No. 419 of 1999).

One would have to raise serious questions regarding the wisdom of inserting (6A). As the offence section appears at subsection (5)(e) it is likely that on prosecution by the *(qv)* regional board under the section a Court would require them to prove that subsection (6A) had been complied with. The prosecution would, after all, be an exercise of a power under subsection (5). This appears to be the intention. It makes nonsense of the new powers given to the regional boards under the section and is in fact more restrictive of their existing powers of prosecution which have only been in place since the F(A)A 1994. If it was unintentional, steps should be taken quickly to remedy the situation by shifting the onus on a defendant to prove failure to comply with subsection (6A).

One would also have to question the status of the *(qv)* Marine Institute in such matters.
See: MARINE INSTITUTE.

Reverting to the amendments under section 19 of the F(A)A 1999 referred to above, as there was some confusion in the minds of those drafting this amendment of section 100 as to the connection between subsection (1), which contains a restriction on the use of certain fishing engines in freshwater, and subsection (5) which deals exclusively with eel fishery authorisations, the following was added by the F(A)A 1994:

Section 19(2) of the F(A)A 1994:

"(2) Subsection (1) of section 100 of the Principal Act shall not apply, and shall be deemed never to have applied, to a fishing engine used in accordance with an authorisation purporting to have been issued by the Minister under the section."

This provision is absolutely meaningless as it is quite obvious that there is no such connection. It was the improper use of fishing engines by persons holding authorisations under section 100, particularly breaches of the conditions attached to same, that necessitated the penalty sections inserted by the F(A)A 1994 for those very breaches.

Section 100(6) permits the Minister to so amend or revoke an authorisation on notice in writing to the holder of at least a fortnight stating that the amendment or revocation is under consideration and setting out the grounds on which such amendment or revocation is being considered and the Minister must consider any representation by the holder before the expiration of the notice.

SECTION 99(5) AUTHORISATION

Section 99(5) of the F(C)A 1959 entitles the Minister, if he thinks fit, by order to authorise a named person to erect, in accordance with plans approved by the Minister, at a specified place in the freshwater portion of a specified river or lake, a specified kind of *(qv)* fishing engine (being a *(qv)* fishing weir, fishing mill dam or *(qv)* fixed engine) for the capture of eels.

See: FIXED ENGINES, FISHING WEIRS, FISHING MILL DAMS, PROHIBITION OF.

EEL FISHING WEIR WITHOUT FREE GAPS, AUTHORISATION OF
(F(C)A 1959, s. 109)

Section 109 of the F(C)A 1959 provides that, despite the provisions of section 107 which requires a (*qv*) free gap in every fishing weir, the Minister, if he thinks fit, may by order authorise the operation of a specified eel fishing weir without a free gap subject to such conditions, if any, as the Minister thinks fit.

Section 109(2) provides for the revocation of such an order, at any time:
(i) if the occupier is convicted of an offence,
(ii) if he fails to comply with any of the conditions.

Subsection (3) provides that during the currency of the order none of the provisions of the Act relating to free gaps in fishing weirs will apply in respect of such weir in so far as it is used for the capture of eels only.

EELS, EXEMPTIONS FROM SECTION 114 (GUIDING WALLS)
(F(A)A 1962, s. 12)

Section 12 of the F(A)A 1962 provides that the Minister may grant exemptions in relation to a specified (*qv*) fishing weir or a (*qv*) fishing mill dam used solely for the capture of eels, from the provisions of section 114 of the F(C)A 1959 requiring the construction of guiding walls appurtenant to fishing weirs and fishing mill dams.

EELS, USE OF FIXED ENGINES IN TIDAL WATERS
(F(A)A 1962, s. 11)

Section 11 of the F(A)A 1962 provides that the Minister may make bye-laws authorising, subject to condition, the placing, erection, fishing with and use of any (*qv*) fixed engine for the capture of eels, at any specified place in tidal waters, notwithstanding the provisions of sections 102 and 103 of the F(C)A 1959. *See:* FIXED ENGINES, FISHING WEIRS, FISHING MILL DAMS, PROHIBITION OF.

EDUCATION AND RESEARCH
(NH 97 Reg. 35)

Regulation 35 of the NH 97 Regulations (S.I. No. 94 of 1997) provides:

"(1) The Minister shall –
(a) promote education and general information on the need to protect species of wild flora and fauna and to conserve their habitats and natural habitats,
(b) encourage the necessary research and scientific work for the purpose of meeting the requirements of Article 11 of the (*qv*) Habitats Directive with particular attention to scientific work necessary for the implementation of Articles 4 and 10 of that Directive,
(c) supply information, where appropriate, for the purpose of proper co-ordination of research carried out at Member State and Community level to other Member States and the Commission."

EFFLUENT, SEWAGE
(LG(WP)A 1977, s. 1(1))

"means effluent from any works, apparatus, plant or drainage pipe used for the disposal to (*qv*) waters of (*qv*) sewage, whether treated or untreated."

EFFLUENT, TRADE
(LG(WP)A 1977, s. 1(1))

"means effluent from any works, apparatus, plant or drainage pipe used for the disposal to waters or to a sewer of any liquid (whether treated or untreated), either with or without particles of matter in suspension therein, which is discharged from premises used for carrying on any trade or industry (including mining), but does not include domestic sewage or storm water."

The discharges of these two effluents to waters are licensed under section 4 of the LG(WP)A 1977. *See:* LICENCE(3).

ELECTION YEAR
(FA 1980, s. 2(1))

"subject to section 15(2), means the year fixed by the Minister under section 12(5) and every fifth successive year thereafter."

ELECTIONS OF MEMBERS OF REGIONAL FISHERY BOARDS
(FA 1980, s. 12)

Section 12 of the FA 1980:

"(1) Elections of members of a (*qv*) regional board, other than the members appointed by the Minister under section 10 of this Act, shall in each (*qv*) election year be held in accordance with this Act as regards each (*qv*) fisheries region and each such election shall be conducted in accordance with this Act and regulations under this section."

See: Election to Regional Fisheries Boards Regulations, 1981 (S.I. No. 361 of 1981) and Election to Regional Fisheries Boards (Amendment) Regulations 1992 (S.I. No. 352 of 1992). The 1992 Regulations deal with the addition of members of *(qv)* fisheries co-operatives to the electorate.

Subsection (2) limits the number of votes to one only per persons in the following instances:

(a) a person holding two licences,

(b) a person who is both a rate payer and a licence holder,

(c) a person who is both registered in a (*qv*) register of sea anglers and is a licence holder

"(3) (a) The Minister may make such regulations as he thinks proper in relation to elections under this section of members of regional boards.

(b) Without prejudice to the generality of paragraph (a) of this subsection, regulations under this subsection may provide for –

(i) the nomination of different classes of candidates for election as members of regional boards and for the election of such candidates by different classes of electors,

(ii) postal voting at elections under this section of members of regional boards."

Subsection (4) provides that where the regulations provide for different classes of candidate for election a person shall be entitled to be nominated for one class only.

Subsection (5) provides that the Minister fixes the first year of election by order.

The first election was held on the third Tuesday of December 1981.

Section 10(4)(ii) of the FA 1980 gives the Minister power to appoint members to the *(qv)* regional fisheries boards. Other members of such boards are elected pursuant to section 12 of the FA 1980. Section 10 of the FA 1980 was extensively amended by section 7 of the F(A)A 1999.

Section 7(2) of the 1999 Act provides that, notwithstanding anything provided in the Act of 1980, the date for holding of the first election of members to *(qv)* regional boards after the commencement of section 7 of the 1999 Act shall be such date, not later than 3 months after the commence, as the Minister may by order fix and that an election shall be held as soon as practicable after each fifth anniversary of that date.

Section 7 of the 1999 Act came into force on 20 December 1999 by virtue of the Fisheries (Amendment) Act, 1999 (Commencement) Order (S.I. No. 419 of 1999). The 20th day of March, 2000 was the date fixed by the Minister under section 7 pursuant to the Regional Fisheries Boards (Date for Holding of First Elections after Commencement of Section 7 of the Fisheries (Amendment) Act, 1999 (Order), 2000 (S.I. No. 30 of 2000).

ELECTORATE FOR ELECTION OF ELECTED MEMBERS OF REGIONAL BOARDS
(FA 1980, ss. 10, 13–17)

Section 13 of the FA 1980 –

"(1) (a) Subject to section 12(2) of this Act, every person who is the holder of an ordinary fishing licence or an oyster fishing licence which is valid for a particular election year and who is ordinarily resident in [Ireland] on the date fixed under this Act for the receipt of nominations at an election to be held under this Act in that year shall be entitled to vote at the election to be held in that year as regards the (*qv*) regional board by which the licence is issued.

(b) (i) Subject to section 12(2) of this Act and to sub paragraph (ii) of this paragraph, every person who is for the time being registered in a Register of Sea Anglers (other than a person who is so registered as a non-voting), and who is ordinarily resident in [Ireland] on the date fixed under this Act for the receipt of nominations at an election to be held under this Act as regards the regional board by which the register is maintained, shall be entitled to vote at the election.

(ii) A person shall be entitled to vote pursuant to this paragraph at an election under this Act which is not the election first held as regards a regional board if, and only if, he has been registered in the register maintained by the board to which the election related for a continuous period of not less than three years ending on the day fixed under this Act for the receipt of nominations at the election".

Subsection (1)*(b)* was amended by section 2(2)*(c)* of the F(A)(No. 2) A 1987 which substituted "Register of Sea Anglers" for "Register of Trout, Coarse Fish and Sea Anglers".

Subsection (2) provides that the holder of a valid (*qv*) special local licence and having the appropriate residency qualifications on the date for receipt of nominations shall be entitled to vote in the (*qv*) fisheries region where the (*qv*) special tidal waters to which the licence relates are situate.

Subsection (3) provides that where a person is a rated occupier of a fishery and has paid his (*qv*) fishery rate the following provision shall have effect –

(a) he or his (*qv*) agent duly appointed under section 328 of the F(C)A 1959 shall be entitled to vote in the fisheries region in which his fishery is situate,

(b) where regulations are in force, the production of the receipt for the current fishery rate is sufficient for the rated occupier, or his attorney or agent to vote.

Subsection (4) provides that references in the Act to the electorate of a fisheries region shall be construed as references to the persons entitled to vote in that year by virtue of this section.

Section 14 of the FA 1980 gives a list of the persons who are not eligible for election: a member of either house of the Oireachtas, an M.E.P., a person not entitled to vote, an undischarged bankrupt, a person who has made a composition with his creditors in the past three years and a person who has been convicted of an offence under the Fisheries Acts within the past seven years.

Section 15 of the FA 1980 entitles the Minister to postpone an election by order under the section if he thinks fit but the order must be laid before both houses of the Oireachtas and approved. Section 36 of the F(A)A 1962, which deals with the annulment of an order under that Act, is stated not to apply to an order made under this section.

Section 16 of the FA 1980 provides for the situation where there are no members elected under section 12, in which event the previous board continue in office, and the section also provides for filling casual vacancies.

DISQUALIFICATION

Section 17 of the FA 1980 provides for the disqualification of a member of a regional board who absents himself during a period of six consecutive months, Subsection (2) allows the board to extend the period of six months if there are special circumstances but to achieve this result two thirds of the members of the board must be present at the appropriate meeting and, of those present, at least two thirds must vote in favour of the extension.

Section 10 of the FA 1980 will be dealt with separately under (*qv*) fisheries regions but the Minister has power, by virtue of section

10(4)*(a)*(ii), to appoint his own nominees to the regional boards. The number of persons he can appoint must be specified in the order establishing the relevant region.

ELECTORATE ENLARGED UNDER F(A)A 1991
(F(A)A 1991, ss. 4 and 14)

Section 4 of the F(A)A 1991 gives the Minister power by order to establish in every fishery region one or more "fisheries co-operative societies". The word "society" is defined in the Election of Fisheries Boards (Amendment) Regulations 1992 (S.I. No. 352 of 1992).
See: FISHERIES CO-OPERATIVES.

Section 14 of the F(A)A 1991 –

"(1) (a) Every ordinary member of a society for a particular year shall, if ordinarily resident in Ireland, be entitled to vote at an election held in that year for members of the (*qv*) regional board for the region which includes the society's area but, in the case of an election for any year subsequent to the first election after the commencement of this Act, only if he had also been an ordinary member for any two years since the previous election.
(b) Every former life member of Iontaobhas Iascaigh Intire Incorptha (the Inland Fisheries Trust Incorporated), who registered under section 58(4) of the Fisheries Act, 1980, in the register of a (*qv*) regional board and who is ordinarily resident in Ireland on the date fixed under the Fisheries Act, 1980, for the receipt of nominations at an election held for members of the regional board by which the register is maintained, shall be entitled to vote at that election.
(c) This subsection shall not prejudice the operation of section 13 of the Fisheries Act, 1980."

Subsection (2) applies the vote once only rule which appears in section 12(2) of the 1980 Act and provides that there cannot be double qualification to vote under that section and this section.

Subsection (3) provides that for the purposes of section 12(3)*(b)*(i) of the FA 1980 all persons who are members of a society in a particular region as trout anglers shall constitute one class and likewise with coarse fish anglers. However, *see:* DUTIES ON ORDINARY FISHING LICENCES.

Subsection (4) provides that section 13 of the FA 1980 is amended by the substitution of "Ireland" for "the State" throughout.

EMISSION,
(APA 1987, s. 7(1))

"means, save where the context otherwise requires, an emission of a (*qv*) pollutant into the atmosphere."

(EPAA 1992, s. 3(1)

"means –
(a) an emission into the atmosphere of a *(qv)* pollutant within the meaning of the Air Pollution Act, 1987,
(b) a discharge of (*qv*) polluting matter, (*qv*) sewage effluent or (*qv*) trade effluent within the meaning of the Local Government (Water Pollution) Act, 1977, to (*qv*) waters or (*qv*) sewers within the meaning of that Act,
(c) (*qv*) waste,
(d) (*qv*) noise."

[*Note:* the words "the disposal of" in paragraph (c) which appeared before the word "waste" were deleted by section 65(1)*(d)* of the WMA 1996].

(WMA 1996, s. 5(1))

"has the meaning assigned to it by the Act of 1992."

"Emission into the atmosphere" is defined by section 5(1) of the WMA 1996 as meaning - "the emission of a (*qv*) pollutant, within the meaning of the Air Pollution Act 1987, into the atmosphere."

As a result of these cumulative definitions of "emission" the word has a specialised meaning in the APA 1987 and for that Act only. The word "emission" in the EPAA 1992 and the WMA 1996 has a much more general meaning which is intended to encompass all environmental legislation up to 1992 and up to the passing of the APAA in 1992 and from 1992, when referring to an emission into the atmosphere within the meaning of the APA 1987 instead of simply using the word "emission" the phrase "emission into the atmosphere" is used.

EMISSION LIMIT VALUE
(APA 1987, s. 6(1)

This is defined in the APA, 1987, section 6(1), as meaning a limit prescribed by the Minister under section 51.

Section 51(1) of the APA 1987 allows the Minister to make regulations specifying limits. emission limit values (ELVs), for emissions and different ELVs may be specified for different areas or classes of areas, different premises or classes of premises, different circumstances or classes of circumstances or for different periods of time.

Subsection (2) provides that the ELV may relate to a particular (*qv*) pollutant or to a combination of pollutants.

Subsection (3) provides that when an elv has been specified by regulation there is an obligation placed on an (*qv*) occupier of any (*qv*) premises from which the pollutant or combination of pollutants is emitted into the atmosphere to take such steps as may be necessary to ensure that such emissions do not exceed the ELV concerned.

offence
A contravention of this section would be dealt with under section 11(1) of the APA 1987 which is the general penalty section.

See: Air Pollution Act 1987 (Combustion Plant) Regulations 1992 (S.I. No. 273 of 1992) which came into operation on the 1st day of October, 1992 whereby the Minister prescribed (*qv*) emission limit values relating to sulphur dioxide and dust for certain combustion plants in accordance with Directive 88/609/EEC on the limitation of emissions of certain pollutants from such plants.

They also gave directions as to the (*qv*) best practicable means for limiting the emissions concerned and specify procedures for monitoring, evaluating and determining emissions.

"Combustion plant" in the Regulations means any industrial plant in which fuels are oxidized in order to use the heat thus generated for the production of energy, other than such plant which makes direct use of the products of combustion in a manufacturing process or which is powered by a petrol, diesel or gas engine or by a gas turbine.

See: Air Pollution Act 1897 (Municipal Waste Incineration) Regulations 1993 (S.I. No. 347 of 1993) which were signed on the December 1, 1993 the Minister prescribed emission limit values relating to Dust, Hydrochloric Acid (HCL), Hydroflouric Acid (HF), Sulphur Dioxide (SO2), Lead (Pb+), Chromium (Cr+), Copper (Cu+), Manganese (Mn), Nickel (Ni+), Arsenic (As), Cadmium (Cd) and Mercury (Hg), as specified in the First Schedule, for municipal waste incineration plants subject, as appropriate, to the conditions specified in the Second Schedule.

"Municipal waste" in the Regulations means domestic refuse, and commercial and trade refuse and any other waste similar in nature and composition to domestic refuse.

"Municipal waste incineration plant" means industrial plant specifically used for the incineration of municipal waste, with or without recovery of the combustion heat generated.

Article 4 directs the best practicable means for preventing or limiting emissions for municipal waste incineration plant under paragraphs (a) to (h). Article 5 provides that the local authority shall make the monitoring results which it receives pursuant to these Regulations available for public inspection.

See: Air Pollution Act 1987 (Emission Limit Value for the use of Asbestos) (Amendment) Regulations, 1990 (S.I. No. 28 of 90) which came into operation on the 1st day of March 1990 and provide for the emission limit value for asbestos in the case of industrial plant concerned with the production and processing of asbestos and manufacture of asbestos related products.

See also: Air Pollution Act 1987 (Emission Limit Value for Combustion Plant) Regulations, 1996 (S.I. No. 264 of 1996) operative date October 1, 1996 revokes the 1992 Regulations, S.I. No. 273 of 1992.

EMISSION LIMIT VALUES AND QUALITY STANDARDS
(EPAA 1992, s. 103)

"(1) The Agency may, at any time, and shall when requested by the Minister to do so, make recommendations to the Minister in relation to –
(a) the specifying of (*qv*) air quality standards under section 50 of the Air Pollution Act, 1987,
(b) the specifying of (*qv*) emission limit values under section 51 of the Air Pollution Act, 1987,
(c) the prescribing of (*qv*) quality standards for (*qv*) waters, (*qv*) trade effluents and (*qv*) sewage effluents and standards in relation to methods of

treatment of such effluents, under section 26 of the Local Government (Water Pollution) Act, 1977.

(2) Before making regulations for any of the purposes referred to in subsection (1) the Minister shall have regard to any recommendations made by the Agency pursuant to that subsection.

(3) Recommendations under subsection (1), other than recommendations made at the request of the Minister, shall be published by the Agency."

EMPLOYEE OF THE AGENCY
(EPAA 1992, s. 3(1)):

"does not include the Director General or other director of the Agency".

ENFORCEMENT
(LG(WP)A 1977/APA 1987/EPAA 1992/ WMA 1996/WLA 1976/NH 97)

The enforcement of environmental law is said to be *proactive* when it attempts to anticipate a future event *e.g.* when an injunction is sought. Injunctive relief at its best is an attempt to prohibit the occurrence of some future event in anticipation of untoward consequences arising from the occurrence.

Environmental law is also described as being *reactive* when the reaction to the event does not take place until after the occurrence and when, more often than not in environmental terms, the damage has been done *e.g.* when a discharge into waters of polluting matter has taken place and fish life and the food of fish has been damaged or destroyed. The only remedy at this late stage is a prosecution in respect of the past event and punishment of the offender by fine, by fine and imprisonment, by forfeiture of his "weapons of destruction" and forfeiture of whatever licence was used to give a semblance of legality to the enterprise which gave rise to the offence. There is also provision for compulsory remedial action at the cost of the offender *e.g.* restocking with fish waters after pollution.

Failure to act can be as damaging as positive action. The person who causes a discharge of polluting matter to waters by omitting to turn off a tap or failing to close a sluice gate is as culpable as the person who physically throws the polluting matter into the waters.

Under this heading of enforcement is included the notices requiring information which need to be served by persons investigating suspicious circumstances to elicit information and which are often a precursor to legal action. Some but not all notices attract a penalty for non-compliance with the terms of the notice as distinct from a penalty which may be imposed for the commission of the offence which may come to light as a result of these inquiries.

The following headings for enforcement have been chosen for the purposes of this book:

(1) By court application for injunctive relief,
(2) By forfeiture of licence,
(3) By notice requiring measures to be taken,
(3a) By notice stating offence committed,
(4) By notices for particulars,
(5) By direction,
(6) By direct intervention without notice,
(7) By a third party property order,
(8) By seizure, detention and forfeiture of fish, things, boats, fishing engines, vehicles and equipment, and
(9) By prohibition by provision of statute.

(1) BY COURT APPLICATION FOR INJUNCTIVE RELIEF

(A) LG(WP)A 1977

Sections 10 and 11 of the LG(WP)A 1977 give a local authority a right to apply to the court for what amounts to injunctive relief when (*qv*) polluting matter has entered, is entering or is likely to enter (*qv*) waters. *See:* PROHIBITION, WATER UNDER LG(WP)A 1977 and LG(WP)(A)A 1990.

(B) APA 1987

Section 28 of the APA 1987 gives a similar right of application where the continuance of an emission would give rise to a serious risk of air pollution, the emission is an emission from industrial plant in contravention of the terms of a licence or a like emission for which a licence is required and in relation to which no licence has been granted.

The order made under the section may provide:

(a) specific measures to eliminate or reduce the risk,
(b) requiring the doing, not doing, or ceasing from doing anything to ensure that the emission is terminated or restricted or complies with a licence under the Act in the case of an activity where a Part IV licence is in force,
(c) in relation to costs.

Section 28A of the APA 1987 (inserted by section 18, Third Schedule, of the EPAA 1992) extends these powers of application to any person where there is an emission from any premises other than an emission under and in accordance with a licence under the Act, or an emission in compliance with an (*qv*) emission limit value under section 51 or directions specifying best practicable means issued by the Minister under section 5.

See: Order 96 Rule 2 District Court Rules, 1997.

The APA 1987 does not provide for offences of failing to comply with sections 28 and 28A.

Extension of powers to agency:

These functions, under sections 28 and 28A of the APA 1987, now apply to the Agency in the circumstances described in Article 10 of the Environmental Protection Agency (Extension of Powers) Order 1996 (S.I. No. 126 of 1996). *See:* EXTENSION OF POWERS.

(C) EPAA 1992 – GMO Regulations

Article 62 Genetically Modified Organisms Regulations, 1994 (S.I. No. 345 of 1994) provides for application by the Agency to the High Court for an order prohibiting or restricting any process or action involving a (*qv*)genetically modified organism where the court is satisfied that:

(a) the continuance of the process or action would constitute a contravention of the Regulations, or
(b) the continuance of the process or action would pose a real and substantial danger to human health or the environment.

(D) WMA 1996

Sections 57 and 58 of the WMA 1996 provide for an application to the High Court in the case of section 57 and any "appropriate Court" in the case of section 58 where waste is being held, (*qv*) recovered or (*qv*) disposed of in a manner causing or likely to cause (*qv*) environmental pollution.

The appropriate court in section 58 by virtue of subsection (1)*(b)* is the District Court where the estimated cost of complying with the order is less than £5,000, the Circuit Court where that value does not exceed £30,000, and thereafter the High Court.

Apart from the different court jurisdictions provided for, the distinction between the two sections would appear to be that section 58 applies when a person is holding or has held in a manner that is causing or has caused environmental pollution whereas section 57 applies when the waste is being held in a manner that causes or is likely to cause environmental pollution. It is the same distinction as is made in the LG(WP)A 1977 between sections 10 and 11. *See:* PROHIBITION, WATERS UNDER THE LG(WP)A 1977 and LG(WP)(A)A 1990.

The orders, however, under subsection (1) in the case of both sections, are worded quite differently as follows:

In section 57 the court may by order:

(a) require the carrying out of specified measures to prevent or limit, or prevent the recurrence of, environmental pollution,
(b) require the doing or restraining from doing any specified act, or the refraining from or ceasing making any specified omission,
(c) make any other provision, including the payment of costs.

In section 58 the court may order:

(a) the discontinuance of the holding, recovery or disposal of waste, or
(b) the mitigation or remedying of the effects of such holding, recovery or disposal.

Offence
In section 57(7) and section 58(4) failure to comply with an order constitutes an offence.

(E) NH 97 Regulations

Regulations 17(3) of the NH 97 Regulations (S.I. No. 94 of 1997) provide that where the Minister is of the opinion that the (*qv*) operation or activity would adversely affect the integrity of the site concerned he can bring an application to the High Court to prohibit the continuance of the operation or activity.
See: POWERS (7).

(F) Foreshore Acts 1933 to 1992

Sections 5 and 6 of the Foreshore (Amendment) Act 1992 provide remedies similar to those in sections 10 and 11 of the LG(WP)A 1977. *See:* FORESHORE.

(2) BY FORFEITURE OF LICENCE

Fisheries Acts

There are a number of sections in the F(C)A 1959 which deal with general powers of forfeiture, apart from the specific provisions for forfeiture as a statutory consequence of conviction which appears in every offence section where a (*qv*) fishing engine is used.

Special local licence

Section 78 of the F(C)A 1959 provides that where the holder of a special local licence is convicted of an offence under the Fisheries Acts the court may, on conviction, direct the licence to be forfeited.

Forfeiture of fishing and oyster fishing licences

Section 90(1) of the F(C) 1959 (substituted by section 51 of the FA 1980) provides that where a person is convicted of an offence under the Act, other than an offence under subsection (3), and is the holder of a fishing licence or oyster fishing licence, the court may, in addition to any other penalty, declare the licence or licences to be forfeited.

Subsection (2) provides that where the person does not hold a licence the Court may disqualify him from holding a licence for a period of not more than one year.

Section 90(3) of the F(C)A 1959 –

"(3) (a) This subsection applies to the following offences, namely –
(i) an offence under section 65, 69, 73, 94, 97, 127, 128, 129, 130, 132, 134, 140, 145, 146, 176, 182, 285A (inserted by section 24 of the Act of 1962) or 301 of this Act,
(ii) an offence under section 29 of the Act of 1962,
(iii) an offence under any bye-law described in subsection (4) (inserted by section 3 of the Act of 1962) of section 9 of this Act which is also a bye-law described in subsection 46(4) of the Fisheries Act, 1980,
[(iv) an offence under regulations made under section 24 of the Fisheries (Amendment) Act, 1999 which is an offence declared by the Minister by regulations to be an offence to which this subsection applies.]
(b) Where a person is convicted of an offence which is both an offence to which this sub section applies and a second or any subsequent such offence [which is the second or subsequent such offence in any period of 12 consecutive months] the court by whom such person is convicted shall make an order (in this Act referred to as a "consequential disqualification order") declaring him to be disqualified for holding an ordinary fishing licence in respect of any scheduled engine mentioned in Part II of the Fourth Schedule to this Act, and such order shall operate so as to disqualify the person to whom it relates during the period of three years commencing on the date on which the order was made."

Subsection (3) was amended by section 26 of the F(A)A 1999.

Subsection (4) provides that in the case of an appeal the appellate court has jurisdiction to make, confirm or annul a consequential disqualification order, and subsection (5) provides that a consequential disqualification order shall not be annulled on appeal unless the conviction by reference to which it was made is reversed.

WLA 1976

Section 75 of the WLA 1976 provides for revocation of a (*qv*) firearms certificate if the holder is convicted of an offence under Part II of the Act. The order is discretionary.

Section 49 of the WLA 1976 provides for the revocation of a (*qv*) wildlife dealer's licence on conviction of an offence under section 31 or an offence under section 69(2) because of a contravention of, or of a failure to comply with, regulations made under sections 41 or 46. The order is discretionary. Although the word "revocation" is used these are properly forfeitures.

(3) BY NOTICE REQUIRING MEASURES

This enforcement procedure is mainly reserved to local authorities except where these functions have been taken over by the Agency under Articles 4 and 10 of the Environmental Protection Agency (Extension of Powers) Order 1996 (S.I. No. 126 of 1996) and except where the Agency has a primary responsibility under section 107 of the EPAA 1992 which deals with noise and the GMO Regulations 1994 (S.I. No. 345 of 1994). *See:* (1) EXTENSION OF POWERS; (2) NOISE; (3) GENETICALLY MODIFIED ORGANISMS.

(A) F(C)A 1959

This function is reserved to the Minister and is rare.
See: DAMS AND NATURAL OBSTRUCTIONS.

(B) LG(WP)A 1977

(1) Notice requiring measures to prevent pollution

Section 12(1) of the LG(WP)A 1977 provides that where it appears to it to be necessary to do so to prevent or control pollution of (*qv*)waters, a local authority may serve notice in writing on any person having the custody or control of any (*qv*)polluting matter on premises.

Subsection (2) provides that the notice shall:

(a) specify such measures as the local authority consider necessary to prevent the polluting matter from entering waters,

(b) direct the person served to take such measures as are specified in the notice, and

(c) specify a period within which such measures are to be taken.

Subsection (2A) (inserted by section 9(a) of the LG(WP)(A)A 1990) provides that, notwithstanding subsection (2), the notice may either in addition to or in lieu of complying with that subsection:

(a) regulate and restrict subject to specified conditions the carrying on of any activity, practice or use of premises that could result in the entry of (*qv*)polluting matter to waters, and

(b) require the provision, re-location or alteration of facilities, for the collection or storage of polluting matter.

Subsection (3) provides that the person receiving the notice has the right to make representations regarding the terms of the notice.

Offence
Subsection (4) creates the offence of failing to comply with the terms of the notice.

Subsection (5) empowers the local authority in default of compliance to have the works carried out and recover the costs from the notice party.

This section was substantially amended by sections 9, 24 and 30 of the LG(WP)(A)A 1990.

EXTENSION OF POWERS TO THE AGENCY

These functions under section 12 of the LG(WP)A 1977 now apply to the Agency in the circumstances described in Article 4 of the Environmental Protection Agency (Extension of Powers) Order 1996 (S.I. No. 126 of 1996). *See:* EXTENSION OF POWERS.

(2) Notice requiring ceasing of contravention

Section 16(13) of the LG(WP)A 1977 provides that a (*qv*) sanitary authority may serve on any person making, causing or permitting a discharge or entry in contravention of section 16(1) or (7) LG(WP)A 1977 a notice in writing requiring the ceasing of the contravention within such period as may be specified in the notice and requiring mitigation or remedying of any effects of the contravention within such period and in such manner as may be specified.

For section 16, *see:* LICENCE(3).

Offence
Subsection (13A), inserted by section 12(b) of the LG(WP)(A)A 1990, creates the offence of failing to comply with a notice under the section.

Subsection (14) empowers the sanitary authority in default of compliance to carry out whatever works are necessary to prevent the discharge or mitigate or remedy its effects and recover the costs of the works from the notice party on satisfying the court that that person is responsible for the contravention.

Subsection (15), amended by the First Schedule to the Environmental Protection Agency (Extension of Powers) Order 1996 (S.I. No. 126 of 1996) provides that a notice may be served under subsection (13) whether or not there has been a prosecution under Part IV of the EPAA 1992 in the case of an (*qv*)activity in respect of which a licence or a revised licence under that part of that Act is in force or, in any other case, a prosecution under this section.

EXTENSION OF POWERS TO AGENCY

Section 16(13), (14) and (15) is affected by Article 4 of the Environmental Protection Agency (Extension of Powers) Order 1996 (S.I. No. 126 of 1996). *See:* EXTENSION OF POWERS.

(C) APA 1987

Notice requiring measures

A notice under section 26(1) of the APA 1987 is similar to a section 12(1) notice under the LG(WP)A 1977, above.

Section 26(1) of the APA 1987 provides that where it appears to a local authority that it is necessary to do so to prevent or limit (*qv*) air pollution, they may serve a notice under this section on the (*qv*) occupier of any premises from which there is an (*qv*) emission.

Unlike the LG(WP)A 1977, which is not so circumscribed, the APA 1987 requires prior consideration by the local authority of the various plans, requirements for different premises, different areas of control and levels and quality of emission before the service of a notice under this section.

There is the same right of making representations under this section as in the LG(WP)A 1977 but no offence is created by section 26 for failing to comply with a notice.

The remedy for failure to comply with the requirements of the notice within the period specified in the notice is for the local authority to take such steps as may be necessary to secure compliance and recover the costs of compliance from the notice party.

EXTENSION OF POWERS TO AGENCY

These functions under section 26 of the APA 1987 now apply to the Agency in the circumstances described in Article 10 of the Environmental Protection Agency (Extension of Powers) Order 1996 (S.I. No. 126 of 1996). *See:* EXTENSION OF POWERS.

(D) EPAA 1992

(1) Notice for prevention or limitation of noise

Section 107 of the EPAA 1992 provides that a local authority, where the source of noise does not constitute an (*qv*) activity, and the Agency, where it does and requires a licence, may serve a notice on the (*qv*) person in charge where it is necessary to do so for the prevention or limitation of (*qv*) noise.

The provisions regarding the service and consequences of the notice are the same as in the LG(WP)A 1977 and APA 1987 except:

(i) There is an offence but it is not specified in the section. It arises under the general offences section, section 8 of the EPAA 1992.

(ii) There is a statutory defence to a prosecution in relation to a contravention of this section.

(iii) The local authority or the Agency must keep a (*qv*) register of notices issued, amended or revoked which must be made available for inspection by the public.

(2) Notice requiring measures under GMO Regulations

Article 63 of the Genetically Modified Organisms Regulations, 1994 (S.I. No. 345 of 1994) –

"(1) Where it appears to the Agency that it is necessary to do so in order to protect human health or the environment, it may serve a notice in writing under this article on any *(qv)* user.

(2) A notice under this article shall –

(a) specify the measures which appear to the Agency to be necessary in order to protect human health or the environment,

(b) direct the user on whom the notice is served to take such measures as may be specified in the notice, and

(c) specify a date by which such measures are to be taken.

(3) A notice under this article –

(a) may be served whether or not there has been a prosecution for an offence under these Regulations in relation to the particular process or action the subject of the notice, and

(b) shall not prejudice the initiation of a prosecution for an offence under these Regulations or under the Act.

(4) A person on whom a notice under this article has been served, may, within such period as may be specified in the notice, make representations in writing to the Agency concerning the terms of the notice and the Agency, having considered the representations, may amend or revoke the notice.

(5) A person on whom a notice is served under this article shall, within the period specified, comply with the notice."

See: Article 3 of these Regulations for definitions.

(*Note:* Section 8 of the EPAA 1992 provides that any person who contravenes any provision of this Act or any regulation made under this Act.....shall be guilty of an offence which renders an offence article in the Regulations superfluous.)

(E) WMA 1996

Notice requiring measures to be taken

Section 55(1) of the WMA 1996 provides that a local authority may serve a notice where it appears to them to be necessary to do so in order to prevent or limit (*qv*) environmental pollution caused, or likely to be caused, by the holding, (*qv*) recovery or (*qv*) disposal of waste.

No such notice can be served where the recovery or disposal is carried out in accordance with a waste licence or a licence or revised licence granted under Part IV of the EPAA 1992 (an Integrated Pollution Control (IPC) licence).

The notice may require:

(a) the taking of specified measures which the local authority considers necessary in order to prevent or limit the environmental pollution concerned or to prevent a recurrence thereof,

(b) the cesser of the holding, recovery or disposal concerned,

(c) the mitigation or remedying of any effects of any activity aforesaid in a specified manner, within a specified period (not less than 14 days), and, without prejudice to the generality of the section a notice may require:

  (a) the removal of waste to any location or locations,

  (b) the disposal of waste in a specified manner or at a specified facility,

  (c) the taking of measures to prevent the continuance of the activity to which the notice relates,

  (d) the treatment of affected lands or waters so as to mitigate or remedy the effects of the activity concerned,

  (e) the taking of such other action as may be necessary to counteract any risk of environmental pollution arising from the activity concerned.

The default provisions are the same as for the LG(WP)A 1977 and the APA 1987 in (B) and (C) above.

The person on whom the notice is served may make representations.

In default of compliance the local authority may take such steps as are reasonable and necessary to secure compliance.

Offence
Section 55(8) of the WMA 1996 provides a specific offence of failing to comply with the notice.

(F) NH 97

Notice requiring (*qv*)restoration of land

Regulation 19(1) of the NH 97 Regulations (S.I. No. 94 of 1997) provides for service by the Minister of a notice requiring a person who carried out an (*qv*)operation or activity on lands within the definitions at Regulations 19(1)(i),(ii) and (iii) of the NH 97 to restore the land in accordance with the Minister's direction. *See:* RESTORATION OF LAND IN A EUROPEAN SITE FOLLOWING DAMAGE.

Offence
Failure to comply with the regulation is not of itself an offence but the Minister has power to have the works directed by him carried out and it is an offence under Regulation 19(3) by act or omission to obstruct or impede a person, authorised to do, from entering on land for the purpose of carrying out those works.

(3A) BY NOTICE STATING OFFENCE COMMITTED

Section 25 of the F(A)A 1999 –

"(1) This section applies to such offences under regulations made under section 24 as may be declared by the Minister by regulations to be offences to which this section applies.

(2) Where an authorised officer has reasonable grounds for believing that a person is committing or has committed an offence to which this section applies, he or she may serve the person with a notice in writing in the prescribed form stating that –

(a) the person is alleged to have committed the offence,

(b) the person may during the period of 21 days beginning on the date of the notice make to the (*qv*) regional board concerned at the address specified in the notice a payment of £100 accompanied by the notice, and

(c) a prosecution in respect of the alleged offence will not be instituted during the period specified in the notice and, if the payment specified in the notice is made during that period no prosecution in respect of the alleged offence will be instituted.

(3) Where notice is given under subsection (2) –

(a) a person to whom the notice applies may, during the period specified in the notice, make to the regional board concerned at the address specified in the notice the payment specified in the notice accompanied by the notice;

(b) the regional board specified in the notice may receive the payment, issue a receipt for it and retain the notice so paid, and any payment so received shall not be recoverable in any circumstances by the person who made it;

(c) a prosecution in respect of the alleged offence shall not be instituted in the period specified in the notice, and if the payment so specified is made during that period, no prosecution in respect of the alleged offence shall be instituted.

(4) in a prosecution for an offence under this section the onus of proving that a payment pursuant to a notice under this section has been made shall lie on the defendant.

(5) The Minister may by regulations vary the amount standing specified for the time being under subsection (2)(b)."

The Fisheries (Amendment) Act, 1999 (save for section 23) came into force on 20 December 1999 by virtue of the Fisheries (Amendment) Act, 1999 (Commencement) Order, 1999 (S.I. No. 419 of 1999). For regulations made under section 24.
*See:*SALMON, WILD SALMON AND SEA TROUT TAGGING SCHEME.

(4) BY NOTICES FOR PARTICULARS

(A) LG(WP)A 1977

Section 23(1) and (2) of the LG(WP)A 1977 (inserted by section 17 of the LG(WP)(A)A 1990) provide for the service by a local authority/sanitary authority of a notice in writing seeking particulars of actions which are actually causing pollution or which they suspect may cause pollution such as the abstraction of water, the discharge of (*qv*) trade or (*qv*) sewage effluent, the having in custody or control (*qv*) polluting matter or the engaging in any activities which may cause pollution.

Subsection (3) provides that as part of the particulars sought the authority can request:

(a) maps, plans, drawings or photographs showing the location, nature, extent and condition of:
   (i) any facilities for the collection, storage, treatment or disposal of the effluent or other polluting matter,
   (ii) any other premises from which polluting matter may enter (*qv*) waters, or
   (iii) any sewer, and showing their relationship to any waters, and

(b) such other particulars as may be specified in the notice of the matters aforesaid, including particulars of the arrangements, systems and methods in use or proposed for the disposal of the effluent or other polluting matter and of the times and rates of disposal.

Offence
Subsection (4) creates the offences of failing to comply with a requirement in the notice or, in purported compliance, giving information that to his knowledge is false and misleading in a material respect.

EXTENSION OF POWERS TO AGENCY

This function under section 23 of the LG(WP)A 1977 is now performed by the Agency in the circumstances described in Article 4 of the Environmental Protection Agency (Extension of Powers) Order 1996 (S.I. No. 126 of 1996).
See: EXTENSION OF POWERS.

(B) APA 1987

Section 16(1) of the APA 1987:

"(1) A local authority may for any purpose relating to their functions under this Act, by notice in writing require –
   (a) the (*qv*) occupier of any (*qv*) premises within their functional area, within such period (being not less than fourteen days after the date of service of the notice) as may be specified in the notice, to furnish in writing to the authority such particulars as to –
      (i) any activity or process being carried out on the premises,
      (ii) any (*qv*) fireplaces in the premises, and
      (iii) the fuels or other materials being burned on the premises,
   as may be so specified.
   (b) the occupier of any premises (other than a (*qv*) private dwelling) within their functional area, within such period as may be specified in the notice, to furnish in writing whether by periodic returns or otherwise, such information concerning any (*qv*) emission from the premises as may be so specified, and
   (c) any person engaged in the production, treatment, importation, placing on the market, distribution or sale of any fuel to furnish in writing to the authority in writing such particulars as to the type and quantity of fuel produced, treated, imported, placed on the market, distributed or sold by such person, as the case may be, within the functional area of the authority concerned as may be specified in the notice."

Subsection (2) provides that a notice shall not

require periodic returns at intervals of less than 3 or more than 12 months.

Offence
Subsection (3) provides for the offence of furnishing information in reply to the notice known to be false and misleading in a material particular.

Subsection (4) provides that information given to a local authority under this section shall not be given by them to any other person.

The section does not provide for a specific offence of failing to comply with the requirements of a notice. Such an offence would be dealt with under the general offence section 11.

EXTENSION OF POWERS TO THE AGENCY

The functions performed under paragraphs (a) and (b) of subsection (1) and subsections (2), (3) and (4) are performed by the Agency in the circumstances described in Article 10 of the Environmental Protection Agency (Extension of Powers) Order 1996 (S.I. No. 126 of 1996). *See:* EXTENSION OF POWERS.

(C) WMA 1996

Section 18(1) of the WMA 1996:

"(1) The Minister, a local authority or the Agency may, for any purpose relating to his or her functions under this Act, by the service of a notice in writing on the person require –
(a) any (*qv*) holder of waste,
(b) any person engaged in the importation, exportation, production, (*qv*) collection, (*qv*) recovery or (*qv*) disposal of waste, or any related or ancillary activity, or
(c) any person acting as a waste broker or dealer, or
(d) the occupier or any person in charge of a (*qv*) waste facility,
to maintain such records and furnish in writing to the Minister , local authority, or the Agency, as the case may be, within such period (being not less than 14 days after the date of service of the notice) and, if appropriate, thereafter at such frequency as may be specified in the notice, such particulars, as to –
(i) any activity or process as aforesaid or any facility concerned,
(ii) provisions proposed to be made or made or measures taken for the importation, exportation, collection, recovery or disposal of any waste concerned,
(iii)the origin, type, quantity, nature, composition and properties of waste concerned, or
(iv)any other related ancillary matter, as may be so specified."

Offence
Subsection (2) provides that failure to comply with a notice is an offence.

Subsection (3) provides for the making of certain Ministerial regulations.

Subsection (4) and (5) provide for the furnishing of any such information to the Minister or the Agency and also the furnishing of a compilation of statistics on any aspect of waste production and management as the Minister may specify in writing.

Subsection (6) provides that the Agency or local authorities may circulate to other local authorities or the Agency, depending on who procured the conviction, of particulars of a conviction of any person of an offence under this Act.

Subsection (7) obliges the Agency when a waste licence is granted, transferred or surrendered to notify within 21 days the local authority within whose functional area the *(qv)* activity the subject matter of the licence is carried on.

Offence
Subsection (8) creates the offence of contravention of provisions of regulations under subsection (3).

(5) BY DIRECTION

Section 14(5) of the WMA 1996 makes the following provisions as to directions:

(a) it entitles an (*qv*) authorised person who has entered any premises or boarded any vehicle pursuant to section 14 of the Act and who considers that waste thereon or therein is being handled or transported in such a manner as to constitute a risk of (*qv*) environmental pollution, to direct such measures as are necessary to remove that risk,
(b) it provides that where there is a failure to comply with the direction the authorised person may do what is necessary and recover the cost as a simple contract debt in any court of competent jurisdiction. *See:* ENTRY AND SEARCH, WMA 1996.

(6) BY DIRECT INTERVENTION WITHOUT NOTICE

(A) F(C)A 1959

Section 300 of the F(C)A 1959:

"Where any (*qv*)authorised person finds –

(a) during the annual close season for salmon or trout or the weekly close time –
   (i) any passage in any (*qv*) fishing weir, (*qv*) fishing mill dam, (*qv*) fixed engine, (*qv*) net or contrivance closed or obstructed, or
   (ii) any net or other contrivance whatsoever placed or used in contravention of this Act or any instrument made thereunder, or

(b) at any time, any obstruction in the (*qv*) free gap of a fishing weir or in a (*qv*) free pass, or

(c) at any time, any obstruction in the waste gate appurtenant to any mill or factory when such waste gate is required, by section 122, to be open,

he may open such passages and remove such obstructions, doing no unnecessary damage, and seize and remove all things so found or used contrary to the provisions of this Act or any instrument made thereunder."

(B) LG(WP)A 1977

Section 13(1) of the LG(WP)A 1977 (substituted by section 10 of the LG(WP)(A)A 1990) provides:

"(1) Where it appears to a local authority or a sanitary authority that for the purpose of

-

(a) preventing the entry of (*qv*) polluting matter to any (*qv*) waters or to any drain or sewer provided solely for the reception or disposal of storm water in its functional area,

(b) removing polluting matter from any such waters, drain or sewer,

(c) preventing polluting matters outside its functional area from affecting such area or any seashore (within the meaning of the Foreshore Act, 1933) adjoining such area, or

(d) mitigating or remedying in relation to its functional area or any such seashore aforesaid, the effects of any polluting matter in any such waters, drain or sewer as aforesaid,

it is necessary to do so, it may take such measures (including the giving of assistance, whether financial or otherwise, to others and the procuring of the taking of measures by others) as it considers appropriate for these purposes and may dispose of such polluting matter as it thinks fit.

For "seashore" *see:* FORESHORE.

(2) To the extent (if any) that any measures taken by a local authority or a sanitary authority under this section were necessitated by acts or omissions of a person (being acts or omissions that the person ought reasonably to have foreseen would or might necessitate the taking of the measures by the authority), the expenditure incurred by the authority in relation to the measures may be recovered by the authority from the person as a simple contract debt in any court of competent jurisdiction."

This is not a section to which the Environmental Protection Agency (Extension of Powers) Order 1996 (S.I. No 126 of 1996) applies. The Agency, if they were dissatisfied with the manner in which the local authority was performing its functions under this section, could invoke section 63 of the EPAA 1992. (*See:* PERFORMANCE OF STATUTORY FUNCTIONS BY LOCAL AUTHORITY) and after going through the various steps required by that section they could invoke the ultimate sanction under section 63(3)(b) of going in and doing the works themselves.

(C) APA 1987

Section 27 of the APA 1987 gives similar powers to local authorities where urgent measures are necessary to prevent or limit (*qv*) air pollution , to "take such steps, carry out such operations or give such assistance as they consider necessary" and to recover the costs.

(D) WMA 1966

Section 56(1) of the WMA 1996 gives similar powers to local authorities "in order to prevent or limit environmental pollution in its functional area caused, or likely to be caused, by the holding, recovery or disposal of waste". The local authority may take such steps, carry out such operations, recover or dispose of, or arrange for the recovery and disposal of, such waste or give such assistance as it considers necessary to prevent or limit such pollution or to mitigate or remedy the effects on the environment of such activity.

Subsection (2) entitles the local authority to recover the costs of the necessary steps from the person whose act or omission necessitated such steps.

Subsection (3) provides that nothing in the Act or other enactment shall prejudice the taking of necessary action by a local authority under this section.

(7) BY A THIRD PARTY PROPERTY ORDER

This procedure appears in the APA 1987 only and one would have to wonder as to its enforceability.

Section 55 of the APA 1987:

"(1) If the occupier of any *(qv)* premises is unable, without the consent of some other person, to carry out works which he is required to carry out in order to comply with the provisions of this Act, and such other person withholds his consent to the carrying out of the works, the occupier may apply to the District Court for an order under this section.

(2) If, on the hearing of an application under subsection (1), the District Court determines that the consent of the other person has been unreasonably withheld, the District Court may, in its discretion, deem the consent to have been given and direct the occupier of the premises to carry out the works."

Subsection (3) provides for an order directing the repayment to an occupier who carries out works under this section of the monies expended by him, by either the owner of the premises, or by some other person having an interest therein or by the owner or occupier of adjoining premises.

See: Order 96 Rule 3, District Court Rules, 1997.

(8) BY SEIZURE, DETENTION AND FORFEITURE OF FISH, THINGS, BOATS, FISHING ENGINES, VEHICLES AND EQUIPMENT

This enforcement option is limited in environmental statutes to seizure, detention and forfeiture of the following:

(a) fish unlawfully captured under the Fisheries Acts,
(a) protected fauna under the WLA 1976,
(b) where instruments are used for the unlawful taking, *e.g.* fishing rods and tackle, nets, guns, snares, decoys, etc, the instrument used.
(c) where vehicles such as boats, motor cars, lorries and other equipment are used in the commission of offences or as an aid to the commission of an offence, *e.g.* boats and motor cars in fisheries, lorries and other equipment in waste, those vehicles and equipment.

(A) F(C)A 1959

Under the Fisheries Acts most offence sections provide that both the instrument used in regard to the offence and the catch are forfeited as a statutory consequence of conviction. *See:* FORFEITURE.

This article deals with seizures and detention after detection but before prosecution.

(i) Fish

AUTHORISED PERSONS

Section 297(2) of the F(C)A 1959, substituted by section 71(b) of the FA 1980, provides that where an *(qv)* authorised person enters a dwelling house or curtilage under warrant under the section he has power to seize and detain anything found in the course of his search if he has reasonable grounds for suspecting that an offence has been or is being committed under the Act. The section provides that authorised person can use force to enter but can only execute a warrant under this section if accompanied by a member of the Garda Síochána and the powers can only be exercised in respect of a dwelling house.

AUTHORISED OFFICERS

Section 301(2)*(e)* of the F(C)A 1959 provides that an *(qv)* authorised officer has power to take, remove and detain any fish (either together with or without any package in which the same may be contained) found while exercising his powers under this section in respect of which an offence is being or is suspected of being committed or which have been or are suspected of having been unlawfully captured.

Subsection (3) provides that steps must be taken, as soon as may be, to have the person believed to be guilty of the offence in respect of which the fish was seized dealt with according to law.

Subsections (4) and (5) deal with procedures which must be adopted in relation to a fish which is detained in custody and is likely to become unfit for human consumption. It must be brought before a Peace Commissioner who must direct in writing as to whether the fish is to be destroyed or sold. *See:* DISPOSAL OF THINGS SEIZED.

Subsection (6) provides that no authorised officer shall be liable for any loss or damage occasioned by him or in the course of the exercise of the powers conferred on him by this section unless such loss or damage was caused by him wantonly or maliciously.

(ii) A (*qv*) Fishing Engine

AUTHORISED PERSONS

Section 296(1)*(f)* of the F(C)A 1959 permits an authorised person or a member of an Garda Síochána, for the purpose of the protection of the fisheries, to seize any unlawful fishing engine or any lawful fishing engine which is being unlawfully used.

WARRANT UNDER SECTION 297

Section 297 of the F(C)A 1959, as amended by section 71 of the FA 1980, entitles a District Justice to grant a warrant to an authorised person to enter and search, if need be by force, the garden, dwellinghouse or curtilage or any structure or building in such garden or curtilage on suspicion that an offence has been or is being committed, to require any person found there or the person in occupation or control to furnish his name and address and to seize and detain anything found which might be required in evidence.

Subsection (2)(b) lists the persons who are authorised to assist an authorised person in the above.

AUTHORISED OFFICERS

Section 301(2)*(f)* of the F(C)A 1959 empowers an authorised officer to take, remove and detain in his custody any fishing engine liable or believed to be liable to forfeiture under the Act.

(iii) A Boat

Section 301(2)*(ff)* of the F(C)A 1959 (inserted by section 25(b) of the F(A)A 1962) provides that an authorised officer is authorised to take, remove and detain in his custody any boat or vehicle liable or believed to be liable to forfeiture under the Act.

Section 301(2)*(da)* and *(db)* of the F(C)A 1959 (inserted by section 53 (a) of the FA 1980) provides:

"(da) if the boat contains or he believes or suspects that it contains fish unlawfully captured he may without summons, warrant or other process take the boat and all persons thereon to the nearest or most convenient port or other place, and if he decides to take the steps mentioned in subsection (2A) of this section, he may, pending the taking of those steps, detain the boat and the persons."

Section 301(2A) of the F(C)A 1959 (inserted by section 53(b) of the FA 1980) provides:

"(2A) Where an authorised officer has in exercise of the powers conferred on him by this section taken any boat and the persons thereon to a port or other place, he shall, as soon as may be, bring the person who at the time the boat was so taken was, or appeared to him to be, in charge of the boat, and any other person thereon, and against whom, in either case, proceedings for an offence under sections 65, 69, 73, 97, 127, 132, 140 and 182 of the Principal Act or section 29 of the Act of 1962 or for the contravention of a bye-law described in paragraph (a), (b), (c) or (d) of section 46 (4) of the Fisheries Act, 1980, are or are about to be instituted before a District Justice or, where no District Justice is immediately available, a Peace Commissioner, and thereupon the District Justice or Peace Commissioner (as the case may be) shall, if he is satisfied that the proceedings are or are about to be instituted against the person, by order directed to an authorised officer or officers require the authorised officer or officers to detain at a specified port or other place in the State either, as may be specified in the order, such boat and the person or persons brought before him or such boat only until the proceedings have been adjudicated upon by a District Justice, and the boat or the boat and such person or persons, as may be appropriate, may be detained accordingly".

All of the sections and the bye-law referred to section 301(2A) above relate to restrictions of one kind or another on fishing for salmon or trout.

See: Order 65 Rule 10, District Court Rules 1997.

This section was passed at a time when the conservation of salmon was being achieved by restriction by bye-laws, intended to be made under section 46(4) of the FA 1980 (*See:* (1)

INDICTABLE OFFENCES; (2) BYE-LAWS), on the use of monofilament nets or drift nets. It contemplated the detention of boats and gear in the same manner as was being done in Sea Fisheries. The section went too far. It is inconceivable that a person charged under Section 65, for example, for using an unlicensed scheduled engine for the taking of salmon trout or eels would be detained under this section. *See:* ANNUAL CLOSE SEASON.

For procedure after seizure of a boat or fishing engine. *See:* DISPOSAL OF THINGS SEIZED.

(iv) A Motor Vehicle.

Section 301(2)*(ff)* of the F(C)A 1959 (as amended by section 25(b) of the F(A)A 1962) authorises an authorised officer to take, remove and detain in his custody any boat or vehicle liable or believed to be liable to (*qv*) forfeiture under this Act.

(B) WMA 1996

Section 61 of the WMA 1996. *See:* DETENTION OF BOATS, VEHICLES AND EQUIPMENT.

(C) WLA 1976

Section 72 of the WLA 1976 gives powers of seizure to the Garda Síochána or authorised person of specimens, documents and things.
See: ENTRY AND SEARCH, WLA 1976.

(9) BY PROHIBITION BY PROVISION OF STATUTE

Under this heading are acts or defaults prohibited by statute which render a person who contravenes the prohibition guilty of an offence under and by virtue of the statute or an instrument made under a statute and liable on conviction to penalty consisting of fine only or imprisonment or both fine and imprisonment and, in some cases, forfeiture of instruments used in the commission of the offence, the fish or fauna taken and, where the accused is a licence holder under the Fisheries Act, forfeiture of licence. The use of the word "offence" denotes an offence section throughout. *See:* (1) PROHIBITION; (2) OFFENCE.

ENGINES, FIXED, FISHING, NON-SCHEDULED, SCHEDULED
(F(C)A 1959)

FIXED ENGINES

Following the decision of the Supreme Court in *North Western Fisheries Board v. McKeown* (unreported, Supreme Court, December 15, 1986) the definition of "scheduled engine" appearing at section 3(1) of the F(C)A 1959 was found to be inoperative so this was corrected by passing in the following year the F(A)A 1987 which deal exclusively with a new and tighter definition of "fixed engine".

This statute is not to be confused with the F(A)A (No. 2)A1987 which deals with the imposition of (*qv*) duties on fishing for trout and coarse fish.

The definition of "fixed engine" from **Section 3(1) of the F(C)A 1959**, as substituted by section 1 of the F(A)A 1987 and as amended by section 27(a) of the F(A)A 1999 is as follows –

"Section 3(1) of the Fisheries (Consolidation) Act 1959 is hereby amended by the substitution of the following definition for the definition of 'fixed engine':
'fixed engine' means any engine being
(a) a stake net
(b) a bag net
(c) a fixed draft net
[(cc) a fixed long line, or]
(d) a head weir
(e) any net, implement, engine or device, fixed to the soil or secured by one or more anchors or by any other means, and used solely for the purpose of facilitating the taking of fish, not being a fishing weir, a fishing mill dam or a drift net."

The section had read "any net, implement engine or device, fixed to the soil or secured by anchors or held by hand or made stationary in any other way and used solely for the purpose, etc". The problem had arisen in the use of the plural for anchors as it had been intended that a net or device secured at one end only would constitute a "fixed engine" but the court apparently decided otherwise.

The importance of the definition becomes apparent when dealing with sections 100 to 113 of the F(C)A 1959. *See:* EELS.

DEFINITIONS UNDER SECTION 3(1) OF THE F(C)A 1959

"'fishing engine' means any engine, net or other instrument whatsoever capable of being used for the taking of fish."

'non-scheduled engine' means an engine of a kind not specified in the Fourth Schedule to this Act."

"'scheduled engine' means any engine of a kind specified in the Fourth Schedule to this Act."

ENTRY INTO WATERS
(LG(WP)A 1977)

See: DISCHARGES.

ENTRY INTO ATMOSPHERE
(APA 1987)

See: EMISSIONS.

ENTRY ON LAND, WITH A FIREARM, HUNTING
(WLA 1976, s. 44)

Section 44 of the WLA 1976:

Offence

"(1) Any person who not being the owner or occupier of land –
(a) with a firearm or with a device, instrument or missile mentioned in section 72(7) of this Act hunts a (*qv*)wild bird or wild animal on the land or moves or drives such a bird or such an animal off the land in order so to hunt it,
(b) enters on the land for the purpose of so hunting wild birds or wild animals,
(c) carries on the land any firearm, net, or other weapon, instrument or device capable of being used for hunting a wild bird or wild animal, or
(d) shoots over or into the land,

without the permission either of the person who is the owner or the occupier of the land or, in case some person is entitled to enjoy sporting rights over the land, that other person, shall be guilty of an offence."

Subsection (2) specifies the classes of persons who may demand of the person so entering their name and address:
(a) owner or occupier or person authorised,
(b) a person who enjoys sporting rights or person authorised,
(c) the holder of a licence under section 29,

and the person making the demand under (c) must produce either a current licence granted to him under section 29 or a firearms certificate containing the endorsement required by section 29(8).

Offence

Subsection (3) creates the offence of refusing a demand under subsection (2) or giving a name and address which is false or misleading.

Subsection (4) specifies the persons who may prosecute under this section, the persons at subsection (2)(a) and (b) and the secretary of a (*qv*) recognised body entitled to sporting rights over the land.

In the case of a prosecution by a recognised body they must prove that they published a notice in a newspaper circulating in the area where the land is situate that sporting rights in the land in respect of which the prosecution is brought are reserved to their body.

Subsection (5) empowers the Minister to declare by regulation that any association, club, society or other body of persons which has among its objects the conservation of game is a recognised body for the purposes of this section.

The Minister has, to date, make two sets of Wildlife Act 1976 (section 44) (Recognised Bodies), Regulations 1977 (S.I. No. 335 of 1977) and the Wildlife Act 1976 (section 44) (Recognised Bodies) Regulations 1980 (S.I. No. 233 of 1980).

Subsection (7) provides that in any proceedings for an offence under this section it shall not be necessary for the prosecution to prove that the defendant was on land without lawful authority; the onus lies on the defendant to prove that he has such authority.

Subsection (8) provides that in the section "game" means any (*qv*) exempted wild mammal or any (*qv*) protected wild bird which is of a species specified in an order under section 24 of the Act.

See: OPEN SEASONS.

ENTRY, UNAUTHORISED, ONTO SEVERAL FISHERY
(F(C)A 1959, ss. 178 to 181)

Offences

Chapter IV Part XI of the F(C)A 1959 deals with offences in respect of private fisheries as follows:

Section 178 of the F(C)A 1959 creates the offence of an unauthorised person entering into or upon a (*qv*)several fishery for the purpose or under the pretence of killing fish therein or taking fish there from or killing any fish therein or taking fish there from.

Section 179(1) of the F(C)A 1959 creates the offence of using or fishing with a (*qv*)net within the limits of a several fishery without authority in writing. Subsection (2) provides for forfeiture of the net on conviction.

Section 180 of the F(C)A 1959 creates the offence of killing, taking or destroying any fish in any pond, private canal or reservoir wherein he has no property without the authority of the owner.

Section 181 of the F(C)A 1959 creates the offence of entering on any land for the purpose or under the pretence of fishing in any water without authority in writing from the owner or occupier.

(Note that the maximum penalties prescribed under sections 178–181 above have been increased. *See:* FINES AND IMPRISONMENT (IMPOSITION OF)).

ENTRY ON LAND FOR FISHERY IMPROVEMENT
(FA 1980, s. 18)

Section 18 of the FA 1980 deals with the powers of the Central Board and *(qv)* regional boards in relation to improvement of fisheries. *See:* FISHERY IMPROVEMENT.

As an adjunct to the exercise of those powers they have various rights under section 18(3) to enter on land as follows:

"(3) Subject to section 43 of this Act, the (*qv*) Central Board or any (*qv*) regional board, or their servants or agents or any contractor employed by the board or any workman employed by such contractor may, with or without vehicles, machinery or other apparatus (including boats or other vessels) or equipment, for the purpose of,
(a) gaining access to the site of fishery improvement works which are completed or which are in the course of being carried out or are to be carried out by the board,
(b) gaining access to a fishery (whether or not the fishery is the property of the board) in order to inspect or maintain it,
enter on land at any reasonable time."

For section 43, *see:* COMPENSATION.

Subsection (4) gives power to the Central Board or any regional board, subject to obtaining all necessary consents from the local authority, the Minister, any other Minister of Government, the Irish Land Commission, (*qv*) the Commissioners or a (*qv*) public authority where appropriate, for the purposes mentioned in subsection (3), to construct on or over any land a bridge, road or pathway and to use and maintain same when constructed.

Subsection (5) provides that a person entering on land under this section may do thereon all things ancillary or reasonably necessary for the purpose for which the entry was made.

Subsection (6) provides that a person authorised to exercise a power mentioned in subsection (1) of this section shall be furnished by the Central Board or the regional board concerned, as may be appropriate, with a certificate of such authorisation and when doing anything pursuant to the authorisation shall, if requested by the person affected, produce the certificate to that person.

For authority to exercise powers, *see:* FUNCTIONS, PERFORMANCE BY CENTRAL BOARD AND REGIONAL BOARDS.

Subsection (7) provides:

"(7) (a) Nothing in this section shall be construed as conferring on any person a power to enter a dwellinghouse, nor except where there is through the garden or curtilage of a dwellinghouse an ordinary road or passage to a fishery, shall it be construed as conferring on any person a power to enter such a garden or dwelling house.
(b) Nothing in this section shall be construed as enabling a regional board to exercise outside its (*qv*) fisheries region any of the powers conferred on it by this section.
(c) Nothing in this section shall be construed as modifying or otherwise affecting the application of any requirement under the Local Government (Planning and Development) Acts, 1963 and 1976."

ENTRY AND SEARCH

(F(C)A 1959/F(A)A 1999/LG(WP)A 1977/APA 1987/
EPAA 1992/WLA 1976/WMA 1996/NH 97)

The powers of private (*qv*) water keepers, authorised persons, (*qv*) authorised officers and members of the Garda Síochána in relation to entry and search, inspection, seizure, taking samples, executing search warrants, giving directions and all other such matters under environmental statutes are as follows:

F(C)A 1959

(1) Powers of (*qv*) Authorised Persons (including private (*qv*) water keepers)

Section 296 of the F(C)A 1959 (as amended by section 11(5), Fourth Schedule, of the FA 1980) and section 14 of the F(A)(No. 2)A 1987, provides:

"(1) Any member of the Garda Síochána or authorised person may, for the purposes of the protection of the fisheries, do all or any of the following things –

(a) enter into or pass through or along or remain on the banks or borders of any lakes or rivers frequented by salmon, trout (including any rainbow trout or char) or their spawn or fry, eels or coarse fish or of the tributaries thereof,

(b) with boats or otherwise enter upon any such lakes or rivers,

(c) enter upon and examine all weirs, sluices, (*qv*) mill dams, mill races and (*qv*) watercourses communicating with such lakes or rivers,

(d) enter any boat engaged or about to engage in fishing,

(e) examine all standing, floating or other nets whatsoever,

(f) seize any unlawful fishing engine or any lawful fishing engine being unlawfully used,

(g) do all such other acts and things as he is authorised to do by or under this Act.

(1A) Any member of the Garda Síochána or authorised person may enter any land for the purpose of enabling him to exercise elsewhere a power conferred on him by subsection (1) of this section.

(2) Nothing in this section shall be construed as authorising any member of the Garda Síochána or authorised person to enter any enclosed garden or any dwelling house or the curtilage thereof except where the ordinary road or passage to any weir, dam or dyke is through such garden or curtilage."

Section 297 of the F(C)A 1959 (as amended by section 71(a) and (b) of the FA 1980) provides:

"(1) Where upon an information on oath it appears to any District Justice or Peace Commissioner that there are reasonable grounds for believing that a breach of the provisions of this Act or any instrument made thereunder has been committed within any enclosed garden or any dwellinghouse or the curtilage thereof, he may by warrant under his hand authorise any authorised person to enter the said garden or dwellinghouse or the curtilage thereof, at such times in the day or night as may be mentioned in the warrant."

See: Order 65 Rule 11, District Court Rules, 1997.

"(2) (a) Subject to subsection (3) of this section, a warrant issued under this section shall operate to authorise the person to whom it is issued (and named therein) at any reasonable time or times within seven days of the issue of the warrant to –

(i) enter and search, if need be by force, the garden, dwellinghouse or curtilage thereof named in the warrant or any structure or building in such garden or curtilage,

(ii) require any person found on such land to furnish to him his name and address,

(iii) require a person who is in occupation or is in control or in concerned in the management of such land to furnish to him his name and address,

and if the person so named has reasonable grounds for suspecting that an offence has been or is being committed under this Act with or in relation to anything found in the course of his search, the person may seize and detain that thing or anything else so found which appears to him to be something which might be required as evidence in proceedings for an offence under this Act.

(b) Subject to subsection (3) of this section, a warrant issued under this section shall operate to enable any one or more of the following, namely, any member of the Garda Síochána, any officer of the Minister and, in case the warrant is issued to an officer of a (*qv*)regional board, any other person employed by that board to accompany and assist the person to whom the warrant is issued in the exercise of the powers thereby conferred on him.

(3) The powers conferred on a person named in a warrant issued under this section shall be exercisable by the person as regards a dwellinghouse only if, and only for so long as, he is accompanied by a member of the Garda Síochána."

Section 298 of the F(C)A 1959 (as amended by section 11(5), Fourth Schedule, of the FA 1980) provides that in respect of a fishing vessel employed in fishing, subject to any directions and regulations given or made by the Revenue Commissioners, a member of an Garda Síochána or officer appointed by the Minister or regional board may board such vessel, examine the register and any *(qv)* fishing engines and seize any unlawful fishing engine or lawful fishing engine being unlawfully used.

Offence
Subsection (2) creates the offence of the master of any fishing vessel refusing to produce his certificate of registry.

(Note that the maximum penalty prescribed under this subsection has been increased. *See:* FINES AND IMPRISONMENT (IMPOSITION OF)).

Section 299 of the F(C)A 1959 (as amended by section 11(5) of the FA 1980, Fourth Schedule) provides:

"(1) In this section the expression 'authorised person' includes any person interested in the fishery in which the relevant offence is committed.

(2) If any person (in this section referred to as the offender) is found using any unlawful fishing engine or unlawfully using any fishing engine or otherwise offending against the provisions of this Act or any instrument made thereunder, the following provisions shall have effect:
(a) any member of the Garda Síochána or authorised person may require the offender to do the following things –
(i) desist from such offence, and
(ii) tell his name and address,
(b) if the offender, after being so required, wilfully continues such offence, refuses to tell his name and address, the authorised person or any other person acting under his directions may apprehend the offender,
(c) where the offender is apprehended under this section, by a person who is not a member of the Garda Síochána, the authorised person shall forthwith deliver him into the custody of a member of the Garda Síochána to be dealt with according to law."

Section 300 of the F(C)A 1959 permits a member of an Garda Síochána or an authorised person to enter on a (*qv*) fishing weir or fishing mill dam and open a passage which has been closed or obstructed by removing the obstruction and may remove any net or other contrivance placed or used in contravention of the Act. *See:* ENFORCEMENT (4)(a).

Section 18 of the FA 1980 confers powers on persons authorised by the Central Board or a regional board in connection with fishery improvement which includes entry. *See:* ENTRY ON LAND UNDER SECTION 18 FA 1980, FISHERY IMPROVEMENT.

(2) Powers of Authorised Officers

Section 301 of the F(C)A 1959, which contains these powers of authorised officers, has been substantially amended by section 25 of the F(A)A 1962 and by section 11(5) and section 53 of the FA 1980.

Section 301(2) of the F(C)A 1959:

"(2) Every authorised officer is authorised to do all or any of the following things –
(a) to stop and search any person conveying or suspected of conveying any fish of any kind or any instrument or substance used or adapted for taking fish unlawfully and to inspect any fish, instrument or substance which such person is found to be conveying and for that purpose to open and search any vehicle or package in which such fish, instrument or substance is or may be or is believed to be conveyed;

(b) at all reasonable times to enter upon and have free access to search –
   (i) any premises in which fish is or is believed to be sold or kept, exposed or stored for sale, or
   (ii) any premises in which poison or explosive intended for the destruction of fish is or is believed to be kept, or
   (iii) the premises of any person engaged in the business of carrying goods for reward, or
   (iv) any aerodrome, pier, quay, wharf, jetty, dock or dock premises, or any hotel, guesthouse, restaurant or other premises or place at which board and lodgings and meals are provided for reward,
   (v) any ship, boat, aircraft, railway wagon, motor lorry, cart or other vessel or vehicle used for the conveyance of goods;
(c) to examine all fish found in any place which he is authorised by this section to enter and for that purpose to open any package found in such place and containing or believed to contain fish;
(d) to stop, enter and search, on any river, lake or estuary, or the shores thereof or any part of the sea or the shores thereof, any boat used or believed to be used for fishing or containing or suspected of containing fish unlawfully captured and to examine all fish and all fishing engines found therein and for that purpose to open any package which contains or is suspected of containing any fish or fishing engine;
(da) if the boat contains, or he believes or suspects it contains, fish unlawfully captured he may without summons, warrant or other process take the boat and all the persons thereon to the nearest or most convenient port or other place, and if he decides to take the steps mentioned in sub section (2A) of this section, he may, pending the taking of those steps, detain the boat and the person;
(db) he may for the purposes of exercising the power conferred on him by paragraph (da) of this subsection use such force as he may consider necessary;
(e) to take, remove and detain in his custody any fish (either together with or without any package in which the same may be contained) found in the course of the exercise of any of the powers conferred by this section in respect of which an offence under this Act is being or is suspected of being committed or which have been or are suspected of having been unlawfully captured;
(f) to take, remove and detain in his custody any fishing engine or any article liable or believed to be liable to forfeiture under this Act;
(g) to demand and take the name and address of the person having custody of the fish or other article which the authorised officer is authorised under this section to examine and also demand and take from such person the name and address of the owner of such fish or other article."

Subsection (2A) is an extensive subsection which deals with the procedures which must be adopted by a person who in exercise of the powers conferred on him by the section takes a boat and the persons therein to a port or other place. It was inserted by section 53 (b) of the FA 1980. *See:* DETENTION AND FORFEITURE OF BOATS AND FISHING VESSELS.

Subsection (3) provides that where an authorised officer detains in his custody under the authority of this section any fish or other article he shall, as soon as may be, take such steps as may be proper to have the person guilty or believed to be guilty of the offence committed or believed to have been committed in relation to such fish or other article dealt with according to law;

Subsections (4) and (5) outline the procedure in relation to the detention of a fish which is likely to become unfit for human food before the matter can conveniently be dealt with by any court. The officer must produce the fish before a Peace Commissioner who, depending on his own opinion, can direct either that the fish be destroyed or sold and his direction must be in writing, in such form as the Minister may direct, describing the fish and any markings, peculiarities or other features and that direction is conclusive evidence in every court of the matters of fact stated therein.

Subsection (6):

"(6) No authorised officer shall be liable for any loss or damage occasioned by or in the course of the exercise of any of the powers conferred on him by this section unless such loss or damage was caused by him wantonly or maliciously."

Offence

Subsection (7) provides that every person who obstructs or impedes an authorised officer in the exercise of any of the powers conferred on him by this section or refuses to give his own name and address or the name and address of any other person (so far as known to him) when lawfully demanded under this section shall be guilty of an offence under this section.

(Note that the maximum penalty prescribed under this subsection has been increased. *See:* FINES AND IMPRISONMENT (IMPOSITION OF)).

Fishery officers believed that subsection (7) gave them *carte blanche* to demand the name and address of any suspect and then to prosecute if there was a refusal but it is well established that the power to demand the name and address must be coupled with the exercise of a particular power conferred under the section and that evidence of that power being exercised must be given in every case. There is no authority bearing on the matter.

EXTENSION OF POWERS BY MINISTERIAL ORDER.

The F(A)A 1983 was intended to and deals almost exclusively with sea fisheries which are not dealt with in this book. Section 4, however, which is the tail end of a long series of amendments to the original section 223 of the F(C)A 1959, at subsection (1) gives the Minister power by order to prescribe and adopt measures of conservation of fish stocks and measures of rational exploitation of fisheries, and provides at subsection (1A)(b) that the Minister's power for the purpose of enabling the order to have full effect, extend any or all of:

(i) the powers conferred by this Act on a sea fisheries protection officer for the purposes of this Act,
(ii) the powers so conferred on an (*qv*) authorised person within the meaning of Part XVIII of this Act,
(iii) the powers so conferred on (*qv*) authorised officers within the meaning of section 301 of this Act.

Section 24(4) and 95) of the F(A)A 1999 –

"(4) For the purposes of enforcing any regulations made under this section, an authorised officer may –

(a) stop and question any person who has or is suspected of having in his or her possession any tag or log book issued, or record kept, under regulations made under this section or any salmon and request the production of and examine such tag, log book record or salmon and search the person whom he has reason to believe has contravened ay regulations made under this section.
(b) at all reasonable times, enter and search any place or premises or boat or vehicle in which the officer believes there is any tag or log book issued, or a register maintained, or record kept, under regulations made under this section or any salmon and there examine and take copies of or extracts from any log book, register or record, found therein,
(c) where he or she finds any wild salmon or sea trout which has not been tagged in accordance with regulations made under this section, the officer may in accordance with such regulations tag the fish or remove any tags affixed to it which do not comply with such regulations or require the person found in the possession of the fish or in charge of the place, premises, boat or vehicle where it is found to tag, or cause it to be tagged, in accordance with such regulations or to remove or cause to be removed any tags affixed to it which do not comply with any such regulations,
(d) take, remove and detain in his or her custody any tag, log book, register or record found in the course of the exercise of any of the powers conferred by this section in respect of which a contravention of any regulation made under this section is being or is suspected of having been committed,
(e) request and take the name and address of the person having custody of any tag, log book, register or record or salmon which the officer is authorised under this section to examine."

Offence

"(5) A person who obstructs or interferes with, or fails to comply with a requirement of, an authorised officer in exercise of any power conferred on the officer under this section or refuses to give his or her name and address when required under this section shall be guilty of an offence."

It is surprising that the authorised officer is not given power to seize under paragraph (d) the salmon in respect of which a contravention of a regulation under the section is being or is suspecting of having been committed although of course he or she would have such a power under section 301(2)(e) of the F(C)A 1959. The Fisheries (Amendment) Act, 1999 (save for section 23) came into force on 20 December 1999 by virtue of the Fisheries (Amendment) Act, 1999 (Commencement) Order, 1999 (S.I. No. 419 of 1999).

It is greatly to be regretted that this section was not constructed so as to form a series of amendments to section 301 of the F(C)A 1959. The proliferation of different authorised officers and different powers of authorised officers under new sections will cause considerable confusion for groups attempting to prosecute. It has got to the stage that there will shortly be a new statute for each new offence which is gravely discourteous to those who drafted the splendid Consolidation Act of 1959.

LG(WP)A 1977

Section 28 of the LG(WP)A 1977, as amended by sections 19, 24 and 30 of the LG(WP)(A)A 1990, provides:

"(1) Subject to this section, an authorised person may at any reasonable time enter premises or vessels for the purposes of –
(a) performance of a function conferred under this Act on a local authority, a sanitary authority, the Minister, the Minister for Fisheries or a (*qv*) board of conservators,
(b) ascertaining whether such a function should be performed,
(c) ascertaining whether there is or has been a contravention of any provision of this Act or of any regulations under this Act, or
(d) carrying out such inspection and taking such samples of waters, effluents or other matter as may be necessary for the performance of such a function under this Act.

(2) Notwithstanding anything in subsection (1), the power of entry to premises or vessels conferred by that subsection may be exercised at any time in relation to a function conferred by section 13.

(3) In any legal proceedings under this Act it shall be presumed until the contrary is shown that any sample of effluent taken by an authorised person at an inspection chamber or manhole or other place provided under and in accordance with a licence under this Act is a sample of what was passing from the premises, works, apparatus, plant or drainage pipe concerned to waters or a sewer at the time the sample was taken.

(3A)(a) Where an (*qv*) authorised person who is on a premises or a vessel in pursuance of the powers conferred by this section reasonably believes that an offence under section 3(1), 4(1) or 16(1) of this Act or section 21(3) of the Local Government (Water Pollution) (Amendment) Act 1990, is being or has been committed in relation to the premises or vessel, he may request from any person he finds on the premises or vessel his name and address and a description of his occupation and his functions and responsibilities as respects the premises or vessel, as the case may be, and any enterprise carried on at the premises or on the vessel and (in so far as they are known to him) the name and address of the occupier of the premises, the owner of the vessel and the person in charge of the premises or vessel."

Offence

(b) A person who fails or refuses to comply with a request under this subsection or, in pursuance of such a request furnishes information to an authorised person that is false or misleading shall be guilty of an offence and shall be liable on summary conviction to a fine not exceeding £1,000 or to imprisonment for a term not exceeding 6 months or both".

"(4) A person who obstructs an authorised person in the performance of his duties under this section shall be guilty of an offence."

Subsection (5) gives guidelines for regulations which the Minister may make for the purposes of the section including the taking of samples, carrying out tests, examinations and analyses of samples, prescribing the persons to do these things and to give certificates of the results, prescribe for the certificate or other evidence and that the certificate is sufficient evidence of the result.

"(6) (a) A person authorised under this section to enter premises or vessels shall, if so required, produce evidence of his authority before so entering and may take with him such other persons and such equipment

as may be necessary.
(b) Entry to any premises or vessel used exclusively for residential purposes, and entry with heavy equipment to any other land, shall not, except for the purpose of exercising a function under section 13, be made under this section unless seven days' notice in writing of the intended entry has been given to the occupier.
(c) Any person who in exercise of the powers under this section enters any premises or vessel which is unoccupied or from which the occupier is temporarily absent shall leave the premises or vessel as effectually secured against trespassers as he found it.

(7) (a) Where it is shown to the satisfaction of a Justice of the District Court on sworn information in writing –
(i) that admission to any premises or vessel which any person is entitled to enter under this section has been refused to that person or that refusal is apprehended, and
(ii) that there is reasonable ground for the entry for the purpose for which entry is required: the Justice may by warrant under his hand authorise that person to enter the premises or vessel.
(b) A warrant granted under this section shall remain in force until the purpose for which the entry is required has been satisfied."

See: Order 96 Rule 6, District Court Rules, 1997.

Subsection (8) of section 28 was repealed by section 30 of the LG(WP)(A)A 1990. Subsection (9) gives the definition of authorised person for the section. *See:* AUTHORISED PERSON.
EXTENSION OF POWERS TO AGENCY

These functions under section 28 of the LG(WP)A 1977 now apply to the Agency in the circumstances described in Article 4 of the Environmental Protection Agency (Extension of Powers) Order, 1996 (S.I. No. 126 of 1996). *See:* EXTENSION OF POWERS.

APA 1987

Section 14 of the APA 1987 provides:

"(1) Subject to subsection (2), an authorised person shall, for any purpose connected with this Act, be entitled, at all reasonable times, to enter into any premises and to bring therein such other persons or equipment as he may consider necessary for the purpose.

(2) A authorised person shall not, other than with the consent of the occupier, enter into a private dwelling unless he has given to the occupier of the dwelling not less than 24 hours notice in writing of his intended entry.

(3) Every authorised officer shall be furnished with a certificate of his appointment and when exercising any power conferred on him by or under this Act, the authorised person shall, if requested by any person affected, produce the certificate to that person.

(4) Whenever an authorised person enters into any premises pursuant to this section he may therein-
(a) make such plans and carry out such inspections,
(b) make such tests and take such samples,
(c) require from the owner or occupier of the premises or from any other person on the premises such information, or
(d) inspect such records or such documents,

as he, having regard to all the circumstances, considers necessary for the purposes of this Act.

Offence

(5) Any person who obstructs an authorised person in the exercise of his powers under this section or who fails to comply with a requisition of an authorised person or who wilfully withholds any information which the authorised person requires shall be guilty of an offence.

WARRANT

(6) Where an authorised person in the exercise of his powers under this section is prevented from entering any (*qv*)premises, the authorised person or the person by whom he was appointed may apply to the District Court for a warrant authorising such entry."

*See:*Order 96 Rule 1, District Court Rules, 1997.

Subsections (7) and (8) provide for Ministerial regulations under the section which are the same as regulations under section 28(5) of the LG(WP)A 1977.

EXTENSION OF POWERS TO AGENCY

These functions under section 14 of the APA 1987 now apply to the Agency in the circumstances described in Article 10 of the Environmental Protection Agency (Extension of Powers) Order 1996 (S.I. 126 of 1996). *See:* EXTENSION OF POWERS.

EPAA 1992

Section 13 of the EPAA 1992 provides:

"(1) An authorised person shall, for any purpose connected with this Act, be entitled, at all reasonable times, to enter any premises and to bring therein such other persons (including members of the Garda Síochána) or equipment as he may consider necessary for the purpose.

(2) Subject to subsection (6), an authorised person shall not, other than with the consent of the occupier, enter into a private dwelling unless he has given the occupier of the dwelling not less than 24 hours notice in writing of his intended entry.

(3) Every authorised person shall be furnished with a certificate of his appointment and, when exercising any power conferred on him by or under the Act, the authorised person shall, if requested by any person affected, produce the certificate to that person.

(4) Whenever an authorised officer enters any premises pursuant to this section, he may therein –
   (a) make such plans, take such photographs and carry out such inspections,
   (b) make such tests and take such samples,
   (c) require from the occupier of the premises or any person employed on the premises or from any other person on the premises such information,
   (d) inspect such plant, vehicles, records and documents,

   as he, having regard to all the circumstances, considers necessary for the purposes of, and exercising any power conferred on him by or under this Act.

Offence

(5) Any person who –
   (a) refuses to allow an authorised person to enter any premises or to take any person or equipment with him in the exercise of his powers under this section,
   (b) obstructs or impedes an authorised officer in the exercise of any of the powers conferred on him by this section,
   (c) gives, either to an authorised person or to the Agency, information which is false and misleading in a material respect, or
   (d) fails or refuses to comply with any requirement under the section,

   shall be guilty of an offence."

WARRANT

Subsection (6) provides for the issue of a warrant by the District Court authorising entry to premises where in the exercise of powers under the section an authorised person is prevented from entering or has reason to believe that evidence related to a suspected offence under the Act may be removed or destroyed.

See: Order 96 Rule 7, District Court Rules, 1997.

Subsections (7) and (8) provide that the Minister may make regulations under the section. These subsections are the same as corresponding provisions provided for in section 25 of the LG(WP)A 1977 and section 12 of the APA 1987.

Subsection (9):

"(9) Any certificate or other evidence given or to be given in respect of any prescribed test, examination or analysis of any sample shall in relation to that sample be evidence, without further proof, of the result of the test, examination or analysis unless the contrary is shown."

ENTRY BY PERSON HOLDING INQUIRY UNDER SECTION 105

Section 105(3)*(b)* of the EPAA 1992 entitles a person holding an (*qv*) inquiry to which section 105 relates to enter premises, entry to which appears requisite for the purposes on the inquiry into the circumstances in which (*qv*) environmental pollution occurred.

ENTRY IN THE CASE OF GENETICALLY MODIFIED ORGANISMS

Section 111(6) of the EPAA 1992, which deals with (*qv*)genetically modified organisms, provides that in addition to the powers conferred by section 13, an (*qv*)authorised officer has the power to require, in relation to any premises or part of a premises which he has power to enter or in relation to any process or action or part of a process or action on such premises or in relation to anything in or on such premises, that it should be maintained without disturbance or in such manner as he may specify for so long as is reasonable to carry out his investigation or tests.

WMA 1996

Section 14 of the WMA 1996 provides:

"(1) An authorised person may, for any purpose connected with this Act –

(a) at all reasonable times, or at any time if he or she has reasonable grounds for believing that there may be an risk of environmental pollution arising from the carrying on of an activity at the premises or that such pollution is occurring, enter any premises and bring there on such other persons (including members of the Garda Síochána) or equipment as he or she may consider necessary for the purpose, and

(b) at any time halt and board any vehicle and require the driver of the vehicle to take it to a place designated by the authorised person, and such a vehicle may be detained at that place by the authorised person for such period as he or she may consider necessary for the purpose.

(2) Subject to subsection (7), an authorised person shall not, other than with the consent of the occupier, enter into a private dwelling under this section unless he or she has given to the occupier of the dwelling not less than 24 hours notice in writing of his or her intended entry.

(3) Every authorised person shall be furnished with a certificate of his or her appointment and when exercising any power conferred on him or her by or under this Act, the authorised person shall, if requested by any person affected, produce the certificate to that person.

(4) Whenever an authorised person enters any premises or boards any vehicle, pursuant to this section, the authorised person may therein, as appropriate –

(a) make such plans, take such photographs and carry out such inspections,

(b) make such tests and take such samples,

(c) carry out such surveys, take such levels, make such excavations and carry out such examinations of depth and nature of subsoil,

(d) require that the premises or vehicle or any part of the premises or anything in the premises or vehicle shall be left undisturbed for such period,

(e) require from the occupier of the premises or any occupant of the vehicle or any person employed on the premises or any other person on the premises, such information,

(f) require the production of and inspect such records and documents, and take copies of or extracts from, or take away if considered necessary for the purposes of inspection or examination, any such records or documents,

as the authorised per-son, having regard to all the circumstances, considers necessary for the purpose of exercising any power conferred on him or her by or under this Act.

(5) (a) An authorised person who, having entered any premises or boarded any vehicle, pursuant to this section, considers that waste thereon or therein is such, or is being handled or transported in such manner, as to constitute a risk of (*qv*) environmental pollution, may direct the (*qv*) holder of such waste to take such measures as are considered by that authorised person to be necessary to remove that risk, including the (*qv*) disposal of the waste, in such manner and place and within such period as the authorised person may specify.

(b) If a holder of waste fails to comply with a direction of an authorised person under this subsection, the authorised person may do all things as are necessary to ensure that the direction is carried out and the costs incurred by him or her in doing any such thing shall be recoverable from the holder of the waste by him or her, or the person by whom he or she was appointed, as a simple contract debt in any court of competent jurisdiction."

Offences

"(6) Any person who –

(a) refuses to allow an authorised person to enter any premises or board any vehicle or to take any person with him or her in the exercise of his or her powers under the section,

(b) obstructs or impedes an authorised person in the exercise of any of his or her powers under this section,

(c) gives either to an authorised person, a relevant local authority or the Agency, information which to his or her knowledge is false or misleading in a material respect, or

(d) fails or refuses to comply with any requirement of this section or of the authorised person,

shall be guilty of an offence.

(7) (a) Where an authorised person in the exercise of his or her powers under this section is prevented from entering any premises or if an authorised person has reason to believe that evidence related to a suspected offence under this Act may be present in any premises and that the evidence may be removed there from or destroyed, the authorised person or the person by whom he or she was appointed may apply to a judge of the District Court for a warrant under this subsection authorising the entry by the authorised person into the premises.

(b) If on application being made to him or her under this subsection, a judge of the District Court is satisfied, on the sworn information of the applicant, that the authorised person concerned has been prevented from entering a premises as aforesaid or that the authorised person has reasonable grounds for believing that other matters aforesaid, the judge may issue a warrant under his or her hand authorising that person, accompanied, if the judge deems it appropriate to so provide, by such number of members of the Garda Síochána as may be specified in the warrant, at any time or times within 1 month from the date of issue of the warrant, on production if so requested of the warrant, to enter, if need be by force, the premises concerned and exercise the powers referred to in subsections (4) and (5)."

Subsection (8) provides that where an authorised person who is exercising a power under the Act involving the bringing of any vehicle to any place anticipates any obstruction he or she may request a member of the Garda Síochána to assist him or her and the member is obliged under the section to comply with such a request.

Subsection (9) provides that an authorised person may enter on land for the purpose of assessing the suitability of the land for waste disposal; such entry shall be subject to the relevant provisions of section 83 other than subsection (6) of the LG(P&D)A 1963 as if the entry were made under that section.

Subsections (10) and (11) provide for the making of Ministerial regulations providing for:

(a) the taking of samples and the carrying out of tests, examinations and analyses,

(b) the specification of the classes of persons to be responsible for the taking of such samples and for the carrying out of such tests, examinations and analyses, or

(c) the specification of the certificate or other evidence to be given as the result of any such tests, examination or analysis and the class or classes of persons by whom such certificate or evidence is to be given.

Subsection (12) provides that any such certificate as is described at (10) and (11) shall, in relation to that sample, be evidence, without further proof, of the result of the test, examination or analysis.

ABANDONED VEHICLES

Section 71(4) of the WMA 1996 provides that a local authority has power to enter on land upon which a vehicle has been abandoned and remove it but must not enter a private dwelling house under the section without giving the occupier 24 hours notice in writing of the intended entry. *See:* VEHICLES, ABANDONED.

WLA 1976 and NH 97

(A) Section 72 Authorised Persons

Section 72(2) and (3) of the WLA 1976:

"(2) A member of the Garda Síochána or (*qv*) an authorised person may, if he has reasonable grounds for suspecting that a person has committed an offence under Part II or under section 45, 47, 51, 52 or 53 of this Act, at all reasonable times stop any person who is suspected by him of being in any way concerned in the offence and require the person to give his name and address and to declare and, if such member or authorised person, as the case may be, considers it necessary, to produce on demand for examination any specimen of (*qv*) fauna or (*qv*) flora or any part or product of any such specimen or any thing which is mentioned in subsection (7) of this section, which is in the person's possession and such member or authorised person may seize and detain any specimen or part or product of a specimen or any thing so produced which appears to him to be something which might be required as evidence in proceedings for an offence under the Act.

(3) A member of the Garda Síochána or an authorised person may, if he has reasonable grounds for suspecting that a person has committed an offence under Part II or under sections 45, 47, 51, 52 or 53 of this Act, at all reasonable times –
  (a) search any vehicle, vessel or aircraft which he reasonably suspects of being used to transport, export or import any specimen of fauna or flora or part or product of such specimen contrary to the said section 51, 52 or 53 and such member or authorised person, for the purpose of carrying out the search, may, if he thinks fit, require the person, for the time is in control of the vehicle, vessel or aircraft to bring it to a stop or refrain from using it,
  (b) open and examine any package, parcel, box or other container which he reasonably suspects is being so used,
  (c) require the person who is for the time being in control of the vehicle, vehicle or aircraft mentioned in paragraph (a) of this subsection or any other person found thereon to furnish to him that person's name and address and to produce for examination any book, record or other document which relates to any specimen of fauna or flora or any part or product of fauna or flora and which is in the person's possession or under his control and, if known to the person, the name and address of the owner of any specimen of fauna or flora or part or product of fauna or flora found in the course of the search.
  (d) inspect and, if he thinks fit, take copies of any entry in any book, record or other document produced pursuant to a requirement under this section,

  and if -
  (i) such member or authorised person has reasonable grounds for suspecting that an offence has been or is being committed under this Act with or in relation to anything found, in the course of the search, or
  (ii) a document so found is a record or other document which the member or person has reason to believe may be required as evidence in proceedings for an offence under this Act,

  the member or authorised person may seize and detain that thing or document and anything else so found that appears to him to be something which might be required as evidence in proceedings for an offence under this Act."

Subsection (4)(a) confers on a member or authorised person the right of entry on any land at any time for the purpose of exercising the powers conferred by subsection (2) and paragraph (a) of subsection (3) of this section. Subsection (4)*(b)* provides that paragraph (a) of this subsection does not confer the right to enter buildings on land.

Subsection (5) provides for the issue to a person exercising powers under the Act of a certificate of authorisation which must be produced on demand.

Subsection (6) provides that the powers conferred of a member of the Garda Síochána under this section does not prejudice his existing powers of seizure and detention of property.

Subsection (7) provides that the "things" referred to in subsection (2) include a firearm, trap, snare, net, line, hook, arrow, dart or spear or a similar device, instrument or missile, calculated or likely to cause death or bodily injury to a *(qv)* wild bird or wild mammal coming into contact with it, birdlime or any substance of a like nature, poisonous, poisoned or stupefying bait, tracer shot or a gun or container mentioned in section 33(2) of the Act and a decoy or electrical or other instrument device or appliance mentioned in section 35(1) or 38 of the Act.

For section 33(2), *see:* FIREARMS, RESTRICTIONS ON USE, for section 35(1), *see:* SCARECROWS, DECOYS, BIRD CALLS AND CALLS and for section 38, *see:* LAMPS, USE OF, IN HUNTING.

(B) Search Warrants

Section 73(1) of the WLA 1976 provides:

"(1) If a Justice of the District Court or a Peace Commissioner is satisfied by information on oath of an (*qv*) authorised person or a member of the Garda Síochána that there are reasonable grounds for suspecting that a person is in possession on any premises or other land of –
(a) a protected wild bird,
(b) a protected wild animal,
(c) the eggs of a protected wild bird,
(d) the carcass or any other part of, or any product of a protected wild bird or protected wild animal, or
(e) any plant or part or product of a plant which is of a species to which an order under section 21 of this Act applies,
and that as regards the bird, animal, plant, part, product or other thing an offence under this Act has been or is being committed, such Justice or Commissioner may issue a search warrant under this section.

(2) Subject to subsection (3) of this section, a warrant issued under this section shall be expressed and shall operate to authorise –
(a) in case the relevant information is sworn by a member of the Garda Síochána, a member of the Garda Síochána named in the warrant, accompanied by such other members of the Garda Síochána or such authorised persons as may be reasonably necessary,
(b) in case the relevant information is sworn by an authorised person, an authorised person named in the warrant, accompanied by such other persons as may be reasonably necessary,
at any reasonable time or times within seven days of the issue of the warrant to –
(i) enter and search, if need be by force, the premises or other land named in the warrant,
(ii) require any person found on such premises or other land to furnish to him his name and address,
(iii) require a person who is in occupation or is in control or is concerned in the management of the premises or other land to furnish to him his name and address and to produce –
(A) any thing mentioned in sub section (1) of this section [should be section 72(7)],
(B) any books, records or other documents which relate to any thing so mentioned and which are in any such person's possession or under his control,
and if known to such person, to furnish to him the name and address of the owner of any thing so produced,
(iv) inspect, and, if he thinks fit, take copies of any entry in any book, record or other document produced in pursuance of a requirement made pursuant to the warrant,
and if the member or authorised person so named has reasonable grounds for suspecting that either –
(A) an offence has been or is being committed under this Act with or in relation to anything found in the course of the search, or
(B) a document so found is a record or other document which the member or authorised person has reason to believe may be required as evidence in proceedings for an offence under this Act,
the member or authorised person may seize and detain that thing or document or anything else so found which appears to him to be something which might be required as evidence in proceedings for an offence under this Act.

(3) The powers conferred on an authorised person by a warrant issued under this section shall be exercisable by the person as regards a dwelling only if, and only for so long as, he is accompanied by a member of the Garda Síochána."

See: Order 89.10, District Court Rules, 1997.

Under Section 46(4) of the WLA 1976 an authorised officer has power to inspect and take copies of entries in documents produced to comply with requirements under regulations made by the Minister under section 46 to regulate and control (*qv*) wildlife dealing.

(C) Section 68 Authorised Persons

These authorised persons are appointed under section 11 of the Forestry Act 1946.

Section 68(1) of the WLA 1976 provides that any person appointed in writing by the Minister under section 11 of the Forestry Act 1946 to be an authorised officer for the purposes of that section (subsequently referred to in this section as an authorised officer) may at any reasonable time enter on, inspect and survey any land for the purpose of ascertaining whether there are (*qv*) fauna on the land which are in need of protecting under section 17 of this Act, or for any other purpose (apart from the purpose mentioned in subsection (2) of this section) in connection with the performance by the Minister of his functions under the Act.

For Reg. 17, *see:* DESIGNATION ORDER.

Subsection (2) provides that an authorised officer may at any reasonable time enter on and inspect any land to which a *(qv)* recognition order relates to ascertain whether or not the objectives indicated in the order are being, or have been, attained, or, where attained, are being maintained.

Subsection (3) provides that an authorised officer entering on land under this section may do thereon all things reasonably necessary for the purpose for which the entry was made.

Subsections (4), (5) and (6) deal with the necessity of giving notice of an intention to make an entry where there is no consent and the right of appeal against that notice to the District Court.

See: Order 89.9, District Court Rules, 1997.

(D) Under **section 42(1) of the WLA 1976** the Minister has power to authorise persons to take steps, including entering on any land and capturing and killing wild birds and wild animals causing damage described in subsection (1).

(E) Authorised Officers under **Regulation 7(5) of the NH Regulations 1997** (S.I. No. 94 of 1997)

"(5) An authorised officer may, for the purposes of these Regulations –
(a) enter and inspect any lands for the purpose of undertaking (*qv*) surveillance of the conservation status of the natural habitats and species under paragraph (1), and generally for the purposes of giving effect to the (*qv*) Habitats Directive and, without prejudice to the generality of the foregoing, may enter and inspect any lands –
(i) for the purpose of the preparation of a (*qv*) candidate list of European sites or of any proposed modification of any such list by virtue of Regulation 3(3) or of any proposed addition to any such list by virtue of Regulation 6,
(ii) to which a candidate list of European sites, a modified list under Regulation 3(3) or a list treated as added to by virtue of Regulation 6(1) relates,
(iii) to which Regulations 8 or 9 relates,
(iv) upon which a notice is erected by virtue of Regulation 11,
(v) which is the subject of an agreement under Regulation 12,
(vi) to which Regulation 14 relates,
(vii) to which Regulation 18 relates,
(viii) to which Regulation 19 relates,
(ix) for the purpose of establishing whether or not Regulation 23 has been complied with,
(x) to which Regulation 24 relates,
(xi) other than a dwelling, upon which the authorised officer has reasonable cause to suspect that an offence under these Regulations is being or has been committed or evidence of any such offence is to be found;
(b) request the owner or occupier of such land so entered to give assistance, to carry our such instructions and to give such information as may be reasonably necessary for the purposes of the performance by the authorised officer of his or her functions.

Offence
(6) A person who obstructs or interferes with an authorised officer when he or she is exercising a function conferred by this Regulation shall be guilty of an offence."

This slightly annoying list of references to various regulations in fact covers almost the entire of the NH 97 Regulations and certainly all that deal with identifying, listing, notifying and designating sites as (*qv*) special areas of conservation including the restrictions on the carrying on of (*qv*) operations and activities and the taking in the wild of the species of (*qv*) fauna and (*qv*) flora set out in Part II of the First Schedule. *See:* SCHEDULES HERETO, WLA 1976 SCHEDULES.

(F) Under **European Communities (Wildlife Act, 1976) (Amendment) Regulations 1986** (S.I. No. 254 of 1986)

Regulation 6(1) provides:

"An authorised person may, for the purposes of these Regulations –

(a) enter on and inspect any lands on which he reasonably believes that killing or capturing of wild birds has taken place,

(b) request the owner or occupier of any lands on which he reasonably believes that killing or capturing of wild birds has taken place to provide him with information about –

(i) the number, if any, of wild birds killed or captured on such lands,

(ii) the means by which such wild birds have been killed or captured,

(iii) any poisons which may have been laid to kill birds including but without prejudice to the generality of the aforesaid information about the quantity, type and frequency of laying of poisons."

Offence

"(2) A person who obstructs or interferes with an authorised person when he is exercising a power conferred by this Regulation or fails to comply with a request under paragraph (1)(b) of this Regulation shall be guilty of an offence and shall be liable on summary conviction to a fine not exceeding £400."

UNDER EC (MAMMALIAN ANIMAL WASTE) AND (PROCESSING ANIMAL WASTE) REGULATIONS 1998

Regulation 8(1) in the **European Communities (Mammalian Animal Waste) Regulations, 1998** (S.I. No. 2 of 1998) and Regulation 9 (1) of the European Communities (Processing Mammalian Animal Waste) Regulations 1998 (S.I. No. 62 of 1998) each provide that an authorised officer may, for the purposes of these Regulations or Commission Decision 96/449/EC of July 18, 1996 (O.J. L184 of July 24, 1996 p. 43) –

"(a) at all reasonable times, enter any premises or place, and any vehicle, wagon, vessel or other means of transport (other than any premises, place or means of transport consisting of a dwelling or other than so much thereof as consists of a dwelling) where he reasonably suspects that any product or document which he considers should be examined or inspected for the purposes of his functions under these Regulations is to be found,

(b) there, or at any other place, examine and inspect any product or document,

(c) take, without payment of compensation, such samples of any product at the premises or place or on or in the means of transport as he may reasonably require for the purposes of his functions under these Regulations and carry out or have carried out on the samples such analyses, examinations, checks and inspections as he considers necessary or expedient for the purposes of such functions,

(d) there, or at any other place, carry out or have carried out such examinations, checks and inspections of the premises, place or means of transport and any equipment, machinery or plant and any product found there as he reasonably considers necessary or expedient for the purposes of such functions,

(e) require any person at the premises or place or on or in the means of transport and the owner or person in charge thereof and any person employed in connection therewith to give to him such information and to produce to him such books, certificates, documents and other records, including any records required to be kept by the Regulations, within the power or procurement of the person as he may reasonably require for the purposes of his functions under the Regulations,

(f) examine and take copies of, or of extracts from, any such records as afore said,

(g) seize and detain anything found there which he reasonably believes to be evidence of an offence under the Regulations."

Offences

Regulation 8(2) of the European Communities (Mammalian Waste) Regulations, 1998 (S.I. No. 2 of 1998) and Regulation 9(2) of the European Communities (Mammalian Waste Processing) Regulations, 1998 (S.I. No. 62 of 1998) provide that a person shall not in purported compliance with a requirement under paragraph (1)(e) above, give information to an authorised officer that he knows to be false or misleading in a material respect and Regulation 9(2) and 10(2) of the above cited regulations provide that a person shall not obstruct or impede an authorised officer in the due exercise of any of the functions of the officer under the Regulations.

ENVIRONMENTAL APPROVAL
(EPAA 1992, s. 73)

As amended by section 81 of the F(A)A 1997. *See:* APPROVAL, ENVIRONMENTAL.

ENVIRONMENTAL AUDIT
(EPAA 1992, s. 74)

See: AUDIT, ENVIRONMENTAL

(WMA 1996, s. 27)

"Environmental audit" has the same meaning as it has in section 74 of the EPAA 1992 above. *See:* WASTE, MEASURES RELATED TO THE RECOVERY OF.

ENVIRONMENTAL IMPACT ASSESS-MENT
(EIA) REGULATIONS, 1989 to 1999
(EPAA 1992)

The Regulations dealt with in this Article are four in number, the European Communities (Environmental Impact Assessment) Regulations 1989 (S.I. No. 349 of 1989, ((herein called "the 1989 Regulations"), the European Communities (Environmental Impact Assessment) (Amendment) Regulations 1994 (S.I. No. 84 of 1994), the European Communities (Environmental Impact Assessment) (Amendment) Regulations 1996 (S.I. No. 101 of 1996), the European Communities (Environmental Impact Assessment) (Amendment) Regulations 1998 (S.I. No. 351 of 1998) (all of which are herein called "the 1994, 1996 and 1998 Regulations") and the European Communities (Environmental Assessment (Amendment) Regulations 1999 (S.I. No. 93 of 1999) (herein called "the 1999 Regulations).

The 1994, 1996 and 1998 Amendment Regulations have been substantially subsumed into the 1989 Regulations and the 1999 Regulations and the Schedules.

The 1989 Regulations, which came into operation on the 1st day of February 1990, implement Council Directive of June 27, 1985, (85/337/EEC, O.J. L175/40, July 5, 1985), on the assessment of of the effects of certain public and private projects on the environment and the 1999 Regulations, which came into operation on the 1st day of May 1999, give effect to Council Directive of March 3, 1997 (No. 97/11/EC, O.J.No. L73/5, March 14, 1997).

Effect was given to Directive 85/337/EEC in respect of motorways by the European Communities (Environmental Impact Assessment) (Motorways) Regulations 1988 (S.I. No. 221 of 1998) which are not dealt with in this book.

Both the 1989 Regulations and the 1999 Regulations modify the provisions of the LG (P&D)A 1963 as amended so as to provide a framework for the application of environmental impact assessment to the planning control procedures under those Acts. The 1989 Regulations contain procedures for the application of Environmental Impact Assessments to development by local authorities.

The 1999 Regulations introduce the concept of a person required to submit an environmental impact assessment for a proposed development applying in advance for a written opinion on the information to be contained in the statement.

Both Acts contain amendments to certain Acts which are specified hereunder.

Significant changes were made to the Planning Regulations by the Local Government (Planning and Development) Regulations, 1999 (S.I. No. 92 of 1999). These Regulations amend the Planning Development Regulations, 1994 to 1998, principally to reflect the provisions of Directive 97/11/EC of 3 March 1997 (O.J. L. No. 73/5, 14 March 1997) relating to environmental impact assessment. The Regulations came into force on 1 May 1999.

The amendments provide for matters of procedure in relation to a request to a planning authority for an opinion on the information which should be contained in an environmental impact statement. These procedures also apply to appeals to An Bord Pleanála and to applications to the Minister for the Environment and Local Government for the certification of proposed local authority development. The amendments also extend the procedures to be followed in the case of a proposed development which would be located on an environmentally sensitive site or be likely to have significant effects on the environment of another Member State of the European Communities.

The regulations also provide that certain fish farming development which is licensed under the Fisheries (Amendment) Act, 1997, is exempted development for the purposes of the Planning Acts.

1989 REGULATIONS

""Environmental impact statement" is defined in the European Communities (Environmental Impact Assessment) Regulations 1989 (S.I. No. 349 of 1989), Regulation 3(1), as meaning a statement, prepared in accordance with a requirement of or under any enactment (including these Regulations), other than the European Communities (Environmental Impact Assessment) (Motorways) Regulations, 1988 (S.I. No. 221 of 1988), of the effects, if any, which proposed development, if carried out, would have on the environment."

Part II (Articles 4 to 11) of the European Communities (Environmental Impact Assessment) Regulations, 1989 (S.I. No. 349 of 1989) deal with the amendments to the Planning Acts which are as follows:

Regulation 5, section 2(1) Local Government (Planning and Development) Act 1963.
Regulation 6, section 4, of the Local Government (Planning and Development) Act 1963.
Regulation 7, section 25 of the Local Government (Planning and Development) Act 1963.
Regulation 8, section 26 of the Local Government (Planning and Development) Act 1963.
Regulation 9, section 41 of the Local Government (Planning and Development) Act 1963.
Regulation 10, section 78 of the Local Government (Planning and Development) Act 1963
Regulation 11, section 20 of the Local Government (Planning and Development) Act 1976.

The Regulations also amend other Statutes as follows:

Public Health (Ireland) Act 1878,
Foreshore Act 1933,
Air Navigation and Transport Act 1936,
Water Supplies Act 1942,
Harbours Act 1946,
Fisheries (Consolidation) Act 1959,
Petroleum and Other Minerals Development Act 1960,
Gas Act 1976,
Fisheries Act 1980 and
Urban Renewal Act 1986.

DEVELOPMENT BY LOCAL AUTHORITY WHO ARE ALSO PLANNING AUTHORITY

The substantive amendment, in so far as the environment is concerned, is to section 78 of the LG(P&D)A 1963. This section is in Part III of the Act which deals with development by local authorities of land which is in their ownership for the purpose of its functions under the Local Government (Planning and Development) Acts.

Section 78 of the LG(P&D)A 1963 provides for regulations made in relation to any specified cases or classes of cases of development proposed to be carried out by local authorities who are planning authorities and specifies that the regulations must require the local authority to give public notice of the proposed development and include in the notice an invitation for the making by interested persons of objections to the development and if these objections persist, require the authority to have the consent of the Minister before carrying out the proposed development.

The new subsection (2) of section 78, inserted by regulation 10, provides for regulations under the section in respect of any specified cases or classes of cases of development proposed to be carried out by or on behalf of local authorities who are planning authorities and then lists the specific requirements to be dealt with under the regulations.

The important requirements can be summarised as follows:

(1) The local authority have to prepare an Environmental Impact Statement (EIS) in respect of "specified proposed development".
Note that Article 24 provides that development of the classes set out in Part I and II of the First Schedule to the regulations is specified development for the purposes of the regulations.
The EIS shall contain the information specified in paragraph 2 of the Second Schedule and may contain the information specified in paragraph 3 of that Schedule.

See: SCHEDULES HERETO, EIA REGULATION SCHEDULES.

(2) The Minister may require an EIS from a local authority in respect of other proposed development.

(3) Where an EIS is required, a local authority must have certification of the Minister that the proposed development (or the proposed development as varied or modified by him) will not, in his opinion, have significant adverse effects on the environment, or will embody the (*qv*) best practicable means to

prevent or limit such effects.

(4) The Minister must, before certifying proposed development, have regard to:
   (a) the EIS prepared in respect of that development,
   (b) any submissions or observations made to him in accordance with the regulations (Art. 10(i)),
   (c) to the views of other Member States of the EC arising from consultation, if any, in accordance with regulations (Art. 10(j)),

(5) The Minister may, by order, where he is satisfied that special circumstances so warrant, grant an exemption from the requirement under the section to prepare an EIS in respect of proposed development but must publish notice of any exemption granted of the reasons for granting it and any other requirements in the Iris Oifigiúil and at least one Irish daily newspaper.

The proposed Regulations under section 78 must also provide for other matters, *e.g.* public access to files, and notices to the public.

EIS AND DEVELOPMENTS BY CERTAIN STATE AUTHORITIES

Part IV of the European Communities (Environmental Impact Assessment) Regulations 1989 (S.I. No. 349 of 1989) deal with the requirement that State Authorities, meaning any authority being a Minister of the Government or the (*qv*) Commissioners of Public Works in Ireland, shall, before undertaking any development of a class specified under Article 24 of the regulations (Parts I and II of the First Schedule) or any development which would be of such a class but for not exceeding a quantity, area or other limit specified in relation to such class and which, in the view of the State authority, would be likely to have significant effects on the environment, prepare a statement of the likely effects on the environment (EIS) of the proposed development.

EIS REQUIRED IN RELATION TO CERTAIN DEVELOPMENTS

Part V of the above Regulations provide at Regulation 24 that development of the classes set out in Part I and II of the First Schedule are specified for the purposes of the regulations and, therefore, require an EIS.

Regulation 25 provides that the EIS must contain the information specified in paragraph 2 of the Second Schedule and may contain the information specified in paragraph 3.
See: SCHEDULES HERETO, EIA REGULATIONS SCHEDULE.

1999 REGULATIONS

Part II (Article 4) amends the following sections of the LG(P&D) Acts:

Section 25 of the 1963 Act, section 78 of the 1963 Act and section 7 of the 1992 Act.

The Regulations also contain amendments to other Statutes as follows:

The Foreshore Act 1933, *see:* FORESHORE, the Arterial Drainage Act 1945, the Harbours Act 1946, the Petroleum and Other Minerals Development Act 1960, the Gas Act 1976, the Roads Act 1993, the Transport (Dublin Light Rail) Act 1996, section 26 of the Dublin Docklands Development Authority Act 1997 and section 10 of the Fisheries (Amendment) Act 1997. *See:* LICENCE (1) AQUACULTURE.

The 1989 Regulations are amended by the 1999 Regulations as follows:

By Article 7 which adds a new Article 27:

"(27) The criteria set out in the Third Schedule are hereby specified for the purposes of this article."

and by Article 8 which provides:

"The 1989 Regulations are hereby amended by:-

(a) the substitution for the First and Second Schedules (as amended by article 7 of the 1998 Regulations) thereto of the First and Second Schedules respectively to these regulations;

(b) the insertion following the Second Schedule thereto of the Third Schedule to these regulations."

And the 1999 Regulations contain substitutions for Schedules 1 and 2 of the 1989 Regulations as amended and the new Third Schedule referred to in the new Article 27.

See: SCHEDULES HERETO, EIA.

Article 1(2) of the 1999 Regulations provides that the four regulations of 1989, 1994, 1996 and 1999 may be collectively cited as the European Communities (Environmental Impact

Assessment) Regulations, 1989 – 1999.

ENVIRONMENTAL IMPACT ASSESSMENT (GUIDELINES)
(EPAA 1992, s. 72)

Section 72 of the EPAA 1992 introduces some changes to the existing law relating to environmental impact assessment contained in:

(1) The European Communities (Environmental Impact Assessment) (Motorways) Regulations 1988 (S.I. No. 221 of 1988),
(2) The European Communities (Environmental Impact Assessment) Regulations 1989 (S.I. No. 349 of 1989),
(3) The Local Government (Planning and Development) Regulations 1990 (S.I. No. 2 5 of 1990), and
(4) the Local Government (Planning and Development) Regulations 1992 (S.I. No. 222 of 1992).

Section 72 provides for the preparation by the (*qv*) Agency of guidelines on the contents of Environmental Impact Statements (EISs) in respect of developments made subject to an EIA under the 1989 Regulations but subject to the existing statutory provisions regarding the contents of an EIS.

Section 72 of the EPAA 1992 provides:

"(1) (a) Subject to Article 25 of the European Communities (Environmental Impact Assessment) Regulations, 1989, and subsections (3) and (3A) of section 4 of the Local Government (Roads and Motorways) Act, 1974, or to any provisions amending or replacing that Article or those subsections, the Agency may, and shall at the request of the Minister, or of any other Minister of the Government in relation to those matters for which that Minister is the competent authority, prepare guidelines on the information to be contained in environmental impact statements in respect of development to which this section applies.

(b) The Agency shall, in preparing such guidelines, consult with the Minister and with any other Minister who in the opinion of the Agency is concerned.

(2) Guidelines under subsection (1) may relate to all development, or to any particular class of development, to which this section applies.

(3) (a) Regard shall be had, in the preparation of an environmental impact statement in respect of development to which this section applies, to any guidelines under subsection (1) which relate to the development concerned.

(b) A competent authority to which an Environmental Impact Statement is submitted in respect of development to which this section applies shall, in considering the said statement, have regard to any guidelines under subsection (1) which relates to the development concerned.

(4) (a) A copy of an environmental impact statement prepared in relation to any development or class of development to which this section applies other than an (*qv*)activity for which a licence or revised licence under Part IV is required, shall be sent to the Agency by the person or body on whose behalf the environmental impact statement is prepared, at such time as may be prescribed.

(b) (i) The Agency may, having considered an environmental impact statement received pursuant to paragraph (a), make to the competent authority concerned such submissions or observations as it considers appropriate within such period as may be prescribed.

(ii) Where an environmental impact statement received by the Agency pursuant to paragraph (a) relates to development other than development by a State authority within the meaning of Article 23 of the European Communities (Environmental Impact Assessment) Regulations, 1989, a copy of any submissions or observations submitted to the competent authority under sub paragraph (i) shall be sent by the Agency to the person or body by whom the Environmental Impact Statement was sent pursuant to paragraph (a).

(c) A competent authority which receives submissions or observations from the Agency under paragraph (b)(i) shall, notwithstanding the provisions of any other enactment as to the matters to which the authority is to have regard in dealing with a case involving an environmental impact statement, have regard to such submissions or observations.

(5) The Agency shall be consulted and regard shall be had to its views, in the case of any development to which this section applies, before –
   (a) a decision is made on an application for an exemption from a requirement of any enactment to prepare an environmental impact statement, or
   (b) a State authority within the meaning of Article 23 of the European Communities (Environmental Impact Assessment) Regulations, 1989, decides that article 23 (1)(a) shall not apply in relation to the proposed development.

(6) Any submissions or observations made by the Agency under subsection (4)(b)(i) or subsection (5) shall be available for inspection by any person free of charge at the Agency's headquarters during office hours.

(7) This section shall apply to –
   (a) development which is of a class for the time being specified under Article 24 of the European Communities (Environmental Impact Assessment) Regulations, 1989, or under any enactment amending or replacing that Article, and
   (b) a motorway which has the meaning assigned to it by the Local Government (Roads and Motorways), Act 1974.

(8) In this section, unless the context otherwise requires –
   'competent authority' means –
   (a) a Minister of the Government or other public authority or body to which an environmental impact statement in respect of development to which this section applies is required by or under any enactment to be submitted, or
   (b) a State authority within the meaning of Article 23 of the European Communities (Environmental Impact Assessment) Regulations, 1989, by which an environmental impact statement in respect of development to which this section applies is required to be prepared;
   'environmental impact statement' includes an 'environmental impact study' for the purposes of the European Communities (Environmental Impact Assessment) (Motorways) Regulations, 1988."

ENVIRONMENTAL IMPACT ASSESSMENT (EIA)
(NH 97, Reg. 2(1))

"means an assessment carried out in accordance with the provisions of any enactment made in connection with the Council Directive No 85/337/EEC of 27 June, 1985 on the assessment of the effects of certain public and private projects on the environment (O.J. No. L 175/40, 5 July 1985), and any Directive amending or replacing the first-mentioned Directive and includes an assessment carried out in accordance with section 51 of the Roads Act, 1993 (No 14 of 1993)."

ENVIRONMENTAL IMPACT STATEMENT (EIS)
(EPAA 1992, s. 3(1))

As amended by insertion by article 12 of the European Communities (Environmental Impact Assessment) (Amendment) Regulations 1994 (S.I. No. 84 of 1994)

"A statement prepared in accordance with a requirement of or under regulations under section 25 (as amended by the European Communities (Environmental Impact Assessment) Regulations, 1989, and 1994) of the Act of 1963 of the effects, if any, which proposed development, if carried out, would have on the environment."

(WMA 1996, s. 5(1))

"means a statement prepared under and in accordance with a requirement of, or made pursuant to, regulations under section 25 (as amended by the European Communities (Environmental Impact Assessment) Regulations, 1989, and Act of 1963 or regulations under section 45, of the effects, if any, which proposed development, if carried out, would have on the environment."

ENVIRONMENTAL MANAGEMENT SYSTEM
(WMA 1996, s. 27)

Under section 27(1) of the WMA 1996 means a system for managing the carrying on of an activity with regard to its effects on the environment.

ENVIRONMENTAL MEDIUM
(WMA 1996, s. 5(1))

Has the meaning assigned to it by the EPAA 1992.

Section 4 of the EPAA 1992 defines "environmental medium" as including "the atmosphere, land, soil and waters".

ENVIRONMENTAL POLLUTION
(WMA 1996, s. 5(1))

"means, in relation to (*qv*) waste, the holding, (*qv*) transport, recovery or (*qv*) disposal of waste in a manner which would, to a significant extent, endanger human health or harm the environment, and in particular –

(a) create a risk to (*qv*) waters, the atmosphere, land, soil, plants or animals,
(b) create a nuisance through (*qv*) noise, odours or litter, or
(c) adversely affect the countryside or places of special interest."

ENVIRONMENTAL MEDIUM ENVIRONMENTAL PROTECTION, ENVIRONMENTAL POLLUTION,

(EPAA 1992)

The terms "environmental protection", "environmental pollution" and "environmental medium" are defined in section 4 of the EPAA 1992. The term "waters" is defined in that section by reference to the Local Government (Water Pollution) Act 1977.

Section 4 of the EPAA 1992:

"(1) In this Act 'environmental protection' means:
(a) the prevention, limitation, elimination, abatement or reduction of environmental pollution, and
(b) the preservation of the quality of the environment.

(2) In this Act 'environmental pollution' means:
(a) 'air pollution' for the purposes of the Air Pollution Act, 1987,
(b) the condition of waters after the entry of polluting matter within the meaning of the Local Government (Water Pollution) Act, 1977,
(c) the disposal of waste in a manner which would endanger human health or harm the environment and, in particular –
(i) create a risk to waters, the atmosphere, land, soil, plants or animals,
(ii) cause a nuisance through noise or odours, or
(iii) adversely affect the countryside or places of special interest, or
(d) noise which is a nuisance, or would endanger human health or damage property or harm the environment.

(3) In this Act –
'environmental medium' includes the atmosphere, land, soil and waters;
'waters' has the meaning assigned to it in the Local Government (Water Pollution) Act, 1977."

See: WATERS.

ENVIRONMENTAL MONITORING PROGRAMME
(EPAA 1992, s. 65)

Section 65 of the EPAA 1992:

"(1) The Agency shall, after consultation with such persons or bodies (if any) as may be prescribed, prepare programmes for monitoring the quality of the environment and a copy of each such programme shall, as soon as may be, be sent by the Agency to the Minister and shall be published by the Agency.

(2) A programme under this section shall specify –
(a) the nature and extent of the monitoring to which the programme relates and the reasons why, in the opinion of the Agency, the monitoring should be carried out,
(b) the persons or bodies (including the Agency) by which the intended the monitoring is to be carried out,
(c) the resources, including equipment, other facilities and staff, required to carry out of the monitoring and the cost thereof,
(d) the arrangements which the Agency considers appropriate for access to, dissemination of, and publication of the results of the monitoring.

(3) It shall be the duty of the Agency to take appropriate steps to ensure that a programme under this section is implement-

ed and for that purpose the Agency may –

(a) give such directions as it considers appropriate to any local authorities in relation to the carrying out of monitoring by that authority,

(b) make arrangements with any public authority, or other person or body, for the carrying out of specific monitoring,

(c) carry out, cause to be carried out, or arrange for, such monitoring as it may consider necessary for the purposes of the programme,

(d) assist any person or body in the carrying out of any part of the approved monitoring programme.

(4) The Minister may make regulations specifying the monitoring, or classes of monitoring in relation to which the Agency shall consult with him or obtain his agreement prior to giving any directions under subsection (3)(a).

(5) Where the Agency is not satisfied with the response of a local authority to a direction under subsection (3)(a), it shall consult with the local authority concerned, and, if the Agency is still dissatisfied with the response following such consultation, the Agency shall carry out, cause to be carried out, or arrange for, the monitoring concerned and the costs of the monitoring may be recovered by the Agency from the local authority as a simple contract debt in any court of competent jurisdiction.

(6) The Agency may, after consultation with the persons or bodies (if any) referred to in subsection (1), amend or revoke a programme."

ENVIRONMENTAL PROTECTION AGENCY, ACT 1992
(EPAA 1992)

"An Act to make further and better provision for the protection of the environment and the control of pollution, to establish an Environmental Protection Agency, for these and other purposes to increase certain existing monetary penalties and to provide for other matters connected with the matters aforesaid. [April 23, 1992]"

ENVIRONMENTAL QUALITY OBJECTIVES
(EPAA 1992, s. 75)

Section 75 of the EPAA 1992:

"(1) The Agency shall, in relation to any (*qv*) environmental medium and without prejudice to its functions under section 103, specify and publish quality objectives which the Agency considers reasonable and desirable for the purposes of environmental protection.

(2) Without prejudice to subsection (1), the Agency may –

(a) prepare guidelines or recommendations on the manner and the period within which the quality objectives could be achieved,

(b) identify the public authorities or other bodies which may contribute to the achievement of such objectives,

(c) assess the resources, including staff and funding, which would be required to achieve such objectives, or

(d) arrange for the dissemination of information on any of the matters provided for in this subsection or any other relevant matter to the Minister or any other Minister of the Government or other public authority or other body which may in the opinion of the Agency contribute to the achievement of such objectives.

(3) Without prejudice to the operation or effect of any standard, limit value, or other matter specified or prescribed or otherwise in force by or under any enactment, the Minister and any other Minister of the Government and any other public authority shall take into account any quality objective drawn up and published by the Agency in the formulation of policy, in the setting of standards or in the exercise of any of their other functions concerning environmental protection."

For section 103, *see:* EMISSION LIMIT VALUES AND QUALITY OBJECTIVES.

ENVIRONMENTAL RESEARCH
(EPAA 1992, s. 171)

Section 71 of the EPAA 1992:

"(1) The functions of the Agency in relation to environmental research shall include the matters specified in this section.

(2) (a) The Agency shall advise the Minister on the need for environmental research and shall, at such intervals as the Minister may specify (or, where for the time being no intervals

are specified by the Minister, at such intervals as it thinks fit) prepare programmes of such research.

(b) Programmes under this section shall specify –
  (i) the subjects in relation to which research is necessary and the objectives of such research,
  (ii) the manner in which and the persons or bodies by which such research could be carried out,
  (iii) the estimated cost of particular research projects or operations.

(c) Programmes under this section shall be prepared after consultation with such persons or bodies as may be prescribed.

(3) (a) The Agency shall, from time to time, prepare and publish registers of environmental research projects and operations being carried out, or proposed to be carried out, in the State and which shall be available for inspection by any person free of charge at the Agency's headquarters during office hours.

(b) The Agency shall, insofar as is practicable, co-ordinate environmental research in the State and, for that purpose, may advise any public authority or any other person or body at the request of such person or body in relation to the allocation of financial support or other facilities for such research.

(4) The Agency may assist in money or in kind, or by the provision of services and facilities (including the services of staff), any person or body carrying out, or proposing to carry out, environmental research.

(5) The Agency may carry out, cause to carry out, or arrange for, environmental research in accordance with a programme prepared in accordance with subsection (2).

(6) The Agency shall, in consultation with the Minister, establish and maintain liaison with the Commission of the European Communities and any other international organisation in relation to programmes of environmental research carried out, promoted, or assisted by the Commission or such other organisation, and shall promote and facilitate, as far as possible, participation in such programmes by persons and bodies in the State."

ESTABLISHED ACTIVITY

(EPAA 1992, s. 3(1))

"means an (*qv*) activity –

(a) in respect of which a permission under Part IV of the Act of 1963 is granted prior to such day (in this paragraph and in paragraph (b) referred to as 'the relevant day') as may be prescribed by the Minister and which on the relevant day has not ceased to have effect, in accordance with the provisions of sections 2 and 4 of the Local Government (Planning and Development) Act, 1982, or

(b) which is, on the day immediately prior to the relevant day, or was, at any time during the period of twelve months ending on the day immediately prior to the relevant day, carried on, other than an activity which involves or is associated with an unauthorised structure or an unauthorised use within the meaning of the Act of 1963."

"The Act of 1963" means the LG(P&D)A 1963.
See: (1) ACTIVITY (2) LICENCES (5) S.82 EPAA 1992.

(WMA 1996, s. 5(1))

"means –

(a) in relation to an activity the carrying on of which requires a waste licence, an activity –
  (i) in respect of which a permission under Part IV of the Act of 1963 is granted before the date prescribed under section 39(1) in respect of that activity ('the relevant date') and which permission on that date has not ceased to have effect in accordance with the provisions of sections 2 and 4 of the Local Government (Planning and Development) Act, 1982, or
  (ii) which is, immediately before the relevant date, or was, at any time during the period of 12 months ending on the said date, carried on, other than an activity which involves or is associated with an unauthorised structure or an unauthorised use within the mean-

ing of the Act of 1963, and

(b) in any other case, an activity which was being lawfully carried on immediately before the commencement of the provision concerned of this Act that requires the use of the (*qv*) best available technology not entailing excessive costs."

ESTABLISHMENT ORDER
(WLA 1976, s. 15)

Section 15 of the WLA 1976:

"(1) This section applies to the following land –
(a) land (including land covered by inland waters) owned by the State, including land in which the Minister has (whether jointly or severally) any interest,
(b) any *(qv)* foreshore which belongs to the State,
(c) land, other than the foreshore mentioned in paragraph (b) of this subsection, which forms part of the seabed under the (*qv*) territorial waters of the State.

(2) Where, after consultation with the Minister for Agriculture and Fisheries, the Minister for Transport and Power and the (*qv*)Commissioners, the Minister is satisfied that –
(a) land to which this section applies –
(i) includes the habitat or forms the habitat or part of the habitat of one or more (*qv*) species or community of flora or fauna being a species or community which are of scientific interest, or
(ii) includes or forms an ecosystem which is of scientific interest,
and that the habitat or ecosystem is likely to benefit if measures are taken for its protection,
(b) it is desirable to establish the land as a nature reserve, and
(c) the proper management of the land as a nature reserve would not be precluded by any interest of any other person (including a person who is an owner with the Minister) in or over the land,

he may by order (in this Act referred to as establishment order) declare that the land shall constitute and that there shall be established by the order a nature reserve: provided that,
(i) in case the *(qv)* Commissioners have any interest in the land, the order shall be made by the Minister only with the concurrence of the Commissioners, and
(ii) in case the Minister's interest in the land is held by him jointly with another person, the Minister in addition to being satisfied as regards the matters aforesaid, shall, before making an establishment order in relation to the land be satisfied that the fact that the other person has an interest in the land will not inhibit the proper management of the land by the Minister as a nature reserve."

Subsection (3) provides that the order must specify the reasons why and the objectives for which the nature reserve is established.

Subsection (4) provides that the lands, the subject of an establishment order are to be managed by the Minister to secure, as best as may be, the objectives having regard to and in accordance with the general protection of the natural environment.

The lands are in fact managed by NPWS (National Parks and Wildlife Service) (now (*qv*) Dúchas).

Subsection (5) provides that the Minister shall not amend an establishment order unless he considers that the objectives, as regards which the nature reserve was established, require revision because of changes in the features or characteristics of the reserve or in any other circumstances which affect the reserve.

Subsection (6) provides that the Minister shall not revoke an order unless he considers that it is no longer practicable to maintain the reserve.

Subsection (7) provides for the transmission of copies of the establishment order to the Commissioners, the (*qv*) Board and the appropriate planning authority.

Sections 59(1)*(c)* and *(d)* of the WLA 1976 provides for regulations permitting public access to lands to which an establishment order applies. *See:* ACCESS TO AN ENTRY ON LAND.

This environmental designation is not to be confused with Special Protection Areas (SPAs) under the (*qv*) Birds Directive of 1979 or Special Conservation Areas under the NH 97 Regulations passed to implement the (*qv*) Habitats Directive of 1992.

See: RESERVES AND REFUGES.

LIST OF ESTABLISHMENT ORDERS TO DATE

Ballydoyle Estuary (1988)
Ballyarr Wood (1986)
Ballinastaig Wood (1983)
Ballygilgan (Lisadell) (1986)

Ballykeefe (1980)
Ballyteige (1986)
Ballyteig Burrow (1990)
Ballyteig Burrows (1987)
Caher (Murphy) (1980)
Capel Island and Knockadoon Head (1985)
Castlemaine Harbour (1990)
Clara Bog (1987)
Coolacurragh Wood (1982)
Coole-Garryland (1983)
Cumeragh River Bog (1994)

Deputys Pass (1982)
Derkmore Wood (1988)
Derryclare (1980)
Derrycrag Wood (1983)
Dromore (1985)
Duntally Wood (1986)

Easkey Bog (1990)
Eirk Bog (1986)

Fiddown Island (1988)

Garryrickin (1980)
Glendalough (1988)
Genealo Valley (1988)
Glengarriff (1991)
Glen of the Downs (1980)
Grantstown Wood
Granston Lough (1982)
Great Skellig (1988)

Keelhilla, Slievecarran (1986)
Kilcolman Bog (1993)
Knockomagh Wood (1989)
Knockmoyle/Shaskin (1986)
Knockmoyle/Sheskin (1990)
Knocksink Wood (1994)
Kyledohir (1980)

Leam West (1991),
Lough Barra Bog (1987)
Lough Hyne (1981)
Lough Knocknamdarrig (1988)
Lough Ganavan (1988)

Meenachullion (1990)
Mount Brandon (1986)

North Bull Island (1988)

Oldhead Wood (1984)
Owenboy (1986)

Pettigo Plateau (1984)
Pollardstown Fen (1980)
Pollknockaun Wood (1983)
Puffin Island (1987)

Raheenmore Bog (1987)
Rathmullen Wood (1986)
Redwood Bog (1991)
Richmond Esker (1985)
Rogerstown Estuary (1988)
Rosturra Wood (1983)

Scragh Bog (1992)
Slieve Bloom Mountains (1985)

Teraght Island (1989)
The Raven (1983),
Timahoe Esker (1985)
Tralee Bay (1989)

Uragh Wood (1982)
Vale of Clara (1983)
Wexford Wildfowl Reserve (1981).

ESTABLISHMENT OF THE ENVIRONMENTAL PROTECTION AGENCY (EPA)
(EPAA 1992, s. 19)

Section 19 of the EPAA 1992 provides:

"(1) There shall be a body to be known as An Ghníomhaireacht um Chaomhnú Comhshaoil or, in the English language, the Environmental Protection Agency (in this Act referred to as the Agency) to perform the functions assigned to it by or under this Act.

(2) The Agency shall stand established on such day as the Minister by order appoints.

(3) The Agency shall consist of a Director General and four other directors."

The Environmental Protection Agency (Establishment) Order 1993 (S.I. No. 213 of 1993) established the Agency on July 26, 1993.

ESTABLISHMENT OF REGIONAL ENVIRONMENTAL UNITS
(EPAA 1992, s. 43)

Section 43 of the EPAA 1992:

"(1) The Agency shall establish such number of units (in this Act referred to as regional environmental units) as may be approved of by the Minister and shall, as far as is practicable, arrange for the performance of its functions, or particular functions, through such units.

(2) Each regional environmental unit shall

comprise such number and types of employees and such facilities for the performance of its functions as the Agency considers necessary."

ESTABLISHMENT OF WATER QUALITY CONTROL AUTHORITIES
(LG(WP)A 1977, s. 25)

Section 25 of the LG(WP)A 1977 deals with the establishment of water quality control authorities. The section was never brought into operation. Section 25 refers to a Water Pollution Advisory Council which not only does not exist but the machinery for establishing it, section 2 of the LG(WP)A 1977, was repealed by section 30 of the LG(WP)A 1990.

ESTUARY
(F(C)A 1959, s. 3(1))

"includes any harbour or roadstead."

EUROPEAN COMMUNITIES
(WMA 1996, s. 5(1))

"has the meaning assigned to it by the European Communities Act, 1972."

EUROPEAN SITE
(NH 97, Reg. 2(1))

"means –

(a) a (*qv*) special area of conservation,
(b) a site of Community importance which has been placed on the list referred to in the third sub paragraph of Article 4(2) of the (*qv*) Habitats Directive,
(c) an area classified pursuant to paragraph (1) or (2) of Article 4 of the Birds Directive."

EUROPEAN WASTE CATALOGUE
(WMA 1996, s. 5(1))

"means the list of waste set out in Commission Decision 94/3/EC of 20 December, 1993 (O.J. No. L 15/5, 7 January 1994) (made pursuant to Article 1(a) of Council Directive 75/442/EEC (O.J. No. L 194/39, 25 July 1995) on waste) and includes such list as amended from time to time."

EVIDENCE
(FDA/LG(WP)A 1977/APA/
EPAA 1992/WMA/WLA)

(1) IN THE F(C)A 1959

PROOF OF EXPENSES INCURRED BY MINISTER

Section 320 of the F(C)A 1959:
"Where the Minister is entitled under section 99, 110, 112, 113, 114, 116, 117 or 129 to recover any expenses a certificate sealed with the official seal of the Minister and certifying the amount of those expenses shall be prima facie evidence of the amount of those expenses."

PROOF OF BYE-LAWS AND INSTRUMENTS MADE UNDER THE ACTS

Section 321 of the F(C)A 1959:

"(1) In any proceedings under the repealed enactments or this Act, a document purporting to be a copy of any instrument in writing made or issued under the repealed enactments or this Act shall, if it is certified by an officer of the Minister to be a true copy of such instrument, be prima facie evidence of such instrument and it shall not be necessary to prove the signature of the person so certifying such document or that he is an officer of the Minister.

(2) Nothing in this section shall be construed as limiting or affecting the operation of section 4 of the Documentary Evidence Act, 1925 (No. 24 of 1925)."

PROOF OF INSTRUMENT OF APPOINTMENT

Section 26 of the FA 1980:

See: INSTRUMENT OF APPOINTMENT.

SEAL AND JUDICIAL NOTICE OF SEAL
Second Schedule of the FA 1980, *see:* SEAL, CENTRAL BOARD AND ANY REGIONAL FISHERIES BOARD.

(2) EVIDENCE SUFFICIENT TO JUSTIFY PROCEEDINGS

F(C)A 1959, sections 171 and 172/
LG(WP)(A)A 1990/APA 1987/
EPAA 1992/WMA 1996

In most of the environmental statutes, including sections 171 and 172 of the F(C)A 1959, but excluding the other enforcement sections of the Fisheries Acts, there is a provision that section 10(4) of the Petty Sessions (Ireland) Act 1851, which requires that summary proceedings must be commenced within six months of the date of commission of the offence, does not apply in certain circumstances and one of these circumstances is where evidence sufficient to justify the proceedings has not come to the knowledge of the person by whom the proceedings are initiated, within that six months period.

Section 70(3) of the WLA 1976 simply provides that, notwithstanding section 10(4) of the Petty Sessions (Ireland) Act 1851, proceedings for any offence under the Act may be instituted at any time within one year from the date of the offence.

Similar provisions are contained in the following enactments:

section 27(d)*(i)* of the LG(WP)(A)A 1990,
section 13(3)*(b)* of the APA 1987,
section 11(3)*(b)* of the EPAA 1992 and
section 11(3)*(c)* of the WMA 1996.

each of which provide that notwithstanding the provisions of section 10(4) of the Petty Sessions (Ireland) Act 1851, summary proceedings may be commenced as follows:

(A) LG(WP)A 1990: six months from the date on which evidence sufficient, in the opinion of the person by whom the proceedings are initiated, to justify the proceeding comes to such persons knowledge, provided that no such proceedings shall be initiated later than five years from the date on which the offence concerned was committed.

(B) APA 1987: 12 months from the date the offence was committed or three months from the date on which evidence sufficient, in the opinion of the person by whom the proceedings are initiated, to justify the proceeding comes to such persons knowledge, whichever is the later, but in any event no later than five years.

(C) EPAA 1992: 12 months from the date on which the offence was committed or six months from the date on which evidence sufficient, in the opinion of the person by whom the proceedings are initiated, to justify the proceeding comes to such persons knowledge, whichever is the later but in any event not later than five years.

(D) WMA 1996: 12 months from the date on which the offence was committed, after the expiry of the 12 months where the person against whom the proceedings are to be brought is outside the State, within six months from the date on which he or she next enters the State, six months from the date on which evidence sufficient, in the opinion of the person by whom the proceedings are initiated, to justify the proceeding comes to such persons knowledge, and in any event not later than five years.

(E) F(C)A 1959: this provision is applied to sections 171 and 172 of the F(C)A 1959 by section 27(d)*(i)* of the LG(WP)A 1977 and the periods of limitation are the same as in the LG(WP)A 1977.

In the case of each statute to which this provision applies there is a further subsection immediately following on the subsections quoted above which provides as follows:

"For the purposes of this paragraph, a certificate signed by or on behalf of the person initiating the proceedings specifying the date or dates on which evidence relating to the offence came to his knowledge shall be prima facie evidence of such date or dates and in any legal proceedings a document purporting to be a certificate under this paragraph and to be so signed shall be deemed to be so signed and shall be admitted as evidence without proof of the signature of the person purporting to sign the certificate, unless the contrary is shown."

(3) PROOF OF ORDERS AND OTHER DOCUMENTS UNDER THE WLA 1976

Section 71 of the WLA 1976:

"In any proceedings for an offence under this Act, it shall not be necessary to

(a) negative by evidence the existence of any order under section 24 or 25 of this Act or any licence or permission under this or any other Act,
(b) prove that any act which is the subject of the proceedings was not caused by or the result or effect of, or was not consequent upon any other thing lawfully done,

and the onus of proving such licence or permission or that such act was so caused or was such a result or effect or was so consequent upon shall be on, in the case of such a licence or permission, the person seeking to avail himself thereof, or in any other case, the person against whom the proceedings are instituted."

(4) PROOF BY CERTIFICATE IN THE EPAA 1992

Section 13(9) of the EPAA 1992 provides that

any certificate or other evidence of a test, examination or analysis of a sample shall be accepted without further proof.

(5) PROOF OF A DOCUMENT UNDER SEAL OF THE AGENCY

Section 77 of the EPA 1992 provides for the receipt in evidence without further proof of a document under seal of the Agency purporting to be a code, or part of a code, of practice published or approved of by the Agency under section 76. *See:* CODES OF PRACTICE.

Section 20(4) of the EPAA 1992 provides for judicial notice being taken of the seal of the Agency and every document purporting to be an instrument made by the Agency and to be sealed with the seal (purporting to be authenticated in accordance with subsection (3)) of the Agency shall be received in evidence and be deemed to be such an instrument without proof, unless the contrary is shown.

(6) PROOF OF ENTRIES IN COMPUTERISED REGISTER

Section 112 of the EPAA 1992 provides for the proof of entries in a register kept in computer or other non-legible form and evidence of those entries. *See:* REGISTERS (4)

(7) PROOF BY CERTIFICATE IN THE WMA 1996

Section 14(12) of the WMA 1996 provides that any certificate or other evidence of any prescribed test, examination or analysis of any sample shall be evidence without further proof.
See: ENTRY AND SEARCH WMA.

Section 23(4)*(b)* of the WMA 1996 provides for the production of a copy of or extract from a (*qv*) waste management plan certified by an officer of the local authority to be accepted as prima facie evidence of the contents.

(8) PRESUMPTIONS IN THE FISHERIES ACTS

Section 96(5) of the F(C)A 1959 and section 10 of the F(A)A 1962 contain presumptions in relation to a prosecution under section 96(2), the first under section 96(5) is the presumption that the person charged had possession or control of the net with intent to use it and the second under section 10 is the presumption that a net, other instrument lure or bait found on his person or in a boat or vehicle belonging to him shall be deemed to be in his possession or control. The presumptions can be rebutted in each case. *See:* NETS, RESTRICTION ON THEIR USE.

Section 182(2)*(b)* of the F(C)A 1959 provides that in any proceedings under section 182(2) where a person is charged with purchasing, selling, exposing for sale, having in his possession, having in his control salmon, trout, eel or molluscan shellfish the onus of proving lawful capture lies on the defendant. *See:* SALMON, TROUT, EELS AND MOLLUSCAN SHELLFISH UNLAWFULLY CAPTURED.

Article 11 of the Salmon and Trout Conservation Bye-law No. 743, 1998 when a person is found using or attempting to use in fishing certain nets the evidence of a sea fisheries protection officer, authorised officer or authorised person in relation to such use creates a rebuttable presumption that the said fishing was for salmon or trout. *See:* SALMON AND TROUT CONSERVATION BYE-LAW.

(9) PRESUMPTIONS IN WLA 1976

Section 21(6) of the WLA 1976 provides that where a person is charged with an offence under the section and it is proved he sold a "plant" to which the offence relates and he claims the plant is from an area to which an order under the section applies then it will be assumed, unless the contrary is shown by him, that the sale was in contravention of subsection (3). *See:* PROTECTION, FLORA, SECTION 21 OF WLA 1976.

Section 22(7) of the WLA 1976 provides that where a person is charged under the section with disturbing a protected wild bird it shall not be necessary for the prosecution to prove that at the time of the alleged offence the defendant was not engaged in ornithology. *See:* PROTECTION, PROTECTED WILD BIRDS.

EXEMPTED WILD ANIMALS
(WLA 1976, s. 25)

See: OPEN SEASONS.

EXEMPTION PERMITS
FOR ARTIFICIAL PROPAGATION
(F(C)A 1959, s. 14(1))

Section 14(1) of the F(C)A 1959, as substituted by section 4 of the F(A)A 1962 –

"(1) Subject to subsection (2) of this section, nothing in this Act or in any instrument made thereunder shall prohibit anything done by the Minister or a person previously authorised in writing by the Minister in that behalf for the purpose of artificial propagation of fish, for some scientific purpose or for the improvement or development of any fishery.

(2) Nothing shall be done pursuant to sub section (1) of this section in relation to a (*qv*) several fishery without the consent of the owner thereof.

(3) A person authorised by the Minister under this section to do anything shall be furnished by the Minister with a certificate of such authorisation and when doing anything pursuant to the authorisation shall, if requested by any person affected, produce the certificate to that person."

The marginal note for section 14 in the 1959 Act read "power of Minister to grant exemption permits for the purpose of artificial propagation, etc." whereas the margin note for the substituted section in the 1962 Act reads "saving for acts done for artificial propagation, scientific purposes or improvement of fisheries."

See: OYSTERS.

EXISTING INDUSTRIAL PLANT
(APA 1987, s. 6)

See: INDUSTRIAL PLANT.

EXPENSES OF MINISTER
(LG(WP)A 1977, s. 35)

Section 35 of the LG(WP)A 1977:

"(1) The expenses incurred by the Minister in the administration of this Act shall be paid out of monies provided by the Oireachtas to such extent as may be sanctioned by the Minister for Finance.

(2) The expenses under this Act of the council of the County of Dublin shall be charged on that County exclusive of the Borough of Dun Laoghaire."

EXPORT OF SALMON, TROUT, EELS OR MOLLUSCAN SHELLFISH
(F(C)A 1959, s. 157)

Section 157 of the F(C)A 1959, amended by substitution of it and the entire of Part X by section 20 of the F(A)A 1994, provides:

"(1) It shall not be lawful for any person to export for sale or attempt to export for sale from any place salmon, trout, eels or molluscan shellfish unless:
(a) such person is the holder of a salmon dealer's licence, eel dealer's licence or molluscan shellfish dealer's licence as appropriate, for the time being in force, and
(b) such place is a place at which he is authorised by such licence to sell salmon and trout, eels or molluscan shellfish as appropriate."

Offence
Subsection (2) creates the offence of contravention of subsection (1).

Subsection (3) provides that the section shall not apply to a fisherman exporting salmon, trout, eels or molluscan shellfish of his own capture. *See:* CERTIFICATE OF FITNESS.

EXPORT, FAUNA AND FLORA
(WLA 1976, s. 53)

Section 53 of the WLA 1976 provides that, subject to section 52(5) of the Act, the Minister may, after consultation with the Minister for Agriculture and Fisheries by regulations prohibit the export, save under and in accordance with a licence granted by or on behalf of the Minister under this section, of protect wild birds, protected wild animals, carcasses or eggs or spawn of protected wild birds and protected wild animals or wild plants (subject to a section 21 order) or any part or product of such plants. *See:* FAUNA AND FLORA, EXPORT OF.

EXTENSION OF POWERS TO AGENCY
(EPAA 1992/LG(WP)A 1977/APA 1987)

EXTENSION OF POWERS IN LG(WP)A 1977

Section 100 of the EPAA 1992 gave the Minister power to apply, by order, any provision of the LG(WP)A 1977 to the Agency, specifying that the function conferred on the local authority or sanitary authority may, in addition to or in lieu of that authority, be exercised by the Agency.

EXTENSION OF POWERS IN APA 1987

Section 101 of the EPAA 1992 gave exactly similar powers to the Minister to apply, by order, any provision of the APA to the Agency.

ENVIRONMENTAL PROTECTION AGENCY (EXTENSION OF POWERS) ORDER, 1996 (S.I. No. 126 of 1996) made under sections 7, 100 and 101 of the EPAA 1992 provides:

"(1) In relation to the Local Government (Water Pollution) Act, 1977 by Article 4, and by reference to the Table to the Order, that the provisions of the Local Government (Water Pollution) Act, 1977 specified in the Table shall apply to the Agency in lieu of the local authority or sanitary authority for the purpose of the prevention or limitation, or the remedying of the effects, as the case may be, of water pollution from an (*qv*) activity, other than an activity to which section 99(2) of the Act applies, in respect of which a licence or revised licence under Part IV of the Act (EPAA 1992) is in force."

Section 99(2) is a transitional section pending the granting of an (*qv*) IPC (Part IV) licence.

The Table lists the following sections of the LG(WP)A 1977 as amended, as being affected by Article 4, the entire sections 3, 10, 11, 12 , 22, 23, 28 and 32 and subsections (7), (8), (13), (14) and (15) of section 16 and sections 26, 27 and 28 of the LG(WP)A Act 1990.

Subsection (2) provides:

"(2) In relation to the Air Pollution Act, 1987 by Article 10 made an order in the same terms as Article 4, for "the Act of 1987", which is the Air Pollution Act, 1987, and the sections of that Act which apply to the Agency in lieu of the local authority for the purposes of the prevention or limitation, or the remedying of the effects, as the case may be, of (*qv*) air pollution from an (*qv*) activity, other than an activity to which section 99(2) of the Environmental Protection Agency Act 1992 applies, in respect of which a licence or revised licence under Part IV of the Environmental Protection Agency Act 1992 is in force, are –

Sections 7(1), 11, 12, 13(1), (3) and (4), 14, 15, 16 (1)(a) and (b) and (2), (3) and (4), 24, 26, 28, 28A (4) and (6) and 54 (1),(2),(3) and (4)."

Article 13 provides in relation to section 29 (notification of incident causing air pollution) that it applies to the Agency in addition to the local authority for the purposes of prevention, limitation or remedying the effects.

Both Articles 4 and 10 apply to the Agency in lieu of the local authority meaning that the Agency alone can exercise the powers conferred by the sections in the Schedules.

Article 16 provides that where, under Articles 4 and 10, powers are to be exercised by the Agency in lieu of the local authority these powers can only be exercised by a local authority with the consent of the Agency.

The First and Second Schedules to the order contain substantial modifications by way of amendments to various sections of the LG(WP)A 1977 and the APA 1987 respectively to give effect to the foregoing.

See: PERFORMANCE OF STATUTORY FUNCTIONS BY LOCAL AUTHORITIES.

EXTINGUISHMENT OF EASEMENTS
(WLA 1976, s. 61)

Section 61 of the WLA 1976 provides that where any lands held by the Minister for the purposes of the WLA 1976 or the Forestry Act 1946 is subject to easements the Minister may apply to the Lay Commissioners of the Land Commission of the Irish Land Commission for an order extinguishing such easements or any one or more of them. Procedures are under the 1946 Act. "Extinguishment order" has the meaning assigned to it by section 19 of that Act.

The Irish Land Commission was dissolved by the Irish Land Commission (Dissolution) Act 1992. *See:* LAY COMMISSIONERS.

F

FACILITY
(WMA 1996, s. 5(1))

"means, in relation to the recovery or disposal of waste, any site or premises used for such purpose."

FALCONRY
(WLA 1976, s. 2(1))

"means hunting by means birds of the order 'falconiformes' which are trained to hawk for sport."

Section 41 of the WLA 1976

(WLA 1976, s. 41)

"(1) The Minister may make regulations –
   (a) regulating hunting by eagles, hawks, falcons and other birds of the order Falconiformes trained to hawk for sport, or otherwise governing the practice of falconry,
   (b) regulating the taking of eagles, hawks, falcons and other birds of the order Falconiformes for training to hawk for sport,
   (c) regulating the possession, breeding, training to hawk for sport, display or exhibition of eagles, hawks, falcons and other birds of the order Falconiformes,
   (d) providing that a person shall not, save under and in accordance with a licence granted in that behalf by the Minister –
      (i) engage in falconry,
      (ii) have in his possession, or under his control, any eagle, hawk or falcon or the eggs or young of any eagle, hawk or falcon,
   (e) provide for the payment of prescribed fees by applicants for licences for the purposes of this section,
   (f) providing for any matters ancillary or incidental to any of the foregoing.

(2) The Minister may grant licences for the purposes of this section."

BIRDS OF PREY REGULATIONS 1984

Wildlife Act 1976 (Birds of Prey) Regulations 1984 (S.I. No. 8 of 1984) were made under and to give effect to section 41 of the WLA 1976. "birds of prey" are defined in the same way as in section 41(a) as being "any eagle, hawk, falcon or other bird of the order falconiformes".

Offences
Regulation 4(1) creates the offence of engaging in falconry or having in possession or control any eagle, hawk or falcon or the eggs or young thereof, save under and in accordance with a licence granted in that behalf by the Minister.

Regulation 5(1) prohibits the taking of a bird of prey for training to hawk for sport or for breeding in captivity by a person who is not the holder of a section 41 licence which is in force.

Regulation 5(2) requires a person holding a licence when taking any bird of prey for training to hawk for sport, to comply with the following–
   (a) the specimen shall only be taken if it is a nestling,
   (b) the nest from which it is taken must contain not less than three nestlings (including the one taken) at the time of taking,
   (c) the taking must be in a manner which will minimise disturbance to the nest, its surroundings, the young and the parent birds.

Regulation 6 prohibits breeding birds of prey other than by the holder of a licence granted under section 41.

Regulation 7 provides:

"(1) A person who possesses, breeds, displays, exhibits any bird of prey shall comply with the following provisions –
   (a) the bird shall kept at all times in accommodation suitable as regards size, shelter, temperature, lighting, ventilation and cleanliness and, when caged, shall be kept only in a cage of sufficient dimensions to enable it to move and exercise freely;
   (b) the bird shall be provided with adequate perches;
   (c) the bird shall be supplied with a sufficient quantity of suitable food and drink;
   (d) all reasonable precautions shall be taken to prevent the bird contracting or spreading any infectious disease;
   (e) the bird shall be adequately safeguarded against fire hazards and predators and shall also be protected against undue disturbance;

(f) where accommodation is provided for two or more birds of prey, each of such birds shall be either tethered separately or separated for the other birds of prey by a partition, but where there is or are one or more pairs of such birds which, or all of which, is or are involved in a captive breeding project, as between the birds forming the pair or pairs, the provisions of this sub paragraph shall not apply as regards such pair or pairs.

(2) The accommodation provided for a bird of prey pursuant to this Regulation may be inspected by an authorised person on demand being made to him in that regard at any reasonable time."

Regulation 8 requires any appliance used for securing a bird of prey to a perch to be of a suitable strength, size and materials and designed to hold the bird securely without causing injury.

Regulation 9 provides that where a licensed bird is being flown free, any appliance attached shall be designed so as not to catch or become entangled in any branch, bush, line, tree, wire or other obstruction.

Regulation 10 provides that a bird of prey shall not be trained in such a manner that its training causes or is likely to cause unnecessary suffering to it.

Regulation 11 provides for payment to the Minister of a fee of £10 for a licence referred to in these regulations.

Section 22 (6) of the WLA 1976 exempts certain protected wild birds which would be of the order falconiformes and are described in Part I of the Fourth Schedule as Buzzards, Eagles, Falcons, Harriers, Hawks, Kites, Osprey and Owls from the capturing and killing of protected wild birds in the case of urgent necessity as is described in section 42(1), on the basis that these birds are so rare they should never be captured or killed.
See: (1) DAMAGE BY PROTECTED WILD BIRDS; (2) PROTECTION PROTECTED WILD BIRDS, SECTION 22(6).

FALSE OR MISLEADING STATEMENTS – AQUACULTURE LICENCES
(F(A) 1997, s. 72)

Section 72 of the F(A)A 1997:

offence
"(1) A person who in or in relation to an application for a licence, or an appeal against a decision on an application for an aquaculture licence or the revocation or amendment of a licence, makes a statement in writing which to the person's knowledge is false or misleading in a material respect shall be guilty of an offence.

(2) Where a person is convicted of an offence under subsection (1), any licence granted to that person, or to some other person on whose behalf the convicted person was authorised to act, consequent on the application or appeal in relation to which the information was furnished, shall be revoked from the date of conviction."

FAUNA
(WLA 1976, s. 2(1))

"means all wild animals (both aquatic and terrestrial) and includes in particular wild birds, wild mammals, reptiles, non-aquatic invertebrate animals and amphibians and all such wild animals' eggs and young, but in relation to fish or aquatic invertebrate animals (or their eggs or spawn or brood or young) only includes fish and such aquatic invertebrate animals which are of a species specified in regulations under section 23 of this Act which are for the time being in force."

(Heritage Act 1995, s. 2(1))

"means all wild birds and all wild animals (both aquatic and terrestrial) and includes in particular fish, wild mammals, reptiles, non-aquatic invertebrate animals and amphibians, and all such wild animals' eggs, larvae, pupae or other immature stage and young, but in relation to fish or aquatic invertebrate animals (or their eggs or spawn or other immature stage or brood or young) only includes fish and such aquatic invertebrate animals of a species specified in regulations under section 23 of the Wildlife Act, 1976, which are for the time being in force."

Regulations under made section 23 are as follows:

Wildlife Act 1976 (Protection of Wild Animals) Regulations 1980 (S.I. No. 282 of 1980) and Wildlife Act 1976 (Protection of Wild Animals) Regulations 1990 (S.I. No. 112 of 1990).

In the WLA 1976 the definition of "wildlife" includes flora and fauna.

Section 11(1) of the WLA 1976 provides:

"It shall be the function of the Minister to secure the protection of wildlife."

The designation of fauna, under the WLA 1976, breaks down into wild birds and wild mammals. Wild birds when protected under the Act are called (*qv*) protected wild birds.

Wild animals when protected become (*qv*) protected wild animals and when they lose their protected status under section 25 of the Act and can be hunted under an (*qv*) open seasons order they become (*qv*) exempted wild mammals.

When a protected wild bird loses its protected status under section 24 and can be hunted under an (*qv*) open seasons order it becomes "a protected wild bird of a species specified in an order under section 24".

For section 23, *see:* PROTECTION, PROTECTED WILD ANIMALS, for section 22, *see:* PROTECTION, PROTECTED WILD BIRDS and for sections 24 and 25, *see:* OPEN SEASONS.

FAUNA, TRANSPORT OF PACKAGES CONTAINING CERTAIN FAUNA
(WLA 1976, s. 51)

"(1) This section applies to any package, parcel, box or other container which contains all or any of the following, namely –
(a) any protected wild bird or protected wild animal,
(b) the dead body, carcass or other part either of a protected wild bird or a protected wild animal,
(c) eggs of a protected wild bird.

(2) Every package, parcel, box or other container to which this section applies shall, if transported, whether by hand or otherwise, be marked conspicuously on the outside thereof or an a label attached thereto, so as clearly to indicate -
(a) that the package, parcel, box or other container contains protected wild birds or protected wild animals, as may be appropriate, and
(b) the name and address of the consignor.

Offence

(3) Any person who consigns or transports a package, parcel, box or other container which is not marked in the manner required by subsection (2) of this section, and who knows that the package, parcel, box or other container, as the case may be, contains any thing mentioned in paragraph (a), (b) or (c) of subsection (1) of this section is guilty of an offence.

Defence

(4) In any proceedings for an offence under this section, it shall be a good defence to show that the package parcel, box or other container to which the alleged offence relates did not contain at the time of the alleged offence protected wild birds or protected wild animals other then the following, namely, a protected wild bird or an exempted wild mammal lawfully hunted by virtue of an order under section 24 or 25 of this Act or the dead body or any part of such protected wild bird of exempted wild mammal."

FAUNA AND FLORA, IMPORT OF
(WLA 1976, s. 52)

Section 52 of the WLA 1976:

"(1) The Minister may, after consultation with the Minister for Agriculture and Fisheries, by regulations prohibit the importation, save under and in accordance with a licence granted by or on behalf of the Minister under this section, of all or any of the following –
(a) any wild animal or wild bird of a species specified in the regulations,
(b) the dead body or the carcass of a wild animal or wild bird which is of a species so specified,
(c) any part, other than the carcass, or any product of a wild animal or wild bird which is a part or product so specified,
(d) the eggs or spawn of a species of wild animal or wild bird which is so specified,
(e) any plant of a species so specified,
(f) the flowers or roots of any such plant,
(g) any part, other than the flowers or roots, or any product of any such plant which is a part or product so specified.

(2) The Minister may grant to a person a licence to import any thing the importation of which is prohibited by regulations made under subsection (1) of this section.

(3) The Minister may authorise a person to grant on his behalf a licence mentioned in subsection (2) of this section.

Offence

(4) Where an animal, plant or other thing is imported in contravention of this section, an officer of Customs and Excise may require any person (being the importer or carrier concerned) to export the animal, plant or other thing within a specified time, and if such person fails to comply with such requisition he shall be guilty of an offence and the animal, plant or thing shall be killed or otherwise disposed of as the Minister directs.

(5) Nothing in this section or in section 53 of this Act shall restrict, prejudice or affect the functions of the Minister for Agriculture and Fisheries under the Destructive Insects and Pests (Consolidation) Act, 1958 (Act No 11 of 1958), the Diseases of Animals Act, 1966 (Act No 6 of 1966), or the Fisheries Acts 1959 to 1974, or the functions of the Minister for Health under the Health Act, 1947 (Act No 28 of 1947), as amended by section 34 of the Health Act, 1953 (Act No 26 of 1953)."

The statutes referred to in subsection (5) above have been extensively amended and extended since 1976 to an extent that they require specialised study.

The Wildlife Act 1976 (Control of Importation of Wild Birds) Regulations 1989 (S.I. No. 296 of 1989):

"3. Subject to Regulation 4 of these Regulations, the importation of a live wild animal, a live wild bird or the eggs or spawn of a wild animal or wild bird of any species is hereby prohibited save under and in accordance with a licence granted by or on behalf of the Minister.

4. These Regulations shall not apply to live fish or the eggs or young of fish."

FAUNA AND FLORA, EXPORT OF
(WLA 1976, s. 53)

Section 53(1) of the WLA 1976:

"(1) Subject to section 52(5) of this Act the Minister may, after consultation with the Minister for Agriculture and Fisheries, by regulations prohibit the export, save under and in accordance with a licence granted by or on behalf of the Minister under this section, of all or any of the following:

(a) protected wild birds or protected wild animals of a species specified in the regulations,
(b) the dead body or the carcass either of a protected wild bird or protected wild animal of a species so specified,
(c) any part, other than the carcass, or any product of a wild animal or wild bird which is a part or product so specified,
(d) the eggs or spawn of a species of wild animal or wild bird which is so specified,
(e) wild plants which are of a species which is so specified and to which an order under section 21 of the Act for the time being applies,
(f) the flowers or roots of any such wild plants,
(g) any part, other than the flowers and roots, or any product of any such plant which is a part or product so specified.

(2) The Minister may grant to a person a licence to export any thing the export of which is prohibited by regulations made under subsection (1) of this section.

(3) The Minister may authorise a person on his behalf to grant a licence mentioned in subsection (2) of this section.

(4) Any officer of the Minister for Posts and Telegraphs may detain and examine and if necessary open for that purpose any postal packet addressed to a place outside the State and containing, or suspected by him of containing, any thing which is being exported in contravention of this section, and if a postal packet so detained contains any such thing, the officer of the Minister for Posts and Telegraphs shall dispose of the packet and its contents in accordance with the instructions of the Minister.

(5) Nothing in this section shall restrict, prejudice or affect the functions of the Minister for Agriculture and Fisheries under the Agriculture and Fishery Products (Regulations of Export) Act, 1947, or functions which are for the time being transferred to and vested in the Minister for Industry and Commerce by an order under section 5 of that Act."

The statutes referred to in subsection (5) above have been extensively amended and extended since 1976 to an extent that they require specialised study.

The WLA 1976 (Control of Export of Fauna) Regulations, 1979 (S.I. No. 235 of 1979) provide:

"4. Subject to Regulation 5 of these Regulations, the export of any of the following is hereby prohibited save under and in accordance with a licence granted in that behalf by or on behalf of the Minister, namely:

WILD BIRDS
(a) any protected wild bird of any species other than a carrier pigeon or a racing homing pigeon,
(b) the dead body or carcass of any such bird,
(c) the eggs (whether whole or blown) or the feathers of any such bird,
(d) any stuffed specimen of any such bird.

WILD ANIMALS
(e) Any protected wild animal which is of any species of fauna mentioned in the fifth Schedule to the Act,
(f) the dead body or carcass of any such animal,
(g) any stuffed specimen of either any such animal or any part of any such animal,
(h) the skull, antlers or teeth of any deer,
(i) the eggs or spawn of the natterjack toad,
(j) the skin or fur, or any piece or cutting (including the head, tail or paw) of any skin or fur, or any article of wearing apparel or any rug or cover made wholly or partly of any skin or fur, of any badger, deer, fox, otter, pine marten, red squirrel or seal.

5. Regulation 4 of these Regulations shall not apply to –
(a) the export by a person ordinarily resident outside the State of specimens of game which an officer of the Custom and Excise is satisfied –
(i) have been shot and killed by that person under and in accordance with a valid (*qv*) hunting licence, and
(ii) are not being exported in the course of a business.
(b) the export by any person of any article of wearing apparel made wholly or partly of any skin or fur of any of the species specified in paragraph (j) of the said Regulation 4 where such article forms part of the baggage of such person and is shown to the satisfaction of the officer of the Customs and Excise to be a personal effect of such person."

Section 54 of the WLA 1976 provides that no order or regulation made under or thing done in accordance with the provisions of this Act shall absolve the importer, exporter or other person concerned with the import or export of any animal, plant or other thing from complying with the requirements of the Customs Acts in regard to the animal, plant or other thing concerned.

FEES

See: CHARGES.

FINANCIAL ASSISTANCE FOR CERTAIN WORKS, SPECIAL CONTROL AREAS
(APA 1987, s. 45)

Under section 45 of the Air Pollution Act 1987, the Minister, with the consent of the Minister for Finance, may arrange financial assistance for the whole or part of the costs incurred by an owner or occupier of premises in a (*qv*) special control area to enable compliance of the premises with the requirements of a special control area order or a notice under section 44.

FINANCIAL PROVISIONS REGARDING WASTE RECOVERY AND DISPOSAL
(WMA 1996, s. 53)

"(1) The Agency, may, before it does any of the following things, namely –
(a) decides whether to –
(i) grant a waste licence,
(ii) transfer such a licence,
(b) conducts a review of a waste licence,

require the applicant for, or the holder of, the licence or the proposed transferee, as the case may be to,
(i) to furnish to it such particulars in respect of such matters affecting his or her ability to meet the financial commitments or liabilities that the Agency reasonably considers will be entered into or incurred by

him or her in carrying on the activity to which the licence relates, or will relate, as the case may be, in accordance with the terms of the licence or the consequences of ceasing to carry on that activity, as it may specify and

(ii) make, and furnish evidence of having so made, such financial provision as it may specify (which may include the entering into of a bond or other form of security) as will, in the opinion of the Agency, be adequate to discharge the said financial commitments or liabilities.

Offence

(2) A person who, pursuant to a requirement made of him or her under subsection (1), furnishes to the Agency any particulars or evidence which he or she knows to be false or misleading in a material respect shall be guilty of an offence.

(3) The Minister may make regulations for the purposes of this section.

(4) Without prejudice to the generality of subsection (3), regulations under this section may specify by reference to the type of activity to which the waste licence concerned relates or will relate –

(a) the nature of the financial provision that the Agency may require a person to make under subsection (1)(ii).

(b) the matters to be had regard to by the Agency in determining the amount of financial provision that it may require a person to make under subsection (1)(ii)."

FINES AND IMPRISONMENT (IMPOSITION OF)

(F(C)A 1959/LG(WP)A 1977/WLA 1977
APA 1987/EPAA 1992/WMA 1996)

This entry covers fines and terms of imprisonment which may be imposed on conviction of offences under in Fisheries Acts 1959–1999, the Local Government (Water Pollution) Acts 1977 and 1990, the Wildlife Act 1976, the Environmental Protection Agency Act 1992 , the Foreshore Act 1933, the Waste Management Act 1996, the NH 97 Regulations and the Mammalian Animal Waste Regulations.

The following categories of headings have been chosen for this entry:

(1) Fines Imposed Under Fisheries Act 1959
(2) Indictable Offences Under F(A)A 1962 and FA 1980
(3) Pollution Offences – Sections 171 and 172 of the F(C)A 1959
(4) Increase of Penalties under the F(A)A 1994
(5) Table of offences and penalties imposed under Fisheries (Consolidation) Act 1959, as amended.
(6) New offences created by F(A)A 1991 F(A)A 1997 and F(A)A 1999.
(7) Penalties under LG(WP)A 1977 and LG(WP)(A)A 1990
(8) Penalties under WLA 1976
(9) Penalties under APA 1987
(10) Penalties under EPAA 1992
(11) Increase of certain Penalties under the EPAA 1992
(12) Penalties under WMA 1996
(13) Penalties under Foreshore Acts.
(14) Penalties for offences under NH 97 Regulations
(15) Penalties under Mammalian Animal Waste Regulations.

(1) FINES ORIGINALLY IMPOSED UNDER FISHERIES ACT 1959

The monumental Fisheries (Consolidation) Act 1959 contains a large number of offence sections and each section which creates an offence provides in the same section for the penalties and statutory consequences of conviction as was then customary.

All but a handful of these penalties have been increased, first by section 32 of the F(A)A 1962 and then by section 50 of the FA 1980. Both section 32 and section 50 achieved these increases by reference to a Schedule within each section the format of which was similar.

In the few cases where there was no increase of penalty, due mainly to the fact that the section was never if ever used, the penalty is given in the actual text accompanying the offence section.

(2) INDICTABLE OFFENCES UNDER F(A)A 1962 AND FA 1980

Indictable offences created by Fisheries (Amendment) Act 1962:

Offences triable on indictment and the penalties on conviction under the Fisheries Acts are as follows:

(a) By virtue of section 16 of the F(A)A 1962, section 164 of the F(C)A 1959. Penalty: Fine of £500 or two years imprisonment or both.
(b) By virtue of section 24 of the F(A)A

1962, section 285A of the F(C)A 1959. Penalty: Fine of £500 or two years imprisonment or both.

(c) By virtue of section 46(1) of the FA 1980, sections 56, 66, 69, 73, 94, 96, 97, 127, 128, 129, 130, 132, 134, 135, 137, 140, 145, 146, 156, 176, 177 and 182. Penalty: Fine of £2,000 or two years imprisonment or both. These penalties are imposed by section 50(3) of the FA 1980.

(d) By virtue of section 46(2) of the FA 1980, section 28 of the F(A)A 1962. Penalty: fine of £2,000 together with an amount not exceeding £50 for each salmon and £5 for each trout in respect of which the offence was committed or two years imprisonment or both.

(e) By virtue of section 46(4) of the FA 1980, certain specified bye-laws made under section 9 of the F(C)A 1959 dealing with the use of drift nets and monofilament nets. penalty: £2,000 or two years imprisonment or both.

(f) By virtue of section 25 of the LG(WP)(A)A 1990, sections 171 and 172 of the F(C)A 1959 dealing with water pollution. Penalty: £25,000 or five years imprisonment or both.

Section 46(5) provides that any reference to summary conviction in any section of the 1959 Act mentioned in section 46(1) above, or in section 28 or 29 of the 1962 Act, shall be construed as if the reference therein to summary conviction included a reference to conviction on indictment. Section 46(6) makes similar provision as regards section 9(4) of the 1959 Act (which makes offences under bye-laws made under that section subject to summary conviction).

Section 46(7) provides that subsections (1)–(4) above are in addition to and not in substitution for section 309(1) of the 1959 Act (as inserted by section 49 of the 1980 Act). The effect of this provision is to ensure that offences, though triable on indictment, can also be tried summarily.

This ramshackle structure of indictable offences which was so laboriously introduced in the 60s and 80s to answer the then perceived threat to salmon and trout stock at sea was never used or if it was the prosecutions were a rarity. The only exception to this is (f) where recent decisions have copperfastened prosecutions under sections 171 and 172 as the really effective style of prosecution in respect of water pollution.
See: PROHIBITION (1) WATERS UNDER THE F(C)A 1959

The protection of salmon and trout at sea is now effectively controlled by the *(qv)* Salmon and Trout Conservation Bye-law of 1998.

(3) POLLUTION OFFENCES – SECTIONS 171 AND 172 OF THE F(C)A 1959

Sections 171 and 172 of the Fisheries (Consolidation) Act 1959 relate to the protection of fishing waters from pollution. These sections were not affected by the Fisheries (Amendment) Act 1962 or the Fisheries Act 1980.

Section 25 of the Local Government (Water Pollution) (Amendment) Act 1990 made offences under sections 171 and 172 of the 1959 Act triable on indictment with greatly increased penalties, being a maximum fine of £25,000 or imprisonment for a term not exceeding 5 years, or both. The maximum penalties and imprisonment which may be imposed on summary conviction were set at £1,000and six months or both.

(4) INCREASE OF PENALTIES UNDER F(A)A 1994

Section 19 of the F(A)A 1994 amends section 100 of the F(C)A 1959 by substituting subsection (3) and (4) which provide on summary conviction, in the case of subsection (3), for the use of a fishing weir, fishing mill dam or a *(qv)* fixed engine in contravention of the section a maximum fine of £1,000 and if after conviction the offence is continued on each day during which the contravention continues to a fine not exceeding £500 and, in the case of subsection (4)*(e)*, where there is a failure by the holder of an eel fishery authorisation to comply with the conditions attached to the authorisation a fine not exceeding £1,000. There is also provision for forfeiture of catch and fishing engine as a statutory consequence of conviction.

Section 20 of the F(A)A 1994 increases penalties imposed under sections 157(2), 162 and 163(4) of the F(C)A 1959 as follows:

Section 163A(1) of the F(C)A 1959, inserted into Part X of the F(C)A 1959 by section 20(1) of F(A)A 1994, buying, when not the holder of a Part X licence, salmon, trout, eels or molluscan shellfish, on summary conviction to a fine not exceeding £1000 in all, of an amount not exceeding £500 together with an amount not exceeding £50 for each salmon, £50 for each kilogram of eels or molluscan shellfish and £100 for each other fish.

Section 163A(3) of the F(C)A 1959 a person buying who purports to be an agent of the holder of a Part X licence who refuses or fails to produce his authorisation or to permit the inspector to read same on summary conviction to a fine not exceeding £500 and subsection (5) a person selling who gives a false or misleading statement in writing on summary conviction to a fine not exceeding £500. *See:* CERTIFICATE OF FITNESS.

Section 21 of the F(A)A 1994 amends section 182(4) of the F(C)A 1959, which subsection, as amended, now provides:

"(4) Every person guilty of an offence under subsection (1), (2), or (3) of this section shall be liable on summary conviction thereof to a fine not exceeding £500 together with an amount not exceeding £50 for each salmon, £50 for each kilogram of eels or molluscan shellfish and £10 for each trout in respect of which the offence under the section is committed, not exceeding in all £1000 or at the discretion of the court, or imprisonment for a term not exceeding twelve months or to both such fine and such imprisonment.."

Section 22 of the F(A)A 1994 amends sections 183(4) of the F(C)A 1959, which provides for breach of that section. It provides in the case of summary conviction for a first offence to a fine not exceeding £500 and in the case of a second or subsequent offence to a fine not exceeding £1000 or 6 months imprisonment or both. *See:* MARKING PACKAGES.

(5) TABLE OF OFFENCES AND PENALTIES IMPOSED UNDER FISHERIES (CONSOLIDATION) ACT, 1959 AS AMENDED

The following is a table of offences and penalties imposed on summary conviction for various offences under the Fisheries (Consolidation) Act 1959, as amended by the Fisheries (Amendment) Act 1962, the Fisheries Act 1980, the Fisheries (Amendment) Act 1991 and the Fisheries (Amendment) Act 1994.

This table is based on the similar such table set out in the table to section 50 of the Fisheries Act 1980.

The penalties imposed on conviction on indictment (where applicable) are specified in parenthesis in the table with the section number(s) indicated by means of an asterisk. Where penalties on conviction for existing offences in the 1959 Act have been increased under the F(A)A 1994, the section numbers and fines so increased are indicated by means of an asterisk and material in bold type.

Part I of the table relates to sections of the F(C)A 1959.

Part II of the table relates to sections of the F(A)A 1962.

TABLE

PART I

12, 13, 80, 289, 305
A fine not exceeding £50

49, 105, 106, 152,
153, 162*, 240, 241,
242, 243, 255, 265,
286, 287, 288, 290,
294, 298, 303, 304,
306, 323.
A fine not exceeding £200 (a fine not exceeding £500)
17, 65*, 66*, 73*,
91, 92, 93, 112, 113,
119, 120, 121, 122,
125, 130*, 140*, 141,
143, 144, 145*, 146*,
163*, 167, 168, 169,
178, 179, 180, 181,
237, 238, 239, 253,
273, 274, 277, 285,
291.
A fine not exceeding £500
(£2,000.00/two years or both)
(a fine not exceeding £500 or, in the case of a second or any subsequent offence, to a fine not exceeding £1000)

69*, 123*, 128*, 129*.
A fine not exceeding £500 and in the case of a continuous offence, a further fine (not exceeding in all £600) not exceeding £50 for each day during which the offence is continued.
(£2000.00/two years or both)

100
A fine not exceeding £500 and in the case of a continuing offence, a further fine (not exceeding in all £600) not exceeding £100 for each day during which the offence is continued.

111
A fine not exceeding £500 and a further fine (not exceeding in all £600) not exceeding £10 per day until the defendant restores the bed of the river in respect of which the offence under the said section 111 is committed to its original state.

124
A fine not exceeding £500 and a further fine (not exceeding in all £600) not exceeding £50 for each day during which the neglect referred to in the said section 124 continues.

172*
A fine not exceeding £500 and a further fine (not exceeding in all £600) not exceeding £50 for each day during which the failure referred to in the said section 172 continues.

(For s. 172 see s. 25 of the LG(WP)(A)A 1990 above).

127*, 134*, 135*, 136,
137*, 138, 177*
A fine (not exceeding in all £600) of an amount not exceeding £500 together with an amount not exceeding £50 for each salmon and £10 for each other fish in respect of which the offence under the section is committed.
(£2000.00/two years or both)
94*
A fine (not exceeding in all £600) of an amount not exceeding £500 together with an amount not exceeding £50 for each salmon and £10 for each other fish caught by means of any net used in the commission of the offence under the said section 94.
(£2000.00/two years or both)

95*, 96*, 97*, 99, 102,
103, 104, 107, 110,
114, 116, 131, 132*,
164*, 165, 166, 170,
171*, 173, 174, 183*,
285A*, 301, 308.
A fine not exceeding £500 or, at the discretion of the court, imprisonment for any term not exceeding six months or both such fine and such imprisonment.
(£2000.00/two years or both)
(in case of the first offence, a fine not exceeding £500 and in the case of a second or a subsequent offence a fine not exceeding £1000 or six months imprisonment or both)

(for s. 171 see s. 25 of the LG(WP)(A)A 1990)

156*, 157*, 176*, 182**
A fine (not exceeding in all £600) of an amount not exceeding £50 for each salmon and £10 for each other fish in respect of which the offence under the section is committed or, at the discretion of the Court, imprisonment for a term not exceeding six months or both such fine and such imprisonment.
(£2000.00/two years or both)
(a fine not exceeding £500 together with an amount not exceeding £50 for each salmon, or each kilogram of eels or molluscan shellfish and £10 for each other fish not exceeding £1000 in all or 12 months imprisonment or both)

PART II

27
A fine not exceeding £100

28(1)*
A fine (not exceeding in all £600) of an amount not exceeding £200 together with an amount not exceeding £50 for each salmon and £10 for each trout in respect of which the offence is committed.
(£2000.00/two years or both)

28(3), 28(5)
A fine not exceeding £200.

29*
A fine not exceeding £500 or, at the discretion of the court, imprisonment for any term not exceeding six months or both such fine and such imprisonment.
(£2000.00/two years or both)

(6) NEW OFFENCES CREATED BY F(A)A 1991 AND F(A)A 1997

The Fisheries (Amendment) Act 1991 and Fisheries (Amendment) Act 1997 created new offences and some increased penalties as follows:

Section 15 of the F(A)A 1991, sets out the penalties which may be imposed for offences under sections 9 and 12(3) of that Act, provides on summary conviction for a fine not exceeding £1,000 and imprisonment for a term not exceeding 12 months or both. On conviction on indictment, the section provides for a fine of such amount as the court may impose or imprisonment for a term not exceeding five years or both. *See:* FISHERIES CO-OPERATIVE.

Section 6(2) of the F(A)A 1997 provides in relation to an offence an offence under section 6(1) of that Act (engaging in aquaculture without appropriate licence) which attracts the general penalty under section 65 that if the offence is continued for every day on which it continues and for each further offence on summary conviction to a fine not exceeding £200 and on conviction on indictment to a fine not exceeding £1,000.

Section 65(2) of the F(A)A 1997 provides for conviction of an offence under subsection (1) or any other provision of the Act for which no other penalty is prescribed, a penalty:

(a) on summary conviction, to a fine not exceeding £1,500, or to imprisonment for a term not exceeding 12 months, or both, or
(b) on conviction on indictment, to fine not exceeding £100,000 or to imprisonment for a term not exceeding two years, or both.

(Subsection (1) of section 65 of the F(A)A 1997 provides that a person who contravenes or fails to comply with a term of a licence or a condition subject to which it is issued will be guilty of an offence).

Under **section 24(5) of the F(A)A 1999** for obstructing or impeding an authorised officer, failing to comply with a requirement or refusing to give name and address on summary conviction to a fine not exceeding £1,500. Under **section 24(6)(b) of the F(A)A 1999** for failure to comply with an regulation or provision thereof made under the section on summary conviction of a fine not exceeding £1,500 or imprisonment for a term not exceeding 6 months or to both. The Fisheries (Amendment) Act, 1999 (save for section 23) came into force on 20 December 1999 by virtue of the Fisheries (Amendment) Act, 1999 (Commencement) Order, 1999 (S.I. No. 419 of 1999).

(7) PENALTIES UNDER LG(WP)A 1977 AND LG(WP)(A)A 1990

In the LG(WP)A 1977, various offences and penalties are prescribed.

Section 24 of the LG(WP)(A)A 1990 increased all of the penalties on conviction on indictment under the 1977 Act.

Section 24 provides:

"(1) A person guilty of an offence under section 3, 4 or 16 of the Principal Act shall, in lieu of the penalty specified in the section concerned, be liable –
(a) on summary conviction a fine not exceeding £1,000 or imprisonment for a term not exceeding six months imprisonment, or both, or
(b) on conviction on indictment to a fine not exceeding £25,000 or a term not exceeding five years imprisonment, or both.

(2) A person guilty of an offence under section 6, 12, 19, 27 or 28(4) of the Principal Act shall, in lieu of the penalty specified in the section concerned, be liable on summary conviction to a fine not exceeding £1,000 or imprisonment for a term not exceeding six months, or both.

(3) A person guilty of an offence under section 14 of the Principal Act shall, in lieu of the penalty specified in the section concerned, be liable on summary conviction to a fine not exceeding £1,000.

(4) This section shall have effect as respects offences committed after the commencement of this section."

Sections 3(2)*(b)*, 4(8)*(b)* and 16(8)*(b)* of the Local Government (Water Pollution) Act 1977 refer to conviction on indictment. The Principal Act is the LG(WP)A 1977.

Section 21(3) of the LG(WP)(A)A 1990, which is the only provision that provides for an offence and penalty under the 1990 Act, provides as follows:

"(3) (a) A person who contravenes or fails to comply with bye-laws under subsection (2) shall be guilty of an offence.
(b) A person guilty of an offence under this subsection shall be liable –
(i) on summary conviction, a fine not exceeding £1,000 or imprisonment for six months or to both,
(ii) if the offence is a contravention of or failure to comply with a bye-law prohibiting the carrying on of a specified activity or a bye-law relating to a matter referred to in subsection (2)(c), on conviction on indictment, to a fine not exceeding £25,000 or to imprisonment for a term not exceeding five years or to both."

Subsection (2)*(c)* relates to breaches of conditions attached to bye-laws made under section 21 of the 1990 Act.
See: AGRICULTURAL ACTIVITIES.

Section 21A(11) of the LG(WP)(A)A 1990, inserted by section 66(3) of the WMA 1996, provides for a penalty on summary conviction of a failure to comply with a notice under section 21A(1) or (8) of the LG(WP)(A)A 1990 of £1,000 or imprisonment for a term not exceeding six months, or both.

(8) PENALTIES UNDER WLA 1976

In the WLA 1976 the section providing for the penalty is separate from the section creating the offence.

Section 74 of the WLA 1976 provides, in subsection (1), that in cases of a person being found guilty of an offence under the 1976 Act not being an offence mentioned in subsection (2) or (3) of that section, he shall be liable on summary conviction:

(a) in the case of a first offence under the particular section or subsection a fine not exceeding £50,
(b) in the case of a second such offence a fine not exceeding £100,
(c) in the case of a third or subsequent such offence a fine not exceeding £200.

Section 74(2) provides that in the case of all offences under section 69(2) because of a contravention of, or for failure to comply with regulations under section 59 or an offence committed under the Act on land to which an (*qv*) establishment order, a (*qv*) recognition order, a (*qv*) designation order or a (*qv*) management agreement under section 18 relates, the penalty on summary conviction is a fine of £250 and on conviction on indictment a fine of £500.

Section 74 provides, in subsection (3), that where offences are committed under section 21(4), 22(4),23(5), 44(1), 45, 51, 52 or 53 and the flora or fauna in relation to which the offence was committed is of a species for the time being declared by regulations under this section to be a species to which this subsection relates and the particular species to which the offence relates is of a species to which such regulations apply, the penalty on summary conviction is a fine of £250 and on conviction on indictment a fine of £500.

(9) PENALTIES UNDER APA 1987

In the APA 1987 the section providing for the penalty is separate from the section which creates the offence. This section is section 12.

Section 12 of the APA 1987 provides that the penalty on summary conviction is a fine not exceeding £1000, a continuing fine not exceeding £100 a day for a continuing offence, but not exceeding in all £1,000, and imprisonment for a term not exceeding six months.

The penalty on conviction on indictment is a fine not exceeding £10,000, a continuing fine of £1,000 a day or imprisonment for any term not exceeding two years.

(10) PENALTIES UNDER EPAA 1992

Section 8 deals with offences under the EPAA 1992 and section 9 specifies the penalties under that Act. Section 9(1)*(b)* of the EPAA 1992 provides for conviction on indictment.

Section 9(1)(a) provides that the penalty on summary conviction is a fine not exceeding £1000, or 12 months imprisonment or both; Section 9(1)(b) provides that the penalty on conviction on indictment is a fine not exceeding £10,000,000 or to imprisonment for any term not exceeding 10 years or both.

Section 9(2) provides that in imposing a penalty under subsection (1) the court shall, in particular, have regard to the risk or extent of damage to the environment arising from the act or omission constituting the offence.

Section 9(3) provides that the penalty for a continuing offence, for every day, on summary conviction is a fine not exceeding £200 a day and on conviction on indictment, for every day, a fine not exceeding £100,000 a day.

(11) INCREASE OF CERTAIN PENALTIES UNDER THE EPAA 1992

Section 113 of the EPAA 1992 provides for the increase of certain penalties by reference to the Table to the section as follows:

The Waterworks Clauses Act 1847, sections 55, 58 and 60 increased to £1,000. The Dublin Corporation Waterworks Act 1861, section 51 increased to £1000. The Waterworks Clauses Act 1863 sections 17, 18, 19 and 20 increased to £1,000. The Public Health (Ireland) Act 1878, sections 70 and 112 increased to £1,000, section 114 increased to £200 and sections 119, 171, 220, 272 and 273 increased to £1,000. The Local Government (Sanitary Services) Act 1948 sections 31, 33, 34, 37, 42, 44, 46, 47, 4, 8, 3, and 16 increased to £1,000.

Section 113(2)*(b)* provides that in the case of a continuing or further offence the penalty for each day on which the contravention continues shall, in lieu of any other monetary penalty, forfeiture or fine provided in respect thereof, be a fine not exceeding £200.

Section 113(3) provides that the section shall have effect in relation to offences committed after the date of commencement of the section.

(12)PENALTIES UNDER WMA 1996

Section 10 of the WMA 1996 provides the following penalties:

Under subsection (1):

(a) on summary conviction, to a fine not exceeding £1,500, or to imprisonment for a term not exceeding 12 months or both such fine and such imprisonment, or
(b) on conviction on indictment, to a fine not exceeding £10,000,000 or to imprisonment for a term not exceeding 10 years or to both such fine and such imprisonment above.

Section 10(2) provides for summary conviction only under sections 16(5), 32(6) (where the offence consists of a contravention of regulations under subsection (4) of that section), 33(8), 38(7) or 40(13) and a fine of £1,500 or twelve months imprisonment or both.

Section 10(3) provides for a penalty for continuing offences after conviction, the person shall be guilty of a further offence on every day on which the contravention continues, and for each such offence the person shall be liable, on summary conviction to a fine not exceeding £200 or (in a case to which subsection (1) applies) on conviction on indictment to a fine nor exceeding £100,000.

Section 10(4) provides that in imposing any penalty the court shall, in particular have regard to the risk or extent of *(qv)* environmental pollution arising from the act or omission constituting the offence.

(13) PENALTIES UNDER FORESHORE ACTS

Section 6(5) of the Foreshore Act 1933, as amended by section 3 of the Foreshore (Amendment) Act 1992, provides the following penalties for contravention of the subsection -

(a) on summary conviction, to a fine not exceeding £1,000 or to imprisonment for a term not exceeding six months, or both,
(b) on conviction on indictment, to a fine not exceeding –
    (i) £100,000, in the case of a first offence under the section, and
    (ii) £200,000 in the case of a second or subsequent offence under the section, or to imprisonment for a term not exceeding five years, or to both.

Section 7(3) of the Foreshore Act 1933, as amended by section 4 of the Foreshore (Amendment) Act, 1992, provides the same penalties as in section 6(5) above for contravention of the subsection.

Sections 13(2) and 14(2) of the Foreshore Act 1933, as amended by section 5(2) of the Fisheries and Foreshore (Amendment) Act 1998, for an offence under section 13(2) or (4) or section 14 (2), provides for the following penalties:

(a) on summary conviction to a fine not exceeding £1,500 or to imprisonment for a term not exceeding 12 months, or to both, or
(b) on conviction on indictment, to a fine not exceeding £100,000, or to imprisonment for a term not exceeding two years, or to both.

Section 6(2) of the Foreshore (Amendment) Act 1992 provides for failure to comply with an order under subsection (1) on summary conviction a penalty of a fine not exceeding £1,000 or imprisonment for a term not exceeding six months, or to both.

(14) PENALTIES FOR OFFENCES UNDER NH 97 REGULATIONS

Regulation 39 of the NH 97 Regulations (S.I. No. 94 of 1997) provides penalties for offences as follows:

(a) under Regulation 11 on summary conviction to a fine not exceeding £1,000, or
(b) under any other provisions on summary conviction to a fine not exceeding £1,500 or to six months imprisonment or to both.

(15) PENALTIES UNDER MAMMALIAN ANIMAL WASTE REGULATIONS

See: WASTE, MAMMALIAN ANIMAL.

Regulation 10 of the European Communities (Mammalian Animal Waste) Regulations 1998 (S.I. No. 2 of 1998) and Regulation 11 of the European Communities (Processing of Mammalian Animal Waste) Regulations 1998 (S.I. No. 62 of 1998) provide for contravention of any of the Regulations on summary conviction a fine of £1,500 or imprisonment for a term not exceeding six months or both.

FINES (DISPOSAL OF)

FISHERIES ACTS

Section 314 of the F(C)A 1959 provides that every fine imposed under the Act shall be paid into or disposed of for the benefit of the Exchequer as the Minister for Finance shall direct and if a fine has been remitted after it has been paid into the Exchequer it shall be repaid out of the Exchequer as the Minister for Finance shall direct.

Section 315(1) of the F(C)A 1959, having first excluded from its provisions offences under various specified Parts and sections of the Act, provides for a system in relation to the disposal of fines as follows –

(a) where it appears to the Minister that a member of the Garda Síochána was the means of bringing to justice the person by whom the offence was committed then one-third of the fine is paid to the Garda Síochána Reward Fund and two-thirds to the local fisheries board,

(b) in any other case the fine is paid to the fisheries board.

Subsection (2) provides that the monies payable under this section are paid by the Minister out of monies provided by the Oireachtas as he thinks fit.

LG(WP)(A)A 1990

Section 26 of the LGWP(A)A 1990 provides for payment of the fine imposed under the LG(WP)A 1977 and the LG(WP)(A)A 1990 to the prosecutor of the offence *i.e.*, (*qv*) local authority, (*qv*) sanitary authority or (*qv*) regional fisheries board, but only by order following an application made before the time of imposition of the fine and further provides that the order for payment of the fine can be enforced by the authority or board, as the case may be, as if it were due on foot of a decree or order made by a court in civil proceedings.

EPAA 1992

Section 10 of the EPAA 1992 also contains a provision for an application for the payment of the fine to the prosecutor who, under the EPAA 1992, is the (*qv*) Agency to whom the fines are ordered to be paid. Again the application must be made before the imposition of the fine and again it can be recovered by the Agency as if it were a civil decree.

WMA 1996

Section 13 of the WMA 1996 has a similar provision. In the WMA 1996 the prosecutor can be the Agency, a local authority or a person specified under section 11(2).

FIREARM
(WLA 1976, s. 2(1))

"means any lethal firearm or other lethal weapon of any description (including an airgun) from which any shot, bullet, slug or other missile can be discharged."

**FIREARMS,
RESTRICTIONS
ON USE OF**
(WLA 1976, s. 33)

Offences
provides for a series of offences in relation to firearms and other guns as follows –

(1) It shall be an offence for a person to kill or injure–
  (a) with a repeating or automatic shotgun (other than a repeating or automatic shotgun which is adapted or modified so as to render it incapable of carrying more than three shotgun cartridges), with an (*qv*) airgun, air-rifle, gas-rifle, pistol or revolver, or with any firearm fitted with a silencer device, any (*qv*) wild bird,
  (b) with a rifle, any (*qv*) protected wild bird.

(2) It shall be an offence for a person to kill or injure any wild bird or (*qv*) wild mammal with a spring gun, or with tracer shot or with a floating container containing an explosive substance.

(3) It shall be an offence for a person to kill or injure with a shotgun a protected wild animal other than a hare.

(4) Subject to the foregoing subsections of this section, the Minister may make regulations specifying the type and calibre of firearms and ammunition which may be used to hunt wild birds and wild mammals and providing that firearms and ammunition of any other type and calibre shall not be used to hunt such birds or mammals.

(5) In this section 'rifle' includes both a gas-rifle and an air-rifle.

**FIREARMS,
HUNTING OR KILLING**
(WLA 1976, s. 28)

Deals with restrictions on hunting or killing with firearms.

See: PROTECTION, HUNTING OR KILLING WITH FIREARMS.

FIREARMS AND AMMUNITION REGULATIONS 1977
(WLA 1977)

Wildlife Act, 1976 (Firearms and Ammunition) Regulations 1977 (S.I. No. 239 of 1977) provide that:

"(2) (a) The firearms and ammunition of the type and calibre specified in the Schedule to these Regulations may be used to hunt deer species.
(b) Firearms and ammunition of any type and calibre other than the type and calibre specified in the Schedule to these Regulations shall not be used to hunt deer species

SCHEDULE

Firearms
Centre-fire rifles of not less than .22 calibre with a muzzle energy of not less than 1,700 foot pounds.

Ammunition
Any bullet for use in such rifles, weighing not less than 55 grains."

FIREARMS, LICENCE TO HUNT WITH
(WLA 1976, s. 29)

"(1) Subject to section 75(1) of this Act, the Minister may, if he thinks fit, grant to a person ordinarily resident in the State, who when making the application makes a declaration in a form approved of for the purposes of this section by the Minister, a licence (operating in the manner specified in subsection (4) of this section) to hunt and kill with firearms, subject to the restrictions contained in section 33 of this Act, (*qv*) exempted wild mammals, (other than hares)."

For section 75, *see:* REVOCATION OF LICENCES, PERMITS AND CERTIFICATES. For section 33, *see:* FIREARMS, RESTRICTIONS ON USE OF.

Subsection (2) provides for the grant, in the same circumstances, to a person ordinarily resident outside the State, who makes the same declaration as is provided for in subsection (1), of a licence to hunt and kill with firearms, subject also to section 33, exempted wild mammals and protected wild birds to which an order under section 24 for the time being applies.

For section 24, *see:* OPEN SEASONS.

Subsection (3) provides that in determining an application for a licence or renewal under subsections (1), (2) or (6) of this section, the Minister shall have regard to the conservation requirements of the species of protected wild birds or exempted wild mammals concerned and to the suitability of the applicant having regard to those requirements or to the purposes of this Act.

Subsection (4) provides that a licence granted or renewed under the section remains in force until the next following July 31 and operates to authorise the holder of the licence to hunt and kill with firearms any (*qv*) fauna to which the licence relates pursuant to and in accordance with such orders (if any) made under sections 24 or 25 of this Act as are for the time being in force.

For sections 24 and 25, *see:* OPEN SEASONS.

Subsection (5) provides:

"(5) Where a person applies to a Superintendent of the Garda Síochána for the grant under section 3 of the Firearms Act, 1925, of a firearm certificate or the renewal under section 9 of the Firearms Act, 1964, of such a certificate and when making the application for such certificate or renewal the person makes a declaration referred to in subsection (1) of this section, the certificate shall, if it is endorsed in the manner described in subsection (8) of this section, for the purposes of sections 22(4) and 23(5) of this Act be deemed to be a licence granted by the Minister under this section and, subject to section 75(1) and to the restrictions contained in section 33 of this Act, such certificate shall, for so long as it is in force, operate to authorise the person to whom it is granted, with the firearm to which the certificate relates –
(a) to hunt and kill pursuant to any order under section 24 of this Act which is for the time being in force any protected wild bird,
(b) to hunt and kill pursuant to and in accordance with any order under section 25 of the Act which is in force any hare."

For section 22, *see:* PROTECTION, PROTECTED WILD BIRDS; for section 23, *see:* PROTECTION, PROTECTED WILD ANIMALS.

Subsection (8) provides for the indorsement

required by subsection (g) as follows:

"(8) Where a firearm certificate is granted to a person described in subsection (5) of this section, there shall be endorsed on the certificate the following:

"This certificate, for so long as it is in force, authorises the person to whom it is granted, with the firearm to which it relates –

(a) to hunt and kill pursuant to any order under section 24 of the Wildlife Act, 1976 which is for the time being in force any protected wild bird,

(b) to hunt and kill pursuant to and in accordance with any order made under section 25 of the said Act which is so in force any hare."

Subsection (9) provides for recognition by Ministerial regulation of licences of other countries or territories or their recognition of our licences in accordance with any convention, protocol or agreement between the State and those countries or territories.

Subsection (10) places an obligation on a licence holder to give the Minister certain information such as a statement of the number of species of protected wild birds and protected wild animals shot and taken by him during a specified period in such place as may be specified when required either by notice in writing or publication in a daily newspaper.

Offence

Subsection (11) provides that failure to comply with a requirement of the Minister under subsection (10) constitutes an offence.

Subsection (12) provides that nothing in the section shall be construed as affecting anything contained in the Firearms Acts.

FIREARMS (TEMPORARY PROVISIONS) ACT 1998

In 1998, following on successful action brought in the High Court by the National Association of Regional Gun Clubs against the Minister and the Minister for Tourism, who had been issuing licences to non-nationals in blatant contravention of section 29 of the WLA 1976, it became necessary to pass the Firearms (Temporary Provisions) Act.

The Firearms (Temporary Provisions) Act 1998

Section 4 provides for the construction of the Act as one with both the Firearms Acts 1925 to 1990 (other than the Firearms (Proofing) Act 1998) and the WLA 1976 and that the Act shall expire on the day that is 12 months after the date of its passing, July 13, 1998, but the Government (not the Minister) can by order extend the Act for a period not exceeding 12 months from the date on which it ceases to have effect.

Section 2 deals with section 29 of the WLA 1976 as follows:

"(1) Notwithstanding subsection (3) of section 29 of the Wildlife Act, 1976, and subject to this section, the Minister, before granting a licence under subsection (2), or renewing a licence under subsection (6), of that section to a person ordinarily resident outside the State, shall be of the opinion that the application is bona fide and that there is no good reason to refuse to grant the licence or renew it.

(2) The Minister may, for the purpose of establishing that there is no good reason to refuse to grant or renew a licence under section 29 of the Wildlife Act, 1976, treat any of the following as *prima facie* evidence of suitability to so grant or renew:

(a) where the person is resident in a Member State of the European Community other than the State, any European Firearms Pass duly issued to such person to which paragraphs (4) and (5) of Regulation 7 of the European Communities (Acquisition and Possession of Weapons and Ammunition) Regulations, 1993 (S.I. No. 362 of 1993) relate, or

(b) In any case, any other permit, licence, authorisation or other document duly issued by an appropriate authority or body outside the State which the Minister considers acceptable.

(3) The Minister may make such enquiries as he or she considers appropriate as to the suitability of any applicant ordinarily resident outside the State for a licence under section 29 of the Wildlife Act, 1976.

(4) In this section 'the Minister' means the Minister for Arts, Heritage, Gaeltacht and the Islands."

'The Minister' in section 1 of the Act which deals with a similar "loosening" of procedures under sections 4 and 8 of the Firearms Act 1925, as amended, is the Minister for Justice, Equality and Law Reform.

The result of this Act is that firearms certificates can now be issued at will by local Tourist offices to any person who is ordinarily resident outside the State on production, for example, of any foreign driving licence if the Minister considers this to be appropriate.

FISH
(F(C)A 1959, s. 3(1))

As amended by section 16 of the F(A)A 1978, fish

"includes all marine invertebrates, all crustaceans and molluscs found in the sea, and brood and spawn of fish, and references to a fish shall be construed as including references to part of a fish."

(LG(WP)A 1977, s. 1(1))

Has the same meaning as in the Fisheries Acts 1959 to 1976.

FISH CULTURE LICENCES
(F(C)A 1959, ss. 15 and 15A)

Repealed by section 5(1) and (2) respectively of the F(A)A 1997. *See:* OYSTERS.

FISH, LIVE, RESTRICTION ON IMPORT
(F(C)A 1959, s. 17)

"(1) The Minister may, whenever and so often as he thinks fit, by order (in this section referred to a restriction on import (fish) order) prohibit the import of any specified kind of article to which this section applies otherwise than under and in accordance with a licence in that behalf issued under this section."

Subsection (2) provides that the Minister may by order under this subsection revoke or amend any order made by him under this section.

Offence
Subsection (3) creates the offence of importing in contravention of an order under the section.

Subsection (4) provides for the issue of a licence and subsection (5) provides that the section applies to the following articles, live fish or other aquatic animals, and the eggs or young of fish or other aquatic animals.

FISH PASS
(F(C)A 1959, s. 3(1))

"means a channel for the free run or migration of fish in, over or in connection with an obstruction in a river, lake or watercourse and includes a fish ladder or any other contrivance which facilities the passage of fish." *See:* DAMS.

FISHERIES ACTS, 1959 AND 1980 AND AMENDING ACTS
(F(C)A 1959)

The long title of the Fisheries (Consolidation) Act 1959 (No. 14 of 1959) is:

"An Act to consolidate the Fisheries Acts 1842 to 1958, and certain other enactments relating to fisheries [8th July 1958]".

By virtue of section 2(1), the 1959 Act came into operation, except for the provisions postponed by section 2(2), on the October 1, 1959.

The postponed provisions are, sections 16, 24(3), 39, 61, 72, 79 to 84, 185 to 191, 192(1), 194(2) 195, 196, 198 to 209, 216, 218 and 305. All of these postponed sections except for section 16(1) and (2) (which deal with leases of fisheries for research purposes) have been repealed over the years.

The long title of the Fisheries Act 1980 (Act No. 1 of 1980) is:

"An Act to establish a body to be known as the Central Fisheries Board and to define its functions, to enable regional fisheries boards to be established and the define their functions, to dissolve Iontaobhas Iascaigh Intíre Ioncorportha (The Inland Fisheries Trust Incorporated) and certain boards of conservators established by the Fisheries (Consolidation) Act, 1959, to amend section 59 of the Foyle Fisheries Act, 1952, to provide for other matters connected with the foregoing and otherwise to amend and extend the Fisheries Acts 1959 to 1978 [18th March 1980]."

Unless otherwise specified, the provisions of the FA 1980 entered into force on the date of passing of the Act. However, various provisions in the Act are stated to take effect only as from the "appointed day". The "appointed day" under section 3 of the FA 1980 was October 29, 1980 by virtue of the Fisheries Act 1980 (Appointed Day) Order 1980 (S.I. No. 323 of 1980).

Section 69 of the FA 1980, the operation of

which was postponed by section 69(4), came into operation on January 1, 1981 by virtue of Fisheries Act 1980 (Section 69) Commencement Day, Order 1980 (S.I. No. 414 of 1980).

FISHERIES (AMENDMENT) ACTS DATING FROM 1959 TO 1999

There were Fisheries Amendment Acts in 1959S, 1962, 1963S, 1964, 1970S, 1974, 1976, 1978S, 1983, 1987, 1987(No. 2), 1991, 1994, 1995, 1997 and 1999. In addition, sections 1, 2, 3, 4 and 7 of the Fisheries and Foreshore (Amendment) Act 1998 amend the Act of 1997.

The Fisheries Acts indicated above followed by the letter S deal exclusively with Sea Fisheries. There were also a number of Acts called Sea Fisheries (Amendment) Acts in the same period. Part XIII (sections 219 to 243) of the F(C)A 1959 is the basis of the law relating to Sea Fisheries. This subject is not dealt with in this book.

FISHERIES CO-OPERATIVES
(F(A)A 1991)

Fisheries co-operatives are creatures of the F(A)A 1991 and were devised as a means of breaking the deadlock in the rod licence dispute. *See:* DUTY ON ORDINARY FISHING LICENCES.

The dispute arose over an attempt to introduce, by the F(A)(No. 2)A 1987, a new system of licensing for angling for trout and coarse fish as a means of raising funds for fisheries.

The matter was compromised after lengthy negotiations in 1991 by the Fisheries Act of that year and these fisheries co-operatives were devised as a means of having the trout anglers raise revenue without the crude imposition of a tax or duty which they found objectionable. It was central to the scheme that it would be an offence for a person to fish for trout or coarse fish without becoming a member of the co-operative and the monies raised from selling membership was to constitute the replacement revenue. Membership of the co-operative also conferred the right to vote in the election for membership of the regional fisheries boards. *See:* ELECTORATE FOR ELECTION.

1992 ORDER

Article 3 of the F(A)A 1991 (Fisheries Co-operative Societies) Order 1992 (S.I. No. 126 of 1992), which came into operation on the May 18, 1992, established the following co-operatives: Eastern Fisheries Development Society, Southern Fisheries Development Society, South-Western Fisheries Development Society, Lower Shannon Fisheries Development Society, Upper Shannon Fisheries Development Society, Western Regional Fisheries Development Society, North Western Fisheries Development Society and Northern Fisheries Development Society.

These correspond with the Regional Fisheries Boards except in the case of the Shannon Board which was divided into Upper and Lower Shannon. Article 4 of the order defines "society" as meaning a fisheries co-operative society established under section 4(1) of the F(A)A 1991.

F(A)A 1991

Section 4 of the F(A)A 1991 provides that the co-operatives are established to raise and disburse for the public benefit funds for the development of trout or coarse fisheries or both in a specified area in each *(qv)* fisheries region and subsection (3) provides that the society be deemed to be established for charitable purposes.

Section 5 of the F(A)A 1991 provides for the making of rules by the Minister and two orders have been made under the section.

(1) Fisheries (Amendment) Act, 1991 (Fisheries Co-operative Societies) Order 1992 (S.I. No. 126 of 1992), and

(2) Fisheries (Amendment) Act, 1991 (Fisheries Co-operative Societies) Rules 1992 (S.I. No. 127 of 1992).

Sections 6 and 7 of the F(A)A 1991 deal firstly with the running of the society by the trustees appointed under the section 4 order until the first election of a management committee and secondly with the identification of the ordinary membership after the election. Section 7(3) provides that the holder of an annual share certificate of the society for any one year shall be a member of the society for that year on the grant of the certificate.

Section 8 of the F(A)A 1991 deals with the admittance of angling clubs or other bodies as corporate members and the club can nominate individual members from the members of the club. In fixing fees for corporate members "particular regard must be had to the outlay of the body concerned on fishery development work of public benefit in the area in which the society operates".

Offence
Section 15(1) of the F(A)A 1991 creates two offences:

By reference to section 9(1) which provides that where a society has so decided by a vote of 60 per cent of its ordinary members entitled to vote and voting, a person shall not be entitled to angle for trout or coarse fish in any area unless:

(a) he holds a current share certificate in a society,
(b) he is under 18 or over 66,
(c) he is unemployed and in receipt of social welfare, or
(d) he is in receipt of an invalidity pension.

It is assumed that the intention is that a person angling for trout or coarse fish who does not come within one of the above qualifications commits an offence. The section is so oddly drafted it doesn't in fact say this. Section 15 provides that a person who contravenes section 9 commits an offence.

Subsection (2) requires publication of the notice of the making of the request to the regional board in Iris Oifigiúil and one or more newspapers circulating in the area and subsection (6) provides that its production constitutes prima facie evidence of the making of the request.

Subsection (3) empowers the authorised officers to request of any person angling with rod and line for trout or coarse fish:

(a) their name and address,
(b) production on the spot or within 7 days of a current share certificate.

It is assumed that in accordance with the terms of section 15 failure to comply with these requests constitutes an offence.

Subsection (4) exempts the same persons exempted under section 9(1) above *(b)*, *(c)* or *(d)*.

Subsection (5) provides that it is a good defence if the rod and line was in the defendant's possession as a manufacturer or seller thereof and not for his own use.

Some, certainly the Western Region Development Society, did not pass by a 60 per cent vote the provisions of section 9(1) which means that in that region that entire portion of the Act is a nullity.

Although the F(A)A 1991 resolved the rod licence dispute politically it left the trout anglers and the fishery boards farther apart than they had ever been. Things were said at meetings and in court during the dispute that will never be forgiven or forgotten and some dark and despicable deeds were done.

The 1991 Act failed completely to reconcile these two powerful fishing bodies and has been totally ineffective in introducing the concept of policing by the regional boards at the request of the societies which was to be the main prop of the new system of fishery protection.

AMENDMENT BY F(A)A 1999

Section 28 of the F(A)A 1999 makes minor adjustments to the F(A)A 1991. The most significant of these adjustments was to be the amendment of section 5 of the 1991 Act which deals with the rules of societies established under that Act by section 28 of the F(A)A 1999. Under section 5(4), the Minister was entitled to appoint two members of the management committee of a society. The Bill when introduced to the Dáil provided that the Minister could appoint 7 persons to these committees which would have been "swamped" by the Minister. The entire structure of the co-operatives could have been re-arranged to suit the Department who would at this stage be perfectly happy to see them disappear altogether. They were only invented as a sop to the rod anglers and as a clumsy device to settle the *9(qv)* rod licence dispute. They never worked out and had no real impact. Following publication of the Bill there was uproar from the fisheries co-operatives and it was hastily re-drafted. The amendment which now appears in the 1999 Act as passed and which is totally unnecessary merely reiterates the provisions of section 5(4), that is, that the Minister can appoint two members and adds a provision to the effect that one of the two persons appointed by the Minister shall be a member of staff of the local fishery board appointed on the nomination of that board. The Fisheries (Amendment) Act, 1999 (save for section 23) came into force on 20 December 1999 by virtue of the Fisheries (Amendment) Act, 1999 9Commencement) Order, 1999 (S.I. No. 419 of 1999).

Section 28 rather oddly mixes amendments and new provisions in one section. The subsections which amend the F(A)A 1991 are firstly dealing with section 5(4) which is covered above and secondly dealing by substitution with section 13. Section 13 dealt with grants by the Minister to the societies which no longer applies and in its place there is provision for repayment to the fisheries boards in respect of funds disbursed by the societies in the development of the public interest of trout or coarse fisheries.

Subsection 2 deals with the election of members in 2000 subject to rule 9(4) of the Fisheries (Amendment) Act 1991 (Fisheries Co-operative Societies) Rules, 1992 (S.I. No. 127 of 1992). This would have been easier to follow if this was done by amendment of the rules by further order under section 5 rather than by burying it in this Statute.

Subsection (4) deals further with section 5(4) with respect to the continuance in office of an officer appointed by the Minister immediately before the commencement of section 28. Again this should properly have been dealt with by amendment of the rules.

This confused section adds more confusion to the general confusion created by the F(A)A 1991.

FISHERIES,
LEASE FOR RESEARCH
(F(C)A 1959, s. 16)

"(1) The Minister, with the consent of the Minister for Finance may, for the purposes of any scheme of research into the life-history and habits of salmon or any freshwater fish and the economic conditions affecting the commercial development of fisheries, take on lease any fishery."

Subsection (2) refers to a Part of the F(C)A 1959 dealing with vested fisheries which has been repealed by section 6 of the FA 1980 and subsection (3) has been repealed by section 6 of the FA 1980.

FISHERIES REGIONS AND
REGIONAL FISHERIES BOARDS
(FA 1980)

On the dissolution of the boards of conservators and the Inland Fisheries Trust under Chapter V (sections 34, 35 and 36) of the FA 1980 it became necessary to establish regional fisheries boards and the Central Board to take over their functions and to create new administrative regions to be called fisheries regions.

"Fisheries region" is defined in the FA 1980, section 2(1), as having the meaning assigned to it by section 10.

CREATION OF FISHERIES REGIONS AND FISHERIES BOARDS

Section 10(1), (2) of the FA 1980 provide:

"(1) (a) Subject to paragraph (b) of this sub section and to compliance with the requirement of subsection (2) of this section, the Minister may by order create, either by union, sub-division or otherwise, such regions (each of which is in this Act referred to as a 'fisheries region') as appear to him to be appropriate having regard to the purposes of this Act and such order shall specify the name of each fisheries region so created.

(b) An order under this section, other than the order referred to in subsection (2) of this section, shall not made without the consent of the Minister for the Public Service.

(2) As soon as may be after the passing of this Act, an order shall be made by the Minister under subsection (1) of this section creating seven, and only seven, fisheries regions in the State and such order shall be the first order made under this section and will come into force on the appointed day."

The Fisheries Act 1980 (Appointed Day) Order 1980 (S.I. No. 323 of 1980), fixed the October 29, 1980 as the appointed day.

Subsection (3) provides that where an order is made under this section, there shall, by virtue of the order, be established in relation to any fisheries region created by the order a board (a "regional board") and such board shall be known as "The ------ Regional Fisheries Board" (the name of the fisheries region being inserted) and shall perform as regards the fisheries region in relation to which it is established the functions assigned to a regional board by the Act.

Subsection (4) provides that the number of members elected pursuant to section 12 and members nominated by the Minister shall be specified in the order and that the elected members are to hold office, unless they are removed by the Minister under section 24 or they resign or become disqualified, from the day after the day they are elected until midnight on the day the results of the next election are declared and that appointed members are to hold office for such term as is fixed by the Minister when making the appointment but in the case of an appointed member for not more than five years.

Subsection (5) provides that the Minister shall appoint the first members of the regional boards in the order under section 10(1) creating the boards who hold office until the first election.

Subsection (6) provides that a member of either House of the Oireachtas or an M.E.P is ineligible for appointment as a member of a fisheries board.

Subsection (7) provides that Part II of the Second Schedule to the FA 1980 gives regulations for the election of members, appointments by the Minister and conduct of the meetings of the board.

Subsection (8) provides that the order under the section creating a fisheries region must specify the boundaries by reference to a map specified in the order.

Subsection (9) provides that:

(a) a fisheries region may include waters comprising a (*qv*) fishery district and any other waters which are
  (i) in any area of the sea to which the internal or inland waters of the State extend by virtue of section 5 of the Maritime Jurisdiction Act 1959,
  (ii) in the portion of the sea which lies between the baseline for the purposes of the said Act and a line every point of which is on the seaward side and at a distance of 12 nautical miles from the nearest point of that base-line.

Paragraphs (b), (c) and (d) of this subsection deal with an adjustment by the Minister by order specifying a number of nautical miles other than 12 as in (a)(ii) above.

Subsection (10) provides that the Minister may by order alter the boundaries by reference to the map referred to at subsection (8).

See: Fisheries Regions (Alteration of Boundaries) Order 1994 (S.I. No. 208 of 94)).

Subsection (11) provides that he may make an order:

(a) for the alteration of the number of both elected and appointed members of a regional board by Ministerial order, and
(b) entitles the Minister when making an order under subsection (1), to reduce the number of members other than that established by the order, and notwithstanding subsection (4)*(b)*(i) of this section such an order may provide for the termination in a specified manner of the term of office of specified members (whether elected or appointed) of such other regional board.

Subsection (12) provides:

"(12)(a) The Minister shall cause to be prepared maps showing, in such manner as the Minister thinks fit and indicates thereon, the boundaries of each of the several fisheries regions in existence for the time being.
(b) Paragraphs (b) to (e) of section section 19(3) of the Principal Act shall apply in relation to maps prepared under this subsection as they apply to maps prepared under that section and for the purposes of the foregoing each of the references in those paragraphs to the official maps shall be construed as including a reference to a map prepared under this subsection."

Section 19(3) of the F(C)A 1959 sets out the protocol to be observed in preparing maps of fishery districts under that Act.

Subsection (13) provides that the Minister when making an order under section 10 creating a fisheries region (whether by union, subdivision or otherwise) may provide in the order for the vesting in the regional board specified in the order of all the property held as is provided at paragraph (a).

Subsection (14) provides that where the Minister by order under this section creates a fisheries region by the union of two or more fisheries regions the boards of the united regions shall stand dissolved from the commencement of the order.

Subsection (15) provides that on the making of an order under this section notice must be published in an Iris Oifigiúil and one or more newspapers circulating in the region created and copies must be lodged with the County Registrar and the District Court Clerk of the court areas where the fisheries region is situated.

AMENDMENT BY THE F(A)A 1999

Section 7 of the F(A)A 1999 makes a number of amendments to section 10 of the FA 1980. As in the article FISHERIES CO-OPERATIVES, where section 28 of the 1999 makes amendments to sections of the F(A)A 1991, the legislators are purporting to amend provisions which are contained in orders made under sections instead of amending or altering the provisions of the relevant order by subsequent order.

The Fisheries (Amendment) Act, 1999 (save for section 23) came into force on 20 December 1999 by virtue of the Fisheries (Amendment) Act 1999 (Commencement) Order, 1999 (S.I. No. 41) of 1999).

The Fisheries Regions Orders made under section 10 of the FA 1980 9referred to supra) fixed the number of members to be appointed by the Minister in respect of each of the seven regions at 5. The number of elected members varied from region to region. The amending section 7 of the F(A)A 1999 ignores the existence of these orders and subsection (4) itself fixes the number of elected members at 8 but to be appointed after such consideration as the Minister considers appropriate.

You now have a situation in relation to section 10(4) that the provisions of the orders establishing the fisheries region dealing with numbers of elected members and appointed members of boards have been "side stepped" and left in limbo. The orders cannot be simply ignored as they perform other important functions in relation to fisheries regions.

Section 7(1)(b) of the new Act further amends section 10(4) by inserting before paragraph (b) a new paragraph (aa) which provides that where the Minister is appointing members to a regional board he must appoint persons representing agriculture, protection and preservation of the environment, regional tourism, national heritage within the meaning of the national Heritage Act, 1995 and promoters of regional or local development. There are detailed provisions in this regard and there must be at least 4 of either sex on the board.

"national heritage" is not defined in this Act or the Heritage Act, 1985 but section 6 of that Act provides in relation to the functions of the *(qv)* Heritage Council –

"the functions of the Council shall be to propose policies and priorities for the identification, protection, preservation, and enhancement of the national heritage, including monuments, archaeological objects, heritage objects, architectural heritage, flora, fauna wildlife habitats, landscapes, seascapes, wrecks, geology, heritage gardens and parks and inland waterways."

Most of these terms are defined in section 2(1) of the Heritage Act 1995.

The Minister is also given power under amending section 7(c), substituting a new subsection 10(11), to alter by order the number of members of a regional board. This provision for new Ministerial orders under section 10 when nothing has been done about the old orders will cause confusion.

There follows in section 7 subsections (2), (3), (4), (5) and (6) a series of provisions in relation to the election of members of regional boards, Ministerial power by order to revoke or vary an order made under the section, the manner for presenting orders before the House and provision, similar to that contained at section 28(2) of the F(A)A 1999 relating to section 5 of the F(A)A 1991, dealing with the election of members in the year 2000 subject to the eligibility of candidates as it set out at section 15 of the FA 1980. The orders required under the Act to hold these elections, The Commencement Order (S.I. No. 30 of 2000), have been rushed through and the elections are to be held on 20 March 2000.

See: FISHERIES CO-OPERATIVES.

FISHERIES REGIONS ORDERS
(FA 1980)

It is worth quoting the explanatory note to the 1980 Fisheries Order, dealt with hereunder, which provides as follows:

"The main effects of this order is to –

(a) create seven fisheries regions and specify the geographical area and the name of each region,
(b) establish a regional fisheries board for each fisheries region and specify the name of the board and the number of members of the board,
(c) specify –
    (i) the classes of electorate for elections to regional fisheries boards and
    (ii) the number of members to be elected to each regional board by each class of the electorate,
(d) provide for the transfer of the properties of boards of conservators to the appropriate regional fisheries board, and
(e) provide that any legal proceedings, contracts or debts, instituted, entered into or incurred by a board of conservators shall become the responsibility of the appropriate regional board."

In fact to date three orders have been required under section 10(1) of the FA 1980 and these are as follows:
The Fisheries Regions Order 1980 (S.I. No. 324 of 1980), the Fisheries Regions (Amendment) Order, 1981 (S.I. No. 373 of 1981) and the Fisheries Regions (Amendment) Order 1992 (S.I. No. 353 of 1992) which are described in the 1992 Order as "the Fisheries Regions Orders, 1980 to 1992".

The 1981 Order was necessary because of an error in the 1980 Order which had understated the number of elected members pursuant to section 10(4)*(a)* and columns (5) and (8) of the First Schedule reference number 2 was increased from 18 to 19 members, the omitted member being the member elected by licensed eel fishermen of the Southern Fisheries Region and the 1992 Order became necessary to change the classes of electorate for election to the regional fisheries boards and to change the number of members following on the provisions of the F(A)A 1991 and the enfranchisement of members of the fisheries co-operatives.

The fisheries regions are created by the

Orders numerically and sequentially, the reference number for each fisheries region is given in column (1) of the Second Schedule to the order which sets out the seven Regions and gives the area or physical limits of the fishery at column (4).

The Regions are:
1. Eastern Fisheries region,
2. Southern Fisheries Region,
3. South Western Fisheries Region,
4. Shannon Fisheries Region,
5. Western Fisheries Region,
6. North western Fisheries Region and
7. Northern Fisheries Region.

Article 3 of the Fisheries Region Order 1980 provides:

"(1) Each area described in column (4) of the First Schedule to this Order at any reference number shall be a fisheries region within the meaning of and for the purposes of the Act of 1980 and shall be known by the name mentioned in column (2) of that schedule opposite the description of the area.
(2) The boundaries of each fisheries region created by this order shall be the boundaries indicated on the map of such region prepared pursuant to section 10(8) of the Act of 1980 and for the purposes of this Order, which map is deposited in the office of the Minister."

Articles 4, 5 and 6 deal with, by reference to columns (5), (6) and (7) of the First Schedule and column (2) of the Second Schedule, the numbers of elected members and nominated members in each fisheries board and the classes of electorate for elected members.

Article 7 (3) to (7) deals with properties and choses in action.

FISHERY, A, POWER TO OPERATE
(FA 1980, s. 60)

"(1) The Minister may, for the purpose of operating a fishery owned by him, do all such things as he may consider necessary for carrying on such fishery as a commercial undertaking and which he could do if he were a private individual and the owner of such fishery, and without prejudice to the generality of the foregoing provisions he may do all or any of the following:
(a) buy and sell fish anywhere;
(b) buy or manufacture any article required in connection with the capture, storage, transport, treatment, purchase or sale of fish;
(c) carry on any business which is ancillary or incidental to the operation of such fishery;
(d) enter into contracts;
(e) employ such and so many persons as he thinks fit;
(f) purchase fishing licences."

Subsections (2) and (3) provide for incidents of the employment of persons by the Minister.

FISHERY DISTRICTS AND AND ELECTORAL DIVISIONS
(F(C)A 1959)

These were the jurisdictional foundation for the establishment and functioning of the old (*qv*) boards of conservators, and although the boards were abolished by the FA 1980 both the fishery districts and electoral divisions were retained for various administrative functions in respect of the (*qv*) regional fisheries boards which were established by the FA 1980 to take over most of the functions of the boards of conservators.

FISHERY DISTRICTS UNDER F(C)A 1959

Section 19(1) of the F(C)A 1959 provides that, subject to an order under section 20, each area mentioned in column (4) of the Second Schedule to this Act at any reference number shall be a fishery district for the purposes of this Act and shall be known by the number and name mentioned in columns (2) and (3) respectively of the said Schedule at that reference number.

Section 20 empowered the Minister to create new fishery districts.

REPEALS BY SECTION 6 OF THE FA 1980

Section 6 of the FA 1980 repealed subsection (2) of section 19 and subsections (1), (2) and (5) of section 20 of the F(C)A 1959. Section 19(1) of the 1959 Act was unaffected by this repeal.

The result of these changes is that the Minister may no longer create new fishery districts but may alter the boundaries of existing fishery districts by means of orders made under section 19(1) of the 1959 Act.

Section 20(4) of the F(C)A 1959 as amended by section 64 of the FA 1980 provides:

"(4) The Minister may by regulations alter the boundaries of a fishery district by the inclusion therein of any specified waters which are in the area or portion of the sea described in sub paragraph (i) or (ii) of section 10(9) of the Fisheries Act, 1980, and regulations under this subsection shall, by reference to a map specified in the regulations, indicate the boundaries of the relevant fishery district or districts as altered by the regulations."

See: FISHERIES REGIONS AND REGIONAL FISHERIES BOARDS.

Section 10(9)(a) of the FA 1980 is dealt with hereunder under (q*v*)Fisheries Regions.

What remains of sections 19 and 20 of the F(C)A 1959 keeps alive the Second Schedule to the 1959 Act which is still the basis for the issue of district licences and for the fisheries rating system. They have transitional functions between the 1959 and the 1980 Fisheries Acts and are a mapping reference in relation to the creation of the new fisheries regions under the 1980 Act.

There is a further function by way of definition under Articles 2 and 8 of the Salmon and Trout Conservation Bye-law (No. 743 of 1998) for some of the fishery districts. *See:* (1) SALMON AND TROUT CONSERVATION BYE-LAW 1998; (2) FISHERY REGIONS.

FISHERY IMPROVEMENT
(FA 1980, s. 18)

"(1) Subject to the following subsections of this section, for the purpose of improving any fishery (whether or not the fishery is the property of the (*qv*) Central Board or the (*qv*) regional board concerned) the Central Board or a regional board may do all or any of the following namely –
(a) take fish from a fishery by any means whatever,
(b) implement any other measure intended to alter or regulate the stock in a fishery of fish of one or more particular species,
(c) keep under surveillance and from time to time ascertain by any means the quality of water in a fishery,
(d) alter, repair, remove or demolish any fence, hedge, tree or wall,
(e) dig, break or otherwise temporarily close, cross, extend, divert or otherwise interfere with or alter any navigable waterway, river, stream or other watercourse, bridge, tunnel, culvert, pipe, drain or other thing,
(f) notwithstanding section 327 of the Principal Act, take materials from any river, stream or other watercourse,
provided that a (*qv*) board shall only exercise a power under paragraph (e) or (f) of this subsection after consultation with the (*qv*) Commissioners and provided also that in relation to a fence, hedge, tree or wall which is adjacent to the public road or any property of a public authority, the board shall only exercise a power under this subsection with the consent of the authority concerned, and in case there is a dispute as to whether a particular fence, hedge, tree or wall is adjacent to a public road or any such property, the matter shall be referred by the board concerned to the Minister to determine, whose decision, after consultation with the Minister for the Environment, or such other Minister of the Government as he considers appropriate, shall be final.

(2) (a) Subject to paragraph (b) of this subsection, a board shall not, in relation to a (*qv*) several fishery or other thing exercise a power mentioned in subsection (1) of this section without the consent of the owner thereof, and for the avoidance of doubt it is hereby declared that in case the owner of the several fishery or other thing is a Minister of the Government, the Irish Land Commission, (*qv*) the Commissioners or a public authority, the said Minister, the said Commission, the Commissioners or the public authority in giving such consent may attach such reasonable conditions as he or they think fit, and in addition to the forgoing, the board shall not enter on or take possession of any fishery or land without giving the occupier thereof one month's previous notice in writing of its intention so to do,
(b) Where, on application made to him by a board, the Minister is satisfied that the owner of a several fishery or other thing cannot by diligent enquiry be found or ascertained, he may issue an authorisation under this section as regards the several fishery or other thing and for so long as an authorisation under this section is in force paragraph (a) of this subsection shall not apply as regards the several fishery or other thing to which the

authorisation relates,

(c) The Minister may at any time withdraw an authorisation under this section either on his own motion or on the application of any other person."

For Irish Land Commission *see:* LAY COMMISSIONERS.

FISHERY RATE

(F(C)A 1959, s. 3(1))

"means a rate

(a) struck by a regional board and confirmed by the Minister under section 55, or

(b) struck by the Minister under the same section."

Fishery rates are dealt with under Part V of the F(C)A 1959 which was amended by the repeal firstly of section 60 and 61 by section 6 of the FA 1980 and then section 63 by section 3 of the F(A)A 1994. This brought Part V down to two sections 55 and 56.

There have been minor amendments to section 55 by section 2 of the F(A)A 1964 and Articles 4 and 5 of the Fisheries (Alteration of Fishery Year) Order, 1982 (S.I. No. 32 of 1982) which brought the date of striking the rate into line with the financial year. The (*qv*) fishery year had been the twelve months commencing on October 1, in any year.

Section 55(1) of the F(C)A 1959, as amended, provides for the striking of a fishery rate by the regional board as regards every fishery year and within the period (beginning on the 1st day of October preceding the commencement of that fishery year and ending on the 31st day of January next following), on all fisheries within its fishery region (as appear in the revised valuation lists prepared by the Commissioner for Valuation by the 1st December immediately preceding such commencement) a rate of such amount percentage of their valuations as will, with the estimated amount of other income, be sufficient to meet the estimated amount of the regional board's expenditure for that fishery year.

Although the words in brackets in the above have not been repealed the period of time specified should now correspond with the financial year.

Subsection (2) provides that the rate struck is subject to confirmation by the Minister.

Subsection (3) provides that if the regional board fail to strike a rate the Minister may do so and the rate is then dealt with as if it was struck by the regional board.

Subsection (4) entitles either the regional board or the Minister, when either have struck a rate, to make such departure, not affecting value, from the particulars in the revised valuation list as may be necessary to make a valid rating.

Subsection (5) provides that rates are payable in two moieties on the 1st May and 1st September.

Subsection (6) provides that a person paying a fishery rate is not liable to pay a rate to the council on the same fishery.

Subsection (7) was repealed by section 17 of the F(A)A 1994

Section 56 of the F(C)A 1959 deals with valuations by reference to which fishery rates are struck and appeals against valuations.

Section 57 of the F(C)A 1959 deals with minor amendments in the rate such as correcting occupiers names, misdescriptions, arithmetical and other errors. These corrections can be made by the regional board on notice to the rated occupier.

Section 58 of the F(C)A 1959 provides that the person liable to pay a rate in respect of a fishery is the occupier thereof.

Section 59 of the F(C)A 1959 deals with the collection of the rates, when, by whom and from whom the fishery rate may be recovered.

Section 62 of the F(C)A 1959 deals with grants by the Minister to (*qv*) regional boards in a (*qv*) fishery year within whose (*qv*) fishery districts there are for that year or part thereof (*qv*)special tidal waters.

FISHERY YEAR

(F(C)A 1959, s. 3(1))

"means the period of twelve months commencing on the 1st day of October in any year."

This was amended by Article 3 of the Fisheries (Alteration of Fisheries Year) Order, 1982 (S.I. No. 328 of 1982) which provided that any reference to a fishery year in the F(C)A 1959 shall, on or after the 31st day of December 1982 be construed and have effect as a reference to a period which is co-extensive with the calendar year.

FISHING ENGINES

(F(C)A 1959)

For definition, *see:* ENGINES, FIXED, FISHING.

FISHING LICENCES
(F(C)A 1959, s. 3(1))

"when used without qualification, means a licence being either
(a) an *(qv)* ordinary fishing licence or
(b) a *(qv)* special local licence."

For grant of new fishing licences under section 11(6)(b) of the FA 1980, *see:* FUNCTIONS OF REGIONAL FISHERIES BOARDS, GRANT OF NEW FISHING LICENCES.

FISHING MILL DAM
(F(C)A 1959, s; 3(1))

"means a dam used or intended to be used partly for the purpose of taking or facilitating the taking of fish and partly for the purpose of sustaining water for milling or other purposes."

FISHING WEIR
(F(C)A 1959, s. 3(1))

"means any erection, structure or obstruction, which –
(a) is fixed to the soil across or partly across a river,
(b) is used solely for the purpose of taking or facilitating the taking of fish,
(c) incorporates one or more openings wherein fish may be taken, and
(d) is not a (*qv*) head weir."

FISHING WEIRS AND FISHING MILL DAMS, REQUIREMENTS FOR A FREE GAP
(F(C)A 1959, ss. 107 TO 114)

REQUIREMENTS FOR A FREE GAP

Section 107(1) of the F(C)A 1959.

"(1) In every fishing weir there shall be a free gap or opening in accordance with the following provisions –
(a) the free gap shall be situate in the deepest part of the stream,
(b) the sides of the free gap shall be in line with and parallel to the direction of the stream at the weir,
(c) the bottom of the free gap shall be level with the natural bed of the stream above and below the gap,
(d) the width of the free gap in its narrowest part shall not in any case be narrower than three feet, and, subject to that limitation, shall not be narrower than one-tenth part of the width of the stream or fifty feet whichever is the less,
(e) no existing free gap in any fishing weir shall be reduced in width or a gap of less width substituted therefor or any alteration made therein so as to reduce the flow of water through such gap,

(2) (a) Subsection (1) of this section shall not apply to any *(qv)* fishing weir in respect of which an order has been made under paragraph (b) of this subsection.
(b) Where the breadth of the river, where there is a chartered or patent fishing weir (being a fishing weir existing on the 28th day of July, 1863), does not exceed forty feet and it might be inexpedient to require a free gap to be made therein, the Minister may, if he thinks fit, instead thereof, direct by his order the extension the (*qv*)weekly close time for a period of twenty four hours.

Offence
(3) Where a free gap has been made in a fishing weir but is not maintained in accordance with subsection (1) of this section, the owner of the fishing weir shall be guilty of an offence under this section and shall be liable on summary conviction thereof to fine not exceeding five pounds for each day he is in default".

(Note that the maximum penalty prescribed under this subsection has been increased. *See:* FINES AND IMPRISONMENT (IMPOSITION OF)).

OPERATION OF FISHING WEIR WITHOUT FREE GAP BY MINISTERIAL ORDER

Section 108 of the F(C)A 1959 entitles the Minister by order to authorise the operation of a specified fishing weir belonging to him or to the ESB without a free gap subject to conditions as to the release upstream of a sufficient number of fish to adequately maintain a stock of such fish as he thinks proper.

Subsection (2) provides that before making an order under the section notice must be published of the Minister's intention to make the order and draft of the order in a newspaper circulating in the locality affected and the Minister must consider objections and subsection (5) provides that the order must be laid before both houses of the Oireachtas and shall be annulled on resolution to annul passed within 21 days.

Subsection (6) provides that after the making of the order notice must again be published both in an Iris Oifigiúil and in one or more local newspapers and a copy of the order must be deposited with the County Registrar, the District Court Clerk and every station of the Garda Síochána in the area affected.

Subsection (7) and (8) provide that the Minister can cause a public inquiry to be held into the desirability of making a particular order on notice under section 322.

Section 109 of the F(C)A 1959 entitles the Minister to make an order authorising the operation of a specified eel fishing weir without a free gap.

Subsections (2) and (3) provide for revocation of the order on conviction of the occupier of an offence under the Act or the failure of the occupier to comply with conditions attaching to the authorisation on notice to the occupier and also there is provision for an exemption from the provisions of the Act for an eel fishing weir in respect of which an order has been made under the section.

CONSTRUCTION OF FREE GAPS IN FISHING WEIRS

Section 110(1) of the F(C)A 1959 provides that where there is not in a fishing weir a gap in accordance with section 107, the Minister may serve a notice on the occupier requiring the construction of a free gap in the fishing weir in accordance with section 107 within a period of not less than one month from the date of service.

Subsection (2) provides that the notice party may apply to the Circuit Court for an order quashing the notice on the grounds that there is already a free gap in accordance with the section and the subsection gives detail of the procedures for and consequences of such an application.

Subsection (3) provides that where a notice has been served by the Minister under the section and it has not been referred to the Court in accordance with subsection (2), when the time specified in the notice has expired and the specified work has not been carried out then the following provisions shall have effect:

Offence

(I) the occupier is guilty of an offence, and
(II) the Minister may, whether or not there has been a prosecution under (I), enter on the fishing weir and the lands adjoining and construct a free gap in such weir.

(Note that the maximum penalty prescribed under this subsection has been increased from the amount originally set under the 1959 Act. *See:* FINES AND IMPRISONMENT (IMPOSITION OF)).

Subsection (4) provides that the Minister can recover as a simple contract debt from the occupier the expenses incurred in constructing such free gap and subsection (5) provides that any consequential damage arising out of the construction by the Minister shall be the responsibility of the occupier.

Subsection (6) provides that the section does not apply to a fishing weir the subject of an order under section 107(2).

ALTERATION OF BED OF RIVER AFFECTING FLOW OF WATER

Offence

Section 111 of the F(C)A 1959 creates the offence of making alterations to the bed of a river so as to reduce the flow of water to a free gap.

(Note that the maximum penalty prescribed under this subsection has been increased from the amount originally set under the 1959 Act. *See:* FINES AND IMPRISONMENT (IMPOSITION OF)).

FISHING IN OR NEAR FREE GAPS AND OBSTRUCTING SAME

Offences

Section 112 of the F(C)A 1959 provides for the offences of:

(a) using a fishing engine in a free gap,
(b) using a fishing engine (not being a rod and line) within fifty yards above or below any part of a fishing weir,
(c) using a contrivance or doing any act whereby fish may be scared, deterred or in any way prevented from freely entering and passing up and down a free gap at all times of the year,
(d) placing any bridge, board, cloth or any other thing whatsoever in, over or across a free gap in a fishing weir, except a temporary bridge or board during the time only when the persons engaged in the fishing of the said weir are passing over the free gap.

Subsection (2) provides that where there is a prosecution against the occupier of a fishing weir for obstruction of the free gap, the onus lies on the defendant to prove that he did not place the obstruction there.

(Note that the maximum penalty prescribed under this subsection has been increased from the amount originally set under the 1959 Act. *See:* FINES AND IMPRISONMENT (IMPOSITION OF)).

Subsection (3) provides that after a conviction under the section for an obstruction, the Minister can remove the obstruction and recover the expense of doing so from the defendant.

BOXES IN SALMON FISHING WEIRS AND FISHING MILL DAMS

Section 113 of the F(C)A 1959 deals with rules as to boxes in salmon fishing weirs and fishing mill dams. Section 113 provides:

"(1) In this section the expression 'salmon weir' means any weir being –
  (a) a fishing weir used for taking salmon, or
  (b) a fishing mill dam used for taking salmon.

(2) The following rules shall be observed in relation to the construction and use of boxes in salmon weirs –
  (a) the surface of the floor of the box shall be level with the natural bed of the river,
  (b) the (*qv*)inscales and the (*qv*)heck of the box shall be capable of being removed and opened up,
  (c) the bars of the heck of the box shall be placed perpendicularly,
  (d) the inscales and heck of the box shall be so constructed that no bar or part of a bar is nearer to any other bar or part of a bar than two inches,
  (e) the box shall not be built over or in any other manner hidden from public inspection.

(3) Where the Minister is satisfied that sea-trout form the principal part of the fish caught in a salmon weir, the Minister may, if he thinks fit, by order declare that paragraph (d) of subsection (2) of this section shall, in relation to such salmon weir, have effect as if the words "one and a quarter inches" were substituted for 'two inches'.

Offence
(4) If any person uses or constructs any box in a salmon weir in contravention of subsection (2) of this section, he shall be guilty of an offence under this section and shall be liable on summary conviction thereof to a fine not exceeding twenty pounds."

(Note that the maximum penalty prescribed under this subsection has been increased from the amount originally set under the 1959 Act. *See:* FINES AND IMPRISONMENT (IMPOSITION OF)).

CONSTRUCTION OF GUIDING WALLS

Section 114(1) of the F(C)A 1959 provides:

"(1) In this section, the expression 'guiding wall' means any spur or tail wall, leader or outrigger."

Offence
Subsection (2)(a) prohibits the attachment to a fishing weir or a fish mill dam of a guiding wall of greater length than 20 feet measured as is provided in the section. Paragraph (b) of that subsection prohibits the attachment of a guiding wall which has the effect of narrowing up or preventing the ingress and discharge of water through or from the free gap in the fishing weir. Paragraph (c) of that subsection provides:
  (c) If an occupier is in breach of (2)(a) or (b)
    (i) he commits an offence,
    (ii) the Minister may alter or remove the guiding wall and recover the expenses from the occupier as a simple contract debt."

(Note that the maximum penalty prescribed under this subsection has been increased from the amount originally set under the 1959 Act. *See:* FINES AND IMPRISONMENT (IMPOSITION OF)).

Offence
Subsection (3) provides that if the occupier of a fishing mill dam or a fishing weir in a river makes such use of any island or natural obstruction in the river as secures to him the advantage he would have obtained by attaching a guiding wall in contravention of section 114(2)*(a)* he shall be guilty of an offence under this subsection.

(Note that the maximum penalty prescribed under this subsection has been increased from the amount originally set under the 1959 Act. *See:* FINES AND IMPRISONMENT (IMPOSITION OF)).

Subsection (4) provides that if a fishing mill dam is used partly to sustain water for a mill or factory or for navigation nothing in this section shall be construed to extend to such fishing mill dam so as to affect injuriously the necessary supply of water to such mill, factory or navigation.

EXEMPTIONS FROM SECTION 114 (EELS)

Section 12(1) of the F(A)A 1962 provides that the Minister may, if he thinks fit and subject to such conditions (if any) as he may specify grant exemptions either for a limited time or without limitation as to time in relation to a specified fishing weir or fishing mill dam used solely for the capture of (*qv*)eels from the provisions of section 114 F(C)A 1959 and subsection (2) provides that he may, at any time, revoke or amend an exemption given under this section.

FIXED ENGINE
(F(C)A 1959, s. 3(1))

"Means an engine, being –
(a) a stake net,
(b) a bag net,
(c) a fixed draft net,
[(cc) a fixed long line, or]
(d) a head weir, or
(e) any net, implement, engine or device, fixed to the soil or secured by one or more anchors, or by any other means, and used solely for the purpose of taking or facilitating the taking of fish, not being a *(qv)* fishing weir, a *9qv)* fishing mill dam or a *(qv)* drift net."

This definition was substituted by section 1 of the F(A)(No. 2)A 1987 and amended (by the insertion of (cc) by section 27(a) of the F(A)A 1999.
See: ENGINES, FIXED, FISHING, NON-SCHEDULED.

FIXED ENGINES,
FISHING WEIRS,
FISHING MILL DAMS,
PROHIBITION OF
(F(C)A 1959, ss. 97 to 101)

Chapter I of Part VIII of the F(C)A 1959 contains a number of sections, 97 to 101, which deal with the prohibition of fishing with fixed (*qv*) engines, (*qv*) fishing weirs and (*qv*) fishing mill dams. Some of these headings refer to certificates granted under the Salmon Fishery (Ireland) Act 1863 and the form of certification under the Act which must have very limited, if any, application at this stage. The F(C)A 1959 could do with a judicious but vigorous pruning. However, the Chapter deals with an important eel authorisation under section 100(5).

These prohibitory sections are as follows:

Offence
Section 97(1) of the F(C)A 1959 prohibits fishing with, making use of or erecting any fixed engine for the capture of salmon without a certificate under the Salmon Fishery (Ireland) Act 1863 in force and granted prior to December 31, 1923. Contravention of subsection (1) creates the offence under subsection (2).

(Note that the maximum penalty prescribed under this subsection has been increased from the amount originally set under the 1959 Act. *See:* FINES AND IMPRISONMENT (IMPOSITION OF)).

Subsection (3) provides for the forfeiture of the fixed engines as a statutory consequence of conviction.

Section 98 of the F(C)A 1959 provides that the production of a certificate under section 6 of the 1863 Act shall be conclusive evidence that the person named therein is the person entitled to exercise the right therein given, but it shall not render any fixed engine lawful which would otherwise be unlawful by reason of its being injurious to navigation, a common nuisance to the right of fishing or otherwise in violation of the common law or an enactment.

Offence
Section 99(1) of the F(C)A 1959 creates the offence of erecting in the freshwater portion of any river or lake, a fishing weir, fishing mill, dam or fishing engine and contravention of section 99(1) creates the offence under section 99(2).

(Note that the maximum penalty prescribed under this subsection has been increased from the amount originally set under the 1959 Act. *See:* FINES AND IMPRISONMENT (IMPOSITION OF)).

Subsection (3) gives the Minister power to demolish (apparently without notice) any such engine erected in contravention of the section and may recover the cost of doing so from the occupier as a simple contract debt in any court of competent jurisdiction.

Subsection (4) exempts from the provisions of the section long lines used solely for the capture of (*qv*) eels or engines used for the capture of fish other than salmon, trout and eels.

Subsection (5) deals with a specific eel

authorisation granted by the Minister to erect, in accordance with plans approved by the Minister, at a specified place in the freshwater portion of a specified river or lake, a specified kind of fishing engine (being a fishing weir, fishing mill dam or fixed engine) for the capture of eels.

This authorisation is quite separate and to be distinguished from an eel authorisation under section 100(5). *See:* EELS.

Subsection (6) exempts from the provisions of the section the erection of certain fishing engines by the ESB or under a section 99(5) eel authorisation.

Section 100(1) of the F(C)A 1959 is distinguishable from section 99 in that it prohibits the use rather than the erection of such fishing engines in the freshwater portion of any river or in any lake, unless such fishing engine was in lawful use during the open fishing season of one of the years 1936, 1937 or 1938.

Subsection (2) provides that where one or more boxes in a fishing weir were used during these years it or they shall be deemed to have been lawfully used.

Subsection (3) creates an offence in contravention of subsection (1).

(Note that the maximum penalty prescribed under this subsection has been increased from the amount originally set under the 1959 Act by virtue of the FA 1980 and further increased by section 19 of the F(A)A 1994. *See:* FINES AND IMPRISONMENT (IMPOSITION OF)).

Subsection (4) was also amended by section 19 of the F(A)A 1994. It provides that the provisions of this section shall not apply to engines used for the capture of fish other than salmon, trout or eels.

Subsection (5) provides for the granting by the Minister of an eel fishery authorisation under the section to the occupier of a fishing engine (being a fishing weir, fishing mill dam or fixed engine) subject to conditions and for the revocation of such an authorisation and subsection (6) provides for the steps required to be taken in relation to amendment or revocation of an authorisation. *See:* EEL FISHERY AUTHORISATION UNDER SECTION 100(5).

Subsection (7) provides for the exemption from the provisions of the section, of:

(a) fishing weirs erected by the ESB for the capture of eels or in exercise of the powers conferred on them by section 101, or
(b) the use of fishing engine (fishing weir, fishing mill dam or fixed engine) in respect of which there is an eel fishery authorisation under subsection (5) so long as it is used in accordance with such authorisation.

Section 101 of the F(C)A 1959 deals with an entitlement of the ESB in respect of fisheries acquired by them under Part III of the Electricity Supply (Amendment) Act 1945 to construct and maintain a fishing weir for the purposes of the fisheries with the consent of the Minister.

FIXED ENGINES, RESTRICTIONS ON SITES

(F(C)A 1959, ss. 102 to 105)

Offence

Section 102(1) of the F(C)A 1959 prohibits the placing, erecting, fishing with or using a fixed engine in any part of the estuary of the tidal part of any river where the breadth of the channel at low water is less than three-quarters of a mile by a person who is not the owner of the several fishery in the whole of such estuary and river and subsection (2)*(a)* creates the offence and *(b)* provides the court shall order the stakes thereof to be pulled down and destroyed.

(Note that the maximum penalty prescribed under this subsection has been increased from the amount originally set under the 1959 Act. *See:* FINES AND IMPRISONMENT (IMPOSITION OF)).

Subsection (3) provides for forfeiture of the fixed engine as a statutory consequence of conviction.

Subsection (4) exempts certain stake nets and other contrivances established 20 years before the August 10, 1842 and stake nets, head weirs and other contrivances established in a lawfully constituted (*qv*)several fishery for 10 years before that date and any head weir, not fished by means of a fixed net.

Section 103(1) of the F(C)A 1959 prohibits the same activity within one mile seaward, coastward or inward from or on either side of the mouth of any river (being a river the inland portion of which is frequented by salmon and the mouth whereof is at low water at ordinary spring tide less in breadth than half a mile) other than the proprietor of a several fishery within the limits thereof and as part of the order on conviction the court shall order the stakes thereof to be pulled down or destroyed at the expense of the defendant.

(Note that the maximum penalty prescribed under this subsection has been increased from the amount originally set under the 1959 Act.

See: FINES AND IMPRISONMENT (IMPOSITION OF)).

Subsection (2) provides for forfeiture of the fixed engine as a statutory consequence of conviction.

Subsection (3) provides that references to the mouth of any river where there is an order under the Act defining the mouth of any tributary river shall be construed as including a reference to the mouth of such tributary river. *See:* DEFINITIONS OF MOUTHS OF RIVERS.

Section 104(1) of the F(C)A 1959 prohibits the placing or allowing to continue in any river or estuary or within a distance of three miles from the mouth of a river of a (*qv*) bag net.

Offence
Subsection (2) provides:

(a) that any bag net placed in contravention of this section shall be deemed to be a common nuisance and may be taken possession of or destroyed and
(b) that the owner of the bag net will be guilty of an offence under the section.

(Note that the maximum penalty prescribed under this subsection has been increased from the amount originally set under the 1959 Act *See:* FINES AND IMPRISONMENT (IMPOSITION OF)).

Subsection (3) provides for forfeiture of the bag net as a statutory consequence of conviction.

Subsection (4) exempts a bag net lawfully existing on the July 28, 1863 where the owner has salmon fishing right in the whole of the river.

Section 105(1) of the F(C)A 1959 creates the offence of placing or erecting, or maintaining and using any stake net or any leader, outrigger or other work of any kind or description whatsoever connected therewith or adjacent thereto in such a manner that it will extend to a greater distance than from high water mark to low water mark at ordinary spring tides.

(Note that the maximum penalty prescribed under this subsection has been increased from the amount originally set under the 1959 Act. *See:* FINES AND IMPRISONMENT (IMPOSITION OF)).

Subsection (2) provides that the section does not apply to any head weir not fished by means of a fixed net.

FIXED ENGINES, CONSTRUCTION AND USER
(F(C)A 1959, s. 106)

Offences
Section 106 of the F(C)A 1959 creates the offence of:

(a) constructing, maintaining, or using a stake net which is capable of taking undersized fish or the fry of salmon or any such fish, or
(b) maintaining or using any stake net, the meshes of the nets whereof are not stretched to their full opening, or
(c) maintaining or using a stake net which is so constructed that a clear opening or of least four feet cannot be made in the pouches, traps and chambers of such stake net, from the top to the bottom thereof, or
(d) maintaining or using any bag net, the meshes of the nets of any leader whereof are not stretched to their full opening, or
(e) maintaining or using any bag net which is so constructed that the leader thereof cannot be raised and kept out of the water.

(Note that the maximum penalty prescribed under this subsection has been increased from the amount originally set under the 1959 Act. *See:* FINES AND IMPRISONMENT (IMPOSITION OF)).

FLORA
(WLA 1976, s. 2(1))

"means all plants (both aquatic and terrestrial) which occur in the wild (whether within or outside the State) and are not trees, shrubs or other plants being grown in the course of agriculture or horticulture and includes in particular lichens, mosses, liverworts, fungi, algae and vascular plants, namely flowering plants, ferns and fern allied plants and any community of such plants."

(Heritage Act 1995, s. 2(1))

Flora is the same as in the WLA 1976 except that "forestry" appears between "agriculture" and "or horticulture" and the use of the words "other than" instead of "and are not" so that phrase in the Heritage Act reads "other than trees, shrubs or plants being grown in the course of agriculture, forestry or horticulture".

FORAS FORBARTHA, AN
(EPAA 1992, s. 32)

Section 32(1) of the EPAA 1992 provides for the abolition of the National Institute for Physical Planning and Construction (An Foras Forbartha Teoranta) by Ministerial Order (1 August 1983, S.I. No. 215 of 1993) and subsection (2) provides that an order under subsection (1) may, inter alia, provide for the transfer of or distribution of property, rights and liabilities to the *(qv)* Agency, the Environmental Research Unit established under the Environmental Research Unit (Establishment) Order 1998 (S.I. No. 20 of 1998) No. 20 of 1998 the Minister , or any other public authority specified in the Order.

FORESHORE

(Foreshore Acts, 1933 and 1992)

DEFINITIONS

Section 1(1) of the Foreshore Act 1933:

"The word 'foreshore' means the bed and shore, below the line of high water of ordinary or medium tides, of the sea and of every tidal river and tidal estuary and of every channel, creek and bay of the sea or of any such river or estuary;"

The expression "tidal lands" means the bed and shore, below the line of high water of ordinary spring tides, of the sea and of every tidal river and tidal estuary and of every channel, creek, and bay of the sea or of any such river or estuary;

The word "seashore" means the foreshore and every beach, bank and cliff contiguous thereto and includes all sands and rocks contiguous to the foreshore;

The expression "beach material" means sand, clay, gravel, shingle, stones, rocks, and mineral substances on the surface of the seashore and includes outcrops of rock or any mineral substance above the surface of the seashore and also includes bent grass growing on the seashore and also seaweed whether growing or rooted on the seashore or deposited or washed up thereon by the action of tides, winds and waves or any of them;

The expression "sea defence work" means any wall, pier, groyne, stakes, bank, or other work constructed for the purpose of protecting any land, building, or other structure from injury by the sea or the waves or tides thereof;

The word "lease" includes a letting for one year or for any period less than one year;

The word "term" includes a period of one year and any period less than one year:

The expression "development" has the meaning assigned to it by section 3 of the LG(P&D)A 1963.

References to foreshore belonging to Saorstát Éireann shall be construed as references to foreshore which for the time being belongs to Saorstát Éireann whether by virtue of Article 11 of the Constitution or by any other means (present or future) whatsoever.

The definition "development" was inserted by Article 13(b) of the European Communities (Environmental Impact Assessment) Regulations 1989 (S.I. No. 349 of 1989). *See:* DEVELOPMENT.

Section 1 of the Foreshore (Amendment) Act 1992 gives the same definition for "local authority" as section 3(1) of the EPAA 1992. *See:* LOCAL AUTHORITY.

In the same section 1 "the Minister" means the Minister for the Marine. In the Foreshore Act, 1933 the responsible Minister was the Minister for Industry and Commerce.

LEASES AND LICENCES BY THE MINISTER UNDER THE FORESHORE ACT 1933

(1) Leases

Section 2(1) of the Foreshore Act 1933, as amended by section 3 of the Foreshore (Amendment) Act 1992, provides for the demising by the Minister, if he is of the opinion that it is in the public interest to do so, of foreshore with buildings and other structures (if any) thereon by lease for a period of not more than 99 years.

Subsection (2) provides for the payment (unless the Minister is of the opinion that it is in the public interest that it should be free of any payment) of a fine or other preliminary payment or rent or other periodic payment or by way of royalty on materials removed or by all or any of such ways, as the Minister shall think proper and agree.

Subsection (3) provides that the sanction of the Minister for Finance must be obtained where the rent or other periodic payment exceeds £10 a year.

Subsection (4) provides that every lease must contain a power of re-entry for breach, non-performance or non-observance by the lessee of any of the lessee's covenants.

Subsection (5) provides that no lease made under the section shall contain any covenant or agreement for renewal.

Subsection (6) provides that every lease shall contain such covenants, conditions and agreements as the Minister shall consider proper and desirable and shall agree.

Subsection (7) provides:

"(7) A lease made under the section may include all minerals on or in the demised foreshore to a depth of thirty feet from the surface of such foreshore, together with the right to get and take such minerals, but no such lease shall extend to or include any mines or minerals more than thirty feet below the surface of the demised foreshore."

Subsection (8) provides that when application is made to the Minister for a lease under the section he may, if he thinks fit, hold a public inquiry into the making of such lease.

(2) Licences

Section 3(1) of the Foreshore Act, 1933, as amended by section 3 of the Foreshore (Amendment) Act 1992, provides for the Minister granting licences of foreshore belonging to Saorstát Éireann, under seal for a term not exceeding 99 years, if in his opinion it is in the public interest, authorising any person to place any material, or to place or erect any articles, things, structures or works in or on such foreshore, to replace or remove any beach material from [or to disturb any beach material in] such foreshore, to get and take any minerals in such foreshore and not more than 30 feet below the surface thereof, or to use or occupy such foreshore for any purpose.

Subsection (2) corresponds with section 2(2) above in (1) Leases.

Subsection (3) provides that where the licence owing to its nature, duration or otherwise is of a trivial nature it may be granted by way of permission in writing without payment or subject to a nominal payment only.

Subsection (4) corresponds with section 2(3) above.

Subsection (5) corresponds with section 2(4) in (1) Leases above except that this subsection deals with termination of a licence following a breach rather than re-entry for a breach as in section 2(4).

Subsection (6) corresponds with section 2(5) above in (1) Leases.

Subsection (7) corresponds with section 2(6) above in (1) Leases.

Subsection (8) of section 3 provides:

"(8) No licence granted under the section shall extend to or authorise the removal of any minerals lying more than thirty feet below the surface of the foreshore to which such licence relates."

Subsection (9) in (1) Leases corresponds with section 2(8) above.

PURPORTED AQUACULTURE LICENCES UNDER THE FORESHORE ACT 1933

Section 3 of the Fisheries and Foreshore (Amendment) Act 1998, *inter alia* deals with a strange hybrid, a foreshore licence for aquaculture purposes under the Foreshore Act 1933.

This arose because of deficiencies which became apparent in the aquaculture section 54 of the FA 1980. To get over the difficulty and because of pressure from applicants for aquaculture licences the Department of the Marine with the compliance of the Department of Industry and Commerce, which was the Department responsible for the granting of foreshore licences until the Foreshore (Amendment) 1992, granted what is now being called in the Fisheries and Foreshore (Amendment) Act 1998 "a foreshore licence for aquaculture purposes". After 1992 these licences were granted by the Minister for the Marine. The fact that there was no provision for the granting of such licences under section 3 of the Foreshore Act 1933 did not appear to concern either Government Departments. The foreshore licence granted gave some semblance of authority to the activities of the grantees. *See:* (1) LICENCES(1) AQUACULTURE LICENCES; (2) OYSTERS.

SURRENDERS, RELEASES AND WAIVERS IN RELATION TO LEASES AND LICENCES

Section 4 of the Foreshore Act 1933 provides in subsection (1) for the Minister accepting a surrender of any lease or licence of foreshore, in subsection (2) for the Minister waiving or releasing any covenant or condition contained in any lease or licence and waiving any breach of such covenant or condition and in subsection (3) such a waiver or release may be either without any consideration or be for such consideration as the Minister considers proper.

ACQUISITION OF FORESHORE

Section 5 of the Foreshore Act 1933 entitles the Minister, with the consent of the Minister for Finance, to either:

(a) purchase by agreement any foreshore, any easement, *profit-a-prendre*, or other

right over any foreshore, or any right of wreck not belonging to Saorstát Éireann, or
(b) take same on lease by agreement.

PROHIBITORY ORDER

Section 6 of the Foreshore Act 1933 as amended by section 3 of the Foreshore (Amendment) Act 1992:

"(1) In this Act the expression 'prohibitory order' means an order made or deemed to have been made under section 6 prohibiting the removal of beach material from, or disturbance of beach material in, an area of seashore.

(2) Whenever the Minister is of opinion that, in relation to beach material of any kind or kinds of beach material –
(a) the removal, the unrestricted removal or the removal by specified means from, or
(b) the disturbance or the disturbance in one or more on (intended to read 'one') specified manner in, any particular area, or class or classes of areas, of seashore
(i) has affected or is likely to affect a any flora or fauna of such area or areas, as the case may be, of seashore or of any area in the neighbourhood thereof, or
(ii) has affected or is likely to affect prejudicially any amenities or public rights in respect of any such area or areas, as the case may be, of seashore or any lands or water in the neighbourhood there of, or
(iii) has caused or is likely to cause injury to any land or to any building, wall, pier, or other structure,
the Minister may prohibit by order any such removal or disturbance by any person of beach material either (as the case may require) of any kind or of the said particular kind or kinds from or in (as appropriate) the said area or classes of area of foreshore.

(3) The Minister may by order at any time at his discretion, revoke or amend a prohibitory order."

Subsection (4) provides that the Minister may at his discretion hold a public inquiry relating to the continuation, making, amendment or revocation of a prohibitory order.

Offence
Subsection (5), substituted by section 3(c) of the Foreshore (Amendment) Act 1992, provides for the offence of removing any beach material from, or disturbing any beach material in, any foreshore or seashore in contravention of a prohibitory order. *See:* FINES AND IMPRISONMENT.

Subsection (6) provides for the continuance in force of orders made under section 14 of the Harbours Act 1814 in force at the passing of the Foreshore Act 1933 notwithstanding the repeal of that section and such orders shall be deemed to have been made under section 6 of the Foreshore Act 1933 on the date on which it was actually made.

Subsection (7), substituted by section 3(d) of the Foreshore (Amendment) Act 1992:
"a prohibitory order shall not operate to prevent the granting under this Act of a licence to remove beach materials from, or disturb beach materials in, foreshore to which such order applies or to prevent such removal or disturbance under and in accordance with a licence granted (whether before or after the making of such order) under this Act."

Subsection (8), added by section 3(d) of the Foreshore (Amendment) Act 1992, gives definitions for "fauna" and "flora" which approximate to definitions given elsewhere in this book. *See:* (1)FAUNA; (2)FLORA.

PROHIBITORY NOTICE

Section 7 of the Foreshore Act 1933, substituted by section 4 of the Foreshore (Amendment) Act 1992:

"(1) Whenever the Minister is of the opinion that the removal of beach material from, or the disturbance of beach material in, any area of the foreshore belonging to the State in respect of which no prohibitory order is in force should be restricted or controlled, the Minister may serve on any person a notice (in this Act referred to as a prohibitory notice) in writing prohibiting such person from –
(a) removing or removing by any specified means, or
(b) disturbing or disturbing in more than one specified manner,
beach material of any kind or of any specified kind or kinds from or in (as appropriate) the said area of foreshore.

(2) It shall not be lawful for any person on who a prohibitory notice has been served –
(a) to remove or disturb, or
(b) cause to be removed or disturbed,
otherwise than in accordance with a licence granted under this Act, any beach material to which such notice applies from or in (as appropriate) the area of foreshore to which such notice applies.

Offence
(3) Every person who removes any beach material from, or disturbs any beach material in, any foreshore in contravention of a prohibitory notice, or connives in such contravention, shall be guilty of an offence under this section."

See: FINES AND IMPRISONMENT.

Section 8 provides for regulations prohibiting, restricting, regulating or controlling, either permanently or temporarily, the public entry to and use of the foreshore and creates an offence of breaching the regulations.

Section 9 provides for authorisation by the Minister of sea defence works necessary for the protection of the property of any person.

Section 10, as amended by Article 13(b) of the European Communities (Environmental Impact Assessment) Regulations 1989 (S.I. No. 349 of 1989) provides that:
(1) the erection on tidal lands not the property of the State of any building, pier, wall or other permanent structure is prohibited unless approved by the Minister,
(2) the Minister can only refuse an application if the structure would cause or be likely to cause (either directly or indirectly) an obstruction to navigation or fishing [or would have or be likely to have significant adverse effects on the environment,]
(3) the Minister can serve a notice requiring the pulling down or removal of the structure and may in default so pull down or remove and recover the costs from the notice party.

Section 11 gives the Minister power to pull down and remove dilapidated structures from the foreshore which cause or are likely to cause an obstruction to navigation or to fishing.

Section 12, as amended by section 5(1)*(a)* of the Fisheries and Foreshore Act 1998, deals with the procedure for obtaining court orders in relation to structures unlawfully erected on State foreshore.

Offences
Section 13 prohibits the deposit of material of any kind on the foreshore without the consent of the Minister. The section creates an offence and gives a court power to order the removal of the material. It creates a further offence of failure to comply with an order for removal.

Section 13A, inserted by Article 13(c) of the European Communities (Environmental Impact Assessment) Regulations 1989 (S.I. No. 349 of 1989) (hereinafter referred to a "the 1989 Regulations"), provides that:

(1) An application for a development of a class specified under Article 24 of the 1989 Regulations shall be accompanied by an environmental impact statement of the likely effects on the environment of such development.

(2) The Minister may request an environmental impact statement, where the development would be of a class referred to in Article 24 but for not exceeding a quantity, area or other limit for the time being specified in relation to that class, where he considers it would be likely to have a significant effect on the environment.

(2A), (2B) and (2C) inserted by Article 9 of the European Communities (Environmental Impact Assessment) (Amendment) Regulations 1999 (S.I. No. 93 of 1999) (hereinafter referred to as "the 1999 Regulations"):

(2A) where the application would involve a development which would:
(a) be of a class specified under Article 24 of the 1989 Regulations but for not exceeding a quantity, area, or other limit for the time being specified in relation to that class, and
(b) be located on:
(i) a special area of conservation *See:* CONSERVATION, SPECIAL AREAS OF,
(ii) a site notified in accordance with Regulation 4 of the NH 97 Regulations. *See:* CONSERVATION, SPECIAL AREAS OF,
(iii) an area classified pursuant to paragraph (1) or (2) of Article 4 of the Birds Directive. *See:* BIRDS DIRECTIVE,
(iv) a site where consultation has been initiated in accordance with Article 5 of the Habitats Directive. *See:* CONSERVATION, SPECIAL AREAS OF,
(v) land established or recognised as a

nature reserve within the meaning of section 15 or 16 of the WLA 1976. *See:* RESERVES AND REFUGES,

(vi) land designated as a refuge for fauna under section 17 of the WLA 1976. *See:* RESERVES AND REFUGES,

the Minister shall decide whether the said development would or would not be likely to have significant effects on the environment.

(2B) The Minister shall, where he is deciding whether or not a development would be likely to have a significant effect on the environment, have regard to the criteria specified in Article 27 of the 1989 Regulations.

(2C) The Ministers decision under the section shall be made available for inspection by the public.

(3) An Environmental impact statement shall contain the information specified in Article 25 of the 1989 Regulations.

(3A) inserted by Article 9(b) of the 1999 Regulations:

(a) provides for the Minister giving, on request in advance of the submission of an environmental impact assessment and after consultation with the person requesting and prescribed bodies, a written opinion on the information to be contained in such statement,

(b) the giving of such an opinion shall not prejudice the Minister's powers to require the person making the request to provide further information in relation to the effects on the environment of the development.

(4) (a) substituted by Article 9(c) of the 1999 Regulations, the Minister may exempt, after consultation with the Minister for the Environment and Local Government, by order in exceptional circumstances an application from the requirements of section 13A(1),

(b) the Minister in granting an exemption may by order apply other requirements as he considers necessary or appropriate,

(c) notice of the exemption granted and the reasons for granting it must be published in Iris Oifigiúil and a newspaper circulating in the district where the foreshore is situated,

(d) inserted by Article 9(d) of the 1999 Regulations, an exemption shall not be granted if a Member State, having been informed pursuant to section 19(c), indicates that it intends to furnish views on the said effects.

Article 4 of the Foreshore (Environmental Impact Assessment) Regulations 1990 (S.I. No. 220 of 1990) prescribes for the purpose of the section:

(a) the Commissioners of Public Works in Ireland where the development which is to take place is of archaeological, scientific or ecological interest,

(b) the local authority in whose functional area the development is to take place,

(c) An Taisce where the development is to take place in an area of special amenity value or special interest, and

(d) Bord Fáilte Éireann.

Offences

Section 14, as amended by section 5(1)*(b)* of the Fisheries and Foreshore (Amendment) Act, 1998, prohibits the deposit of articles such as glass, china, earthenware, metal or other article which would or might cause injury to a person bathing or wading or otherwise using an injurious material or substance. It creates an offence and gives a court power to order removal of the article, material or substance. It creates a further offence of failure to comply with an order for removal.

Section 15 deals with the prohibition of the use of certain evidence of title to foreshore as against the State.

Section 16 confers jurisdiction on the Circuit Court to deal with matters where there is no poor law valuation.

Section 17 deals with notices required to be given to the Minister in respect of certain conveyances of or declarations of title in relation to the foreshore.

Section 18 deals with the holding of public inquiries held by the Minister under the Act.

Section 19 deals with discretionary public notice to be given by the Minister of a proposal or application for an order, lease or licence under the Act.

Section 19A, inserted by Article 13(d) of the 1989 Regulations, provides for:

(1) the publication of a notice in a newspaper circulating in the district where the foreshore is situated

(a) stating that the application has been made and the location and nature of the proposal,

(b) stating that an environmental impact statement has been prepared in relation to the proposal,

(c) naming a place where a copy of the statement may be inspected or purchased,

(d) the time when this can be done,
(e) stating that any person may during the prescribed period make objections and representations to the Minister in relation to the effects on the environment of the proposal;

(2) the making available of copies for purchase;

(3) the furnishing of copies to prescribed bodies indicating that objections and representations may be made to the Minister;

(4) "prescribed" means prescribed by regulations by the Minister.

Section 19B (1), was inserted by Article 13(d) of the 1989 Regulations and amended by substitution of a new subsection (1) by Article 9(e) of the 1999 Regulations:

"Where an environmental impact statement has been submitted in accordance with a requirement of or under or under Section 13A of this Act, the Minister shall have regard to the said statement, to any objections and representations made to him during the prescribed period in relation to the effects on the environment of the proposal, and to the views, if any, furnished by other Member States of the European Communities pursuant to section 19C of this Act."

Subsection (2) provides for requests by the Minister for further specified information in relation to the effects of the proposal on the environment.

Section 19C, was inserted by Article 13(d) of the 1989 Regulations and amended by substitution of a new section by Article 9(f) of the 1999 Regulations:

"(1) Where the Minister considers that proposed development, which is the subject of an environmental impact statement in accordance with a requirement of or under section 13A of this Act, would be likely to have significant effects on the environment in another Member State of the European Communities, or where another Member State of the European Communities considers that the said development would be likely to have the said effects and so requests, he shall as soon as possible, send to that other Member state:-
(a) a description of the proposed development and any available information on its possible effects on the environment of the Member State, and
(b) information on the nature of the decision which may be taken,

and shall give to that Member State a reasonable time to indicate whether it wishes to furnish views on the said effects."

Subsection (2) provides that where a Member State indicates that it wishes to furnish views the Minister shall, if he has not already done so, furnish a copy of the environmental impact statement and information on the procedure for making a decision.

Subsection (3) provides for consultation between the Minister and the Member State regarding the potential effects of the proposed development on the environment in that Member State and the measures envisaged to reduce or eliminate such effects.

Subsection (4) provides for the Minister notifying the Member State of his decision on the application in respect of which information was sent.

Section 20 deals with the laying by the Minister before each House of the Oireachtas of an annual statement of leases and licences made and granted and rents and other periodic payments collected.

Section 21 provides for the publication by the Minister in Iris Oifigiúil, by advertisement and by the erection of warning notices of orders made by him under the Act.

Section 21A, was inserted by Article 13(e) of the 1989 Regulations and amended by Article 9(g) of the 1999 Regulations:

"When a decision is taken on a relevant application in respect of which an environmental impact statement was submitted in accordance with a requirement of or under section 13A of this Act, the Minister shall:-
(a) publish notice of the decision in Iris Oifigiúil and in one or more newspapers circulating in the district in which is situated the foreshore to which the relevant application relates,
(b) make arrangements to make the said statement and information on the decision available for inspection by members of the public during a period to be specified by him."

Section 22 provides for financial provisions of the Minister of expenses incurred in the execution of the Act.

Section 23 provides for the recovery of expenses of making orders from the person requesting same as a civil debt.

Section 24 excludes the application of the State Lands Act 1924 to the foreshore and the Mines and Minerals Act 1931 in or under the foreshore and not more than 30 feet below the surface.

Section 25 repeals the entire of the Public Harbours Act 1806 and section 14 of the Harbours Act 1914.

CITATION OF FORESHORE ACTS

Section 26 provides that the Act may be cited as the Foreshore Act 1933.

Section 10(2) of the Foreshore (Amendment) Act 1992 provides that the 1933 Act and that Act may be cited together as the Foreshore Acts 1933 and 1992 and shall be construed together as one.

Section 7(3) of the Fisheries and Foreshore (Amendment) Act 1998 provides that the Foreshore Acts, 1933 and 1992, section 5 of that Act and, so far as they relate to that section, section 1 of that Act and this section may be cited together as the Foreshore Acts 1933 to 1998, and shall be construed together as one Act.

See: ENVIRONMENTAL IMPACT ASSESSMENT; EUROPEAN COMMUNITIES, REGULATIONS 1989–1999.

ADDITIONAL ENFORCEMENT PROVISIONS SECTIONS 5 AND 6 FORESHORE (AMENDMENT) ACT 1992.

Comparison: Sections 5 and 6 of the Foreshore (Amendment) Act 1992 are modelled on sections 10 and 11 of the LG(WP)A 1977. *See:* PROHIBITION, WATERS UNDER THE LG(WP)A 1977.

Section 5 of the Foreshore (Amendment) Act 1992:

"(1) Where, on application to the High Court by –
(a) the Minister,
(b) a local authority in respect of any area of seashore which is in whole or in part within its functional area or contiguous thereto, or
(c) any other person, whether or not that person has an interest in the seashore concerned,
that Court is satisfied that there has occurred, is occurring or is likely to occur any removal or disturbance of beach material or any kind or kinds of beach material in contravention of –
(i) a licence under section 3 of the Principal Act,
(ii) a prohibitory order under section 6 of the Principal Act, or
(iii) a prohibitory notice under section 7 of the Principal Act,
the High Court may by order –
(I) prohibit any person from removing or disturbing beach material of any kind or kinds of beach material in contravention of the licence, prohibitory order or prohibitory notice concerned,
(II) for the purpose of preventing, or preventing the continuance or recurrence of such a contravention, require any person concerned to do, refrain from or cease doing any specified act or to refrain from or cease making any specified omission, and
(III) make such other provisions as the Court considers appropriate."

Sections 3, 6 and 7 of the Foreshore Act 1933 referred to are dealt with above under this heading FORESHORE.

"(2) An application may be brought under subsection (1) of this section notwithstanding that a prosecution under the Principal Act has been brought in relation to the matters to which the application relates.

(3) An application for an order under this section shall be in a summary manner, and the High Court when considering the matter may make such interim or interlocutory order as it considers appropriate.

(4) The order by which an application under this section may be determined may contain such terms and conditions as to payment of costs as the High Court considers appropriate."

Section 6 of the Foreshore (Amendment) Act 1992:

"(1) (a) Where on application to the appropriate court by –
(i) the Minister,
(ii) a local authority in respect of any area of seashore which is in whole

or in part within its functional area or contiguous thereto, or

(iii) any other person, whether or not that person has an interest in the seashore concerned,

that court is satisfied that there has occurred or is occurring any removal or disturbance of beach material or any kind or kinds of beach material by another person (in this paragraph referred to as 'the second-mentioned person') in contravention of –

(I) a licence granted under section 3 of the principal Act,

(II) a prohibitory order under section 6 of the Principal Act, or

(III) a prohibitory notice under section 7 of that Act,

that court may make an order directing the second- named person to do any one or more of the following, that is to say –

(A) to refrain from or cease such removal or disturbance within such period as may be specified in the order, or

(B) to mitigate or remedy any effects of such removal or disturbance in such manner and within such period as may be specified in the order, or

(C) to pay to the applicant or such other person as may be specified in the order a specified amount to defray all or part of any costs incurred by the applicant or that other person in investigating, mitigating or remedying the effects of such removal or disturbance."

Subsection (1)*(b)*, *(c)*, *(d)* and *(e)* and subsections (2), (3) and (4) are exactly the same as section 10(1)*(b)*, *(c)*, *(d)* and *(e)* and subsections (2), (3) and (4) of the LG(WP)A 1977. *See*: PROHIBITION, WATERS UNDER THE LG(WP)A 1977.

Subsection (5)*(a)* and *(b)* deal with the jurisdiction of the District Court – the district in which the seashore concerned is in whole or in part situated or in which the defendant ordinarily resides – and the Circuit Court – the circuit in which the seashore concerned is situated or where the defendant ordinarily resides.

Subsection (6) provides that section 16 of the Principal Act, which deals with the jurisdiction of the Circuit Court by reference to the poor law valuation of the foreshore, shall not apply in proceedings under this section.

"(7) An application may be made under subsection (1) of this section notwithstanding that a prosecution under the Principal Act has not been brought in respect of the matters to which the application relates."

PROSECUTION OF OFFENCES

Section 7 of the Foreshore (Amendment) Act 1992:

"(1) A summary offence under the Foreshore Acts, 1933 and 1992, may be prosecuted by –

(a) the Minister, or

(b) a local authority in respect of any area of seashore which is in whole or in part within its functional area or contiguous thereto.

(2) Notwithstanding the provisions of section 10(4) of the Petty Sessions (Ireland) Act , 1851, summary proceedings for an offence under this Act may be commenced at any time within twelve months from the date on which the offence was committed."

Section 9 of the Foreshore (Amendment) Act 1992:

"Every licence granted under section 3 of the Principal Act, every prohibitory order made under section 6 of that Act and every prohibitory notice served under section 7 of that Act, which is a subsisting licence, order or notice (as the case may be) immediately before the commencement of this Act shall, as respects acts committed or omissions after the commencement of this Act which contravene such a licence, order or notice (as the case may be), continue in force as if granted, made or served under the said section 3, 6 or 7 (as the case may be) as amended by this Act."

FORFEITURE OF LICENCE

(F(C)A 1959, ss. 90 and 316)

Section 90 of the F(C)A 1959, amended by substitution by section 51 of the FA 1980 deals with forfeiture of licence as one of the ways of enforcing environmental law. *See:* ENFORCEMENT(2)(A).

Section 316 of the F(C)A 1959:

"Where –

(a) a person is convicted by a District Justice of an offence under any provision of this Act, and

(b) the said provision provides that a particular thing shall, as a statutory consequence of conviction, stand forfeited,

then, notwithstanding any rule of law, it shall not be necessary for the said Justice -

(i) to pronounce the fact of such forfeiture at the time of adjudication, or

(ii) to record the fact of such forfeiture in the Justice's Minute Book or the Charge Sheet or in the order of conviction."

FORFEITURE OF BOATS, VEHICLES AND EQUIPMENT
(F(C)A 1959, s. 301/WMA 1996, s. 6)

Section 301(2)(da) F(C)A 1959 inserted by section 53(a) of the FA 1980 in respect of boats and section 61(1)*(a)* of the WMA 1996 in respect of vehicles and equipment. *See:* (1) DETENTION AND FORFEITURE OF BOATS, VEHICLES AND EQUIPMENT; (2) ENFORCEMENT (7).

FUEL, REGULATIONS
(APA 1987, s. 53)

See: REGULATIONS IN RELATION TO FUEL SECTION 53 OF THE APA 1987.

FUNCTIONS
(WMA 1996, s. 5(1))

"includes powers and duties and references to the performance of functions include, as respects powers and duties, references to the exercise of the powers and the carrying out of the duties."

(F(A)A 1999, s. 2(1))

"Includes powers and duties."

FUNCTIONS OF THE CENTRAL BOARD AND TRANSFER OF PROPERTIES
(FA 1980, ss. 8 and 9)

Section 8 of the FA 1980, as substituted by section 5 of the F(A)A 1999 –

"(1) The general functions of the Central Board are to promote, support, facilitate and co-ordinate where necessary, and to advise the Minister on policy relating to, the conservation, protection, management, development and improvement of inland fisheries and the efficient and effective performance by the regional boards of their functions under this Act.

(2) Without prejudice to the generality of subsection (1) the Central Board shall –

(a) provide and undertake such co-ordination, specialist and support services to or for regional boards as are necessary for the efficient performance by the regional boards of their functions,

(b) co-ordinate and consult with the regional boards on the preparation and regular review of national inland fisheries development plans, incorporating regional inland fisheries development plans, and submit such plans to the Minister for the Minister's consideration in such form and at such intervals as the Minister may require,

(c) administer such schemes, grants and other financial facilities requiring the disbursement of European Union and such other funds as may from time to time be authorised by the Minister with the consent of the Minister for Finance,

(d) support, and co-ordinate where necessary, the angling promotion and marketing activities of the regional boards in respect of their fishery regions, and co-operate and co-ordinate with Bórd Fáilte in developing international promotion and marketing strategies and activities in relation to game, coarse and sea tourism angling,

(e) undertake the efficient and effective management, conservation, protection, development and improvement of any fishery, hatchery or fish farm in its possession or occupation in accordance with the direction, if any, of the Minister, and

(f) in the performance of it's functions have regard to the need for the sustainable development of the inland fishery resource (including the conservation of fish and other species of fauna and flora habitats and the biodiversity of inland water ecosystems) and as far as possible ensure that its activities are carried out so as to protect the national heritage, within the meaning of the Heritage Act, 1995.

(3) The Central Board may provide education courses or facilities for training or otherwise instructing persons in matters relating to the management, conservation, protection, development or improvement of fisheries and charge such fees for the provision of those courses or facilities as it thinks fit.

(4) The Central Board may provide such services for the management, conservation, protection, development, improvement or promotion

of fisheries or matters relating to fisheries, and charge such fees in relation to the provision of such services (other than those provided by the regional board or the Minister), as it thinks fit.

(5) (a) The Central Board may, in relation to an inland fishery, carry out such research or experimental work as it considers necessary for the performance of its functions but this paragraph shall not be construed as enabling the Board to carry out research or experimental work on or in relation to any species of sea-fish, within the meaning of Part XIII of the Principal Act, other than research similar or analogous to research in relation to sea-fish being carried out by the Central Board immediately before the commencement of section 5 of the Fisheries (Amendment) Act, 1999.
(b) In the carrying out of work under paragraph (a) of this subsection the Central Board shall, as appropriate, co-operate with any regional board in whose region the fishery is situated and shall also co-operate and co-ordinate, as appropriate, with the *(qv)* Marine Institute.

(6) For the purpose of performing its functions under this Act, but subject to the directions, if any, of the Minister, the Central Board may enter into such partnership or other arrangements with such persons or bodies as it thinks fit.

(7) The Central Board may make recommendations to the Minister as to the exercise by the Minister of the powers conferred on the Minister by section 29 of the Fisheries (Amendment) Act, 1962, the levels of fishery rates and fishery licence duties payable under the Fisheries Acts, 1959 to 1999.

(8) The Minister may, if he or she thinks fit, authorise the Central Board to engage in the processing and marketing of such species of fish as are specified in the authorisation.

(9) The Central Board shall have regard to the particular role and contribution of angling clubs and associations in the sustainable management and development to the public benefit of State, public and inland fisheries."

For Heritage Act 1995 *See:* COUNCIL, THE, HERITAGE COUNCIL, THE.

This new section 8 FA 1980, inserted by section (5) of the F(A)A 1999, when read in conjunction with the new section 11 of the FA 1980, inserted by section 8 of the F(A)A 1999, basically changes the structure of management of inland fisheries laid down in Part II of the FA 1980 of which sections 8 and 11 form part.

The FA1980 had dismantled the old *(qv)* boards of conservators and substituted therefor the non-elected Central Board and the democratically elected regional fisheries boards. Under the 1980 Act it was intended that the Central Board would have an umbrella role over the activities of the regional boards and was given specific power under the old section 8 to direct the functions of the regional boards.

The F(A)A 1999 downgrades the Central Board and it is now relegated to being no more than an advisory body, and aide to tourism promotion, a conduit between the Minister and the regional boards and a promoter of fishing competitions. It used to be the regional boards who had responsibility for angling under the old section 11(1)(c)9iv).

An important function of the Central Board under the old section 8 had been the preparation and submission to the Minister at specified intervals of an "inland fisheries development programme". The title to this exercise has been altered in the new section 8 of the F(A) 1999 to a "national inland fisheries development plan". The Central Board is not now involved in the preparation of the development plan. Its function under section 8(1)(b) is to co-ordinate and consult with the regional boards on it's preparation and review. They are still, however, responsible under the same paragraph for the submission of the development plan to the Minister.

The foregoing surely creates a problem. There has been no clear appointment of any other body to do the work of preparation of the development plan. The regional boards are enjoined under section 11(b) to prepare and submit a plan for its region for incorporation in the development plan to be submitted to the Minister but that is as far as its responsibilities go. The function of preparing a national plan should have been clearly and decisively designated.
See: FUNCTIONS OF REGIONAL FISHERIES BOARDS

Section 9 of the FA 1980 provides that certain properties specified in the section and which were occupied by or on behalf of the *(qv)* boards of conservators shall be transferred to the Central Board on the appointed day (October 29, 1980) and that they will on that day be vested in the Central Board without conveyance or assignment.

Chapter IV of the FA 1980 (sections 19 to 33) contains provisions relating to the protocol and administration of the Central Board as does Part I of the First Schedule. The sections deal with annual reports to the Minister, yearly estimates of income and expenditure for presentation to the Minister, grants payable to the Central Board out of monies provided by the Oireachtas and the (*qv*) Salmon Conservancy Fund, preparation of accounts for and requirements in relation to the audit by the Comptroller and Auditor General, and power of borrowing of both central and regional boards.

COMMITTEES OF THE CENTRAL BOARD

Section 8A of the FA 1980 (inserted by section 6 of the F(A)A 1999) –

"(1) The Central Board may establish committees to assist and advise in relation to the performance of its functions.

(2) A committee may, if the Board thinks fit, include among its members persons who are not members of the Board.

(3) The Central Board shall appoint a member of the Board to be chairperson of a committee.

(4) The Central Board may at any time dissolve a committee.

(5) The Central Board may regulate the procedure of its committees but, subject to any such regulations, a committee may regulate its own procedure."

FUNCTIONS OF REGIONAL FISHERIES BOARDS

(FA 1980, s. 11)

Section 11 of the FA 1980 as amended by section 8 of the F(A)A 1999 –

"(1) A regional board shall –

(a) subject to this Act, protect the fisheries in its fisheries region and generally enforce the Fisheries Act, 1959 to 1999, in the region,

(b) prepare and submit to the Central Board a plan for the development of inland fisheries in its *(qv)* fisheries region, in such form and at such intervals as the Minister may from time to time direct, for incorporation in any inland fisheries development plan to be submitted to the Minister under paragraph (b) of section 8(2) of this Act,

(c) ensure that any fishery in the possession or occupation of the *(qv)* board, or any fishery, hatchery or fish farm which by virtue of section 8(2) of this Act is under the care and management of the board, is managed, conserved, protected, developed and improved, or otherwise dealt with, in accordance with both the current development plan prepared under this section by the board and any direction of the Minister referred to in paragraph (c) of section 8(2) of this Act and which is for the time being in force,

(d) in accordance with such development plan, promote and encourage the management, conservation, protection, development and improvement of the fisheries which are not in its possession or occupation in its fisheries region,

(e) ensure that any oyster or other mollusc fishery in its fisheries region is protected in accordance with such direction of the Minister as relates to a fishery of that kind,

(f) encourage, promote, organise and co-ordinate angling for salmon, trout, coarse fish and sea-fish and, for the purposes of any or all of those kinds of angling, provide such facilities and amenities, if any, as it thinks fit,

(g) encourage, promote, organise, and co-ordinate together with the inland fisheries owners, bodies and organisations in its fisheries region, the voluntary development of inland fisheries catchment management plans in its fisheries region and for that purpose have regard to the distinctive circumstances which pertain in each of the catchment systems in its region and consult with and involve local authorities and other interested bodies and organisations and comply with any directions the Minister may from time to time give to it,

(h) co-operate and co-ordinate with the Central Board or any one or more of the regional boards where necessary to ensure the effective and efficient deployment of resources, performance of functions, drawing up of estimates and the provision of services within and between the fishery regions and in this regard comply with any directions the Minister may from time to time give to it, and

(i) in the performance of its functions, have regard to the need for the sustainable d evelopment of the inland fisheries resource (including the conservation of fish and other species of fauna and flora habitats and the biodiversity of inland water ecosystems) and as far as possible ensure that its activities are carried out so as to protect the national heritage within the meaning of the Heritage Act 1995.

(2) A regional board may provide such services (including education or training courses or facilities for training or instruction) for the management, conservation, protection, development and improvement of fisheries, or such other matters relating to fisheries, as it thinks fit and to charge such fees in relation to those services (other than those provided for (by?) another board or the Minister) as it thinks fit.

(2A) For the purpose of performing its functions under this Act, but subject to the directions, if any, of the Minister, a regional board may enter into such partnership or other arrangements with such persons or bodies as it thinks fit.

(2B) A regional board shall have regard to the particular role and contribution of angling clubs and associations in the sustainable management and development to the public benefit of State, public and other inland fisheries in its region."

The Fisheries (Amendment) Act, 1999 (save for section 23) came into force on 20 December 1999 by virtue of the Fisheries (Amendment) Act, 1999 (Commencement) Order, 1999 (S.I. No. 419 of 1999).

"(3) (a) Subject to Article 1(b) of the Fourth Schedule to this Act, the power under Part V of the Principal Act of striking a rate on fisheries, in so far as before the commencement of this section it was exercisable by a board of conservators, and the powers under that Part to amend, collect and recover such a rate are, in so far as they apply to a fishery district, hereby assigned to the (*qv*) regional board concerned.

(b) Where a regional board strikes a rate on fisheries, the Minister in considering whether to confirm the rate with or without modification or to exercise the power conferred on him by section 55 of the Principal Act to strike a rate shall have regard to any relevant recommendation made by the (*qv*) Central Board under section 8(1)(d) of this Act.

(4) The powers under the Principal Act to issue licences, for fishing for salmon or eels (other than salmon rod (twenty-one day) ordinary licences) and to issue oyster fishing licences, which, immediately before the passing of this Act, were exercisable by a board of conservators shall, on and from the appointed day, be exercisable by a (*qv*) regional board.

(4A) The powers exercisable by a (*qv*) regional board by virtue of subsection (4) of this section of issue certain types of licences shall, upon the coming into operation of section 19 of the Fisheries (Amendment) (No. 2) Act, 1987, extend to licences to which that Act relates and the references in the said subsection (4) to 'salmon rod (twenty-one day) ordinary licences' shall not be construed as referring to salmon rod (twenty-one day) ordinary licences issued by virtue of that Act."

Subsection (4A) was inserted by section 19 of the F(A)(No. 2)A 1987. This subsection is now meaningless. *See:* DUTIES ON ORDINARY FISHING LICENCES).

Article 3 of that Schedule was amended by section 23 of the F(A)A 1999. Section 23 of the Fisheries (Amendment) Act, 1999 came into force on 24 January 2000 by virtue of the Fisheries (Amendment) Act, 1999 (Section 23) (Commencement) Order, 2000 (S.I. NO. 21 of 2000).

Section 11 of the FA 1980 deals, *inter alia*, with oyster fishery orders. Section 5(6) of the FA 1997 repealed the Part of the F(C)A 1959 which dealt with the making of oyster fishing orders. However, section 278 of the F(C)A 1959, which allowed the boards of conservators to issue oyster fishing licences (as distinct from the making of oyster fishery orders) is unchanged and the power to issue such licences passes by virtue of section 10(4) to the regional boards.

Section 11(5) of the FA 1980:

"(5) The amendments to the Principal Act or the Act of 1962 specified in the Fourth Schedule to this Act shall have effect as on and from the appointed day."

The appointed day for the purposes of this Act was October 29, 1980. *See:* The Fisheries Act 1980 (Appointed Day) Order 1980 (S.I. No. 323 of 1980).

Section 11(6) of the FA 1980:

"(6) (a) The Minister may, if he thinks fit, authorise a (*qv*) regional board to engage in the processing and marketing of such species of fish as are specified in the authorisation.

(b) (i) The Minister may by order provide for the issue by any regional board, on payment of such duty (if any) as may be specified in the order, of licences for fishing of a class or description specified in the order.

(ii) In case an order under this section provides for the issue of licences for fishing with engines which are not scheduled engines, then so long as the order is in force the following provisions shall have effect, namely, any engine which is of a kind described in the order shall for the purposes of section 65 of the Principal Act be regarded as being a scheduled engine, and any such licence shall for the said purposes be regarded as being an ordinary fishing licence.

(iii) In case an order under this paragraph is for the time being in force, the power conferred by the order on (*qv*) regional boards shall be in addition to and not in substitution for the power conferred on such boards under subsection (4) of this section.

(c) The Minister may by order assign to –

(i) regional boards generally,

(ii) regional boards of a particular class or description,

(iii)one or more particular regional boards,

such functions relating to fisheries (being functions additional to those assigned by this Act) as the Minster thinks fit).

(d) Duties payable as regards licences issued by virtue of this section shall be paid to the regional board by whom the licence is issued.

(e) In this Act 'fishing licence', when used without qualification, shall include a licence issued pursuant to an order under paragraph (b) of this subsection."

FUNCTIONS, PERFORMANCE BY CENTRAL BOARD AND REGIONAL BOARDS

(FA 1980, 2nd Schedule)

Part I of the Second Schedule to the FA 1980 concerns the performance by the (*qv*) Central Board and any (*qv*) regional board of its functions came into force on 20 December 1999 by virtue of the Fisheries (Amendment) Act, 1999 (Commencement) Order 1999 (S.I. No. 419 of 1999).

Article 20 of that Schedule provides:

"The Central Board may perform any of its functions through or by any of its officers or servants or any other person duly authorised by the Central Board in that behalf, but nothing in this Article shall be construed as enabling any person to execute on behalf of the Central Board any document under seal."

See: SEAL, CENTRAL BOARD AND REGIONAL FISHERIES BOARDS.

FUNCTIONS OF THE ENVIRONMENTAL PROTECTION AGENCY

(EPAA 1992, ss. 52 to 57)

The overall function of the Agency is the protection of the environment and in so far as a greater part of the exercise of this function involves supervising, advising and, at times, admonishing other bodies, it is only concerned with the environmental functions of those bodies.

Section 52 of the EPAA 1992:

"(1) The functions of the (*qv*) Agency shall, subject to the provisions of this Act, include –

(a) the licensing, regulation and control of (*qv*) activities for the purposes of (*qv*) environmental protection,

(b) the (*qv*) monitoring of the quality of the environment, including the establishment and maintenance of (*qv*) data bases of information related to the environment and making arrangements for the dissemination of such information and for public access thereto,

(c) the provision of support and advisory services for the purposes of environmental protection to local authorities and other public authorities in relation to the performance of any function of those authorities,

(d) the promotion and co-ordination of (*qv*) environmental research, the provision of assistance and advice in relation to such research and the carrying out, causing to be carried out, or arranging for, such research,
(e) liaison with the European Environment Agency provided for under Council Regulation 1210/90/EEC (O.J. No. L 120, 11.05.90, p.1),
(f) such other functions in relation to environmental protection as may be assigned or transferred to it by the Minister under sections 53 or 54 including functions arising from any obligations under any treaty governing the European Communities or an act adopted by the institutions of those Communities or other international convention or agreement to which the State is, or becomes, a party.

(2) In carrying out its functions, the Agency shall –
(a) keep itself informed of the policies and objectives of (*qv*) public authorities whose functions have, or may have, a bearing on matters with which the Agency is concerned,
(b) have regard to the need for a high standard of environmental protection and the need to promote sustainable and environmentally sound development, processes or operations,
(c) have regard for the need for precaution in relation to the potentially harmful effects of (*qv*) emissions, where there are, in the opinion of the Agency, reasonable grounds for believing that such emissions could cause significant (*qv*) environmental pollution,
(d) have regard to the need to give effect, insofar as it is feasible, to the (*qv*) 'polluter pays' principle, as set out in Council Recommendation 75/436/EURATOM, ECSC, EEC of 3 March, 1975 (O.J. No. L 194, 25.7.75 P.1), regarding cost allocation and action by public authorities on environmental matters,
(e) ensure, in so far as is practicable, that a proper balance is achieved between the need to protect the environment (and the cost of such protection) and the need for infrastructural, economic and social progress and development."

Section 53 of the EPAA 1992 concerns the assignment of additional functions to the Agency. Subsections (1) and (2) of that section provide that the Minister may, following consultation with the Agency and such government department as are deemed appropriate, assign by regulation to the Agency additional functions and as a consequence of that assignment modify existing functions as he considers appropriate and particularly those functions which relate to environmental protection and arise from or are necessary to implement European acts and treaties and international conventions or agreements to which the State is, or becomes a party.

Subsection (3) of section 53 provides for the assignment to the Agency of such ancillary, incidental and supplemental functions as are necessary for such implementation. Subsection (4) provides for charges for these functions and recovery of those charges

Section 54 of the EPAA 1992 provides that those functions relating to environmental protection conferred on a public authority, which for the purposes of this Act includes a local authority, specified in the Second Schedule and which the Minister considers could be more effectively performed by the Agency, may, by regulation, be performed by the Agency in lieu of the authority.

Comparison: Sections 100 and 101 of the EPAA 1992 which provide for specific orders in relation to statutory functions under the LG(WP)A 1977 and the APA 1987. *See:* EXTENSION OF POWERS.

Section 55(1) of the EPAA 1992 provides that for the purposes of (*qv*) environmental protection, the Agency may, of its own volition and must when requested by the Minister so to do, give advice or make recommendations on any matter relating to the functions or responsibilities of any Minister of the Government. The recipient is obliged by the section to have regard to the advice or recommendation.

Subsection (2) provides that the advices and recommendations may include the assessment of the environmental factor of any proposal for the amendment or implementation of European law, any change in Irish law generally, any change in Irish environmental law, overall advices and recommendations in relation to guidelines, standards and other matters including management of coastal areas, in respect of (*qv*) environmental protection and generally keeping the Government abreast of particular issues and problems in relation to environmental protection

Section 56 of the EPAA 1992 provides for the

advisory functions of the Agency to local authorities generally or to a particular local authority in the performance of their functions and they stand in the same position to the Agency as do government departments in section 55 above. These advices may be proffered by the Agency on their own initiative and must be given when requested by the Minister.

Subsection (2) provides that the advice and recommendations may include the provision of scientific facilities and services, the preparation of legal proceedings for prosecution for breach of any environmental law, the formulation of standards and procedures in relation to any particular development or process or generally, the management of coastal areas, the monitoring of emissions and environmental quality and sampling, measuring and analysis and the equipment to be used for sampling, measuring and analysis.

Subsection (3) provides that the Agency may organise or assist in organising conferences, seminars, lectures, demonstrations, training courses or publications for staff or members of local authorities involved in environmental protection.

Subsection (4) provides that in the section "local authority" has the meaning assigned to it by the Local Government Act 1941.

Section 57 of the EPAA 1992 provides that the Agency shall provide general support, assistance and services to local authorities as the Agency considers necessary and feasible.

FUNCTIONS OF HERITAGE COUNCIL
(Heritage Act 1995, s. 6)

See: COUNCIL, THE, HERITAGE COUNCIL, THE.

FUNCTION OF LOCAL AUTHORITIES

See: (1) COUNTY COUNCILS; (2) PERFORMANCE OF STATUTORY FUNCTIONS BY LOCAL AUTHORITIES.

FUNCTIONS OF LOCAL AUTHORITIES IN RELATION TO WASTE
(WMA 1996, s. 59)

Section 59 of the WMA 1996:

"(1) Each local authority shall, save in a particular case where a provision of this Act provides to the contrary, be responsible for the supervision of, and the enforcement of the relevant provisions of this Act in relation to the holding, (*qv*) recovery and (*qv*) disposal of waste by persons within its functional area.

(2) Nothing in subsection (1) shall be construed as prejudicing the right of the (*qv*) Agency or any other person to perform any other functions conferred on it or him or her by or under any provision of this Act."

FUNCTIONS OF THE MINISTER UNDER WLA 1976
(WLA 1976, s. 11)

Section 11 of the WLA 1976:

"(1) It shall be the function of the Minister to secure the conservation of (*qv*)wildlife.

(2) Without prejudice to the generality of subsection (1) in this section, the Minister may in particular do all or any of the following –

(a) give assistance or advice to any person on any matter affecting wildlife,

(b) where the Minister considers that the management, or supervision of the management by him or on his behalf, in any land in which he has not an interest, is desirable in the interests of wildlife, he may manage or cause to be managed, or supervise or cause to be supervised the management of the lands upon such terms and subject to such conditions as may be agreed upon between him and a person having an interest in the land,

(c) enter into and carry out an agreement with another person to participate in a scheme, undertaking or project for the conservation of wildlife and for the purposes of such scheme, undertaking or project to perform any one or more of the functions assigned to him under this Act,

(d) make grants or loans to further projects or activities which have as their object the conservation of wildlife generally, a particular aspect of such conservation or the development and proper use of hunting amenities and resources,

(e) promote, either directly or indirectly, whether alone or in conjunction with other persons, schemes or projects for the better conservation and use of wildlife or for the prevention, reduction or removal of any damage, or source of damage, to wildlife.

(3) The Minister may, either directly or in association with or through the agency of another person –
(a) carry out or cause to be carried out research which he considers desirable for the performance of his functions under this Act,
(b) promote the knowledge and understanding of matters to which the functions assigned to him under this Act are related.

(4) Nothing in this section shall restrict, prejudice or affect the performance by the Minister for Agriculture and Fisheries of any function which could have been performed by him immediately before the commencement of this section."

FUNCTIONS, TRANSFER OF
(APA 1987, s. 21)

The Minister can by regulation provide that any function conferred on a local authority by the APA, in addition or in lieu of performance by the local authority, can be performed by such person or body as he may specify. *See:* TRANSFER OF FUNCTIONS.

(EPAA 1992, s. 54)

The Minister may by regulation transfer from any public body to the Agency any function relating to environmental protection. *See:* TRANSFER OF FUNCTIONS.

(WMA 1996, s. 21)

The Minister may transfer any function conferred on a local authority to the Agency. *See:* TRANSFER OF FUNCTIONS FROM LOCAL AUTHORITY TO AGENCY.

(WMA 1996, s. 69)

Transfer of functions from the Agency to a local authority in relation to waste licences. *See:* TRANSFER OF FUNCTIONS IN RELATION TO WASTE LICENCES.

FUNCTIONAL AREA

See: LOCAL AUTHORITY.

G

GAME
(WLA 1976)

The designations "game species", "game birds" and "game animals" are used extensively and loosely in literature on the WLA 1976. In fact the word "game" is defined in the Act for the purposes of one section only, section 44, and even then its application is to one subsection only, subsection (5), which provides for Ministerial regulations declaring a club or association which has among its objects the preservation of game to be a "Recognised Body" and these recognised bodies have power to prosecute for breach of section 44 under section 44(4)(c).

"Game" is defined in the WLA 1976, section 44(8), as meaning any (*qv*) exempted wild mammal or any (*qv*) protected wild bird which is of a species specified in an order under section 24 of the Act.

Section 24 refers to (*qv*) open seasons when the Minister may by order provide it is permitted to shoot not "game" birds but any protected wild bird which is of a species specified in the order.

GARDA SÍOCHÁNA
(F(C)A 1959/WLA 1976)

Members of the Garda Síochána share wide powers with authorised officers appointed under the Fisheries Acts and the WLA 1976 under sections 296, 298, 299, 300 and 301 of the F(C)A 1959 and section 72 of the WLA 1976. *See:* ENTRY AND SEARCH (1) AND (6). They are also obliged by section 14(8) of the WMA 1996 to assist an authorised person where that person is being obstructed on bringing a vehicle to any place in exercise of powers under the section.

GEOLOGY
(Heritage Act 1995, s. 2(1))

"Geology" means the study of the planet Earth as a whole or in part, the materials of which it is made, the processes that act and have acted upon these materials and the products and structures formed by such action, the physical and biological history of the planet since its origin including the history of life preserved as fossils in rocks and deposits at the surface or in layers beneath the surface of the earth, stratigraphic succession, caves, fossil content or any other items of scientific interest, and includes geomorphology, lithology and mineralogy.

GRANT OF LICENCE
(F(C)A 1959/WLA 1976/LG(WP)A 1977/APA 1987/EPAA 1992/WMA 1996)

See: (1) LICENCES; (2) CONDITIONS.

GRANTS, SPECIAL TIDAL WATERS
(F(C)A 1959, s. 62)

Section 62(1) of the F(C)A 1959 refers to certain grants which must be made by the Oireachtas to regional fishery boards within whose region during a fishery year there are *(qv)* special tidal waters by reference to a percentage of the fishery rate for that year.

Subsection (2) provides for a discretionary disbursement by the Minister, again in the case of a regional board within whose region there are special tidal waters, of a grant equal to an estimated deficit. The consent of the Minister for Finance must be obtained.

GRANTS, TO THE AGENCY
(EPAA 1992, s. 46)

Section 46 of the EPAA 1992 provides that the Minister may in each financial year, after consultation with the Agency in relation to its proposed work programme and expenditure for that year, make grants of such amounts as may be sanctioned by the Minister for Finance out of monies provided by the Oireachtas towards the expenditure incurred by the Agency in the performance of its functions.

GENETICALLY MODIFIED ORGANISMS
(EPAA 1992, s. 111)

Section 111 of the EPAA 1992:

"(1) The Minister may, for the purposes of (*qv*) environmental protection, for the prevention of danger to health or damage to property or for the preservation of amenities and, in particular, for the purpose of giving full effect to Council Directives 90/219/EEC (of 23 April 1990 on the contained use of genetically modified organisms (O.J. No. L 117, 8.05.90 p 1)) and 90/220/EEC (of 23 April 1990 on the deliberate release into the environment of genetically modified organisms (O.J. No. L 117, 8.05.90, p.15) following consultation with the Minister for Industry and Commerce and any other Minister of the Government who in the opinion of the Minister is concerned, make regulations for the control, management, regulation or prohibition of any process or action or classes of processes or actions, involving a genetically modified organism."

MATTERS TO BE DEALT WITH UNDER REGULATIONS MADE UNDER SECTION 111(2) OF EPAA 1992

Subsection (2) provides that regulations may make various provisions relating to activities concerning genetically organisms.

The conditions set out in subsection (2) follow the well-established pattern in the Act for the grant of and conditions attaching to an (*qv*) Integrated Pollution Control Licence at sections 83 and 84 (*See:* CONDITIONS) but here the emphasis is on the dangers inherent in dealing with unknown quantities and the danger of what is called a "release" to an (*qv*) environmental medium. The word is not defined but it is used in conjunction with "emission" which is defined in section 3(1) of the EPAA 1992 *See:* EMISSIONS.

The phrase "(*qv*) deliberate release" is used in the Genetically Modified Organisms Regulations 1994 (S.I. No. 345 of 1994).

The matters that may be covered by regulations can be summarised as follows:

Assignment by the Minister of his functions, general duties and obligations and consultation.

Paragraphs (a), (b) and (c) deal with the Minister's power to assign his functions under subsection (1), and placing duties and obligations on a person genetically modifying an organism or "importing, acquiring, keeping, using or releasing to the environment any genetically modified organism" and consultation between the Minister and specified persons, whether in or outside the State.

Licensing, Regulation and Prohibition

Paragraphs (d) and (e) deal with licensing a person engaged in genetically modifying any organism, or who is importing, acquiring, keeping, using or releasing to the environment any genetically modified organisms (GMO) and regulating, including licensing, the establishment and operation of any process or action involving a GMO and prohibiting any such process or action unless a licence has been obtained.

Information

Paragraph (f) deals with the information including information on personnel, premises and waste management to be furnished with an application for a licence and provision for seeking additional information.

Suggested Conditions to be attached to a Licence

Paragraph (g) (i) to (vi) covers period of licence, organisms covered by licence, limitations or prohibitions, continuance of conditions after expiry, cancellation or suspension or when process or action is completed, restrictions and limits on releases and emissions or specified methods for their treatment or disposal and monitoring and making available the results.

Grant, Review, Cancellation and Suspension of Licences

Paragraph (h) provides for the specification of procedures for grant review, cancellation and suspension of licences and for the making and consideration of representations in relation thereto.

Studies and Assessments

Paragraph (i) deals with studies and assessments of the nature of, the process or action involving a GMO, the possible risks to the environment either from the organism or from the process or action and the potential effects of a release whether planned or accidental.

Precautions and Reacting to an Emergency

Paragraph (j) deals with the setting up of biosafety committees, the information to be provided to the public, emergency response arrangements, notification to proper authorities, the urgent measures to be taken by those authorities to protect the environment, measures for the prevention of danger to health or damage to property or the preservation of amenities, the recovery of the costs of such measures and generally the controls to be observed in relation to particular organisms or classes of organisms, processes or classes of processes or actions or classes of actions, involving a GMO.

Applications to the High Court

Paragraph (k) contemplates an application by the Minister "or such other person as may be prescribed under subsection (1)" for an order prohibiting or restricting any process or action involving a GMO in such circumstances as may be specified.

This is now regulated for by Article 62 of the GMO Regulations, 1994.
See: ENFORCEMENT (1)(C).

Prohibition of Specified Process

Paragraph (l) allows the prohibition of any specified process or action involving, or any importation, acquisition, keeping, using or releasing to the environment, a specifically genetically modified organism, of any specified genetic modification of an organism.

Grant of Exemptions

Paragraph (m) proposes the grant:

(i) to a specified class of persons,
(ii) for specified research or in specified circumstances, or
(iii) as regards specified organisms or classes of organisms, processes or classes of processes or actions or classes of actions involving specified organisms or classes of organisms, exemptions from any requirements of the regulations in specified circumstances and subject to specified conditions.

Notices, records and registers regulations in respect of notices, records, keeping a register, advices and charges are dealt with in paragraphs (n), (o), (p), (q) and (r) following on the spirit of openness and transparency which permeates this Act and which puts the public on notice of every application of substance to the Agency under this and other headings and allows the public access to the information regarding these applications in the register but, as in other sections throughout, the Minister can control the precise information made available and there is a provision for restricted information.

The making of charges is in line with all modern environmental administration. *See:* CHARGES.

Offence
Subsection (3) provides that it shall be an offence not to comply with any condition attached to a licence issued pursuant to regulations made under this section.

BATNEEC

Subsection (4) requires of a person in charge of any process or action above to apply the (*qv*) BATNEEC principle for the purposes of environmental protection, for the prevention of danger to health or damage to property, or for the preservation of amenities, arising from any process or action involving a GMO.

Subsection (5) provides that regulations under this section may contain such incidental, supplementary, consequential and transitional provisions (including provisions modifying any provision of this Act or of any other enactment) as appear to the Minister to be necessary for the purposes of, in consequence of, or to give full effect to, the regulations. The GMO Regulations are dealt with hereunder.

POWERS OF AUTHORISED PERSONS EXTENDED

Subsection (6) provides for the purposes of this section, in addition to the powers given under section 13 to an authorised person, that that person may require, in relation to any premises or part of premises which he has power to enter or in relation to any process or action or part of a process or action on such premises, or in relation to anything in or on such premises, that it should be maintained without disturbance or in such manner as he may specify for so long as is reasonable in order to carry out his investigations or tests.

INTERPRETATION

Subsection (7) provides that in this section –
"genetically modified organism" means:

(a) an organism derived from the formation of a combination of genetic material by artificial techniques, or
(b) an organism inheriting such combination of genetic material, or
(c) an organism that results from the replication of an organism described in paragraph (a), or
(d) such other matter as may be prescribed by the Minister.

"Organism" means any multicellular, unicellular, subcellular or acellular entity capable of replication or of transferring genetic material whether by natural or artificial processes or such other matter as may be prescribed by the Minister.

"Environment" includes atmosphere, land, soil, water and all living organisms.

"Licence" includes a consent or any other form of authorisation and cognate words shall be construed accordingly.

In the Genetically Modified Organisms

Regulations 1994 (S.I. No. 345 of 1994)

"“genetically modified micro-organism” means any microbiological entity, cellular or non-cellular, capable of replication or of transferring genetic material in which the genetic material has been altered in a way that does not occur naturally by mating and/or natural recombination."

GENETICALLY MODIFIED ORGANISMS REGULATIONS 1994

The appropriate regulations are the Genetically Modified Organisms Regulations 1994 (S.I. No. 345 of 1994) and two Amendment Regulations made in 1996 and 1997 (S.I. Nos. 348 of 96 and 332 of 97).

The 1994 Regulations which are made under sections 6 and 11 of the EPAA 1992 are expressed in their explanatory note to give effect to Council Directive 90/219/EEC of April 23, 1990 on the (*qv*) contained use of genetically modified organisms (O.J. L117, May 8, 1990 p.1)) and 90/220/EEC of April 23, 1990 on the deliberate release into the environment of genetically modified organisms (O.J. L117, May 8, 1990, p.15).

The Regulations provide for various procedural matters in relation to the contained use, deliberate release and (*qv*) placing on the market of genetically modified organisms. They provide for notifications for consent, application of principles on good microbiological practice, risk assessment, reviews of consents, accidental procedures and the contents of a register of notifications.

Users of genetically modified organisms are required under the Regulations to ensure that all appropriate measures are taken to avoid adverse effects on human health and the environment. A consent to place a product, containing or consisting of a genetically modified organism, on the market must include conditions relating to the labelling and packaging of the product.

Offence
Article 29 provides:

"Subject to the provisions of Article 5, a person shall not (*qv*) deliberately release a genetically modified organism, or a combination of genetically modified organisms, for the purpose of research and development, or for any purpose other than for (*qv*) placing on the market, unless the written consent of the Agency has been received and the conditions attached to the consent have been complied with in respect of that release."

Article 5 provides:

"A person who carries out a (*qv*) contained use, (*qv*) deliberate release or a (*qv*) placing on the market, or any other (*qv*) use, shall ensure that all appropriate measures are taken to avoid adverse effects on human health and the environment."

Article 39 provides:

"A person shall not (*qv*) place on the market any (*qv*) product containing or consisting of genetically modified organisms unless -

(a) consent in writing has been received under this Part, or
(b) consent in writing has been received from the competent authority of another Member State of the European Communities in accordance with Part C of Council Directive 90/220/EEC,

and the conditions attached to the relevant consent have been complied with."

Article 40 provides:

"(1) Notwithstanding the provisions of Article 39, the Agency may by notice in writing provisionally restrict or prohibit the (*qv*) use or (*qv*) placing on the market of a (*qv*) product containing or consisting of genetically modified organisms where there are reasonable grounds to believe that the product constitutes a risk to human health or the environment.

(2) Where the Agency decides provisionally to restrict or prohibit the placing on the market of a product containing genetically modified organisms, that has received a written consent under these Regulations or from the competent authority of another Member State of the European Communities which satisfies the provisions of Part C of Council Directive 90/220/EEC, it shall, as soon as practicable, inform the Commission of the European Communities and the other Member States of the European Communities of its decision and the reasons therefor.

Offence

(3) It shall be an offence to contravene a provision of any notice in writing made under sub-article (1).

(4) A decision taken under article 16(2) of Council Directive 90/220/EEC shall be accepted by the Agency in respect of any notice in writing given by it under sub-

article (1)."

See: (1) AUTHORISED PERSONS, EPAA 1992; (2) PROSECUTION, POWERS OF, (3) ENFORCEMENT (1)(C); and (4) ENFORCEMENT (3)(D).

In an action entitled *Clare Watson (applicant) v. the Environmental Protection Agency and Monsanto (respondents)* (Action No. 168J of 1997) which arose out of the consent of the EPA for limited trials for genetically modified organisms and in proceedings for judicial review the applicant sought to have the consent quashed.

The High Court refused the relief sought and held that the EPA, in deciding whether to consent to a (*qv*) deliberate release of a GMO into the environment, is not required to be satisfied beyond reasonable doubt that the risk of adverse effects has been reduced to an effective zero level. The standard to be applied is set out in the 1994 Regulations (S.I. No. 345 of 1994) and is the same as that contemplated by the 1992 Act and as established by the 1990 Directive and requires the (*qv*) Agency to ensure that all appropriate measures are taken to avoid adverse effects.

GIFTS
(WLA 1976/EPAA 1992/Heritage Act 1995)

WLA 1976

Section 6 of the WLA 1976 provides that the Minister may accept any gift made to him for all or any of the purposes of this Act, and subject to the terms thereof, may apply it for those purposes.

EPAA 1992

Section 48(1) of the EPAA 1992 provides that the Agency may accept gifts of money, land or other property upon such trusts or conditions (if any) as may be specified by the donor.

Subsection (2) provides that the Agency shall not accept a gift if the trusts or conditions attached to it would be inconsistent with, or prejudice, the effective performance of its functions.

Subsection (3) provides that the Agency shall publish in its annual report details of all gifts accepted by it during the period of the report.

Heritage Act 1995

Section 12(1) of the Heritage Act 1995 provides that the (*qv*) Council may accept any gift for any purpose which relates to the functions of the Council.

Subsection (2) provides that a gift which is inconsistent with performance of its functions is not acceptable by the Council.

Subsection (3) provides that the Council may provide for the housing and study of, and may exhibit and dispose of non-pecuniary gifts as it deems appropriate.

GUIDING WALLS
(F(C)A 1959)

See: FISHING WEIR, GUIDING WALLS, CONSTRUCTION OF.

H

HABITAT
(NH 97, Reg. 2(1))

""Habitat of a species" means an environment defined by specific abiotic and biotic factors, in which the species lives at any stage of its biological cycle."

This definition is taken verbatim from the (*qv*) Habitats Directive (92/43/EEC of May 21, 1992 (O.J. L206, July 22, 1992, p.7)), Article 1(f)).

""Natural habitats" means terrestrial or aquatic areas distinguished by geographic, abiotic and biotic features, whether entirely natural or semi-natural."

This definition is from the same source, Article 1(b) of the Habitats Directive.

HABITATS DIRECTIVE, NATURAL HABITATS REGULATIONS
(WLA 1976/NH 97)

The Habitats Directive is Council Directive 92/43/EEC of May 21, 1992 on the conservation of natural habitats and of wild fauna and flora (O.J. L206, July 22, 1992. p.7).

The European Communities (Natural Habitats) Regulations, 1977 (S.I. No. 94 of 1997) were made on the February 26, 1997 for the purpose of giving effect to the Habitats Directive. They are referred to in this work as the "NH 97".

Regulation 2, as amended by the European Communities (Natural Habitats) (Amendment) Regulations 1998 (S.I. No. 233 of 1998), provides:

"The Habitats Directive" means Council Directive No. 92/43/EEE of May 21, 1992 (O.J. L206, July 22, 1992, p7) as amended by Council Directive No. 97/62/EC of October 27, 1997 (O.J. L305, November 8, 1997 p.42)."

The 1998 Regulations were required to correct Regulation 2 of the 1997 Regulations which had neglected to recite the amending Directive 97/62/EC.

Article 2 of the Habitats Directive as a general statement of the overall objectives of the Directive provided that –

"1. The aim of this Directive shall be to contribute towards ensuring bio-diversity through the conservation of natural habitats and of wild (*qv*) fauna and (*qv*) flora in the European territory of the Member States to which the Treaty applies.

2. Measures taken pursuant to this Directive shall be designed to maintain or restore, at favourable conservation status, natural habitats and species of wild fauna and flora of Community interest.

3. Measures taken pursuant to this Directive shall take account of economic, social and cultural requirements and regional and local characteristics."

HABITATS, PRIORITY NATURAL HABITAT TYPES
(NH 97, Reg. 2(1)))

See: PRIORITY NATURAL HABITAT TYPES.

HARE'S ORDER
(WLA 1976 s. 2(1))

"means an order made by the Minister under section 25 of the WLA 1976 and in which any species of hare is specified."

Section 25 of the WLA 1976 provides for the making by the Minister of an order permitting the hunting as specified in the order of specified protected wild animals during open seasons.

The hare species is a (*qv*) protected wild animal. It and deer are the only protected wild animals permitted or likely to be permitted by order to be hunted under section 25. *See:* OPEN SEASONS.

HARMFUL SUBSTANCE
(LG(WP)A 1977)

The Local Government (Water Pollution) Regulations 1992 (S.I. No. 271 OF 1992) as amended by the Local Government (Water Pollution)(Amendment) Regulations 1999 (S.I. No. 42 of 1999). *See:* DISCHARGES TO AQUIFERS, CONTROL OF.

HAZARDOUS WASTE
(WMA 1996, s. 4(2))

"(a) In this Act, 'hazardous waste' means –
- (i) hazardous waste for the time being mentioned in the list prepared pursuant to Article (1) (4) of Council Directive 91/689 of 12 December, 1991 (O.J. No. L 377/20, 31.12.1991) being either –
  - (I) Category I waste that has any of the properties specified in Part III of the Second Schedule, and
  - (II) Category II waste that –
    - (A) contains any of the constituents specified in Part II of the Second Schedule, and
    - (B) has any of the properties specified in Part III of the said Schedule,
- (ii) such other waste, having any of the properties specified in Part III of the Second Schedule, as may be prescribed for the purposes of this definition."

(b) For the purposes of the definition in this subsection –
'Category I waste' means waste specified in any of the following paragraphs of Part I of the Second Schedule, namely paragraphs 1 to 18;
'Category II waste' means waste specified in any of the following paragraphs of the said Part I, namely paragraphs 19 to 40."

Paragraphs 1 to 40 in fact comprise the entire of Part 1 of the Second Schedule. *See:* (1) WASTE MANAGEMENT PLAN; (2) SCHEDULES HERETO, WASTE SCHEDULES; (3) WASTE.

HAZARDOUS WASTE MANAGEMENT PLAN
(WMA 1996, s. 26)

Section 26(1) and (2) of the WMA 1996 provides for the making by the Agency of a national hazardous waste management plan.

Section 26 provides:

"(1) The Agency shall, as soon as may be after the commencement of this section, but not later than such date as may be prescribed, make a national plan (in this Act referred to as 'the hazardous waste management plan') with regard to –
- (a) the prevention and minimisation of hazardous waste,
- (b) the recovery of hazardous waste,
- (c) the collection and movement of hazardous waste, and
- (d) the disposal of such hazardous waste as cannot be prevented or recovered.

(2) The hazardous waste management plan shall have regard to, and incorporate such information contained in, any (*qv*) waste management plan as the Agency considers appropriate and shall –
- (a) describe the type, quantity, and origin of hazardous waste arising in the State, the movement of hazardous waste within, into or out of the State, and (*qv*) facilities available for the collection, (*qv*) recovery or (*qv*) disposal of such waste in the State, and such description shall indicate the likely position with respect to each of those matters for such period after the making or review under subsection (3) of the plan as the Agency thinks appropriate;
- (b) specify objectives and, where appropriate, targets which in the opinion of the Agency are practicable or desirable in relation to the prevention and minimisation of the production of hazardous waste, the minimisation of the harmful nature of such waste and the recovery and disposal of such waste, over such periods as may be specified;
- (c) provide for, as appropriate, the identification of sites at which waste disposal activities, being activities that to a significant extent involved hazardous waste, have been carried on, the assessment of any risk of (*qv*) environmental pollution arising as a result of such activities, the taking or recommendation of measures in order to prevent or limit any such environmental pollution, the identification of necessary remedial measures in respect of such sites, and the recommendation of measures to be taken to achieve such remediation, having regard to the cost-effectiveness of available remediable techniques;
- (d) have regard to the need to give effect to the (*qv*) polluter pays principle;
- (e) have regard to the need for precau-

tion in relation to the potentially harmful effect of (*qv*) emissions, where there are, in the opinion of the Agency, reasonable grounds for believing that such emissions could cause significant environmental pollution;

(f) make recommendations, as respects the management of hazardous waste, regarding -
   (i) priorities, measures or programmes which could be pursued,
   (ii) infrastructures, waste facilities or other physical resources considered by the Agency to be necessary throughout the State or any area of the State,
   (iii) the functions of any relevant public authorities;

(g) specify policies which the Agency proposes to pursue, having regard to its functions under this Act and any other enactment."

Under section 22 of the WMA 1996:

It is the appropriate local authority who makes a waste management plan within its functional area but subsection (8) of section 22 of that Act provides that that there must be included in a waste management plan but separate from the other information, information as respects the implementation of measures consequential on or incidental to the hazardous waste management plan or any recommendations made by the Agency under section 26(6).

Section 26(3) provides for five yearly reviews of the plan and making revisions therein by the Agency.
See: REVIEW (4) WMA 1996(C)

Subsection (4)(a) provides for publication in at least one national newspaper of a notice of intention to make the hazardous waste management plan or a revision thereof consequent on a review and paragraph (b) provides that subsection (2), (3) and (4) of section 23 which deals with the publication of notices for a waste management plan shall apply in relation to a hazardous waste management plan with modifications.

Subsection (5) provides that a Minister of the Government, a local authority and any other public authority in whom are vested functions relating to (*qv*) environmental protection shall, where appropriate, take measures to implement or otherwise give effect to, recommendations contained in the hazardous waste management plan and subsection (6) provides that the Agency may make such recommendations which will be regarded as having been issued by them under section 63 of the EPAA 1992 which gives the Agency extensive powers to implement its recommendations. *See:* PERFORMANCE OF STATUTORY FUNCTIONS BY LOCAL AUTHORITIES.

Subsection (7) obliges a local authority and any public authority to furnish to the Agency when making or reviewing a hazardous waste management plan, any relevant information which is available to or can be reasonably obtained by them.

Subsection (8) provides that the Agency are not required to provide or assume a direct role in the provision of waste facilities, equipment or related resources nor have they a duty to any person to identify such a site as is referred to in subsection (2)(c).

Subsection (9) provides for the publication of notices of the making of a hazardous waste management plan and that copies are available and at what cost and for furnishing copies of the plan to the Minister, each local authority and any other public body having interest.

HAZARDOUS WASTE REGULATIONS AND MOVEMENT OF HAZARDOUS WASTE REGULATIONS 1998
(WMA 1996)

The Waste Management (Hazardous Waste) Regulations 1998 (S.I. No. 163 of 1998) came into operation on the May 20, 1998.

Regulation 3 provides:

"The purposes for which these Regulations are made include the purpose of giving effect to provisions of –

(a) Council Directive 75/439/EEC of 16 June 1975 on the disposal of waste oils, as amended by Council Directive 87/101/EEC of 22 December, 1986 (O.J. L 194/23 25.07.1975 and O.J. No. 42/43, 12.02.1987),
(b) Council Directive 87/217/EEC of 19 March, 1987 on the prevention and reduction of environmental pollution by asbestos (O.J. No. 85/40, 28.03.1987),
(c) Council Directive 91/157/EEC of 18 March, 1991 on batteries and accumulators containing dangerous substances (O.J. No. 78/38, 26.03.1991),
(d) Council Directive 91/689/EEC of 12 December, 1991 on hazardous waste (O.J. No. 377/20, 31.12.1991) and

(e) Council Directive 96/59/EC of 16 September, 1996 on the disposal of polychlorinated biphenyls and polychlorinated terphenyls (O.J. No. 243/31, 24.09.1996)."

These Regulations replace and update a number of Regulations made under the European Communities Act 1972 which are revoked by virtue of Sections 1 and 6 of the WMA 1926.

Offence

"23. A person shall not compile information which is false or misleading to a material extent or furnish any such information in any notice or other document used for the purposes of these Regulations."

The Waste Management (Movement of Hazardous Waste) Regulations 1998 (S.I. No. 147 of 1998) came into operation on the May 20, 1998.

Article 2 provides that the purpose for which these Regulations made include the purposes of giving effect to provisions of –

(a) Council Directive 91/689/EEC of 12 December, 1991 on hazardous waste (O.J. No. L 377/20, 31 December, 1991), and
(b) Council Regulation (EEC) No. 259/93 of 1 February, 1993 on the supervision and control of shipments of waste within, into and out of the European community (O.J. No. L 30/1, 6 February, 1993).

Offences

"4. A person shall not consign, move from the premises where it is being held, or accept, or facilitate by consent, connivance or neglect the consignment, movement or acceptance of, hazardous waste otherwise than in accordance with the requirements of these Regulations."

"13. A person shall not furnish information which is false or misleading to a material extent in any consignment note, report, notice or other document used for the purposes of these Regulations."

HAZARDOUS WASTE, INCINERATION OF, REGULATIONS 1998

(EPAA 1992)

The European Communities (Licensing of Incinerators of Hazardous Waste) Regulations, 1998 (S.I. No. 64 of 1998) which were signed on the March 11, 1998 are intended to implement Council Directive 94/67/EC of December 16, 1994 on the incineration of hazardous waste (O.J. No. L365/34, 31 December, p.15) by reference to sections 83(1) and 84 of the EPAA 1992 which deal respectively with the grant of (*qv*)Integrated Pollution Control Licences under Part IV of the 1992 Act (*See:* LICENCE) and conditions attaching to IPC licences (*See:* CONDITIONS).

Article 3 –

"3. (1) Subject to sub-article (2) of this Article, these Regulations apply to an activity which comprises the incineration of hazardous waste by oxidation, with or without the recovery of the combustion heat generated, including pre-treatment of such waste prior to incineration, the burning of such waste as a regular or additional fuel for any industrial process, pyrolysis or other thermal treatment process (insofar as the products of such processes are subsequently incinerated).
(2) These Regulations do not apply to an activity which comprises –
(a) the incineration of hazardous waste of a type which is excluded from the scope of Council Directive by virtue of article 2.1 of that Directive, or
(b) the incineration of hazardous waste at an incinerator of a type which is excluded from the scope of the Council Directive by virtue of article 2.2 of that Directive."

Without prejudice to Section 83(3) of the Act of 1992, the Agency shall not grant a licence or revised licence in relation to an *(qv)* activity to which these regulations apply unless it is satisfied that the activity will be carried out in a manner, and in a premises, which comply with the requirements of Articles 3.1 and 3.4 of the Council Directive.

Articles 5 and 6 –

"5. Notwithstanding sections 83(1) and 84 of the Act of 1992, the Agency shall attach to any licence or revised licence that may be granted by it in relation to an activity to which these Regulations apply such conditions as are, in the opinion of the Agency necessary to give effect to Articles 3 to 12 of the Council Directive.

(6) Notwithstanding section 88(1) of the Act of 1992, the Agency shall, as soon as may be but in any event not later than the 1st day of July, 2000, review any licence or revised licence granted in relation to an activity to which these Regulations apply in case where such licence or revised licence was granted by the Agency prior to the 31st day of December 1996."

Section 83 deals with the grant of *(qv)* licences and section 88 with the *(qv)* review of licences in the EPAA 1992.

"HEAD WEIR"
(F(C)A 1959, s. 3(1))

"Means the fixed engine commonly called a head weir or an ebb and flow weir."

"HECK"
(F(C)A 1959, s. 3(1))

"Means a grating mounted at the upstream end of a box in a (*qv*) fishing weir or (*qv*) fishing mill dam and so constructed as to prevent the passage of fish without obstructing the flow of water."

HEDGES
(LG(P&D)A 1963, s. 44)

"(1) If it appears to the (*qv*) planning authority that it is expedient in the interests of amenity that any hedge should be removed or altered, the planning authority may serve on the owner and on the occupier of the land on which the hedge is situate a notice requiring the carrying out of such removal or alteration and, in the case of a removal, any replacement appearing to the planning authority to be suitable.

(2) Where a notice is served under this section, any person may, at any time before the day (not being earlier than one month after such service) specified in that behalf in the notice, appeal to the Minister against the notice.

(3) Where an appeal is brought under this section from a notice, the Minister may confirm the notice with or without modification, or annul the notice.

(4) A notice under this section (other than a notice which is annulled) shall take effect –
 (a) in case no appeal against it is taken or every appeal against it is withdrawn before the expiration of the period for taking an appeal – on the expiration of the period for taking an appeal,
 (b) in case an appeal or appeals is or are taken against it and the appeal or appeals is or are not withdrawn during the period for making an appeal – when every appeal not so withdrawn has been either withdrawn or determined.

(5) If within the period specified in a notice under this section, or within such extended period as the planning authority may allow, the removal or alteration required by the notice has not been effected, the planning authority may enter on the land on which the hedge is situate and may effect such removal or alteration and any replacement specified in the notice.

(6) Where a notice under this section is complied with, the planning authority shall pay to the person complying with the notice the expenses reasonably incurred by him in carrying out the removal or alteration and any replacement specified in the notice.

(7) Particulars of a notice served under this section shall be entered in the register (planning register S.8)."

(WLA 1976, s. 40(2)*(a)*)

In relation to hedges or hedgerows section 40(2)*(a)* of the WLA 1976 exempts the destruction, in the ordinary course of agriculture or forestry, of any vegetation growing in or on any hedge or ditch from the protective terms of section 40(1) which makes it an offence to cut, grub, burn or otherwise destroy during the period beginning on the 15th day of April and ending on the 31st day of August any vegetation growing on any land not then cultivated or in the course of cultivation for agriculture or forestry. *See:* DESTRUCTION OF VEGETATION.

HERITAGE COUNCIL
(Heritage Act 1995)

The Heritage Council was established by section 5(2) of the Heritage Act 1995 and by virtue of section 6 it took over the functions of the National Monuments Advisory Council, The Historic Monuments Council and the Wildlife Advisory Council which are now under the control of the Minister for (*qv*) Arts, Heritage, Gaeltacht and the Islands. *See:* COUNCIL, THE, HERITAGE COUNCIL.

HOLDER
(WMA 1996, s. 5(1))

"Means, in relation to waste, the owner, person in charge, or any other person having, for the time being, possession or control, of the waste."

HOLDER OF WASTE, GENERAL DUTY OF A
(WMA 1996, s. 32)

Section 32 of the WMA 1996 deals with this important regulatory matter which, together section 39 (9), constitute the main enforcement sections of the WMA 1996.

Section 32 provides:

"(1) A person shall not hold, recover or dispose of waste in a manner that causes or is likely to cause (*qv*) environmental pollution.

(2) A person shall not, except in such circumstances as may be specified under subsection (4), transfer the control of waste to any person other than an appropriate person.

(3) A holder of waste shall, without delay, inform –
   (a) the local authority in whose functional area the loss, spillage or other matter mentioned in this subsection occurs, or
   (b) in the case of (*qv*) hazardous waste, both the said local authority and the Agency,

   of any loss, spillage, accident or other development concerning that waste which causes, or is likely to cause, environmental pollution.

(4) The Minister may by regulations –
   (a) provide that the holder of a specified class or classes of waste shall effect and maintain a policy of insurance insuring him or her to a specified extent as respects any liability on his or her part to pay damages or costs on account of injury to person or property arising from the holding by him or her of waste,
   (b) provide that on the transfer of waste, in specified circumstances, the holder of the waste shall provide to the transferee specified particulars in writing of the waste so as to enable that person to avoid a contravention of the relevant provisions of this Act,
   (c) provide that subsection (2) shall not apply in specified circumstances.

(5) In this section 'an appropriate person' means a local authority, the corporation of a borough that is not a county borough, the council of an urban district, or a person otherwise authorised under and in accordance with this Act or the Act of 1992 to undertake the collection, recovery or disposal of the class of waste in question.

Offence

(6) (a) A person who contravenes subsection (1), (2) or (3) or a provision of regulations under subsection (4) shall be guilty of an offence.
   (b) In a prosecution for a contravention of subsection (1) it shall be a good defence to prove that the activity concerned was carried on in accordance with a (*qv*)waste collection permit or (*qv*)waste licence under this Act or a licence or revised licence under Part IV of the Act of 1992.

(7) Without prejudice to subsection (6), where a person transfers the control of waste to another person in contravention of subsection (2) –
   (a) any act done or instrument made by a person to transfer title in the waste for that purpose shall not operate to transfer that title,
   (b) the first-mentioned person shall, for the purposes of this Act, be deemed to be a holder, in addition to the second-mentioned person, of the waste:

   Provided that nothing in this paragraph shall be construed as requiring either of the said persons to be held to be a holder of the waste on or after the date on which a subsequent transfer (if any), of the control of the waste in accordance with subsection (2) is effected."

"Part IV of the Act of 1992" is the part of the EPAA 1992, sections 88 to 99, dealing with Integrated Pollution Control and most significantly the grant of (*qv*) Integrated Pollution Control Licences.

The Waste Management (Miscellaneous Provisions) Regulations 1998 (S.I. No. 164 of 1998), provide:

"5. Section 32(2) of the Act shall not apply in respect of the transfer of waste to a person who is not prohibited under this Act or the Act of 1992 from undertaking the collection, recovery or disposal of the category of waste in question."

HOUSEHOLD WASTE
(WMA 1996, s. 5(1))

"Means waste produced within the curtilage of a building or self-contained part of a building used for the purposes of living accommodation."

HUNT
(WLA 1976, s. 2(1))

"means stalk, pursue, chase, drive, flush, capture, course, attract, follow, search for, lie in wait for, take, trap or shoot by any means whether with or without dogs, and, except in sections 28 and 29, includes killing in the course of hunting, but does not in this Act include stalking, attracting, searching for or lying in wait for any fauna by an unarmed person solely for the purpose of watching or of taking or making photographic or other pictures, and kindred words shall be construed accordingly."

Section 28 of the WLA 1976 prohibits the hunting or killing with firearms of an (*qv*) exempted wild mammal or protected wild bird with two exceptions, one in the case of hunting pursuant to licence under the Act, or, two, where the person hunting is a qualified person as defined in the section. Section 29 of that Act deals with the granting by the Minister of a licence to hunt with firearms. *See:* HUNTING, HUNTING OR KILLING WITH FIREARMS.

(NH 97, Reg. 2(1))

"means stalk, pursue, chase, drive, flush, capture, course, attract, follow, search for, lie in wait for, take, trap or shoot by any means whether with or without dogs and, except in sections 28 and 29 of the Principal Act, includes killing in the course of hunting and cognate words shall be construed accordingly."

There is no new provision in the Regulations in relation to hunting as such. The regulations use the phrase "capturing and killing" but there is one mention of the word hunting in Regulation 24(2)(b) which deals with Ministerial control of taking in the wild certain species of fauna and flora. "The Principal Act" is the WLA 1976. for section 28 *see:* PROTECTION, PROTECTED WILD ANIMALS/PROTECTED WILD BIRDS. For section 29 *see:* FIREARMS, LICENCE TO HUNT WITH.

HUNT, LICENCE TO WITH FIREARMS
(WLA 1976, s. 29)

See: FIREARMS, LICENCE TO HUNT WITH.

HUNTING BY NIGHT
(WLA 1976, s 37(1))

"(1) Notwithstanding anything contained in this Act apart from this section but subject to section 42, a person shall not hunt:
 (a) a woodcock at any time between sunset and sunrise,
 (b) any other protected wild bird, other than a wild duck or a wild goose, or any protected wild animal at any time during any period beginning one hour after sunset and ending one hour before sunrise.

(2) Subsection (1) of this section shall not apply to:
 (a) hunting protected wild birds pursuant to and in accordance with a licence granted by the Minister under section 22(9) of this Act for a purpose mentioned in paragraph (a) or (d) of that section, or,
 (b) hunting protected wild animals pursuant to and in accordance with a licence granted by the Minister under section 23(6) of this Act.

Offence
"(3) A person who contravenes subsection (1) of this section shall be guilty of an offence."

HUNTING OR KILLING WITH FIREARMS
(WLA 1976, s. 28)

See: HUNTING, HUNTING OR KILLING WITH FIREARMS

HUNTING ON FORESHORE BELONGING TO STATE
(WLA 1976, s. 30)

"(1) It shall not be lawful for a person, without the permission of the Minister, to hunt (*qv*) fauna on or over foreshore belonging to the State or on or over land belonging to the State and which is either covered by any inland waters or comprised in the lakeshore accretion from any lake.

(2) Any person who contravenes subsection (1) of this section shall commit a trespass and may, if the Minister thinks fit, be

sued by the Minister for trespass in any court of competent jurisdiction.

(3) Nothing in this section shall operate to prejudice any legal proceedings which may be instituted apart from this section."

HUNTING, HUNTING OR KILLING WITH FIREARMS

(WLA 1976, s.28)

"(1) A person shall not with firearms hunt or kill on any land an exempted wild mammal or a protected wild bird of a species specified in an order under section 24 of the Act which is for the time being in force unless –
(a) the exempted wild mammal or protected wild bird is hunted or killed pursuant to and in accordance with a licence granted under this Act, or deemed to have been granted under section 29 of this Act, and
(b) the person is in relation to the land a qualified person for the purposes of this section.

(2) A person shall be in relation to land a qualified person for the purpose of this section if he is at least 16 years of age and –
(a) is entitled to sporting rights over the land, or
(b) is the guest, invitee, servant or agent, or possesses the written authority of a person who is entitled to sporting rights over the land, or
(c) is a member of a body of persons which is entitled to sporting rights over the land or which has such authority, or
(d) is a person who is of a class or description which the Minister by regulations declares to be a qualified class or description for the purposes of this section."

Offence

"(3) A person who contravenes subsection (1) of this section shall be guilty of an offence."

HUNTING ON TERRITORIAL SEAS BELONGING TO STATE

(WLA 1976, s. 58)

"(1) It is hereby declared that the right to hunt (qv) fauna in or over portion of the sea which is the (*qv*) territorial seas of the State belongs to the State.

(2) It shall not be lawful for a person without the permission of the Minister, to hunt fauna on, in or over any part of the portion of the sea mentioned in subsection (1) of this section.

(3) Any person who contravenes subsection (2) of this section shall commit a trespass.

(4) Nothing in this section shall operate to prejudice any legal proceedings which may be instituted apart from this section and a person who contravenes subsection (2) of this section may, if the Minister thinks fit, be sued by the Minister for trespass in any court of competent jurisdiction and for the purpose of giving jurisdiction under this Act the trespass shall be deemed to have been committed where the person complained against may be."

HYDROMETRIC PROGRAMME

(EPAA 1992, s. 64)

"(1) The Agency shall, after consultation with such persons or bodies (if any) as may be prescribed, prepare a national programme for the collection, analysis and publication of information on the levels, volumes and flows of water in rivers, lakes and groundwaters in the State (in this Act referred to as 'hydrometric data'), and a copy of such programme shall, as soon as may be, be sent by the Agency to the Minister.

(2) A programme under this section may, after consultation with the persons or bodies (if any) referred to in subsection (1), be revised from time to time by the Agency and shall be reviewed at least every five years.

(3) It shall be the duty of the Agency to take appropriate steps to ensure that a programme under this section is implemented and for that purpose the Agency may –
(a) direct a local authority to provide, operate and maintain such gauges and other equipment as it may specify and to furnish specified information to the Agency and in such manner at such times as it may specify,
(b) make arrangements with any public authority, or other person or body to provide, operate and maintain gauges and other equipment as it such

may specify and furnish specified information to the Agency at such manner and in such times as it may specify,

(c) provide, operate and maintain gauges and other equipment for recording hydrometric data.

(4) Where the Agency is not satisfied with the response of a local authority to a direction under subsection (3)(a), it shall consult with the local authority concerned, and, if the Agency is still dissatisfied with the response following such consultation, the Agency shall carry out, cause to be carried out, or arrange for, the monitoring concerned and the costs of the monitoring may be recovered by the Agency from the local authority as a simple contract debt in any court of competent jurisdiction."

I

IDENTITY
PROOF OF
(F(A)A 1962, s. 27)

Offence
Section 27 of the F(A)A 1962 provides that any person who produces to an (*qv*)authorised person a fishing licence or an oyster fishing licence, as the case may be, shall on demand furnish the authorised person then and there, or as soon as may be thereafter, with evidence of his identity and, in default, the person shall be guilty of an offence under this section.

(Note that the maximum penalty prescribed under this section has been increased. *See:* FINES AND IMPRISONMENT (IMPOSITION OF)).

IMMUNITY
FROM ACTION
(F(C)A 1959, s.301(6))

"No (*qv*) authorised officer shall be liable for any loss or damage occasioned by him or in the course of the exercise of any of the powers conferred on him by this section unless such loss or damage was caused by him wantonly or maliciously."

(EPAA 1992, s. 15)

"No action or other proceedings shall lie or be maintainable against the (*qv*) Agency or any body referred to in section 44 or 45 for the recovery of damages in respect of any injury to persons, damage to property or other loss alleged to have been caused or contributed to by a failure to perform or to comply with any of the functions conferred on the said Agency or body."

Section 44 deals with the provision by the Minister and local authorities or other public authorities of services to the Agency and section 45 deals with agreements regarding such provision.

(WMA 1996, s.67)

"(1) No action or other proceeding shall lie or be maintainable against the Agency or a local authority for the recovery of damages in respect of any injury to persons, damage to property or other loss alleged to have been caused or contributed to by a failure to exercise any power or carry out any duty conferred or imposed on the Agency or local authority by or under this Act.

(2) Where a local authority or the Agency is satisfied that any (*qv*) authorised person appointed by that Local authority or the Agency, or any officer or employee of that local authority or the Agency, has carried out his or her duties in relation to the performance by that local authority or the Agency of its functions under this Act in a bona fide manner, the local authority or the Agency, as the case may be, shall indemnify the authorised person, officer or other employee against all actions or claims howsoever arising in respect of the carrying out by him or her of his or her said duties."

IMPEDE
(F(C)A 1959/WLA 1976/
EPAA 1992/WMA 1996)

See: OBSTRUCT, IMPEDE.

IMPORT OF
FAUNA AND FLORA
(WLA 1976, s.52)

See: FAUNA AND FLORA, IMPORT OF.

INCORPORATION
OF AGENCY
(EPAA 1992, s.20)

"(1) The (*qv*) Agency shall be a body corporate with perpetual succession and a seal and power to sue and be sued in its corporate name and to acquire, hold and dispose of land.

(2) The Agency shall provide itself with a seal.

(3) The seal of the Agency shall be authenticated by the signature of the Director General or some other director or of a person, being an employee of the Agency or a person whose (*qv*) services are availed of by, or supplied to, the Agency under section 44, authorised by the Agency to act in that behalf.

(4) Judicial notice shall be taken of the seal of the Agency and every document purporting to be an instrument made by the Agency and to be sealed with the seal (purporting to be authenticated in accordance with subsection (3)) of the Agency shall be received in evidence and be deemed to be such instrument without proof, unless the contrary is shown."

INDEMNIFICATION OF DIRECTOR GENERAL
(EPAA 1992, s.16)

"Where the (*qv*) Agency is satisfied that the Director General or other director or authorised person appointed by the Agency, or any other employee of the Agency has discharged his duties in relation to the enforcement of the relevant statutory provisions in a bona fide manner, it shall indemnify the Director General or other director or authorised person of the Agency or any other employee of the Agency, against all actions or claims howsoever arising in respect of the discharge by him of his duties."

INDUSTRIAL PLANT AND EXISTING INDUSTRIAL PLANT
(APA 1987, s.6)

"(1) "Industrial Plant" in this Act means any plant, equipment, appliance, apparatus, machinery, works, building or other structure or any land or any part of any land which is used in the course of trade, business or industry for the purposes of, or incidental to, any industrial process specified in the Third Schedule."

See: SCHEDULES HERETO, APA SCHEDULE.

"(2) In this Act "existing industrial plant" means industrial plant:

(a) in respect of which a permission under Part IV of the Local Government (Planning and Development) Act, 1963, is granted prior to such day (in this subsection referred to as 'the relevant day') as may be prescribed by the Minister, or
(b) which is, on the day immediately prior to the relevant day, or was, at any time during the period of twelve months ending on the day immediately prior to the relevant day, used for the purposes, of or incidental to, any industrial process specified in the Third Schedule, other than industrial plant which is an unauthorised structure or the use of which constitutes an unauthorised use."

Industrial plant is required to be licensed under the APA 1987, section 30.

Section 6 of the APA 1987 came into operation on the November 1, 1988 by virtue of the Air Pollution Act, 1987 (Commencement Day) Order 1988 (S.I. No. 265 of 1988).

INDUSTRIAL PROCESS
(APA 1987, s.7)

"includes any process which is carried on in the course of trade, business or industry and which is for, or incidental to, the making or production of any article, part of an article, substance, energy or thing or the altering, repairing, ornamenting, finishing, cleaning, washing, packing or canning, or the adapting for sale, or breaking up or demolition of any article, substance or thing; including in particular, the getting, raising, taking, carrying away and processing (including size reduction, grading and heating) of minerals, the storage of mineral wastes and the incineration, treatment or recovery of other wastes"

INFORMATION, NOTICES REQUIRING
(WMA 1996, s.18)

Section 18 of the WMA 1996 deals extensively with the service of notices requiring information by local authorities and the Agency and the dissemination of information procured by these notices and otherwise. *See:* ENFORCEMENT (4)(C).

INLAND WATERWAYS
(Heritage Act 1995, s.2(1))

"includes canals, canalised sections of rivers and lakes, navigation channels in rivers and lakes, and their associated navigational features."

INSCALES
(F(C)A 1959, s.3(1))

"means a pair of gratings mounted at the downstream end of a box in a *(qv)* fishing weir or a (*qv*) fishing mill dam and converging towards the centre in the upstream direction to form between the upstream ends a vertical gap, the effect of the arrangement being to permit the passage of fish into the box and hinder their escape there from."

INSPECTION
(F(C)A 1959/LG(WP)A 1977/
APA 1987/EPAA 1992/
WLA 1976/WMA 1996/NH 97)

As one of the powers of authorised persons, authorised officers and others. *See:* ENTRY AND SEARCH.

INSTRUMENTS OF APPOINTMENT
(FA 1980, s.26)

Section 26 of the FA 1980 provides that every instrument of appointment by the Central Board or a regional board of an officer or other person to be an *(qv)* authorised person for the purposes of Part XVIII of the Principal Act shall be:

(a) prepared and printed in the prescribed form, and
(b) sealed with the seal of the board,

and every document purporting to be such an instrument and to be sealed with the seal of such board as is appropriate in the circumstances shall be admissible in any legal proceedings as prima facie evidence of such appointment.

See: the FA 1980 (Section 26) Regulations, 1983 (S.I. No. 71 of 1983) for the prescribed form.

INSURANCE
(WMA 1996, s.34(7)(h))

Provides that conditions in relation to insurance indemnifying the permit holder as respects any liability for injury to person or property may be attached by a local authority to a *(qv)* waste collection permit.

INQUIRY, PUBLIC
(Foreshore Acts 1933 and 1992)

The holding by the Minister of public inquiries is dealt with under sections 2(8), 13(9) and 18 of the Foreshore Act 1933. *See:* FORESHORE.

INQUIRIES INTO FISHERIES
(F(C)A 1959, ss. 8, 50)

Section 8 of the F(C)A 1959:

"(1) The Minister may from time to time cause an inquiry to be held in any fisheries district in relation to the fisheries therein or any of them and the best means to be adopted for the regulation, improvement or protection thereof, and for this purpose may appoint an officer of the Minister to hold such inquiry.

(2) The Minister shall cause to be given, in accordance with section 322, notice of the holding of an inquiry under this section."

This section does not appear to have been amended by the FA 1980 to take account of the new designations under that Act. One would have thought that the inquiry would be held in a *(qv)* fisheries region rather than a fisheries district.

Section 50 of the F(C)A 1959, amended as indicated in square brackets by section 65 of the FA 1980, provides:

"(1) The Minister may at any time, if he thinks fit, order an inquiry into the performance of its duties by [the Central Board or any regional board] and may appoint any person to hold such inquiry.

(2) Where a person (not being an officer of the Minister) is appointed to hold an inquiry under this section, such person shall be paid such remuneration and such allowances for expenses as the Minister may with the consent of the Minister for Finance determine.

(3) Where an inquiry in relation to [the Central Board or a regional board] has been held under this section, the Minister shall certify the amount of the expenses incurred by the Minister in relation to such inquiry, and the amount so certified shall be recovered by the Minister from the revenue of such board.

(4) Any sum recovered by the Minister under subsection (3) of this section shall be paid into or disposed of for the benefit of the Exchequer in such manner as the Minister for Finance shall direct."

NOTICE OF INQUIRY

Section 322 of the F(C)A 1959 deals with the circumstances in which notice is required under this Act of the holding of an inquiry. Section 322 provides:

"Where notice of the holding of an inquiry is required by this Act to be given that requirement shall be complied with if not less than fourteen days before the holding of such inquiry, the following things are done –

(a) there are distributed, in such manner as the Minister may direct, printed notices announcing the time and place at which the inquiry is to be held and the matters to be inquired into thereat, and

(b) there is published in one or more newspapers circulating in the fishery district in which the inquiry is to be held an advertisement stating the time and place at which the inquiry is to be held and the matters to be inquired into thereat."

POWERS IN RELATION TO THE HOLDING OF INQUIRIES

Section 323 of the F(C)A 1959 deals with the powers of persons appointed by the Minister to hold inquiries who can summon witnesses to attend, examine witnesses on oath and require witnesses to produce documents.

Offence
Subsection (3) creates a series of offences arising out of the inquiry, a witness defaulting in attending, a witness refusing to take the oath, failing to produce a document and failing to answer a question.

(Note that the maximum penalty prescribed under this subsection has been increased. *See:* FINES AND IMPRISONMENT (IMPOSITION OF)).

COMMISSION UNDER THE F(A)A 1995

For power of Minister to establish a commission under section 3 of the F(A)A 1995 to perform a similar function in relation to the Central Board or a regional fisheries board. *See:* (1) COMMISSION; (2) BYE-LAWS, SECTIONS 95 (3), AND (4).

INQUIRIES UNDER
EPAA 1992
(EPAA 1992, s.105)

Section 105 of the EPAA 1992 deals with inquiries to be held under that Act. Section 105 provides:

"(1) (a) The Agency may, where after consultation with the Minister if it considers it necessary to do so, arrange for an inquiry to be held into any incident of (*qv*)environmental pollution or any other matter related to (*qv*) environmental protection.

(b) The Minister may direct the Agency to arrange for an inquiry to be held into any specified instance of environmental pollution or any other matter related to environmental protection and the Agency shall comply with such direction.

(2) The inquiry shall be conducted by a person appointed in that behalf by the Agency in such manner as the person thinks appropriate.

(3) The person conducting the inquiry may, for the purposes of the inquiry –

(a) investigate the circumstances in which the incident of environmental pollution or any other matter related to environmental protection occurred,

(b) enter (on production of the confirmation of his appointment if so demanded by the occupier or person in charge of the premises) at any reasonable time any premises, entry to which appears requisite for the said purposes,

(c) carry out such inspection and examination and do such things and make such enquiries as appear to him to be reasonably necessary for the said purposes and, in particular —

(i) require, by summons, any person to attend as a witness to give evidence,

(ii) require any person to produce such books, papers, other documents and any articles (being in that person's custody or under his control) which the person conducting the inquiry may consider relevant and retain such books, papers, documents and articles for such time as he may reasonably require them,

(iii) administer or cause to be administered an oath and take evidence under oath.

Offences
(4) If a person –

(a) on being duly summoned as a witness before an inquiry without just cause or excuse disobeys the summons,

(b) being in attendance as a witness refuses to take an oath or to make an affirmation when legally required by the person conducting the inquiry to do so, or to produce any documents or articles in his custody or control legally required by the person conducting the inquiry to be produced by him, or to answer any question to which the person conducting the inquiry may legally require an answer,

(c) wilfully gives evidence which is material to the inquiry and which he knows to be false or does not believe to be true,

(d) by act or omission, obstructs or hinders the person conducting the inquiry in the performance of his functions,

(e) fails, neglects or refuses to comply with any requirement provided for under subsection (3)(c)(ii), or

(f) does or omits to do any other thing and if such doing or omission would, if the inquiry had been in the High Court, have been contempt of that Court,

the person shall be guilty of an offence.

(5) A statement or admission made by a person before a person conducting an inquiry under this section shall not be admissible in evidence against that person in any criminal proceedings other than proceedings in relation to an offence under subsection (4).

(6) Persons attending as witnesses at the inquiry shall be allowed such expenses to be paid out of moneys available to the Agency as would be allowed to witnesses attending before a court of record and, in case of dispute as to the amount to be allowed, the dispute shall be referred by the person conducting the inquiry to a taxing master of the High Court, who, on request signed by the person conducting the inquiry, shall ascertain and certify the proper amount of the expenses.

(7) The person conducting the inquiry shall make a report to the Agency stating the causes and circumstances of the subject of the inquiry and may add any observation which he thinks right to make.

(8) The Agency may cause the report of a person who conducted an inquiry under this section to be made public at such time and in such manner as it thinks fit.

(9) The Agency may require that all or part of the expenses incurred by the Agency in relation to an inquiry under this section shall be paid in whole or in part by any person who appears to the Agency to be, by reason of any act or default on the part of such person or on the part of any servant or agent of his, responsible in any degree for the subject of the inquiry.

(10) The Agency shall give notice of an inquiry under this section by a notice published in Iris Oifigiúil and in at least one daily newspaper circulating in the State setting out the terms of reference of the inquiry.

(11) The Minister may make regulations for the purpose of this section."

INQUIRIES IN RELATION TO SPECIAL AMENITY AREA ORDERS
(LG(P&D)A 1963)

See: SPECIAL AMENITY AREA ORDERS.

INQUIRIES INTO FORESHORE LEASES AND LICENCES
(Foreshore Acts 1933 and 1992)

See: FORESHORE.

INTEGRATED POLLUTION CONTROL LICENCE,
(EPAA 1992, Part IV)

An integrated pollution control licence is a licence granted under Part IV of the EPAA 1992, sections 82 to 99. Eventually this licence will encompass all activities of consequence requiring to be licensed under the LG(WP)A 1977 and the APA 1987. *See:* LICENCE (5).

J

JUDICIAL REVIEW
(F(A)A 1997, s.73)

Section 73(1) of the F(A)A 1997 provides that a person shall not question:

(a) a decision on an application for a licence or the revocation or amendment of a licence, or

(b) a determination of the (*qv*) Board on an appeal otherwise than by way of an application for judicial review under Order 84 of the Rules of the Superior Courts.

Subsection (2) outlines the procedure which is that which is already set out in Order 84.

Subsection (3) provides that the determination of the High Court on the matter shall be final and no appeal shall lie except with the leave of the High Court, which leave shall only be granted where the High Court certifies that its decision involves a point of law of exceptional public importance and that it is desirable in the public interest that an appeal should be taken to the Supreme Court.

Subsection (4) provides that subsection (3) shall not apply to a determination of the High Court in so far as it involves a question as to the validity of any law having regard to the provisions of the Constitution.

Subsection (5) provides that references to Order 84 shall include references to the Order as amended or re-enacted (with or without modification) by rules of court.

JURISDICTION
(FA 1980, s.47)

Whereas each environmental statute makes specific provision for the precise person or body entitled to bring proceedings to enforce the statute, which in some statutes is open to "any person", it is unnecessary to give specific jurisdiction to particular courts to hear and determine such proceedings. The jurisdiction of the courts is well established.

Under the FA 1980, however, it was deemed necessary to confer jurisdiction where the ordinary rules relating to jurisdiction would not apply in respect of certain specified offences in certain circumstances as follows:

Section 47(1) of the FA 1980 provides, in relation to offences under sections, 65, 69, 97, 127, 140, 176, 182 or 285A (inserted by section 24 of F(A)A 1962) of the F(C)A 1959 or section 29 of the F(A)A 1962 or any offence against a bye-law described in section 46(4) of the FA 1980, all of which offences are among those offences which can be tried on indictment by virtue of section 46(1), (3), and (4) of the FA 1980, that proceedings to enforce their provisions may be taken in any District Court District and...

"in case such proceedings are taken and apart from this section the Justice before whom the proceedings are brought would not have jurisdiction to hear and determine the proceedings, then for the purpose of conferring such jurisdiction the offence may be treated as having been committed within the District Court District to which such Justice is assigned".

Subsection (2) makes the same provision for offences triable on indictment in the Circuit Court in relation to the same specified offences.

L

LABELLING PRODUCTS AND SERVICES
(EPAA 1992, s.78)

Section 78 of the EPAA 1992 provides:

"(1) The Agency shall, if it considers it necessary or desirable to do so, having regard to any act of an institution of the European Communities relating to a Community labelling scheme, establish or arrange for the establishment of a scheme or schemes for the use of a special symbol or symbols on the labels of specified products or in connection with specified services which meet specified criteria and standards as to their impact on the environment."

Subsection (2) sets out the suggested steps which the Agency may take, without prejudice to the generality of subsection (1), including they themselves setting the appropriate criteria and standards, procedures in relation to the use, refusal and withdrawal of a special symbol, the testing of products or services related to their use as a special symbol to ensure compliance with criteria and standards, charging for those tests, monitoring the use of a special symbol, determining the product categories or services for the scheme and publishing periodic reports and details of the scheme.

Subsection (3) provides that the Agency shall consult with such public authorities and such other persons and bodies as may be prescribed, in the preparation, amendment or revocation of a scheme under this section.

Offence
"(4) It shall be an offence-
(a) to use a symbol provided for in a scheme under this section, or under a Community environmental labelling scheme in force in the State, or a similar symbol, on the labelling of a product or in connection with a service which has not been approved under the scheme or for which the approval has been withdrawn or, if approved, no longer meets the standards and criteria of the scheme, or
(b) for a person to make a statement or claim in writing or otherwise in connection with the use, or an application or an appeal against a refusal for the use, or for the withdrawal, of a special symbol which to his knowledge is false or misleading in a material respect.

Subsection (5) provides that the Agency may amend or revoke a scheme under subsection (1).

LABELLING
(WMA 1992, s.29)

Section 29 of the WMA 1996 deals with the measures related to the (*qv*)recovery of waste, and subsection (4), when suggesting the contents of regulations under the section, provides at paragraph (a) that the regulations may, *inter alia*, provide for:

"requiring the labelling or marking of a product or substance or its packaging, in a specified manner, so as to identify or specify —
(i) the composition of the product, substance or packaging,
(ii) the potential hazards of the product, substance or packaging in the event of its being recovered or disposed of,
(iii) the potential of the product, substance or packaging to be recovered,
(iv) such other information as may be specified."

LAMPS, USE OF, IN HUNTING
(WLA 1976, s.38)

Section 38 of the WLA 1976 prohibits the use of any lamp, light, torch, mirror or other artificial light-reflecting or dazzling device or appliance in hunting any protected wild bird or protected wild animal, otherwise than while either:
(a) attaching thereto any band, ring, tag or other marking device, or
(b) hunting for educational or scientific purposes, pursuant to and in accordance with a licence granted under this Act by the Minister.

Offence
The use of the above devices without a licence constitutes an offence under the section.

LAND
(WLA 1976, s.2(1))

"Where the context admits, includes land covered by water and in relation to the acquisition of land

also includes any easement, *profit a prendre* or other right in, to or over land or water (including any easement, *profit a prendre* or other right granted to or held by the Minister)."
See: ACQUISITION.

(NH 97, Reg. 2(1))

has the same meaning as in the WLA 1976.

(WMA 1996, s.5(1))

"Includes any subsoil thereunder and structure thereon."

LAND DRAINAGE SCHEME
(WLA 1976, s.43)

Section 43 of the WLA 1976 provides that:

"(1) Where the (*qv*) Commissioners propose to undertake either –
(a) a drainage scheme within the meaning of the Arterial Drainage Act, 1945 (Act No. 3 of 1945), which is one to which this section applies, or
(b) any other land drainage scheme,
in respect of an area which includes land to which an (*qv*) establishment order, a (*qv*)recognition order or a (*qv*) designation order applies, or land to which an agreement made under section 18 of the Act applies, the Commissioners shall, before commencing the scheme, consult the Minister to ascertain if and to what extent the proposed scheme if carried out would affect or interfere with the suitability of the land affected by the scheme for a nature reserve or refuge, as may be appropriate, and take all practicable steps including, where appropriate, the limitation of the drainage scheme to minimise or avoid such effect or interference.

(2) This section applies to any drainage scheme within the meaning of the Arterial Drainage Act, 1945, not being a scheme of which a copy has been exhibited in accordance with section 5 of that Act before the commencement of this section."

"LANDFILL"
(WMA 1996, s.5(1))

"Means a waste disposal (*qv*) facility used for the deposit of waste onto or under land."

LANDFILL SITES FOR WASTE DISPOSAL
(EPAA 1992, s.62)

Section 62 of the EPAA 1992 provides:

"(1) The Agency shall, as soon as is practicable, for the purposes of (*qv*) environmental protection, specify and publish criteria and procedures for the selection, management, operation and termination of use of landfill sites for the disposal of domestic and other wastes.

(2) Without prejudice to the generality of subsection (1), specified criteria and procedures may relate to –
(a) site selection,
(b) design and bringing into operation of sites,
(c) impacts on the environment,
(d) (*qv*) leachate management, treatment and control,
(e) control and recovery of landfill gas,
(f) operational guidelines, including classification of wastes and establishment of acceptance criteria for landfill,
(g) acceptance of different classes of waste at different classes of sites,
(h) fire, pest and litter control,
(i) appropriate recovery, reuse and recycling facilities,
(j) co-disposal of industrial and other wastes,
(k) monitoring of leachate, other effluents and emissions,
(l) termination of use and subsequent monitoring.

(3) (a) A local authority which manages or operates a landfill site to which specified criteria and procedures apply shall carry out, cause to be carried out, or arrange for, such monitoring in connection with the management or operation of the landfill site as the Agency shall direct, and shall transmit the results of such monitoring and such information on the management or operation of the site to the Agency in such manner and at such times as the Agency shall direct.
(b) The Agency shall carry out, cause to be carried out, or arrange for, such monitoring as it considers necessary to verify results transmitted to it

under paragraph (a).

(4) Where the Agency is not satisfied with the response of a local authority to a direction under subsection (3)(a), it shall consult with the local authority concerned, and, if the Agency is still dissatisfied with the response following such consultation, the Agency shall carry out, cause to be carried out, or arrange for, the monitoring concerned and the costs of the monitoring may be recovered by the Agency from the local authority as a simple contract debt in any court of competent jurisdiction.

(5) Where criteria and procedures specified under this section relate to a landfill site managed or operated by a local authority, the authority shall, where necessary, take steps as soon as is practicable to ensure that the management or operation of such landfill site complies with the specified criteria and procedures.

(6) The Agency shall, from time to time, prepare and publish reports on the management and operation of local authority landfill sites and shall include in such reports such recommendations as it considers appropriate.

(7) In this section 'local authority' means a public waste collector for the purposes of the European Communities (Waste) Regulations, 1979."

Subsection (7) refers to the European Communities (Waste) Regulations 1979 (S.I. No. 390 of 1979). *See:* PERFORMANCE BY LOCAL AUTHORITIES OF THEIR STATUTORY DUTIES, S. 63 OF THE EPAA 1992.

(WMA 1996, s.68)

Section 68(3) of the WMA 1996 provides that the provisions of section 62 of the EPAA 1992 shall, in so far as they apply or have effect in relation to a particular landfill facility cease to have effect upon a grant of a waste licence under section 40 in relation to that facility.

LANDSCAPE
(Heritage Act 1995, s.2(1))

"Includes areas, sites, vistas and features of significant scenic, archaeological, geological, historical, ecological or other scientific interest."

LAY COMMISSIONERS
(WLA 1976, s.55)

The Lay Commissioners who performed an important function in compensation for acquisition of land under section 55(8) of the WLA 1976, no longer exist. The Irish Land Commission was dissolved by section 2 of the Irish Land Commission (Dissolution) Act 1992 and section 4 of that Act provided that any power or duty vested by law in the Commission or the Lay Commissioners should, so far as is not inconsistent, be exercised by the Minister, who for the purposes of the Act is the Minister for Agriculture and Food, or by an officer of the Minister for the time being authorised, whether specifically or by reference to a class of such officers, in that behalf by the Minister.

SECTION 14 OF THE IRISH LAND COMMISSION (DISSOLUTION) ACT 1992

Section 14 (3) of the Irish Land Commission (Dissolution) Act 1992 provides that the Act shall come into operation on such day as the Minister may by order appoint. The Irish Land Commission (Dissolution) Act, 1992 (Commencement) Order, 1999; (S.I. No. 75 of 1999) appointed the March 31, 1999 as the day on which the Act shall come into operation.

"LEACHATE"
(WMA 1996, s.5(1))

"Means any liquid percolating through deposited waste and emitted from or contained within a landfill."

LEASES UNDER FORESHORE ACT 1933
(Foreshore Act 1933, s.3)

See: FORESHORE.

LEASES OF FISHERIES FOR RESEARCH PURPOSES
(F(C)A 1959, s.16)

"(1) The Minister, with the consent of the Minister for Finance, may, for the purposes of any scheme of research into the life-history and habits of salmon or any freshwater fish and the economic conditions affecting the commercial development of fisheries, take on lease any fishery."

Subsection (2) although still extant does not appear to be relevant as it refers to Part XII of the F(C)A 1959 relating to the operation of (*qv*) vested fisheries which Part has been repealed by section 6, First Schedule of the FA 1980.

Subsection (3) was repealed by section 6 of the FA 1980.

LICENCE
(F(A)A 1997, s.3(1))

"means an (*qv*) aquaculture licence or a (*qv*) trial licence."

"LICENCE DUTY"
(1)DUTIES ON ORDINARY LICENCES
(2) SPECIAL LOCAL LICENCES
(F(C)A 1959, s.3(1))

"Means:

(a) in relation to an ordinary fishing licence, the licence duty payable for such licence.
(b) in relation to a (*qv*) special local licence, in respect of special tidal waters, the special local licence duty payable for such licence."

LICENCED WILDLIFE DEALER
(WLA)

See: WILDLIFE DEALER, LICENSED.

LICENCES
(F(C)A 1959/LG(WP)A 1977/APA 1987/ WLA/EPAA 1992/WMA 1996)

The number of licences granted for the Minister for the Marine under section 171 of the F(C)A 1959 must be virtually nil and if any were granted they are now totally irrelevant. Yet a section 171 licence is being mentioned as late as the WMA 1996.

It is important when reading the licensing Parts of the F(C)A 1959, the LG(WP)A 1977 and the Air Pollution Act 1987 to remember that by virtue of section 82 of the EPAA 1992, it is the Agency under Part IV of that Act who will be receiving, processing and ultimately granting licences in respect of "activities" as defined by reference to the First Schedule and not the Minister for the Marine or the local authorities under the various licensing sections of the other Acts.

There are exceptions. Under section 18 of the LG(WP)A 1977 a sanitary authority remains the sole grantor in respect of a licence to discharge trade effluent or other matter (excluding sewage or storm water) to a sewer which is vested in or controlled by that sanitary authority. Under the F(A)A 1997 the Minister and Licensing Authority are sole grantors of an (*qv*) aquaculture licence and under section 40 of the WMA 1996 the Agency was the original and remains sole grantor of waste licences though local authorities have powers to issue permits and other authorisations under that Act. *See*: PERMIT, WASTE COLLECTION PERMIT AND WASTE PERMIT.

(1) FISHERIES

LICENCING FIXED ENGINES/SCHEDULED ENGINES

Fishery law differs from other branches of environmental law in that, except in the case of (*qv*) aquaculture licences, and licences under section 171 licencing control in fisheries is mainly exercised by licencing the implement used to fish which is described as a (*qv*) fishing engine and particularised by reference to the Fourth Schedule to the F(C)A 1959 whence it becomes a (*qv*) scheduled engine. The appearance of scheduled engines/fishing engines in this Schedule is also used as the basis for levying duty. *See:* SCHEDULES HERETO, F(C)A 1959 SCHEDULES.

Section 67(1) of the F(C)A 1959 as amended provides for the issue of fishing licences in respect of scheduled engines by the (*qv*) regional fisheries board for the appropriate (*qv*) fishery district. *See:* DUTIES ON ORDINARY FISHING LICENCES.

LICENCING UNDER SECTION 171 OF F(C)A 1959

Section 171(1) of the F(C)A 1959:

The only part of the licencing procedures in the Fisheries Acts which resembles the general anti-pollution measures under the LG(WP)A 1977 and the APA 1987 is under Section 171 of the F(C)A 1959 which provides for the licensing of steeping flax or hemp and throwing, emptying, permitting to fall and causing to fall into waters (*qv*) deleterious matter. This would be a sister section to sections 4 and 16 of the LG(WP)A 1977 in that they are all concerned with discharges of various substances to waters and in fact by virtue of section 27 of the WP(A)A 1990 regional fisheries boards share with local authorities the right to prosecute under sections 3 and 4 of the LG(WP)A 1977 in addition to their right to prosecute under section 171 of the F(C)A 1959. Conversely local authorities could, if they wished, prosecute under any provision of the F(C)A 1959.
See: PROHIBITION (1) DISCHARGES TO

WATERS UNDER F(C)A 1959 where this section is dealt with in detail.

EFFECT OF SECTION 40 OF THE WMA 1996

Section 40(5) of the WMA 1996 provides that where a waste licence is granted in relation to an activity, a licence under section 171 shall not be granted in relation to such an activity and if there is an existing licence it will cease to have effect on the granting of the waste licence.

LICENSING OYSTER FISHING ENGINES

Section 278 of the F(C)A 1959, as partially repealed by section 6 of, and the First Schedule to, the FA 1980, and amended by section 11(5) of the FA 1980, –

"(1) Regional fishery boards shall, in accordance with this section, issue licences (in this Act referred to as (*qv*) oyster fishing licences) in respect of (*qv*) oyster fishing engines.

(2) The period for which oyster fishing licences are to be issued shall be one year.

(3) An oyster fishing licence shall be valid and in force for the year specified in that behalf in the licence.

(4) A separate oyster fishing licence shall be issued for each separate oyster fishing engine.

(5) Every oyster fishery licence issued by the regional fisheries board for a (qv)fisheries district shall -
   (a) be in such form as the Minister may direct,
   (b) state thereon -
      (i) the year for which it is to be valid and in force,
      (ii) the number or name of that fishery district,
      (iii) ...
      (iv) the oyster fishing engine to which it relates,
      (v) the name of the person to whom it is issued,
   (c) be sealed with the seal of such fisheries board."

Sub-paragraph (iii) of paragraph (b) above was repealed by section 6 of, and the First Schedule to, the FA 1980. It had read "the electoral division (being an electoral division of such fishery district) in which it is issued".

"(6) An oyster fishing licence shall be available for use in the fishery district of the regional board by which it was issued and in no other fishery district.

(7) Every oyster fishing licence shall operate to authorise, during the year specified therein and in the fishery district specified therein, the use of the oyster fishing engine specified therein, but subject to the provisions of the Acts and any instrument made thereunder."

DUTY

Section 279 of the F(C)A 1959 as amended by sections 3(b) and 4 of the F(A)A 1976 provided for a licence duty on an oyster fishing licence.

OFFENCE OF FISHING OTHERWISE THAN WITH LICENSED DREDGE

Offence
Section 277 of the F(C)A 1959 creates the offence of taking in a fishery district any oysters from an oyster fishery otherwise than by means of an oyster fishing engine in respect of which there is for the time being in force an oyster fishing licence authorising the use of such oyster fishing engine in that fishery district.

(Note that the maximum penalty prescribed under this section has been increased. *See:* FINES AND IMPRISONMENT (IMPOSITION OF)).

RIGHT TO ISSUE OF A LICENCE

Section 280 of the F(C)A 1959, which provided that where a person applied for an oyster fishing licence and tendered the licence duty that person was to be issued with such a licence, was regrettably repealed by section 6 of, and the First Schedule to, the FA 1980.

LICENSING SALMON DEALERS, TROUT DEALERS, EEL DEALERS AND MOLLUSCAN SHELLFISH DEALERS

Part X of the F(C)A 1959, as amended by insertion of a new Part X by section 20 of the F(A)A 1994, deals with the licensing of salmon dealers, trout dealers, eel dealers and molluscan shellfish dealers *See:* CERTIFICATE OF FITNESS.

LICENCING AQUACULTURE UNDER F(A)A 1997

Section 6(1) of the F(A)A 1997 :

Offence

"(1) A person who, at any place or in any (*qv*) waters, engages in (*qv*) aquaculture except under and in accordance with an (*qv*) aquaculture licence, a (*qv*) trial licence, or an (*qv*) oyster bed licence or an (*qv*) oyster fishery order shall be guilty of an offence."

AQUACULTURE LICENCES

Section 7 of the F(A))A 1997:

"(1) Subject to section 8, the (*qv*) licensing authority may, if satisfied that it is in the public interest to do so, licence a person, at a place or in waters specified in the licence, to engage in aquaculture or such operations in relation to aquaculture, and subject to such conditions, as it thinks fit and specifies in the licence.

(2) A licence may be granted notwithstanding the existence of any public right to fish in any waters to which the licence relates."

Subsection (3) provides for conditions subject to which the licence may be granted. *See:* CONDITIONS.

LIMITATION ON LICENSING TO ENGAGE IN AQUACULTURE

Section 8(1) of the F(A)A 1997:

"(1) The licensing authority shall not licence a person to engage in aquaculture within the limits of an oyster bed or oyster fishery the property of any private person or to which an oyster bed licence or oyster fishery order relates, without the consent of that private person or of the person who for the time being is beneficially entitled to the oyster bed or oyster fishery.

(2) The licensing authority may licence a person to engage in aquaculture within the limits of a (*qv*)several fishery, as defined by section 3 of the Principal Act, only -

(a) if the person is the owner of the fishery, or

(b) with the consent in writing of the owner.

(3) An aquaculture licence shall not be construed as taking away or abridging any right on, to or over any portion of the seashore enjoyed by a person under a local or special Act, or any charter, letters patent, prescription or immemorial usage, or a right of several fishery, with out the consent of that person."

TRIAL LICENCES

Section 9 of the F(A)A 1997:

"(1) The Minister may licence a person, other than in freshwater –

(a) to carry on, at a place or in waters specified in the licence, such operations for the the purpose of investigating the suitability of the place or waters for aquaculture, or for any activity forming part of an aquaculture operation, or

(b) to carry out any other trials and experiments (including trials in the culture or farming of novel species),

for such period –

(i) in the case of salmon, not exceeding one year, and

(ii) in all other cases, not exceeding 3 years,

and subject to such conditions, which may include or relate to all or any of the matters specified in section 7(3), as the Minister sees fit and specifies in the licence.

(2) Without limiting the generality of subsection (1), a trial licence may specify, by means of a map or otherwise, the boundaries or limits of the place or waters in relation to which the licensee is licensed.

(3) A trial licence is not capable of being renewed.

(4) The Minister may revoke a trial licence when he or she considers that there has been a contravention of or failure to comply with the terms of the licence or of a condition subject to which it is granted."

Subsection (4) seems pretty draconian but then so did section 266 of the F(C)A 1959 which gave the Minister a similar right, from which there was no appeal, to determine an oyster fishery order. *See:* OYSTERS.

APPLICATIONS FOR LICENCES

Section 10(1) of the F(A)A 1997:

"(1) A person may, in accordance with the application regulations, apply to the Minister for an aquaculture licence or a trial licence."

Subsection (2) provides for Ministerial Regulations in relation to the making of applications and their consideration and may contain different provisions in respect of different classes of applications.

Subsection (3) provides that, without limiting the generality of subsection (2) these regulations may provide the form of application, require publication of notices and the furnishing of information to specified persons, make specific requirements in relation to EC Directive 85/337/EEC on the furnishing of environmental impact statements (O.J. L175, July 5, 1985), provide for the making available of documents for inspection and copying, provide for consultation with prescribed bodies, provide for the making of submissions and the time within which they are to be made, requiring additional information with evidence to verify and the publication and the giving of notices by the licensing authority on applications and decisions on applications.

Subsection (4), as inserted by Article 17 of the European Communities (Environmental Impact Assessment) Regulations 1999 (S.I. No. 93 of 1999), provides:

"(a) Without prejudice to subsection (3)(d) of this section, if a person, before making an application for a licence in respect of which an environmental impact assessment must be submitted in accordance with regulations under this section, so requests, the Minister shall, after consulting such person and such bodies as may be prescribed for that purpose, give a written opinion on the information to be contained in such statement.

(b) The giving of a written opinion in accordance with paragraph (a) of this subsection shall not prejudice the exercise by the Minister of his or her powers under this Act or regulations made thereunder to require the person concerned to furnish further information in relation to the effects on the environment of the aquaculture concerned."

The current regulations relating to application for aquaculture licences are the Aquaculture (Licence) Application Regulations, 1998 (S.I. No. 236 of 1998).

These Regulations, which came into force on 30 June 1998, make comprehensive provision relating to various matters concerning the application for licences including: –

the making of an application (Regulation 4), environmental impact statements required for such applications (regulation 5), procedure on receipt of application (regulation 6) and further information which may be required (regulation 7), public notice to be give by applicant of the application (regulation 8), right to make submissions concerning the application (regulation 9), notice to certain bodies of receipt of application (regulation 10) and of the environmental impact statement (regulation 11), consideration of submissions and furnishing of information (regulation 12), notice to Member States of EU (regulation 13), applicant's comments on submissions (regulation 14), power to request further submissions and to declare them withdrawn (regulation 15), revised plans (regulation 16), withdrawal of application (regulation 17), advising applicant of Minister's decision (regulation 18), publication of Minister's decision (regulation 19), additional notice in certain cases (regulation 20), revocation or amendment of aquaculture licences (regulation 21) and consequences of failure to comply with Regulations (regulation 22).

The First Schedule to these Regulations concerns the information to be contained in an Environmental Impact Statement. The Second Schedule deals with public notices of applications for an aquaculture licence, Environmental Impact Statements and applications for a foreshore licence under the Foreshore Act, 1933 (Act No. 12). The Third Schedule deals with public notices for applications for an aquaculture licence under the Fisheries (Amendment) Act, 1997 and for a foreshore licence under the Foreshore Act, 1933. The Fourth Schedule deals with public notice and publication of further information received in respect of an Environmental Impact Statement published in connection with an application for an aquaculture licence under the 1997 Act.

These regulations were followed by the Aquaculture (Licence Application and Licence Fees) Regulations, 1998 (S.I. No. 270 of 1998) and the Aquaculture (Licence Application and Licence Fees) (N.o 2) Regulations, 1998 (S.I. No. 324 of 1998).

Section 11 of the F(A)A 1997, which provided

for rejection of the application if the applicant pre-empted his application by engaging in aquaculture was repealed by section 4(2) of the Fisheries and Foreshore (Amendment) Act, 1998 which is dealt with hereunder.

These commencement dates are:

February 26, 1998: sections 2, 3, 4(1) (in so far as it repeals section 54A of the FA 1980), 5(2), 10, 23, 63, 64, 65(2)(3), 66 and 67 (S.I. No.46 of 1998).

June 16, 1998: sections 19, 22, 24 to 39, 68 and 70 and the Schedule (S.I. No. 203 of 1998).

June 30, 1998: all remaining provisions except sections 11 and 13 (S.I. No. 203 of 1998).

DETERMINATION OF APPLICATIONS FOR LICENCES

Determination is important as the time for lodging an appeal is dependent on the time when the written notice of determination is served on the applicant. It is modelled on the procedure under the LG(P&D)A 1963 of notification of an intention to make a decision, followed by a period within which an appeal can be lodged and it is only when the time allowed for appeal has elapsed that the actual planning decision issues.

Section 12 of the F(A)A 1997:

"(1) The licensing authority shall determine an application for a licence by deciding to -
- (a) grant the licence or a variation of the licence,
- (b) refuse to grant the licence.

(2) A variation referred to in subsection (1)(a) may be a variation of the term of the licence or of a condition to which the licence is to be subject, or the inclusion or omission of a term or condition.

(3) The licensing authority shall, as soon as practicable after determining an application, advise the applicant in writing of its decision."

PERIOD FOR DETERMINATION OF APPLICATION FOR LICENCES

Section 13 of the F(A)A 1997:

"(1) The Minister shall endeavour to determine an application for a licence –
- (a) in the case of an application for a trial licence, as soon as practicable, but in any case not later than four months after all requirements of or under the application regulations relating to the application have been complied with, and
- (b) in the case of an application for an aquaculture licence received on after the commencement of this section –
  - (i) within four months from the date on which all requirements of or under the application regulations relating to the application have been complied with, or
  - (ii) such other period as the Minister may prescribe, either generally or in respect of a particular class of applications to which the application belongs.

(2) Where it appears to the Minister that it would not be possible or appropriate, because of the particular circumstances relating to an application for a licence, to determine the application within the period referred to in subsection (1), the Minister shall, by notice in writing served on the applicant and any person who has made submissions or observations in relation to the application in accordance with the application regulations, inform the applicant and those persons of the reasons why it would not be possible or appropriate to determine the application within that period and shall specify the date before which, or the period within which, the Minister intends that the application shall be determined.

(3) Where a notice has been served under subsection (2), the Minister shall take such steps as are open to him or her to ensure that the application is determined before the date, or within the period, specified in the notice.

(4) The Minister may make regulations –
- (a) providing that subsection (1) shall not have effect for such period as is specified in the regulations, or
- (b) varying a period mentioned in that subsection, either generally or in respect of a particular class or particular classes of applications,

where it appears to the Minister to be necessary, because of exceptional circumstances to do so and, for so long as the regulations are in force, this section shall be construed and have effect accordingly.

(5) In the section 'application for a licence' shall include an application for a review of an aquaculture licence."

GRANTING OF LICENCES

Section 14 of the F(A)A 1997:

"(1) Where the Minister determines an application for a trial licence by deciding to grant the licence, the Minister shall grant the licence as soon as practicable after so deciding.

(2) Where the Minister determines an application for an aquaculture licence by deciding to grant the licence or a variation of the licence and no appeal is lodged against the decision within the time allowed by section 40(1) for the lodging of such appeals, the Minister shall grant the licence or licence as so varied as soon as practicable after the last day on which such appeal could be lodged.

(3) Where the Minister determines an application for an aquaculture licence by deciding to grant the licence or a variation of the licence and an appeal is lodged against the decision within the time allowed by section 40(1) for the lodging of such appeals, the Minister shall not grant the licence or licence as so varied unless the appeal is, or where more than one appeal is lodged against the decision all the appeals are —
(a) withdrawn, or
(b) determined by the (*qv*) Board pursuant to section 48 by confirming under section 40(4)(a) the decision of the Minister, or
(c) dismissed by the Board pursuant to section 51,
but shall grant the licence as soon as practicable thereafter.

(4) In this section, a reference to a case in which the Minister decides to grant an aquaculture licence shall include a reference to a case in which the Minister, following a (*qv*) review of an aquaculture licence in accordance with section 70, decides to alter any or all of the terms of the licence, or to amend or delete any conditions to which the licence is subject, or to impose conditions or additional conditions in relation to the licence."

EFFECT OF LICENCE

Section 16 of the F(A)A 1997:

"(1) A licence is binding on the State and on all persons whomsoever, and subject to section 8(3), shall operate to enable the licensee to carry on, in accordance with the licence, such operations as are specified in the licence, free from all prior or other rights, titles, estates or interests, if any.

(2) In addition to his or her entitlement under subsection (1), and notwithstanding anything contained in the Fisheries Acts 1959 to 1995, or any instrument under those Acts, a licensee and any person acting under the directions of a licensee shall by virtue of, but subject to the conditions of, the licence and the requirements of any (*qv*) regulations made under section 71, have the exclusive right to do within the boundaries or limits specified in the licence anything authorised by the licence or necessary or expedient to conduct the operations specified in the licence."

For matters to which licensing authority shall have regard in determining aquaculture licences and appeals, *see*: APPEALS F(C)A 1959 (2).

For duration (Section 15), *see:* DURATION, for renewal (Section 19), *see:* RENEWAL, for application of sections 263 and 264 F(C)A 1959, *see:* OYSTERS, for offence of interfering with licencees right under licence, *see:* AQUACULTURE LICENCE, INTERFERING WITH, for delegation of functions by Minister, *see:* DELEGATION.

FISHERIES AND FORESHORE (AMENDMENT) ACT 1998

The Minister was given power under section 54 of the FA 1980 to grant aquaculture licences. For many complex reasons they ceased to do so. Section 54 of the FA 1980 was repealed by section 5 of the F(A)A 1997. *See:* OYSTERS.

In the period between the ban on issuing aquaculture licences under section 54 and the repeal of that section in 1997 the Minister prevailed on the Minister for Industry and Commerce to issue in lieu of aquaculture licences foreshore licences under section 3 of the Foreshore Act 1933 "purporting to be aquaculture licences". These licences were legally ineffective but they were not questioned and the grantee had some semblance of authority to carry out aquaculture activities. *See:* FORESHORE.

After the F(A)A 1997, section 75 of which provided for the granting of a new aquaculture licence, it became necessary to validate these section 3 foreshore licences. This was not done properly in the F(A)A 1997 so it was necessary to pass the Fisheries and Foreshore (Amendment) Act, 1998 which attempts to validate these section 3 Foreshore Act 1933 licences and also fish culture licences granted under section 15 of the F(C)A 1959.

Section 3 of the Fisheries and Foreshore (Amendment) Act 1998:

"(1) Subject to subsection (2) of this section, where before the commencement of section 75 of the Act of 1997 there was purported to be granted –
(a) a foreshore licence for aquaculture purposes under the Act of 1933, or
(b) a fish culture licence under section 15 of the Principal Act,
then such purported grant of the licence concerned shall be deemed to have been duly made and, accordingly, shall be deemed by virtue of the said section 75 to be an aquaculture licence granted under the Act of 1997."

Subsection (2) deals with the procedures for "converting" these licences into section 75 aquaculture licences and subsection (3) with the liability of the grantees for such fees as are prescribed by the Minister under the Act of 1977.

"(4) Notwithstanding subsection (1) of this section, in the case of a foreshore licence which is deemed to be an aquaculture licence under the said subsection (1), the provisions of the Foreshore Acts, 1933 and 1992, shall apply to such foreshore licence.

(5) Where a licence is deemed under subsection (1) of this section to be an aquaculture licence and such deeming would, but for this subsection, conflict with the constitutional right of any person, then the licence concerned shall be subject to such limitation as is necessary to secure that it does not so conflict but shall be otherwise of full force and effect."

For fish culture licences, *see:* FISH CULTURE LICENCES.

COMMENCEMENT DATES FOR F(A)A 1997

The commencement date for sections 11 and 13 of the F(A)A 1997 was postponed by the F(A)A 1997 (Commencement) (No 2) Order 1998 (S.I. No. 203 of 1998). The repeal of section 11 by section 4(2) of the Fisheries and Foreshore (Amendment) Act 1998 leaves section 13 the only section which does not have a commencement date.

The commencement dates for the F(A)A 1997 are as follows:

February 26, 1998: (for sections 2, 3, 4(1) (in so far as it repeals section 54A of the FA 1980), 5(2), 10, 23, 63, 64, 65(2) and (3), 66 and 67) – S.I. No. 46 of 1998.

June 16, 1998: (for sections 19, 22, 24 to 39, 68 and 70 and the Schedule) – S.I. No. 203 of 1998

June 30, 1998: (for all remaining provisions except sections 11 and 13) – S.I. No. 203 of 1998

Section 4 of the Fisheries and Foreshore (Amendment) Act 1998:

"(1) On and from the 10th day of December, 1998, an application for an aquaculture licence shall not be accepted, or if accepted shall not be determined, if the applicant or any person on behalf of the applicant commences to engage in (*qv*) aquaculture at the place or waters to which the application relates before a licence is granted under the Act of 1997.

(2) Section 11 of the Act of 1997 is hereby repealed."

(2) LICENCING UNDER THE WLA 1976 AND NH 97 REGULATIONS

Although it is obviously not invariably so, it does appear from the WLA 1976 that every section which provides for the protection of (*qv*) fauna or (*qv*) flora contains a subsection which enables the Minister to authorise by licence the very activity which is prohibited in the first instance.

The awkward layout of the Act does not help nor does the fact that it has not had an amendment of substance by statute. All of the amendments have been by Ministerial order and regulation mainly driven by the two great European nature Directives, the (*qv*) Birds Directive and the (*qv*) Natural Habitats Directive.

(A) FORBIDDEN IMPLEMENTS WHICH CAN BE LICENCED

Section 29 of the WLA 1976 authorises the Minister to licence the use for hunting of firearms. The Firearms (Temporary Provisions) Act 1998 extends his powers under the section. *See:* FIREARMS, LICENCE TO HUNT WITH.

Section 32 of the WLA 1976 licenses the use of band, ring, tag or other marking device, net or trap for the purposes of subsection (1) of section 32, and for a like purpose licenses the import of cannon-nets, mist-nets, rocket-nets or similar appliances. *See:* RINGING OF BIRDS AND TRAPPING OFFENCES.

Section 35(4) of the WLA 1976 entitles the Minister to licence scarecrows, decoys live birds as decoys and birdcalls, under subsection (4) decoys and electrical devices imitating birdcalls for scientific research or another purpose approved by the Minister and, under subsection (5) the use of a live bird as a decoy for hunting birds of the same species subject to rigorous conditions. *See:* SCARECROWS, DECOYS, BIRD CALLS AND CALLS.

Section 36(2) of the WLA 1976 permits the licensing of mechanically-propelled vehicles, vessels or aircraft, used to capture or kill protected wild birds and protected wild animals. *See:* USE OF MECHANICALLY-PROPELLED VEHICLE, VESSEL OR AIRCRAFT IN HUNTING.

Section 34(2) of the WLA 1976 permits the licensing of traps, snares, nets, lines, hooks, arrows, darts, spears or similar devices, instruments or missiles or birdlime or poisonous, poisoned or stupefying bait for certain uses, excepting those uses described in subsection (3), under section 34(2) but use for taking or killing protected wild birds and protected wild animals are excluded. *See:* TRAPS, SNARES, NETS, PROHIBITION OF.

Section 38 of the WLA 1976 permits the licensing of lamps, lights, torches, mirrors or other artificial light-reflecting or dazzling devices or appliances used in hunting protected wild birds or protected wild animals for –

- (a) attaching thereto any band, ring, tag or other marking device, or
- (b) hunting for educational or scientific purposes.

See: LAMPS, USE OF LAMPS, MIRRORS ETC. IN HUNTING.

(B) FORBIDDEN HUNTING WHICH CAN BE LICENSED

Sections 22(9) and 23(6) of the WLA 1976 permit the licensing of hunting protected wild birds and protected wild animals at night, between one hour after sunset and one hour before sunrise, a time otherwise prohibited under section 37(1) of the WLA 1976, in the circumstances mentioned in the appropriate subsections. *See:* HUNTING BY NIGHT.

OTTER AND DEER

Section 26(1) of the WLA 1976 empowers the Minister to grant periodic licences to hunt:

(i) otters with an otter pack,
(ii)deer with a pack of stag hounds.

HARES

See: HARES ORDER.

HARES WITH A PACK

Section 26(2) of the WLA 1976 allows the Minister to grant to a pack of beagles or harriers a licence to hunt hares (other than on a day specified in a hares order).

COURSING FOR HARES

Section 26(3) of the WLA 1976 empowers the Minister to grant to a coursing club affiliated to the Irish Coursing Club, a licence to hold regulated coursing matches.

OPEN SEASON

By means of the "open season" system the shooting of certain wild birds and wild animals is permitted which is licensing of a kind. *See:* OPEN SEASON.

(C) LICENCING FOR EDUCATION AND RESEARCH AND DEROGATION

There is provision in both the WLA 1976 and in the NH 97 Regulations for licencing under the headings of education, research and the introduction of non-native species in certain very limited circumstances.

Section 22(9) of the WLA 1976 provides that the Minister may grant a licence:

- (a) to capture or kill humanely a protected wild bird as specified for such educational, scientific or other purposes as may be specified,

(b) to hunt protected wild birds which are both pen-reared and of a species so specified,
(c) to hunt protected wild birds for the purpose of training gun dogs for any field sport or holding gun dog trials,
(d) to take the eggs or nests of protected wild birds for educational, scientific or other purposes.

Regulation 25 of the NH 97 Regulations (S.I. No. 94 of 1997) allows the Minister to grant licences permitting persons to derogate from the provisions of certain regulations for conservation and other purposes. *See:* DEROGATION.

(D) MISCELLANEOUS LICENCES AND PERMISSIONS

TERRITORIAL SEAS OF THE STATE

Section 58(1) of the WLA 1976:

"(1) It is hereby declared that the right to hunt (*qv*) fauna in or over the portion of the sea which is the (*qv*) territorial seas of the State is the property of the State.

(2) It shall not be lawful for a person without the permission of the Minister to hunt fauna on, in or over any part of the portion of the sea mentioned in subsection (1).

(3) Any person who contravenes subsection (2) of this section shall commit a trespass.

(4) Nothing in this section shall operate to prejudice any legal proceedings which may be instituted apart from this section and a person who contravenes subsection (2) of this section may, if the Minister thinks fit, be sued by the Minister for trespass to any court of competent jurisdiction and for the purpose of giving jurisdiction under this Act the trespass shall be deemed to have been committed where the person complained against may be."

This latter provision must be intended to refer to the place of residence of the defendant but even this is unclear in a very muddy section.

LICENCE TO REGULATE FALCONRY

Section 41(2) of the WLA 1976.

See: FALCONRY.

WILDLIFE DEALER'S LICENCE

Section 48 of the WLA 1976 provides for the grant by the District Court of a (*qv*) wildlife dealer's licence. It is an offence under section 47 of the WLA 1976 to carry on the business of a wildlife dealer except under and in accordance with such a licence.
See: WILDLIFE DEALING.

LICENCE FOR IMPORT AND EXPORT OF FAUNA AND FLORA

Section 52 of the WLA 1976 authorises an import licence (*See:* FAUNA AND FLORA, IMPORT) and section 53 of the WLA 1976 provides for an export licence. *See:* FAUNA AND FLORA, EXPORT.

"PERMISSION" UNDER SECTION 42 (3), (4), (5) AND (6)

Section 42 of the WLA 1976 gives the Minister the power to give permission to an owner or occupier of land, where damage as described in subsection (1) is being caused, to capture or kill protected wild birds and protected wild animals or take other steps to stop the damage. *See:* DAMAGE BY PROTECTED WILD BIRDS AND PROTECTED WILD ANIMALS (1).

(3) LICENCING UNDER THE LG(WP)A 1977

LICENCING OF TRADE AND SEWAGE EFFLUENT

Section 4 of the LG(WP)A 1977 provides:

"(1) (a) Subject to subsection (2), a person shall not, after such date as may be fixed for the purpose of this subsection by order made by the Minister, discharge or cause or permit the discharge of any (*qv*) trade effluent or (*qv*) sewage effluent to any (*qv*) waters except under and in accordance with a licence under this section.
(b) A licence under this section may be granted –
(i) in the case of a discharge to waters in the functional area of a local authority, by that local authority, and
(ii) in any other case, by a local authority in whose functional area

any premises, works, apparatus, plant or drainage pipe from which the effluent is discharged is situated.

(2) Subsection (1) does not apply to discharges –
(a) to tidal waters from vessels or marine structures,
(b) from a sewer, or
(c) the subject to regulations under sub section (10)."

"(3) (a) A local authority may at its discretion refuse to grant a licence under this section or may grant such a licence subject to such conditions as it thinks appropriate and specifies in the licence.
(b) In considering whether or not to grant a licence under this section a local authority shall have regard to the objectives contained in any relevant plan under section 15.

(4) A local authority shall not grant a licence under this section in respect of the discharge of an effluent which would not comply with, or would result in the waters to which the discharge is made not complying with, any relevant standard prescribed under section 26."

Subsections (5) and (6) deal with conditions attaching to licences under the section. *See:* CONDITIONS.

Subsection (7) provides that where no discharge of the type authorised by the licence has been made, or having commenced has ceased for 3 years the licence shall cease to have effect.

Offence
Subsection (8) provides that a person who con travenes subsection (1) shall be guilty of an offence.

Subsection (10) gives the Minister power, after consultation with the Minister for Fisheries (and the (*qv*) Water Pollution Advisory Council), by regulations to grant exemptions from subsection (1).

Subsection (11) provides that it is a good defence to a prosecution for any enactment under this Act that the act constituting the offence is authorised by licence under this section.

Subsection (12) provides that a person shall not be entitled solely by reason of a licence under this section to discharge, or cause or permit the discharge of (*qv*) trade effluent or (*qv*) sewage effluent to (*qv*) waters.

PROVISIONS CONSEQUENTIAL ON SECTION 4

Section 5 of the LG(WP)A 1977:

"(1) A person shall be deemed not to have contravened section 4(1) in relation to an existing discharge of (*qv*) trade effluent or (*qv*) sewage effluent made before he is granted or refused a licence under section 4, if before the relevant date, he applies for such a licence and complies with the requirements of any regulations under section 6 regarding the furnishing of information to a local authority.

(2) In a prosecution for an offence under section 4 it shall be presumed, until the contrary is shown by the person charged, that the discharge concerned is not an existing discharge of trade effluent or sewage effluent made in the circumstances specified in subsection (1).

(3) Where regulations under section 26 relate to an existing discharge of trade effluent or sewage effluent being made in the circumstances specified in subsection (1) or to waters to which such discharge is being so made, the local authority concerned shall grant or refuse (as the case may require) a licence under section 4 in respect of the discharge as soon as may be after the regulations are made.

(4) In this section –
'existing discharge' means a discharge which is similar in nature, composition and temperature to, and is of a similar volume and is made at a similar rate to, a discharge made during any corresponding period in the period of twelve months ending on the relevant date.
'relevant date' means the date fixed by order under section 4(1)."

(The relevant date was October 1, 1978 by virtue of S.I. No. 16 of 1978.)

LICENCING OF DISCHARGES TO SEWERS

Section 16 of the LG(WP)A 1977:

"(1) A person other than a sanitary authority shall not, after such date as may be fixed for the purposes of this section by order made by the Minister, discharge or cause or permit the discharge of any trade effluent or other matter (other than domestic sewage or storm water) to a sewer, except under and in accordance with a licence under this section granted by the sanitary authority in which the sewer is vested or by which it is controlled.

(2) (a) A sanitary authority may at its discretion refuse to grant a licence under this section or may grant such a licence subject to such conditions as it thinks appropriate and specifies in the licence.
(b) In considering whether or not to grant a licence under this section a sanitary authority shall have regard to the objectives contained in any relevant plan under section 15.

(3) A (*qv*) sanitary authority shall not grant a licence under this section in respect of the discharge of a trade effluent which would not comply with any relevant standard under section 26."

For the text of subsections (4) and (5), *see:* CONDITIONS.

Subsection (6) provides that where no discharge of the type authorised by the licence has been made, or having commenced has ceased for three years the licence shall cease to have effect.

"(7) A person shall not permit or cause the entry of any (*qv*) polluting matter including (*qv*) sewage, to any drain or sewer provided solely for the reception or disposal of storm water."

Offence

"(8) A person who contravenes subsection (1) shall be guilty of an offence."

Subsection (9) which had provided for the persons entitled to prosecute was repealed by section 30 of the LG(WP)(A) 1990 which now contains those provisions.
See: PROSECUTION, POWERS OF (2).

"(10) The Minister may, after consultation with the Minister for Fisheries, by regulations exempt from subsection (1) such classes of discharge as he specifies in the regulations."

"(11) It shall be a good defence to a prosecution for an offence under any enactment other than this Act that the act constituting the offence is authorised by a licence under this section."

"(12) A person shall not be entitled solely by reason of a licence under this section to make, cause or permit a discharge to a sewer."

Subsections (13), (13A), (14) and (15) deal with notices under the section. *See:* ENFORCEMENT (3)(B)(2).

For section 15 *see:* WATER QUALITY MANAGEMENT PLANS. For section 26 *see:* QUALITY STANDARDS, WATERS, TRADE AND SEWAGE EFFLUENT.

EXTENSION OF CERTAIN FUNCTIONS UNDER SECTION 16 TO AGENCY

These functions under section 16(7), (8), (13), (14) and (15) now apply to the Agency in the circumstances described by Article 4 of the Environmental Protection Agency (Extension of Powers) Order 1996 (S.I. No. 126 of 1996). *See:* EXTENSION OF POWERS.

PROVISIONS CONSEQUENTIAL ON SECTION 16

Section 18 of the LG(WP)A 1977:

"(1) A person shall be deemed not to have contravened section 16(1) in relation to an existing discharge of (*qv*) trade effluent or other matter made before he is granted or refused a licence under section 16 if, before the relevant date, he applies for such a licence and complies with the requirements of any regulations under section 19 regarding the furnishing of information to a local sanitary authority.
(2) In a prosecution for an offence under section 16 it shall be presumed, until the contrary is shown by the person charged, that the discharge concerned is not an existing discharge of trade effluent or other matter made in the circumstances specified in subsection (1).

(3) Where regulations under section 26 relate to an existing discharge of trade effluent being made in the circumstances specified in subsection (1), the sanitary authority concerned shall grant or refuse (as the case may require) a licence under section 16 in respect of the discharge as soon as may be after the regulations are made.
(4) In this section:
'existing discharge' means a discharge which is similar in nature, composition and temperature to, and is of a similar

volume and is made at a similar rate to, a discharge made during any corresponding period in the period of twelve months ending on the relevant date;
'relevant date' means the date fixed by order under section 16(1)."

(The relevant date was October 1, 1978 by virtue of S.I. No. 16 of 1978.)

EFFECT OF SECTION 40(5) OF THE WMA 1996

Sections 4 and 16 of the LG(WP)A 1977 are affected in the same way as is section 171 under Fisheries (1). On the granting of a waste licence under the WMA 1996, the licences under sections 4 and 16 cease to have effect.

REGULATIONS: Local Government (Water Pollution) Regulations 1978 (S.I. No. 108 of 1978), Licensing of discharge to waters by local authority Part II; by sanitary authority Part III and for exempted effluents under section 4(1) Part II Article 4 First Schedule. Local Government (Water Pollution) Regulations 1992 (S.I. No. 271 of 1992) licence applications and reviews Part III.

CONTROL OF DISCHARGES TO AQUIFERS

The 1992 Regulations quoted above deal extensively in Part VI with the Control of Discharges to Aquifers *See:* DISCHARGES TO AQUIFERS.

(4) LICENCING UNDER THE APA 1987

Section 32 of the APA 1987 –

"(1) Where
(a) an application is made to a local authority in accordance with regulations under section 31 for a licence under this Act,
(b) the requirements of, or made pursuant to, such regulations have been complied with,
The local authority may, subject to section 35(2), decide to grant the licence subject to, or without, conditions or to refuse the application.

(2) In considering an application for a licence under this Act, the local authority shall have regard to –
(a) any (*qv*) air quality management plan in force in relation to the area concerned, and
(b) any (*qv*) special control area order in operation in relation to the area.

(3) A local authority shall not grant a licence in relation to (*qv*) industrial plant unless they are satisfied that -
(a) the (*qv*) best practicable means will be used to prevent or limit any emissions from the plant,
(b) any emissions from the plant will comply with any relevant (*qv*) emission limit value,
(c) any emissions from the plant will not result in the contravention of any relevant air quality standard,
(d) any emissions from the plant will not cause significant air pollution

and, where appropriate, the local authority shall attach conditions relating to the matters specified in paragraphs (a),(b),(c) and(d) to the licence."

Subsection (3) was amended by section 18, Third Schedule, 3, of the EPAA 1992

For the form of application for a licence and procedures on application under section 31, referred to supra in section 32(1), refer to the Air Pollution Act, 1987 (Licensing of Industrial Plant) Regulations, 1988 (S.I. No. 266 of 1988) which are not dealt with in detail in this book.

For subsection (4) *See:* CONDITIONS.

"(5) Whenever a local authority, having considered an application for a licence undor the Act, decide that -
(a) the licence shall be granted, they shall forthwith notify the applicant of the decision and of any conditions which may be attached to the licence and of the reasons for the attachment of any such conditions, or
(b) the licence shall not be granted, they shall forthwith notify the applicant of the decision and of the reasons for the decision."

For sections 31 and 35 APA 1987, *see:* REGULATIONS APA 1987 ss. 31 and 35.

EFFECT OF SECTION 40(5) OF THE WMA 1996

Licences under Section 32 of the APA 1987, are affected in the same way are licences under section 171 of the F(C)A 1959 dealt with under

FISHERIES (1) supra. On the granting of a waste licence the licence under section 32 ceases to have effect.

(5) LICENCING UNDER THE EPAA 1992

Section 82 of the EPAA 1992:

"(1) A person shall not carry on an (*qv*) activity, other than an (*qv*) established activity, on or after such day as may be prescribed unless a licence or revised licence under this Part is in force in relation to the activity.

(2) The Minister may, by order, provide that an established activity of any class specified in the order shall not be carried on, on or after such date as may be specified in the order, unless a licence or revised licence under this Part is in force in relation to the activity."

See: (*qv*) "established activity" definition which was originally and properly part of this section but which was moved after debate in the Dáil to section 3(1).

See: EPA (Established Activities) Orders 1994, (S.I. No. 83 of 1994) 1995, (S.I. No. 58 of 1995, (No. 2) 1995, (S.I. No. 204 of 1995, and 1997 (S.I. No. 140 of 1997).

"(3) Where an order under subsection (2) comes into operation, the carrying on of an established activity to which the order relates shall, in the period before a licence in relation to the activity is granted or refused, be deemed not to have contravened the provisions of this Part provided that, before the date specified in the order an application has been made for a licence in respect of that activity and the requirements of regulations for a licence made under section 87 in relation to the application for the licence have been complied with by the applicant therefor."

Comparison: Section 30 APA 1987. *See: Angus Fine Chemicals Ltd. v. Cork County Council [1990] 2 I.R. 365*)

GRANT OF LICENCES

Section 83 of the EPAA 1992, as amended by Article 13 of the European Communities (Environment Impact Assessment) Regulations 1994 (S.I. No. 84 of 1994) which inserted subsection (2)(cc) and section 65(1)(b) and (c) of the WMA 1996 which inserted subsection (IA) and (3)(a).

"(1) Where an application is made to the Agency in the prescribed manner for a licence under this Part it may, subject to section 94 and to compliance with any regulations under section 87, grant the licence subject to, or without, conditions or refuse the application.

Prior to, and for the purpose of considering an application for, the grant of a licence or a revised licence, the Agency shall carry out or cause to be carried out such investigations as it considers necessary or as may be prescribed."

(Subsection (1A) was inserted by section 65 (1)*(b)* of the WMA 1996.)

"(2) In considering an application for a licence or the review of the licence or revised licence under this Part, the Agency shall have regard to –

(a) any relevant (*qv*) air quality management plan under section 46 of the Air Pollution Act, 1987, or (*qv*) water quality management plan under section 15 of the Local Government (Water Pollution) Act, 1977, or (*qv*) waste management plan,

(b) any relevant (*qv*) noise regulations under section 106,

(c) any (*qv*) special control area order under section 39 of the Air Pollution Act, 1987, in operation in relation to the area concerned, and

(cc)(i) the environmental impact statement, if any, submitted with the application,

(ii) any submissions or observations made to the Agency in relation to the environmental impact statement,

(iii) any further information or particulars submitted in relation to the environmental impact statement in compliance with a notice given under (*qv*) regulations under section 87, and

(iv) where appropriate, the views of other Member States of the European Communities in relation to the effects on the environment of the proposed (*qv*) activity, insofar as the statement, submissions, views, observations, information or particulars relate to the risk of (*qv*) environmental pollution from the activity,

(d) such other matters related to the prevention, limitation, elimination, abatement or reduction of environmental pollution as it considers necessary.

(3) The Agency shall not grant a licence or revised licence for an activity unless it is satisfied that –

(a) any (*qv*) emissions from the activity will not result in the contravention of any relevant (*qv*) air quality standard specified under section 50 of the Air Pollution Act, 1987, and will comply with any relevant (*qv*) emission limit value specified under section 51 of the Air Pollution Act, 1987,

(b) any emissions from the activity will comply with, or will not result in the contravention of, any relevant quality standard for waters, trade effluents and sewage effluents and standards in relation to treatment of such effluents prescribed under section 26 of the Local Government (Water Pollution) Act, 1977,

(c) any emissions from the activity or any (*qv*) premises, (*qv*) plant, methods, processes, operating procedures or other factors which affect such emissions will comply with, or will not result in the contravention of, any relevant standard including any standard for an (*qv*) environmental medium prescribed under regulations made under the European Communities Act, 1972, or under any other enactment,

(d) any (*qv*) noise from the activity will comply with, or will not result in the contravention of, any regulations under section 106,

(e) any emissions from the activity will not cause significant (*qv*) environmental pollution, and

(f) the (*qv*) best available technology not entailing excessive costs will be used to prevent or eliminate or, where that is not practicable, to limit, abate or reduce an emission from the activity,

and where appropriate, the Agency shall attach conditions relating to the matters specified in the foregoing paragraphs to the licence or revised licence.

(3A) Section 53 of the Waste Management Act 1996, shall apply in relation to a licence or revised licence under this Part, with the substitution for references in that section to the grant or review of a waste licence of references to the grant or review of a licence or revised licence under this Part and with any other necessary modifications."

(Subsection (3A) was inserted by section 65(1)*(c)* of the WMA 1996.)

"(4) A person shall not be entitled solely by reason of a licence or revised licence under this part to make, cause or permit an emission to any *(qv)* environmental medium.

(5) Where a licence or revised licence is required under this Part in respect of an activity –

(a) a licence under

(i) Part III of the Air Pollution Act, 1987,

(ii) Section 4 or 16 of the Local Government (Water Pollution) Act, 1977, or

(iii) Section 171 of the Fisheries (Consolidation) Act, 1959, or

(b) a permit under –

(i) the European Communities (Toxic and Dangerous Waste) Regulations, 1982, or

(ii) the European Communities (Waste) Regulations, 1979,

shall not be granted in relation to such activity."

Both regulations (S.I. No. 33 of 1983) and (S.I. No. 390 of 1979) mentioned in sub-paragraphs (i) and (ii) were revoked by section 6 of the WMA 1996.

The WMA 1996 provides for the licensing of the disposal and recovery of waste under its Part V by way of waste licence which is totally separate from the IPC licence system under the EPAA 1992.

See: LICENCES (6).

"(6) Where a licence or revised licence has been granted under this Part in respect of an activity –

(a) a licence under –

(i) Part III of the Air Pollution Act, 1987,

(ii) section 4 or 16 of the Local Government (Water Pollution) Act, 1977, or

(iii) section 171 of the Fisheries (Consolidation) Act, 1959, or

(b) a permit under –
(i) the European Communities (Toxic and Dangerous Waste) Regulations, 1982 (S.I. No. 33 of 1982), or
(ii) the European Communities (Waste) Regulations, 1979 (S.I. No. 390 of 1979),
shall cease to have effect in relation to such activity.

(7) It shall be a good defence –
(a) to a prosecution for an offence under any enactment other than this Part, or
(b) to proceedings under –
(i) section 10 or 11 of the Local Government (Water Pollution) Act, 1977, or
(ii) section 20 of the Local Government (Water Pollution) (Amendment) Act, 1990, or
(iii) section 28, 28A or 28B of the Air Pollution Act, 1987,
to prove that the act complained of is authorised by a licence or revised licence granted under this Part."

Section 84 of the EPAA 1992 provides for conditions attaching to a licence *See:* CONDITIONS.

Note: The provisions of European Communities (Licensing of Incinerators of Hazardous Waste) Regulations 1998 (S.I. No. 163 of 1998) in relation to the grant of a licence or attachment of conditions to a licence in respect of an activity to which the regulations refer. *See:* HAZARDOUS WASTE, INCINERATION OF, REGULATIONS, 1998.

Section 40(5) of the WMA 1996 does not apply to integrated pollution control licences under Part IV of the EPAA 1992.

PROCESSING OF APPLICATIONS FOR LICENCES OR REVIEWS OF LICENCES

Section 85 of the EPAA 1992:

"(1) (a) Where an application is to be made to the Agency for a licence under section 83 the applicant shall notify the (*qv*)planning authority in whose functional area the activity is or will be situate and such other person (if any) as may be prescribed, and shall publish or give such notices as may be prescribed under section 87.

(b) Where the Agency proposes to review a licence or revised licence under section 88, it shall publish or give such notice as may be prescribed under section 87, and shall notify in writing the licensee and the planning authority in whose functional area the activity is situate and such other person (if any) as may be prescribed, of its intention to review the licence or revised licence.

(2) Before making its decision under section 83(1) on an application for a licence, or under section 88(2) on the review of a licence or revised licence, the Agency shall notify –
(a) the planning authority in whose functional area the activity is or will be situate,
(b) the applicant or the licensee, as the case may be, and
(c) any person who made a written submission in relation to the application or the review,
indicating the manner in which it proposes to determine the application or the review and, where it is proposed to grant a licence or revised licence, specifying where a copy of the proposed licence or proposed revised licence may be obtained.

(3) A notification provided for under subsection (2) shall be given within two months of the date of the application for a licence under section 83 or the date of the publication of a notice under subsection (1)(b), as the case may be.

(4) The Agency shall, in relation to an application for a licence, or the review of a licence or a revised licence –
(a) in case no objection is taken against the proposed determination as indicated under subsection (2), or
(b) in case an objection or objections is or are taken against the proposed determination as indicated under subsection (2) and the objection or objections is or are withdrawn,
make its decision in accordance with the proposed determination as indicated under subsection (2) and, where it is proposed to grant a licence or revised licence, grant the licence or revised licence as soon as may be after the expiration of the appropriate period.

(5) Any person may, subject to compliance with the requirements of any regulations under sections 87 and 94 at any time before the expiration of the appropriate period, object to the proposed determination as indicated under subsection (2), and shall include with the objection the grounds for the objection.

(6) Where an objection has been lodged, the Agency shall have an absolute discretion to hold an (*qv*)oral hearing and, if it so decides, the Agency shall notify, in writing, the applicant or, in the case of a review, the licensee, the planning authority in whose functional area the activity the subject of a licence application or review will be or is situate and all those from whom objections in compliance with subsection (5) were received.

(7) It shall be a duty of the Agency to ensure that a decision by it to hold an oral hearing, and a decision by it on the application for a licence or on the review of a licence or revised licence whether or not an oral hearing has been held, shall be given as expeditiously as may be and for that purpose the Agency shall take all such steps as are open to it to ensure that, in so far as is practicable, there are no avoidable delays at any stage in the consideration of objections.

(8) A person shall not by any application for judicial review or in any other legal proceedings whatsoever question the validity of a decision of the Agency to grant or refuse a licence or revised licence unless the proceedings are instituted within the period of two months commencing on the date on which the decision is given.

(9) The provisions of this section shall not, to such extent as may be prescribed, apply to an application for a licence or to the review of a licence or revised licence to discharge to a sewer.

(10) In the section — 'the appropriate period' means–
(a) in the case of the applicant or the licensee, the period of 28 days beginning on the day of the giving of the notification under subsection (2),
(b) in any other case, the period of 21 days beginning on the day of the giving of the notification under subsection (2)."

ORAL HEARING

Section 86 of the EPAA 1992 provides for oral hearings and written reports on same *See:* ORAL HEARINGS.

(6) LICENCING UNDER THE WMA 1996

Section 40 of the WMA 1996:

"(1) (a) On application being made in that behalf to it, the Agency may grant to the applicant a waste licence subject to, or without, conditions or refuse to grant to the applicant such a licence.
(b) This subsection is subject to sections 42 and 50 and regulations under section 45.

(2) Subject to subsection (5), in considering an application for a waste licence or in reviewing, pursuant to this Part, a waste licence, the Agency shall –
(a) carry out or cause to be carried out such investigations as it deems necessary or as may otherwise be prescribed for the purposes of such consideration or review,
(b) have regard to –
(i) any relevant (*qv*) air quality management plan under section 46 of the Act of 1987, or (*qv*) water quality management plan under section 15 of the Local Government (Water Pollution) Act, 1977, or (*qv*) waste management plan or (*qv*) hazardous waste management plan under Part II;
(ii) (I) any (*qv*) environmental impact statement in respect of proposed development comprising or for the purposes of the waste activity concerned, which is submitted to the Agency under and in accordance with a requirement of, or made pursuant to, regulations under section 45,
(II) any submissions or observations made to the Agency in relation to the environmental impact statement,
(III) such supplementary information (if any) relating to such statement as may have been furnished to the Agency by the applicant or licence holder under and in accordance with a requirement of, or made

pursuant to, regulations under section 45,

(IV) where appropriate, the views of other Member States of the European Communities in relation to the effects on the environment of the proposed activity,

(iii) such other matters related to the prevention, limitation, elimination, abatement or reduction of (*qv*) environmental pollution from the activity concerned as it considers necessary, and

(iv) such other matters as may be prescribed.

(3) (a) For the purpose of subsection (2)(b)(ii), the Agency shall, other than in the case of an environmental impact statement in respect of development proposed to be carried out by or on behalf of a local authority within the functional area of the authority, have regard to the matters mentioned in the environmental impact statement and any submissions, observations or supplementary information relating to such statement made or furnished to the Agency under and in accordance with a requirement of, or made pursuant to, regulations under section 45, only in so far as they relate to the risk of environmental pollution from the activity in question.

(b) The reference in this subsection to a local authority's functional area is a reference to its functional area — in its capacity as a (*qv*) planning authority.

(4) The Agency shall not grant a waste licence unless it is satisfied that –

(a) any emissions from the recovery or disposal activity in question ('the activity concerned') will not result in the contravention of any relevant standard, including any standard for an (*qv*) environmental medium, or any relevant (*qv*) emission limit value, prescribed under any other enactment,

(b) the activity concerned, carried on in accordance with such conditions as may be attached to the licence, will not cause (*qv*) environmental pollution ,

(c) the (*qv*) best available technology not entailing excessive costs will be used to prevent or eliminate or, where that is not practicable, to limit, abate or reduce an emission from an activity concerned,

(d) if the applicant is not a local authority, the corporation of a borough that is not a county borough, or the council of an urban district, subject to subsection (8), he or she is a fit and proper person to hold a waste licence,

(e) the applicant has complied with any requirements under section 53.

(5) Where a waste licence is granted in relation to an activity, a licence under –

(a) Part III of the Act of 1987,

(b) section 4 or 16 of the Local Government (Water Pollution) Act, 1977, or

(c) section 171 of the Fisheries (Consolidation) Act, 1959,

shall not be granted in relation to such an activity, and any such licence that is in force in relation to such an activity shall thereupon cease to have effect in relation thereto.

(6) (a) Where a waste licence is granted in relation to an activity, and a foreshore licence has been granted under the Foreshore Act, 1933, in relation to the same activity, any conditions attached to that foreshore licence shall, in so far as they are for the purpose of preventing environmental pollution, cease to have effect.

(b) The grant of a licence under the Foreshore Act, 1933, in relation to any activity shall not prejudice, affect or restrict in any way the application of any provision of this Act to such an activity.

(7) For the purpose of this Part, a person shall be regarded as a fit and proper person if –

(a) neither that person nor any other relevant person has been convicted of an offence under this Act prescribed for the purposes of this subsection,

(b) in the opinion of the Agency, that person or, as appropriate, any person or persons employed by him or her to direct or control the carrying on of the activity to which the waste licence will relate has or have the requisite technical knowledge or qualifications to carry on that activity in accordance with the licence and the other requirements of this Act,

(c) in the opinion of the Agency, that person is likely to be in a position to meet any financial commitments or liabilities that the Agency reasonably considers wil be entered into or incurred by him or her in carrying on the activity to which the waste licence will relate in accordance with the terms thereof or in consequence of ceasing to carry on that activity.

(8) The Agency may, if it considers it proper to do so in any particular case, regard a person as a fit and proper person for the purposes of this Part notwithstanding that that person or any other relevant person is not a person to whom subsection (7)(a) applies.

(9) The references in subsections (7) and (8) to a relevant person are references to a person whom the Agency determines to be relevant for the purposes of considering the application concerned having had regard to any criteria that the Minister by regulations provides it is to have regard to in determining such a matter.

(10) A waste licence granted to a person under this Part may not be transferred to another person, other than under and in accordance with section 47.

(11) A person shall not be entitled solely by reason of a waste licence under this part to make, cause or permit an emission to any environmental medium.

(12) It shall be a good defence –
- (a) to a prosecution for an offence under any enactment other than this Part, or
- (b) to proceedings under –
  - (i) section 10 or 11 of the Local Government (Water Pollution) Act, 1977,
  - (ii) section 20 of the Local Government (Water Pollution) (Amendment) Act, 1990,
  - (iii) section 28, 28A and 28B of the Act of 1987,
  - (iv) section 57 or 58,

to prove that the act complained of is authorised by a waste licence granted under this Part.

[(13A) A holder of a waste licence shall, within a period of 1 month after the cesser of the activity to which the licence relates, give notice in writing of that fact to the Agency.

Offence

(b) A person who fails to comply with paragraph (a) shall be guilty of an offence].”

OFFENCES PRESCRIBED UNDER SECTION 40(7)

Article 47 of the Waste Management (Licensing) Regulations 1997 (S.I. No. 133 of 1997):

“For the purpose of section 40(7) of the Act –
- (a) a contravention of section 32(1), 32(3) or 39(1) of the Act, or
- (b) an offence under section 14(6), 15(3), 34(1), 36(1), 45(4), 57(4) or 58(7) of the Act,

shall be a prescribed offence.”

CONDITIONS

Section 41 of the WMA 1996 which deals with conditions attached to a waste licence is dealt with under a separate heading *See:* CONDITIONS.

PROCESSING OF APPLICATIONS FOR LICENCES AND REVIEWS OF LICENCES

See: PARTS II, III AND IV WASTE MANAGEMENT (LICENSING) REGULATIONS, 1997 (S.I. No. 133 of 1997).

Section 42 of the WMA 1996

“(1) (a) Where a person proposes to make an application to the Agency for the grant of a waste licence under section 40 or for the review of a waste licence under section 46, he or she shall publish or give notice of his or her intention to do so in such form and to such persons if any as may be prescribed under section 45.

(b) Where the Agency proposes to review a waste licence under section 46(1), it shall publish such notice as may be prescribed under section 45 for the purposes of this section, and shall give notice in writing to the holder of the licence and, where appropriate, to the local authority in whose functional area the activity, the subject matter of the licence, is carried on, and to such other persons (if any) as may be so prescribed, of its intention to conduct such a review"

Subsection (2) provides that before making a decision under section 40 for either a grant or review the Agency must give notice in writing to the same persons as in section 85, that is, the applicant or licence holder, any person who has made a written submission in relation to the application or review, where relevant, the appropriate local authority and one additional one, such person as may be prescribed.

As in section 85, the notice given is of the decision the Agency proposes to make under the section and if it be a grant rather than a refusal it must specify where a copy of the licence or proposed licence may be obtained.

Unlike section 85(3), which places a time limit on the giving of the notice, there is no limit on the Agency under this section.

Whereas section 85(4) itself provides for the actual making of the decision in relation to the application or review this section is silent on this and we rely of the section that deals with the decision, section 40, for the actual grant or refusal.

OBJECTION – ORAL HEARING

Sections 42(3) to (12) of the WMA 1996 deal with objections and oral hearings.

Subsection (3) provides that any person may, subject to compliance with the requirements of regulations under sections 45 and 50, and at any time before the expiration of the appropriate period, make an objection to the Agency in relation to a decision referred to in subsection (2) (of section 42) that it proposes to make.

Subsection (4) provides that an objection shall:

(a) be made in writing,
(b) state the name and address of the objector,
(c) state the subject matter of the objection,
(d) state in full the grounds of the objection and the reasons, considerations and arguments on which they are based, and
(e) be accompanied by such fee (if any) as may be payable in accordance with regulations under section 50.

Subsection (5) provides that failure to comply with these requirements renders the objection invalid and that the requirements under subsection (4) apply whether or not an oral hearing has been requested under subsection (9).

Subsection (6) provides that the objection shall be accompanied by such documents, particulars or other information relating to the objection as the objector considers necessary or appropriate.

Subsection (7) provides that the objector shall not be entitled to elaborate in writing upon, or make further submissions in writing in relation to his objection and subsection (8) precludes the furnishing of any further documents, particulars or information unless required by the Agency.

Subsection (9)*(a)* provides that a person making an objection under subsection (3) may request an oral hearing of the objection and 9*(b)*(i) and (ii) provide that such an application must be accompanied by such fee as may be prescribed under section 50 and that if it is not so accompanied the Agency are not obliged to consider the request. Subsection (9)*(c)* provides that the request must be made within the "appropriate period".

Subsection (10) provides for further formalities in relation to an objection under (3) or a request for an oral hearing under (9). The objection or request shall be made:

(a) by prepaid post sent to the Agency, or
(b) by leaving (by hand) with an employee of the Agency at the principal offices of the Agency during office hours, or
(c) by such other means as may be prescribed.

Subsection (11)(a) gives the Agency as absolute discretion to hold an oral hearing in relation to the objection. If it does decide to hold such a hearing it shall give notice in writing of that decision to:

(i) the applicant or holder of the licence,
(ii) where relevant, the local authority in whose functional area etc.,
(iii) any person who requested an oral hearing, and
(iv) such other person as may be prescribed,

Subsection (11)(b) provides that where the Agency decides not to hold an oral hearing it shall give notice in writing of its decision to the person who requested the oral hearing.

Subsection (12) provides that in the section "the appropriate period" means the period of 28 days beginning on the day on which notification is sent under subsection (2) {of section 42} in respect of the matter concerned.

Section 44 of the WMA 1996 deals with the conduct of oral hearings and the written report thereon. *See:* ORAL HEARINGS.

The protocol for dealing with the foregoing is contained at Part V (Article 25 to 36) of the Waste Management (Licensing) Regulations 1997 (S.I. No. 133 of 1997).

SUPPLEMENTARY PROVISIONS TO APPLICATION FOR WASTE LICENCE

Section 43 of the WMA 1996:

"(1) (a) Where –
(i) no objection is made in accordance with section 42(3) to the Agency in relation to a decision that it proposes to make in respect of an application made to it for the grant of a waste licence or in consequence of a review conducted by it of a waste licence, or
(ii) any objection or objections that has or have been so made to it in relation thereto is or are withdrawn,
the decision of the Agency in relation to that application or in consequence of the review shall be that as notified by it under section 42(2).
(b) Where the decision of the Agency is to grant a waste licence or a revised waste licence, such a licence shall be granted by it as soon as may be after the making of the decision.

(2) Without prejudice to section 40(4), where an objection has been made in accordance with section 42(3) in relation to a decision referred to in section 42(2) which it proposes to make, and has not been withdrawn, the Agency shall consider such objection and any submissions, plans, documents or other information and particulars furnished to the Agency in accordance with regulations under section 45 in relation to such objection and, where an (*qv*)oral hearing has been held in relation to the objection, to the report on the hearing, and as soon as may be thereafter the Agency shall decide to grant or refuse to grant the relevant licence in accordance with section 40(1).

(3) For the purposes of subsection (2), the Agency may consider an objection in relation to a decision referred to in section 42(2), notwithstanding a default of compliance on the part of an objector with a requirement of, or made pursuant to, regulations under section 45 to furnish any submissions, plans, documents or other information and particulars, without further notice to that person.

(4) It shall be the duty of the Agency to ensure that –
(a) a decision by it under section 42(11) to hold an oral hearing, or
(b) a decision by it in respect of an application made to it for the grant of a waste licence or in consequence of a review that has been conducted by it of a waste licence, whether or not an oral hearing has been held in relation to any objection made to it in accordance with section 42(3) in respect of that decision,

shall be given as expeditiously as may be, and for that purpose the Agency shall take all such steps as are open to it to ensure that, in so far as is practicable, there are no unavoidable delays at any stage in the determination of any such application or the completion of any such review.

(5) (a) A person shall not question the validity of a decision of the Agency on an application made to it for the grant of a waste licence, or in consequence of a review conducted by it of such a licence, otherwise than by way of an application for judicial review under Order 84 of the Rules of the Superior Courts (S.I. No. 15 of 1986) (hereafter in this subsection referred to as 'the Order').
(b) An application for leave to apply for judicial review under the Order in respect of a decision referred to in paragraph (a) shall –
(i) be made within the period of 2 months commencing on the date on which the decision is given,
(ii) be made by motion on notice (grounded in the manner specified in the Order in respect of an ex parte motion for leave) to –
(I) the Agency,
(II) where the applicant for leave is not the applicant for, or the holder of, the waste licence concerned, the applicant for or holder of that licence,
(III) any person who has made an objection in accordance with section 42(3) to the Agency in relation to the matter concerned,
(IV) any other person specified for that purpose by order of the High Court,
and such leave shall not be grant-

ed unless the High Court is satisfied that there are substantial grounds for contending that the decision is invalid or ought to be quashed.

(c) (i) The determination of the High Court of an application for leave to apply for judicial review as aforesaid or of an application for such judicial review shall be final and no appeal shall lie from the decision of the High Court to the Supreme Court in either case save with the leave of the High Court which leave shall only be granted where the High Court certifies that its decision involves a point of law of exceptional public importance and that it is desirable in the public interest that an appeal should be taken to the Supreme Court.

(ii) This paragraph shall not apply to a determination of the High Court in so far as it involves a question as to the validity of any law having regard to the provisions of the Constitution.

(d) References in this subsection to the Order shall be construed as including references to the Order as amended or re-enacted (with or without modification) by rules of court."

There have been two sets of Regulations passed under the Act relating to licensing.

The Waste Management (Licensing) Regulations, 1997 (S.I. No. 133 of 1997) and the Waste Management (Licensing) (Amendment) Regulations 1998 (S.I. No. 162 of 1998).

(7) LICENCE UNDER SECTION 3 OF THE FORESHORE ACT 1933.
See: FORESHORE.

LICENSEE
(F(A)A 1997 s 3(1))

"Means a person to whom a license is granted, or that person's heirs, executors, administrators or assigns to whom the benefit of the licence has devolved."

LICENSING AUTHORITY
(F(A)A 1997, s. 3(1))

"Means:

(a) the Minister,
(b) an officer to whom functions have been delegated under section 21(1) by the Minister, or
(c) the (*qv*)Board."

LIMITS ON DURATION OF LICENCES
(LG(WP)A 1977/APA 1987/EPAA 1992)

The sections given hereunder do not deal with the (*qv*) duration of licences where the operation authorised by the licence has been activated and has been uninterrupted. They are designed to get rid of licences which, having been granted, have not been activated at all or where no authorised operation has been carried on under the licence for a period of three years.

(LG(WP)A 1977, ss. 4(7) and 16(6))

Deal respectively with licensing of (*qv*) trade effluent and (*qv*) sewage effluent and discharges to (*qv*) sewers and provide that where after three years from the date on which a licence under the section has been granted no discharge of the type authorised by the licence has been made, or where such a discharge has ceased for a period of three years, the licence shall cease to have effect.

(APA 1987, s. 36(1))

Section 36(1) of the APA 1987 provides that, subject to subsection (2), where (*qv*) industrial plant to which a licence under the Act relates:

(a) has not commenced operations within three years after the date on which the licence was granted, or
(b) has ceased operations for a period of not less than three years,

the licence shall cease to have effect.

Subsection (2) provides that subsection (1) shall not have effect if a licence was granted prior to the construction, or to the commencement of the operations, of industrial plant and the local authority, having regard to the nature and extent of the construction works and any other relevant consideration, are satisfied that the licence should continue to be in force for such period as the local authority consider reasonable, having regard to the circumstances.
(EPAA 1992, s.90(1))

Section 90(1) of the EPAA 1992 provides that, subject to subsection (2), where an (*qv*) activity to which a licence or revised licence under this Part (IV) relates:

(a) has not commenced within three years after the date on which the licence or

revised licence was granted, or
(b) has ceased for a period of not less than three years,

the licence or revised licence shall cease to have effect.

Subsection (2) provides that, without prejudice to subsection (1), the Agency may, having regard to the nature of the works and arrangements necessary in connection with the activity and any other relevant consideration:

(a) specify a period being a period of more than three years during which the licence or revised licence is to have effect,
(b) on an application which complies with the requirements (if any) which may be prescribed, extend the period so specified.

(WMA 1996, s. 49(1))

Section 49(1) of the WMA 1996 provides that where an activity to which a waste licence relates has not been substantially commenced within the period of three years beginning on the date on which the licence was granted or, as may be appropriate, the period referred to in paragraph (a) or (b) of subsection (2) (of this section), then that licence shall cease to have effect on the expiry of that period.

Subsection (2) provides that the (*qv*) Agency may, having regard to the nature of the activity to which a waste licence to be granted or granted by it will relate or relates, as the case may be, and any arrangements necessary to be made or made in connection with the carrying on of the activity and any other relevant consideration:

(a) specify for the purposes of subsection (1) a period of more than three years beginning on the date on which the licence is to be granted,
(b) in the case of a waste licence granted by it, on an application which complies with such requirements (if any) as may be prescribed being made by the holder of the licence in that behalf, extend for the purposes of subsection (1) the period referred to in that subsection or specified by in under paragraph (a), as may be appropriate.

LITTER
(LPA 1997, s. 2(1))

"Means a substance or object, whether or not intended as waste (other than waste within the meaning of the Waste Management Act, 1996, which is properly consigned for disposal) that, when deposited in a place other than a litter receptacle or other place lawfully designated for the deposit, is or is likely to become unsightly, deleterious, nauseous or unsanitary, whether by itself or with any other such substance or object, and regardless of its size or volume or the extent of the deposit."

LITTER POLLUTION ACT, 1997

The Litter Pollution Act, 1997 was enacted on 18 April 1997 and revoked and replaced the Litter Act of 1982. Comprised of seven Parts and some 36 sections, it constitutes a useful and novel code on the law relating to litter.

Section 3 contains the offence of littering and section 4 imposes obligations on certain persons to prevent litter. Section 5 provides that section 3 shall not be construed as prohibiting the deposit of waste in a litter or waste receptacle provided for the purpose of such waste, or the deposit of commercial, household, municipal or industrial waste for collection by or on behalf of a local authority or by another authorised waste collector within the meaning of the Waste Management Act, 1996 or the deposit of waste at a civic waste facility within the meaning of section 36 of that Act, provided, however, that reasonable care is taken to prevent the creation of litter. Section 6 of the Litter Pollution Act, 1997, imposes duties on occupiers of public places (or land appurtenant thereto and footways adjacent thereto) to keep such places free of litter.

Part III of the 1997 Act (sections 7-14) relate to local authority functions and duties generally in relation to the prevention of, and dealing with, litter. Section 7 requires that a local authority shall ensure that each public road in its functional area is, so far as practicable, kept free of litter. Section 8 requires the local authority to take all practicable measures for the prevention of the creation of, and the overcoming of the polluting effects of, litter in its functional area. Section 9 allows local authorities to serve notices on persons requiring the removal of litter. Section 10 requires local authorities to make and implement litter management plans. Section 11 sets out the requirements to be contained in such plans. Section 12 specifies the procedures for making, amending or replacing of such plans. Section 13 provides that duties of local authorities under sections 10 and 12 shall be a reserved function for the purposes of the County Management Acts, 1949 to 1994 (in the case of a council or an elective body) or the Acts relating to the management of a county borough (in the case of a corporation of a county borough). Section 14 grants immunity to local authorities in respect of the exercise or failure to exercise functions conferred or imposed under this Act.

Part IV of the Litter Pollution Act, 1997 contains miscellaneous provisions dealing with certain operations. Section 15 covers litter receptacles to be provided by operators of mobile outlets used for the sale of produce, food or drink and section 16 allows the local authority to impose special measures on the occupier to premises to which the section applies. Such premises are listed in subsection (9) of section 16 and the terms "land" and "land in the vicinity" are given specialised definitions for the purposes of that section. Section 17 grants local authorities powers to require taking of measures by the promoters or organisers of major public events and section 18 gives local authorities power to take measures to prevent or limit litter creation by such major public events. Section 19 contains prohibitions of articles and advertisements and defacement on certain structures without prior authorisation and section 20 gives local authorities powers to take actions to remove or other steps to deal with articles and advertisements and defacement of certain structures. Section 21 allows local authorities to make bye-laws prohibiting or regulating the distribution to the public of advertising material. Dog faeces removal and disposal are dealt with in section 22 of the 1997 Act.

Part V (Enforcement) of the Litter Pollution Act, 1997 imposes a number of offences in relation to creation of litter. Section 23 sets out offences relating to obstruction of a litter warden or member of the Garda Síochána who is exercising functions under the 1997 Act. Section 24 provides that a person guilty of an offence under this Act shall be liable on summary conviction to a fine not exceeding £1,500 and, where the contravention is continued, that the person shall be liable on summary conviction to a fine not exceeding £100 for each day during which the contravention continues. Section 25 gives local authorities power to prosecute offences under this Act. Section 26 provides that where the contents of litter that has been deposited in contravention of this Act shall give rise to reasonable suspicion as to the identity of the person from whom the litter or waste emanated, that such contents shall constitute evidence, in the absence of evidence to the contrary, that the litter or waste emanated from the person before the deposit or placement and that the person made the contravening deposit or placement. Section 27 creates offences relating to the commission of offences under this Act by the owner or hirer or operator of motor vehicles. Section 28 allows litter warden or member of the Garda Síochána to issue notices of offences under this Act in circumstances specified under that section (the so-called "on the spot" fines for litter offences).

Part VI (General) of the Litter Pollution Act, 1997 contains various miscellaneous provisions. Section 29 gives the Minister (of the Environment) power to issue policy directions and guidelines to local authorities in relation to the prevention and control of litter. Section 30 extends the purposes for which regulations may be made under sections 28 and 29 of the Waste Management Act, 1996, to include the limiting, minimising or controlling of litter under this Act. Section 31 gives the Minister power to make regulations prescribing any matter or thing referred to in this Act and for the purposes of enabling any provision of the Act to have full effect. Section 32 relates to the service of notices under the Act. Section 33 provides that the expenses incurred by the Minister in administration of this Act shall be paid out of moneys provided by the Oireachtas. Section 34 provides that moneys received by local authorities under this Act shall be lodged to the credit of the municipal fund or the county fund (as the case may be) and that such moneys may be expended for the same purposes as other moneys credited to that fund. Section 35 of the Litter Pollution Act, 1997 amends section 37(3) of the Local Government Act, 1994, repeals paragraph (a) of section 17(2) of the Control of Dogs Act, 1986, and repeals the Litter Act, 1982. Section 36 provides that the Act shall come into operation on such day as may be fixed by order of the Minister. The Litter Pollution Act, 1997, came into operation on 1st day of July, 1997, by virtue of the Litter Pollution Act, 1997 (Commencement) Order 1997 (S.I. No. 213 of 1997).

LITTER POLLUTION REGULATIONS

The first regulations made under the Litter Pollution Act, 1997 were the Litter Pollution Regulations 1997 (S.I. No. 214 of 1997). These regulations set out Forms A and B (in the Schedule) as the prescribed forms for purposes of notices in relation to offences which may be issued by a litter warden or member of the Garda Síochána pursuant to section 28(1) of the Litter Pollution Act, 1997 (the so-called "on the spot" fines for litter offences).

The Litter Pollution Regulations 1999 (S.I. No. 356 of 1999) revoked and replaced S.I. No. 214 of 1997 and prescribed new versions of Form A and B (set out in the Schedule thereto) to be used for the purposes of section 28(1) of the 1997 Act. The 1999 Regulations came into force on the 3rd of January 2000. Regulation 3 provides that the "prescribed amount" for the purposes of section 28(1) shall be £50. Form A relates to offences committed with the use of a motor vehicle. Form B lists the offences to which a notice under section 28(1) of the Litter

Pollution Act, 1997, including offences under section 3(1), (2), (3), 4(1), (2), 6,(1), (2), (3), (4), (5), 15(1), 15(2), 19(1), (2), 21 and 22.

LITTER RECEPTACLE
(LPA 1997, s. 2(1))

"Means a receptacle designated or otherwise apparently intended to be used for the deposit of litter."

LITTER WARDEN
(LPA 1997, s. 2(1))

"Means a person authorised by a local authority to perform, on behalf of the local authority, the functions of the local authority and of a litter warden under this Act."

LOCAL AUTHORITY

The phrase "local authority" is variously described throughout in environmental statutes but the most up-to-date definition is that given at section 3(1) of the EPAA 1992 as follows:

"'local authority' means –
(a) in the case of the administrative county of Dublin, other than the borough of Dun Laoghaire, the council of the county of Dublin,
(b) in the case of the borough of Dun Laoghaire, the corporation of the borough,
(c) in the case of a county borough, the corporation of the county borough, and
(d) in the case of any other administrative county, the council of the county,
and references to the functional area of a local authority shall be construed accordingly."

Note that this definition does not include Urban District Councils and Town Commissioners who do not have a "hands on" function in relation to environmental matters although they have considerable power in relation to the administration of their functional areas.

See: LOCAL GOVERNMENT ACT, 1941.

LOCAL AUTHORITY, PERFORMANCE OF ITS STATUTORY FUNCTIONS, AGENCY'S POWERS
(EPAA 1992, s.63)

"(1) Where the Agency is of opinion that a local authority has failed to perform a statutory function of that authority in relation to (*qv*) environmental protection, or has performed that function in an unsatisfactory manner, the Agency may request a report within a specified period from the authority in relation to the matter and the local authority shall comply with the request.

(2) The Agency, having considered any report of the local authority may, with a view to ensuring the satisfactory performance of the function in question –
(a) issue such advice and recommendations to the local authority as it considers necessary, or
(b) provide, on such terms and conditions as may be agreed, such assistance or support as the Agency considers, in consultation with the local authority concerned, would be helpful.

(3) (a) Where the Agency is of the opinion that the response of the local authority to advice or recommendations issued or assistance or support offered under subsection (2) is inadequate for the purpose of environmental protection it may, without prejudice to any of its powers under this Act or any other enactment direct the local authority to carry out, cause to be carried out, or arrange for, such action related to the function in question as the Agency considers necessary for the purposes of environmental protection within such period as may be specified.
(b) Where a local authority fails without reasonable cause to comply with a direction under paragraph (a) the Agency shall carry out, cause to be carried out, or arrange for, such action related to the function in question as it considers necessary to ensure compliance with the direction and the costs of such action may be recovered by the Agency from the local authority as a simple contract debt in any court of competent jurisdiction.
(c) The Agency shall not give a direction under paragraph (a) unless the local authority, with due regard to its other statutory functions, has the necessary funds to comply with the direction or those funds can reasonably be made available by it.

(4) Nothing in this section shall be construed as enabling the Agency to exercise any power or control under this section in relation to the making of a decision on an application for a permission under Part IV of the Act of 1963.

(5) In the section 'local authority' has the meaning assigned to it by the Local Government Act, 1941."

M

MAMMALIAN ANIMAL WASTE REGULATIONS 1998

See: WASTE, MAMMALIAN ANIMAL.

MANAGEMENT AGREEMENTS, USE AND MANAGEMENT OF LAND
(WLA 1976, s.18)

Section 18 of the WLA 1976 provides:

"(1) The Minister or, with his prior approval, any other person, may enter into an agreement with a person having an interest in or over land ensuring that the management of the land shall be conducted in a manner (to be specified in the agreement) which will not impair wildlife or its conservation.

(2) An agreement under this section shall be entered into only after consultation with the Minister for Agriculture and Fisheries, the (*qv*) Commissioners and any (*qv*) planning authority in whose area the relevant land or any part of it is situate.

(3) An agreement under this section may provide for the payment by the Minister or any other person who is party to the agreement of consideration, either by way of single payment or by way of payment of an annual sum, to a person having, or claiming to be entitled to, an interest in or over the land to which the agreement relates.

(4) An agreement under this section may provide that the agreement shall be enforceable against persons deriving title to the land under the person having the interest in or over the land, and, in case such provision is included in the agreement, subject, where appropriate, to the agreements being registered under section 69 of the Registration of Title Act, 1964, as amended by section 66 of this Act, and to compliance with any rules made under section 126 of that Act which are relevant, it shall be so enforceable in respect of the person's former interest as if the Minister, or the person who with the Minister's approval entered into the agreement, was possessed of adjacent land and as if the agreement had been expressed to be made for the benefit of that land.

(5) The Commissioners, the*(qv)* Board and any planning authority within whose area the land, or any part of the land, to which an agreement made under this section relates, shall be notified by the Minister of the agreement, and if the agreement is terminated and the Minister is aware thereof, of the termination.

(6) Where an agreement under this section to which the Minister is not a party is terminated, the parties to the agreement shall cause notice of the termination to be given to the Minister.

(7) In this section 'management' in relation to land means use of the land for agriculture or forestry, the carrying out of works on, in or under the land, the making of any change in the physical, topographical or ecological nature or characteristics of the land and the use of the land for educational or recreational purposes."

(WLA 1976, s.59)

Section 59(5) of the WLA 1976 provides for regulations permitting public access to land to which an agreement under section 18 of the Act applies where all the parties (other than the Minister, where the Minister is such a party) agree. *See:* ACCESS TO AND ENTRY ON LAND.

REPS

It is under section 18 that the Rural Environmental Protection Scheme (REP) is administered by (*qv*) Dúchas in conjunction with the Department of Lands.

(NH 97, Reg. 12)

Regulation 12(1) of the NH 97 Regulations (S.I. No. 94 of 1997) permits the Minister to enter into management agreements in accordance with section 18 of the WLA 1976 with any owner, lessee or occupier of land forming part of a (*qv*) European site or land adjacent to such a site for the management, conservation, restoration or protection of the site or any part of it.

Regulation 12(2) provides that any agreement previously entered into under section 18 of the WLA 1976 in relation to land which on or after the coming into force of these Regulations becomes part of a European site or is near such a site shall also have effect as if entered into under this Regulation.

MANAGEMENT OF LAND BY MINISTER
(WLA 1976, s.56)

Section 56(1) of the WLA 1976 provides for the permitted uses by the Minister of certain lands acquired, vested in, held or used by him under the Forestry Acts, other than land which he considers to be land to which section (1) and (2) of this section should apply, and in relation to which a direction (which the section empowers him to give) that those subsections shall not apply to the land is given by him and is in force, and such land may, as he considers appropriate, be used:

(a) for the growth of forest crops,
(b) the conservation of wildlife,
(c) the management or exploitation of hunting and fishing resources,
(d) other purposes ancillary to the foregoing, including the promotion of scientific knowledge, amenity, or recreational or educational purposes.

Subsection (2) provides that land which is not considered suitable for the purposes in subsection (1) may be used by the Minister in such manner as he thinks fit.

Subsection (3) provides for the levying of charges to the public for access to such lands used as described at subsection (1).

In the WLA 1976, as presently constituted, an (*qv*) establishment order under section 15 is the only order in Part II Chapter II of the WLA 1976, Reserves and Refuges, which relates to land owned by the State. Section 57, therefore, can only apply to such lands as have been designated as nature reserves under section 15. *See:* (1) ESTABLISHMENT ORDER; (2) RESERVES AND REFUGES.

MANAGEMENT PLANS, AIR, WATER, WASTE
(EPAA 1992, s.102)

Section 102(1) of the EPAA 1992, as amended by section 68 of the WMA 1996, provides that without prejudice to the generality of sections 100 and 101, which provide for the extension of powers of local authorities to the Agency under the LG(WP)A 1977 and the APA 1987, the Minister may, by order, provide that the Agency may make an (*qv*) air quality management plan under section 46 of the APA 1987, or a (*qv*) water quality management plan under section 15 of the LG(WP)A 1977 or a (qv)waste management plan under section 22 WMA 1996.

Subsection (2) provides that an order under this section may contain such incidental and consequential provisions as the Minister considers appropriate, including provision for the modification of sections 46, 47 and 48 of the APA 1987 or section 15 of the LG(WP)A 1977 [or sections 22, 23 and 25 of the WMA 1996] as they apply in relation to the Agency and in particular:

(i) the procedures to be followed by the Agency in making the plan,
(ii) consultation by the Agency with any local authority concerned in regard to the making of a plan,
(iii) provisions relating to the consent of a local authority before a plan is made,
(iv) provisions for the determination of matters where the Agency considers that the consent of a local authority is unreasonably upheld,
(v) provisions relating to the recovery of costs of making a plan from the local authorities concerned.

The sections of the APA 1987 quoted above refer to (*qv*) air quality management plans and standards, the sections of the LG(WP)A 1977 refer to (*qv*) water quality management plans and the sections in the WMA 1996 to (*qv*) waste Management plans.

MARINE INSTITUTE

Foras na Mara, the Marine Institute was established by section 3(1) of the Marine Institute Act, 1991.

Section 4 of the Marine Institute Act, 1991 provides –

"(1) The Institute shall have the following general functions, namely, to undertake, to co-ordinate, to promote and to assist in marine research and development and to provide such services related to marine research and development, that in the opinion of the Institute, will promote economic development and create employment and protect the marine environment."

This subject should not strictly be referred to in a work devoted to inland waters but for the definition of "marine" in section 1 of the Act:

"'Marine' means of, in, near, concerned with or belonging to the sea and tidal waters, inhabiting, found or got from the sea or from non-tidal waters."

This definition is intended to include fish such as salmon or eels which are " found or got from the sea". The definition is ambiguous and unclear. In recent legislation, particularly section 27 of the F(A)A 1999 where it amends section 100 of the F(C)A 1959 by adding subsection (6A), the Marine Institute is being used as an arbiter in respect of inland fisheries matters which, because of the ambiguity of the definition of "marine", are arguably outside its scope of operation.

MARINE STRUCTURES
(LG(WP)A 1977, s.1(1))

"Means a platform or other man-made structure at sea."

MARKING OF PACKAGES CONTAINING SALMON, TROUT, EELS AND MOLLUSCAN SHELLFISH
(F(C)A 1959, s.183)

Section 183 of the F(C)A 1959, as substituted by section 22 of the F(A)A 1994:

"(1) Every package or container containing salmon, trout, eels or molluscan shellfish in course of transit in the State shall be marked conspicuously on the outside with the words '(*qv*) salmon, (*qv*) trout, (*qv*) eels and molluscan shellfish' or the words 'salmon, trout and eels' or the words 'salmon, trout and molluscan shellfish' or the words 'salmon, eels and molluscan shellfish' or the words 'trout, eels and molluscan shellfish' or the words 'salmon and trout' or the words 'salmon and eels' or the words 'salmon and molluscan shellfish' or the words 'trout and eels' or the words 'trout and molluscan shellfish' or the words "'eels and molluscan shellfish' or the word 'salmon' or the word 'trout' or the word 'eels' or the words 'molluscan shellfish', as the case may require, and shall have marked thereon or on a label affixed thereto the name and address of the consignor.

Offences

(2) Every person who sends or consigns for transit in the State any package or container containing salmon, trout, eels or molluscan shellfish which is not marked in the manner required by this section shall be guilty of an offence under this section.

(3) Every person who carries for reward, by land in the State, by sea from any port in the State or by air from anywhere in the State, any package or container containing salmon, trout, eels or molluscan shellfish which is not marked in the manner required by this section shall be guilty of an offence under this section unless he proves that he did not know or could not reasonably have known that such package or container contained salmon, trout, eels or molluscan shell fish."

Subsection (4) provides for penalties under the section. *See:* FINES AND PENALTIES.

"(5) For the purpose of the section a package or container shall be deemed to be in the course of transit in the State when the same is being carried by any means whatsoever from any premises or place in the State to any other premises or place within or outside the State or is in any place, public or private, in the course of or for the purpose of such carriage."

MASS BALANCES
(EPAA 1992, s.96A)

Section 96A of the EPAA 1992, inserted by section 64 of the WMA 1996, provides:

"(1) The Minister may, for the purposes of –

(a) determining the extent of, and making available to members of the public information in relation to, the release of substances to (*qv*) environmental media resulting from the use or consumption of any specified class or classes of substance in any specified class or classes of process, development or operation (whether or not comprising an (*qv*) activity to which Part IV applies),

(b) determining, and making available information in relation to, the relationship ('the mass balance') between such a release of substance and the use or consumption of a substance aforesaid in a process, development or operation aforesaid,

make regulations requiring a person who carries out a process, development or operation aforesaid to make such determination of, and provide to the

Agency or specified *(qv)*public authorities, or publish, such information in relation to, the matters referred to in paragraphs (a) and (b) as may be specified in the regulations.

(2) Without prejudice to the generality of subsection (1), regulations under this section may provide for all or any of the following –
(a) requiring the person concerned to make on specified dates or at specified intervals measurements, calculations, estimates or projections of the release of substances to environmental media,
(b) prescribing the methods or procedures to be used in the making of such measurements, calculations, estimates or projections,
(c) requiring records or registers in a specified form to be kept by the person concerned of, or in which there shall be entered by him or her, specified particulars as respects the release of substances to environmental media and the use or consumption of any substance in a process, development or operation that gives rise to such a release,
(d) the intervals and the manner in which information as respects the matters aforesaid shall be provided by the person concerned to the Agency or other public authorities or be published,
(e) matters consequential on, or incidental to, the foregoing.

(3) The *(qv)* Agency and any prescribed *(qv)* public authority shall each publish information that has been provided to it pursuant to regulations under this section in such manner and subject to such conditions as may be prescribed."

MATERIALS FROM STREAMS
(F(C)A 1959, s.327)

Section 327 of the F(C)A 1959:

"Nothing in this Act shall prejudice the right of any owner thereof to take materials from any stream."

Under section 174 of the F(C)A 1959 it is an offence, *inter alia*, to disturb spawning fish or fish on the spawning beds. The act of removing gravel from a stream where there are spawning beds or spawning fish must give rise to circumstances in which the owner is likely to commit an offence under section 174. "Stream" is not defined in the 1959 Act but is included in the definition of *(qv)*"rivers" at section (3)(1) of that Act.

(Note that the maximum penalty prescribed under this section has been increased. *See:* FINES AND IMPRISONMENT (IMPOSITION OF)).

MEETINGS, MEMBERSHIP AND PROTOCOL OF AGENCY
(EPAA 1992, Pt. III)

Part III of the EPAA 1992 in the following sections from that Part, which are listed in sequence, provides:

Section 25: Director General and directors have one vote each, meetings chaired by Director General, Deputy Director or director chairs meeting, questions decided by majority vote and chairman has casting vote.

Section 26: Quorum not less than two. Minister to fill vacancies from established civil servants not serving for more than six months and on not more than three occasions.

Section 27: *See:* ADVISORY COMMITTEE.

Section 28: *See:* ADVISORY COMMITTEE.

Section 29: Employment of Agency staff.

Section 30: Transfer of staff of public authorities to the Agency with their consent on notice to trade unions or staff association.

Section 31: Conditions of employment of staff transferred under sections 30 and 32.

Section 32: Dissolution of an Foras Forbartha Teoranta transfer of staff to Agency, transfer or distribution of property.

Section 33: Superannuation scheme for Director General and directors.

Section 34: Superannuation scheme for Director General and directors.

Section 35: Agency directors and staff cannot be members of or candidates for either house of the Oireachtas or the European Parliament.

Section 36: Likewise in relation to membership of local authorities.

Section 37: *See:* DECLARATION OF INTERESTS.

Section 38: *See:* DISCLOSURE OF INTERESTS.

Section 39: *See:* CONFIDENTIAL INFORMATION, DISCLOSURE OF.

Section 40: *See:* COMMUNICATIONS, PROHIBITION AGAINST.

Section 41: *See:* COMMITTEES AND CONSULTATIVE GROUPS, CONSULTANTS AND ADVISORS.

Section 42: *See:* COMMITTEES AND CONSULTATIVE GROUPS, CONSULTANTS AND ADVISORS.

Section 43: *See:* ESTABLISHMENT OF REGIONAL ENVIRONMENTAL UNITS.

Section 44: *See:* PROVISION OF SERVICES.

Section 45: *See:* AGREEMENTS BETWEEN AGENCY AND OTHER PUBLIC BODIES.

Section 46: *See:* GRANTS TO AGENCY.

Section 47: Agency may borrow with the consent of the Minister and the Minister for Finance

Section 48: *See:* GIFTS, ACCEPTANCE OF THE AGENCY OF.

Section 49: *See:* CHARGES/FEES FOR SERVICES.

Section 50: *See:* ACCOUNTS, AUDITS AND ANNUAL REPORTS.

Section 51: *See:* ACCOUNTS, AUDITS AND ANNUAL REPORTS.

MESH OF NETS AND ENGINES

(F(C)A 1959, ss. 92 and 93)

NETS OF RIGID AND NON-RIGID MATERIAL

Sections 92 and 93 of the F(C)A 1959 deal with nets and engines not formed of rigid material (section 92(1)) and engines formed of a rigid material (section 93(1)) used for the taking of salmon on any part of the coast or within any bay, estuary or tideway by any person (other than the proprietor of the whole of the fishery of the river flowing into such bay, estuary or tideway from the mouth of the source thereof, including its tributary streams).

PROHIBITION IN SECTION 92

Section 92(2) of the F(C)A 1959 prohibits the use of nets with a mesh of less size than one and three-quarter inches from knot to knot, to be measured along the side of the square or seven inches to be measured all around each such mesh, such measurements being taken in the clear when the net is wet.

Subsections (4) and (5) permits the Minister by bye-law to alter, in respect of any particular district or locality, the size of the mesh specified above.

PROHIBITION IN SECTION 93

Section 93(2) of the F(C)A 1959 prohibits the use of engines with meshes or openings of less width than three inches on three sides on each side of the square, and, where no meshes or openings of the nature of reticulations are used, of less width between the bars than two inches.

Offences

Subsection (2) of each section creates the offences and there is the usual consequential forfeiture of the net.

Neither of these sections were regarded as sufficiently important in 1980 to warrant trial on indictment under section 46 of the FA 1980. It is unlikely that they will ever be invoked since the arrival on the scene of monofilament nets some time in the 1980s.

MONOFILAMENT NETS

The (*qv*) Salmon and Trout Conservation Byelaw 743, 1998 now effectively deals with the control of the use of nets.

METHODS OF FISHING, PROHIBITION OF

(F(C)A 1959, ss.164 to 170)

Chapter 1 of Part XI of the F(C)A 1959, sections 164 to 170 deals with the prohibition of certain methods of fishing for, and of practices liable to destroy salmon and other fish.

USE OR POSSESSION OF DELETERIOUS MATTER

Section 164 of the F(C)A 1959 prohibits the use of (*qv*)deleterious matter in any waters for the capture, destruction or injury of fish or its possession or control on the bank of or near any waters with intent to use.

(Note that the maximum penalty prescribed under this section has been increased. *See:* FINES AND IMPRISONMENT (IMPOSITION OF)).

LIGHT OR FIRE FOR TAKING FISH

Section 165 of the F(C)A 1959 prohibits the use or possession or control in or on or near the banks of any lake, river or estuary of any light or fire of any kind for the purpose of taking any fish.

(Note that the maximum penalty prescribed

under this section has been increased. *See:* FINES AND IMPRISONMENT (IMPOSITION OF)).

STROKEHAULS AND OTHER ILLEGAL IMPLEMENTS

Section 166 of the F(C)A 1959 amended by section 17 of the F(A)A 1962:

"(1) In this section the expression 'instrument to which the section applies' means any otter, spear, (*qv*) strokehaul, [snare, tailer], gaff or other instrument of a similar kind.

Offence

(2) If, for the purpose of taking any fish, any person uses or has in his possession or control in any lake, river, or estuary or on or near the banks thereof any instrument to which this section applies, such person shall, subject to subsection (3) of this section, be guilty of an offence under this section ..."

(Note that the maximum penalty prescribed under this subsection has been increased. *See:* FINES AND IMPRISONMENT (IMPOSITION OF)).

Section 17(2) of the F(A)A 1962 –

"(2) Where a person is charged with an offence under the said section 166 in relation to an instrument to which that section applies, found on his person, in a boat or vehicle belonging to, or any lands, tenements or hereditaments occupied by, him, he shall (unless he satisfies the Court that, without his knowledge or consent, another person put the instrument in the place where it was found) be deemed, for the purposes of the said section 166, to have the instrument in his possession or control."

Section 166(3) of the F(C)A 1959 –

"(3) Subsection (2) of this section shall not apply to the use, possession or control of –

(a) a [tailer or gaff] used or to be used solely as an auxiliary to lawful angling between sunrise and one hour after sunset, or

(b) a gaff used or to be used by the holder of a fishing licence in respect of any (*qv*) box in a (*qv*) fishing weir or (*qv*) fishing mill dam solely for the purpose of lawfully removing fish therefrom, or

(c) an eel spear used for taking eels."

CROSS LINES

Section 167 of the F(C)A 1959 prohibits taking, catching or fishing for any salmon, trout or coarse fish by means of cross lines in any river.

(Note that the maximum penalty prescribed under this section has been increased. *See:* FINES AND IMPRISONMENT (IMPOSITION OF)).

The words "or coarse fish" were added by section 9 of the F(A)(No. 2) A 1987 as part of the abortive attempt to introduce a rod licence duty for trout and coarse fish.

TAKING SALMON OR TROUT IN AN EEL WEIR

Section 168 of the F(C)A 1959 prohibits the owner or occupier of an eel weir taking or suffering to be taken therein any salmon, trout or coarse fish.

(Note that the maximum penalty prescribed under this section has been increased. *See:* FINES AND IMPRISONMENT (IMPOSITION OF)).

The words "or coarse fish" were added by section 10 of the F(A)(No. 2) A 1987 as part of the abortive attempt to introduce a rod licence duty for trout and coarse fish.

DAMS, TEEMS OR EMPTIES RIVER OR MILLRACE

Section 169 of the F(C)A 1959 prohibits the damming, teeming or emptying any river or millrace for the purpose of taking or destroying salmon, trout or coarse fish.

(Note that the maximum penalty prescribed under this section has been increased. *See:* FINES AND IMPRISONMENT (IMPOSITION OF)).

The words "or coarse fish" were added by section 11 of the F(A)(No. 2) A 1987 as part of the abortive attempt to introduce a rod licence duty for trout and coarse fish.

REMOVING DEAD OR UNLAWFULLY KILLED FISH

Section 170 of the F(C)A 1959 prohibits removing or causing the removal from any river or lake -

(a) salmon, trout or coarse fish not killed by lawful means, or

(b) salmon, trout or coarse fish found dead.

(Note that the maximum penalty prescribed under this section has been increased. *See:* FINES AND IMPRISONMENT (IMPOSITION OF)).

Subsection (2) provides that the section does not apply to:

(a) any person acting with the authority of the Minister, or
(b) any officer of a regional board acting under the instructions of that board, or
(c) any owner of a fishery or his agent acting under the written authority of a regional board, or
(d) a member of the Garda Síochána or a Sanitary Officer, when the salmon trout or coarse fish is diseased or was found dead.

The words 'or coarse fish' were added by section 12 of the F(A)(No. 2) A 1987 as part of the abortive attempt to introduce a rod licence duty for trout and coarse fish.

MINISTER, THE
(FA/LG(WP)A 1977/APA 1987/
EPAA 1992/WLA 1976/NH 97/
WMA 1996)

(1) F(C)A 1959

"The Minister" is defined in the F(C)A 1959, as the Minister for Lands, but is now the Minister for Marine and Natural Resources.

(1A) F(A)A 1999

"The Minister" is defined in the F(A)A 1999, section 2(1) as meaning the Minister for the Marine and Natural Resources.

(2) LG(WP)A 1977

"The Minister" is defined in the LG(WP)A 1977, section 1(1), as meaning the Minister for Local Government, now the Minister for the Environment.

(3) APA 1987

"The Minister" is defined in the F(C)A 1959, section 7(1), as meaning the Minister for the Environment.

(4) EPAA 1992

"The Minister" is defined in the EPAA 1992, section 3(1), as meaning the Minister for the Environment.

(5) WLA 1976

"The Minister" is defined in the WLA 1976, section 2(1), as meaning the Minister for Lands, now the Minister for Arts, Heritage, Gaeltacht and the Islands.

(6) NH 97

"The Minister" is defined in the NH 97 Regulations (S.I. No. 94 of 1997), Regulation 2(1), means Arts, Culture and the Gaeltacht now Arts, Heritage, Gaeltacht and the Islands.

(7) WMA 1996

"The Minister" is defined in the WMA 1996, section 5(1), as meaning the Minister for the Environment.

(8) MAMMALIAN ANIMAL WASTE REGULATIONS

"The Minister" is defined in Regulation 2(1) of both the European Communities (Mammalian Animal Waste) Regulations 1998 (S.I. No. 2 of 1998) and the (European Communities) (Processing of Animal Waste) Regulations 1998 (S.I. No. 62 of 1998) as meaning the Minister for Agriculture and Food.

MOLLUSCS
(OTHER THAN OYSTERS)
(F(C)A 1959, ss. 281 to 284)

A mollusc, which is not defined under the Fisheries Acts, can be rather crudely but simply described as a soft-bodied invertebrate usually with a hard shell.

Part XV of the F(C)A 1959 uses as a general heading "Molluscs (other than oysters)".

Section 281 of the F(C)A 1959 –

"(1) Section 245 shall extend to and include mussel beds, periwinkle beds and cockle beds and the Minister is hereby empowered to grant in respect of the said beds the licences mentioned in the said section 245.

(2) Sections 246 to 253 shall extend to and include mussel beds and mussel fisheries, periwinkle beds and periwinkle fisheries, and cockle beds and cockle fisheries."

Section 245 deals with the granting by the

Minister of (*qv*) oyster bed licences. It survived the extensive amendments in the F(A)A 1997 although it does appear that anyone intending to farm molluscs (other than oysters) would now require an (*qv*) aquaculture licence.

Section 282, as amended by section 5(7) of the F(A)A 1997, provides that sections 261 to 268 shall apply to mussels, mussel beds and mussel fisheries as they respectively apply to oysters and oyster beds and oyster fisheries.

The amendment to this section consisted of replacing sections 256 to 269 with sections 261 to 268 as sections 256 to 260 which dealt with the making by the Minister of an oyster fishery order.

Although section 5(6) of the F(A)A 1997 in repealing sections 256, 257, 258, 260 and 269 of the F(A)A 1959 and, inter alia, repealing the Minister's power to make a new order, which lay under section 256, it was important to leave in place the regulatory sections governing the operation of existing oyster fishery (1959) Act order and most significantly the Minister's own powers to determine those orders under section 266. *See:* OYSTERS.

BYE-LAW FIXING CLOSE SEASONS FOR MOLLUSCS

Section 283(1) of the F(C)A 1959 empowers the Minister to make, if he thinks fit, a bye-law fixing a period or periods in each year during which it shall not be lawful to take molluscs (other than oysters) of the kind specified in the bye-law from any locality specified in the bye-law.

Subsection (2) refers to the provisions of the Fifth Schedule which apply to the making of these as they do to the making or alteration of all bye-laws made under the Act except by omission, section 9. *See:* BYE-LAWS, FIFTH SCHEDULE.

In fact almost all bye-laws since the passing of the 1959 Act would appear to have been made under section 9. These section 283 bye-laws would have a purely local application.

BYE-LAWS FOR AN EXTENDED PERIOD

Section 284(1) empowers the Minister to make bye-laws, on the application of any person interested or on his own motion, fixing a period (not exceeding three years) during which it shall not be lawful to take or attempt to take molluscs (other than oysters) of the kind specified in the bye-law from any locality specified in the bye-law.

Subsection (2) provides that the provisions of the Fifth Schedule again apply.

These bye-laws would usually apply only in the locality affect by the bye-law. Bye-laws which apply nationally are rare

MINISTER'S POWERS TO DEAL WITH MOLLUSCS UNDER FA 1980

Section 2(3) of the FA 1980 excludes molluscs from the prohibition under that section against the Minister dealing with sea fish or stocks of sea fish and specifically refers to the power of the Minister under section 9(1)(b) of the 1980 Act to give directions to the *(qv)* Central Board for the protection of molluscs. Section 3 of the F(A)A 1999 amends this section by removing the words relating to section 8(1)(b) which has been made irrelevant by amendment by substitution of section 8 by section 5 of the F(A)A 1999. The Fisheries (Amendment) Act, 1000 (save for section 23) came into force on 20 December 1999 by virtue of the Fisheries (Amendment) Act, 1999 (Commencement) Order, 1999 (S.I. No. 419 of 1999).

In its place section 2(2) of the FA 1980 now refers to section 18(A)(1), inserted by section 10 of the F(A)A 1999 as Division 1A after Division I of Chapter IV of Part II of the FA 1980, which enables the Minister to give the Central Board or a *(qv)* regional board policy directions for the management, conservation, protection, development or improvement of inland fisheries or for the protection of molluscs, either in general terms or in relation to specific matters.

MONITORING
(LG(WP)A 1977, s.22)

"Monitoring includes inspection, measurement, sampling or analysis, whether periodically or continuously."

Section 22 of the LG(WP)A 1977 –

"(1) A local authority or sanitary authority
  (a) shall carry out or cause to be carried out or arrange for such monitoring of waters and discharges of trade effluents and sewage effluents and other matter to *(qv)*waters (in the case of a local authority) or to *(qv)*sewers (in the case of a sanitary authority) as it considers necessary for the performance of any of its functions under this Act or as may be directed by the Minister,
  (b) may collect, cause to be collected or arrange for the collection of such information as it considers necessary for the performance of any of its functions under this Act or as may be directed by the Minister.

(2) A local authority or a sanitary authority may provide meters, gauges, manholes, or inspection chambers or any other apparatus for any of the purposes of this section."

These functions under section 22 of the LG(WP)A 1977 now apply to the Agency since May 27, 1996 in lieu of the local authority/sanitary authority for the purposes of the prevention or limitation, or remedying the effects, as the case may be of water pollution in respect of an activity other than an activity to which section 99(2) of the EPAA 1992 applies, in respect of which a licence or a revised licence under Part IV of the EPAA 1992 is in force by virtue of Article 4 of the Environment Protection Agency (Extension of Powers) Order 1996 (S.I. No. 126 of 1996). Section 99(2) deals with transitional powers of the Agency between the date of commencement of the EPAA 1992 and the grant of an (*qv*)IPC licence. *See:* EXTENSION OF POWERS.

(APA 1987, s.7(1))

"Monitoring includes the inspection, measurement, sampling or analysis, for the purposes of the Act, of any (*qv*) emission or of the ambient air in any locality, whether periodically or continuously."

Section 54 of the APA 1987 –

"(1) A local authority shall carry out, or cause to be carried out, such monitoring of -
(a) air quality,
(b) the nature, extent and effects of emissions,
as the local authority may consider necessary for the performance of their functions under this Act or as they may be directed by the Minister to carry out.

(2) A local authority shall keep and maintain, or cause to be kept or maintained, such records of any monitoring carried out under subsection (1) as they consider reasonable and necessary."

By virtue of article 4 of the Air Pollution Act 1987 (Municipal Waste Incineration) Regulations 1993 (S.I. No. 347 of 1993) the local authority must make available for public inspection monitoring results which it receives pursuant to the Regulations. *See:* EMISSION, EMISSION LIMIT VALUE.

"(3) A local authority may require the (*qv*) occupier of any premises, other than a (*qv*) private dwelling, from which there is an emission to carry out such monitoring of the nature, extent and effect of the emission and of the air quality as the local authority consider necessary and to keep and to supply to the local authority such records of the monitoring as the local authority consider necessary.

(4) A local authority shall, if so directed by the Minister, supply to him or to any person specified by him at such intervals and in such manner as the Minister may direct records of any monitoring carried out under this section.

(5) Where an (*qv*) air quality standard applies to their functional area or to any part thereof, the local authority shall, in relation to the area of application of the air quality standard, make such arrangements for monitoring as may be necessary so that the local authority can determine if the air quality standard is being complied with.

(6) The Minister may give directions to the local authority in relation to –
(a) the number and location of places within an area at which monitoring is to be carried out,
(b) the manner in which sampling, measuring and analysing for the purposes of this section is to be carried out,
(c) the equipment to be used for the purposes of such sampling, measuring and analysing,
and the local authority shall comply with every such direction of the Minister.

(7) The Minister may monitor, or make such arrangements for the monitoring of, (*qv*) air pollution as seem to him to be necessary or desirable."

EXTENSION OF POWERS TO AGENCY

The functions under subsections (1), (2), (3) and (4) of section 54 of the APA 1987 now apply to the Agency in the circumstances described in Article 10 of the Environmental Protection Agency (Extension of Powers Order) 1996. *See:* EXTENSION OF POWERS.

(EPAA 1992, s.(3)1)

"Monitoring includes the inspection, measurement, sampling or analysis for the purposes of this

Act of any (*qv*) emission, or of any (*qv*) environmental medium in any locality, whether periodically or continuously."

MONITORING IN RELATION TO SANITARY AUTHORITIES TRADE EFFLUENT

Section 61 of the EPAA 1992 –

"(1) (a) A (*qv*) sanitary authority in which is vested or which has control over, or the use of, any plant, (*qv*) sewer or drainage pipe from which effluent is discharged to (*qv*) waters and in respect of which standards or other requirements have been prescribed or an authorisation issued under section 59, or criteria and procedures have been specified under section 60, shall carry out, cause to be carried out, or arrange for, such monitoring of the effluent or of the waters concerned or in connection with the management or operation of the plant, sewer or drainage pipe –

(i) as may be necessary or prescribed under section 59(2)(e) to assess compliance with standards or other requirements prescribed, or authorisation issued, under section 59, or

(ii) as the Agency shall direct in relation to criteria and procedures specified under section 60, and shall transmit the results of such monitoring to the Agency in such manner and at such times as the Agency shall direct.

(b) The Agency shall carry out, cause to be carried out, or arrange for, such monitoring as it considers necessary to verify results transmitted to it under paragraph (a).

(2) Where the Agency –

(a) is the opinion that the monitoring being carried out in accordance with the provisions of subsection (1)(a)(i) is inadequate for the purpose of assessing compliance with standards or other requirements prescribed, or authorisation issued, under section 59, or

(b) is not satisfied with the response of a sanitary authority to a direction under subsection (1)(a)(ii),

it shall consult with the sanitary authority concerned, and if the Agency is still dissatisfied with the response following such consultation, the Agency shall carry out, cause to be carried out, or arrange for, the monitoring concerned and the costs of the monitoring may be recovered by the Agency from the sanitary authority as a simple contract debt in any court of competent jurisdiction."

Comparison: powers of Agency in relation to the performance by a local authority of its statutory functions under section 63 where the direction cannot be given where the local authority lacks the funds to do the work. *See:* PERFORMANCE OF STATUTORY FUNCTIONS BY LOCAL AUTHORITY.

"(3) The Agency shall, from time to time, or at such intervals not exceeding two years and in such manner as may be prescribed for the purposes of monitoring compliance with specified standards or other requirements prescribed or authorisations issued under section 59, prepare and publish reports on the quality of effluents being discharged from plant, sewers or drainage pipes vested in, or controlled or used by, sanitary authorities and shall include in such reports such recommendations as it considers appropriate."

For monitoring by local authorities and by the Agency of certain landfill sites, section 62 of the EPAA 1992. *See:* LANDFILL SITES FOR WASTE DISPOSAL.

For section 59 *see*: SEWAGE AND OTHER EFFLUENTS.

For section 60 *see*: FUNCTIONS OF THE ENVIRONMENTAL PROTECTION AGENCY, SECTION 60.

Environmental monitoring programme is dealt with in section 65 of the EPAA 1992. *See:* ENVIRONMENTAL MONITORING PROGRAMME.

MONITORING OF ACTIVITIES OF PUBLIC AUTHORITIES

Section 68 of the EPAA 1992 provides:

"(1) The Agency shall exercise general supervision over the monitoring carried out by local authorities (and such other (*qv*) public authorities as may be prescribed) for the purposes of any enactment relating to (*qv*) environmental protection.

(2) The Agency shall keep itself informed of the nature and extent of the monitoring carried out by each local authority and by each public authority prescribed under subsection (1).

(3) For the purposes of subsection (2), the Agency may require a local authority or other public authority prescribed under subsection (1) to provide information within a specified period on –
(a) the number and location of places within an area at which monitoring is being carried out and the frequency of such monitoring,
(b) the manner in which samples and measurements are taken and analyses are carried out,
(c) the equipment being used for the purposes of taking such samples or measurements or for carrying out such analyses,
(d) the results of such monitoring,
and the authority shall not unreasonably withhold the information sought.

(4) The Agency may, for the purposes of subsection (1), of its own volition, or at the request of a local authority or other public authority prescribed under subsection (1), advise the authority in relation to –
(a) the number and location of places within an area at which monitoring is should be carried out and the frequency of such monitoring,
(b) the manner in which samples and measurements are to be taken and analyses are carried out,
(c) the equipment to be used for the purposes of taking such samples and measurements or of carrying out such analyses,
(d) the manner in which the results of such monitoring should be published or otherwise made available.

(5) The Agency may provide such services including general support, back-up, advice and assistance, as it considers necessary for the discharge by a local authority or other public authority prescribed under subsection (1) of its monitoring operations.

(6) The Agency may make arrangements with a local authority or other public authority prescribed under subsection (1) on such terms and conditions as may be agreed, for the provision of services under subsection (5).

(7) The Agency shall, at intervals not exceeding three years, prepare and publish a report on the monitoring operations of local authorities and other public authorities prescribed under subsection (1) and may, at more frequent intervals, report on monitoring operations related to particular environmental issues, or to particular areas, or to particular local authorities or to particular public authorities prescribed under subsection (1).

(8) A report under subsection (7) shall be laid by the Minister before each house of the Oireachtas."

MONITORING OF ENVIRONMENTAL QUALITY AND EMISSIONS

Section 96 of the EPAA 1992 provides:

"(1) The Agency shall, in relation to an (*qv*) activity, carry out, cause to be carried out, or arrange for, such monitoring of –
(a) environmental quality, and
(b) the nature, extent and effects of emissions to the environment,
as the Agency may consider necessary for the performance of its functions under this Part.

(2) The Agency may, as it considers necessary, require the person in charge of an activity from which there is an emission to the environment to carry out such monitoring of the nature, extent and effect of the emission, and of the quality of any environmental medium likely to be affected by such emission, and to keep and to supply to the Agency such records of the monitoring as the Agency considers necessary.

(3) The Agency shall carry out, cause to be carried out, or arrange for, such monitoring or other measures as it considers necessary to verify the monitoring or records of such monitoring provided for under subsection (2).

(4) ...

(5) The Agency shall, if so directed by the Minister, supply to him or to any person specified by him, at such intervals and in such manner as the Minister may direct, records of any monitoring carried out

under this section."

(Subsection (4) was repealed in its entirety by section 6(1) of the WMA 1996 by reference to column (3), Part 1 Fifth Schedule).

See: MASS BALANCES.

(Genetically Modified Organisms Regulations, 1994, Reg. 64)

Regulation 64 of the Genetically Modified Organism Regulations, 1994 (S.I. No. 345 of 1994) provide for monitoring, inspections or other measures for the purpose of the performance of any of the Agency's functions and reporting, as directed by the Minister, to the Minister or any other person.

(WMA 1996, s.5(1))

"Monitoring includes the inspection, measurement, sampling or analysis, whether periodically or continuously, for the purpose of this Act, of waste, a premises at which waste is produced, or a (*qv*) facility at which waste is held, (*qv*) recovered or (*qv*) disposed of, and of any (*qv*) emissions there from, or any (*qv*) environmental medium which is affected by or which, in the opinion of the local authority concerned or the Agency may be affected by, such emissions."

Section 15 of the WMA 1996 provides:

"(1) (a) Each local authority and the Agency shall carry out, or cause to be carried out, such monitoring of the nature, extent and effects of emissions to the environment arising from the holding, recovery or disposal of waste as it consider to be necessary for the performance of its functions under this Act.

(b) Each local authority and the Agency shall carry out such periodic inspection of facilities for the holding, recovery or disposal of waste, premises where hazardous waste is produced, and the activities of persons otherwise holding or dealing in waste as it considers to be necessary for the performance of its functions under this Act.

(2) Each local authority and the Agency shall keep and maintain or cause to be kept and maintained, such records of any monitoring or inspections carried out by it under subsection (1) as it considers reasonable and necessary.

(3) (a) Where it appears necessary to do so for any purpose of this Act, a local authority or the Agency may require any person who holds or is in control of the recovery or disposal of any waste to carry out or arrange to have carried out such monitoring in relation to the activity concerned as the local authority or the Agency may specify and to keep and supply to the local authority or the Agency such records of the said monitoring as the local authority or the Agency may specify.

Offence

(b) A person who fails to comply with a requirement under this subsection shall be guilty of an offence.

(4) Each local authority and the Agency shall, if so requested by the Minister, supply to the Minister or to any person specified by the Minister, at such intervals and in such manner as the Minister may require, records of any monitoring carried out under this section that are in its possession or control.

(5) Each local authority and the Agency shall carry out or take or cause to be carried out or taken such monitoring or other measures as it considers necessary to verify that any monitoring or records of such monitoring required by it under subsection (3) to be carried out or kept are carried out or kept.

(6) Without prejudice to any other provisions of this Act, the Minister shall make regulations requiring the making of payments to the Agency or a local authority by any person holding, dealing in, or in control of the recovery or disposal of, waste for the purpose of defraying costs which may be incurred by the Agency or local authority in carrying out any monitoring or inspection or taking other measures under this section in relation to the activities aforesaid of that person.

(7) A defrayment, the payment of which is required under regulations under this section, shall be payable on demand and, in default of being so paid, shall be recoverable from the person concerned by the Agency or local authority con-

cerned as a simple contract debt in any court of competent jurisdiction."

MONITORING ON SURRENDER OF A WASTE LICENCE

Section 48(4) of the WMA 1996 provides that notice requiring additional monitoring may be served by the Agency on surrender of a waste licence under the section. *See:* SURRENDER OF A WASTE LICENCE.

MONOFILAMENT NETS
(F(C)A 1959)

See: SALMON AND TROUT CONSERVATION BYE-LAW

MOUTH OF A RIVER
(F(C)A 1959 s.3(1))

"References to the mouth of that river shall be construed as references to the mouth of that river as defined by an order under section 10."

MOVEMENT OF WASTE, REGULATIONS
(WMA 1996, s.36)

Section 36 of the WMA 1996 provides:

"(1) For the purpose of preventing (*qv*) environmental pollution there from, the Minister may by regulations provide for the supervision and control of the movement of waste within, into or out of the State.

(2) Without prejudice to the generality of subsection (1), regulations under this section may provide for all or any of the following –
(a) the prohibition, prevention, limitation or control of the movement of waste and, in particular –
(i) requiring that any movement of waste or waste of a specified class or classes be authorised by the Agency or a local authority,
(ii) enabling conditions of a kind specified in the regulations to be attached by the Agency or a local authority, as the case may be, to any such authorisation;
(b) notifications, including documentation, to be given before and after the movement of waste, the form and content of such notifications, the persons required to give such notifications and the persons to whom such notifications are to be given;
(c) information, including documentation, to accompany any movement of waste, the form and content of such information and the persons required to prepare, hold or submit such information;
(d) enabling the inspection of consignments of waste and documentation relating thereto by persons authorised in that behalf by the Agency or a local authority,
(e) requirements as to segregation, handling, packaging and labelling of waste and the containers in which waste may be moved;
(f) a requirement that shipments of waste may enter or leave the State at a specified place or places only with in the State,
(g) requiring a person who undertakes the movement of waste to effect and maintain a policy of insurance insuring him or her as respects any liability on his or her part to pay damages or costs on account of injury to person or property arising from the movement of the waste;
(h) requiring an agreement or agreements to be entered into with one or more appropriate persons by a person exporting or importing waste whereby the first-mentioned person or persons agrees or agree to recover or dispose of the waste;
(i) the seizure, taking in charge, recovery or disposal of a consignment of waste or a part thereof by the Agency or a local authority or a person authorised by the Agency or a local authority in that behalf where any provision of regulations under this section or of any specified enactment has not been complied with as respects the consignment or a part thereof, as the case may be;
(j) the keeping of records by specified persons of the source of, and particulars concerning the movement, delivery and receipt of, waste and, as the case may be, the recovery or disposal thereof, and the persons to whom such records should be made available;
(k) the prevention and control of litter and nuisance from odours that may arise from the movement of waste

and generally with respect to the handling of waste whilst it is being moved;

(l) the imposition by the Agency or a local authority on a person undertaking the movement of waste of such charges as are necessary to defray any costs reasonably incurred by the Agency or the local authority in performing any function under regulations under this section with respect to the waste;

(m) requiring a person to give such security to the Agency or a local authority for the payment of any charges he or she may be liable to pay to the Agency or the local authority (as the case may be) pursuant to regulations under paragraph (l) as the Agency or the local authority may request;

(n) requiring a person who undertakes the movement of waste to give security of a specified nature to the Agency, a local authority or any other specified person in respect of costs which may be incurred by the Agency, local authority or other person aforesaid in taking steps in relation to the waste in the event of the contravention by the first-mentioned person of any provision of regulations under this section as respects that waste;

(o) requiring a person who undertakes the movement of waste or who is the consignee of waste imported into the State or moved within the State to return, where the Agency or a local authority directs him or her to do so, the waste to its place of origin or to such other place as may be specified in the direction and to take such measures as may be so specified in relation to the waste, including the recovery or disposal of the waste in such manner or at such facility as may be so specified;

(p) specifying the circumstances in which the Agency or a local authority may give a direction to a person pursuant to paragraph (o);

(q) any matters consequential on, or incidental to, the foregoing.

Offence

(3) A person who contravenes a provision of regulations under this section shall be guilty of an offence."

The Waste Management (Transfrontier Shipment of Waste) Regulations 1998 (S.I. No. 149 of 1998) made under sections 7, 15 and 36 of the WMA 1996 which came into operation on the May 20 1998 give effect to Council Directive 259/93/EEC of February 1, 1993 on the supervision and control of shipments of waste within, in and out of the European Community, as amended (O.J. L30/1, February 6, 1993).

MOVEMENT OF HAZARDOUS WASTE REGULATIONS 1998
(WMA 1996)

Regulation 4 of the WMA (Movement of Hazardous Waste) Regulations 1998 (S.I. No. 147 of 1998), passed under sections 7, 15, 18 and 36 of the WMA 1996, which came into operation on the May 20, 1998, and which give effect to provisions of:

(a) Council Directive 91/689/EEC of December 12, 1991 on hazardous waste (O.J. L377/20, 31 December, 1991), and

(b) Council Regulation EEC No 259/93 of 1 February 1993 on the supervision and control of shipments of waste within, and into and out of the European Community (O.J. No. L30/1, February 6, 1993) as amended,

"4. A person shall not consign, move from the premises where it is being held, or accept, or facilitate by consent, connivance or neglect the consignment, movement or acceptance of, hazardous waste otherwise than in accordance with the requirements of these Regulations."

"13. A person shall not furnish information which is false or misleading to a material extent in any consignment note, report, notice or other document used for the purposes of these Regulations."

The general office section, section 36(3), already quoted supra, makes contraventions of provisions of regulations under the section an offence.

MUNICIPAL WASTE
(WMA 1996, s.5(1))

"Means household waste as well as commercial and other waste which, because of its nature and composition, is similar to household waste."

N

NAMES ON FISHING BOATS
(F(C)A 1959, s.289(1))

Section 289 of the F(C)A 1959:

"(1) Every fishing boat shall have upon some conspicuous part thereof the name of the owner, or of one of the owners where more than one, and his place of residence, painted in clear legible characters or letters of not less than two inches in length.

Offence

(2) If in respect of a fishing boat the provisions of subsection (1) of this section are not complied with, the owner or any person using the fishing boat shall be guilty of an offence under this section."

(Note that the maximum penalty prescribed under this subsection has been increased. *See:* FINES AND IMPRISONMENT (IMPOSITION OF)).

The requirement for a name applies both to fishing boats used in inland waters and sea fishing boats.

NATURA 2000
(NH 97, Reg. 2(1))

"Means the European network of (*qv*) special areas of conservation and special protection areas under the Birds Directive provided for by paragraph 1 of Article 3 of the (*qv*) Habitats Directive." 92/43/EEC (O.J. L206 July 22, 1992 p7).

HABITATS DIRECTIVE, ARTICLE 3

"1. A coherent European ecological network of *(qv)* special areas of conservation shall be set up under the title Natura 2000. This network, composed of sites hosting the natural habitat types listed in Annexe 1 and habitats of the species listed in Annexe II, shall enable the natural habitat types and the species habitats concerned to be maintained or, where appropriate, restored at a favourable conservation status in their natural range. The Natura 2000 network shall include the *(qv)* special protection areas classified by the Member States pursuant to Directive 79/409/EEC."

The Directive quoted in the Directive known is the *(qv)* Birds Directive.
See: BIRDS DIRECTIVE.

The annexes quoted are very extensive and apply to habitat types and habitats throughout the EC.

"2. Each member State shall contribute to the creation of Natura 2000 in the proportion to the representation within its territory of the natural habitat types and the habitats of species referred to in paragraph 1. To that effect each Member State shall designate, in accordance with Article 4, sites as special areas of conservation taking account of the objectives set out in paragraph 1.

3. Where they consider it necessary, Member States shall endeavour to improve the ecological coherence of Natura 2000 by maintaining, and where appropriate developing, features of the landscape which are of major importance for wild fauna and flora, as referred to in Article 10."

NATURAL HABITATS
(NH 97, Reg. 2(1))

"Means terrestrial or aquatic areas distinguished by geographic, abiotic and biotic features, whether entirely natural or semi-natural."

NATURE RESERVE
(WLA 1976, ss.15 and 16)

Sections 15 and 16 of the WLA 1976 provide for nature reserves. *See:* (1) ESTABLISHMENT ORDER; (2) RECOGNITION ORDER; (3) RESERVES AND REFUGES.

NETS
(F(C)A 1959)

Nets are included in a number of important definitions under the Fisheries Acts, *e.g.* (*qv*) fixed engines, (*qv*) fishing engines and (*qv*) scheduled engines, but are not separately defined in respect of their use in inland waters as they are for their use in the sea. They are of course the same nets. There is really no such thing as a "freshwater net".

Section 219 of the F(C)A 1959 defines "net" for the purposes of Part XII Sea Fisheries which is outside the scope of this book but the definition is helpful. It was amended by section 17 of the F(A)A 1978, a Sea Fisheries Act, and appears in the table to that section as:

"The word "net" means any trawl, seine or other net towed or hauled or intended to be towed or hauled, in the sea, whether on or near the bottom thereof or otherwise.

(In fishing with nets in inland waters the net is often held or drawn by hand or affixed to poles)"

In the Fifth Schedule to the F(C)A 1959, referred to in section 68 as the basis for assessing the amount of duty on ordinary fishing licences at Part II there is a list of types of engines/scheduled engines used for fishing and among these are the following nets:

> "1: stake net or fly net, 2: bag net, 4: draft net, 5: drift net, 6: snap net, 7: pole net, 8: loop net, 13: coghill net for eels and 14: fyke net for eels."

DEFINITIONS OF NETS IN SALMON AND TROUT CONSERVATION BYE-LAW No. 743, 1998

This important bye-law contains definitions which are peculiar to the particular bye-law but which are also helpful.

2. In this bye-law:

"'drift net' includes a single sheet of netting attached to a floating head rope and a weighted ground rope, designed to drift freely at the surface of waters for the purpose of taking or fishing or attempting to take or fish for, or take salmon or trout, to which net or ropes no weights or anchoring devices are attached which in any way hinder or prevent the free movement of the net in those waters.

'draft net' includes a single wall of netting attached to a floating head rope and a weighted ground rope, designed so that a bag is formed into which the catch is drafted or hauled, for the purpose of taking or fishing for, or attempting to take or fish for, salmon or trout.

'snap net' includes a single wall of netting attached to a floating head rope and a weighted ground rope, designed to suspend between two boats and into which the catch is drawn, for the purpose of taking or fishing for or attempting to take or to fish for salmon or trout

'other net' means any fishing engine not being a drift net, a draft net, a snap net or a rod or a line, capable of being used for the purpose of taking or fishing for, attempting to fish for salmon or trout.

'monofilament' means a single filament of synthetic material having a diameter equal to or greater than 0.1 millimetres and which is strong enough to function alone as a yarn for the construction of nets without having to undergo any further processing;

'multistrand monofilament' means filaments of synthetic material, comprised of two or more monofilaments twisted together, where any single filament has a diameter equal to or greater than 0.1 millimetres."

See: SALMON AND TROUT CONSERVATION BYE-LAW 1998.

NETS, RESTRICTIONS ON THEIR USE

(F(C)A 1959, ss.91 to 96)

The (*qv*) Salmon and Trout Conservation Bye-law 1998 is now the main enforcement instrument in relation to nets. It replaces two long serving bye-laws and no doubt it will itself be replaced as fashions and circumstances change.

The F(C)A 1959 contains the following restrictions but they are mainly of historic interest except for sections 95 and 96 which are still commonly prosecuted:

Section 91(1) of the F(C)A 1959 provides:

"(1) If any person –
- (a) makes use of or fishes with any net formed with a false bottom (except nets for the taking of eels), or
- (b) places two or more nets one behind the other, or
- (c) uses any nets covered with canvas, hide, or other substance for the taking of undersized fish, or
- (d) affixes or keeps up continued nets stretched across any river,

Offence

such person shall be guilty of an offence under this section ..."

(Note that the maximum penalty prescribed under this subsection has been increased. *See:* FINES AND IMPRISONMENT (IMPOSITION OF)).

"(2) Where a person is convicted of an offence under this section, the net in respect of which the offence was committed shall, as a statutory consequence of conviction, stand forfeited."

Offence
Section 92 of the F(C)A 1959 applies to nets formed of a non-rigid material and which is illegal because its mesh is less than a certain specified size. *See:* MESH OF NETS AND ENGINES.

(Note that the maximum penalty prescribed under this subsection has been increased. *See:* FINES AND IMPRISONMENT (IMPOSITION OF)).

Offence
Section 93 of the F(C)A 1959 creates the offence of using nets of a rigid material with an illegal mesh. *See:* MESH OF NETS AND ENGINES.

(Note that the maximum penalty prescribed under this subsection has been increased. *See:* FINES AND IMPRISONMENT (IMPOSITION OF)).

Offence
Section 94(1) of the F(C)A 1959 creates the offence for any person (other than the owner of a (*qv*) several fishery within the limits thereof) to shoot, draw or use any net for taking salmon at the mouth of any river or within half a mile seaward or half a mile inwards or along the coast from the mouth of any river.

(Note that the maximum penalty prescribed under this subsection has been increased. *See:* FINES AND IMPRISONMENT (IMPOSITION OF)).

Offence
Section 94(2) of the F(C)A 1959 creates the offence for any person (other than the owner of a several fishery in the whole of a river and its tributaries within the limits of such several fishery) to shoot, draw or stretch any net entirely across the mouth or across any other part of a river.

(Note that the maximum penalty prescribed under this subsection has been increased. *See:* FINES AND IMPRISONMENT (IMPOSITION OF))

In the case of each of these offences there is the usual provision for forfeiture in subsection (4) and subsection (5) provides where an order defines the mouth of any tributary river, references in the preceding subsections of this section to the mouth of any river shall be construed as including references to the mouth of any tributary river.

Offence
Section 95(1) of the F(C)A 1959 amended by section 18 of the F(A)A 1994 shown in square brackets.

"It shall not be lawful for any person to use any net for the capture of fish in the freshwater portion of any river or in any freshwater lake, unless:
(a) such net is used under and in accordance with bye-laws made under this section, or
(b) such net is a landing net and is used solely as auxiliary to lawful fishing with rod and line, or
(c) such net is used solely for the purpose of removing fish from traps in a weir, or
[(d) such net is constructed for the capture of eels and is operated in accordance with the conditions set out in an authorisation issued under section 100 of this Act]."

For Subsection (1)(d) which is the section substituted by section 18 *see:* EELS.

Offence
"(2) If any person uses any net in contravention of this section such person shall be guilty of an offence under this section."

(Note that the maximum penalty prescribed under this subsection has been increased. *See:* FINES AND IMPRISONMENT (IMPOSITION

Subsection (3) and (4) deal with the making of bye-laws permitting the use of nets in specified areas despite the provisions of section 95(1) *See:* BYE-LAWS, SECTION 95(3) AND (4).

Offence
Section 96(1) of the F(C)A 1959
"If any person has in his possession or control in any waters or on or near the bank of any waters –
(a) any net, the use of which in such waters for the purpose of taking fish is prohibited by any provision (other than section 95) of this Act or by any bye-law made thereunder, or
(b) any instrument (other than a net) or lure or bait, the use of which in such waters for the purpose of taking fish is prohibited by any provision of this Act or by any bye-law made thereunder,

such person shall be guilty of an offence under this subsection."

Offence

"(2) If any person has in his possession or control in, or in the vicinity of, a freshwater lake or the freshwater portion of any river any net constructed or mounted so as to be capable of being used for the capture of fish with intent to use it in contravention of section 95, such person shall be guilty of an offence under this subsection."

(Note that the maximum penalty prescribed under this subsection has been increased. *See:* FINES AND IMPRISONMENT (IMPOSITION OF)).

Subsection (4) provides that the net, other instrument, lure or bait in respect of which the offence was committed shall, as a statutory consequence of conviction, stand forfeited.

Subsection (5) provides that where a person is charged under subsection (2) and it is proved that he was in possession or control of a net in, or in the vicinity of, a freshwater lake or the freshwater portion of any river it shall be presumed that such possession or control was with intent to use it contrary to section 95 unless he can prove that at the time the offence is alleged to have been committed:

(i) he came within the exceptions in section 95(1) or, if the net is a draft net, its use was permitted under bye-laws made under section 95(4), or

(ii) if he was in possession of the net on the boundary between the tidal and freshwater portions of such river he held a licence to use that net in that fishery district and intended to use it in the tidal portion.

Section 10 of the F(A)A 1962 provides in relation to a charge for an offence under section 96 which alleges possession or control of a net, other instrument, lure or bait found on his person or in a boat or vehicle belonging to, or on any lands, tenements or hereditaments occupied by him, that the defendant shall (unless he satisfies the court that, without his knowledge or consent, another person put the net, other instrument, lure or bait in the place where it was found) be deemed, for the purposes of the said section 96, to have in his possession or control the net, other instrument, lure or bait, as the case may be.

NETS, PROHIBITION AGAINST SALE

(FA 1980 s.57)

Section 57(1) of the FA 1980 provides that the Minister may by order prohibit the sale of nets or netting of a prescribed class or description.

Offence

Subsection (2) provides that a person who sells a net or netting in contravention of an order under this section shall be guilty of an offence.

Subsection (3) provides for a complicated defence to proceedings under this section based on the proposition that the defendant notifies the Minister in writing in advance of the sale of his intention to sell nets or netting of the prescribed class or description, having enquired, again in advance, of the purchaser as to the purposes for which the relevant net or netting was to be used and having kept a record in the manner prescribed by the Minister under subsection (4).

If the court is satisfied that the inquiries were made in good faith and that in the circumstances of the case it would have been reasonable for the defendant, as a result of his inquiries, to have believed that such net or netting was not to be used for or in relation to fishing, then the defendant is entitled to an acquittal.

No order would ever appear to have been made under the section. It would have been almost impossible to prosecute.

NOISE

(EPAA 1992 ss.106, 107, 108)

"Noise" is defined in the EPAA 1992, section 3(1), as including vibration.

REGULATIONS FOR CONTROL OF NOISE

Section 106 of the EPAA 1992:

"(1) The Minister may, following consultation with any Minister of the Government who in the opinion of the Minister is concerned and with the Agency, make regulations for the purpose of the prevention or limitation of any noise which may give rise to a nuisance or disamenity, constitute a danger to health, or damage property.

(2) Without prejudice to the generality of subsection (1), that regulations under this section may provide for all or any of the following –

(a) controlling sources of noise,

(b) (i) specifying maximum limits for noise either generally or in specified areas of classes of areas,

(ii) specifying maximum limits for noise emissions, from or into premises or classes of premises, either generally or at specified periods, or

(iii) specifying maximum limits of noise levels in prescribed premises,

(c) regulating the operation, including licensing, of trades, processes or works, including the timing and control of movement of vehicles and the operation of engines and plant which are, or may be, sources of noise.

(d) limiting or prohibiting the use of loud speakers in or adjoining public places, including different provisions for different places or classes of places and at different times, and subject to such exceptions as may be specified.

(e) the measurement of noise and the investigation of noise effects, or

(f) the imposition of charges or the payment of fees for the purpose of the regulations or for services performed thereunder.

(3) The Act of 1963 is hereby amended by the addition at the end of Part IV of the Third Schedule of the entry: 14. Securing the reduction or prevention of noise."

The Third Schedule to the LG(P&D)A 1963 sets out the purposes for which objectives may be indicated in the (*qv*) development plan. Part IV of this Schedule refers to amenities. This amendment will entitle the reduction or prevention of noise to be included as an objective. Regulation 26 of the NH 97 Regulations (S.I. No. 94 of 1997) amended the same Schedule to give effect to the (*qv*) Birds Directive.

NOTICE REQUIRING MEASURES TO PREVENT OR LIMIT NOISE

Section 107 of the EPAA 1992 provides:

"(1) Where it appears to –

(a) a local authority in relation to any premises, processes or works, other than an activity for which a licence is required under Part IV, or

(b) the Agency in relation to an (*qv*) activity for which a licence is required under Part IV but has not been issued,

that it is necessary to do so for the prevention or limitation of noise, the local authority of the Agency, as the case may be, may serve a notice on the person in charge.

(2) A notice pursuant to this section shall indicate requirements for the prevention of limitation of noise and may –

(a) specify the measures which appear to the local authority or the Agency, as the case may be, to be necessary in order to prevent or limit the noise,

(b) direct the person on whom the notice is served to take such measures as may be specified in the notice to prevent or limit the noise, and

(c) specify a period, which the local authority or the Agency, as the case may be, considers reasonable in all the circumstances of the case, within which such measures are to be taken.

(3) A person on whom a notice under this section has been served may, within such period as may be specified in the notice, make such representations in writing as he thinks fit to the local authority or the Agency, as the case may be, concerning the terms of the notice, and the local authority or the Agency, as the case may be, having considered any such representations, may amend a provision of the notice (including the provision relating to subsection (2)(c)) or may confirm or revoke the notice, and shall inform the person of such amendment, confirmation or revocation.

(4) A person on whom a notice under this section has been served shall, within the period specified, comply with the requirements of the notice, or as the case may be, the notice as amended.

(5) If a person on whom a notice under this section has been served by a local authority or the Agency, as the case may be, does not, within the period specified in the notice or in the notice as amended, as the case may be, comply with the requirements of the notice or the notice as amended, the local authority or the Agency, as the case may be, may take such steps as it considers reasonable and necessary to secure compliance with the notice and may recover any costs and expenses incurred thereby from the person on whom the notice was served as a simple contract debt in any court of competent jurisdiction."

Although there is no specific provision in the section for prosecution for contravention, The Agency may prosecute under the general contravention section 8. *See:* OFFENCES.

"(6) It shall be a good defence, in a prosecution for a contravention of this section in the case of noise caused in the course of a trade or business, for the accused to prove that –
(a) he took all reasonable care to prevent or limit the noise to which the charge relates by providing, maintaining, using, operating and supervising facilities, or by employing practices or methods of operation, that, having regard to all the circumstances, were suitable for the purposes of such prevention or limitation, or
(b) the noise is in accordance with –
(i) the terms of a licence under this Act, or
(ii) regulations under section 106.

(7) A register of notices issued, amended or revoked by the local authority or the Agency shall be kept at the office of the local authority or the Agency, as the case may be, and be available for public inspection free of charge during office hours and copies of entries shall be provided on request to any person on payment by him to the local authority or the Agency, as the case may be, of such fee (if any) as the local authority or the Agency, as the case may be, shall fix not exceeding the reasonable cost of making the copy."

DISTRICT COURT PROSECUTION UNDER SECTION 108 NOISE AS A NUISANCE

Section 108 of the EPAA 1992 provides:

"(1) Where any noise which is so loud, so continuous, so repeated, of such duration or pitch or occurring at such times as to give reasonable cause for annoyance to a person in any premises in the neighbourhood or to a person lawfully using any public place, a local authority, the Agency or any such person may complain to the District Court and the Court may order the person or body making, causing or responsible for the noise to take the measures necessary to reduce the noise to a specified level or to take specified measures for the prevention or limitation of the noise and the person or body concerned shall comply with such order."

Regulation 5 of Environmental Protection Agency Act 1992 (Noise) Regulations 1994 (S.I. No. 179 of 1994), gives the form of complaint prescribed.

See: Order 96 Rule 8, District Court Rules, 1997.

DEFENCE

"(2) It shall be a good defence, in the case of proceedings under subsection (1) or in a prosecution for a contravention of this section, in the case of noise caused in the course of a trade or business, for the accused to prove that –
(a) he took all reasonable care to prevent or limit the noise to which the complaint relates by providing, maintaining, using, operating and supervising facilities, or by employing practices or methods of operation, that, having regard to all the circumstances, were suitable for the purposes of such prevention or limitation, or
(b) the noise is in accordance with –
(i) the terms of a licence under this Act, or
(ii) regulations under section 106."

NOTICE OF COMPLAINT

"(3) Before a complaint is made to the District Court under subsection (1) the local authority or the person concerned, as the case may be, shall serve a notice in the prescribed form of the intention to make such a complaint, within such time as may be specified in the notice, on the person alleged to have made or have caused or have been responsible for the noise.

(4) This section shall not apply to noise caused by –
(a) aircraft, or
(b) such statutory undertaker or local authority, as may be prescribed, in the exercise of powers conferred on it by or under any enactment in such circumstances as may be prescribed."

NON-APPLICATION OF APA 1987
(APA 1987, s.3)

Section 3 of the APA 1987 provides:

"This Act shall not apply in relation to an (*qv*) emission arising from –

(i) the disposal at sea of a substance by deliberate combustion for thermal destruction, or

(ii) the use of any radioactive substance or device."

NON-APPLICATION OF WMA 1996
(WMA 1996, s.3)

See: WASTE, NON-APPLICATION OF WMA 1996.

NON-SCHEDULED ENGINE
(F(C)A 1959, s.3(1))

Means an engine of a kind not specified in the Fourth Schedule to the Act. *See:* ENGINES.

NOTICES REQUIRING MEASURES — AND NOTICES REQUIRING INFORMATION
(LG(WP)A 1977, ss.12 and 16)

There is provision for two notices requiring measures served by local authorities under section 12(1) of the LG(WP)A 1977. *See:* ENFORCEMENT (3)(B)(1), and section 16(13) of the LG(WP)A 1977. *See:* ENFORCEMENT (3)(B)(2) and one notice requiring particulars section 23(1) of the LG(WP)A 1977. *See:* ENFORCEMENT (3)(B)(3).

(APA 1987, ss. – 26 and 16)

There is one of each. A notice requiring measures to be taken section 26(1) of the APA 1987, *see:* ENFORCEMENT (3)(C)(1) and a notice requiring information/particulars section 16(1) of the APA 1987, *see:* ENFORCEMENT (3)(C)(2).

(EPAA 1992, s.107)

There is only one notice for the prevention or limitation of noise under section 107(1) of the EPAA 1992. *See:* ENFORCEMENT (3)(D).

(WMA 1996, s.55)

Again there is one of each. A notice requiring measures to be taken, section 55(1) of the WMA 1996. *See:* ENFORCEMENT (3)(E))(1) and a notice requiring information, section 18(1) of the WMA 1996. *See:* ENFORCEMENT (3)(E)(2)

(NH 97, Reg.18)

A notice served by the Minister requiring the restoration of land after an operation or activity has been carried out on the land Regulation 18 NH 97 Regulations. *See:* ENFORCEMENT (3)(F).

NOTICES, SERVICE OF
(LG(WP)A 1977, s.32)

Subsection (1) provides that any notice required to be given or served by or under this Act shall be addressed to the person concerned and given or served in one of the following ways:

(a) by addressing it to him by name and delivering it to him,

(b) by leaving it at the address at which he ordinarily resides,

(c) by sending it by post in a prepaid registered letter addressed to him at the place where he ordinarily resides,

(d) where the address where he ordinarily resides cannot be ascertained by reasonable inquiry and the notice is required to be given in respect of any premises or vessel by delivering it to a person over 16 years of age resident or employed on the premises or vessel or by affixing it in a conspicuous position on or near the premises or vessel.

Subsection (2) provides that where the name of the occupier cannot be ascertained by reasonable inquiry notice under this section can be addressed to "the occupier".

Subsection (3) provides that for the purposes of this section a company registered under the Companies Act 1963, shall be deemed to be ordinarily resident at its registered office, and every other body corporate and every unincorporated body shall be deemed to be ordinarily resident at its principal office or place of business.

EXTENSION OF FUNCTION TO AGENCY

These functions under section 32 of the LG(WP)A 1977 now apply to the Agency in the circumstances described in Article 4 of the Environmental Protection Agency (Extension of Powers) Order 1996 (S.I. No. 126 of 1996). *See:* EXTENSION OF POWERS.

(APA 1987, s.15)

Provisions as to notices are the same as in the LG(WP)A 1977 above except that for the following:

There is an additional mode of service after

subsection (1)*(c)*, which stands in the place of subsection (1)*(d)* of section 32, which provides that if an address for the service of notices has been furnished by the person concerned, by leaving it at, or by sending it by prepaid registered post addressed to him at, that address.

Paragraph *(e)* of subsection (1) which follows is the same as *(d)* above in the LG(WP)A 1977 except that the words "or vessel" where they occur in paragraph (d) supra are omitted from paragraph *(e)* in section 15 of the APA 1987.

In subsection (2) the words "of a premises" appear after the word "occupier" in the first line.

EXTENSION OF POWERS TO AGENCY

These functions under section 15 of the APA 1987 now apply to the Agency in the circumstances described in Article 10 of the Environmental Protection Agency (Extension of Powers) Order 1992 (S.I. No. 126 of 1996). *See:* EXTENSION OF POWERS.

(EPAA 1992, s.14)

Subsection (1) is the same as an amalgam of the LG(WP)A 1977 and the APA 1987 except, paragraph (1)*(e)* of section 14 in the EPAA 1992 is worded differently and reads:

> "(e) where the address at which he ordinarily resides cannot be ascertained by reasonable inquiry and notice is required to be served on, or given to, him in respect of any premises, process, works or development, by delivering it to a person over the age of 16 years employed thereon or resident in the premises, or by affixing it to a conspicuous position on or near the premises, process, works or development."

The wording in subsection (2) is also different:

> "(2) Where the name of the person concerned cannot be ascertained by reasonable inquiry, a notice under this Act may be addressed to 'the occupier', 'the owner' or '(*qv*) the person in charge', as the case may be."

Subsection (3) is the same as in the LG(WP)A 1977 and APA 1987.

Subsection (4) is new and provides that a person shall not at any time during the period of three months after a notice is affixed under subsection (1)*(e)* remove, damage or deface the notice without lawful authority. (A contravention would be dealt with under section 8.)

(WMA 1996, s.16)

Is the same as an amalgam of the LG(WP)A 1977, the APA 1987 and the EPAA 1992, above, except that paragraph (1)*(e)* of this section is the same as (1)*(e)* in the EPAA 1992 and there is a specific offence subsection:

Offence
Subsection (5) of section 15 provides that a person who contravenes subsection (4) shall be guilty of an offence.

Offences arise only under section 14(4) and section 8 of the EPAA 1992 and section 16(5) of the WMA 1996.

NOTICE OF THE HOLDING OF INQUIRIES
(F(C)A 1959, s.322)

Notices in relation to the holding of inquiries. *See:* INQUIRIES.

NOTICE OF DESIGNATION AS SPECIAL AREA OF CONSERVATION (SAC)
(NH 97, Reg. 11)

Provides for the erection of a notice on land designated under Regulation 9 as a *(qv)* special area of conservation indicating the existence of the designation.

Paragraph (1) confers a right of entry on such land or any other land on the person authorised by the Minister under the Regulation.

Offence
Paragraph (2) creates the offence of a person destroying, altering, defacing, disfiguring, marking or otherwise interfering with the notice referred to in paragraph (1).

NOTICE OF NOTIFIABLE ACTIONS
(NH 97)

The material quoted hereunder (which is taken from a sample Notices of Notifiable Actions) was made pursuant to provisions of Chapter III of the NH 97 Regulations which deal with (*qv*) operations and activities on (*qv*) European sites.

These sample notices appear to be administrative acts indicating the form and content of the notices required to be given under Regulation 4 of the NH 97 Regulations.

The sample notices refer both to specific habitats (Notices 1.1–7.1) and specific species of flora and fauna (Notices 8.1–8.9).

Each of the sample notices is headed as follows:

"Under S.I. No. 94 of 1997, made under the European Communities Act, 1972 and in accordance with the obligations inherent in Council Directive 92/43/EEC of 21 May 1992 (the Habitats Directive) on the conservation of natural habitats and species of wild fauna and flora, all persons must obtain the written consent of the Minister for Arts, Culture and the Gaeltacht before performing any of the operations listed below on, or affecting the habitat of ..."

Then, in each notice, there follows the specific habitat appropriate to the particular notice being served and it is chosen from the following habitats:

open marine waters, inlets and bays, tidal rivers and estuarine channels (1.1)

mudflats and sandflats, sandy coastal beaches, shingle beaches, boulder beaches, bedrock shores (1.2)

saltmarshes (1.3)

sand dunes or machairs (1.4)

brackish lakes (1.5)

rocky sea cliffs, clay sea cliffs, sea stacks and islets (stacks, holms and skerries) (1.6)

upland grassland, scree and inland cliff (2.1)

dry lowland grasslands (2.2)

wet lowland grasslands (2.3)

limestone pavements (2.4)

turloughs (2.5)

blanket bog (3.1)

heath (3.2)

raised bog, cutaway bog and bog woodland (4.1)

fens (4.2)

woodlands (5.1)

scrub (5.2)

rivers or streams (6.1)

lakes, ponds, canals (6.2)

marshes and reedbanks (6.3)

ditches, hedges, cereals and intensive grasslands, walls, buildings, waste ground, bare soil, parkland, grassland, bracken, caves or quarries (7.1)

THE SAMPLE NOTICES THEN DEAL WITH THE FOLLOWING SPECIES:

lesser horseshoe bat (8.1)

grey seal, common seal, bottle-nosed dolphin, harbour porpoise (8.2)

river lamprey, sea lamprey, brook lamprey, salmon, twaite shad, white-clawed cray-fish, fresh water pearl mussel (8.3)

killarney shad (8.4)

vertigo species, shining sickle moss (8.5)

killarney fern, otter, marsh fritillary, kerry slug (8.6)

slender naiad (8.7)

marsh saxifrage (8.8)

petalwort (8.9)

Each of the sample notices continues as follows:

"Where a landowner has a current approved plan under the Rural Environmental Protection Scheme (REPS) or any scheme which the Minister considers to be equivalent s/he need only notify the Minister of activities not covered in the plan"
and then continues:

"The activities which should not be undertaken before consent are-".

These are too extensive to list here and they vary from habitat to habitat and from species to species.

They range from "causing erosion by any means (*e.g.* driving vehicles, riding horses, etc.)" which is one of the activities for which consent is required for the species of flora "petalwort" to "grazing of livestock" for which consent is required for the habitats "raised bog, cutaway bog and bog woodland".

At this stage the notices would appear to

have partially complied with Regulation 4(2) and (3) of the NH 97 Regulations which deals with notification.

There would, however, appear to be serious inconsistencies between the contents of the notice and the requirements of the Regulations, notably Regulation 4(3)(c) which requires that the notice should indicate the procedure by which a person may object.

The sample notices continue, in the cases of fauna and flora only, and that a trifle erratically, as follows:

"Please note that it is an offence under the Wildlife Act, 1976 to pick, collect, damage this species or disturb or destroy their breeding places."

The sample notices continues, in all cases, that is, fauna and flora and habitats:

"Please note that the activities listed below may require a licence or consent from another statutory authority (e.g. the local planning authority, the Minister for the Environment, or the Minister for Agriculture, Food and Forestry). The activities listed below must be notified to the Minister for Arts, Culture and the Gaeltacht when they are not regulated by another statutory authority."

Again the listed activities vary from habitat/habitat of species to habitat/habitat of species. By way of example, in the case of the habitat "raised bog, cutaway bog and bog woodland", used above, the activities requiring licence or consent and which are notifiable to the Minister, include":

"developing leisure facilities including golf courses, sports pitches, caravan and camping facilities" and "removal of soil, mud, gravel, sand or minerals".

This last list of of activities which may require a licence or consent from another statutory authority is not a notifiable matter under the NH 97 Regulations.

What they state is in fact correct but in so far as the NH 97 Regulations are concerned it is a piece of gratuitous information.

What appears to be an error appearing in these notices is the substantial deviation from the wording of the NH 97 Regulations which refer throughout to "operation or activity" and not "activity" simpliciter as do the sample notices.

The words "operation or activity" are defined at Regulation 2(1), the word "activity" is not defined. *See:* CONSERVATION, SPECIAL AREAS OF.

NOTIFICATION OF ACCIDENTAL DISCHARGE
(LG(WP)A 1977, s.14)

See: ACCIDENTAL DISCHARGE.

NOTIFICATION OF INCIDENT CAUSING AIR POLLUTION
(APA 1987, s.29)

See: ACCIDENTAL DISCHARGE.

NUTRIENT MANAGEMENT PLANS
(LG(WP)(A) 1990, s.21A)

Nutrient Management Plans is the title given to a complex section, section 21A, inserted into the LG(WP)(A), 1990 by section 66(3) of the WMA 1996. As the two sections 21 and 21A share a common interpretation section, section 21(1) and (2) (a) of the LG(WP)(A), 1990, and particularly the dense, unique and highly significant definition of "activity" which is central to and has an extensive application in both sections it is essential that the two sections, separated as they are by six years of total inactivity in the face of the National "nutrient crisis" in inland waters, are put together for the better understanding of what is one of the most ambitious and far-reaching attempts to resolve the crucial national problem in relation to farm activities adjoining inland waters and the prevention, elimination or minimising the entry of nutrients from farming activities. One would have to question the will and expertise of local authorities to take on this problem in view of their state of total stasis from 1990 to date but no doubt the EPA will watch them like the proverbial hawks they have come to resemble. Its juxtaposition immediately after section 21 of the LG(WP)(A)A, 1990 would suggest some belated acknowledgment of that much neglected section. *See:* AGRICULTURAL ACTIVITIES.

Comparison: Sections 21 and 21A are both designed to give greater control to local authorities over the discharge of (*qv*) polluting matter to (*qv*) waters from "activities" arising out of the use of land and they share a common definition of that word. The new section 21A adopts the original definition appearing in section 21 of the LG(WP)(A)A, 1990.

Section 21 of the 1990 Act was never invoked successfully by a local authority or activated by the Minister whereas section 21A becomes law effectively with the passing of the WMA 1996.

Section 21A of the LG(WP)(A)A 1990, inserted by section 66(3) of the WMA 1996, provides:

"(1) Subject to subsection (2), whenever a local authority considers that, for the purposes of preventing, eliminating or minimising the entry of (*qv*) polluting matter to waters from an (*qv*) activity referred to in section 21 (1)(b) (being an activity that is carried on in its functional area) it is necessary to do so, it may serve a notice in writing under this section on –
(a) the owner of the land on which the activity is carried on, or
(b) if the occupier of the said land is not in occupation of the said land, the person who is in occupation thereof, requiring the person to prepare and furnish to it for its approval under this section a plan (in this section referred to as a 'nutrient management plan') in relation to the activity within a specified period, being a period of not less than 5 months beginning on the date of service of the notice."

Subsection (2) provides that a notice shall not be served where there is an IPC ((*qv*) Integrated Pollution Control) licence in force in relation to the activity.

Subsection (3) provides for consultation by the local authority with bodies to be prescribed before exercising the power under subsection (1) either generally in its functional area or in a particular part.

Note that Article 2 of the Local Government (Water Pollution) (Nutrient Management Planning Consultation) Regulations 1998 (S.I. No. 257 of 1998) prescribes the (*qv*) Environmental Protection Agency for consultation purposes for the purpose of section 21A(3) of the Act.

"(4) A notice under this section –
(a) shall require that the nutrient management plan –
(i) provide such particulars of the activity concerned as are specified in the notice,
(ii) specify the quantities of such nutrients in animal and other waste as are specified in the notice (which may include nutrients in waste as aforesaid produced from sources other than the land concerned) which it is estimated will be used in each year of the relevant period on the land concerned.
(iii) provide that a determination of the types and concentration of nutrients in the soil of the land concerned shall be made in accordance with a programme of sampling and analysis to be determined by the local authority after consultation with the person on whom the notice is served (hereinafter in this section referred to as "the relevant person"),
(iv) specify the maximum quantities of such nutrients as are specified in the notice that, in the opinion of the relevant person, having regard to each of the matters referred to in subsection (5), ought, in each year of the relevant period, to be applied to, or injected into, the land concerned, or such parts thereof as are specified in the notice, or applied to crops growing on that land or such parts are are so specified,
(v) specify the times during the relevant period when the application to, or the injection into, the land concerned, or the application to crops growing there on, of animal and other waste and chemical fertiliser ought, and ought not, in the opinion of the relevant person, to be carried out, having regard to any crop requirements and the objective of preventing, eliminating or minimising the loss of nutrients to waters,
(vi) require the keeping and maintenance of records in respect of each year, or, in the case of the matters referred to in clause (III), the year or years concerned, of the relevant period, containing such particulars as may be determined by the local authority after consultation with the relevant person in relation to –
(I) the doing of the following things during the year concerned by the said person namely –
(A) the production, treatment, receiving from, or transfer to, another person by him of animal or other waste,
(B) the application to, or the injection into, the land concerned or the application to crops growing thereon, by him of animal or other waste and the times and rates at which such application or injection is carried out,
(II) the types and quantities of chemical fertiliser applied to the land concerned during the year concerned and the times and rates at which such application is carried

out,

(III) the results of the determination referred to in sub paragraph (ii) made in relation to the land concerned and, as the case may be, of any further determination of such kind made, pursuant to a requirement under paragraph (b) (ii), during the year concerned,

(vii) require such information in relation to the matters referred to in this paragraph, and, or as the case may be, paragraph (b), as is, specified in the notice to be furnished to the local authority.

(b) may require that the nutrient management plan –

(i) shall require the keeping and maintenance of records in respect of each year of the relevant period containing particulars as may be determined by the local authority after consultation with the relevant person of the concentration of such nutrients in animal or other waste as are specified in the notice that have been applied to, or injected into, the land concerned during the year concerned,

(ii) shall provide that a further determination of the kind referred to in paragraph (a) (iii) (whether in respect of nutrients generally or nutrients of a class specified in a notice served by the local authority on the relevant person for the purposes of this paragraph) shall be made at specified intervals after the determination referred to in that provision has been made,

(iii) shall address such other matters as the local authority considers necessary fo the purpose of preventing, eliminating or minimising the entry of nutrients to waters from the activity concerned and specifies in the notice.

(5) The matters referred to in subsection (4)*(a)*(iv) are:

(a) the nature of the activity concerned,

(b) the type of soil concerned and the types and concentration of nutrients in that soil,

(c) the types of crop previously grown on the land concerned and the types of nutrient previously applied to, or injected into, that land and the rates of such application or injection, where relevant,

(d) the types of crop grown or to be grown on the land concerned,

(e) the intensity of the stocking of animals (if any) on the land concerned and of any other agricultural activities carried on on that land, and,

(f) the need to make efficient use of nutrients having regard to any crop requirements and the objective of preventing, eliminating or minimising the loss of nutrient to waters."

Subsection (6) provides that in subsection (4) and the subsequent provisions of this section "the relevant period" means the period of 12 months, or such longer period as may be specified in the notice concerned under subsection (1) or (8), as appropriate, beginning on the date that is two months after the approval of the nutrient management plan concerned under this section by the relevant local authority.

Subsection (7) provides that a local authority may, as respects a nutrient management scheme prepared and furnished to it in accordance with subsection (1), refuse to approve of the plan or approve thereof without modifications or make such modifications therein as it considers proper and approve of the plan as so modified.

"(8) (a) A local authority, where it refuses to approve of a nutrient management plan under subsection (7), may, by service of a notice in writing on the person who furnished the plan to it, require that person to prepare and furnish to it another such plan and subsection (3) and the other provisions of this section shall apply to such a notice and such a plan as they apply to a notice under subsection (1) and a plan pursuant to a notice under that subsection.

(b) The reference in subsection (2) to a notice under subsection (1) includes a reference to a notice under this subsection."

"(9) If, on the expiration of the period of two months from the date of the receipt by it of a nutrient management plan prepared and furnished in accordance with a notice under this section, the local authority concerned has neither given a decision under subsection (7) to refuse to approve of the plan nor a decision thereunder to approve of the plan (by either of the means referred to in that subsection), the local authority shall be deemed to have approved of the plan under that subsection.

(10) A nutrient management plan may, with the prior written consent of the local authority which approved of the plan under this section,

be varied during the relevant period."

Offence

Subsection (11) provides that a person who fails to comply with a notice under subsection (1) or (8) within the period specified in the notice shall be guilty of a summary offence.

Subsection (12) provides that proceedings for an offence under the section may be brought by the local authority which served the notice concerned. For Penalties *see:* FINES AND IMPRISONMENT.

The Local Government (Water Pollution) (Nutrient Management Planning Consultation) Regulations 1998 (S.I. No. 257 of 1998) by Article 2 prescribed the (qv) EPA for the purposes of section 21(A)(3) of the L6(WP)(A)A 1990.

O

OBJECTION
(EPAA 1992 s.85(5)/
LG(P&D)A 1963, s.43/
WMA 1996, s.42(3)/
NH 97, Reg.5)

Section 85(5) of the EPAA 1992 provides that the applicant has 28 days and any other person 21 days within which to object to the proposed determination under section 85 indicated under section 85(2) and shall include with the objection the grounds for same. The objector must comply with regulations under sections 87 and 94 of the EPAA 1992. There is provision for an oral hearing of the objection. *See:* (1) LICENCE(5); (2) ORAL HEARING(2).

Section 43 of the LG(P&D) A 1963 provides for a right of objection to the making of a special amenity area order under section 42. *See:* SPECIAL AMENITY AREA ORDER.

Section 42(3) of the WMA 1996 provides that a person may object within the "appropriate period" to the proposal by the Agency to make a decision under section 40 — notified under section 42(2) and subject to compliance with regulations under section 45 and 50.
See: (1) LICENCE (6), PROCESSING OF APPLICATIONS FOR LICENCES AND REVIEW OF LICENCES; (2) ORAL HEARINGS (3).

Regulation 5 of the NH 97 Regulations (S.I. No. 94 of 1997) provides that a person, on being notified under Regulation 4(2), can object on scientific grounds to the inclusion of a site on the candidate list of (*qv*) European sites. *See:* CONSERVATION, SPECIAL AREAS OF.

OBLIGATIONS IN RELATION TO RESERVES AND REFUGES
(WLA 1976, s.12)

Section 12 of the WLA 1976, *see:* RESERVES AND REFUGES, OBLIGATIONS IN RELATION TO.

OBSTRUCT, IMPEDE
(F(C)A 1959/EPAA 1992/
WMA 1996/WLA 1976/NH 97)

The most common offence against the person of an officer authorised to enforce environmental legislation is the offence of obstructing or impeding him/her in the exercise of powers conferred on him/her. Each statute has a specific section creating the offence. In some sections, the offence is obstruction only. *See:* OBSTRUCT.

The following are a list of the provisions dealing with the offence of obstructing, impeding:

F(C)A 1959, s. 301(7)
F(C)A 1959, s. 287 (the protection afforded by this section is for a member of the public and not an authorised officer),
F(A)A 1997, s.57(3),
F(A)A 1999, S.28(4),
APA 1987, s. 14(5),
EPAA 1992, s. 13(5)(b),
WLA 1976, s.69(3)(b),
WMA 1996, s. 14(6)(b),
NH 97, reg. 7(6),
European Communities (Mammalian Animal Waste) Regulations 1998 (S.I. No. 2 of 1998),
European Communities (Processing of Mammalian Animal Waste) Regulations 1998 (S.I. No. 2 of 1998).
See: ENTRY AND SEARCH.

OCTOBER, CLOSE PERIOD FOR ANGLING
(F(C)A 1959, s.3(1))

Means the period commencing on the 13th day of October and ending on the "31st day of that month".

This no longer has any relevance. Refer to local bye-laws for close season.

OFFENCES
(F(A)A 1997, s.65(1)/
APA 1987, s.11(1)/
EPAA 1992, s.8(1)/
WLA 1976, s.69)

In most of the environmental statutes with which this work is concerned the offences are treated individually and each provision, the breach or contravention of which is an offence, so provides within the section itself. They appear in thus work after the word *offences*.

F(C)A 1959

This is particularly so in the Fisheries Acts which have over 100 individual offences. Although the F(A)A 1997 adheres to the Fisheries Acts system of treating each offence individually, section 65(1) of the F(A)A 1997 provides that a person who contravenes or fails to comply with a term of a licence or a condition subject to which a licence is issued will be guilty of an offence.

LG(WP)A 1977

In the LG(WP)A 1977 each section creates its own offence.

APA 1987, EPAA 1992 and WLA 1976

In the APA 1987 and the EPAA 1992 and to a limited extent in the WLA 1976 each section creates the offence, however, there are specific and separate omnibus "offence" sections as follows -

Section 11(1) of the APA 1987 provides that any person who contravenes any provision of this Act or of any regulation made under this Act or of any notice served under this Act shall be guilty of an offence.

Subsection (2) provides for offences by bodies corporate. *See:* OFFENCES BY BODIES CORPORATE.

Subsection (3) provides that in this section, a reference to the contravention of a provision includes, where appropriate, a reference to a refusal, or a failure to comply with that provision.

EXTENSION OF FUNCTIONS UNDER S. 11 OF THE APA 1987 TO AGENCY

These functions, under section 11 of the APA 1987 now apply to the Agency in the circumstances described in Article 10 of the Environmental Protection Agency (Extension of Powers) Order 1996 (S.I. No. 126 of 1996). *See:* EXTENSION OF POWERS.

EPAA 1992

Section 8(1) of the EPAA 1992 provides that any person who contravenes any provision of the Act or of any regulation made under the Act or of any order made under this Act or of any notice served under this Act shall be guilty of an offence.

Subsection (2) provides for offences by bodies corporate. *See:* OFFENCES BY BODIES CORPORATE.

Subsection (3) provides that in the section, a reference to a contravention of a provision includes, where appropriate, a reference to a refusal, or a failure, to comply with that provision.

WLA 1976

In the WLA 1976 offences are specified from section to section and there is also an omnibus offence section 69 which deals with general offences and particularly offences involving failure to cooperate with (*qv*) authorised officers and members of the Garda Síochána.

Section 69 of the WLA 1976

See: ATTEMPTS, MISCELLANEOUS OFFENCES. WMA 1996

WMA 1996

The WMA 1996 reverts to the system of providing for the offence in each section separately so that the offence constitutes a breach or contravention of a provision or a failure to perform in accordance with or comply with a direction contained in the section.

OFFENCES BY BODIES CORPORATE

(F(C)A 1959, s.311/NH 97, Reg. 38/ LG(WP)A 1977, s.23(1)/APA 1987, s.11(2)/ EPAA 1992, s.8(2)/WMA 1996, s.8(1), (2)/ Foreshore (Amendment) Act 1992, s.3)

FISHERIES ACTS

Section 311 of the F(C)A 1959

"Where an offence under any provision of this Act was committed by a body corporate and is proved to have been so committed with the consent or approval of, or to have been facilitated by any neglect on the part of, any director, manager, secretary or other officer of such body corporate, such director, manager, secretary or other officer shall also be deemed to be guilty of such offence and shall be liable to be proceeded against and punished accordingly."

NH 97

Regulation 38 of the NH 97 Regulations (S.I. No. 94 of 1997) provides that where an offence under the regulations has been committed by a body corporate and it is proved to have been so committed with the consent or connivance of, or, to be attributable to any neglect on the part of any person who, when the offence was committed, was a director, manager, secretary or other officer of the body corporate, or a person purporting to act in such capacity, that person, as well as the body corporate, shall be guilty of an offence and shall be liable to be proceeded

against and punished as if guilty of the first-mentioned offence.
LG(WP)(A)A 1990

Section 23(1) of the GL(WP)(A)A 1990

"Where an offence under the Principal Act or this Act has been committed by a body corporate and is proved to have been committed with the consent or connivance of or to be attributable to any neglect on the part of a person being a director, manager, secretary or other officer of that body corporate, or a person who was purporting to act in any such capacity, that person shall be guilty of an offence and shall be liable to be proceeded against and punished as if he were guilty of the first mentioned offence."

Subsection (2) provides that where the affairs of a body corporate are managed by its members, subsection (1) shall apply to the acts and defaults of a member in connection with his functions of management as if he were a director or manager of the body corporate.

APA 1987

Section 11(2) of the APA 1987

"Where an offence under this Act is committed by a body corporate or by a person acting on behalf of a body corporate and is proved to have been so committed with the consent, connivance or approval of, or to have been facilitated by any neglect on the part of, any director, manager, secretary or other official of such body, such person shall also be guilty of an offence."

EPAA 1992

Section 8(2) of the EPAA 1992 makes provisions in exactly similar terms to those of the APA 1987 above.

WMA 1996

Section 9(1) and (2) of the WMA 1996 makes provisions in exactly similar terms to those of the LG(WP)(A)A 1990, supra.

MAMMALIAN ANIMAL WASTE AND PROCESSING MAMMALIAN WASTE REGULATIONS 1998.

In these two regulations, the European Communities (Mammalian Waste) Regulations, 1998 (S.I. No. 2 of 1998) and the European Communities (Processing of Mammalian Waste) Regulations, 1998 (S.I. No 64 of 1998). At Reg. 9(3) in S.I. No. 2 and at Reg. 10(3) in S.I. No. 64 provide in exactly similar terms to those at section 23(1) of the LG(WP)(A)A 1990.

OFFER AND MAKE AVAILABLE FOR RECOVERY
(WMA 1996)

Article 4(3) of the Waste Management (Packaging) Regulations 1997 (S.I. No. 242 of 1997) made under sections 7, 19, 27, 28 and 29 of the WMA 1996, to give effect to Articles 6 and 11 of European Parliament and Council Directive 94/62/EC of 20 December, 1994 on packaging and packaging waste (O.J. No. L 365/10, 31 December, 1944) provides, in relation to packaging that "offer and make available for recovery" means to –

"(a) segregate such packaging waste into appropriate categories for the purpose of facilitating the recovery of said waste, and at a minimum into the specified categories, and
(b) take reasonable steps to notify persons engaged in waste recovery (in these Regulations referred to as 'recovery operators') of the availability, nature, amount and location of such packaging waste, and
(c) offer to provide such packaging waste to a recovery operator free of charge, and
(d) store such waste for a period of not less than four weeks after notification under paragraph (b), or until it is collected by a recovery operator, whichever is the earlier."

"Recovery operator" for the purposes of the regulations means a person referred to in the definition of "offer and make available for recovery". *See:* (1) PRODUCER (2) PRODUCER RESPONSIBILITY OBLIGATION.

OFFICER OF THE MINISTER
(F(C)A 1959, s.3(1))

"Includes a servant of the Minister."

OPEN SEASON
(WLA 1976, ss.24 and 25)

To understand fully how the "open season" system under the WLA 1976 works it is helpful to review the basic structures in the Act for the protection of (*qv*) wildlife as the main exemption from this protection is the creation of "open seasons" which mean a specified period of the year when the rules for protection are suspended for some specified species of wildlife.

The open season exemption is not to be confused with parallel exemptions from the protection rules which exist for scientific and educational purposes and the protection afforded to growing crops and other agricultural activities which are at risk from damage from wildlife, particularly wildbirds. *See:* DAMAGE TO PROTECTED WILD BIRDS AND PROTECTED WILD ANIMALS.

PROTECTION OF PROTECTED WILD BIRDS AND PROTECTED WILD ANIMALS

Section 19 of the WLA 1976 provides that wild birds and their nests and eggs, other than wildbirds of the species mentioned in the Third Schedule to the Act, shall be protected.

Section 20 of the WLA 1976 provides that animals which are of the species of (*qv*) fauna in relation to which section 23 of the Act applies, which are the species of fauna specified in the Fifth Schedule, shall be protected.

The wild birds EXCLUDED from the THIRD SCHEDULE are protected wild birds and the enforcement of this protection is contained at section 22 of the WLA 1976 (*See:* PROTECTION, PROTECTED WILD BIRDS), and the animals INCLUDED in the FIFTH SCHEDULE are protected wild animals and the enforcement of this protection is contained in section 23 of the WLA 1976 (*See:* PROTECTION, PROTECTED WILD ANIMALS).

The Protection of Flora is under section 21 of the WLA 1976. *See:* PROTECTION OF FLORA.

OPEN SEASONS ORDERS -SECTIONS 24 AND 25 OF THE WLA 1976

Section 24(1) of the WLA 1976:

"Subject to sections 27 and 28 of this Act, the Minister may by order provide that any protected wild bird which is of a species specified in the order, may be hunted either throughout the State or in any part thereof specified in the order on a day or during a period of days so specified."

Section 25(1) of the WLA 1976:

"Subject to sections 27 and 28 of this Act, the Minister may by order provide that any wild mammal (being a protected wild animal) which is of a species specified in the order (in this Act referred to as an exempted wild mammal) may be hunted in a manner so specified either throughout the State or in any part thereof specified in the order on a day or during a period of days so specified."

In fact the Minister makes a separate order under each section for each hunting season, one under section 24 in respect of protected wild birds entitled Wildlife (Wild Birds) (Open Seasons) Order and the other under section 25 in respect of protected wild animals entitled Wildlife (Wild Mammals) (Open Seasons) Order. The orders for the 1998/1999 season are S.I No. 332 (protected wild birds) and S.I. No. 331 (protected wild animals)

Subsection (2) is the same in both sections 24 and 25 and provides:

"(2) An order under this section may contain different provisions in relation to different areas and different species of protected wild birds /exempted wild mammals, including provisions limiting the total number of any particular such species (any particular species of such mammal) which may, during a period of days be specified in the order, be killed by individuals in hunting in accordance with the order either in relation to the area as a whole to which the order applies or to part of such area."

The following fauna, protected wild birds and protected wild animals appear on the National Parks and Wildlife Service (NPWS) (now Dúchas) information handout for the 98/99 hunting season.

Species Open Season

Red grouse
1 September to 30 September

Mallard, Teal, Gadwall,
Widgeon, Pintail, Shoveler,
Scaup, Tufted Duck, Pochard,
Goldeneye, Golden Plover,
Snipe, Jacksnipe
1 September to 31 January

Red-legged Partridge
1 November to 31 January

Cock Pheasant, Woodcock
1 November to 31 January

Curlew
1 November to 31 January

Canada Geese
1 September to 30 September

Canada Geese (Co. Cavan
and Co. Leitrim only) and
excluding the following
townlands: Eonish Island,
Rinn and Deramfield (Cavan)
and the River Shannon (Leitrim)
1 October to 31 January

Greylag Geese
1 September to 30 September

Greylag Geese (Lady's Island,
Co. Wexford and Gearagh West
in Co. Cork only)
1 October to 31 January

Woodpigeon
1 June to 31 January

The open season for hares is from September 26 to February 28th excluding the Co. Wexford townlands North East Slob, North West Slob, Big Island, Beggerin Island and the Raven.

Methods of hunting for hares include shooting with firearms, coursing and hunting with packs of beagles or harriers.

Also included in the NPWS information sheet is a heading "Trade" which prohibits dealing in gadwall, goldeneye, curlew and shoveler either live or dead birds or any easily recognisable parts or derivatives of such birds. *See:* WILDLIFE DEALING.

Deer are more complicated again and distinctions are made between seasons for male and female deer, and between County Kerry, where there are large herds, and the rest of the State excluding Kerry. Culling is an important part of deer management and is strictly controlled.

TEMPORARY SUSPENSION OF OPEN SEASONS

Section 27 of the WLA 1976 deals with the Minister's power to provide when, because of the severity of the weather conditions in the State or elsewhere or for any other specified reason, it is desirable to do so in the interests of conserving (*qv*) fauna, to make an order suspending the open season order for one month only and by virtue of subsection (3) this order may be extended by the Minister by further order for not longer than two months.

A number of orders have been made under this section. In 1982 a great number of species of fauna were included in the first order which ran from January 13th to January 22nd of that year because of the severity of the weather and a further order was made on the January 22nd extending the protection for the Greenland White-fronted Goose only from January 23rd to 31st January. These orders were WLA 1976 (section 27) Order, 1982 (S.I. No. 3 of 1982) and WLA 1976 (Section 27)(No.2) Order, 1982 (S.I. No. 15 of 1982) and the appropriate Ministry at the time was Fisheries and Forestry.

OPERATION OR ACTIVITY
(NH 97, Reg. 2(1))

"Means any use of:
(a) land (including the foreshore and the seabed out to the exclusive fishery limits of the State), and
(b) water covering such land, other than
(i) development which is not exempted development within the meaning of the Local Government (Planning and Development) Acts, 1963 to 1993, or
(ii) development by a local authority, or,
(iii) an operation or activity which requires consent or other authorisation, pursuant to any enactment set out in Part I or II of the Second Schedule."

See: SCHEDULES HERETO, WLA 1976 SCHEDULES.

By virtue of Regulation 17 of the NH 97 regulations the Minister has powers to obtain orders prohibiting operations and activities on certain lands *See:* PROHIBITION AGAINST WORKS (OPERATIONS OR ACTIVITIES) ON CERTAIN PROTECTED LANDS.

ORAL HEARINGS
(LG(WP)A 1977/APA 1987/EPAA 1992/WMA 1996/F(A)A 1997)

Certain statutes provide for oral hearings of certain matters such as the making of an order which is of particular public concern to members of a specific community.

These hearings are invariably open to the public. The manner of conduct of the hearing is determined by the relevant statute or, as is more usual, by regulation made under the statute.

LG(WP)A 1977

Sections 8(1)*(a)* and 20(1)(A) of the LG(WP)A 1977 provide for appeals to an Bord Pleanála *See:* APPEALS/LG(WP)A 1977(1) and (2). Articles 24 to 30 in Part IV of the Local Government (Water Pollution) Regulations 1992

(S.I. No. 271 of 1992) (which replace the Local Government (Water Pollution) Regulations 1978 (S.I. No. 108 of 1978)) and provide for the protocol in relation to oral hearings under the LG(WP)A 1977.

Offence
Article 27(3)*(c)* of the Local Government (Water Pollution) Regulations 1992 (S.I. No. 271 of 1992) provides for prosecution by an (*qv*) Bord Pleanála of offences by a person on whom a notice under Article 27(a) been served and who wilfully refuses or neglects to attend, wilfully alters, suppresses, conceals or destroys documents, particulars or other information to which the notice relates or having so attended fails to produce any documents, particulars or other information to which the notice relates.

APA 1987
SPECIAL CONTROL AREA ORDER

Section 42 of the APA 1987 provides:

"(1) An oral hearing in relation to a (*qv*)special control area order held pursuant to section 41(3) or (4) shall be conducted by a person appointed for that purpose by the Minister.

(2) A person conducting an oral hearing may require any officer of a local authority concerned to give him any information which he reasonably requires for the purpose of the hearing, and it shall be the duty of the officer concerned to comply with the requirement.

(3) (a) A person conducting an oral hearing may visit and inspect premises for any purpose he considers necessary in relation to the special control area order which is the subject of the hearing.

Offence

(b) Any person who obstructs the exercise of the power conferred by this subsection shall be guilty of an offence.

(4) A person conducting an oral hearing may take evidence on oath and for that purpose may administer oaths, and a person giving evidence shall be entitled to the same immunities and privileges as if he were a witness before the High Court.

(5) (a) Subject to paragraph (b), a person conducting an oral hearing may, by giving notice in that behalf in writing to any person, require that person to attend at such time and place as is specified in the notice to give evidence in relation to any matter in question at the hearing and to produce any books, deeds, contracts, maps, plans or other documents in his possession, custody or control which relates to any such matter.

(b) The following provisions shall have effect for the purposes of the foregoing paragraph:

(i) it shall not be necessary for a person to attend in compliance with a notice at a place more than ten miles from his ordinary place of residence unless such sum as will cover his reasonable and necessary expenses of the attendance have been paid or tendered to him;

(ii) the local authority shall, at the request of the person conducting the oral hearing, pay or tender to any person whose attendance is required such sum as the person conducting the hearing considers will cover the reasonable and necessary expenses of the attendance;

(iii) any person who in compliance with a notice has attended at any place shall, save in so far as the reasonable and necessary attendance expenses of the attendance have already been paid to him, be paid those expenses by the local authority, and those expenses, save as aforesaid, shall, in default of being so paid, be recoverable as a simple contract debt in any court of competent jurisdiction.

Offence

(iv) every person to whom a notice has been given who refuses or who wilfully neglects to attend in accordance with the notice or who wilfully alters, suppresses, conceals or destroys any document to which the notice relates or who, having so attended, refuses to give evidence or refuses or wilfully fails to produce any document to which the notice relates shall be guilty of an offence.

(6) Where an oral hearing is conducted by

or on behalf of the Minister under this Act by a person appointed for the purpose by the Minister, the person so appointed shall make to the Minister a written report on the hearing and shall include in his report a recommendation relating to the matter with which the hearing was concerned."

EPAA 1992

Section 85(5) of the EPAA 1992 provides for an objection to a determination by the Agency (*See:* OBJECTION) and subsection (6) provides for an oral hearing of that objection at the absolute discretion of the Agency.

Section 86 of the EPAA 1992 provides:

"(1) An oral hearing provided for in section 85 shall be conducted by a person appointed for that purpose by the Agency.

(2) The person appointed under subsection (1) shall make a written report on the hearing to the Agency and shall include in the report a recommendation relating to the grant or refusal of a licence or to the grant of a revised licence and, where appropriate, the conditions (if any) to be attached to the licence or revised licence.

(3) The Agency shall consider a report made under subsection (2) before making a decision on the application for a licence or on the review of a licence or a revised licence.

(4) The Minister may make regulations in relation to the conduct of an oral hearing and the procedures at such a hearing."

WMA 1996: OBJECTION TO THE GRANT OR REVIEW OF A WASTE LICENCE

Section 44 of the WMA 1996 provides:

"(1) (a) An oral hearing under section 42 shall be conducted by a person appointed for that purpose by the Agency,
(b) Subject to any regulations under subsection (4), the manner in which the hearing aforesaid is conducted shall be at the discretion of the person appointed under this subsection but it shall be the duty of that person to ensure that the hearing is conducted without undue formality.

(2) A person appointed under subsection (1) may take evidence on oath at the oral hearing and for that purpose may administer oaths, and a person giving evidence at such a hearing shall be entitled to the same immunities and privileges as if he were a witness before the High Court.

(3) The person appointed under subsection (1) shall make a written report on the hearing to the Agency and shall include in the report a recommendation relating to the grant of a waste licence or a revised waste licence, as the case may be (including the conditions to be attached to such a licence) or to the refusal of such a licence.

(4) (a) The Minister may make regulations in relation to the conduct of an oral hearing under section 42 and the procedures at such a hearing.
(b) Without prejudice to the generality of paragraph (a), regulations under this subsection shall provide for all or any of the following -
(i) matters that may be raised at an oral hearing;
(ii) the persons who may be heard at an oral hearing;
(iii) enabling the person conducting an oral hearing to require any person to attend the hearing and give evidence in relation to any matter in question at the hearing;
(iv) the publication or giving notice of the holding of an oral hearing;
(v) the alteration of the time and place of the holding of an oral hearing;
(vi) the provision of submissions, plans, documents or other information and particulars to persons;
(vii) the adjournment or re-opening of an oral hearing, and the publication or giving notice regarding such am adjournment or re-opening;
(viii) the replacement of a person appointed to conduct an oral hearing or the conduct of a new oral hearing;
(ix) the withdrawal of a request for an oral hearing, and the matters consequential thereon."

Section 42(9) of the WMA 1996 provides for a request for an oral hearing arising out of an objection to a decision of the Agency under section 40.

F(A)A 1997 – ORAL HEARING OF APPEAL

Section 49 of the F(A)A 1997

"(1) Subject to subsections (2) and (3), the (*qv*) Board of its own motion or at the request of a party, shall have an absolute discretion to hold an oral hearing of an appeal under this Chapter.

(2) An oral hearing may be conducted on behalf of the Board by one or more members of the Board, or other persons, authorised by the Board for that purpose.

(3) A request by a party for an oral hearing of an appeal –
  (a) shall be made in writing to the Board and shall be accompanied by such fee, if any, as may be payable in respect of such request in accordance with (*qv*)regulations under section 63;
  (b) if not accompanied by that fee, if any, shall not be considered by the Board;
  (c) subject to paragraph (d), shall be made within the period of one months referred to in section 40(1); or
  (d) in the case where the party is not the appellant, shall be made within the period referred to in section 44(2)."

(Both sections provide the same period of one month).

"(4) The Board shall not consider a request for an oral hearing of an appeal received later than the time referred to in subsection (3)(c) or (d) for making a request.

(5) Where a Board is requested to hold an oral hearing of an appeal and decides to determine the appeal without an oral hearing, it shall serve notice of its decision on the person who requested the hearing, on each other party to the appeal and on each person who, in accordance with section 45, made submissions or observations to the Board in relation to the appeal."

See: APPEALS.

Section 57 of the F(A)A 1997

"(1) In conducting an oral hearing of an appeal, the Board may require any officer of the Minister or an officer of the Marine Institute to give to the Board such information in relation to the appeal as the Board may reasonably require, and the officer shall comply with the requirement.

(2) The Board may visit and inspect any land, foreshore or area of water to which the appeal relates.

Offence
(3) Any person who obstructs the Board in its performance of a function under sub section (2) shall be guilty of an offence.

(4) The Board in conducting an oral hearing of an appeal, may take evidence on oath and for that purpose may administer oaths, and a person giving evidence at an oral hearing shall be entitled to the same immunities and privileges as if he or she were a witness before the High Court.

(5) Subject to subsection (6), a person conducting an oral hearing of an Appeal may, by giving notice in that behalf in writing to any person, require the person to attend at such time and place as is specified in the notice to give evidence in relation to any matter in question at the hearing and to produce any books, deeds, contracts, accounts, vouchers, maps, plans or other documents in his possession, custody or control which relates to any such matter.

Subsection (6) provides for attendances by persons at the oral hearing and their expenses for so doing and for other expenses and by whom they are to be paid and is in the same terms as those contained at section 42(5) of the APA 1987 quoted in *extenso supra*.

Offence
"(6) (d) every person to whom a notice has been given who -
  (i) refuses or who wilfully neglects to attend in accordance with the notice,
  (ii) wilfully alters, suppresses, conceals or destroys any document to which the notice relates,
  (iii) having so attended, refuses to give

evidence or refuses or wilfully fails to produce any document to which the notice relates,

shall be guilty of an offence and shall be liable on summary conviction to a fine not exceeding £500.

(7) In this section 'the Board' includes a person appointed by the Board to conduct an oral hearing on its behalf."

ORDERS, REVOCATION AND AMENDMENT OF ORDERS AND DIRECTIONS

(F(C)A 1959/EPAA 1992/WMA 1996)

This entry covers orders made under the following Acts: Fisheries Acts 1959–1997, the EPAA 1992, the WMA 1996 and the WLA 1976.

FISHERIES ACTS 1959–1997

Section 11(2) of the F(C)A 1959 provides that the section applies to the following instruments:

(a) All bye-laws made under the Act. *See:* BYE-LAWS.

(b) Orders made under section 10 of the Act by the Minister which are orders defining the mouths of rivers. *See:* DEFINITION OF MOUTHS OF RIVERS.

(c) A licence granted under sections 245 or 281 of the Act, which deals with the licensing of oyster beds, mussel beds and mussel fisheries, periwinkle beds and cockle beds. *See:* OYSTERS, and

(d) Orders under sections 251, 256, 266 or 275 which deal with oysters and the revocation of oyster fishery licences and determination of oyster fishery orders. *See:* OYSTERS.

Section 11 of the F(C)A 1959 provides:

"(1) The following provisions shall apply in relation to any instrument to which this section applies –

(a) notwithstanding any appeal which may be pending, but without prejudice to any order which may be made on such appeal, such instrument shall come into operation on the day specified in that behalf therein, or if no such day is specified, on the twenty-eighth day after the day on which it is made;

(b) such instrument shall, as soon as may be after it is made, be published in the Iris Oifigiuil and in one or more newspapers circulating in the district affected thereby:

(c) A copy of such instrument shall within one month after it comes into operation be deposited –

(i) with the county registrar for every county or county borough which or part of which is affected thereby, and

(ii) with the District Court Clerk of every Court District or part of which affected thereby; and

(iii) in every station of the Garda Síochána within the area affected thereby;

(d) Any person aggrieved by such instrument may, within twenty-eight days after the publication in the Iris Oifigiúil, appeal against such instrument to the High Court, and the following provisions shall apply in relation to such appeal –

(i) the appeal may be heard by one or more judges of the High Court as may be convenient,

(ii) The High Court may on appeal confirm or annul such instrument, but if such instrument is annulled, such annulment shall be without prejudice to the validity of anything done under or in pursuance of such instrument before such annulment,

(iii) the decision of the High Court on the appeal shall be final and conclusive,

(iv) The order made by the High Court on such appeal shall be published in like manner as such instrument is required by paragraph (b) of this subsection to be published and shall be deposited in like manner as such instrument is required by paragraph (c) of this subsection to be deposited."

Apart from sections 10 and 11 and certain sections which contain specific powers to make orders in relation to the activities of the section itself (*See:* POWERS), there is one other provision in the Fisheries Acts, section 5 of the FA 1980, which gives the Minister power to make orders amending or revoking orders made by him under the Act.

Section 5 of the FA 1980:

"(1) Subject to sections 10(1)(b) and 54(6) of this Act and to subsection (5) of this section, the Minister may by order amend or revoke an order made under section

8(3)(b), 10, 11, 15, 24(6), 54, 55, 56 or 57 of this Act, this subsection or section 81(3) or 159(6) of the Principal Act (inserted by sections 68 and 69, respectively, of this Act).

(2) (a) Subject to paragraph (b) of this subsection, the Minister may –

(i) by order amend an order made under section 37, 38, 39 or 42 of this Act,

(ii) by order amend an order made under sub paragraph (i) of this paragraph.

(b) In case the Minister proposes to amend an order under sections 37, 38 or 39 of this Act or this subsection, the following provisions shall apply:

(i) the Minister shall as soon as may be give notice in writing of his intention to amend the order to the (*qv*) Arbitrator who shall cause to be published a notice of the Minister's said intention in such newspapers and in such manner as the Arbitrator shall determine,

(ii) the Minister shall give notice in writing of his said intention to any person by whom an appeal relating to the order proposed to be amended was brought under this Act, or, in case the order is an order under sub paragraph (ii) of paragraph (a) of this subsection, to any person by whom an appeal relating either to the original order under section 37, 38 or 39 of this Act or to any order under the said paragraph (a) which relates to such original order was so brought, or, if in either case any such person is deceased, to his personal representative,

(iii) the Minister shall not make the order unless a draft thereof has been submitted to and approved of under this paragraph by the Arbitrator,

(iv) the Arbitrator shall not determine an application under this paragraph by the Minister before the expiration of the period of thirty days beginning on the day on which the relevant notice is published pursuant to this subparagraph, or in case such publication is made on different days the day of the first such publication,

(v) any one or more of the following may within such period of thirty days, or such longer period as the Arbitrator may determine, serve on the Minister a notice of his intention to make an application to the Arbitrator in relation to the proposed order, namely:

(I) any person by whom such an appeal was so brought, or, in case such person is deceased, his personal representative, or

(II) the person who, immediately before the making of the order proposed to be amended, was the owner of the fishery or land acquired by that order or the successor in title of such person, or, if any right has been acquired by such order, the person who immediately prior to the making of the said order was entitled to the enjoyment of such right or the successor in title of such person, or, if such order was made under section 39 of the Act, the owner of the relevant servient tenement,

(vi) in case a notice is served on the Minister pursuant to this paragraph the Arbitrator shall, before deciding whether or not to approve of the proposed order, give the person by whom the notice was served an opportunity of being heard (either in person or through counsel or a solicitor), and

(vii) the Arbitrator may in determining the matter approve of the draft of the order in the form proposed by the Minister, approve of such draft subject to such amendments as the Arbitrator shall specify or refuse to give his approval.

(3) (a) The (*qv*) Commissioners may by order under their seal amend an order made by them under section 40 of this Act.

(b) The Irish Land Commission may by order under their seal amend an order made by them under section 41 of the Act.

See: LAY COMMISSIONERS

(4) If in relation to an application under sub section (2)(b) of this section the Arbitrator is satisfied that after diligent inquiry a person to whom notice is

required by subsection (2)(b)(ii) of this section to be given by the Minister can not be found or ascertained, the Arbitrator may determine the application, notwithstanding the fact that such person cannot be found or ascertained.

(5) Subsection (7) of section 68 of the Principal Act (inserted by section 3 of the Fisheries (Amendment) Act 1976) shall apply as regards an order under this section by which it is proposed to amend an order made under section 81(3) or 159(6) of the Principal Act (inserted by sections 68 and 69, respectively, of this Act), as it applies as regards an order made under section 68 of the Principal Act."

"The Principal Act" is the F(C)A 1959.

Section 5(1) is amended by section 4 of the F(A)A 1999 which substitutes "section 55A, 55B, 55C and 55D" for "54, 55".
See: SALMON LEVY.

Section 109 of the F(C)A 1959 contains an important specific power to revoke an order made by the Minister under section 109 F(C)A 1959 authorising the operation of an eel fishing weir without a free gap. The revocation is made under section 109(2). *See:* EELS, EEL FISHERY AUTHORISATION.

Section 9 of the F(A)A 1995 confers rights on the Minister to make or revoke orders under that Act. *See:* BOARD.

Section 62 of the F(A)A 1997 subsection (1) gives the Minister power to issue directives as to policy in relation to (*qv*)aquaculture and subsection (4) gives him power to amend or revoke a directive. *See:* POLICY, F(C)A 1959.

LG(WP)A 1977

There is no provision for the making of orders.

Section 40 of the APA 1987 provides for the making of (*qv*) special control area orders. *See:* SPECIAL CONTROL AREA ORDERS.

EPAA 1992

Section 7 of the EPAA 1992 provides:

"(1) The Minister may, by order, revoke or amend any order made by him under this Act, other than an order under section 2, 19(2) or 32(1).

(2) The Minister may, by order, after consultation with the (*qv*) Agency, revoke or amend the First Schedule or the Second Schedule.

(3) Where it is proposed to make an order under subsection (2) or under section 21(6)(a), 100, 101 or 102 a draft of the order shall be laid before each House of the Oireachtas and the order shall not be made until a resolution approving of the draft has been passed by each such House.

(4) Every order made under this Act, other than an order made under subsection (2) or (3), shall be laid before each House of the Oireachtas as soon as may be after it is made."

WMA 1996

Section 7(3) and (4) of the WMA 1996 require that an order under section 8 or section 7(5) amending or revoking such an order shall not be made until a resolution approving of a draft laid before both houses of the Oireachtais has been passed by each such house.

Section 7 of the WMA 1996 provides:

"(5) (a) The Minister may by order amend or revoke an order made by him under this Act (including an order under this paragraph) and by direction amend or revoke a direction given by him or her under this Act (including a direction under this paragraph).

(b) The Agency may by direction amend or revoke a direction given by it under this Act (including a direction under this paragraph).

(c) An order or direction under this subsection shall be made or given in the like manner and its making or giving shall be subject to the like (if any) consents and conditions as the order or direction that it is amending or revoking.

(6) If in any respect any difficulty arises in bringing any provision of this Act into operation or in relation to the operation of any such provision, the Minister may be regulations do anything which appears to him or her to be necessary or expedient for removing that difficulty, for bringing that provision into operation, or for securing or facilitating its operation, and any such regulations may modify any provision of this or any other enactment so far as

may be necessary or expedient for the purposes aforesaid but no regulations may be made under this subsection in relation to a provision of this Act after the expiration of 2 years from the commencement of that provision."

ORDERS IN RELATION TO THIRD AND FOURTH SCHEDULES TO WMA 1996

Section 8 of the WMA 1996 provides that the Minister may make an order amending the Third Schedule or the Fourth Schedule by adding or deleting anything from either of the said Schedules. *See:* SCHEDULES.

WLA 1976

Section 8 of the WLA 1976 provides in relation to orders:

"(2) Subject to subsection (3) of this section and to sections 14(5), 15(5), 15(6), 16(4), 17(3) and 17(13) of this Act, the Minister may by order revoke or amend an order (other than a purchase order within the meaning of section 55 of this Act) made by him under this Act (including an order made under this subsection).

(3) Where this Act requires the Minister, before making an order or regulation under this Act, to consult any other Minister of State, the (*qv*) Commissioners, a (*qv*) planning authority or any other body, the order or regulation shall be revoked or amended by the Minister only after a like consultation.

(4) Every regulation and every order made under this Act by the Minister, other than an order under section 1(2) or a purchase order within the meaning of section 55 of this Act, shall be laid before each House of the Oireachtas as soon as may be after it is made and, if a resolution annulling the regulation or order is passed by either such House within the next twenty-one days on which that House has sat after the regulation or order is laid before it, the regulation or order shall be annulled accordingly but without prejudice to the validity of anything previously done thereunder."

ORDINARY FISHING LICENCE
(F(C)A 1959, s.3(1))

"Means a fishing licence granted under Chapter 1 of Part VI."

An ordinary fishing licence is one issued in respect of a (*qv*) fishing engine appearing in the fourth Schedule to the F(C)A 1959 which because of its appearance there becomes a (*qv*) scheduled engine. *See:* (1) DUTIES ON ORDINARY FISHING LICENCES; (2) SCHEDULES HERETO, F(C)A 1959 SCHEDULE.

ORDINARY LICENCE DUTY
(F(C)A 1959, s.3(1))

"Means the duty payable under Chapter 1 of Part VI for an ordinary fishing licence."

See: DUTIES ON ORDINARY FISHING LICENCES.

ORNITHOLOGY
(WLA 1976)

In Article 3(a) of the European Communities (Wildlife Act, 1976) (Amendment) Regulations, 1985 (S.I. No. 397 of 1985).

"Means any study of wild birds for the purposes of research or teaching which leads to a better understanding of the biology, ecology and conservation requirements of wild birds."

OWNER
(F(C)A 1959, s.3(1))

"Means any person who is in actual possession or use and enjoyment of any land or fishery (as the case may be)"

(WLA 1976, s.2(1));

"in relation to land means –
(a) where the land is vested under the Land Purchase Acts in the Irish Land Commission, but not in the tenant-purchaser or purchaser thereof, the person who is for the time being the tenant-purchaser or the purchaser, as the case may be, of such land, and
(b) in any other case, the owner of the lowest estate in the land constituting an estate under the Land Purchase Acts."

OYSTER FISHING LICENCE
(F(C)A 1959, s.3(1))

"Means a fishing licence granted under Chapter VI of Part XIV."

OYSTERS
(F(C)A 1959)

An oyster is a bivalve mollusc of the families Ostreidae and Aviculidae and the "ostrea edulus (or edulis)" is the oyster native to Ireland. This oyster was commonly called the "flat" oyster to distinguish it from "crassostrea angulata" and "crassostrea virginica" imported to Ireland for farming from France and America since 1974 which were called "cupped" oysters.

Oyster beds in Ireland have been held by individuals under Charter and by grant and prescription since the 18th century and these private beds received statutory recognition and protection since the Fisheries (Ireland) Act 1842.

This Act was repealed by section 5 of the F(C)A 1959, by reference to the First Schedule, and the 1959 Act set aside an entire part – Part XIV – exclusively for the oyster.

POSITION BETWEEN 1959 AND 1980 AFTER THE F(C)A 1959

The following provisions relating to the farming, propagation and storing of oysters were in place.

OYSTER BED LICENCES

Chapter II (of Part XIV) sections 245 to 255 of the F(C)A 1959.

OYSTER FISHERY ORDERS

Chapter III (of Part XIV) sections 256 to 270 of the F(C)A 1959.

SAVING FOR ACTS DONE FOR ARTIFICIAL PROPAGATION

Section 14 of the F(C)A 1959 amended by section 4 F(A)A 1962. This applies to any fish.

A FISH CULTURE LICENCE

Section 15 of the F(C)A 1959 and section 15A of that Act (inserted by Article 18 of the European Communities (Environment Impact Assessment) Regulations 1989 (S.I. No. 349 of 1989) and the Fisheries (Environmental Impact Assessment) Regulations 1990 (S.I. No. 40 of 1990)). These sections applied to fish of a kind specified in the licence.

POSITION BETWEEN 1980 AND 1997

AQUACULTURE LICENCES UNDER FA 1980

The FA 1980 established by section 54 of the first "aquaculture" licence although the term was not defined in that Act. *See:* (1) AQUACULTURE (2) AQUACULTURE LICENCE.

Section 54(1) of the FA 1980 made it unlawful to engage in aquaculture save under and in accordance with a fish culture licence, a licence granted under section 54 or an oyster fishery order. Section 54(10)*(h)* prohibited the Minister from granting new oyster bed licences or making new oyster fishery orders.

AQUACULTURE LICENCES UNDER F(A)A 1997

Section 14 of the F(A)A 1997 established new types of *(qv)* aquaculture licences.

Section 4(1) of the F(A)A 1997 repealed sections 54 and section 54A of the FA 1980 thereby dismantling the whole structure for granting aquaculture licences under that Act which had in any event ceased to function for some time.

Section 54A was inserted by Regulation 18 of the European Communities (Environmental Impact Assessment) Regulations 1989 (S.I. No. 349 of 1989). Section 4(2) revoked orders made under section 54 of the FA 1980. Section 4(3) provides that such revocation did not affect the validity of any aquaculture licence issued under section 54 of the 1980 Act.

Sections 15 and 15A of the F(C)A 1959 were repealed by section 5(1), (2) of the F(A)A 1997 (with effect as from June 30, 1998).

Section 247 (inquiries into oyster bed licences) and sections 256–260 (oyster fishery orders) of the F(C)A 1959 were repealed by section 5(4), (5) of the F(A)A 1997.

The combined effect of sections 4(1) and 5(2) of the F(A)A 1997 was to remove the power of the Minister to make oyster fishery orders under sections 256–260 of the 1959 Act or to grant fish culture licences under section 15 of the 1959 Act or aquaculture licences under section 54 of the 1980 Act.

Sections 4(1) and 5(2) were brought into operation on March 26, 1998 by the Fisheries (Amendment) Act 1997 (Commencement) Order 1998 (S.I. No. 46 of 1998).

PRESERVATION OF EXISTING ORDERS AND LICENCES BY F(A)A 1997

Existing orders and licences granted prior to the coming into force of certain provisions of the F(A)A 1997 were preserved together with all applications for such licences pending on that date.

Section 74 of the F(A)A 1997 provides that such applications will be deemed to have been applications for aquaculture licences under that Act. Section 74(2)–(4) concern the application of the 1997 Act to such applications and dispense with the necessity of public notification or making of further submissions if the Minister is satisfied that sufficient information has been provided.

Section 75(1) deems existing fish culture licences issued under section 15 of the F(C)A 1959 and aquaculture licences issued under section 54 of the FA 1980 to be aquaculture licences granted under the 1997 Act. Section 75(2) ensures that the repeals of section 15 of the 1959 Act and section 54 of the 1980 Act do not affect the duration of licences issued thereunder.

Sections 74 and 75 were brought into operation on June 30, 1998 by the Fisheries (Amendment) Act 1997 (Commencement) Order 1998 (S.I. No. 205 of 1998).

Despite extensive provisions contained in the F(A)A 1997, the position regarding applications for, and licences issued, regarding foreshore licences under section 19 of the Foreshore Act 1933, fish culture licences under section 15 of the F(C)A 1959 and aquaculture licences under section 54 of the FA 1980 remained unclear in relation to such applications made or licences granted prior to June 30, 1998.

This uncertainty was resolved by sections 2 and 3 of the Fisheries and Foreshore (Amendment) Act 1998.

Section 2 of the Fisheries and Foreshore (Amendment) Act 1998:

"(1) Where before the commencement of section 74 of the Act of 1997 an application was made for a fish culture licence under section 15 of the Principal Act such application shall –
(a) be deemed always to have been capable of being so made under the said section 15 notwithstanding the enactment of section 54 of the Act of 1980, and
(b) be determined in accordance with the said section 74.

(2) Where pursuant to section 19 of the Act of 1933 the Minister has caused notice of an application for a licence for the purposes of aquaculture to be published in accordance with the said section 19, then such notice shall be deemed to be a public notice for the purposes of subsection (3) of section 74 of the Fisheries (Amendment) Act, 1997."

Section 3 of the Fisheries and Foreshore (Amendment) Act, 1998:

"(1) Subject to subsection (2) of this section, where before the commencement of section 75 of the Act of 1997 there were purported to be granted –
(a) a foreshore licence for aquaculture purposes under the Act of 1933, or
(b) a fish culture licence under section 15 of the Principal Act,
then such purported grant of the licence concerned shall be deemed to have been duly made and, accordingly, shall be deemed by virtue of the said section 75 to be an aquaculture licence granted under the Act of 1997.

(2) Where a foreshore licence is deemed to be an aquaculture licence under subsection (1) of this section then the following shall apply:
(a) the Minister shall, as soon as practicable, issue a draft aquaculture licence to the licensee concerned and shall give by post to the licensee not less than 28 days notice in writing stating that the Minister proposes to grant the licence subject to such terms and conditions as are contained in the draft licence;
(b) the Minister shall consider any representations in relation to the draft licence made to the Minister by the licensee before the expiration of the notice;
(c) the Minister shall notify the licensee in writing of his or her decision in respect of the draft licence and shall publish notice of the decision –
(i) as soon as practicable after making the decision in a newspaper circulating in the vicinity of the aquaculture, and
(ii) in addition, in the Irish Oifigiúil if an environmental impact statement was required;
(d) sections 14 and Chapter II of the Act of 1997 shall apply to the decision of the Minister in respect of the draft licence as if it was a determination or a decision in respect of an application for an aquaculture licence."

Section 14 of F(A)A 1997 deals with the grant of licences and Part II with what is called in the Chapter heading "Regulation of Aquaculture and Related Matters" but which really means regulation by licence.

"(3) Where a licence is deemed to be an

aquaculture licence under –
(a) subsection (1) of this section, or
(b) section 75 of the Act of 1997,
then the licences shall be liable for such fees as are prescribed by the Minister under the Act of 1997 including fees payable –
(i) on each anniversary of the granting of the licence while the licence is in force,
(ii) in respect of an application for the renewal of the licence, and
(iii) in respect of an application under section 70 of the Act of 1997 for a review of the licence.

(4) Notwithstanding subsection (1) of this section, in the case of a foreshore licence which is deemed to be an aquaculture licence under the said subsection (1), the provisions of the Foreshore Acts, 1933 and 1992, shall apply to such foreshore licence.

(5) Where a licence is deemed under subsection (1) of this section to be an aquaculture licence and such deeming would, but for this subsection, conflict with a constitutional right of any person, then the licence concerned shall be subject to such limitation as is necessary to secure that it does not so conflict but shall otherwise of full force and effect."

SURVIVING LEGISLATION CONCERNING OYSTER BEDS AND AQUACULTURE LICENCES

At present, the following statutory provisions relating to oyster bed licences and aquaculture licences remain in force.

OYSTER BED LICENCE –

Part II (Sections 245-255) of the F(C)A 1959

SAVING OF ACTS DONE FOR ARTIFICIAL PROPAGATION –
section 14 of the F(C)A 1959

AQUACULTURE LICENCES –
section 14 of the F(A)A 1997

A number of old oyster fishery licences and orders issued under Part XIV of the F(C)A 1959 have not yet been determined. Accordingly, sections 264–269 of the 1959 Act remain in effect. Section 17 of the F(A)A 1997 applies sections 263 and 264 of the F(C)A 1959 to licences issued under the 1997 Act as they apply to an oyster fishery licence granted under an oyster fishery order.

OYSTER BED LICENCE

Section 245 of the F(C)A 1959 –

"(1) The Minister may, subject to section 11 and to the provisions of this Chapter –
(a) grant to the owner of any (*qv*) several fishery or the owner of the bed and soil of any estuary, a licence to form or plant an oyster bed within the limits of such several fishery or over such bed and soil above or below the lowest water mark of spring tides,
(b) grant to the owner or occupier of any land bordering on the sea or any estuary or, with the consent of such occupier, to any person, a licence to form or plant an oyster bed on the shore adjacent to such land above or below the lowest water mark of spring tides,
(c) grant to any person a licence to form or plant an oyster bed below the lowest water mark of spring tides.

(2) No oyster bed licence shall be granted to lay or plant an oyster bed –
(a) in any place where the Minister is of opinion that the public exercise and enjoy bona fide a substantially profitable fishing for oysters, or
(b) within the limits of any oyster bed or oyster fishery the property of any private person, or
(c) within the limits of any several fishery without the consent in writing of the owner of such fishery.

(3) Where an oyster bed licence is granted to any occupier of land bordering on the sea or any estuary or to any person with the consent of such occupier, such licence shall remain in force only during the continuance in occupation of the person who was in occupation at the time of granting such licence.

(4) Where a licence is granted to any person with the consent of any owner, such licence shall remain in force only for such period as shall be named in such consent.
(5) An oyster bed licence shall not, except for the purpose of forming or planting oyster beds or layings, affect any rights

in or over the shore or bed of the sea."

Section 70(1), (2) of the FA 1980:

"(1) The placing in or on, or in or on the water above, an oyster bed of any device or other thing which is used, or intended for use, in the cultivation of oysters shall, for the purposes of section 245 of the Principal Act, be regarded as planting an oyster bed in a manner described in that section, and any licence under that section, whether granted before or after the passing of this Act, shall be construed and have effect in accordance with the foregoing.

(2) Subsection (1) of this section shall not be construed as affecting the power conferred on the Minister for Tourism and Transport by section 10 of the Foreshore Act, 1933."

Section 10 of the Foreshore Act 1933 which deals with the consent or refusal of the Minister to the erection of permanent structures on the foreshore was substantially amended by Article 13(b) of the European Communities (Environmental Impact Assessment) Regulations, 1989 (S.I. No. 349 of 1989).
*See:*FORESHORE.

Section 14 of F(A)A 1997 Part II deals with the grant of licences and what the Chapter calls "Regulation of Aquaculture and Related Matters" which really means regulation by licence.

FORM OF OYSTER BED LICENCE

Section 246 of the F(C)A 1959 provides that every licence shall, by reference to a map or otherwise as to the Minister seems best, define the position and limits of the oyster bed to which it relates and may be made subject to such conditions and limitations and subject to the provisions of subsections (3) and (4) of section 245 (above), and may be perpetual or terminable as to the Minister shall seem proper.

INQUIRY

Section 247 which provided for the holding of a public inquiry on the application of a person of a licence was repealed by section 5(4) of the F(A)A 1997.
NOTICES OF GRANTING

Section 248 of the F(C)A 1959 provides for the publication of notice of grant in a local paper and lodgment of a true copy with the county registrar of the county where the licence is to operate and a copy certified by the county registrar shall be evidence of the licence.

EFFECT OF LICENCE

Section 249 of the F(C)A 1959:

"Every oyster bed (1959 Act) licence, if unappealed from under section 11 or if confirmed on such appeal, shall be binding on the State and on all persons whatsoever and shall operate to vest in the licensee, his heirs, executors, administrators and assigns, such rights and privileges as shall be thereby given, according to the tenor thereof, free from all prior or other rights, titles, estates or interests whatsoever."

Note: An oyster bed licence in this section is called "an oyster bed (1959) Act licence" to distinguish it from older licences granted under the 1845 Act, the 1850 Act, the 1866 Act and the 1869 Act: see section 244 of the F(C)A 1959.

DETERMINATION OF LICENCE

Section 250(1) of the F(C)A 1959 provides that the licence is determinable by certificate of the Minister that he is not satisfied that the licensee is properly cultivating the oyster ground within the limits of such licence and on the certificate being made the rights conferred by the licence absolutely determine.

Comparison: with the wording for the determination of an oyster fishery order under section 266 where the test is the failure to maintain the oyster fishery granted. The use of the phrase "oyster ground" in section 250 is confusing as the phrase has no reference and does not appear elsewhere in the Fisheries Acts.

REVOCATION OF LICENCE

Section 251(1) of the F(C)A 1959 provides that the Minister may by order revoke an oyster fishery licence where it appears to him that the licensee or his assigns has not within the period of three years from the date of the licence taken steps proper in the opinion of the Minister to form the oyster bed mentioned in the licence.

Subsection (2) provides that before he makes the revocation order the Minister must cause notice in writing of his intention to make such an order to be served on the person for the time being entitled to such licence, or if that person cannot be found by publishing the notice three times in a newspaper circulating in the district in which the licence is situate and no such order can be made until one month after the service of the notice or the date of the last advertisement.

ALTERATION OF LICENCE TO GIVE EFFECT TO AGREEMENT

Section 252 of the F(C)A 1959, as amended by section 5(5) of the F(A)A 1997, provides:

"The Minister may alter any oyster bed (1845 Act) licence or oyster bed (1850 Act) licence or oyster bed (1959 Act) licence so as to give effect to any agreement or undertaking which may have been given or entered into by or on behalf of such licensee with any person subsequent to the date of such licence."

PENALTY FOR INJURING LICENSED OYSTER BEDS

Section 253 of the F(C)A 1959, as amended by section 70(3) of the FA 1980, provides:

"If any person (other than the licensee or his assigns, his agents, servants and workmen) knowingly does, within the limits of a licensed oyster bed, any of the following things –

(a) uses any implement of fishing, except a line and hook or net adapted solely for catching free swimming fish and so used as not to disturb or injure in any manner any oyster bed or oysters or the oyster fishery,
(b) dredges for any ballast or other substance except under lawful authority for improving navigation,
(c) deposits any ballast, rubbish or other substance,
(d) places any implement, apparatus or thing prejudicial or likely to be prejudicial to any oyster bed or oysters or brood or spawn thereof, or to the oyster fishery, except for a lawful purpose of navigation or anchorage,
(e) disturbs or injures in any manner, except as mentioned in paragraph (d) of this section, any oyster bed or oysters or brood or spawn thereof or the oyster fishery,
(f) interferes with or takes away any of the oysters from such bed without the consent of the licensee or owner or occupier of such bed,
[(g) without such consent removes, damages or otherwise interferes with any device or thing which is placed in or on, or in or on the water above, such bed and is used for the cultivation of oysters.]

the following provisions shall have effect;-

Offences

(1) such person shall be guilty of an offence under this section and shall be liable on summary conviction thereof –
    (i) in the case of the first offence, to a fine not exceeding two pounds,
    (ii) in the case of a second offence, to a fine not exceeding five pounds,
    (iii) in the case of a third or any subsequent offence, to a fine not exceeding ten pounds;
(2) such person, whether or not he has been prosecuted or convicted of such offence, shall be liable to make full compensation to the licensee for all damage sustained by the licensee by reason of such person's unlawful act, and such compensation shall be recoverable in any court of competent jurisdiction."

(Note that the maximum penalty prescribed under this section has been increased. *See:* FINES AND IMPRISONMENT (IMPOSITION OF)).

EFFECT ON 1845 ACT AND 1850 ACT LICENCES

Section 254 of the F(C)A 1959

"Every oyster bed (1845 Act) licence or oyster bed (1850) Act licence in force at the date of the passing of this Act shall be deemed to have been effectual to vest in the licensee, his heirs and assigns, the exclusive right of laying and planting oysters and fishing for oysters in the oyster bed or laying by such licence authorised to be formed, according to the tenor and effect of such licence free from all prior or other rights, titles, estates or interests whatsoever."

TRESPASS ON LICENSED OYSTER BED

Offence

Section 255 of the F(C)A 1959 provides that if any person wilfully trespasses on any licensed oyster bed or oyster layings (the licence in respect whereof was granted before the 7th day of August 1884) such person shall be guilty of an offence under this section.

(Note that the maximum penalty prescribed under this section has been increased. *See:* FINES AND IMPRISONMENT (IMPOSITION

OF)).

OYSTERS (MINIMUM SIZE) BYE-LAW NO. 628 OF 1982

The main offence prosecuted nationally in relation to oysters is for under-sized oysters under this bye-law which came into operation on the October 22, 1982.

The problem with the local bye-laws, which had existed up to that time and still do to a limited extent and which are set out in the schedule to this bye-law, was that it had been an essential proof when prosecuting under the bye-law to prove that the oysters came from a specific oyster bed in the specific locality to which the bye-law applied and this was often difficult and sometimes impossible to prove as when the oysters, for example, were found in the back of a lorry on the way to Dublin.

Accordingly, the 1982 bye-law provided:

"2. Any person engaged in fishing for or taking oysters shall immediately throw back into the sea any oyster which measures less than 76 millimetres at its greatest dimension.

Offence

3. A person shall not sell, expose for sale, give, transfer, purchase, receive, carry or have in his custody or possession any oyster which measures less than 76 millimetres at its greatest dimension.

4. This bye-law shall not apply to oyster cultivation operations which are carried on in accordance with an aquaculture licence, an oyster bed licence or an oyster fishery order granted by the Minister for Fisheries and Forestry.

5. The Bye-laws specified in the Schedule to this bye-law are hereby revoked insofar as they –
   (a) require oysters of less than a specified minimum size taken or caught by any person to be thrown back into the sea,
   (b) prohibit the sale, exposure for sale, giving, transfer, purchase receiving or having in custody or possession of oysters of less than the minimum size."

The practical test for undersized oysters is to put them through a metal ring, the inside rim of which is certified by the Department of the Marine to measure 76 millimetres in diameter. If they pass freely through the ring they are deemed to be undersized for the purposes of the bye-law. There is no statutory or indeed any authority for this method of proof but it is the standard and accepted method.

OYSTER, PROTECTION OF, SUMMARY

(1) The appropriate (*qv*) close season bye-law,
(2) The Minimum Size Bye-law, 628 of 1982,
(3) Fishing for oysters other than by means of a licensed oyster fishing engine, contrary to section 277 of the F(C)A 1959. (This offence is known as "hand picking" oysters.)
(4) Injuring or trespassing on a licensed oyster bed, sections 253 and 255 of the F(C)A 1959.

P

PACKAGES,
MARKING OF
(F(C)A 1959, s.183)

As amended by section 22 of the F(A)A 1994 *See:* MARKING OF PACKAGES CONTAINING SALMON, TROUT, EELS OR MOLLUSCAN SHELLFISH.

PACKAGING
(WMA 1996, s.5(1))

"Means any material, container or wrapping, used for or in connection with the containment, transport, handling, protection, promotion, marketing or sale of any (*qv*) product or substance, including such packaging as may be prescribed."

"Packaging" in the Waste Management (Packaging) Regulations, 1997 (S.I. No. 242 of 1997) Article 4 constitutes packaging within the meaning of section 5 of the Act which is –

"(a) sales or primary packaging, that is packaging conceived so as to constitute a sales unit to the final user or consumer at the point of purchase, or
(b) grouped or secondary packaging, that is to say packaging conceived so as to constitute at the point of purchase a grouping of a certain number of sales units (whether the latter are sold as such to the final user or consumer or whether the packaging serves only as a means to replenish shelves at the point of sale), and which can be removed from a product without affecting the product's characteristics, or
(c) transport or tertiary packaging, that is packaging conceived so as to facilitate handling and transport of a number of sales units or grouped packagings in order to prevent damage from physical handling and transport (but not including road, rail, ship and air containers)."

The wording of the above is confusing. it is obviously intended that the definition of "packaging" in the regulations should be in addition to and an extension of the definition of the Act. There are two other useful definitions in Article 4 of the Regulations.

"Packaging destined for reuse" in the same Regulations means: "packaging which has been conceived and designed to accomplish within its life cycle a minimum of two trips or rotations, and which is subject to operations by which it is refilled or used for the same purpose for which its was conceived, with or without the support of auxiliary products present on the market enabling the packaging to be refilled."

"Packaging material" means:

"material used in the manufacture of packaging and includes raw materials and processed materials prior to their conversion into packaging."

The 1997 Regulations were amended by the Waste Management (Packaging)(Amendment) Regulations, 1998 (S.I. No. 382 of 1998) which inserted definitions for "European standard", deleted the definitions for "imports, manufactures" and added article 26 and a Third Schedule to those Regulations. The Third Schedule sets out the essential requirements on the composition and the reusable and recoverable, including recyclable, nature of packaging.

See: (1) PRODUCER, MAJOR PRODUCER; (2) PRODUCER RESPONSIBILITY OBLIGATION; (3) WASTE, MEASURES TO REDUCE PRODUCTION AND PROMOTE RECOVERY OF WASTE.

PARKS,
NATIONAL

There are three statutes dealing with parks as follows:

The Phoenix Park Act, 1925,
The Bourn Vincent Memorial Park Act 1932 (Muckross Estate, Co. Kerry) and
An Blascod Mor National Historic Park Act 1989 (The Greater Blasket Island, Co. Kerry). The latter Act has been declared to be unconstitutional in the recent past.

See: COMMISSIONERS, COMMISSIONERS OF PUBLIC WORKS IN IRELAND

PAYMENT OF FINES
(LG(WP)A 1977, s.26)

A court may, on the application of the prosecuting body, direct payment of any fine imposed to that body. *See:* FINES (DISPOSAL OF).

**PENALTIES,
FINES AND IMPRISONMENT**

See: FINES AND IMPRISONMENT (IMPOSITION OF).

PENALTIES (MEANING MISCELLANEOUS OFFENCES) UNDER F(C)A 1959
(F(C)A 1959, Pt. XVII)

(i) **Section 286 of the F(C)A 1959**
Three or more persons by violence, intimidation or menace, who impede or obstruct a person lawfully prosecuting a fishery and every person there and then aiding and abetting them.

(ii) **Section 287 of the F(C)A 1959**
Obstructing a person lawfully fishing. *See:* OBSTRUCT, IMPEDE.

(iii) **Section 288(1) of the F(C)A 1959**
Wilfully or maliciously placing any fishing engine with intent to prevent fish entering nets lawfully set and placed in a lawful manner. On conviction the fishing engine will stand forfeited as a statutory consequence.

(iv) **Section 289 of the F(C)A 1959**
Name painted on fishing boat. *See:* NAMES ON FISHING BOATS.

(v) **Section 290 of the F(C)A 1959**
Discharging ballast in improper place. *See:* DISCHARGING BALLAST.

(vi) **Section 291 of the F(C)A 1959**
Every person who makes or causes to be made or aids or assists in making any signal or warning to any person engaged in fishing unlawfully of the approach of any water keeper, officer of a regional fisheries board or member of the Garda Síochána shall be guilty of an offence.

(Note that the maximum penalties prescribed under sections 286–291 have been increased. *See:* FINES AND IMPRISONMENT (IMPOSITION OF)).

**PERFORMANCE OF
STATUTORY FUNCTIONS
BY LOCAL AUTHORITIES**
(EPAA 1992, s.63)

It is under this section that the Agency can take over and carry out any statutory function of a local authority in relation to environmental protection which the authority has failed to perform or has performed in an unsatisfactory manner. It is not to be confused with the extensive powers the Agency has to extend to it; a whole range of functions under the LG(WP)A 1977 and the APA 1987 under sections 100 and 101 and the Extension of Powers Order 1996 (S.I. No. 126 of 1996). *See:* EXTENSION OF POWERS TO AGENCY.

Section 63 of the EPAA 1992 provides:

"(1) Where the Agency is of opinion that a local authority has failed to perform a statutory function of that authority in relation to environmental protection, or has performed that function in an unsatisfactory manner, the Agency may request a report within a specified period from the authority in relation to the matter and the local authority shall comply with the request.

(2) The Agency, having considered any report of the local authority may, with a view to ensuring the satisfactory performance of the function in question –
(a) issue such advice and recommendations to the local authority as it considers necessary, or
(b) provide, on such terms and conditions as may be agreed, such assistance or support as the Agency considers, in consultation with the local authority, would be helpful.

(3) (a) Where the Agency is of the opinion that the response of the local authority to advice or recommendations issued or assistance or support offered under subsection (2) is inadequate for the purposes of environmental protection it may, without prejudice to any of its powers under this Act or any other enactment, direct the local authority to carry out, cause to be carried out, or arrange for, such action related to the function in question as the Agency considers necessary for the purposes of environmental protection within such period as may be specified.
(b) Where a local authority fails without reasonable cause to comply with a direction under paragraph (a) the Agency shall carry out, cause to be carried out, or arrange for, such action related to the function in question as it considers necessary to ensure compliance with the direction and the costs of such action may be recovered by the Agency from the local authority as a simple contract debt in any court of competent jurisdiction.

(c) The Agency shall not give a direction under paragraph (a) unless the local authority, with due regard to its other statutory functions, has the necessary funds to comply with the direction or those funds can reasonably be made available to it.

(4) Nothing in this section shall be construed as enabling the Agency to exercise any power or control under this section in relation to the making of a decision on an application for a permission under Part IV of the Act of 1963.

(5) In this section "local authority" has the meaning assigned to it by the Local Government Act, 1941."

PERMIT, WMA 1996, (TRANSITIONAL)
(WMA 1996, s.68)

Section 68(1) of the WMA 1996 provides:

"(1) References in any enactment (other than this Act) to a permit under –
(a) the European Communities (Waste) Regulations, 1979,
(b) the European Communities (Toxic and Dangerous Waste) Regulations, 1982 or
(c) the European Communities (Waste Oils) Regulations, 1992,
shall be construed as references to, as appropriate –
(i) such a permit that is for the time being in force by virtue of subsection (6),
(ii) a (*qv*) waste collection permit under Part IV,
(iii) a (*qv*) waste licence under Part V."

Section 68 of the WMA 1996 as amended by the addition of the words in square brackets by Article 5 of the European Communities (Amendment of Waste Management Act, 1996) Regulations 1998 (S.I. No. 166 of 1998) provide:

"(6) (a) A permit issued under the European Communities (Waste) Regulations, 1979, the European Communities (Toxic and Dangerous Waste) Regulations, 1982 or the European Communities (Waste Oils) Regulations, 1992, being a permit to which this subsection applies, shall, notwithstanding the revocation of the said Regulations by this Act, continue in force in accordance with its terms but shall cease to have effect upon, as the case may be –
(i) the grant to the (*qv*) holder of the permit of, as appropriate –
(I) a (*qv*) waste collection permit referred to in paragraph (b), or
(II) a (*qv*) waste licence referred to in the said paragraph, or
(ii) the making of a decision by the Agency or the local authority concerned to refuse to grant to the said holder such a permit or licence.
(b) This subsection applies to an aforesaid permit if –
(i) the holder thereof has applied before the appropriate date referred to in section 39(1) for the grant of a waste licence, or, as the case may be, applied before the date referred to in section 34(1) for a waste collection permit, in respect of the activity to which the first-mentioned permit relates, and
(ii) the said application is made in accordance with the requirements of regulations under this Act [and has not been withdrawn by the applicant.
(c) A permit which is continued in force by virtue of this subsection shall not cease to have effect solely by reason of the expiry of the period in relation to which the permit was granted and paragraph (a) shall be construed accordingly.

(7) A reference in subsection (1) or (6) to a waste licence shall be construed as including a reference to a waste permit or such other authorisation or certificate as may be prescribed under section 39(4).]"

PERMIT, WASTE COLLECTION PERMIT AND WASTE PERMIT
(WMA 1996)

Distinguish between a waste collection permit under section 34 of the WMA 1996 (*See:* HOLDING, COLLECTION AND MOVEMENT OF WASTE, WASTE COLLECTION PERMIT) and a waste permit and certificate of registration under Waste Management (Permit) Regulations, 1998 (S.I. No. 165 of 1998) (*See:* WASTE PERMITS AND CERTIFICATES OF REGISTRATION).

PERSON IN CHARGE
(EPAA 1992, s.3(1))

"Includes the occupier of a premises or a manager, supervisor or operator of an activity."

(WMA 1996, s.5(1))

"Includes, in relation to any premises, the occupier of the premises or a manager, supervisor or operator of an activity relating to the holding, disposal or recovery of waste which is carried on at the premises."

PLACING ON THE MARKET
(GMO Regs. 1994, Art. 3(1))

"Means supplying or making available to third parties, and cognate words and expressions shall be construed accordingly."

See: GENETICALLY MODIFIED ORGANISMS.

PLANNING AUTHORITY
(LG(P&D)A 1963)

"Planning authority" in the LG(P&D)A 1963 and by virtue of section 2(2) means:

"(a) in the case of a County exclusive of any Borough or Urban District there in, the Council of the County,
(b) in the case of a County or other Borough, the Corporation of the Borough, and
(c) in the case of an Urban District, the Council of the District."

PLANNING LG(P&D)A 1963 NOTICE OF DISCONTINUANCE, COMPENSATION, WATER POLLUTION
(LG(P&D)A 1963, ss.37 and 19)

Section 37 of the LG(P&D)A 1963 gives the planning authority power to serve a notice requiring the discontinuance of the unauthorised use of land.

"(1) If the (*qv*) planning authority decide, as respects any use of land, that –
(a) the use should be discontinued, or
(b) any conditions should be imposed on the continuance thereof,
the planning authority may serve a notice, requiring discontinuance of that use or imposing those conditions, on the owner and on the occupier of the land and on any other person who in their opinion will be affected by the notice."

Section 19 of the LG(P&D)A 1990, when dealing with the question of compensation arising out the service of such a notice, provides that no compensation shall be paid under the section in relation to damage arising from the imposition under section 37 of the LG(P&D)A 1963 of conditions on the continuance of the use of land, being conditions imposed in order to avoid or reduce serious water pollution or the danger of such pollution.

PLANNING AND DEVELOPMENT, APPLICATION OF PART IV LICENCE TO SECTION 26 OF LG(P&D)A 1963 OR LEASE UNDER THE MINERAL DEVELOPMENT ACTS
(EPAA 1992, s.98)

"(1) Notwithstanding section 26 of the Act of 1963, or any other provision of the Local Government (Planning and Development) Acts, 1963 to 1991, where a licence or a revised licence under this Part has been granted or is or will be required in relation to an (*qv*) activity, a (*qv*) planning authority or an (*qv*) Bord Pleanála shall not, in respect of any (*qv*) development comprising or for the purposes of the activity –

(a) decide to refuse a permission or an approval under Part IV of the Act of 1963 for the reason that the development would cause (*qv*) environmental pollution, or
(b) decide to grant such permission subject to conditions which are for the purposes of the prevention, limitation, elimination, abatement or reduction of environmental pollution from the activity,

and, accordingly –

(i) a planning authority in dealing with an application for permission or an approval for any such development shall not consider any matters relating to the risk of environmental pollution from the activity;
(ii) An Bord Pleanála shall not consider any appeal made to it against a decision of a planning authority in respect of such an application, or any submissions or observations made to it in relation to any such appeal, so far as the appeal, or the submissions or observations,

as the case may be, relates or relate to the risk of environmental pollution from the activity.

(2) Notwithstanding the provisions of the Mineral Developments Acts, 1940 to 1979, where a licence or a revised licence under this Part has been granted or is or will be required in relation to an activity, a lease granted by the Minister for Energy under the said Acts in respect of the same activity shall not contain conditions which are for the purpose of prevention, limitation, elimination, abatement or reduction of environmental pollution from the activity.

(3) Without prejudice to subsections (1) and (2), where a licence or a revised licence under this Part is granted in relation to an activity and –

(a) a permission under Part IV of the Act of 1963, or

(b) a lease under the Mineral Development Acts 1940 to 1979,

has been granted in respect of the same activity, any conditions attached to that permission or contained in that lease, as the case may be, shall, so far as they are for the purposes of the prevention, limitation, elimination, abatement or reduction of environmental pollution, cease to have effect.

(4) The grant of a permission or lease under any of the Acts referred to in subsections (1) and (2) in relation to any activity shall not prejudice, affect or restrict in any way the application of any provision of this Act to such activity."

PLANNING AND DEVELOPMENT, APPLICATION OF SECTION 56 APA 1987 TO LG(P&D)A 1963
(APA 1987, s.56)

"(1) Where a licence under this Act is granted in relation to (*qv*) industrial plant and a permission under Part IV of the Local Government (Planning and Development) Act, 1963, has been granted in respect of the same plant, any conditions attached to that permission shall, in so far as they relate to air pollution, cease to have effect.

(2) The grant of permission under Part IV of the Local Government (Planning and Development) Act, 1963, in relation to any (*qv*) premises shall not prejudice, affect or restrict in any way the application of any provision of this Act to such premises."

PLANNING AND DEVELOPMENT, APPLICATION OF SECTION 54 WMA 1996 TO LG(P&D)A 1963
(WMA 1996, s.54)

"(1) Where a (*qv*) waste licence is granted under this Act in relation to an (*qv*) activity, and a permission has been granted under Part IV of the Act of 1963 in respect of (*qv*) development comprising or for the purposes of that activity, any conditions attached to that permission shall, in so far as they are for the purposes of the prevention, limitation, elimination, abatement or reduction of (*qv*) environmental pollution, cease to have effect.

(2) The grant of permission under Part IV of the 1963 Act in relation to any development comprising or for the purposes of waste (*qv*) recovery or (*qv*) disposal (*qv*) activity shall not prejudice, affect or restrict in any way the application of any provision of this Act to such an activity.

(3) Notwithstanding section 26 of the Act of 1963 or any other provision of the Local Government (Planning and Development) Acts, 1963 to 1993, where a waste licence has been granted or is or will be required in relation to an activity, a planning authority or an Bord Pleanála shall not, in respect of any development comprising or for the purposes of the activity –

(a) decide to refuse a permission or an approval under Part IV of the Act of 1963 for the reason that the development would cause environmental pollution, or

(b) decide to grant such permission subject to conditions which are for the purposes of prevention, limitation, elimination, abatement or reduction of environmental pollution from the activity,

and accordingly –

(i) a planning authority in dealing with an application for a permission or an approval for any such development shall not consider any matters relating to the risk of environmental pollution from the activity;

(ii) An (*qv*) Bord Pleanála shall not

consider any appeal made to it against a decision of a planning authority in respect of such an application, or any submissions or observations made to it in relation to any such appeal, so far as the appeal, or the submissions or observations, as the case may be, relates or relate to the risk of environmental pollution from the activity.

(4) Where a permission under Part IV of the Act of 1963 has been granted or an application has been made for such permission in relation to any development comprising or for the purposes of waste recovery or disposal activity, the carrying on of which requires a waste licence, the Agency –
 (a) shall consult with the planning authority in whose functional area the activity is or will be carried on in relation to any development which –
  (i) is necessary to give effect to any conditions to be attached to a waste licence in respect of the activity, and
  (ii) the Agency considers is not the subject of a permission or an application for a permission under Part IV of the Act of 1963, and
 (b) may attach to the waste licence such conditions related to the development aforesaid as may be specified by the said planning authority for the purposes of the proper planning and development of its functional area, or more stringent conditions as the Agency may consider necessary for the prevention, limitation, elimination, abatement or reduction of environmental pollution from the activity.

(5) Works consisting of or incidental to the carrying out of development referred to in subsection (4)(a) and the provision of waste collection receptacles in accordance with regulations under section 29(4)(o) shall each be exempted development within the meaning, and for the purposes of, the Local Government (Planning and Development) Acts, 1963 to 1993, and a condition attached to a permission granted under Part IV of the Act of 1963 shall not prejudice, affect or restrict in any way the provision of waste collection receptacles as aforesaid.

(6) References in sections 25, 26 and 41 of the Act of 1963 to an activity in relation to which a licence under Part IV of the EPAA 1992 is required shall be construed as including references to an activity in relation to which a waste licence under this Act is required.

(7) (a) Where a development is proposed to be carried out by or on behalf of a local authority in its functional area, being development which comprises or is for the purposes of a waste recovery or disposal activity requiring the grant by the Agency to the local authority of a waste licence, the Minister may by order grant an exemption (if he or she is satisfied that exceptional circumstances warrant the granting of such an exemption) in respect of such development from a requirement of regulations under section 45 to furnish an environmental impact statement.
 (b) The Minister in making an order under this subsection shall comply with the provisions of Article 2(3) of Council Directive 85/337/EEC of 27 June 1985 (O.J. No. L 175/40, July 5 1985).
 (c) Without prejudice to paragraph (b), the Minister shall, where he or she considers it necessary to do so for the purpose of paragraph 3(a) of Article 2 of the aforesaid Directive, specify in an order under this subsection requirements to be complied with by the local authority concerned or, as the case may be, the person who proposes to carry out the development on its behalf in relation to the matters specified in the said paragraph.
 (d) The Minister shall cause an order under this section to be published in the Iris Oifigiúil.
 (e) The reference in this subsection to a local authority's functional area is a reference to its functional area as a planning authority.

(8) The Minister may make regulations specifying the time within which an application for a waste licence shall be made relative to an application for a permission under Part IV of the Act of 1963."

PLANNING AND DEVELOPMENT, AMENDMENT OF THE LG(P&D)A 1963 TO GIVE EFFECT TO BIRDS DIRECTIVE AND NH 97 REGULATIONS (PART IV)
(NH 97)

Part IV of the NH 97 Regulations (S.I. No. 94 of 1997) contains a series of amendments of substance to the LG(P&D)A which give effect to certain basic changes in the approach to planning introduced by the Regulations. These mainly consist of the introduction into the Act of key words and phrases which occur in the Regulations which are part of the central theme of the Regulations and the (*qv*) Habitats Directive from which they emanate, and the addition of a new development objective in the development plan and a new exempted development class in Part IV of the Third Schedule to the Act.

Regulation 26 of the NH 97 Regulations provide:

"The Local Government (Planning and Development) Act, 1963 is hereby amended –

(a) In section 2 –
   (i) by the insertion of the following after the definition of 'appointed day':
   'the 'Birds Directive' means Council Directive No.74/409/EEC of 2 April 1979 on the conservation of wild birds'
   (ii) by the insertion of the following after the definition of 'environmental impact statement' (inserted by the European Communities (Environmental Impact Assessment) Regulations 1989 (S.I. No. 349 of 1989)):

'European site' means –
(a) a special area of conservation;
(b) a site of Community importance which has been placed on the list referred to in the third sub paragraph of Article 4(2) of the Habitats Directive;
(c) an area classified pursuant to paragraph (1) or (2) of Article 4 of the Birds Directive'; and
   (iii) by the insertion of the following after the interpretation given to 'functions':
   'the Habitats Directive' means Council Directive No. 92/43/EEC of 21 May, 1992, on the conservation of natural habitats and of wild fauna and flora;",

(b) In subsection (2) of section 19 -

   (i) by the insertion in paragraph (a) of the following after sub paragraph (iv):
   '(v) for the conservation and protection of European sites in the area to which the development plan relates.
   (ii) by the insertion in paragraph (b) of the following after sub-paragraph (iii):
   (iv) for the conservation and protection of European sites in the area to which the development plan relates;
(c) in Part IV of the Third Schedule, by the insertion of the following paragraph after paragraph 8 –
8A. Protection of features of the landscape which are of major importance for wild fauna and flora in accordance with the Habitats Directive."

These amendments are designed to fit into the alphabetically listed sequence of definitions appearing at section 2 of the LG(P&D)A 1963 which is the interpretation section. Their inclusion there attaches very considerable importance to the NH 97 Regulations as it places the words of those Regulations in the very heart of the planning process.

Section 19 is the section which provides that every planning authority must make a plan indicating the development objectives for their area (*See:* DEVELOPMENT PLAN) and subsection (2) of that section (as amended) now provides:

"(2) A development plan shall consist of a written statement and a plan indicating the development objectives for the area in question, including objectives –
   (a) with respect to county boroughs, boroughs, urban districts and schedules towns –
      (i) for the use solely or primarily (as may be indicated in the development plan) of particular areas for particular purposes (whether residential, commercial, industrial, agricultural or otherwise,
      (ii) for securing the greater convenience and safety of road users and pedestrians by the provision of parking places or road improvements or otherwise,
      (iii) for development and renewal of obsolete areas,
      (iv) for preserving, improving and extending amenities,
      [(v) for the conservation and protection of European sites in the area to which the development plan relates,]
   (b) with respect to other areas –
      (i) for development and renewal of obsolete areas,
      (ii) for preserving, improving and extend-

ing amenities,

(iii) for the provision of new water supplies and sewerage services and the extension of existing such supplies and services,

[(iv) for the conservation and protection of European sites in the area to which the development plan relates]."

PLANNING AND DEVELOPMENT AMENDMENT OF LG(P&D)A 1963 BY EPAA 1992 IN RELATION TO NOISE
(EPAA 1992, s.106(3))

See: NOISE.

PLANT
(EPAA 1992, s.3(1))

"Includes any equipment, appliance, apparatus, machinery, works, building or other structure on any land or any part of any land which is used for the purposes of, or incidental to, any activity specified in the First Schedule."
See: SCHEDULES HERETO, EPAA 1992 SCHEDULES.

(WMA 1996, s.5(1))

"Includes any equipment, appliance, apparatus, machinery, vehicle, skip, works, building or other structure used for the purpose of, or the provision of which is incidental to, the holding, disposal or recovery of waste."

POLICY
(F(C)A 1959/EPAA 1992/
WMA 1996)

AQUACULTURE: F(A)A 1997

Section 62 of the F(A)A 1997:

"(1) The Minister may from time to time issue such general directives as to policy in relation to aquaculture as the Minister considers necessary and the (*qv*)licensing authority shall, in performing its functions, have regard to any such directives.

(2) Nothing in this section shall be construed as enabling the Minister to exercise any power or control in relation to a particular case with which the Board or an officer to whom functions have been delegated under section 21(1) is or may be concerned.

(3) Where the Minister gives a directive under subsection (1), the following provisions shall apply:

(a) as soon as practicable after issuing it the Minister shall cause a copy of the directive to be laid before each House of the Oireachtas;

(b) the directive shall be published in Irish Oifigiúil; and

(c) the Minister shall cause a copy of the directive to be sent to the Board and to each officer, if any, to whom a function has been delegated under section 21(1).

(4) The Minister may amend or revoke a directive under this section and subsection (3), with the necessary modifications, shall apply as if the amendment or revocation were a directive under sub section (1)."

APA 1987

Section 52 of the APA 1987 provides for the issue by the Minister of general directions as to policy in relation to the prevention and limitation of (*qv*) air pollution and a local authority and Bord Pleanála shall have regard to such directions when performing their functions under the Act. Unlike the directives in other statutes dealt with under this heading a direction under this section has no legislative force. Copies of the direction are to be transmitted to each local authority and Bord Pleanála and notice of the issue of a direction must be published in Iris Oifigiúil and the notice must specify where a copy may be obtained and the fee (if any) payable.

EPAA 1992

Section 79 of the EPAA 1992:

"(1) The Minister may, whenever he thinks proper, give such general directives in writing to the Agency as to policy in relation to (*qv*) environmental protection.

(2) In performing its functions the Agency shall have regard to any directives given by the Minister under this section.

(3) Nothing in this section shall be construed as enabling the Minister to exercise any power or control in relation to the performance in particular circumstances by the Agency of a function assigned to it by or under this Act.

(4) Where the Minister gives a directive under this section he shall –
(a) as soon as may be cause a copy of the directive to be laid before each House of the Oireachtas,
(b) cause a notice of the issue of the directive to be published in Iris Oifigiúil and at least one daily news paper circulating in the State, and
(c) cause a copy of the directive to be transmitted to the Agency and to each planning authority.

(5) A notice under subsection (4)(b) shall specify where a copy of the directive to which it relates may be obtained and the fee (if any) payable in respect of such copy which shall not exceed the reasonable cost of making the copy."

WMA 1996

Section 60 of the WMA 1996:

"(1) The Minister may, whenever he or she thinks proper, give general directions in writing to the Agency or each local authority as to policy in relation to, as appropriate –
(a) the making or review of the (*qv*) hazardous waste management plan or a (*qv*) waste management plan,
(b) the management of waste (*qv*) recovery or (*qv*) disposal activities carried on otherwise than under a (*qv*) waste licence,
(c) the granting of waste licences,
(d) the performance by the Agency or local authorities of its functions under this Act with respect to (*qv*) movements of waste,
(e) matters related to matters aforesaid."

Subsections (2) to (5) correspond with (2) to (5) in section 79 of the EPAA 1992 above except that a reference to local authorities is added after a reference to the Agency. Whenever there is such a reference in this section and in subsection (2) the matters referred to at subsection (1)(a) of this section are excepted from the subsection.

POLLEN/
POLLAN
(F(C)A 1959, s.175)

"(1) In this section, the expression 'under sized pollen' means pollen of less size than eight inches in length, measured from the nose to the utmost length of the tail.

Offence
(2) If any person wilfully takes, kills, destroys, buys, sells, exposes for sale, sends or has in his custody or possession any undersized pollen, such person shall be guilty of an offence under this section and shall be liable on summary conviction thereof to a fine not exceeding one shilling for each undersized pollen in relation to which the offence is committed.
(3) Each undersized pollen stands forfeited as a statutory consequence of conviction."

This section has been disregarded in that it has passed through both the F(A)A 1962 and the FA 1980 without increase of penalty. The species of fish would appear to be incorrectly spelt and should be "pollan".
See: PROTECTION, TAKING FLORA AND FAUNA IN THE WILD.

The late A. Whilde in *Threatened Mammals, Birds, Amphibians and Fish in Ireland*, (Irish Red Data Book 2: Vertebrates, Belfast: HMSO 1993) devoted an entire chapter to the Pollan whose Irish population, he states, is the only one in Western Europe, is almost unique in being non-migratory, confined to freshwater lakes and so far outside the rest of its world range. It was apparently to be found as far south as Killaloe (Lough Derg) but is now confined to Lough Neagh.

POLLUTANT
(APA 1987, s.7(1))

As amended by section 18 (Third Schedule) of the EPAA 1992,

"Means any substance specified in the First Schedule or any other substance (including a substance which gives rise to odour) or energy which, when emitted into the atmosphere either by itself or in combination with any other substance, may cause air pollution."
See: SCHEDULES HERETO, APA 1987 SCHEDULES.

"THE POLLUTER PAYS" PRINCIPLE
(WMA 1996)

"The polluter pays principle" means the principle set out in Council Recommendation 75/436/Euratom, ECSC, EEC of March 3, 1975 regarding cost allocation and action by public authorities on environmental matters (O.J. L164,

July 25, 1975. p.1). *See:* WASTE MANAGEMENT PLAN, s.22(5)*(d)* of the WMA 1996 (hazardous waste management plan) and s. 26(2)*(d)* of the WMA 1996.

POLLUTING MATTER
(LG(WP)A 1977, s.1(1))

"Includes any poisonous or noxious matter, and any substance (including any explosive, liquid or gas) the entry or discharge of which into any waters is liable to render those or any other waters poisonous or injurious to fish, spawning grounds or the food of any fish, or to injure fish in their value as human food, or to impair the usefulness of the bed and soil of any waters as spawning grounds or their capacity to produce the food of fish or to render such waters harmful or detrimental to public health or to domestic, commercial, industrial, agricultural or recreational use."

Comparison: (*qv*) "deleterious matter" in section 3(1) F(C)A 1959 and (*qv*) "environmental pollution" in section 4(2) of the EPAA 1992.

POWER/POWERS
(F(C)A 1959/LG(WP)A 1977/APA 1987/ EPAA 1992/WMA 1996/WLA 1976/NH 97)

To a large extent the powers conferred by the various Statutes are powers of (*qv*)Enforcement and are dealt with under that heading.

(1) UNDER THE F(C)A 1959

(A) Powers of the Minister
Section 7 of the F(C)A 1959 in special tidal waters. *See:* SPECIAL TIDAL WATERS.

Section 8 of the F(C)A 1959 to hold inquiries into fisheries. *See:* INQUIRIES.

Section 9 of the F(C)A 1959 to make bye-laws. *See:* BYE-LAWS.

Section 14 of the F(C)A 1959 on exemption permit for artificial propagation. *See:* EXEMPTION PERMITS FOR ARTIFICIAL PROPAGATION.
Section 15 of the F(C)A 1959 fish culture licences. *See:* OYSTERS.

Section 16 of the F(C)A 1959 on lease of fisheries for research. *See:* FISHERIES, LEASE FOR RESEARCH.

Section 17 of the F(C)A 1959 on restriction on import of live fish. *See:* FISH, LIVE.

Section 60 of the FA 1980 on power to operate a fishery. *See:* FISHERY, POWER TO OPERATE.

RESTRICTION ON MINISTER'S POWERS

Section 217 of the F(C)A 1959, which was the one section excluded from the sweeping repeal of Part XII of the F(C)A 1959, which dealt with the transfer of certain fisheries to the Minister, by section 6 of the FA 1980, provides that nothing in this Act shall operate to authorise the Minister:

"(a) to construct or erect on tidal lands (within the meaning of the Foreshore Act, 1933 (No. 12 of 1933), any work or structure, other than a *(qv)* fixed engine for the capture of salmon, trout or eels lawfully existing, or for which a certificate granted under section 6 of the Salmon Fishery (Ireland) Act, 1863, existed, in the year 1939, without the consent of the Minister for Industry and Commerce or otherwise than in accordance with the terms of conditions of such consent;

(b) to erect any buildings or structures which may interfere with the amenities of the residence or pleasure grounds of a person who was the owner or occupier of a fishery vested in the Minister under Chapter II of this Part or operate such fishery in such a way as to interfere with such amenities."

(2) UNDER THE LG(WP)A 1977

(A) Powers of all courts in relation to entry to waters.

Section 10 of the LG(WP)A 1977. *See:* PROHIBITION, WATERS UNDER THE LG(WP)A 1977.

(B) High Court's power to prohibit continuance of contravention of sections 3(1) or 4(1)

Section 11 of the LG(WP)A 1977. *See:* PROHIBITION, WATERS UNDER THE LG(WP)A 1977.

(C) Local Authority's power to require measure to be taken to prevent pollution.
Section 12 of the LG(WP)A 1977. *See:* ENFORCEMENT (3)(B).

(D) Local Authority's power to prevent or abate pollution in certain circumstances.

Section 13 of the LG(WP)A 1977. *See:* ENFORCEMENT (4)(B).

(3) UNDER THE APA 1987

(A) Power of Local authority to require measures to be taken to prevent or limit air pollution.

Section 26 of the APA 1987. *See:* ENFORCEMENT (3)(C).

(B) Power of Local Authority to take steps to prevent or limit air pollution.

Section 27 APA 1987. *See:* ENFORCEMENT (4)(C).

(C) Power of High Court in relation to air pollution.

Section 28 APA 1987. *See:* ENFORCEMENT (1)(C).

(4) UNDER THE EPAA 1992

As the Agency has taken over most of the powers of enforcement of local authorities under the LG(WP)A 1977 and the APA 1987, the powers of the local authorities under the LG(WP)A 1977 and the APA 1987 have become their powers. However, they do have powers in their own right under the EPAA 1992 as follows -

(A) Power to require measures to be taken to prevent or limit noise. Section 107 EPAA 1992. *See:* NOISE.

(B) Power of Agency to apply to the High Court for an order to prohibit or restrict a process or action involving a Genetically Modified Organism (GMO). *See:* ENFORCEMENT (1)(C).

(5) UNDER THE WMA 1996

(A) Powers of local authority to require measures to be taken in relation to the holding, recovery and disposal of waste, section 55(1)*(a)*. *See:* ENFORCEMENT (3)(e).

(B) Powers of local authority to take measures without notice to prevent or limit environmental pollution, section 56(1). *See:* ENFORCEMENT (5)(D).

(C) Power of the High Court in relation to the holding, recovery and disposal of waste, section 57. *See:* ENFORCEMENT (1)(D).

(D) Power of "appropriate court" to remedy unauthorised holding, recovery or disposal of waste on the application of any person, section 58. *See:* ENFORCEMENT (1)(D).

(6) UNDER THE WLA 1976

The Minister has extensive powers under the Act but none that would constitute powers of enforcement as are contemplated under other environmental statutes dealing with the prohibition and control of various kind of pollution.

(7) UNDER THE NH 97

Power of court to prohibit operation or activity under Regulation 17, which deals with the prohibition of operations and activities on certain lands. *See:* PROHIBITION, WORKS, OPERATIONS OR ACTIVITIES.

PREMISES
(LG(WP)A 1977, s.1(1))

"Includes land, whether or not there are structures on the land."

(APA 1987, s.7(1))

"Includes any messuage, building, structure or land (whether or not there are structures on the land or whether or not the land is covered with water) or any hereditament of any tenure, together with any out-buildings and curtilage."

(EPAA 1992, s.3(1))

Is the same definition as that in the APA 1987 above except the word "vessel" appears between the words "building" and "structure".

(WMA 1996, s. 5(1))

Is the same definition as that in EPAA 1992 with the addition of the words "and any land or vehicles on such land" between the) and the words "or any hereditaments ...".

PRESCRIBED
(EPAA 1992, s. 3(1))

Means prescribed by regulations made by the Minister.

PRIORITY NATURAL HABITAT TYPES
(NH 97, Reg. 2(1))

"Means natural habitat types in danger of disappearance, which are present on the territory referred to in Article 2 of the (*qv*) Habitats Directive and for the conservation of which the

Community has particular responsibility in view of the proportion of their natural range which falls within the territory referred to in the said Article 2 and which are indicated in each case by an asterisk in Annex I to the Habitats Directive."

(Of Irish interest, under the heading "Raised Bogs and Mires and Fens": 51.1 *Active raised bogs and 52.1 and 52.2 blanket bog (*active only))

PRIORITY SPECIES
(NH 97, Reg. 2(1))

"Means species referred to in Article 1(g)(i) of the (*qv*) Habitats Directive for the conservation of which the Community has particular responsibility in view of the proportion of their natural range which falls within the territory referred to in Article 2 of the Habitats Directive and which are indicated in each case by an asterisk in Annex II to the Habitats Directive."

Article 1(g) of the Habitats Directive deals with species which are (i) endangered, (ii) vulnerable, (iii) rare, or, (iv) endemic and requiring particular attention.

PRIVATE DWELLING
(APA 1987, s.7(1))

"Means any building or structure or any part of any building or structure (including any ancillary building or structure) which is used, or intended to be used, solely for human habitation but does not include:

(a) a curtilage or garden, or
(b) an ancillary building or structure, or part of a building or structure, having a fire place with a maximum heating capacity exceeding 45kw which serves more than one dwelling."

PRIVATE FISHERY, PROTECTION OF
(F(C)A 1959)

Chapter IV of Part XI of the F(C)A 1959, sections 178 to 181 deals with the protection of private fisheries otherwise called (*qv*)several fisheries. *See:* ENTRY, UNAUTHORISED ONTO SEVERAL FISHERY.

PRODUCER
(WMA 1996, s.5(1))

"Means, in relation to waste, any person whose activities produce waste or who carries out pre-processing, mixing or other operations resulting in a change in the nature or composition of waste."

(Waste Management (Packaging) Regulations, 1997 (S.I. No. 242 of 1997), article 4(4))

For the purpose of these Regulations "producer" is hereby specified under and in accordance with section 27 of the Waste Management Act, 1996, to mean a person who, for the purpose of trade or otherwise in the course of business, imports, manufactures, sells or otherwise supplies to other persons packaging material, packaging or packaged products and "produce" shall be construed accordingly.

"Major producer":

"Article 4(5)

(a) for the purposes of these Regulations, "major producer", means a producer who, for the purpose of trade or otherwise in the course of business, imports, manufactures, sells or otherwise supplies to other persons packaging material, packaged or packaging or packaged products, where the aggregate weight of packaging material and packaging supplied by such major producer exceeds or may be expected to exceed 25 tonnes in a calendar year, and who has an annual turnover of more than £1,000,000.
(b) For the purpose of determining whether or not a producer is a major producer:
    (i) the aggregate weight of packaging material and packaging concerned shall, subject to paragraph (c), be the aggregate weight arising from all relevant activities of the producer within the State, and
    (ii) the turnover of the producer concerned shall be the turnover derived from the producer's activities within the State (including the export of goods and services).
(c) For the purpose of determining whether or not a producer is a major producer, account shall not be taken of:
    (i) packaging destined for reuse, or
    (ii) packaging material and packaging where such material and packaging is supplied by, or used in the supply of products by, that producer to persons outside the State."

"'Turnover' in relation to any producer, means the amounts derived from the provision (including the export) of goods and services falling within the producer's ordinary activities, after deduction of:

(a) trade discounts, and
(b) value added tax."

PRODUCER RESPONSIBILITY OBLIGATION
(WMA 1996, s.27(1))

"Means a requirement to take steps for the purpose of the prevention, minimisation, limitation or recovery of waste as respect the class or classes of product to which the requirement relates and may include a requirement to achieve specified targets in relation to these matters."

This is a specialised meaning for the purpose of Part III of the WMA 1996. Part II of the Waste Management (Packaging) Regulations, 1997 (S.I. No. 242 of 1997) is devoted to the same subject.

PRODUCT
(WMA 1996, s.5(1))

"Includes any naturally occurring or manufactured thing."

(GMO Regs, Art. 3(1))

"Means a preparation consisting of, or containing, a Genetically modified organism or a combination of Genetically modified organisms, which is (*qv*) placed on the market."

PROHIBITION

The environmental statutes the subject matter of this book each contain a specific prohibitory section or a number of such sections which are dealt with hereunder. The section or sections chosen in respect of each statute or regulation are intended to epitomise or typify the functions of that Act or Regulation intended to protect the environment.

(1) WATERS UNDER F(C)A 1959

SUBSTANCE/OBJECT: (*qv*) deleterious matter.
PROHIBITION: against throwing, falling, permitting to fall, causing to fall into....any waters.
PROVISIONS: section 171 (1)*(b)* of the F(C)A 1959.

(2) WATERS UNDER LG(WP)A 1977

SUBSTANCE/OBJECT: (*qv*) polluting matter.
PROHIBITION: against causing or permitting to enter...any waters
PROVISIONS: section 3 LG(WP)A 1977 substantially amended by various sections of the WP(A)A 1990.

(3) CERTAIN EMISSIONS INTO THE ATMOSPHERE (APA 1987)

SUBSTANCE/OBJECT: *(qv)* emission/air pollution/smoke.
PROHIBITION; against causing or permitting... not limiting or preventing...into the atmosphere...so as to be a nuisance.
PROVISIONS: sections 23, 24(1) and (2) and 25 of the APA 1987.

(4) SEWAGE/TRADE EFFLUENT (LG(WP)A 1977)

SUBSTANCE/OBJECT: trade or sewage effluent.
PROHIBITION: discharging, emitting without licence.
PROVISIONS: Sections 4(1)and 16(1) of the LG(WP)A 1977.

(5) OPERATION OF INDUSTRIAL PLANT (APA 1987)

SUBSTANCE/OBJECT: operation of industrial plant.
PROHIBITION: without licence.
PROVISIONS: section 30(6) of the APA 1987.

(6) HOLDING, RECOVERING, DISPOSING OF, WASTE (WMA 1996)

SUBSTANCE/OBJECT: (*qv*) waste.
PROHIBITION: against holding, recovering or disposing of...in a manner that causes or is likely to cause environmental pollution.
PROVISION: section 32(1) of the WMA 1996.

(7) DISPOSING OF OR RECOVERY OF WASTE WITHOUT LICENCE (WMA 1996)

SUBSTANCE/OBJECT: (*qv*) waste.
PROHIBITION: (*qv*) disposing or undertaking the recovery of waste at a (*qv*) facility without a *(qv)* waste licence.
PROVISIONS: section 39(1) of the WMA 1996.

(8) PROTECTION OF FAUNA AND FLORA (WLA 1976)

The subheadings which follow each refer to PROTECTION rather than PROHIBITION as they all relate to the WLA 1976 or to the NH 97 Regulations both of which are predicated on protection of wildlife and wildlife habitats rather than the prohibition of acts which damage the environment. Each will be found under the headings PROTECTION in the text rather than in the sequence of articles on specific PROHIBITION which are contained with this Article.

These instances of protection of fauna and flora are as follows:

(a) SUBSTANCE/OBJECT: birds
PROHIBITION: against hunting, injuring...protected wild birds.
PROVISIONS: Section 22 (4) WLA 1976.
See: PROTECTION, PROTECTED WILD BIRDS.

(b) SUBSTANCE/OBJECT: animals
PROHIBITION: against hunting, injuring...protected wild animals.
PROVISIONS: Section 23(5) WLA 1976.
See: PROTECTION, PROTECTED WILD ANIMALS.

(c) SUBSTANCE/OBJECT: flora
PROHIBITION: against cutting, picking uprooting etc. flora declared to be protected.
PROVISIONS: Section 21(3) WLA 1976 as amended by regulation 21 of the NH 97 Regulations.
See: PROTECTION, OF FLORA

(d) SUBSTANCE/OBJECT: species of fauna in First Schedule Part I to NH 97 Regulations.
PROHIBITION: capture, killing, disturbance.
PROVISIONS: Regulation 23 of the NH 97 Regulations.
See: PROTECTION OF FAUNA, NH 97 REGULATIONS

(e) SUBSTANCE/OBJECT: species of wild flora and fauna in the First Schedule Part II to NH 97 Regulations.
PROHIBITION: taking in the wild.
PROVISIONS: Regulations 24 of the NH 97 Regulations.
See: PROTECTION, TAKING FLORA AND FAUNA IN THE WILD.

(9) OPERATIONS OR ACTIVITIES WITHOUT CONSENT OR AGREEMENT (NH 97)

SUBSTANCE/OBJECT: operations or activities without consent of Minister or in accordance with (*qv*) management agreement.
PROHIBITION: Carrying out.
PROVISIONS: Regulation 14(1) of the NH 97 Regulations.

(10) WORKS (OPERATIONS AND ACTIVITIES) ON CERTAIN PROTECTED LANDS, COURT APPLICATION (NH 97)

SUBSTANCE/OBJECT: (*qv*) operations or activities.
PROHIBITION: against adversely affecting integrity of European site...by carrying out operation or activity.
PROVISIONS: Regulation 17(3) of the NH 97 Regulations (10) NH 97.

(11) WORKS (OPERATIONS OR ACTIVITIES) ON LANDS OUTSIDE A EUROPEAN SITE, COURT APPLICATION (NH 97)

SUBSTANCE/OBJECT: (*qv*) operations or activities.
PROHIBITION: against adversely affecting integrity of site other than a European site...by carrying out an operation or activity.
PROVISIONS: Regulation 18 of the NH 97 Regulations.

(12) FORESHORE, FORESHORE ACT 1933
SUBSTANCE/OBJECT: beach materials
PROHIBITION: against removal or disturbance.
PROVISIONS: Sections 6 and 7 of the Foreshore (Amendment) Act 1992.
See: FORESHORE.

A detailed analysis of these measures, excluding (8) and (12), follows. (8) is dealt with elsewhere under PROTECTION followed by the particular topic, e.g. BIRDS, ANIMALS, FLORA and (12) is dealt with under FORESHORE.

See detailed analysis of each which follows:

(1) WATERS UNDER THE F(C)A 1959

In the F(C)A 1959 there are in fact three sections concerned with water pollution as follows:

"(1) Section 164

Offences
Section 164(1) which creates offences (a) of using in or near waters for the capture, destruction or injury of fish or (b) having in possession or control on the bank or near waters with intent to use for the same purposes, deleterious matter.

(Note that the maximum penalty prescribed under this section has been increased. *See:* FINES AND IMPRISONMENT (IMPOSITION OF)).

(2) Section 171(1)

Offence
Section 171 –
"(1) Any person who –
(a) steeps in any waters any flax or hemp, or
(b) throws, empties, permits or causes to fall into any waters any deleterious matter,
shall, unless such act is done under and in accordance with a licence granted by the Minister under this section, be guilty of an offence under this section ..."

This section is not one of the sections which may be tried on indictment under section 46 of the FA 1980 but section 25 of the LG(WP)(A)A 1990 provides for conviction on indictment.

In *Maguire v. Shannon Regional Board* [1994] 2 I.L.R.M. 253 it was held that an offence under section 171 is an offence of strict liability, being regulatory in essence, that the section does not create an offence of a truly criminal character and therefore proof of *mens rea* is not a requirement for conviction. This judgment was followed in an unreported case of the same year, 1994, *Shannon Regional Fisheries Board v. Cavan County Council.*

Comparison: Section 171 should be compared with section 3 of the LG(WP)A 1977 which is dealt with hereunder and which should be the main tool for enforcing basic reactive pollution control but is not because of the Maguire judgment. Fishery protection officers, who are the main and sometimes only enforcers of the law relating to water pollution, are familiar with the section and regard it as being their own. There are difficulties in prosecuting section 3 of the LG WP(A)A 1977 as there is a statutory defence under subsection (3) if the defendant can prove that he took all reasonable care to prevent the entry to waters. This defence does not apply to section 171 of the F(C)A 1959. By virtue of section 27 of the LG(WP)(A)A 1990 regional fishery boards are entitled to prosecute section 3 as well as the local authority but in practice it is just not prosecuted by anyone because of the defence.

(3) Section 172, which is a little used section, provides that the owner of any receptacle used for containing or conveying any deleterious matter which is within 30 yards of waters, must provide and maintain suitable means as will effectively prevent the passage of the deleterious matter from that receptacle into such waters.

Offence
Section 172(2)*(b)* provides that a person who fails to carry out the duty imposed on him under the section is guilty of an offence.

In this section the definition of "deleterious liquid" in respect of this offence was repealed by section 18 of the F(A)A 1962 leaving "deleterious matter" in place in both sections.

See: LICENCE (1) F(C)A 1959

(2) WATERS UNDER THE LG(WP)A 1977

Section 3 of the LG(WP)A 1977:

"(1) Subject to subsection (5), a person shall not cause or permit any polluting matter to enter waters.

Offence
(2) A person who contravenes subsection (1) shall be guilty of an offence ..."

Subsection (3), as inserted by section 3(1)*(a)* of the LG(WP)(A)A 1990 and section 66(2) of the WMA 1996, provides for the defence of taking all reasonable care to prevent the entry to (*qv*)waters to which the charge relates by providing, maintaining, using, operating and supervising facilities, or by employing practices or methods of operation, that are suitable for the purpose of such prevention and, where appropriate, that the entry to waters to which the charge relates arises from an activity carried on in accordance with a (*qv*) nutrient management scheme approved under section 21A (inserted by the WMA 1996) of the LG(WP)(A)A 1990.

Subsection (4) was repealed by section 30 of the LG(WP)A 1977A 1990. For persons entitled to prosecute, *see:* POWERS OF PROSECUTION. Section 3(5) was amended by section 3(1)(b) of the LG(WP)(A)A 1990 and the First Schedule to the Environmental Protection Agency (Extension of Powers) Order, 1996 (S.I. No. 126 of 1996):

"(5) Subsection (1) does not apply to –
(a) (i) discharge of a trade effluent or a sewage effluent which is made under and in accordance with a licence under section 4 or an emission made under and in accordance with a licence or revised licence under Part IV of the Environmental Protection Agency Act. 1992,
(ii) a discharge of a sewage effluent from a sewer: Provided that, where a standard applying to the

effluent stands prescribed under section 26, the discharge complies with that standard,

(iii) a discharge of a trade effluent or sewage effluent to which regulations under section 4(10) apply: Provided that, where a standard applying to the effluent stands prescribed under section 26, the discharge complies with that standard,

(aa) any entry authorised by or under an enactment specified in the table to subsection (6),

(b) entry to tidal waters of any matter from vessels, from apparatus for transferring any matter to or from vessels, or from marine structures,

(c) any deposit authorised under section 3 or 13 of the Foreshore Act, 1933, or section 48 the Harbours Act, 1946,

(d) any substance or thing authorised under section 88 of the Harbours Act, 1946, to be put in waters,

(e) any works authorised by an order under section 134 of the Harbours Act, 1946,

(f) any entry authorised under the Fisheries Acts, 1959 to 1976."

Subsection (6) of section 3 of the LG(WP)A 1977 was repealed by section 30 of the LG(WP)(A)A 1990 except for the table to the section which provides:

"TABLE
Section 16 of the Shannon Electricity Act, 1925,
Section 16 of the Liffey Reservoir Act, 1936,
Section 10 of the Arterial Drainage Act, 1945,
Section 11 of the Electricity Supply (Amendment) Act, 1945,
Section 27 of the Turf Development Act, 1946,
Section 6 of the Local Authorities (Works) Act, 1949."

EXTENSION OF THESE FUNCTIONS TO AGENCY

These functions under section 3 of the LG(WP)A 1977 now apply to the Agency in certain circumstances by virtue of Article 4 of the Environmental Protection Agency (Extension of powers) Order 1996. *See:* EXTENSION OF POWERS.

REMEDIES UNDER SECTIONS 10 AND 11 LG(WP)A 1977 – COURT ORDERS

Under Section 10 of the LG(WP)A 1977, in any court and under section 11 of the LG(WP)A 1977 in the High Court, an order can be obtained where there is a discharge of (*qv*) polluting matter or (*qv*) trade effluent or (*qv*) sewage effluent to any waters:

(a) Under section 10 to terminate the discharge and mitigate the effects, and

(b) Under section 11 prohibiting the entry and requiring the carrying out of works to prevent the entry.

Section 10 of the LG(WP)A 1977 was substituted by section 7 of the LG(WP)(A)A 1990.

Section 10 is designed for a discharge which is happening or has happened. Section 11 is designed for a discharge which is happening, has happened or is likely to happen.

Sections 10 and 11 do not apply to discharges which are exempted from the provisions of section 3 by section 3(5) (above) or from the provisions of section 4 by section 4(5) or where there is a licence under section 171 of the F(C)A 1959 and section 11 does not apply where the polluting matter has escaped accidentally.
See: (1) LICENCE, LG(WP)A 1977; (2) LICENCE, F(C)A 1959.

Subsection (1)(a) of both sections provides that orders can be sought whether or not the person has an interest in the waters concerned. By virtue of Article 4 of the Environmental Protection Agency (Extension of Powers) Order 1996 (S.I. No. 126 of 1996) where the discharge is from an (*qv*)activity enforcement of both sections applies to the (*qv*) Agency in lieu of the local authority or sanitary authority.

SECTION 10 ORDER

Section 10(1) of the LG(WP)A 1977, as amended by substitution by section 7 of the LG(WP)A A 1990, provides that –

"(1) (a) Where, on the application by any person to the appropriate court, whether or not the person has an interest in the waters concerned, that court is satisfied that another person –

(i) is causing or permitting, or has caused or permitted, pollution matter to enter waters and the entry is or was not one to which section 3(5) applies and is or was not one under and in accordance with a licence under section 171 of the Act of 1959, or

(ii) is discharging or causing or permitting to be discharged, or has discharged or caused or permitted to be discharged, trade effluent to waters and the discharge is or was not one to which subsection (2) of section 4 applies and is or was not one under and in accordance with a licence under that said section 171,

that court may make an order directing that other person to do one or more of the following:

(I) to terminate the entry or discharge within such period as may be specified in the order, or

(II) to mitigate or remedy any effects of the entry or discharge concerned in such manner and within such period as may be specified in the order, or

(III) to pay to the applicant or such other person as may be specified in the order, a specified amount to defray all or part of any costs incurred by the applicant or that other person in investigation, mitigating or remedying the effects of the entry or discharge concerned."

See: Order 10 Rule 5, District Court Rules 1997.

Offence

Subsection (2) creates a summary offence of failure to comply with an order under subsection (1).

Section 10 also provides at subsection (3) that the person named in the order must be given the opportunity of being heard before an order is made, and at subsection (4) that the local authority or regional fisheries board may, where there is failure to comply with the order, take any steps specified in the order to mitigate or remedy the effects and recover the expenditure incurred as a simple contract debt in any court of competent jurisdiction.

SECTION 10 NOTICE

Subsections (5) and (6) provide that where the entry or discharge persists the local authority may serve on the person responsible a notice requiring the cesser of the entry or discharge within a specified period and in a specified manner and on failure to comply can themselves mitigate or remedy and recover the expenditure incurred.

CONTENTS OF SECTION 10 ORDER

Subsection 10(8) provides that without prejudice to the generality of subsections (1) and (5) an order under subsection (1) or a notice under subsection (5) may require:

(a) the replacement of fish stocks,

(b) the restoration of spawning grounds,

(c) the taking of measures to prevent the continuance of the entry or discharge,

(d) the removal of polluting matters from waters,

(e) the treatment of affected waters so as to mitigate or remedy the effects of the entry or discharge concerned,

(f) the making of alternative arrangements for the supply of waters for domestic, commercial, industrial, fishery (including fish farming), agricultural or recreational purposes or the payment of a specified amount to the (*qv*) sanitary authority or other person concerned to defray all or part of the costs of the arrangements,

(g) the making good of any damage to plant or equipment or to any water abstraction or treatment works and any consequential losses incurred by any person.

Subsection (9) provides that an application may be made under subsection (1) and a notice may be served under subsection (5) notwithstanding that a prosecution under section 3 or section 4 has been brought in respect of the relevant entry or discharge.

SECTION 11 ORDER

Section 11 of the LG(W)A 1977, as amended by substitution by section 8 of the LG(WP)A A 1990, provides that:

(1) where, on the application of any person to the High Court, whether or not that person has an interest in the (*qv*) waters concerned, that Court is satisfied that:

(a) (*qv*) polluting matter is being, has been or is likely to be caused or permitted to enter waters,

(b) (*qv*) trade effluent or (*qv*) sewage effluent is being, has been or is likely to be discharged to waters, or

(c) polluting matter has escaped, is escaping or is likely to escape accidentally from premises to waters,

CONTENTS OF SECTION 11 ORDER

The High Court may by order:

(i) prohibit any person from causing or permitting or continuing to cause or permit the entry of polluting matter to the waters or the discharge aforesaid of trade effluent or sewage effluent to the waters,

(ii) require the carrying out of specified

measures by any person having the custody or control of polluting matter or trade effluent or sewage effluent to prevent an entry or discharge or a continuance or recurrence,

(iii) for the purpose of preventing such entry or discharge or avoiding a risk from a person having custody or control of polluting matter, require the person to do, refrain from or cease doing any specified act or to refrain from or case making any specified omission,

(iv) for the purpose of preventing the escape aforesaid or its continuance or recurrence, require the carrying out of specified measures by the occupier of the premises as aforesaid and for the purpose of avoiding any risk of such escape, require the occupier to do, refrain from or cease doing any specified act or to refrain from or cease making any specified omission, and

(v) make such other provision as that court considers appropriate.

Section 11(1A) provides that an application may be brought under section 11 notwithstanding a prosecution under section 4.

Sections 11(1) and (1A) were substituted by section 8 of the LG(WP)(A)A 1990.

Section 11(2) provides that a application may be made by motion and the court may make such interim or interlocutory motions as it considers appropriate and subsection (3) provides for the order including the payment of costs as appropriate.

Article 4 of the Environmental Protection Agency ((*qv*)Extension of Powers) Order 1996 (S.I. No. 126 of 1996) applies to this section in the same manner as it does to section 10 above.

(3) CERTAIN EMISSIONS INTO THE ATMOSPHERE (APA 1987)

In the APA 1987 under the heading "General Provisions Relating to Air Pollution" there are a number of prohibitory sections as the control of emission covers a range of functions and depends to a large extent on specific regulations prohibiting the burning of specific fuels in specified areas. *See:* REGULATIONS RELATING TO FUEL, SECTION 53 OF THE APA 1987.

Section 23 of the APA 1987 is one prohibitory section dealing with the Minister's powers to make, for the purpose of preventing or limiting air pollution, general regulations prohibiting either absolutely or subject to specified exceptions, specified emissions or the production, treatment, use, import, placing on the market, distribution or sale of any substance (other than fuel) which may cause air pollution.

Section 25 is another such section and it deals with the Minister's power by regulation to prohibit or restrict emissions of smoke into the atmosphere from any specified premises.

Section 24 of the APA 1987, however, is the key regulatory and enforcement section and it differentiates between subsection (1) a private dwelling and subsection (2) a premises other than a private dwelling and provides:

"(1) The occupier of any premises, other than a private dwelling, shall use the *(qv)* best practicable means to limit and, if possible, to prevent an emission from such premises.

(2) The occupier of any premises shall not cause or permit an emission from such premises in such quantity, or in such manner, as to be a nuisance.

(3) In any prosecution for contravention of the section, it shall be a good defence to establish that –

(a) the *(qv)* best practicable means have been used to prevent or limit the emission concerned, or

(b) the emission concerned was in accordance with a licence under the Act, or

(c) the emission concerned was in accordance with an (*qv*) emission limit value, or

(d) the emission concerned was in accordance with a (*qv*) special control area order in operation in relation to the area concerned, or

(e) in the case of an emission of smoke, the emission concerned was in accordance with regulations under section 25, or

(f) the emission did not cause air pollution."

STATUTORY DEFENCES

The APA 1987 provides at section 24(3) and section 25(3) the same statutory defence to a prosecution under either section as follows:

(a) the best practicable means have been used to prevent the *(qv)* emission concerned, or

(b) the emission concerned was in accordance with a licence under this Act, or

(c) the emission concerned was in accordance with an *(qv)* emission limit value, or

(d) the emission concerned was in accordance with an *(qv)* special control area order in operation in relation to the area concerned, or
(e) in the case of an emission of smoke, the emission concerned was in accordance with *(qv)* regulations under section 25, or
(in section 24(3) only)
(f) the emission did not cause *(qv)* air pollution.

EXTENSION OF THESE FUNCTIONS TO THE AGENCY

These functions under section 24 of the APA 1987 now apply to the Agency in certain circumstances by virtue of Article 10 of the Environmental Protection Agency (Extension of Powers) Order 1996 (S.I. No. 126 of 1996). *See:* EXTENSION OF POWERS.

(*See Truloc Ltd. v. District Justice Liam McMenamin and Donegal County Council* (Notice Party) High Court 1992 38 J.R. (O'Hanlon J.) June 17, 1993, [1994] I.L.R.M. 151 where O'Hanlon J. discussed the elements of a prosecution under section 24(2) APA 1987)

(4) TRADE/SEWAGE EFFLUENT (LG(WP)A 1977)

Section 4(1) of the LG(WP)A 1977 prohibits after a date (1.10.78) discharge of any trade effluent or sewage effluent except under and in accordance with a licence under this section and section 16(1) of the LG(WP)A 1977 prohibits the discharge of any trade effluent or other matter (other than domestic sewage and storm water) to a sewer except under and in accordance with a licence under this section.

By virtue of S.I. No. 16 of 1978 the operative dates for the sections were fixed at 1st October 1978 for section 4 and 1st January 1979 for section 16.
See: DISCHARGES UNDER LG(WP)AA 1977.

(5) OPERATION OF INDUSTRIAL PLANT (APA 1987)

Section 30(1) of the APA 1987 prohibits the operation of industrial plant, other than existing industrial plant, on or after such day as may be prescribed (November 1, 1988) save under and in accordance with a licence under this Act that is in force in relation to the plant.

Section 30(2) of the APA 1987 provides that the Minister may, by regulations, provide that existing industrial plant of such class as may be specified in the regulations shall not be in operation on or after such date as may be specified.

Section 30(3) contains the usual provision to give legality to an existing industrial plant in the period between the coming into operation of the regulations and the granting of a licence where an application for a licence has been made and the applicant has complied with requirements of regulations under section 31.

(6) HOLDING, RECOVERING, DISPOSING OF, WASTE (WMA 1996)

Section 32(1) of the WMA 1996 provides:

"A person shall not hold, transport, recover or dispose of waste in a manner that causes or is likely to cause environmental pollution.
See: HOLDER OF WASTE, GENERAL DUTY OF.

(7) DISPOSING OF OR RECOVERY OF WASTE WITHOUT LICENCE (WMA 1996)

Section 39 of the WMA 1996, which has been substantially amended by the European Communities (Amendment of Waste Management Act 1996) Regulations 1988 (S.I. No. 166 of 1998), which amendments are shown in square brackets, provides:

"(1) Subject to subsections (4) and (7), a person shall not dispose of or undertake the *(qv)* recovery of waste at a *(qv)* facility, or or after such date as may be prescribed, save under and in accordance with a licence under this Part (in this Act referred to as a waste licence) that is in force in relation to the carrying on of the activity concerned at that facility.

(2) For the purpose of subsection (1), different dates may be prescribed in respect of different waste disposal or recovery activities, different classes of facility and different classes of waste.

(3) The recovery or disposal of waste shall, in the period before a waste licence in relation to such recovery or disposal is granted or refused, be deemed not to have contravened the provisions of this Part if, before the date prescribed under subsection (1) in respect of the activity concerned –
(a) an application has been made for a waste licence in respect of that activity and the requirements of regulations under sections 45 and 50 in relation to the application for a waste

licence have been complied with by the applicant therefor, and

(b) in the case of disposal of waste, other than one carried out by a local authority, the corporation of a borough that is not a county borough, or the council of an urban district, is carried out in accordance with a permit issued under the European Communities (Waste) Regulations, 1979, the European Communities (Toxic and Dangerous Waste) Regulations, 1982 or [the European Communities (Waste Oils) Regulations, 1992,].

[(4) The Minister may by regulations provide that subsection (1) shall not apply in respect of the recovery or disposal in a specific manner of a specified class or classes of waste, if and for so long as the person carrying out the recovery or disposal of the waste, as the case may be, complies with specified conditions in relation to the carrying out of such recovery or disposal.]

(5) Without prejudice to the generality of subsection (4), regulations under that subsection may specify conditions in relation to the following matters –

(a) the quantity of waste concerned which may be recovered or disposed of in a particular period,

(b) the use of the *(qv)* best available technology not entailing excessive costs to prevent or eliminate or, where that is not practicable, to limit, abate or reduce, an emission from the recovery or disposal activity concerned,

[(c) a requirement that the person concerned obtain from a local authority or the Agency a waste permit or such other authorisation or certificate as may be prescribed in respect of the carrying on by him or her of the activity concerned,

(d) the specification of controls to be exercised or measures to be taken by a local authority or the Agency in relation to the carrying on of an activity in respect of which such a permit, authorisation or certificate is required (which controls and measures a local authority or the Agency is hereby empowered to exercise or take, as the case may be),

(e) a requirement regarding the payment to a local authority or the Agency of a fee of a specified amount in respect of an application for such a permit, authorisation or certificate, or of such charges as are necessary to defray or contribute towards the cost of any investigation carried out or caused to be carried out by the local authority or the Agency in relation to such application,

(f) such other matters as the Minister considers are appropriate to ensure that the recovery or disposal activity concerned will not cause (*qv*) environmental pollution.]

(6) The Minister may by regulations –

(a) require the producer of a specified class or classes of waste other than household waste, to –

(i) comply with specified conditions in relation to the treatment or temporary storage by him or her of the waste at the premises where it is produced, including the obtaining of the prior written consent of the relevant local authority to such treatment or storage,

(ii) make a plan with respect to the taking of such measures, in the event of an incident occurring that involves a loss or release of the waste, as will prevent or minimise the risk of environmental pollution there from,

(iii) effect and maintain a policy of insurance insuring him or her to a specified extent as respects any liability on his or her part to pay damages or costs on account of injury to person or property arising from the production or holding of the waste,

(b) enable a local authority to attach specified conditions to a consent granted by it pursuant to regulations under paragraph (a)(i) and to revoke such a consent where any of the conditions so attached are not complied with,

(c) specify the maximum period for which the waste may be stored as aforesaid and deem storage of the waste beyond that period to be a disposal or recovery, as appropriate, of the waste.

(7) In addition to the exemption from its terms provided for by section 51, subsection (1) shall not apply in respect of -

(a) the recovery or disposal of waste at a facility connected with an activity in respect of which a licence or a revised licence under Part IV of the Act of 1992 is in force, where such recovery or disposal is subject to the said licence or revised licence,
(b) household waste produced and disposed of within the curtilage of a dwelling,
(c) the deposit of litter in a litter bin,
(d) ...
(e) the transfer of waste to a local authority, the corporation of a borough that is not a county borough, the council of an urban district or any other person for the purpose of its being recovered or disposed of in accordance with this Act or a licence or revised licence under Part IV of the Act of 1992,
(f) the disposal of animal by-products within the meaning of the European Communities (Disposal, Processing and Placing on the Market of Animal By-Products) Regulations, 1994, and
(g) such other activities as may be prescribed.

(8) The Minister may make regulations amending the First Schedule to the Act of 1992 by the addition thereto, subject to such modifications, if any, as he or she may determine and specifies in the regulations, of any of the activities specified in the Third Schedule or the Fourth Schedule.

Offence
(9) A person who contravenes subsection (1) of this section or a provision of regulations under subsection (4) or (6) shall be guilty of an offence."

The Act of 1992 is the EPAA 1992.

Paragraph (d) of subsection (7) was revoked by the European Communities (Amendment of Waste Management Act, 1996) Regulations 1988 (S.I. No. 166 of 1998).

See: (1) WASTE, RECOVERY AND DISPOSAL OF, REQUIREMENT TO HOLD WASTE LICENCE AND (2) WASTE, WASTE PERMIT REGULATIONS.

(7) PROTECTION OF FAUNA AND FLORA (WLA 1976)

See:
(1) PROTECTION, PROTECTED WILD BIRDS,
(2) PROTECTION, PROTECTED WILD ANIMALS
(3) PROTECTION, FLORA
(4) PROTECTION OF FAUNA NH 97 REGULATIONS
(5) PROTECTION, TAKING FAUNA AND FLORA IN THE WILD.

(9) OPERATIONS OR ACTIVITIES WITH OUT CONSENT OR AGREEMENT (NH 97)

Regulation 14 of the NH 97 Regulations provides:

"(1) A person shall not carry out, cause to be carried out or continue to carry out, on any land included in a (*qv*)special area of conservation or a site placed on a list in accordance with Chapter 1 of this Part, an operation or activity mentioned in a notice issued under Regulation 4(2) unless the operation or activity is carried out, or caused or permitted to be carried out, or continued to be carried out, by the owner, occupier or user of the land and –
(a) one of them has given the Minister written notice of a proposal to carry out the operation, or activity, specifying its nature and the land on which it is proposed to carry it out, and
(b) one of the conditions specified in paragraph (2) is fulfiled.

(2) The conditions referred to in paragraph (1) are as follows –
(a) that the operation or activity is carried out with the written consent of the Minister, or
(b) that the operation or activity is carried out in accordance with the terms of a (*qv*) management agreement provided for under Regulation 12.

Offence
(3) A person who, without reasonable excuse, contravenes paragraph (1) shall be guilty of an offence.

(4) The provisions of this Regulation shall not apply to an operation or activity to which Regulation 15(2) relates."

See: ASSESSMENT. This prohibitory or restrictive Regulation is very easily confused with Regulation 17 which follows: -

(10) WORKS (OPERATIONS AND ACTIVITIES) ON CERTAIN PROTECTED LANDS, COURT APPLICATION (NH 97)

Regulation 17 of the NH 97 Regulations

"(1) Where the Minister considers that an *(qv)* operation or activity is being carried out or may be carried out on –
(a) a site placed on a list in accordance with Chapter I of this Part, or
(b) a site where consultation has been initiated in accordance with Article 5 of the Habitats Directive, or
(c) a European site,
which is neither directly connected with nor necessary to the management of such sites but likely to have a significant effect thereon either individually or in combination with other operations and activities the Minister shall ensure that an appropriate assessment of the implications of the site in view of the site's conservation objectives is undertaken.

(2) An environmental impact assessment in respect of a proposed operation or activity shall be an appropriate assessment for the purposes of this Regulation.

(3) If the Minister, having regard to the conclusions of the assessment undertaken under paragraph (1), is of the opinion that the operation or activity will adversely affect the integrity of the site concerned, the Minister shall make application to a court of competent jurisdiction to prohibit the continuance of the operation or activity.

(4) An application to a court of competent jurisdiction for a prohibition under this Regulation shall be in a summary manner and the Court when considering the matter may make such interim or interlocutory order (if any) as it considers appropriate having regard to paragraph 4 of Article 6 of the *(qv)*Habitats Directive and to the overall requirement of safe guarding the integrity of the site concerned and ensuring that the overall coherence of NATURA 2000 is protected."

(Article 6 (4) applies where compensatory measures are necessary to protect the overall coherence of Natura 2000 where, in spite of a negative assessment of the implications for the site and in the absence of alternative solutions, a plan or project must nevertheless be carried through for imperative reasons of overriding public interest, including those of a social or economic nature.)

"(5) For the purposes of this section "a court of competent jurisdiction" means either a Judge of the Circuit Court within whose Circuit the lands are part of the lands are situate or the High Court."

(11) WORKS (OPERATIONS OR ACTIVITIES) 0N LANDS OUTSIDE A EUROPEAN SITE, COURT APPLICATION (NH 97)

Regulation 18(1) of the NH 97 Regulations makes provision for lands which are not within (a), (b) and (c) of Regulation 17 above but where an operation or activity is being carried out which is liable to have an adverse affect on the integrity of the site concerned either alone or in combination with other operations or activities in which case the Minister shall ensure that an appropriate assessment is undertaken as in Regulation 17

Regulation 18(2) provides that having regard to the conclusion of the assessment undertaken under paragraph (1) the provisions of paragraphs (2) to (5) of Regulations 17 shall apply meaning the minister has the same right as under that regulation to adopt the procedures and obtain an order prohibiting the continuance of the operation or activity.

(12) FORESHORE

The main enforcement sections are sections 5 and 6 of the Foreshore (Amendment) Act 1992 which are closely modelled on sections 10 and 11 of the LG(WP)A 1997 dealt with at (2) above WATERS UNDER THE WP(A)A 1997.
See: FORESHORE.

PROHIBITORY NOTICE, PROHIBITORY ORDER
(Foreshore Acts 1933 and 1992)

See: FORESHORE.

PROOF OF DOCUMENTS
(F(C)A 1959/WLA 1976/EPAA 1992)

See: EVIDENCE.

PROSECUTION, POWERS OF
(F(C)A 1959/LG(WP)A 1977/APA 1987/ EPAA 1992/WMA 1996/WLA 1976)

(1) **Sections 309 and 312 of the F(C)A 1959:**

Section 309 which deals with the prosecution of offences is dealt with extensively elsewhere. *See:* TRIAL OF OFFENCES.

By virtue of section 309 any person can bring a summary prosecution except under the F(A)A 1997 where by virtue of section 65(3) only the Minister or the Director of Public Prosecutions (DPP) can prosecute under that Act.

Section 312, which entitled the Minister to prosecute under any provision of the Act, was amended by section 72 of the FA 1980 which reworded it to read, in the table to the section, "An offence under any provision of this Act, may, if prosecuted summarily, be prosecuted by the Minister."

Section 5(8) of the F(A)A 1997 provided "for the avoidance of doubt, section 312 of the Principal Act, to the extent if any that, by virtue of the Act of 1980 and the table to the section, it is in force, is hereby repealed."

(2) **Section 31 of the LG(WP)A 1977:**

Section 31 of the LG(WP)A 1977 and individual subsections which had dealt with powers to prosecute under that Act were repealed by section 30 of the LG(WP)(A)A 1990.

Section 27 of the LG(WP)(A)A 1990 now contains the law which provides at *(a)*, *(b)* and *(c)* for prosecution of the various enforcement sections of the LG(WP)A 1977 and section 21 of the LG(WP)(A)A 1990, which is the only enforcement section in the 1990 Act, in accordance with Parts 1 and II of the table to the section.

Accordingly depending on whose or adjoining whose functional area the waters concerned are situate either the local authority or sanitary authority prosecute sections 3, 4, 6, 12, 14, 16, 19, 23 and 27, a regional fisheries board sections 3 and 4, the person who applies to the court for the order to which the offence relates section 10, the person who appointed the authorised person concerned section 28, all being sections of the LG(WP)A 1977, and the local authority concerned prosecutes section 21 LG(WP)(A)A 1990 which was the only offence created by that Act.

EXEMPTIONS FROM SECTION 10 PETTY SESSIONS (IRELAND) ACT 1851

Paragraph (d) of section 27 of the LG(WP)(A)A 1990 deals with certain exemptions from the provisions of section 10 (4) of the Petty Sessions (Ireland) Act 1851. *See:* EVIDENCE (2).

EXTENSION OF FUNCTIONS UNDER S. 27 OF THE LG(WP)(A)A 1990 TO AGENCY

These functions under section 27 of the LG(WP)(A)A 1990 now apply to the Agency in the circumstances described in Article 4 of the Environmental Protection Agency (Extension of Powers) Order, 1966 (S.I. No. 126 of 1996). *See:* EXTENSION OF POWERS.

(3) **Section 13 of the APA 1987**:

As amended in square brackets by the Second Schedule to the Environmental Protection Agency (Extension of Powers) Order 1996 (S.I. No. 126 of 1996) provides:

"13 (1) (a) An offence under this Act may be prosecuted summarily by the local authority in whose functional area the offence is committed or, in the case of an offence arising from an order made, or a notice served, by a local authority, by the local authority concerned.

(b) Where a local authority are of opinion that an emission from any premises [other than an activity in respect of which a licence or a revised licence under Part IV of the Environmental Protection Agency Act, 1992, is in force] may cause air pollution affecting any part of their functional area, the local authority may, notwithstanding that the emission is from a premises which is situate outside the functional area of the local authority concerned, initiate summary proceedings for an offence under this Act in relation to the emission concerned.

(2) The Minister may, by regulations under this section, prescribe that such an offence as may be specified in the regulations may be prosecuted summarily by such person (including the Minister) as may be so specified in addition to, or in lieu of, the relevant local authority."

EXEMPTIONS FROM SECTION 10 PETTY SESSIONS (IRELAND) ACT 1851.

Sections 13(3) and (4) deal with certain exemptions from the provisions of section 10(4) of the Petty Sessions (Ireland) Act 1851. *See:* EVIDENCE (2)

EXTENSION OF FUNCTIONS UNDER S. 13 TO THE AGENCY

Sections 13(1), (2) and (4), 14, 16(3) and 24 now apply to the Agency in the circumstances described by Article 10 of the Environmental Protection Agency (Extension of Powers) Order 1996 (S.I. No. 126 of 1996). *See:* EXTENSION OF POWERS.

(4) **Section 11 of the EPAA 1992**:

"(1) An offence under this Act may be prosecuted summarily by the Agency.

(2) Notwithstanding subsection (1), the Minister may, by regulations, provide that an offence under this Act, specified in the regulations, may be prosecuted summarily by such person (including the Minister) as may be so specified."

Part VII of the Genetically Modified Organisms Regulations 1994 (S.I. No. 345 of 1994) provides at Article 61 for prosecution of an offence under the Regulations or an offence arising from the exercise of powers under the Act by (*qv*) authorised persons appointed pursuant to Article 60, by the Agency. *See:* GENETICALLY MODIFIED ORGANISMS, OFFENCES.

EXEMPTIONS FROM SECTION 10 PETTY SESSIONS (IRELAND) ACT 1851

Sections 11(3) and (4) of the EPAA 1992 deal with certain exemptions from the provisions of section 10 of the Petty Sessions (Ireland) Act 1851. *See:* EVIDENCE (2).

(5) **Section 11 of the WMA 1996**

Subsection (1) of section 11 of the WMA 1996 provides that a summary prosecution may be brought by the local authority in whose functional area the offence was committed or by the Agency, but subsection (5) of that section provides that the Agency only, subject to any order under section 69, can prosecute summarily for an offence in respect of failure to comply with a condition attached to a waste licence or any other requirement under the Act in relation to the carrying on of an activity the subject of such a licence.

Subsection (2) of section 11 permits the Minister by regulation to provide for prosecution of a summary offence under regulations by any person (including the Minister).

Subsection (3) deals with certain exemptions from the provisions of the Petty Sessions (Ireland) Act 1851 and subsection (4) deals with prima facie evidence of proof by certificate. *See:* EVIDENCE (2).

Subsection (6) provides that the Minister may by regulation provide that in specified circumstances summary proceedings may be brought by a local authority in respect of an offence committed other than in the functional area of the local authority.

There has been a substantial change under Article 4 of the Waste Management (Miscellaneous Provisions) Regulations, 1998 (S.I. No. 164 of 1998) which provides that since the May 20, 1998 summary proceedings for an offence under the Act may be brought by any person. *See:* PROSECUTION BY ANY PERSON.

The Article does not, however, purport to amend section 11 of the WMA 1996. The Regulations in question are expressed to be made under section 11 as well as other sections of the WMA 1996.

(6) **Section 70 of the WLA 1976:**

"(1) Summary proceedings for any offence under this Act may be prosecuted by the Minister.

(2) Subject to section 44(4) of this Act, summary proceedings for any offence under this act may be prosecuted by a person who is neither the Minister nor a member of the Garda Síochána with the consent of the Minister, or an officer of the Minister not below the rank of Assistant Secretary, nominated by the Minister for the purpose.

(3) Notwithstanding section 10(4) of the Petty Sessions (Ireland) Act, 1851, proceedings for an offence under this Act may be instituted at any time within one year after the date of the offence."

(7) **NH 97**

As there is no separate provision in the regulations for prosecutions they would be brought as is provided under the WLA 1976 as Regulation 1(2) of the NH 97 Regulations provides that the WLA 1976 and the Regulations (other than Part IV) shall be construed together as one.

(8) **Mammalian Animal Waste Regulations 1998**

Regulation 10 of the European Communities (Mammalian Waste) Regulations 1998 (S.I. No. 2 of 1998) and Regulation 11 of the European

Communities (Processing of Mammalian Waste) Regulations 1998 (S.I. No. 62 of 1998) provide that offences under the Regulations may be prosecuted by the Minister.

PROSECUTION BY ANY PERSON
(F(C)A 1959/LG(WP)A 1977/APA 1987, EPAA 1992/WLA 1976/Foreshore Acts 1933 and 1992)

(1) **Section 312 of the F(C)A 1959:**

Prosecutions may be brought by any person under any provision of the Fisheries Acts except under the F(A)A 1997, section 65(3). *See:* PROSECUTION, POWERS OF.

(2) **Sections 10 and 11 of the LG(WP)A 1977**

Any person may bring an application to the court.

(3) **Sections 28 and 28A of the APA 1987**

Any person may bring an application to the court.

(4) **Section 108 of the EPAA 1992**

Any person may bring an application to the District Court under section 108.

(5) **Section 44(1) and (3) of the WLA 1976**

A person who at the time the offence is alleged to have taken place is the owner of land may bring a prosecution in relation to an offence alleged under the section in respect of that land. The secretary of a (*qv*) recognised body which is entitled to enjoy sporting rights over the relevant land can bring a prosecution under the same section.

(6) **Article 4 of the Waste Management (Miscellaneous Provisions) Regulations 1998 (S.I. No. 164 of 1998)**

Article 4 of the Waste Management (Miscellaneous Provisions) Regulations, 1998 (S.I. No. 164 of 1998) provides that summary proceedings for an offence under the Act may be brought by any person.

(7) **Sections 5 and 6 of the Foreshore (Amendment) Act 1992**

Sections 5 and 6 of the Foreshore (Amendment) Act 1992 each provide for prosecution by "any person" as well as other persons.

PROTECTED WILD ANIMAL
(WLA 1976, s.2(1))

Has the meaning assigned to it by section 23(4) of this Act. *See:* PROTECTION, PROTECTED WILD ANIMALS.

PROTECTED WILD BIRD
(WLA 1986, s.2(1))

Has the meaning assigned to it by section 22(3) of this Act. *See:* PROTECTION, PROTECTED WILD BIRDS.

PROTECTION, PROTECTED WILD BIRDS
(WLA 1976, ss.19 and 22)

Section 19 of the WLA 1976:

"Wild birds and their nests and eggs, other than wild birds of the species mentioned in the Third Schedule to to this Act, shall be protected."

See: SCHEDULES HERETO, WLA 1976 SCHEDULES. ENFORCEMENT OF PROTECTION OF WILD BIRDS

Section 22 of the WLA 1976:

"(1) Subject to subsection (2) hereof, this section applies to every wild bird other than a wild bird of a species specified in the Third Schedule to this Act.

(2) The Minister may by regulations provide that –
  (a) a wild bird of a species specified in the Third Schedule to this Act shall be a wild bird to which this section applies,
  (b) this section shall not apply to a wild bird which is of a species specified in the regulations,
  (c) in such places or areas as are specified in the regulations and as regards such period or periods as are so specified, subsection (4) of this section shall not have effect, either, as may be so specified, generally or as regards such species of wild birds as are so specified,
  (d) this section shall not have effect in relation to the taking or removing by persons of a specified class of the eggs and nests of wild birds so specified,

  and in case any regulations under this subsection are for the time being in force, this section shall be construed and have effect subject to and in accordance with them; provided that regulations made by the Minister under this subsection and which deal with any matter mentioned in paragraph (a), (b) or (c) of this subsection shall be so made after consultation with the Minister for Agriculture and Fisheries."

(3) A wild bird to which this section for the time being applies is in this Act referred to as a protected wild bird.

The Minister has made a number of regulations under this section as follows:

(1) Wildlife Act 1976 (Protection of Bullfinches) Regulations 1980 (S.I. No. 283 of 1980

Article 3 declared the bullfinch to be a protected wild bird (PWB) to which section 22 of the WLA 1976 applies.

(2) European Communities (Wildlife Act 1976) (Amendment) Regulations 1985 (S.I. No. 397 of 1985)

Article 3(f) deletes the following species of birds from the Third Schedule:

Carrion Crow
Greater Black-backed Gull
Herring Gull
Hooded (Grey) Crow
House Sparrow
Jackdaw
Jay
Lesser Black-backed Gull
Magpie
Pigeons including wood pigeon
Rook
Starling

Effectively, after 1985, all wild birds are protected wild birds but the Minister has power by declaration to permit the killing and capture of certain protected wild birds in the circumstances described in European Communities (Wildlife Act 1976) (Amendment) Regulations, 1986 (S.I. No. 254 of 1986). *See:* DAMAGE BY PROTECTED WILD BIRDS.

Offences

"(4) Subject to the exceptions specified in subsection (5) of this section, any person who –

(a) (i) hunts a protected wild bird, other than a protected wild bird which is of a species specified in an order under section 24 of this Act, otherwise than under and in accordance with a permission or licence granted by the Minister under this Act, or

(ii) hunts a protected wild bird which is of a species specified in an order under section 24 of this Act, otherwise than –

(A) under and in accordance with such a permission or licence granted by the Minister under this Act other than section 29

(B) under and in accordance with a licence granted under section 29 of this Act and (also) on a day or during a period of days, specified in a relevant order under the said section 24.

(b) Injures a protected wild bird otherwise than while hunting it –

(i) in case the protected wild bird is of a species other than a species specified in an order under section 24 of this Act, under and in accordance with a licence or permission granted by the Minister under this Act,

(ii) in case the protected wild bird is of a species so specified, either in the manner mentioned in clause (A) of paragraph (a)(ii) of this subsection, or in the manner and on a day or during a period of days, mentioned in clause (B) of the said paragraph (a)(ii),

(c) wilfully takes or removes the eggs or nest of a protected wild bird otherwise than under and in a accordance with such a licence,

(d) wilfully destroys, injures or mutilates the eggs or nest of a protected wild bird,

(e) wilfully disturbs a protected wild bird on or near a nest containing eggs or unflown young, shall be guilty of an offence."

The following subsection, section 22(5) has been substantially amended by Regulation 3(b), (c) and (d) of the European Communities (Wildlife Act 1976) (Amendment) Regulations 1985 (S.I. No. 397 of 1985) and the amendments are given in square brackets.

"(5) It shall not be an offence for a person –

(a) while engaged in ornithology wilfully

to disturb a protected wild bird, or

(b) while so engaged or engaged in agriculture, fishing or forestry unintentionally to injure or kill a protected wild bird, or

[(c) to remove for conservation purposes or to destroy unintentionally the eggs or nest of a protected wild bird in the ordinary course of agriculture or forestry,] or

(d) to capture an injured or disabled protected wild bird for the purpose of killing it humanely or with the intention of tending it and of later releasing it, or

(e) to kill humanely a protected wild bird which has been injured in the manner described in paragraph (b), or captured in the manner described in paragraph (d) or injured in the circumstances described in paragraph (h) of this subsection, or

[(f) to take eggs of a protected wild bird for the purpose of having them hatched out for re-population, or re-introduction into the wild, or, for such purpose, to move such eggs from the nest (misprinted 'next' in the regs.) of such a bird to that of another bird of the same species, or]

(g) to destroy or remove any such nest which is built in or on an occupied building, or

[(h) while constructing a road or while carrying on any archaeological operation, building operation or work of engineering construction or while constructing or carrying on such other such other operation or work as may be prescribed, unintentionally to kill or to injure a protected wild bird or to remove for conservation purposes or unintentionally to destroy, injure or mutilate the eggs or nest of a protected wild bird.]

and nothing in this section shall make unlawful anything which is duly done pursuant to a statute (other than this Act) or statutory instrument, which is permitted to be done under such a statute or instrument or which is done pursuant to and in accordance with a licence or other permission granted or issued pursuant to such a statute or instrument or anything caused by or which results from, or is consequent upon or the effect of any other act or thing which is lawfully done.

(6) In any proceedings for an offence under this section relating to a protected wild bird which is of a species other than specified in Part I of the Fourth Schedule to this Act, it shall be a defence for the defendant to prove that any capturing or killing complained of was urgently necessary for the purpose of stopping damage described in section 42 of this Act being caused and that in the particular circumstances of the case it was not practical for him to apply to the Minister beforehand for a permission under section 42 of this Act and that the defendant reasonably believed that damage mentioned in the said section 42 (1) was being caused by the protected wild bird to which the alleged offence relates or by protected wild birds of the same species as that of such protected wild bird."

The species of bird set out at Part 1 of the Fourth Schedule, are protected wild birds which are Buzzards, Eagles, Falcons, Harriers, Hawks, Kites, Osprey and Owls.

These scheduled protected wild birds receive special protection over and above the ordinary protected wild bird because of their extreme rarity.

The subsection provides for a defence to a prosecution under section 22(5) where the protected wild bird is not one of the species at Part 1 of the Fourth Schedule and where the capture or killing was urgently necessary to stop damage described in section 42(1) that in the particular circumstances it was not practical to apply to the Minister beforehand for a permission under section 4 and that the defendant reasonably believed that damage was being caused by the protected wild bird to which the alleged offence relates or by protected wild birds of the same species.

This kind of damage would be more likely be dealt with by declarations by the Minister under Regulation 3(1) of the European Communities (Wildlife Act 1976) (Amendment) Regulations 1986.

For Section 42(1) *See:* DAMAGE BY PROTECTED WILD BIRDS.

"(7) In any proceedings for an offence under this section in which it is alleged that a defendant wilfully disturbed a protected wild bird described in subsection (4)(e) of this section, it shall not be necessary for the prosecution to prove that at the time of the alleged defence the defendant was not engaged in ornithology.

(8) Proceedings for an offence under this section may be taken in any District Court District, and in case such proceedings are taken and apart from this section the Justice before whom the proceed-

ings are brought would not have jurisdiction to hear and determine the proceedings, then for the purpose of conferring such jurisdiction the offence may be treated as having been committed within the District Court District to which such Justice is assigned.

(9) The Minister may grant a licence to a person –
  (a) at any time to capture or kill humanely or capture and humanely kill a protected wild bird of a species specified in the licence for such educational, scientific or other purposes as shall be so specified,
  (b) to hunt, in accordance with the licence, on such day or during such periods of days as is specified in the licence, protected wild birds which are both pen-reared and of a species so specified,
  (c) to so hunt, one such day or during such period of days, protected wild birds or a species so specified for the purpose of either training gun dogs for any field sport or holding gun dog trials,
  (d) to take the nests or eggs of protected wild birds of a species so specified for such educational, scientific or other purposes as shall be so specified.

(10) The Minister may by regulations provide that –
  (a) subsection (6) of this section shall have effect in relation to any proceedings for offences under this section relating to protected wild birds of a species specified in Part I of the Fourth Schedule to this Act and in the regulations,
  (b) the said subsection (6) shall not have effect in relation to any such proceedings relating to protected wild birds of a species specified in the regulations,

  and the said subsection (6) shall have effect accordingly."

No such regulation has ever been made and it is highly unlikely that any ever will be made because of the rarity of the species concerned.

PROTECTION, PROTECTED WILD ANIMALS SS.20 AND 23 WLA 1976
(WLA 1976)

Section 20 of the WLA 1976:

"Animals which are of a species of fauna in relation to which section 23 of this Act applies shall be protected."

ENFORCEMENT OF PROTECTION OF PROTECTED WILD ANIMALS (OTHER THAN PROTECTED WILD BIRDS)

Section 23 of the WLA 1976:

"(1) Subject to subsection (2) hereof, this section applies to any animal which is of a species of fauna specified in the Fifth Schedule to this Act."

This is the opposite to what is provided in section 22 above.

The animals in the Fifth Schedule are protected. They are protected by inclusion in the Fifth Schedule and become protected wild animals.

See: SCHEDULES HERETO, WLA 1976 SCHEDULES.

This Fifth Schedule has been amended twice as follows.

(1) Wildlife Act 1976 (Protection of Wild Animals) Regulations 1980 (S.I. No. 282 of 1980),
Regulation 3. The Common Frog, Common Lizard, Common Newt, Pygmy Shrew and Stoat are each hereby declared to be an animal to which section 23 applies.

(2) Wildlife Act 1976 (Protection of Wild Animals) Regulations 1990 (S.I. No. 112 of 1990)
Regulation 3. Animals of a species of fauna specified in the Schedule to these Regulations shall be animals to which section 23 applies:

Schedule Part 1:
Freshwater crayfish
Freshwater pearl mussel

Schedule Part 2:
Kerry slug
Marine turtle.

Regulation 23 of the NH 97 Regulations protects the additional species of fauna described at

Part I of the First Schedule to those Regulations rather than by reference to this section, section 23 of the WLA 1976, thereby creating another "two tier" system of protection. *See:* PROTECTION OF FAUNA IN NH 97 REGULATIONS.

"(2) Subject to subsection (3) of this section, the Minister may, after consultation with the Minister for Agriculture and Fisheries by regulations provide that –
(a) an animal of a species of fauna specified in the regulations (not being a species specified in the Fifth Schedule to this Act) shall be an animal to which this section applies,
(b) an animal of a species of fauna specified both in the regulations and in the said Fifth Schedule shall not be an animal to which this section applies,
(c) in such places or areas as are specified in the regulations and as regards such period or periods as are so specified, subsection (5) of this section shall not have effect either, as may be so specified, generally or as regards species of animal as are so specified,
and in case any regulations under this subsection are for the time being in force, this section shall be construed and have effect subject to and in accordance with them.

(3) Regulations under this section –
(a) which provide that an animal of any species of fish or aquatic invertebrate shall be an animal to which this section applies, or
(b) the effect of which when made would be that this section would, for so long as the regulations are in force, cease to apply to animals of such a species,
shall be made or amended by the Minister only with the concurrence of the Minister for Agriculture and Fisheries who shall indicate his concurrence by signing the regulations.

(4) An animal to which this section for the time being applies is in this Act referred to as a protected wild animal."

What is called a 'wild animal" and then a "protected wild animal" by virtue of section 23(4) becomes a "protected wild mammal" when it is the subject matter of an order under section 25(1) which permits its hunting during a period of days known as an open season.
See: OPEN SEASONS.

Offences
"(5) Any person who –
(a) hunts a protected wild animal which is not an exempted wild mammal otherwise than under and in accordance with a permission or licence granted by the Minister under this Act,
(b) hunts an exempted wild mammal otherwise than –
(i) under and in accordance with such a permission or a licence granted by the Minister under this Act other than section 29, or
(ii) under and in accordance with a licence granted by the Minister under section 29 of this Act and (also) on a day, or during a period of days, specified in a relevant order under section 25 of this Act,
(c) injures a protected wild animal otherwise than hunting it,
(i) in case the protected wild animal is not a exempted wild mammal, under and in accordance with such a permission or licence granted by the Minister under this Act,
(ii) in case the protected wild animal is an exempted wild mammal, either
(A) under and in accordance with such a permission or licence granted by the Minister other than section 29, or
(B) in the manner and on a day or during a period of days, mentioned in sub paragraph (ii) of paragraph (b) of this subsection,
(d) wilfully interferes with or destroys the breeding place of any protected wild animal,
shall be guilty of an offence.

(6) The Minister may grant a licence to a person to capture or humanely kill and capture and humanely kill at any time a protected wild animal of a species specified in the licence for such educational, scientific or other purpose as shall be specified in the licence.

(7) Notwithstanding subsection (5) of this section, it shall not be an offence for a person –
(a) while engaged in agriculture, fishing or forestry, or in zoology or in any other scientific pursuit, unintentional-

ly to injure or kill a protected wild animal, or

(b) while so engaged to interfere with or destroy the breeding place of such an animal, or

(c) while constructing a road or while carrying on any archaeological operation, building operation or work of engineering construction, or while constructing or carrying on such operation or work as may be prescribed, to kill or injure such an animal or to destroy or injure the breeding place of such an animal, or

(d) to capture an injured or disabled protected wild animal for the purpose of killing it humanely or with the intention of tending it and later releasing it, or

(e) to kill humanely a protected wild animal which is either injured in the manner described in paragraph (a) of this subsection or captured in the manner described in paragraph (d) of this subsection, or so to kill a protected wild animal injured in the circumstances described in paragraph (c) of this subsection,

and nothing in this subsection shall make unlawful,

(i) the taking and killing of hares by coursing at a regulated coursing match which is held both during a period specified as regards hares in a (*qv*) hares order and in a place to which such order applies,

(ii) the hunting of hares by means of a pack of beagles or harriers both during a period specified as regards hares in a hares order and in a place to which such order applies

(iii) anything which section 3(3) of the Whale Fisheries Act, 1937, permits to be done, or

(iv) anything which is duly done pursuant to statute (other than this Act) or statutory instrument, which is permitted to be done under such a statute or instrument or which is done pursuant to and in accordance with a licence or other permission granted or issued pursuant to such such a statute or instrument or anything caused by or which results from, or is consequent upon or the effect of any other act or thing which is lawfully done."

Subsection (8) provides for the defence of urgent necessity where damage is being occasioned as is described in section 42(1) in the case of an offence relating to a protected wild animal which is not of the species protected as is specified in Part II of the Fourth Schedule where it was not practical to apply to the Minister beforehand for permission under section 42. *See:* DAMAGE BY PROTECTED WILD BIRDS.

"(9) In any proceedings for an offence under this section it shall not be necessary for the prosecution to prove that any act constituting (whether in whole or in part) the alleged offence was done otherwise than while the defendant was engaged in agriculture, fishing or forestry, or in zoology or in another scientific pursuit.

(10) Proceedings for an offence under this section may be taken in any District Court District, and in case such proceedings are taken and apart from this section the Justice before whom the proceedings are brought would not have jurisdiction to hear and determine the proceedings, then for the purpose of conferring such jurisdiction the offence may be treated as having been committed within the District Court District to which such Justice is assigned.

(11) The Minister may by regulations provide that –

(a) subsection (8) of this section shall have effect in relation to any proceedings for offences under this section relating to protected wild animals of a species specified both in Part II of the Fourth Schedule to this Act and in the regulations,

(b) the said subsection (8) shall not have effect in relation to any such proceedings relating to protected wild animals of a species specified in the regulations,

and the said subsection (8) shall have effect accordingly."

PROTECTION, FAUNA IN NH 97 REGULATIONS

(NH 97, Reg. 23(1))

The fauna listed in the First Schedule Part 1 of the NH 97 Regulations to which Regulation 23(1) applies are:

1. Mammals: *Lutra lutra* (otter), Cetacean

species and Bat species.
2. Amphibians: *Bufo calamita* (Natterjack toad).

Regulation 23

"(1) The Minister shall take the requisite measures to establish a system of strict protection for the fauna consisting of the animal species set out in Part I of the First Schedule prohibiting –
(a) all forms of deliberate capture or killing of specimens of those species in the wild,
(b) the deliberate disturbance of those species particularly during the period of breeding, rearing, hibernation and migration,
(c) where relevant, the deliberate destruction or taking of eggs of those species from the wild,
(d) the deterioration or destruction of breeding sites or resting places of those species.

Offences
(2) A person who in respect of the species set out in Part 1 of the First Schedule -
(a) deliberately captures or kills any specimen of these species in the wild,
(b) deliberately disturbs these species particularly during the period of breeding, rearing, hibernation and migration,
(c) deliberately takes or destroys the eggs from the wild,
(d) damages or destroys a breeding site or resting place of such an animal,
shall be guilty of an offence.

(3) The prohibitions referred to in subparagraph (a) and (b) of paragraph (1) shall apply to all stages of life of fauna to which this Regulation applies.

(4) The Minister shall establish a system to monitor the incidental capture and killing of fauna consisting of the animal species set out in Part I of the First Schedule, and, having regard to the information gathered, the Minister shall make further research or conservation measures as required to ensure that incidental capture and killing does not have a significant negative impact on the species concerned.

(5) This Regulation is in addition to, and not in substitution for, the provisions of section 23 of the Principal Act."

See: PROTECTION, PROTECTED WILD ANIMALS.

PROTECTION OF FLORA S.21 WLA 1976

(WLA 1976, s.21)

Section 21 of the WLA 1976 amended by Regulation 21 of the NH 97 Regulations as shown surrounded by square brackets:

"(1) Where the Minister considers that a particular species, or particular species, of flora should be protected, he may by order declare the species to be protected throughout the State or in a particular area or areas thereof and an order made under this section shall apply –
(a) in case the order declares a species of flora protected throughout the State, as regards any specimen of that species in every part in the State,
(b) in case the order declares a species of flora protected in a particular area or areas of the State, as regards any specimen of that species in every place in an area specified in the order;
provided that in case the Minister proposes to make an order under this section declaring a species of flora protected in a particular area or in particular areas, of the State, he shall, before making the order, consult any planning authority in relation to whose area, or any part of such area, the proposed order would, if made, apply."

"(2) The Minister shall, as soon as may be after it is made, cause a copy of an order under this section to be sent to the Board and to any (*qv*)planning authority in relation to whose area, or any part of such area, the order applies.

(3) Subject to subsection (5) of this section, a person shall not, save under and in accordance with a licence granted by the Minister under this section –
[(a) cut, pick, collect, uproot or otherwise take, injure damage or destroy any specimen to which this section applies or the flowers, roots, seeds, spores or other part of such specimen,

(b) purchase, sell, keep for sale, transport for sale or exchange, offer for sale or exchange or be in possession of any such specimen whether alive or dead or the flowers, roots, seeds, spores or other parts thereof,]

(c) wilfully alter, damage, destroy or interfere with the habitat or environment of any species of flora to which an order under this section for the time being applies."

Offence

(4) A person who contravenes subsection (3) of this section shall be guilty of an offence.

(5) The Minister may grant a licence to a person for such scientific, educational or other purposes as shall be specified in the licence to do any or all of the following:

(a) to cut, pick, uproot or otherwise take flora of a species specified in the licence and which is of a species to which an order under this section for the time being applies or the flowers, roots or other part of a specimen of the species so specified,

(b) to alter or otherwise interfere with the habitat or environment of any such specimen.

(6) Where in any proceedings for an offence under this section it is proved by the prosecutor that the person accused of the offence:

(a) sold a plant, or the flowers, roots or other part of a plant, which is of the same species as the plant, flowers, roots or other part of a plant, as the case may be, to which the alleged offence relates, and

(b) claimed, either expressly or by implication and whether by advertising or otherwise, that the plant, flowers, roots or other part sold came from or was wholly or partly grown in a particular place, and the place is an area to which an order under this section applied at the time when the alleged offence was committed,

it shall be assumed, until the contrary is shown by the defendant, that the sale was in contravention of subsection (3) of this section.

(7) In any proceedings or an offence under this section, it shall be a defence for the defendant to show that the plant, flowers, roots or other thing to which the alleged defence relates was lawfully imported.

(8) A person shall not be convicted under this section and under section 46 of the Local Government (Planning and Development) Act, 1963, as amended by section 40*(b)* of the Local Government (Planning and Development) Act 1976, in respect of the same act.

(9) In this section:
'Plant' includes a tree or shrub;
'Specimen to which this section applies' means any specimen of a species of flora which is a species to which an order for the time being under this section applies."

FLORA (PROTECTION) ORDER 1999 (S.I. No. 94 of 1999)

"The Minister in exercise of the powers conferred on her by section 21 supra –

2 (1) declared each of the species of flora specified in column (1) of the Schedule to the Order to be protected throughout the State.

(2) The common name of each of the species of flora specified in column 91) of the Schedule to the Order is set out in column (2) of that Schedule opposite the mention of the species.

Article (3) has the effect of excluding form the operation of the order any plants of the named species which are cultivated as vegetables e.g. asparagus.

Article (4) revokes the Flora (Protection) Order 1987 (S.I. No. 274 of 1987). The Order of 1987 had revoke the first Flora (Protection) Order which was made in 1980 (S.I. No. 338 of 1980).

VASCULAR PLANTS.

(1) Scientific name	(2) Common name
Acinos arvensis (Lam.) Dandy	Basil Tyhme
Allium schoenoprasum L.	Chives
Alopecuruis aequalis Sobol.	Orange Foxtail
Arenaria ciliata L. (including ssp. hibernica Ostenf & O.C.Dhal)	Fringed Sandwort
Arthrocnemum perenne (Miller) Moss (syn. Salicornia perennis Mill.)	Perennial Glasswort
Asparagus officinalis L.	Wild Asparagus
Asplenium obovatum Viv. Subsp.	

lanceolatum (Fiori) P.Silva (syn. A. billotii F.W.Schultz)	Lanceolate Spleenwort
Asplenium septentrionale (L.) Hoffm.	Forked Spleenwort
Astragalus danicus Retz.	Purple Milk Vetch
Calamagrostic spigejos (L.) Roth	Wood small-reed
Callitriche truncata Guss.	Short-leaved Water-Starwort
Cardamine impatiens L.	Narrow-leaved Bitter Cress
Cardaminopsis petraea (L.) Hiitonen	Northern Rockcress
Carex depauperata Curtis ex With.	Starved Wood Sedge
Carex divisa Hudson	Divided Sedge
Centaurium pulchellum (Swartz.) Druce.	Lesser Centaruy
Cephalanthere longifolia (L.) Fritsch	Narrow-leaved Helleborine
Colchicum autumnale L.	Autumn Crocus
Cryptogramma crispa (L.) R.Br. Ex Hooker.	Parsley Fern
Deschampsia setacea (Hudson) Hackel	Bog Hair Grass
Epilobium alsinifolium Vill.	Chickweed Willow Herb
Equisetum X moorei Newman	Moore's Horsetail
Eriophorum gracile Koch ex Roth.	Slender Cotton Grass
Galeopsis angustifolia Ehrh. ex Hoffm.	Red Hemp Nettle
Groenlandia densa (L.) Fourr, (syn. Potamogeton densus L.)	Opposite-leaved Pondweed
Gymnocarpium robertianum (Hoffm.) Newman (syn. Thelypteris robertiana (Hoffm.) Slosson	Limestone Fern
Hammarbya paludose (L.) O.Kuntze (syn. malaxis paludosa (L.) Swartz	Bog Orchid
Helianthemum nummularium (L.) Miller	Common Rockrose
Hordeum secalinum Schreber	Meadow Barley
Hydrilla verticillata (L.fil.) Royle	Irish Hydrilla
Hypericum canadense L.	Canadian St. John's Wort
Hypericum hirsutum L.	Hairy St. John's Wort
Inula salicina L.	Irish Fleabane
Lathyrus japonicus Willd.	Sea Pea
Limosella aquatica L.	Mudwort
Logfia minima (Sm.) Dumort. (Syn. Filago minima (Sm.) Pers.)	Slender Cudweed
Lotus subbiflorus Lag. (syn. L.hispidus Desf. ex DC 1815)	Hairy Birdsfoot Trefoil
Lycopodiella inundata Holub (syn. Lycopodium inundatum L.)	Marsh Clubmoss
Mentha pulegium L.	Penny Royal
Mertensia maritima (L.) S.F. Gray	Oyster Plant
Minuartia recurva (All.) Schinz & Thell	Recurved Sandwort
Misopates orontium (L.) Rafin	Lesser Snapdragon
Najas Flexilis (Willd.) Rostk & W.L.E. Schmidt	Slender Naiad
Omalotheca sylvatica (L.) Schultz Bip. & F.W. Schultz (syn. Gnaphallium sylvaticum L.)	Wood Cudweed
Otanthus maritimus (L.) Hoffmans & Link (syn. Diotis maritima (L.) Desf ex Cass.)	Cottonweed
Papaver hybridum L.	Round Prickly-headed Poppy
Pilularia globulifera L.	Pillwort
Polygonum viviparum L.	Alpine Bistort
Pseudorchis albida (L.) A.&D. Love. (syn. Leucorchis albida (L.) E.F.H. Meyer)	Small-white Orchid
Puccinellia fasciulata (Torrey) E.P. Bicknell	Tufted Salt-marsh Grass
Pyrola rotundifolia L.ssp. maritima (Kenyon) E.F. Warburg	Round-leaved Wintergreen
Sanguisorba officinalis (L.)	Great Burnet
Saxifraga granulata L.	Meadow Saxifrage
Saxifraga hartii D.A. Webb	Hart's Saxifrage
SAxifraga hirculus L.	Yellow Marsh Saxifrage
Saxifrage nivalis L.	Alpine Saxifrage
Scirpus triqueter L.	

(syn. Schoenoplectus triqueter (L.) Palla	Triangular Club Rush
Scleranthus annuus L.	Annual Knawel
Simethis planifolia (L.) Gren.	Kerry Lily
Spiranthes romanzoffiana Cham.	Drooping Lady's Tresses
Stachys officinalis (L.) Trevisan (syn. Betonica officinalis L.)	Betony
Trichomanes speciosum Willd.	Killarney Fern
Trifolium glomeratum L.	Clustered Clover
Trifolium subterraneum L.	Subterranean Clover
Trollius europeaus L.	Globe Flower
Vicia orobus DC.	Bitter Vetch
Viola hirta L.	Hairy Violet
Viola lactea Sm.	Pale Heath Violet

MOSSES

Bryum calophyllum R.Br.
Bryum marratii Wils.
Cacoscopium nigritum (Hedw.) Brid.
Drepanocladus vernicosus (Mitt.) Warnst.
Leptobarbula berica (De Not.) Schimp.
Orthrotrichum pallens Brid.
Sorhrotrichum sprucei Mont.
Orthrotrichum stramineum Hornsch. ex. Brid.
Paludella squarrosa (Hedw.) Brid
Pottia wilsonii (Hook.) Br. Eur.
Tetraplodon angustatus (Hedw.) Br. Eur.
Tortella inclinata (Hedw.f.) Limpr.
Weissia longifolia Mitt.
Weissia rostellata (Brid.) Lind.

LIVERWORTS

Leiocolea gillmanii (Aust.) Evans syn. Lophozia gillmanii (Aust.) Schust.	
Leiocolea rutheana (Limpr.) K.Mull. syn. Lophozia rutheana (Limpr.) Howe	Fen flapwort
Petalophyllum ralfsii (Wils.) Nees & Gott.	
Plagiochila atlantica F. Rose	

LICHENS

fulgensia fulgens (Sw.) Elenkin

STONEWORTS

Lamprothamnium papulosum (Wallr.) J. Groves	Foxtail Stonewort
Nitella gracilis (Smith) Agardh	Slender Stonewort

PROTECTION
TAKING FLORA AND FAUNA IN THE WILD,
SPECIES IN PART II
FIRST SCHEDULE REG. 24
(NH 97, Reg. 24)

Part II of the First Schedule to the NH 97 Regulations refers to the following species of fauna and flora:

1. Mammals:
   Martes martes (pine marten),
   Lepus timidus (Irish hare),
   Halichoerus grypus (Grey seal) and
   Phota vitinula (Common seal).
2. Amphibians: *Rana temporaria* (Frog).
3. Fish:
   Lampetra fluviatilis (Lampern),
   Coregonus autumnalis spp. (Pollan),
   Alosa alosa (Allis shads),
   Alosa fallax (Twaite shad) and
   Salmo salar (Salmon) (only in freshwater).
4. Molluscs:
   H*elix pomatia* (Edible snail)
   and *Margaritifera margartifera* (freshwater pearl mussel).
5. Crustaceans:
   Austropotamobius pallipes (White-clawed crayfish)
6. Lichens:
   Cladonia subgenus Cladina: (Reindeer moss).
7. Mosses:
   Leucobryum glaucum,
   All Sphagna
8. Ferns and relatives:
   Lycopodium spp. (Clubmosses).

Regulation 24 of the NH 97 Regulations provide:

"(1) Having regard to the surveillance provided for in Regulation 7(1) –
(a) the Minister, in the case of any wild flora or fauna (to the extent, if any, specified therein) set out in Part II of the First Schedule, and
(b) the Minister for the Marine, in respect of the fish species (to the extent, if any, specified therein) set out in paragraph (3) of that Part,
may each by direction take measures to ensure that the taking in the wild of specimens of species of wild fauna (including those fish species to the extent so specified, if any) and flora set out out in that Part as well as their exploitation is compatible with their being maintained at a favourable conservation status.

(2) Without prejudice to the generality of paragraph (1), the measures to which that paragraph relate may include –
(a) directions regarding access to certain propertiy,
(b) directions regarding the temporary or local prohibition of the taking of specimens in the wild and exploitation of certain populations,
(c) the regulation by direction of either or both the periods or methods of taking of specimens,
(d) application, when specimens are taken, of any other statutory provision relating to either or both hunting and fishing which take account of the conservation of such populations,
(e) establishment of a system of licences for taking specimens or quotas,
(f) such other directions as the Minister, or the Minister for the Marine in respect of the fish species stipulated in Part II of the First Schedule, consider appropriate.

(3) The Minister, and the Minister for the Marine in respect of the fish species stipulated in Part II of the First Schedule, shall publish or cause to be published in the Iris Oifigiúil a copy of every direction under this Regulation.

(4) This Regulation is in addition to, and not in substitution for, the provisions of –
(a) section 23 of the Wildlife Act, 1976
(b) Parts II, VI, VII, VIII, IX, XI, XVII, XVIII and XIX of, and paragraph 2 of the Fifth Schedule to the Fisheries (Consolidation) Act, 1959,
(c) sections 28, 29 and 33 of the Fisheries (Amendment) Act, 1962,
(d) Parts IV and VI of the Fisheries Act, 1980, and
(e) the Foyle Fisheries Acts, 1952 to 1983.

It is difficult to reconcile these two regulations, 24 which is quoted here and 7 to which it refers.

Regulation 7 deals with an obligation on the Minister and the Minister for the Marine to undertake the surveillance of the conservation status of natural habitats and species as defined in Article 2 of the *(qv)* Habitats Directive. Article 2 of the Directive states its aim to be "the conservation of natural habitats and of wild fauna and flora in the European territory...".

Is this surveillance an ongoing thing or is it intended merely as an adjunct to the process of establishing the "conservation status" with regard to its inclusion or exclusion of a site from the list of special areas of conservation as the regulation suggests when it specifies "In the adaption of the list transmitted to the Commission under Regulation 5(4)."?

The use of the word surveillance is not helpful. To keep something under surveillance means to keep under close observation. For how long? Regulation 7 provides that in the course of this surveillance particular regard must be had to *(qv)* priority natural habitat types and *(qv)* priority species.

The Regulation also provides as one of its main functions for the appointment of *(qv)* authorised officers among whose functions under the Regulations are the carrying out of this surveillance. Why is it not described as being one of the functions of an authorised person appointed under section 72(1) of the WLA 1976 who are fully competent to police the NH97 Regulations? This is possibly just clumsy draughtmanship but the functionary is described in WLA 1976 as an "authorised person" and in the Regulations as an "authorised officer".

At the end of the day the functions of an authorised officer appointed under Regulation 7 seem so circumscribed by the terms of that Regulation that it is difficult to see him performing the broad function contemplated by Regulation 24. Should some other functionary be appointed or should there not be a reference here to the person appointed under the WLA 1976 and should they not be designated to carry out the Regulation 24 functions?

Offence

(5) (a) A person who fails to comply with a

direction under this Regulation shall be guilty of an offence,

(b) In a prosecution for an offence under sub paragraph (a), it shall be a good defence for the accused to prove that he or she was not aware of the direction at the relevant time and that he or she could not be reasonably be expected to have known of the direction at the time."

With regard to the defence quoted above in Regulation 24(5)(a) to a prosecution for an offence under 24(5)(a) it is drafted in such unusually generous terms for a defendant that comment has to be made. It could render what is an important offence unenforceable.

FAUNA IN THE FIRST SCHEDULE (REG 23), TAKING IN THE WILD (REG 24) AND PROTECTION OF FLORA (S 21 WLA 1976), DEROGATION FROM

See: DEROGATION.

PROTECTION OF ANIMALS (AMENDMENT) ACT 1965
(WLA 1976, s.67)

"Part V of the he Protection of Animals (Amendment) Act 1965 shall be deemed to apply neither to protected wild birds nor to protected wild animals."

PROTECTION OF SALMON AND OTHER FISH
(F(C)A 1959)

Various sections, *see:* SALMON AND OTHER FISH, PROTECTION OF.

PROTECTION OF YOUNG AND BREEDING FISH
(F(C)A 1959, s.173)

Offence

"(1) If any person –

(a) wilfully takes, sells, purchases, or has in his possession the spawn, smolts or fry of salmon, trout or eels, or
(b) wilfully obstructs the passage of the smolts or fry of salmon, trout or eels, or
(c) injures or disturbs the spawn or fry of salmon, trout or eels, or
(d) injures or disturbs any spawning bed, bank or shallow where the spawn or fry of salmon, trout or eels may be,

such person shall be guilty of an offence under this section.

(2) Where a person is convicted of an offence under this section any device or fishing engine used in the commission of the offence shall, as a statutory consequence of conviction, stand forfeited."

(Note that the maximum penalty prescribed under this subsection has been increased. See: FINES AND IMPRISONMENT (IMPOSITION OF)).

PUBLIC AUTHORITY
(EPAA 1992/Heritage Act 1995)

"Public authority" in the EPAA 1992 and by virtue of section 3(1) of same means –

(a) a Minister of the Government,
(b) the Commissioners of Public Works in Ireland,
(c) a local authority for the purposes of the Local Government Act 1941,
(d) a harbour authority within the meaning of the Harbours Act 1946,
(e) a health board established under the Health Act 1970,
(f) a board or other body established by or under statute,
(g) a company in which all the shares are held by, or on behalf of, or by directors appointed by, a Minister of the Government, or
(h) a company in which all the shares are held by a board, company, or other body referred to in paragraph (f) or (g) of this definition.

The same definition of "public authority" appears in section 2(1) of the Heritage Act 1995 for the purposes of that Act.

PUBLIC HEALTH, EXCLUSION OF CERTAIN ENACTMENTS
(WMA 1996, s.70)

Section 107 of the Public Health (Ireland) Act 1878 and **section 27 of the Public Health Acts Amendment Act, 1890** shall not apply in relation to waste within the meaning of this Act.

PUBLIC PLACE
(EPAA 1992, s.3(1))

"Includes any place to which the public have access, whether by right or by permission, or whether subject to, or free of charge."

PUBLICATION AND DEPOSIT,
BYE-LAWS, ORDERS, ETC.
(F(C)A 1959)

See: BYE-LAWS.

Q

QUALIFIED PERSON
(WLA 1976, s.28(2))

A qualified person within the meaning of section 28(2) of the WLA 1976, who is the holder of a section 29 hunting licence, is entitled with a firearm to hunt and kill on any land an "*(qv)* exempted wild mammal" or a protected wild bird of a species specified in an order under section 24. *See:* (1) HUNTING, HUNTING OR KILLING WITH FIREARMS.

QUALITY STANDARDS, WATERS, TRADE AND SEWAGE EFFLUENT
(LG(WP)A 1977, s.26)

Section 26 of the LG(WP)A 1977 subsection (1A) of which was inserted by section 59(8) of the EPAA 1992 and subsection (4) was substituted by section 18 of the LG(WP)(A)A 1990:

"(1) The Minister may, after consultation with the Minister for Fisheries, the Minister for Industry and Commerce, and any other Minister who appears to him to be interested and the *(qv)* Water Pollution Advisory Council, prescribe for the purposes of this Act quality standards for *(qv)* waters, *(qv)* trade effluents and *(qv)* sewage effluents and standards in relation to methods of treatment of such effluents.

[(1A) Regulations under this section shall not relate to sewage or other effluents from any works, apparatus, treatment plant, sewer or drainage pipe vested in, or controlled or used by, a sanitary authority for the disposal of sewage or other effluents to any waters.]

(2) Regulations under this section may relate to -
(i) all or specified, or specified classes of, waters, trade effluents or sewage effluents,
(ii) waters, trade effluents or sewage effluents in specified areas, or
(iii) waters specified by reference to their use.

(3) Where regulations under this section relate to sewage effluent from a sewer or to waters to which sewage effluent from a sewer discharges, it shall be the duty of the sanitary authority in which the sewer is vested or by whom it is controlled to take steps as soon as practicable to ensure that the sewage effluent complies with, or does not result in the waters to which the effluent is discharged not complying with, any relevant standard prescribed under this section.

[(4) (a) Regulations under this section may require persons to take such steps as may be specified in the regulations to secure compliance with quality standards prescribed under subsection (1) and may contain such incidental, supplementary and consequential provisions as appear to the Minister to be necessary or expedient for the purpose of the regulations (including provisions modifying any provision of the Local Government (Water Pollution) Acts, 1977 and 1990).
(b) Where it is proposed to make regulations under this section modifying a provision of this Act, a draft of the regulations shall be laid before each house of the Oireachtas and the regulations shall not be made until a resolution approving of the draft shall be passed by each such House.]"

Section 26A of the LG(WP)A 1977 as amended by insertion of section 66(1) of the WMA 1996:

"26A(1) For the purpose of preventing or limiting water pollution, the Minister may, by regulations, prohibit or limit or control in a specified manner and to a specified extent, the production, treatment, use (in a process or otherwise), importation, distribution, storage, transport, supply or sale of any specified substance or of any article containing any specified substance.

(2) Without prejudice to the generality of subsection (1), regulations under this section may –
(a) make different provisions for different substances and articles,
(b) require local authorities or other specified persons to take specified steps for the purpose of securing

compliance with the regulations,
(c) contain such incidental, consequential and supplementary provisions as appear to the Minister to be necessary or expedient for the purposes of such regulations.

Offence
(3) (a) A person who contravenes a provision of regulations under this section shall be guilty of an offence.
(b) A person guilty of an offence under this section shall be liable –
(i) on summary conviction to a fine not exceeding £1,00 or imprisonment for a term not exceeding 6 months or, at the discretion of the court, to both such fine and such imprisonment, or
(ii) on conviction on indictment, to a fine not exceeding £25,000 or imprisonment for a term not exceeding 5 years or, at the discretion of the court, to both such fine and such imprisonment.

(4) A prosecution for an offence under this section may be taken by the Minister, a local authority or such other person as may be specified in regulations under this section."

See: Local Government (Water Pollution) Act, 1977 (Water Quality Standards for Phosphorus) Regulations 1998 (S.I. No. 258 of 1998).

EXTENSION OF FUNCTIONS UNDER S.26 OF LG(WP)A 1977 TO THE AGENCY

These functions under section 26 of the LG(WP)A 1977 now apply to the Agency in the circumstances described in Article 4 of Environmental Protection Agency (Extension of Powers) Order 1996 (S.I. No. 126 of 1996). *See:* EXTENSION OF POWERS.

See: EMISSION LIMIT VALUES AND QUALITY STANDARDS.

QUALITY STANDARDS,
AIR
(APA 1987, s.50)

See: AIR QUALITY STANDARDS.

QUALITY MANAGEMENT PLANS,
WATER
(LG(WP)A 1977, s.15)

See: WATER QUALITY MANAGEMENT PLANS.

QUALITY MANAGEMENT PLANS,
AIR
(APA 1987, s.46)

See: AIR QUALITY MANAGEMENT PLANS.

QUALITY,
MONITORING
WATER QUALITY
(LG(WP)A 1977, s.22)

See: MONITORING (1).

QUALITY,
MONITORING
AIR QUALITY
AND EMISSIONS
(APA 1987, s.54)

See: MONITORING (2).

QUALITY,
MONITORING
ENVIRONMENTAL
QUALITY AND
EMISSIONS
(EPAA 1992, s.96)

See: MONITORING (3).

QUALITY
ENVIRONMENTAL QUALITY
DATA STORAGE
(EPAA 1992, s.69)

See: DATA (3).

QUALITY,
ENVIRONMENTAL QUALITY
OBJECTIVES
(EPAA 1992, s.75)

The (*qv*) Agency has a duty to specify and publish. *See:* ENVIRONMENTAL QUALITY OBJECTIVES.

R

RATES ON FISHERIES
(F(C)A 1959 Part V)

See: FISHERY RATES

RECOGNISED BODY
(WLA 1976, s.44(5))

A body recognised by the Minister by order under section 44(5) which confers certain rights in respect of unlawful entry onto land by others hunting with firearms.
See: ENTRY ON LAND, WITH A FIREARM, HUNTING.

RECOVERY
(WMA 1996, s.4(4))

"In relation to waste, means any activity carried on for the purposes of reclaiming, recycling or re-using, in whole or in part, the waste and any activities related to such reclamation, recycling or re-use, including any of the activities specified in the Fourth Schedule, and "waste recovery activity" shall be construed accordingly."
See: SCHEDULES HERETO, WMA 1996 SCHEDULES.

RECOVERY OF WASTE BY LOCAL AUTHORITY
(WMA 1996, s.31)

"(1) A local authority may –
- (a) engage or participate in the recovery of waste, and for that purpose may enter into one or more agreements with any other local authority or any person,
- (b) buy or otherwise acquire waste for the purpose of recovering it,
- (c) use, sell or otherwise dispose of any material or thing, including energy, recovered from waste.

(2) For the purpose of subsection (1), 'local authority' includes the corporation of a borough of any kind and the council of an urban district."

RECOGNITION ORDER
(WLA 1976 s.16)

Is an order made under the provisions of the WLA 1976 recognising a nature reserve where the land, which includes a habitat or an ecosystem described at section 15(2)(a) of the WLA 1976, is already owned by a person who is prepared to dedicate and use and manage the land for that purpose.
See: ESTABLISHMENT ORDER.

Section 16 of the WLA 1976:

"(1) Where a person who is the occupier of land satisfies the Minister that –
- (a) the land includes a habitat or part of a habitat or an ecosystem described in paragraph (a) of section 15(2) of this Act,
- (b) the interest of the person in or over the land is such as to enable the person to establish and manage a nature reserve on the land, and
- (c) the person can, in accordance with any conditions which the Minister sees fit to impose, use or manage the land so as to establish and maintain, or maintain, as may be appropriate, a nature reserve on the land,

then, subject to subsection (2) of this section, the Minister may, by order (in this section referred to as a recognition order) recognise the land as a nature reserve and the recognition shall continue for as long as the order is in force.

(2) Before making a recognition order the Minister shall consult with the Minister for Agriculture and Fisheries, the Minister for Transport and Power, the (*qv*) Commissioners and any (*qv*) planning authority within whose area the land to which the proposed order relates, or any part of such land, is situate.

(3) A recognition order shall state the Minister's reason for recognising the land to which the order relates as a nature reserve and indicate the objectives for which the land is to be used or managed as a nature reserve.

(4) The Minister shall not revoke a recogni-

tion order unless he considers that –
(a) the objectives indicated in the order have not been attained or are not being properly maintained, or
(b) for any other reason, it is no longer appropriate for him to continue to recognise as a nature reserve, by virtue of the order, the land to which the order relates.

(5) The Minister shall, as soon as may be after it is made, cause a copy of the order to be sent to the Commissioners, to the (*qv*) Board and to any planning authority within whose area the land to which the order relates, or any part of such land, is situate."

Section 59(5) of the WLA 1976 provides for regulations permitting public access to land to which a recognition order applies where the owner of the land agrees. *See:* ACCESS TO AND ENTRY ON LAND.

The following is a list of the recognition orders which have been made since the passing of the WLA 1976:

Capel Island and Knockadoon Head (1985), Derrycunihy Wood (1989), Derrymore Island (1989), Kilcolman Bog (1993), Little Skellig (1988), Mangan Bog (1987), North Bull Island (2)(1988), Puffin Island (1987), Sheheree Bog (1990), Teragh Island (1989) and The Gearagh (1987).

See: RESERVES AND REFUGES.

REFUGES,
REFUGES FOR FAUNA
(WLA 1976, s.17)

See: (1) DESIGNATION ORDER; (2) RESERVES AND REFUGES.

RECYCLING
(WMA 1996, s.5(1))

"Means, in relation to waste, the subjection of waste to any process or treatment to make it re-usable in whole or in part."

REGISTERS
(F(C)A 1959/LG(WP)A 1977/APA 1987/ EPAA 1992/WMA 1996)

(1) F(C)A 1959

PART X REGISTER – SECTION 163 OF THE F(C)A 1959

Section 163 of the F(C)A 1959, as amended by substitution by section 20 of the F(A)A 1994, provides for the keeping by holders of a Part X licence of a register of purchases, receipts, sale, exportation, disposal and removals of salmon, trout, eels or molluscan shellfish. *See:* CERTIFICATE OF FITNESS.

REGISTER OF SEA ANGLERS – SECTION 58(1) OF THE FA 1980

"Register of Sea Anglers", for the purposes of section 20(1) of the F(A)A (No. 2) Act 1987, means a register to which section 58(1) of the FA 1980 applies.

Section 58(1) of the FA 1980 had provided for calling the register "Register for Trout, Coarse Fish and Sea Anglers".

Section 58 of the FA 1980, as amended by section 20 of the F(A)A (No. 2) 1987, provides for the establishment and maintenance by each (*qv*) regional fisheries board of a register of sea anglers in which is entered the names of persons applying to be registered. Prior to the 1987 Act there were different categories of anglers for different species of fish, *e.g.* trout angler, coarse fish angler.

The significance of being registered on the register is that by virtue of section 12 of the FA 1980, registration qualifies persons to vote in the election for membership of a regional fisheries board. *See:* ELECTORATE FOR ELECTION.

(2) LG(WP)A 1977

SECTION 9 REGISTER

Section 9 of the LG(WP)A 1977 provides for registers under section 4, trade and sewage effluents, and section 16, discharges to sewers, of that Act and all water (*qv*)abstractions as follows:

"(1) Each (*qv*) local authority shall cause to be established and kept a register of all licences under section 4 granted by it.

(2) Each local authority shall cause to be established and kept a register of abstractions from waters in its functional area.

(3) Each (*qv*) sanitary authority shall cause to be established and kept a register of all licences under section 16 granted by it.

(4) A register under this section shall be kept at the offices of the local authority or sanitary authority and shall at all reasonable times be open to inspection by any person.

(5) Any person shall be entitled to obtain from a local authority or sanitary authority a copy of any entry in a register under this section on payment of a prescribed fee.

(6) Every document purporting to be a copy of an entry in a register under this section and purporting to be certified by an officer of a local authority or a sanitary authority to be a true copy of the entry shall, without proof of the signature of the person purporting so to certify or that he was such officer, be received in evidence in any legal proceedings and shall, until the contrary is proved, be deemed to be a true copy of the entry and to be evidence of the terms of the entry.

(7) The Minister may make regulations for the purpose of this section.

(8) Without prejudice to the generality of subsection (7), regulations under this section may provide that specified classes of abstractions shall be exempt from subsection (2)."

Regulations: Local Government (Water Pollution) Regulations 1978, Part V Registers, Exempted Abstractions (S.I. No. 108 of 1978), Local Government (Water Pollution) Regulations 1992, Part V Register Fee (S.I. No. 271 of 1992).

REGISTER UNDER SALMONOID REGULATIONS 1988.

The European Communities (Quality of Salmonoid Waters) Regulations 1988 (S.I. No. 293 of 1988) (in this work referred to as the "Salmonoid Regulations" are concerned with water quality although these Regulations, for technical reasons, were not made under the LG(WP)A 1977. Regulation 6 of these regulations requires the local authority to keep a register of the results of sampling under the regulations which may be inspected by any person. *See:* SALMONOID REGULATIONS.

(3) APA 1987

SECTION 17 REGISTER

Section 17 of the APA 1987 contains a provision similar to the LG(WP)A 1977:

"(1) Every local authority shall as soon as may be after the commencement of this Act establish and maintain a register (in this Act referred to as 'the register') for the purposes of this Act and shall make therein all such entries and additions as may, from time to time, be prescribed.

(2) The register shall be kept at the offices of the local authority and shall be made available for inspection by any person during office hours.

(3) When a request is made to a local authority for a copy of an entry in the register, the copy shall be issued to the applicant on the payment by him to the local authority of such fee (if any) as they shall fix not exceeding the reasonable cost of making the copy.

(4) Every document purporting to be a copy of an entry in a register and purporting to be certified by an officer of a local authority to be a true copy of the entry shall, without proof of the signature of the person purporting so to certify or that he was such officer, be received in evidence in any legal proceedings and shall, until the contrary is proved, be deemed to be a true copy of the entry and to be evidence of the terms of the entry.

(5) Evidence of any entry in the register may be given by production of a copy thereof certified pursuant to this section and it shall not be necessary to produce the register itself."

Article 37 of the Air Pollution Act 1987 (Licensing of Industrial Plant) Regulations 1988 (S.I. No. 266 of 1988) refers.

(4) EPAA 1992

SECTION 89 REGISTER OF LICENCES

Section 89 of the EPAA 1992:

"(1) The Agency shall, as soon as may be after the coming into operation of this Part, establish and maintain a register (in this Act referred to as the 'register of licences') for the purposes of this Part and shall make therein all such entries and additions as may, from time to time be prescribed.

(2) The register of licences shall be kept at the offices of the Agency and shall be made available for inspection by any person during office hours.

(3) When a request is made to the Agency for a copy of an entry in the register of licence, the copy shall be issued to the person requesting it on the payment by him to the Agency of such fee (if any) as they shall fix not exceeding the reasonable cost of making the copy.

(4) Every document purporting to be a copy of an entry in the register of licences and purporting to be certified by an officer of the Agency to be a true copy of the entry shall, without proof of the signature of the person purporting so to certify or that he was such officer, be received in evidence in any legal proceedings and shall, unless the contrary is shown, be deemed to be a true copy of the entry and to be evidence of the terms of the entry.

(5) Evidence of an entry in the register of licences may be given by production of a copy thereof certified pursuant to this section and it shall not be necessary to produce the register of licences itself.

(6) Every entry in the register of licences relating to an (*qv*)activity in the functional area of a (*qv*)planning authority shall be notified to that planning authority by the Agency as soon as may be and the planning authority shall maintain a copy of these notifications in a register which shall be available for inspection by any person free of charge during office hours."

REGISTER OF INTERESTS

Section 37(7) of the EPAA 1992 provides for the keeping by the (*qv*) Agency of a register to be known as a register of interests containing particulars contained in declarations of interest given to the Agency under section 37 and subsection (8) requires such register to be made available for inspection by the public and copies thereof must be made available at a reasonable cost.

REGISTER OTHERWISE THAN IN LEGIBLE FORM

Section 112(1) of the EPAA 1992 provides that the Agency may keep a register under any provision of the Act otherwise than in legible form so that the register is capable of being used to make a legible copy or reproduction (a "copy record") of any entry in the register.

Subsections (2) and (3) provide for proof by certificate signed by an officer of the Agency, of a copy record of an entry in the register and that a document purporting to be a certificate under subsection (1) is to be accepted without proof of the signature.

Subsection (4) provides that in any proceedings any copy record may be given in evidence and shall be prima facie evidence of any fact therein stated, provided the court is satisfied of the reliability of the system used to make the copy record and the original entry on which it was based.

REGISTER OF NOISE NOTICES

Section 107(7) of the EPAA 1992 requires the keeping of a register of notices under the section with respects to (*qv*) noise which must be available for inspection by the public free of charge and copies of entries must be provided at reasonable cost.

REGISTER UNDER GMO REGULATIONS 1994

Article 8(1) of the Genetically Modified Organisms Regulations, 1994 (S.I. No. 345 of 1994) requires the maintaining by the Agency of a register containing the entries specified in the Article, as appropriate for each notification or record.

(5) WMA 1996

SECTION 19 REGISTER

Section 19 (1) and (2) of the WMA 1996 are in the same terms as the APA 1987 and the EPAA 1992 above except that here it is the local authority who are responsible for the register and subsection (6) differs from subsection (6) in the EPAA 1992 in that it is the local authority who must notify the Agency of such particulars entered in it.

Section 19(7) provides:

"(a) A local authority or the Agency may keep a register under this section otherwise than in legible form so that the register is capable of being used to make a legible copy or reproduction of any entry in the register.
(b) References in the preceding provisions of this section to a copy of an entry in a register under this section shall be construed as including references to such a legible copy or reproduction."

ENTRIES IN RELATION TO PACKAGING IN SECTION 19 REGISTER

Article 21 of the Waste Management (Packaging) Regulations 1997 (S.I. No. 242 of 1977):

"(1) It is hereby prescribed that the register maintained by a local authority under section 19 of the Act shall contain entries specifying the following matters –
(a) the receipt of an application for authorisation under article 5(5) and the decision of the local authority in respect of the application,
(b) the registration or renewal of registration of a major producer by the local authority in accordance with article 6,
(c) the giving of notice under Article 20 (2).
Information received by a local authority in accordance with articles 6, 7 and 20 shall be made available at the principal office of the local authority concerned for inspection by any person during office hours."

WASTE MANAGEMENT REGISTER REGULATIONS 1997

The Waste Management Regulations 1997 prescribe the entries to be made in the registers to be maintained by the Agency and each local authority under section 19 of the WMA 1996 and provides for entries in relation to waste licences, reviews of waste licences and waste collection permits.

It also prescribes entries under the WLA 1996 as to proceedings brought by local authorities for offences under the Act and convictions procured thereunder, requirements under sections 15(3) and 18(1) notices under section 55 applications to the court under sections 57 and 58 and the orders made by the court under those sections.
See: (1)MONITORING, (2) ENFORCEMENT.

FARM PLASTIC

Article 22(1) of the Waste Management (Farm Plastics) Regulations 1997 (S.I. No. 315 of 1997) provides the entries to be made in the section 19 register under those Regulations.

SEWAGE SLUDGE

Article 8(2) of the Waste Management (Use of Sewage Sludge in Agriculture) Regulations 1998 (S.I. No. 148 of 1998) require a local authority to establish and maintain a register known as "the Sludge Register". *See:* WASTE, RECOVERY OF SLUDGES AND AGRICULTURAL WASTE.

It appears that the register contemplated under the Sewage Sludge in Agriculture Regulations is a register separate and apart from a section 19 register above.

WASTE PERMIT

Article 22 of the Waste Management (Permit) Regulations 1998 (S.I. No. 165 of 1998) requires a local authority to maintain a register in accordance with section 19 of the WMA 1996 specifying:

(a) in relation to a waste permit the information specified in Article 10(1)(a) to (d) furnished with the application, and
(b) in the case of a certificate of registration, the location of the (*qv*) facility, the category or categories of (*qv*) hazardous

waste concerned and the volume.

(6) WLA 1976

WILDLIFE REGISTER

Section 46(3)(d) of the WLA 1976 allows the Minister by regulations under the subsection to require the keeping of a register by a wildlife dealer and prescribe entries therein. *See:* WILDLIFE DEALING, REGULATION AND CONTROL

REGULATIONS
(F(C)A 1959/LG(WP)A 1977/APA 1987/
WLA 1976/EPAA 1992/WMA 1996)

A regulation is a formal order made by a designated Minister exercising a power to make subordinate legislation usually within the framework of an existing Act. A regulation is made by statutory instrument and should be distinguished from a (*qv*) bye-law, an (*qv*) order or a Directive.

Section 3 of the European Communities Act 1972 gives a general power to implement European Law by regulation. The two most important European directives on wildlife, the (*qv*) Birds Directive and the (*qv*) Natural Habitat Directive, have both been implemented in Ireland by regulation under this Statute.

These regulations suffer from the disadvantage that they can provide for summary prosecution only for breach or contravention of regulation and not for prosecution on indictment. As summary offences constitute "minor offences" under the Constitution the courts are restricted to the imposition of what are now very significant penalties indeed.

All of the statutes dealing with the environment have a general section empowering the Minister to make regulations for the purposes of the statute as distinct from specific powers to make regulations in individual sections for some particular purpose of that section.

GENERAL POWERS TO MAKE REGULATIONS

General powers to make regulations under the following sections, section 4 of the F(C)A 1959, section 30 of the LG(WP)A 1977, section 10 of the APA 1987, section 6 of the EPAA 1992, section 7 of the WMA 1996 and section 8 of the WLA 1976 share common characteristics and deal broadly with the following:

(1) They are intended to cover:
 (a) all matters referred to as prescribed or to be prescribed, or
 (b) in relation to any matter referred to in the Act as the subject of regulations, or
 (c) for the purpose of giving full effect to the Act/to the provisions of the Act.

The LG(WP)A 1977 lacks (c).

(2) They are intended to relate to different areas, different circumstances and different classes of cases.

The LG(WP)A 1977 lacks this provision also. The provision in section 7(2) of the WMA 1996 is wider. It reads:

"different areas, different circumstances, different classes of persons or waste and different waste management or other activities."

(3) They become law, except in the case of certain specific sections, if no resolution annulling the order is passed by either house of the Oireachtas within 21 days of the order being laid before each house of the Oireachtas, but without prejudice to the validity of anything previously done thereunder.

(4) The excepted sections, which require the actual passing of a resolution approving the draft by each House are:

 (a) Section 6(3) of the APA 1987 which deals, in relation to "industrial plant", with the Minister's power by regulation to vary the Third Schedule by the addition or deletion of an industrial process.
 (b) In the WMA 1996, regulations under sections 7(6), 39(8) or 62 or an order under section 8 or section 69(1) or an order under subsection (5) of section 7 amending or revoking such an order.

(5) **Section 8(3) of the WLA 1976** only requires consultation, between the Minister, any other Minister of State, the (*qv*) Commissioners, a (*qv*) planning authority or any other body before making or revoking or amending a regulation or order.

(6) **Section 7(6) of the WMA 1996** is the only Act which makes provision as follows:

"If in any respect any difficulty arises in bringing any provision of this Act into operation or in relation to the operation of any such provision, the Minister may by regulations do anything which appears to him or her to be necessary or expedient for removing that difficulty, for bringing that provision into operation, or for securing or facilitating its operation, and any such regulations may modify any provision of this or any other enactment so far as may be necessary or expedient for the purposes aforesaid but no regulations may be made under this subsection in relation to a provision of this Act after the expiration of 2 years from the commencement of that provision."

See: ORDERS.

REGULATIONS UNDER SPECIFIC POWERS

F(C)A 1959, s.12

Whereas the Fisheries Acts 1959–1997 refer in a number of headings to "regulations" as described, the word is intended to describe the statutory regulation of the use of certain fishing engines in the section itself and not Ministerial regulations.

Section 12 of the F(C)A 1959 provides, with respects to *(qv)* special local licences, that the Minister may regulate for the times and places for fishing and the keeping of order among the holders of such licences.

Offence
Subsection (2) provides that any act of commission or omission in contravention of such a regulation is an offence.

(Note that the maximum penalty prescribed under this section has been increased. *See:* FINES AND IMPRISONMENT (IMPOSITION OF).)

Section 71 of the F(A)A 1997:

"(1) The Minister may make regulations establishing such requirements in relation to the management and operation of *(qv)* aquaculture as the Minister considers necessary or expedient.

Offence
(2) A person who contravenes or fails to comply with a regulation under subsection (1) shall be guilty of an offence triable summarily."

LG(WP)A 1977, s.6

Section 6 of the LG(WP)A 1977 empowers the Minister to make regulations in respect of licensing of trade and sewage effluent, section 4, and appeals in relation to licensing of trade and sewage effluents, section 8, and reviews of licences under section 4, section 7.

They are concerned with the form and mechanics of application and appeal and not with their merits or demerits. They closely resemble the regulations under section 19 of the LG(WP)A 1977 which appear immediately hereunder.

The main differences are, for "sanitary authority" in section 19 read "local authority" in section 6 and the subsections dealing with the fees payable to An Bord Pleanála in respect of an appeal which were added to both sections by the section 4 of the WP(A)A 1990 do not correspond although they have approximately the same wording.

Subsection (2D) in section 6 is also different because an appeal under section 8(1)*(a)* may be brought by "a person" meaning "any person" whereas in section 20, the subject of the regulations in section 19 hereunder, the appeal can be brought only by the *(qv)* occupier of *(qv)* premises from which a discharge, to which a licence under section 16 relates, is made or, under section 20(1)*(a)* and *(b)*, by a person whose application for a licence under section 16 has been refused. *See:* APPEALS (3)

LG(WP)A 1977, s.19

Section 19 of the LG(WP)A 1977, as amended by the LG(WP)(A)A 1990, provides for regulations under section 16 of the LG(WP)A 1977, Licensing of Discharges to Sewers, and section 20 of the LG(WP)A 1977, Appeals to An Bord Pleanála under section 16, and section 17 Reviews of section 12 Licences.

Section 19(1) of the LG(WP)A 1977:

"(1) The Minister may make regulations for the purposes of section 16 and 20."

The Local Government (Water Pollution)

Regulations 1978 (S.I. No. 108 of 1978) and the Local Government (Water Pollution) Regulations 1992 (S.I. No. 271 of 1992) refer.

Subsection (2) provides that without prejudice to the generality of subsection (1) regulations under this section may make provision for the form of licence, specific information to be furnished and evidence to verify, furnishing the Minister with specific information on applications and their progress and making contributions to the costs of investigating the application.

Subsection (2A) provides for the payment of a fee to the sanitary authority on the application or An Bord Pleanála on an appeal, amounts of fees for different functions, exemptions from and waivers and remissions of fees and the manner in which they may be disposed of.

Subsections (2B), (2C) and (2D) provide that the sanitary authority or An Bord Pleanála are not obliged to consider the matters before them unless and until the fees payable are paid in time whether they be the fees on the initial application, an appeal arising out of that application or an oral hearing of that appeal.

Offence

Subsection (3)(A) and (B) provide that furnishing information when making a statement in writing which is false or to the applicants/appellant's knowledge misleading in a material respect is an offence and that the licence which issues consequent on the application or appeal in relation to which the information was furnished is revoked. Subsection (4) provides that a contribution payable under the section is payable on demand and if unpaid shall be recoverable as a simple contract debt in a court of competent jurisdiction.

LG(WP)A 1977, s.26A

REGULATIONS FOR THE PREVENTION OR LIMITATION OF WATER POLLUTION

Section 26A of the LG(WP)A 1977, inserted by section 66(1) of the WMA 1996, provides:

"[26A(1) For the purpose of preventing or limiting water pollution, the Minister may, by regulations, prohibit or limit or control in a specified manner and to a specified extent, the production, treatment, use (in a process or otherwise), importation, distribution, storage, transport, supply or sale of any specified substance or of any article containing any specified substance.

(2) Without prejudice to the generality of subsection (1), regulations under this section may –
(a) make different provisions for different substances and articles,
(b) require local authorities or other specified persons to take specified steps for the purpose of securing compliance with the regulations,
(c) contain such incidental, consequential and supplementary provisions as appear to the Minister to be necessary or expedient for the purposes of such regulations.

Offence

(3) (a) A person who contravenes a provision of regulations under this section shall be guilty of an offence.
(b) a person guilty of an offence under this section shall be liable –
(i) on summary conviction, to a fine not exceeding £1,000 or imprisonment for a term not exceeding 6 months or, at the discretion of the court, to both such fine and such imprisonment,
(ii) on conviction on indictment, to a fine not exceeding £25,000 or imprisonment for a term not exceeding 5 years or at the discretion of the court, to both such fine and imprisonment.

(4) A prosecution for an offence under this section may be taken by the Minister, a local authority or such other person as may be specified in regulations under this section."

(LG(WP)A 1977, s.27)

RESTRICTING USE OF CERTAIN VESSELS

Section 27 of the LG(WP)A 1977, as amended by sections 24(2) and 30 of the LG(WP)(A)A 1990, provides:

"(1) The Minister may, after consultation with the Minister for Transport and Power, the (*qv*) Commissioners for Public Works in Ireland and the (*qv*) Water Pollution Advisory Council, make regulations to enable local authorities to prohibit, restrict or regulate the keeping or use, in such waters (other than tidal waters) as may be specified in the regulations, of vessels with sanitary appliances from which (*qv*) polluting matter passes or can pass into the waters.

(2) A sanitary authority may provide facilities for the reception and disposal of (*qv*) sewage from vessels and may impose fees or other charges for the use of such facilities."

Offence

Subsection (3) provides for the offence of contravention of a regulation made under the section.

Subsection (4) was repealed by section 30 of the LG(WP)(A)A 1990 and section 27(a) of the LG(WP)(A)A 1990 now provides for persons entitled to prosecute. *See:* PROSECUTION (2).

EXTENSION OF FUNCTIONS TO AGENCY

These functions under section 27 of the LG(WP)A 1977 now apply to the Agency in the circumstances described in Article 4 of the Environmental Protection Agency (Extension of Powers) Order 1996 (S.I. No. 126 of 1996). *See:* EXTENSION OF POWERS.

LG(WP)(A)A 1990, ss.21 and 21A

AGRICULTURAL ACTIVITIES

See: (1) AGRICULTURAL ACTIVITIES; (2) NUTRIENT MANAGEMENT PLANS.

LG(WP)A 1977 REGULATIONS

Hereunder are a list of the statutory instruments to date (with the number and year given in brackets) affecting the LG(WP)A 1977 and the LG(WP)(A)A 1990:

Local Government (Water Pollution) Act 1977 (Commencement) Order 1977 (S.I. No. 117 of 1977);
Water Pollution Advisory Council Order 1977 (S.I. No. 172 of 1977);
Local Government (Water Pollution) Act 1977 (Commencement) (No. 2) Order 1977 (S.I. No. 296 of 1977);
Local Government (Water Pollution) Act 1977 (Sections 4 and 16) (Fixing of Dates) Order 1978 (S.I. No. 16 of 1978);
Local Government (Water Pollution) Act 1977 (Transfer of Appeals) Order 1978 (S.I. No. 96 of 1978);
Local Government (Water Pollution) Regulations, 1978. (S.I. No. 108 of 1978);
Local Government (Water Pollution) Act 1977 Regulations, 1983. (S.I. No. 36 of 1983);
Local Government (Water Pollution) Act 1977 (Transfer of Appeals) Order 1978 (Amendment) Order 1983 (S.I. No. 37 of 1983);
Local Government (Water Pollution) (Fees) Regulations 1985 (S.I. No. 115 of 1985);
Local Government (Water Pollution) Act 1977 (Control of Cadmium Discharges) Regulations 1985 (S.I. No. 294 of 1985);
Local Government (Water Pollution) Act 1977 (Control of Hexachlorocyclohexane and Mercury Discharges) Regulations 1986 (S.I. No. 55 of 1986);
European Communities (Control of Water Pollution by Asbestos) Regulations 1990 (S.I. No. 31 of 1990);
Quality of Bathing Waters Regulations 1992 (S.I. No. 155 of 1992);
Local Government (Water Pollution) (Amendment) Act 1990 (Commencement) Order 1992 (S.I. No. 270 of 1992);
Local Government (Water Pollution) Regulations 1992 (S.I. No. 271 of 1992);
Local Government (Water Pollution) (Transfer of Appeals) (Revocation) Order 1992 (S.I. No. 272 of 1992);
Local Government (Water Pollution) Acts 1977 and 1990 (Control of Aldrin, Dieldrin, Endrin, Isodrin, HCB, HCBD and CHC13 Discharges) Regulations 1993 (S.I. No. 348 of 1993);
Local Government (Water Pollution) Acts 1977 and 1990 (Control of Carbon Tetrachloride, DDT and Pentachlorophenol Discharges) 1994 (S.I. No. 43 of 1994);
Quality of Bathing Waters (Amendment) Regulations 1994 (S.I. No 154 of 1994);
Local Government (Water Pollution) Acts 1977 and 1990 (Control of EDC, TRI, PER and TCB Discharges) Regulations 1994 (S.I. No. 245 of 1994);
Local Government (Water Pollution) (Amendments) Regulations 1996 (S.I. No. 184 of 1996);
Local Government (Water Pollution) Act, 1977 (Water Quality Standards for Phosphorus) Regulations 1998 (S.I. No. 258 of 1998);
Local Government (Water Pollution) (Amendment) Regulations 1999 (S.I. No. 42 of 1999).

EUROPEAN COMMUNITIES REGULATIONS

European Communities (Detergents) Regulations 1984 (S.I. No. 43 of 1984);
European Communities (Detergents) (Amendment) Regulations 1988 (S.I. No. 7 of 1988);
European Communities (Quality of Water Intended for Human Consumption) Regulations 1988 (S.I. No. 81 of 1988);
European Communities (Quality of Salmonoid Waters) Regulations 1988 (S.I. No. 293 of 1988) *See:* SALMONOID REGULATIONS 1988;
European Communities (Quality of Surface Water Intended for the Abstraction of Drinking Water) Regulations 1989 (S.I. No. 294 of 1989). *See:* WATER, SURFACE.
European Communities (Quality of Bathing Water) (Revocation) Regulations 1992 (S.I. No. 154 of 1992).

(APA 1987, s.24)

Provides for regulations prohibiting or restricting the emission into the atmosphere of smoke from any premises.

(APA 1987, s.31)

Section 31 of the APA 1987 –

"(1) The Minister shall, by regulations, provide for the grant of licences by local authorities to persons who apply to the local authority concerned and who comply with the requirements of, or made pursuant to, the regulations in relation to such applications."

Subsection (2) provides that without prejudice to the generality of subsection (1), regulations under this section may make provision for the form of the application and the licence, publication of specified notices, plans, documents and other information and particulars to be submitted, furnishing additional information or particulars and evidence to verify, furnishing the Minister with specified information in relation to applications and their progress, time limits on processing applications and making contribution to the costs of investigating the application.

The Air Pollution Act 1987 (Licensing of Industrial Plant) Regulations 1988 (S.I. No. 266 of 1988) refers.

Offence
Subsection (3) provides that an applicant who makes a statement in writing which to his knowledge is false or misleading in a material respect on an application for a licence or a review or on an appeal is guilty of an offence and the licence issued consequent on the application or appeal in respect of which the information was furnished is revoked.

Subsection (4) provides that any contribution payable under these regulations shall be payable on demand and if unpaid shall be recoverable as a simple contract debt in a court of competent jurisdiction.

(APA 1987, s.33)

See: REVIEW (2).

(APA 1987, s.35)

REGULATIONS RELATING TO FEES

Section 35 of the APA 1987 provides for the making of Ministerial regulations providing for the payment of fees to local authorities in relation to applications for (*qv*) licences and (qv) reviews of licences and to an (*qv*) Bord Pleanála in relation to (*qv*) appeals and the regulations can provide for different fees for different classes or descriptions, exemptions, waiver, remission or refund in specified circumstances and the manner in which fees are disposed of. There is provision that a local authority is not obliged to give a decision until the fee in respect of the application appeal is paid and that an appeal to An Bord Pleanála is invalid until the fee is paid.

(APA 1987, s.53)

REGULATIONS RELATING TO FUEL

Section 53 of the APA 1987:

"(1) The Minister, for the purpose of preventing or limiting (*qv*) air pollution, may make regulations in relation to –
(a) the standard, specification, composition and contents of any fuel of a type which is used in mechanically propelled vehicles or in mechanically propelled vehicles of a particular class or description or mechanically

propelled vehicles in a particular area or a particular class of areas;

(b) the standard, specification, composition and contents of any type of fuel which is burnt in fireplaces or in fire places of a particular class or description or in fireplaces in a particular area or particular class of areas;

(c) the production, treatment, importation, placing on the market, distribution or sale of fuel of any type or description;

(d) the burning, or the prohibition of burning, in fireplaces, or in fireplaces of a particular class or description of a fuel, or of a fuel which does not comply with such requirements as may be specified;

(e) the use, or the prohibition of the use, in mechanically propelled vehicles, or in mechanically propelled vehicles of a particular class or description of a fuel, or of a fuel which does not comply with such requirements as may be specified."

Subsection (3) makes the usual suggestions, without prejudice to the generality of subsection (1), that such regulations should prohibit the use of fuel which does not conform to specified standards, specify different standards for different fuels, specify tests to secure compliance with regulations, provide for exemptions from the regulations, require the display of specified information in a specified place in relation to fuels, provide for enforcement of regulations by specified persons with specified powers, provide for the issue of certificates by specified persons, provide for the keeping and examination of records, provide for examinations of premises, records and vehicles and requirements to be made to persons in charge, provide for the taking of samples, provide for the colouring of different fuels and provide for the admissibility of certificates, tests, examination or analysis of samples and the results thereof in evidence without further proof.

The Air Pollution Act, 1987 (Marketing, Sale and Distribution of Fuel) Regulations, 1998 (S.I. No. 118 of 1998) is now the sole regulations in force made under this section. This regulation revoked and replaced (with effect as from 1st October 1998) the following regulations:

Air Pollution Act, 1987 (Marketing, Sale and Distribution of Fuels) Regulations 1990 (S.I. No. 123 of 1990), the Air Pollution Act, 1987 (Marketing, Sale and Distribution of Fuels) Regulations 1992 (S.I. No. 274 of 1992, the Air Pollution Act, 1987 (Marketing, Sale and Distribution of Fuels) (Cork) Regulations, 1993 (S.I. No. 294 of 1993) and the Air Pollution Act, 1987 (Marketing, Sale and Distribution of Fuels) (Cork) Regulations 1994 (S.I. No. 403 of 1994).

The Schedule to S.I. No. 118 of 1998 sets out restricted areas of marketing, sale and distribution of fuels for Dublin, Cork, Limerick, Arklow, Drogheda, Dundalk and Wexford.

(APA 1987)

APA 1987 REGULATIONS

Air Pollution Act 1987 (Commencement) Order, 1987 (S.I. No. 201 of 1987);
Air Pollution Act 1987 (Commencement) (No. 2) Order, 1987 (S.I. No. 243 of 1987);
Air Pollution Act 1987 (Air Quality Standards) Regulations 1987 (S.I. No. 244 of 1987);
Air Pollution Act 1987 (Commencement) Order, 1988 (S.I. No. 265 of 1988);
Air Pollution Act 1987 (Licensing of Industrial Plant) Regulations 1988 (S.I. No. 266 of 1988);
Air Pollution Act 1987 (Authorised Fireplace) Regulations 1988 (S.I. No. 297 of 1988);
Air Pollution Act 1987 (Authorised Fuel) Regulations 1988 (S.I. No. 298 of 1988);
Air Pollution Act 1987 (Commencement) Order 1989 (S.I. No. 167 of 1989);
Air Pollution Act 1987 (Sulphur Content of Gas Oil) Regulations 1989 (S.I. No. 168 of 1989);
Air Pollution Act 1987 (Authorised Fireplace) (Revocation) Regulations 1989 (S.I. No. 293 of 1989);
Air Pollution Act 1987 (Retail Sale of Fuels) Regulations 1989 (S.I. No. 333 of 1989);
Air Pollution Act 1987 (Emission Limit Value for Use of Asbestos) Regulations 1990 (S.I. No. 28 of 1990);
Air Pollution Act 1987 (Commencement) Order 1990 (S.I. No. 29 of 1990);
Air Pollution Act 1987 (Marketing, Sale and Distribution of Fuels) Regulations 1990 (S.I. No. 123 of 1990);
Air Pollution Act 1987 (Combustion Plant) Regulations 1992 (S.I. No. 273 of 1992);
Air Pollution Act 1987 (Marketing, Sale and Distribution of Fuels) Regulations 1992 (S.I. No. 274 of 1992);

Air Pollution Act 1987 (Marketing, Sale and Distribution of Fuels) (Cork) Regulations 1993 (S.I. No. 294 of 1993);
Air Pollution Act 1987 (Marketing, Sale and Distribution of Fuels) (Amendment) Regulations 1993 (S.I. No. 297 of 1993);
Air Pollution Act 1987 (Municipal Waste Incineration) Regulations 1993 (S.I. No. 347 of 1993);
Air Pollution Act 1987 (Sulphur Content of Gas Oil) Regulations 1994 (S.I. No. 256 of 1994);
Air Pollution Act 1987 (Marketing, Sale and Distribution of Fuels) (Cork) Regulations 1994 (S.I. No. 403 of 1994) ;
Air Pollution Act 1987 (Emission Limit Values for Combustion Plant) Regulations 1996 (S.I. No. 264 of 1996);
Air Pollution Act 1987 (Petroleum Vapour Emissions) Regulations 1997 (S.I. No. 375 of 1997).
Air Pollution Act, 1987 (Marketing, Sale and Distribution of Fuels) Regulations, 1998 (S.I. No. 118 of 1998);
Air Pollution Act, 1987 (Environmental Specifications for Petrol and Diesel Fuels) Regulations, 1999 (S.I. No. 407 of 1999).

(EPAA 1992, s.87)

Section 87 of the EPAA 1992, as amended by substitution by Article 14(b) of the European Communities (Environment Impact Assessment) (Amendment) Regulations 1994 (S.I. No. 84 of 1994) of subsection (2)(f):

"(1) The Minister may make regulations in relation to applications for licences or for the review of licences or revised licences and the grant and review of licences and revised licences."

The Environmental Protection Agency (Licensing) Regulations 1994 (S.I. No. 85 of 1994), Environmental Protection Agency (Licensing Fees) Regulations 1994 (S.I. No. 130 of 1994) and amending regulations: (Licensing) in 1995 (S.I. No. 59 of 1995), (Fees) in 1995 (S.I. No. 60 of 1995), (Licensing)(No. 2) in 1995 (S.I. No. 76 of 1995), (Licensing) in 1996 (S.I. No. 79 of 1996), (Fees) in 1996 (S.I. No. 239 of 1996) and (Licensing) (No. 2) in 1996 (S.I. No. 240 of 1996) refers.

"(2) Without prejudice to the generality of subsection (1), regulations under this section may make provision for all or any of the following –

(a) the form of application and of licence,
(b) the time within which an application for a licence shall be made relative to publication of a notice under section 85(1) and relative to an application for a permission under Part IV of the Act of 1963,
(c) the publication by applicants, licensees or the Agency of such notices as may be prescribed,
(d) specifying the submissions, plans, documents and other information and particulars to be forwarded to the Agency or other specified person by applicants, licensees, objectors, or other persons within such periods as may be specified,
(e) requiring applicants, licensees, objectors or other persons to furnish to the Agency or any other specified person, within such period as may be specified, such additional information or particulars relating to applications, including environmental impact statements or reviews as the Agency may request.

(f) extending the period within which a notification under section 85(3) refers shall be published –
 (i) to two months from the date on which a request for additional information, particulars or evidence under paragraph (e) or (g) is complied with,
 (ii) to any period with the consent of the applicant or licensee,
 [(iii) to such period as the Agency may consider appropriate or as may be requested by the Minister in the case of an application for a licence for an (*qv*) activity which is likely to have significant effects on the environment in another Member State of the European Communities and in respect of which an environmental impact statement has been or will be submitted,
 (iv) to two months after the day on which an exemption under section 25(3) (inserted by the European Communities (Environmental Impact Assessment) Regulations, 1989 and 1994) of the Act of 1963 has been granted by the Minister,
(g) requiring the production, within such period as may be specified, of evidence to verify any information and

particulars given by an applicant, licensee, objector or other person,

[(h) procedures to be followed by the Agency in the processing of applications or reviews, including consultation procedures in relation to an environmental impact statement whether or not an oral hearing is held, and the times within which such procedures shall be carried out,]

(i) the publishing of decisions on applications or reviews and the reasons therefor and of any specified documents or other information in relation thereto, or

(j) requiring an applicant or licensee to defray or contribute towards the cost of any investigation carried out, caused to be carried out, or arranged for, by the Agency in relation to an application or review.

Offence

(3) (a) A person who in relation to an application for a licence, or to a review of a licence or a revised licence, under this Part, makes a statement in writing which to his knowledge is false or misleading in a material respect, shall be guilty of an offence.

(b) Where a person is convicted of an offence under this subsection, any licence or revised licence granted to that person, or to some other person on whose behalf the convicted person was authorised to act, consequent on the application or review in relation to which the information was furnished, shall stand revoked from the date of the conviction.

(4) Regulations under this section may contain such incidental, supplementary, consequential and transitional provisions (including provisions modifying the European Communities (Environment Impact Assessment) Regulations 1989 (S.I. No. 349 of 1989) and the European Communities (Environmental Impact Assessment) (Motorways) Regulations 1988 (S.I. No. 221 of 1988)) as appear to the Minister to be necessary for the purposes of or in consequence of, or to give full effect to, the first mentioned regulations.

(5) A defrayment or contribution the payment of which is required under regulations made under this section shall be payable on demand and, in default, shall be recoverable as a simple contract debt in any court of competent jurisdiction."

(EPAA 1992, s.107)

See: NOISE.

(EPAA 1992)

EPAA REGULATIONS

Environmental Protection Agency (Selection Procedures) Regulations 1992 (S.I. No. 215 of 1992);
Environmental Protection Agency (Advisory Committee) Regulations 1993 (S.I. No. 43 of 1993);
Environmental Protection Agency (Establishment) Order 193 (S.I. No. 213 of 1993);
Environmental Protection Agency Act, 1992 (Dissolution of an Foras Forbartha Teoranta) Order 1993 (S.I. No. 215 of 1993);
Environmental Protection Agency Act 1992 (Commencement) Order 1993 (S.I. No. 235 of 1993);
Environmental Protection Agency Act, 1992 (Commencement) Order 1994 (S.I. No. 82 of 1994);
Environmental Protection Agency Act, 1992 (Established Activities) Order 1994 (S.I. No. 83 of 1994);
Environmental Protection Agency (Licensing) Regulations 1994 (S.I. No. 85 of 1994);
Environmental Protection Agency (Licensing Fees) Regulations 1994 (S.I. No. 130 of 1994);
Environmental Protection Agency Act 1992 (Commencement) (No. 2) Order 1994 (S.I. No. 178 of 1994);
Environmental Protection Agency Act 1992 (Noise) Regulations 1994 (S.I. No. 179 of 1994);
Environmental Protection Agency Act 1992 (Section 36(4)) Order 1994 (S.I. No. 204 of 1994);
Environmental Protection Agency (Declaration of Interests) Regulations 1994 (S.I. No. 205 of 1994);
Environmental Protection Agency (Extension of Powers) Order 1994 (S.I. No. 206 of 1994);
Environmental Protection Agency Act, 1992 (Urban Waste Water Treatment) Regulations 1994 (S.I. No. 419 of 1994);
Environmental Protection Agency Act 1992 (Commencement) Order 1995 (S.I. No. 57 of 1995);
Environmental Protection Agency Act 1992 (Established Activities) Order 1995 (S.I. No. 58

of 1995);
Environmental Protection Agency (Licensing) (Amendment) Regulations 1995 (S.I. No. 59 of 1995);
Environmental Protection Agency (Licensing Fees) (Amendment) Regulations 1995 (S.I. No. 60 of 1995);
Environmental Protection Agency (Licensing) (Amendment No. 2) Regulations 1995 (S.I. No. 76 of 1995);
Environmental Protection Agency Act 1992 (Established Activities) (No. 2) Order 1995 (S.I. No. 204 of 1995);
Environmental Protection Agency Act 1992 (Commencement) (No. 2) Order 1995 (S.I. No. 337 of 1995);
Environmental Protection Agency Act 1992 (Commencement) Order 1996 (S.I. No. 13 of 1996);
Environmental Protection Agency Act 1992 (Commencement) (No. 2) Order 1996 (S.I. No. 77 of 1996);
Environmental Protection Agency Act 1992 (Established Activities) Order 1996 (S.I. No. 78 of 1996);
Environmental Protection Agency (Licensing) (Amendment) Regulations 1996 (S.I. No. 79 of 1996);
Environmental Protection Agency (Extension of Powers) Order 1996 (S.I. No. 126 of 1996);
Environmental Protection Agency (Advisory Committee) Regulations 1996 (S.I. No. 229 of 1996);
Environmental Protection Agency (Licensing Fees) (Amendment) Regulations 1996 (S.I. No. 239 of 1996);
Environmental Protection Agency (Licensing) (Amendment) (No. 2) Regulations 1996 (S.I. No. 240 of 1996);
Environmental Protection Agency Act 1992 (Ozone) Regulations, 1997 (S.I. No. 132 of 1997);
Environmental Protection Agency Act 1992 (Established Activities) Order 1997 (S.I. No. 132 of 1997);
Environmental Protection Agency Act 1992 (Control of Volatile Organic Compound Emissions Resulting from Petrol Storage and Distribution) Regulations 1997 (S.I. No. 374 of 1997);
Protection of Groundwaters Regulations 1999 (S.I. No. 41 of 1999).
Environmental Protection Agency Act, 1992 (Ambient Air Quality Assessment and Management) Regulations, 1999 (S.I. No. 33 of 1999);
European Communities (Control of Emissions of Gaseous and Particulate Pollutants from Non-Road Mobile Machinery) Regulations, 1999 (S.I. No. 396 of 1999).

(WMA 1992, s.36)

Regulations relating to the movement of waste. *See:* MOVEMENT OF WASTE, REGULATIONS IN RELATION TO.

(WMA 1996, s.45)

REGULATIONS REGARDING WASTE LICENCES

Section 45 of the WMA 1996 provides:

"(1) The Minister shall make regulations in relation to applications for the grant of waste licences or for the review of waste licences and in relation to the grant or review of such licences, and such regulations may contain different provisions in relation to different classes of such matters."

Subsection (2) provides, without prejudice to the generality of subsection (1), that the regulations may provide for, the form of the application and the form of the licence, the time of application relative to notice under section 42(1), objections under section 42(3), specified notices to be given by applicant, submissions, plans, information and particulars to be submitted with application including an environmental impact study by the applicant, objectors and others within specified periods, request for additional information, request for verification of the particulars, requirement for Agency to publish or make available to the public copies of documents relating to the application, procedures, including consultation in relation to environmental impact study, to be followed by the Agency in dealing with an application or a review, the period within which a decision may be made, the publication of the decision, the reasons therefor and any documents or other information in relation thereto, the information to be contained in an environmental impact study, requiring contribution towards the costs of investigation in relation to application and specifying the conditions and circumstances under which an application may be deemed to have been withdrawn.

Subsection (3) provides that the regulations may provide such incidental, supplementary and transitional provisions as are necessary to give effect to the regulations.

Offence
Subsection (4) provides that a person who, in relation to an application, makes a statement in writing which to his or her knowledge is false or misleading in a material respect shall be guilty of an offence.

Subsection (5) provides for the recovery of a defrayment or contribution as a simple contract debt in a court of competent jurisdiction in default of payment.

This is the only environmental statute which, when dealing with regulations such as these, does not provide for revocation of the licence on conviction.

(WMA 1996)

WMA 1996 REGULATIONS

Waste Management Act 1996 (Commencement) Order 1996 (S.I. No. 192 of 1996);
Waste Management (Licensing) Regulations 1997 (S.I. No. 133 of 1997);
Waste Management (Planning) Regulations 1997 (S.I. No. 137 of 1997);
Waste Management (Register) Regulations 1997 (S.I. No. 183 of 1997);
Waste Management (Packaging) Regulations 1997 (S.I. No. 242 of 1997);
Waste Management (Farm Plastics) Regulations 1997 (S.I. No. 315 of 1997);
European Communities (Mammalian Animal Waste) Regulations 1998 (S.I. No. 2 of 1998);
European Communities (Processing of Mammalian Animal Waste) Regulations 1998 (S.I. No. 62 of 1998);
European Communities (Licensing of Incinerators of Hazardous Waste) Regulations 1998 (S.I. No. 64 of 1998);
Waste Management (Amendment of Waste Management Act 1996 Regulations 1998 (S.I. No. 146 of 1998);
Waste Management (Movement of Hazardous Waste) Regulations 1998 (S.I. No. 147 of 1998);
Waste Management (Use of Sewage Sludge in Agriculture) Regulations 1998 (S.I. No. 148 of 1998);
Waste Management (Trans-frontier Shipment of Waste) Regulations 1998 (S.I. No. 149 of 1998);
Waste Management (Licensing) (Amendment) Regulations 1998 (S.I. No. 162 of 1998);
Waste Management (Hazardous Waste) Regulations 1998 (S.I. No. 163 of 1998);
Waste Management (Miscellaneous Provisions) Regulations 1998 (S.I. No. 164 of 1998);
Waste Management (Permit) Regulations 1998 (S.I. No. 165 of 1998);
European Communities (Amendment of Waste Management Act 1996 Regulations 1998 (S.I. No. 166 of 1998).
Waste Management (Packaging)(Amendment) Regulations, 1998 (S.I. No 382 of 1998);
European Communities (Processing of Mammalian Animal Waste)(Amendment) Regulations, 1999 (S.I. No. 200 of 1999).

REGULATED COURSING MATCH
(WLA 1976, s.2(1))

"Means a coursing match held in accordance with the rules for such matches which are for the time being both published and approved by the Irish Coursing Club pursuant to the Greyhound Industry Act, 1958."
See: (1) LICENCE (2); (2) COURSING FOR HARES.

RELAXATION OR SUSPENSION OF SPECIAL CONTROL AREA ORDERS
(APA 1987, s.43)

See: SPECIAL CONTROL AREA ORDERS.

RENEWAL OF AQUACULTURE LICENCE
(F(A)A 1997, s.19)

"Subject to section 15(1), an (*qv*) aquaculture licence granted for a period specified in the licence may, on the expiration of the period, be renewed or further renewed by the *(qv)* licensing authority for such period as may be specified by it, after consultation with such bodies, if any, as may be prescribed for that purpose."

REMEDIES FOR UNAUTHORISED HOLDING, RECOVERY OR DISPOSAL OF WASTE
(WMA 1986, s.58)

See: ENFORCEMENT (1)(D).

REMOVAL OF MEMBERS OF CENTRAL BOARD OR A REGIONAL BOARD
(FA 1980, s.24)

"(1) If and whenever the Minister is satisfied that –
(a) the (*qv*) Central Board or a (*qv*) regional board has not, in relation to a direction given by the Minister under section 8(1)(b) of this Act, complied with the requirements of section 8 or 11(1)(c) of this Act, as the case may be, or
(b) after holding under section 50 of the Principal Act, as amended by section 65 of this Act, an inquiry into the performance of the functions assigned to the Central Board or a regional board by or under this Act, the functions so assigned are not being duly and effectively performed by the Central Board or a regional board, or that the performance in general by any such board of the functions so assigned to it has been unsatisfactory,

he may by order remove from office all the members (including the chairman) of the board.

(2) In case the Minister makes an order under subsection (1) of this section, he shall appoint such person or persons as he thinks fit to perform the functions of the board to which the order relates and may from time to time remove the person or persons appointed under this subsection or persons appointed and appoint another or others in his or their place."

Subsection (3)(a) specifies that the appointment under (2) must be in writing. Subsection (3)(a) provides that for so long as the appointment remains in force it shall operate to enable the person or persons thereby appointed to perform the functions of the board in relation to which the appointment was made.

Subsections (4) and (5) specify the duration, basis for remuneration and general terms of the appointment.

Subsections (6) and (7) provide for the Minister's power after removal as aforesaid to cause a new election of members of the board to be held and that whether or not such an election is caused by the Minister the next subsequent election shall be held as if the board had not been dissolved.

Subsection (8) gives the Minister power to make orders or regulations necessary to give full effect to the causing of a new election by him under subsection (6).
See: COMMISSION UNDER F(A)A 1995

REPORTS
(F(C)A 1959, s.18)

See: ANNUAL REPORT BY MINISTER.

(F(C)A 1959, s.209)

REPORT BY MINISTER IN RELATION TO LEASES

The Minister is obliged, within certain time constraints, to lay before each house of the Oireachtas reports containing particulars of every lease for a term exceeding two years.

(EPAA 1992, s.51)

See: ANNUAL REPORT TO MINISTER.
(EPAA 1992, s.70)

See: STATE OF THE ENVIRONMENT REPORTS.

(WLA 1976, s.7)

The Minister shall, as regards each financial year, prepare a report of his proceedings under the Act during that year and he shall cause the report to be laid before both houses of the Oireachtas at the same time as is so laid the report for that year of his proceedings under the Forestry Act 1946.

(NH 97, Reg. 37)

REPORT ON IMPLEMENTATION OF HABITATS DIRECTIVE

"(1) Every 6 years from the date of expiry of the period laid down in Article 17 of the (*qv*) Habitats Directive the Minister shall prepare a report on the implementation of the measures taken under that Directive.

(2) The report under paragraph (1) shall, in particular, include information concerning the conservation measures referred to in Article 6(1) of the Habitats Directive as well as evaluation of the impact of those measures on the (*qv*) conservation status of the (*qv*) natural habitat types in (*qv*) Annex I and species in Annex II, and the main results of the (*qv*) surveillance referred to in Article 11 of, the Habitats Directive."

The time scale in Article 17 is in fact by reference to Article 23 which provides that the Member States shall bring into force the laws, regulations and administrative provisions necessary to comply with this Directive within two years of its notification. They shall forthwith inform the Commission thereof.

The date of the Directive is the May 21, 1992.

REPRESENTATION OF ANGLERS ON FISHERY BOARDS
(FA 1980, s.13)

Provides for full and adequate representation of all licensed fishermen on (*qv*) regional boards *See:* ELECTORATE.

RESEARCH
(LG(WP)A 1977, s.29)

Section 29 of the LG(WP)A 1977 provides that a local authority may contribute to the funds of a person engaged in or proposing to engage in research, surveys or investigation in relation to water pollution, but any such contribution shall not exceed any limit or contravene any condition which may from time to time be prescribed.

(APA 1987, s.18)

Section 18 of the APA 1987 provides:

"(1) A local authority may organise and conduct research, surveys or investigations into the nature and extent, the cause and effect, and the prevention or limitation, of (*qv*) air pollution and may establish and maintain educational programmes relating to such matters and may publish, or cause to be published, any information derived from any such research, surveys, investigations or educational programmes.

(2) A local authority may support or assist, by means of a financial contribution or otherwise, any person, or body of persons, engaged, or proposing to engage, in any research, survey or investigation into the nature and extent, the cause and effect, and the prevention or limitation, of air pollution or in any educational programme in relation to such matters.

(3) The making of a financial contribution pursuant to subsection (2) shall be a (*qv*) reserved function.

(4) The Minister, with the consent of the Minister for Finance, may make a financial contribution to any person, or body of persons, engaged, or proposing to engage, in research, surveys or investigations into the nature and extent, the cause and effect, and the prevention or limitation, of air pollution or in any educational programme relating to such matters."

(EPAA 1992, s.71)

See: ENVIRONMENTAL RESEARCH.

RESERVES AND REFUGES
(WLA 1976)

Part II Chapter II of the WLA 1976 is headed "Reserves and Refuges" and comprises the following:

(1) ESTABLISHMENT ORDER NATURE RESERVE

Section 15 which deals with the constitution and establishment by order of the Minister on land already owned by the State of a nature reserve. *See:* ESTABLISHMENT ORDER.

(2) RECOGNITION ORDER NATURE RESERVE

Section 16 which permits the Minister by Recognition order to recognise land, other than land referred to in section 15, as a nature reserve. *See:* RECOGNITION ORDER.

(3) DESIGNATION ORDER REFUGE FOR FAUNA

Section 17 which permits the Minister to designate land as a refuge for fauna where he considers that a particular species should be specially protected on land which is, or is contiguous to, a habitat of the species. *See:* DESIGNATION ORDER.

(4) AGREEMENTS AS TO THE USE AND MANAGEMENT OF LAND

Section 18 whereby the Minister or any other person with his prior approval may enter into an agreement with a person having an interest in land ensuring that the management of the land shall be conducted in a manner (specified in the agreement) which will not impair wildlife or its conservation. *See:* MANAGEMENT AGREEMENT.

It is useful under this heading to list the legislation which now applies to "Reserves and Refuges" as the terminology has changed since the WLA 1976 and refuges and reserves have become habitats, natural habitats and priority natural habitats. This new language is used in the secondary legislation used to implement European Directives consisting of Regulations made under Statutory Instruments and not under primary legislation like the WLA 1976.

The overall legislation in place at the moment dealing with lands or sites which are protected or species which are protected on such lands or sites is as follows:

(1) UNDER THE WLA 1976

(a) ESTABLISHMENT ORDERS – SECTION 15
(b) RECOGNITION ORDERS – SECTION 16
(c) DESIGNATION ORDERS – SECTION 17
(d) MANAGEMENT AGREEMENTS – SECTION 18

(2) UNDER EUROPEAN DIRECTIVE

(A) SPECIAL PROTECTION AREAS – BIRDS DIRECTIVE – 79/409/EEC (O.J. L103 April 25, 1979 p.1) - Implemented in Ireland by the European Communities (Conservation of Wild Birds) Regulations 1985 (S.I. No. 291 of 1985) and amending Regulations. *See:* BIRDS DIRECTIVE.

(B) SPECIAL CONSERVATION AREAS – NATURAL HABITATS DIRECTIVE – 92/43/EEC (O.J. L206, July 22, 1992, p.7) implemented in Ireland by the European Communities (Natural Habitats) Regulations, 1997 (S.I. No. 94 of 1997). *See:* CONSERVATION, SPECIAL AREAS OF.

(3) AREAS WHICH ARE NOT PROTECTED BUT WHICH HAVE BEEN DESIGNATED INFORMALLY

NATURAL HERITAGE AREAS formerly AREAS OF SCIENTIFIC INTEREST

These are areas of special ecological or geological importance. They represent the remaining areas where wild flora and fauna exist in a relatively natural state and where geological features are well represented. When entitled areas of scientific interest they were specifically identified by An Foras Forbartha in the 1970s and included in their National Heritage inventory. They receive no statutory protection although local authorities give them a special protected designation in development plans.

It is believed they will form a substantial part of the projected Wildlife Bill, that they will be called Natural Heritage Areas and that they will be protected from "works" which will approximate roughly to the system of prohibition of "operations and activities" in the NH 97 Regulations.

(WLA 1976, s.12)

MINISTER'S OBLIGATIONS IN RELATION TO RESERVES AND REFUGES

Section 12 of the WLA 1976 provides:

"(1) This section applies to –
(a) a local authority
(b) The (*qv*) Commissioners,
(c) any other body which is –
(i) established by or under statute and financed wholly or partly by means of loans or grants made by a Minister of State,
(ii) a company (in this section referred to as a State-sponsored company)

within the meaning of the Companies Act, 1963, in which the majority of the shares are held by or on behalf of a Minister of State,

(iii) a company within the meaning of the said Act in which a majority of the ordinary shares are held by a State-sponsored company, or a body established and financed in the manner specified in subparagraph (i) of this paragraph,

as regards which there is in force for the time being a direction given for the purposes of this section by the Minister.

(2) Subject to subsection (3) of this section, a Minister of State other then the Minister and every authority or body to which this section applies shall –

(a) before determining any matter or doing anything which is, in his or their opinion, or is represented by the Minister to the other Minister of State, or the authority or body to be likely or liable to affect, or to interfere with, the suitability for a nature reserve or a refuge, as may be appropriate, of land to which an establishment order, a recognition order or a designation order applies, or the management of land pursuant to and in accordance with an agreement under section 18 of this Act, consult the Minister as regards the avoidance or minimising of such effect or interference, and

(b) take all practicable steps to avoid or minimise such effect or interference.

(3) Subsection (2) of this section shall not apply in relation to –

(a) any determination made or anything done in a an emergency,

(b) the functions of the Minister for Local Government or of a planning authority under Parts III and IV of the Local Government (Planning and Development) Act, 1963, or under Part V of that Act (other than sections 47, 48 and 49) or under the Local Government (Planning and Development) Act, 1976, or

(c) the functions of the (*qv*) Board, or

(d) the functions of the (*qv*) Commissioners under the Arterial Drainage Acts, 1945 and 1955.

(4) The Minister may give in relation to a body described in subsection (1)(c) of this section a direction for the purposes of this section and any such direction shall come into force until cancelled by the Minister."

The application of this section is of little consequence now in the light of certain new provisions of the NH 97 Regulations, *e.g.* the assessment of implications for conservation of certain public bodies – Regulations 27 to 32.

Surprisingly, there is no reference to the section in the Heritage Act, 1995 which laid down a new control structure for the administration of wildlife. *See:* (1) ASSESSMENT OF IMPLICATIONS FOR CONSERVATION; (2) COMMISSIONERS OF PUBLIC WORKS IN IRELAND.

RESERVED FUNCTION

(LG(WP)A 1977, s.1(1))

Means, in the case of the council of a county or the Corporation of Dun Laoghaire a reserved function for the purposes of the County Management Acts 1940 to 1972, or, in the case of the corporation of a county borough, a reserved function for the purpose of the Acts relating to the management of the county borough.

The corporation of Dun Laoghaire as a separate entity was abolished in 1993 by the Local Government (Dublin) Act 1993, section 4(1).

(APA 1987, s.5(1))

Means:

(a) in relation to the council of a county or the corporation of Dun Laoghaire, a reserved function for the purposes of the County Management Acts 1940 to 1985,

(b) in relation to the corporation of a county borough, a reserved function for the purposes of the Acts relating to the management of the county borough.

(WMA 1996, s.5(1))

Means:

(a) in relation to the council of a county, a reserved function for the purposes of the County Management Acts, 1940 to 1994,

(b) in relation to the corporation of a county borough, a reserved function for the purposes of the Acts relating to the management of the county borough.

RESTORATION OF LAND IN A EUROPEAN SITE FOLLOWING DAMAGE
(NH 97, Reg. 19)

"(1) Where an (*qv*) operation or activity has been carried out on –
(i) a site placed on a list in accordance with Chapter I of this Part, or
(ii) a site where consultation has been initiated in accordance with Article 5 of the Habitats Directive, or
(iii) a (*qv*) European site,

and is in contravention of the conditions of Chapter III of this Part the Minister may, by direction issued in writing, require the owner, occupier or user of the land or the person who carried out the operation or activity to restore the land in accordance with the direction.

(b) Every direction shall specify the period within which the land is to be restored;

Offence

(c) Any person who fails to comply with a direction under sub paragraph (a) shall be guilty of an offence.

(2) If within the period specified in the direction or within such extended period as the Minister may allow, any steps required by the direction to be taken have not been taken, the Minister may take such action as the Minister considers necessary, including authorising a person to enter on the land and take those steps, and may recover as a simple contract debt in any court of competent jurisdiction from the person to whom the direction was made any expenses reasonably incurred by the Minister in that behalf.

Offence

(3) Any person who by act or omission impedes or obstructs a person authorised under paragraph (2) from entering on land for the purposes of carrying out any required works under this Regulation shall be guilty of an offence."

Sub-paragraph (i) of paragraph (a) refers to a site placed on a list in accordance with Chapter 1 is a candidate list of European sites. *See:* CONSERVATION, SPECIAL AREAS OF.

Sub-paragraph (ii) of paragraph (a) refers to a site where consultation has been initiated in accordance with article 5 of the Habitats Directive. This is where the Commission find in exceptional circumstances that Ireland have omitted a site from their list at (i) which hosts a (*qv*) priority natural habitat type or (*qv*) priority species which, on the basis of relevant and reliable scientific information, they regard as essential to the maintenance of that priority natural habitat type or for the survival of that priority species and bilateral consultation procedures shall be initiated between Ireland and the Commission for the purpose of comparing the scientific data used by each.

Sub-paragraph (iii) of paragraph (a) refers to a "European site". The definition of a European site includes a (q*v*) special area of conservation, a proposed candidate special area of conservation (pcSAC) and an area classified under Article 4(1) and (2) of the (*qv*) Birds Directive as a (*qv*) special protection area.

See: ENFORCEMENT (3) (F).

RESTRICTIONS ON CARRYING OUT OPERATIONS OR ACTIVITIES
(NH 97, Reg. 14)

See: PROHIBITION (9).

REVIEW OF LICENCES
(F(C)A 1959/LG(WP)A 1977/
APA 1987/EPAA 1992/WMA 1996)

(1) REVIEW UNDER THE LG(WP)A 1977

(A) REVIEW OF LICENCE UNDER SECTION 4 (TRADE AND SEWAGE EFFLUENT)

Section 7 of the LG(WP)A 1977, amended by section 5 of the LG(WP)(A)A 1990, amendments appearing in square brackets, provides:

"(1) A local authority may review a licence under section 4 at intervals of not less than three years from the date of the licence or the last review of the licence, or at any time with the consent of the person making, causing or permitting the discharge.

[(2) Notwithstanding any other provision of this Act or any condition in a licence under section 4, any such licence may be reviewed at any time by the local authority that granted it if –
(a) the local authority has reasonable

grounds for believing that the discharge authorised by the licence is or is likely to be injurious to public health or renders or is likely to render the waters concerned unfit for use for domestic, commercial, industrial, fishery (including fish-farming), agricultural or recreational uses,

(b) there has been a material change in the nature or volume of the discharge,

(c) there has been a material change in relation to the (*qv*) waters to which the discharge is made,

(d) further information has become available since the date of the granting of the licence relating to (*qv*) polluting matter present in the discharge concerned or relating to the effects of such matter, or

(e) the licensee applies to the local authority concerned to review the licence.

(2A) Notwithstanding any other provision of this Act or any condition in a licence under section 4, where regulations are in force under section 26 such a licence relating to an effluent or waters to which the regulations apply shall be reviewed by the local authority that granted it –

(a) in case it was in force before the commencement of the regulations, as soon as may be after such commencement and thereafter at such intervals as may be specified in the regulations, and

(b) in any other case, at such intervals as may be specified in the regulations.

(3) Upon completion of a review under this section, a local authority may amend or delete any condition of the licence or attach conditions or additional conditions to the licence or revoke the licence, and if the local authority proposes to exercise a power aforesaid, it shall do so as soon as may be after the completion of the relevant review under this section.]

(4) (a) The Minister may make regulations for the purpose of this section.

(b) Without prejudice to the generality of paragraph (a), regulations under this subsection may make provision in relation to all or any of the following matters:

(i) the giving of notice by a local authority to a person discharging or causing or permitting a discharge of intention to review a licence,

(ii) requiring a statement in such a notice that representations in relation to the review may be made within a specified period, and

(iii) requiring local authorities to publish any specified notices with respect to amendment or deletion of any condition attached, or attachment of new conditions, to a licence.

[(c) Without prejudice to the generality of paragraph (a), regulations under this subsection may also make provision in relation to any of the following matters:

(i) the payment to local authorities of fees of such amounts as may be specified in the regulations in relation to reviews of licences,

(ii) the payment of fees of different amounts in respect of different classes of such reviews as aforesaid,

(iii) exemptions from the payment of such fees in such circumstances as may be specified,

(iv) the waiver, remission or refund (in whole or in part) of such fees in such circumstances as may be specified, and

(v) the manner in which such fees may be disposed of.

(5) Where, pursuant to regulations under this section, a fee is payable to a local authority, the local authority shall not conduct the review in relation to which it is payable until the receipt thereof by the local authority.]"

(B) REVIEW OF A SECTION 16 LICENCE (DISCHARGES TO SEWERS)

Section 17 of the LG(WP)A 1977, as amended by section 13 of the LG(WP)(A)A 1990, provides for the review of licences issued under section 16 of the same Act.

The provisions of section 17 are similar to those of section 7 above except that "sanitary authority" appears instead of "local authority" throughout and subsection (4)*(b)*(iii) of section 7 does not appear in section 17.

Part III of the Local Government (Water Pollution) Regulations 1992 (S.I. No. 271 of 1992) refers.

(2) REVIEW OF A LICENCE UNDER THE APA 1987

Section 33 of the APA 1987 provides:

"(1) A local authority may review a licence under this Act at any time with the consent of the licensee, or at a time not less than three years from the date on which the licence was granted or, as the case may be, the date of the latest review of the licence.

(2) As soon as may be after they have completed a review under this section, a local authority may decide to grant pursuant to this Act a revised licence in substitution for the licence reviewed.

(3) Notwithstanding any other provision of this Act or any provision in a licence under this Act –
   (a) such licence shall be reviewed by the local authority which granted it if –
      (i) the local authority have reasonable grounds for believing that any *(qv)* emission from the *(qv)* industrial plant to which the licence relates constitutes a serious risk of *(qv)* air pollution, or
      (ii) there has been a material change in the nature or the extent of the emission, or
      (iii) there has been a material change, which could not reasonably have been foreseen when the licence was granted, in the air quality in the area in which the industrial plant to which the licence relates is situate, or
      (iv) further and better evidence, which was not available when the licence was granted, has become available relating to a pollutant present in the emission concerned or the effects of such pollutant, or
      (v) the licensee applies to the local authority concerned to review the licence.
   (b) if –
      (i) a relevant *(qv)* emission limit value is specified in regulations under section 51 in relation to any *(qv)* pollutant emitted from the industrial plant to which the licence relates, or
      (ii) a relevant *(qv)* air quality standard is specified in regulations made under section 50 in relation to any pollutant emitted from the industrial plant to which the licence relates, or
      (iii) a *(qv)* special control area order affecting any pollutant emitted from the industrial plant to which the licence relates comes into operation in relation to the area in which the industrial plant is situate, or
      (iv) any directions are issued by the Minister specifying the *(qv)* best practicable means for prevention or limitation of an emission to which the licence relates,

   the local authority shall, as soon as may be after the regulations are made, the order comes into operation or the directions are given, as the case may be, review the licence,

and subsection (2) shall apply to a review under this subsection.

(4) (a) The Minister may make regulations for the purpose of this subsection.
   (b) Without prejudice to the generality of subsection (a), regulations under this subsection may make provision in relation to all or any of the following matters –
      (i) the giving of notice by a local authority of their intention to review a licence,
      (ii) requiring a statement in such notice that representations relating to the review may be made within a specified period, and
      (iii) requiring local authorities to publish any specified notices with respect to a decision to grant a revised licence.

(5) In the review of a licence under this section, a local authority shall have regard to –
   (a) any change in air quality in their functional area, and
   (b) the development of technical knowledge in relation to air pollution and the effect of pollutants."

(3) REVIEW OF A LICENCE UNDER THE EPAA 1992

Section 88 of the EPAA 1992 provides:

"(2) As soon as may be after it has completed a review under this section, the Agency may grant a revised licence in substitution for the licence reviewed.

(3) Without prejudice to subsection (1), a licence

or revised licence may be reviewed by the Agency, if –

(a) the Agency considers that any emission from the activity to which the licence or revised licence relates constitutes a significant risk of environmental pollution,

(b) there has been a material change in the nature or the extent of an emission,

(c) there has been a material change, which could not have reasonably been foreseen when the licence or revised licence was granted, in the condition of the environment in the area to which the licence or revised licence relates is situate, or

(d) evidence which was not available when the licence or revised licence was granted, has become available, or new standards relating to the contents or nature of the emission concerned or the effects of the emission on the environment or the means for the better control of the emissions are prescribed.

(4) If –

(a) a *(qv)* special control area order under section 39 of the Air Pollution Act, 1987, affecting any emission from the activity to which the licence relates comes into operation in relation to the area in which the activity is situate,

(b) an *(qv)* air quality standard is specified in regulations made under section 50 of the Air Pollution Act, 1987, in relation to any emission from the activity to which the licence relates,

(c) a *(qv)* relevant emission limit value is specified in regulations under section 51 of the Air Pollution Act, 1987, in relation to any emission from the activity to which the licence relates,

(d) regulations under section 26 of the Local Government (Water Pollution) Act, 1977, relate to an effluent the discharge of which is authorised by such a licence or to the waters to which such effluent in discharged,

(e) a *(qv)* relevant standard is prescribed under regulations made under the European Communities Act, 1972, or any other enactment, or

(f) relevant regulations under section 106 are made in relation to any noise emissions from the activity to which the licence relates,

the Agency shall, where necessary, and as soon as may be after the regulations are made, the order comes into operation or the directions are given, as the case may be, review the licence or revised licence.

(5) In the review of a licence or a revised licence under this section the Agency shall have regard to –

(a) any change in environmental quality in the area in which the activity to which the licence or revised licence relates is situate, or

(b) the development of technical knowledge in relation to environmental pollution and the effects of such pollution,

since the licence or revised licence was granted or last reviewed."

Comparison: "serious risk" in APA 1987 becomes "significant risk" in the EPAA 1992 and will become a mere "risk" in the WMA 1996 which immediately follows. The different qualifications of the word "risk" are meaningless except in so far as the local authority are obliged to review under section 33(3)*(a)*(i) whereas the Agency have a discretion in relation to a review under section 88(3)*(a)*. This distinction is probably due to awkward phrasing in the drafting of the APA 1987. The term "significant risk" used in section 88(3)*(a)* of the EPAA 1992 is more efficient.

(4) WMA 1996

(A) REVIEW OF A LICENCE UNDER SECTION 46 OF THE WMA 1996

Section 46 of the WMA 1996 provides:

"(1) The Agency may review a waste licence –

(a) on any of the grounds referred to in subsection (3),

(b) with the consent of, or upon the application in that behalf having been made by, the holder of the licence, or

(c) at a time not less than 3 years from the date on which the licence was granted.

(2) As soon as may be after it has completed a review of a waste licence under this section, the Agency may grant to the holder thereof a waste licence ('a revised waste licence') the terms and conditions of which are, in such respects as the Agency thinks appropriate, different from those of the first- mentioned licence and the revised waste licence shall have effect in lieu of the first-mentioned licence.

(3) The grounds mentioned in subsection

(1)(a) are –

(a) the Agency considers that any (*qv*) emission arising from or as a result of the (*qv*) activity to which the waste licence relates ('an emission concerned') constitutes a risk of (*qv*) environmental pollution,

(b) there has been a material change in the nature of the activity to which the waste licence relates, or in the nature or extent of the emission concerned, or of the location in which the activity is carried on or an adjacent area,

(c) there has been a material change, which could not have been reasonably foreseen when the waste licence was granted, in the condition of the environment in the area in which the activity to which the licence relates is carried on,

(d) evidence, which was not available when the waste licence was granted and would have materially affected the decision of the Agency to grant the licence subject to the conditions to which it was granted, has become available,

(e) new standards or requirements relating to the conduct or control of the activity to which the licence relates, the content or nature of an emission concerned, or their effects on the environment, are prescribed under a provision of this Act or a (*qv*)Community act.

(4) In the review of a waste licence under this section, the Agency shall have regard to –

(a) any change in the quality of the environment in the area in which the activity to which the waste licence relates is carried on, and

(b) the development of technical knowledge in relation to *(qv)* environmental pollution and the effects of such pollution,

since the waste licence was granted or last reviewed.

(5) (a) Without prejudice to subsection (1), the Agency shall review a waste licence upon receipt of a notification under section 40(13), or on otherwise becoming aware of the cessation of the activity to which the licence relates, or following a refusal by it to accept the (*qv*) surrender of the licence under section 48(7).

(b) In a review under this subsection, the Agency shall determine such measures as are in its opinion necessary for the purpose of, as appropriate –

(i) the closure, restoration, remediation or (*qv*) aftercare of any facility concerned for the recovery or disposal of waste,

(ii) environmental protection,

and may grant a revised waste licence accordingly, including such conditions as it deems appropriate as respects the matters aforesaid."

(B) REVIEW OF LICENCE AUTHORISING DISCHARGES TO GROUNDWATER OF DANGEROUS SUBSTANCES

Article 40 of the Waste Management (Licensing) Regulations 1997 (S.I. No 133 of 1997).

"The Agency shall carry out, at least once every four years, a review of a waste licence which authorises the direct or indirect discharge of substances for the time being specified in the Annex to Council Directive 80/68/EEC (17.12.79) on the protection of groundwater against pollution caused by certain dangerous substances" (O.J. No.L 20/43, 26th January 1980)

(C) REVIEW OF A WASTE MANAGEMENT PLAN UNDER SECTION 22 OF THE WMA 1996

Section 22(4) of the WMA 1996 provides for the review of a waste management plan made under section 22 from time to time as occasion may require and at least once in every period of five years from the date of making of the plan. *See:* WASTE MANAGEMENT PLAN.

(5) REVIEW OF AQUACULTURE LICENCE

Section 70 of the F(A)A 1997:

"(1) The Minister may, on the application of the licensee made at any time after the expiration of a period of three years commencing on the granting of the licence or its last renewal under section 19, review an aquaculture licence.

(2) On completion of a review under subsection (1), the Minister may decide to -

(a) alter any or all of the terms of the licence,

(b) amend or delete any condition to which the licence is subject,

(c) attach conditions or additional condi-

tions to the licence, or
(d) do none or all or any of these things.

(3) Part III shall apply to the decision of the Minister on an application for a review of an aquaculture licence in the same manner as it applies to a decision of the Minister on an application for an aquaculture licence.

(4) The application regulations may provide for such procedural matters in relation to applications for reviews of aquaculture licences and decisions on such applications, including the application of (*qv*) environmental impact assessment requirements, as the Minister considers necessary or expedient."

REVOCATION OF LICENCES, PERMITS AND CERTIFICATES

(FA/LG(WP)A 1977/APA 1987 /EPAA/WMA 1996)

It is important to distinguish between (*qv*) forfeiture of a licence, which is part of the penalty imposed by a court for contravention of a provision of a statute and the revocation of a licence, which is effected by the authority granting the licences in certain circumstances when they are reviewing the licences or when a person is convicted of an offence under regulations. The distinction is often a fine one.

REVOCATION ON REVIEW OR FAILURE TO RENEW LG(WP)A 1977, APA 1987, EPAA 1992, AND WMA 1996

Revocation arises in the review sections of each of the above Statutes where, at subsection (1), the licensing body is given the right to review at any time with the consent of the licensee or at an interval of not less than three years. *See:* REVIEW.

The licensing body have the option on review not to renew the licence or to grant a new licence which is tantamount to giving a power of revocation and each section gives a detailed list of the circumstances in which the licensing body shall or may review the licence.

These circumstances can be paraphrased as follows:

(a) where there is a risk of environmental pollution,
(b) where there has been a material change in the (*qv*) emissions or discharges from the licensed premises,
(c) where there has been a material change in the receiving medium which could not have been reasonably foreseen when the licence was granted,
(d) where further and better evidence becomes available which was not available when the licence was granted relating to a (*qv*) pollutant present in the emission or discharge concerned or of the effects of such pollutant.

FISHERIES ACTS 1959–1997

Section 100(6) of the F(C)A 1959 provides that the Minister has power to revoke or amend an eel fishery authorisation on notice. *See:* FIXED ENGINES.

Section 68 of the F(A)A 1997 deals at length with the circumstances in which the Minister is entitled to revoke or amend an *(qv)* aquaculture licence. *See:* REVOCATION OF AN AQUACULTURE LICENCE.

REVOCATION IN THE CASE OF FALSE OR MISLEADING STATEMENTS

The actual word revoke is used sparingly in these statutes. In three of them, LG(WP)A 1977 sections 6(3) and 19(3), APA 1987 section 31(3), and EPAA 1992 section 87(3), where provision is being made for regulations dealing with applications for licences and, in the case of the LG(WP)A 1977, appeals from refusals the word revocation is used.

The sanction arises where a person applying for a licence or the review of a licence, or appealing against a refusal in the case of the LG(WP)A 1977, when furnishing information or verifying information, makes a statement in writing which is false or misleading in a material respect. On conviction under these headings of offence any licence issued to that person consequent on the application or appeal in relation to which the information was furnished shall stand revoked from the date of conviction.

The sections do not specify what agency revokes the licence and indeed it is difficult to distinguish these "revocations" from the statutory forfeiture of a licence by a court.

WMA 1996

Section 39(6) of the WMA 1996 deals with ministerial regulations in relation to the temporary recovery and storage of waste with the consent of the local authority. It is contemplated that under the regulations the local authority will be entitled to regulate for revocation of that consent where conditions attached to the consent have not been complied with.

Section 34(5) and (6) of the WMA 1996 provides that a (*qv*)waste collection permit can be revoked in certain circumstances and under subsection (11) the Minister may regulate for such revocation. *See:* WASTE MANAGEMENT ACT (3) WASTE COLLECTION PERMIT.

WLA 1976

REVOCATION OF FIREARMS CERTIFICATES

Section 75 (1) of the WLA 1976 distinguishes between:

(a) a firearms certificate deemed to be a licence under and by virtue of section 29(5), or

(b) a firearms certificate granted on the production of a current certificate granted under section 29.

Subsection (2) provides that on conviction for an offence under Part II of the Act, (wildlife conservation and protection), the court convicting the holder of either such licence or certificate may, in addition to any other penalty imposed, revoke the licence or certificate and disqualify the holder from holding such a licence or certificate for such period as the court considers appropriate. This section is in addition to any other punishment the Court is entitled to impose.

Subsection (3) provides that revocation of such a certificate as is mentioned at section (1)(a), by virtue of section 6 of the Firearms Act 1925 (inserted by section 8 of the Firearms Act 1964) operates as a revocation under section 5 of the Firearms Act 1925 and if the firearm concerned is a shotgun the appropriate superintendent may, within three months of the revocation, grant under section 12 of the Firearms Act 1964 to such holder in respect of such shotgun a limited certificate within the meaning of said section 12.

Subsection (4) provides for the provision by the registrar or clerk of the court to the Minister of a copy of the order revoking a certificate.

REVOCATION OF A WILDLIFE DEALER'S CERTIFICATE

Section 49 of the WLA 1976 provides that the Minister has power to revoke a wildlife dealer's licence in certain circumstances. *See:* WILDLIFE DEALING.

REVOCATION OR AMENDMENT OF AN AQUACULTURE LICENCE
(F(A)A 1997, s.68)

Section 68 of the F(A)A 1997 provides:

"(1) Subject to subsection (3) and section 69(2), the Minister may, in his or her discretion and, subject to subsection (5), without compensation to the licensee, revoke an aquaculture licence if the Minister –

(a) is satisfied that there has been a breach of any condition specified in the licence,

(b) is satisfied that the aquaculture operation to which the licence relates is not being properly maintained, or

(c) considers that it is in the public interest to do so.

(2) Subject to subsection (3) and section 69(2), the Minister may amend an aquaculture licence if he or she considers it in the public interest to do so.

(3) The following shall apply in relation to the revocation or amendment of an aquaculture licence:

(a) The Minister shall not revoke or amend the licence unless or until he or she has given by post to the licensee not less than 28 days notice in writing stating that the Minister has under consideration the revocation or amendment, as the case may be, of the licence.

(b) the notice shall also state –

(i) where it states the Minister has under consideration the amendment of the licence, the specified amendment under consideration and the grounds on which it is so under consideration, or

(ii) where it states that the Minister has under consideration the revocation of the licence, the grounds on which the revocation is under consideration;

(c) the Minister shall consider any representations in relation to a proposed revocation or amendment made to the Minister by the licensee before the expiration of the notice.

(4) The application regulations may provide for such procedural matters in relation to the revocation or amendment of licences as the Minister considers necessary or expedient.

(5) Where under subsection (1)(c) or (2) the Minister revokes or amends an aquaculture licence, the licensee shall be entitled to be paid by the Minister compensation for any loss suffered by him or her by reason of the revocation or amendment and, in default of agreement, the amount of compensation shall be determined under and in accordance with the Acquisition of Land (Assessment of Compensation) Act, 1919.

(6) Any expenses incurred by the Minister under this section shall, to such extent as may be sanctioned by the Minister for Finance, be paid out of moneys provided by the Oireachtas."

For revocation on two years cesser, *see:* CESSER.

REVOCATION OF A WASTE COLLECTION PERMIT
(WMA 1996, s.34(5))

Section 34(5) of the WMA 1996 provides for the revocation by a local authority of a (*qv*) waste collection permit on conviction of an offence under the WMA 1996 or any other enactment or instrument prescribed for the purposes of the subsection.

REVOCATION OF ORDERS
(FA/EPAA 1992/WMA 1996)

See: ORDERS, REVOCATION OF.

RIGHT TO ISSUE OF LICENCE
(F(C)A 1959, s.71)

Section 71 of the F(C)A 1959 provides for the right of a person who applies for an (*qv*) ordinary fishing licence to use a specified engine for taking fish and who tenders the appropriate licence duty payable, to the issue of a licence. There was a similar right to the issue of an oyster fishing licence at section 280 of the F(C)A 1959.

Regrettably, both sections were revoked by section 6 of and the First Schedule to, the FA 1980.

See: PUBLIC RIGHTS OF WAY.

RIGHTS OF WAY
(F(C)A 1959/WLA 1976)

The (*qv*) Central Board and (*qv*) regional fishery boards have the right to acquire rights of way under certain circumstances. *See:* ACQUISITION (1).

Section 60 of the WLA 1976 has a similar provision but it is confused by the historical dual functions of the Minister for Lands in 1976 when he had charge of both forestry and wildlife. It is difficult to see this section having any application now.

RINGING OF BIRDS AND TRAPPING OFFENCES
(WLA 1976, s.32(1))

Offence
Subsection (1) provides for an offence, unless done under licence, of attaching any band, ring, tag or other marking device to any (*qv*)wild animal or (*qv*)wild bird or the taking by net, trap or by any other means any such animal or bird for the purpose of attaching to it any band, ring, tag or other marking device.

Subsection (2) provides that subsection (1) does not apply to the close ringing of artificially-reared wild birds.

Subsection (3) provides for the offence for a person to import or have in his possession a cannon-net, mist-net, rocket-net or similar appliance for taking or trapping unless he is the holder of a licence granted by the Minister for the purpose of subsection (1) of this section.

Subsections (4) and (5) deal with the grant of licences under the section by the Minister. *See:* LICENCES (2).

Subsection (6) provides that conviction under this section is a bar to conviction under sections 22, 23 or 34 of this Act in respect of the same act. *See:* PROTECTION, PROTECTED WILD BIRDS AND PROTECTION, PROTECTED WILD ANIMALS.

RIVERS
(F(C)A 1959, s.3(1))

"Includes tributaries of rivers and all other streams and watercourses."

ROD AND LINE
(F(C)A 1959, s.3(1))

"Means a single rod and line."

ROD LICENCE DISPUTE
(FISHERIES ACT 1959–1991)

See: DUTIES ON ORDINARY FISHING LICENCES.

S

SAC, SPECIAL AREA OF CONSERVATION
(NH 97)

See: CONSERVATION, SPECIAL AREAS OF.

SAFETY, HEALTH AND WELFARE AT WORK ACT,1989
(EPAA 1992, s.109)

Section 109 of the EPAA 1992 provides that sections 106, 107 and 108 of the EPAA 1992 which deal with (*qv*) noise shall be without prejudice to the provisions of the Safety, Health and Welfare at Work Act 1989.

Section 28 of the Safety, Health and Welfare at Work Act 1989 permits the Minister to make regulations in relation to matters specified in the Fourth Schedule to the Safety, Health and Welfare at Work, Act 1989 and paragraph 25 of that Schedule deals with noise.

SALMON AND ASSOCIATED WORDS AND EXPRESSIONS
(F(C)A 1959)

The salmon species, both commercially and in the sport of angling, is the most important fish species in Ireland and a large part of the Fisheries Acts are devoted to its conservation and protection.

INTERPRETATION

The following words and expressions are interpreted or defined in the F(C)A 1959 by virtue of section 3(1) of that Act as follows:

"salmon" includes all fish of the salmon species, sea trout and the spawn or fry thereof;

"salmon river" means any river frequented by salmon;

"salmon rod licence" means a licence to fish with rod and line for salmon;

"salmon rod ordinary licence" means an ordinary fishing licence to fish with rod and line for salmon;

"salmon rod (annual) ordinary licence" means a salmon rod ordinary licence which is valid for a period of one year and is available for use in every fishery district;

"salmon rod (annual) (district) ordinary licence" means a salmon rod ordinary licence which is valid for a period of one year and is available for use in the fishery district of the (*qv*)regional board by which it was issued and in no other fishery district;

"salmon rod (Foyle Area) licence" means a salmon rod licence issued in pursuance of regulations made under the Foyle Fisheries Act 1952 which is valid for a year;

"salmon rod (twenty-one day) ordinary licence" means a salmon rod ordinary licence which is valid for a period of twenty-one days.

"salmon rod (late season) ordinary licence", "salmon rod (late season)(district) ordinary licence" and "salmon rod (seven day) ordinary licence" do not now appear in Part I of the Fourth Schedule to the F(C)A 1959, as amended.

These phrases, in so far as they define various salmon rod licenses, will have suffered the fate of all such licences at the hands of the F(A) (No. 2)A 1987 and the F(A)A 1991, and are probably now wholly irrelevant. *See:* DUTIES ON ORDINARY FISHING LICENCES.

SALMON AND OTHER FISH, PROTECTION OF
(F(C)A 1959)

Because of its importance the salmon is protected at varying stages of its life, in different places and in the methods of and times for fishing for salmon as are the waters and food which sustain the fish as follows:

(1) Salmon is traditionally caught by two main methods, rod and line and by net.
   (a) The use of rod and line is controlled by

licence and it is an offence to fish for salmon by rod and line without a licence. *See:* DUTIES ON ORDINARY FISHING LICENCES.

(b) Nets are used in fishing for salmon at sea, at the mouths of rivers and within certain fixed distances of the mouths of rivers. The latter form of salmon netting has almost completely disappeared except in the case of some privately owned fisheries. *See:* (1) NETS; (2) MESH OF NETS. When a net is fixed in a certain way it becomes a (*qv*) fixed engine and its use is regulated in a different manner. *See:* FIXED ENGINES, FISHING WEIRS AND FISHING MILL DAMS.

(2) The times within which nets may be used is carefully controlled, usually by bye-law and the period of time within which fishing is prohibited is called a Close Season. *See:* (1) CLOSE SEASONS; (2) SALMON AND TROUT CONSERVATION.

(3) There is special protection in the Fisheries Acts for young and breeding fish and their habitats. *See:* (1) PROTECTION OF YOUNG AND BREEDING FISH; (2) CHASE, INJURE OR DISTURB; (3) POLLEN POLLAN; and (4) UNSEASONABLE SALMON AND TROUT.

(4) Freshwater fishing waters, which must be protected as an environment for salmon, and all fish and the food of fish is protected against poisoning and pollution. *See:* PROHIBITION, WATERS UNDER THE F(C)A 1959.

(5) Apart from the control of nets and rod and line, which are legal methods of fishing when properly used and licensed, there are methods of fishing and practices which are always illegal and strictly prohibited. *See:* METHODS OF FISHING, PROHIBITION OF.

(6) The sale, exposure for sale, keeping for sale, export for sale of salmon, trout, eels or molluscan shellfish and, in certain circumstances, even the purchase of such fish from a person who is not licensed to sell is strictly controlled under Part X of the F(C)A 1959 sections 154 to 163. The entire of Part X was amended by substitution by section 20 of the F(A)A 1994. *See:* CERTIFICATE OF FITNESS.

(7) Apart from the protection afforded by Part X referred to at (6) above there is an additional protection section, section 182, of the F(C)A 1959 which makes it an offence:
   (a) to purchase, sell, expose for sale, keep for sale or have in possession or control any (*qv*) unseasonable salmon or trout, and
   (b) to purchase, sell, expose for sale, keep for sale or have in possession or control any salmon, trout, eel or molluscan shell fish unlawfully captured.

This prosecution of the section under both (a) and (b) is very successful and in the case of a prosecution for unlawful capture, the onus lies on the person accused to prove lawful capture. *See:* SALMON, TROUT, EELS AND MOLLUSCAN SHELLFISH UNSEASONABLE AND UNLAWFULLY CAPTURED, PURCHASE, SALE, POSSESSION.

SALMON CONSERVANCY FUND
(F(C)A 1959, s.49)

The Salmon Conservancy Fund was a scheme established by the Salmon Conservancy Fund Act, 1954. This Act was repealed by the F(A)A 1958 but continued in existence by section 8(2) of that Act.

It consisted of a levy on the exportation of salmon. In 1959 the amount of the levy was fixed at 2 per cent. The monies collected were to be paid into "the Fund" to which was to be added various monies payable by the Oireachtas under section 49(8) of the F(C)A 1959.

Section 49(9) provided for the disbursement of the monies in the Fund:
   (a) (i) to supplement the income of any regional board whose income in any year appears insufficient to defray the expenses of such board in the performance of its duties,
   (ii) towards the expenses incurred in connection with any scheme for the improvement of the inland fisheries

as the Minister thinks proper,
(b) the costs of administration of the Fund,
(c) payments due in respect of advances to the Fund.

Offence
Subsection (10) having provided for Ministerial regulations subsection (11) provides that a contravention of any regulation constitutes an offence.

(Note that the maximum penalty prescribed under this section has been increased. *See:* FINES AND IMPRISONMENT (IMPOSITION OF)).

SALMON LEVY, NATIONAL SALMON COMMISSION

(FA 1980, s.55/F(A)A 1999, s. 22(1))

Section 55 of the FA 1980 provided for a levy on every first and only sale of salmon payable to the Minister to be paid by him into the (*qv*) Salmon Conservancy Fund and the section was brought into operation by the Salmon Levy Order 1980, (S.I. No. 141 of 1980), on the 26th day of May 1980. It is no longer operative.

Section 22(1) of the F(A)A 1999 amends Part V of the FA1980 which comprises section 54, 54A and 55 only by substituting therefor four new sections 55A, 55B, 55C and 55D.

Section 54 and 54A of the FA 1980 (which sections were inserted by Article 18 of the European Communities (Environmental Impact Assessment) Regulations 1989 (S.I. No 349 of 1989) had already been repealed by section 4(1) of the F(A)A 1997.

The Fisheries (Amendment) Act, 1999 (save for section 23) cane into force on 20 December 1999 by virtue of the Fisheries (Amendment) Act, 1999 (Commencement) Order, 1999 (S.I. No. 419 of 1999).

NATIONAL SALMON COMMISSION

The new Part V of the FA 1980, sections 55A, 55B, 55C, and 55, now deals exclusively with what the 1999 Act calls the National Salmon Commission.

Section 55A(1) provides for the establishment by the Minister by order of a committee (the "Commission") to be known as the National Salmon Commission.

Section 55A(2) provides for the composition of the commission by the Minister by order.

Section 55B of the FA 1980 –

"55B The functions of the Commission shall be to assist and advise the Minister in relation to the conservation, management, protection and development of the national salmon resource and, in particular to make recommendations to the Minister on any scheme in relation to the management, development and stocks of wild salmon or sea trout (within the meaning of section 24 of the Fisheries (Amendment) Act, 1998) and in particular the tagging of such fish, and on the setting of a national total allowable catch and quotas for the taking of salmon, in consultation with the boards and the Marine Institute and such other bodies as the Minister directs."

Section 55C provides for the establishment by the Commission of the Standing Technical Committee to advise and assist it on all technical and scientific matters in relation to the performance of its functions.

Section 55D provides for the regulation by the Minister by order of the terms and reference and procedure of the Commission and the Standing Scientific Committee.

Section 22(2) provides for the payment to the Exchequer of all moneys standing to the credit of the Salmon Conservancy Fund and the Fund shall thereupon be closed.

SALMON AND TROUT CONSERVATION BYE-LAW 1998

(F(C)A 1959)

This Bye-law which, by virtue of Article 1(1), may be cited as the Salmon and Trout Conservation Bye-law No. 743, 1998 by virtue of Article 1(2) came into operation on the 14th day of January 1998.

Article 2 is the interpretation Article, the first part of which deals with various definitions of nets and the composition of nets. These definitions are dealt with comprehensively elsewhere.

See: NETS.

The other definitions in Article 2 are as follows:

"'the tidal waters' means –
all the waters of the River Shannon upstream of the mouth of that river as defined and marked out on the 8th day of February, 1864, by the Special Commissioners for Irish Fisheries appointed and acting under the Salmon Fishery (Ireland) Act, 1863, to the weir or dam known as the Corbally Mill Weir;

all the waters of the River Blackwater upstream of the mouth of that river as defined and marked out on the 8th day of February, 1864, by the Special Commissioners for Irish Fisheries appointed and acting under the Salmon Fishery (Ireland) Act, 1863, to the boundary between the tidal and fresh-water portions of that river as defined, determined and marked out on the 15th day of March, 1879, by the Inspectors of Irish Fisheries within the meaning and in pursuance of the Fisheries (Ireland) Act, 1869;

all the waters of the River Liffey upstream of the common estuary of the Rivers Dodder and Liffey as defined and marked out on the 3rd day of March, 1865, by the Special Commissioners for Irish Fisheries appointed and acting under the Salmon Fishery (Ireland) Act, 1863, to the weir on the River Liffey known as the Island Bridge Weir;

'the Waterford estuary' means all the waters of the Rivers Suir, Nore and Barrow upstream of the common mouth of those rivers as defined and marked out on the 8th day of February, 1864, by the Special Commissioners for Irish Fisheries appointed and acting under the Salmon Fishery (Ireland) Act, 1863 –

(a) to the line drawn across the River Suir at and opposite to the most upstream part of the Coolnamuck weir,
(b) to Innishtiogue Bridge on the River Nore,
(c) to the lowest weir or dam used for navigation purposes on the River Barrow near St. Mullin's in Co. Carlow;

'the Slaney Estuary' means all the waters of the River Slaney upstream of the mouth of that river as defined and marked out on the 10th day of February, 1866, by the Special Commissioners for Irish Fisheries appointed and acting under the Salmon Fishery (Ireland) Act, 1863, to the boundary between the tidal and fresh-water portions of that river as defined, determined and marked out by those Commissioners on the 8th day of November, 1865;

'the fishery districts', means all of –

(a) the No. 5 or Cork District,
(b) the No. 7 or Kerry District,
(c) the No. 8 or Limerick District,
(d) the No. 9(1) or Galway District,
(e) the No. 9(2) or Connemara District,
(f) the No. 10(1) or Ballinakill District,
(g) the No. 10(2) or Bangor District,
(h) the No. 11 or Ballina District,
(i) the No. 12 or Sligo District,
(j) the No. 13 or Ballyshannon District, and
(k) the No. 14(1) or Letterkenny District

declared by section 19(1) of the Fisheries (Consolidation) Act, 1959."

These are some only of the fishery districts declared by section 19(1). *See:* FISHERY DISTRICTS AND ELECTORAL DIVISIONS.

This bye-law defers the opening date for commercial salmon fishing, defers the closing time, increases the weekly close time from 48 to 72 hours and introduces day only fishing for drift nets.

It introduces specific arrangements for drift nets in specified estuaries, for draft netting on the Slaney and for snap net fishing in the Waterford estuary.

It also prohibits the possession of specified nets during the annual close season.

"3. (1) Subject to paragraph (2) of this bye-law and notwithstanding anything contained in any Bye-Law varying the weekly close time, it is hereby prohibited –

(a) to take or to fish for or to attempt to take or to fish for, salmon or trout with a drift net, or to aid or assist in such taking, fishing or attempting, during the period commencing at 6 o'clock a.m. on any Friday and ending at 6 o'clock a.m on the next following Saturday, and

(b) to take or to fish for, or to attempt to take or to fish for, salmon or trout with a drift net, or to aid or assist in such taking, fishing or attempting between –

(i) 9 o'clock p.m. on any Monday, Tuesday or Wednesday and 4 o'clock a.m. on the next following Tuesday, Wednesday or Thursday, respectively, and

(ii) 9 o'clock p.m.on any Thursday and 6 o'clock a.m. on the next following Friday.

(2) Paragraph (1) of this bye-law, in so far as it relates to taking or fishing for, or attempting to take or to fish for, salmon or trout with a drift net, or aid-

ing or assisting in such taking, fishing or attempting shall not apply in tidal waters.

4. (1) Subject to paragraphs (2) and (3) of this bye-law and notwithstanding anything contained in any Bye-law varying the (*qv*) weekly close time, it is hereby prohibited to take or to fish for, or to attempt to take or to fish for, salmon or trout with a draft net, snap net or other net or to aid or assist in such taking, fishing or attempting, during the period commencing at 6 o'clock a.m. on any Monday and ending at 6 o'clock a.m. on the next following Tuesday.

(2) Paragraph (1) of this bye-law, in so far as it applies to taking or fishing for, or attempting to take or to fish for, salmon or trout with a snap net, or aiding or assisting in such taking, fishing or attempting, shall not apply in the Waterford estuary during the period commencing on the 12th June, 1998, and ending on the 14th day of August, 1998.

(3) Paragraph (1) of this bye-law in so far as it applies to taking or fishing for, or attempting to take or to fish for, salmon or trout with a draft net, or aiding or assisting in such taking, fishing or attempting, shall not apply in the Slaney estuary during the period commencing on the 12th June, 1998, and ending on the 31st day of August, 1998.

5. (1) Subject to paragraphs (2) and (3) of this bye-law and notwithstanding anything contained in any Bye-law fixing the (*qv*) annual close season for salmon and trout in any locality, it is hereby prohibited to take or to fish for, or to attempt to take or to fish for, salmon or trout with a drift net, or to aid or assist in such taking, fishing or attempting, during the period commencing on the day immediately following the end of the annual close season for salmon and trout and ending on the 31st day of May, 1998.

(2) Paragraph (1) of this bye-law shall not apply to any locality where the annual close season for salmon or trout ends on or after the 31st day of May, 1998.

(3) Paragraph (1) of this bye-law, in so far as it applies to taking or fishing for, or attempting to take or to fish for, salmon or trout with a drift net, or aiding or assisting in such taking, fishing or attempting, shall not apply in the tidal waters.

6. (1) Subject to paragraph (2) of this bye-law and notwithstanding anything contained in any Bye-law fixing the (*qv*)annual close season for salmon and trout in the tidal waters, it is hereby prohibited to take or to fish for, or to attempt to take or to fish for, salmon or trout with a drift net in the tidal waters, or to aid or assist in such taking, fishing or attempting, during the period commencing on the day immediately following the end of the annual close season for salmon and trout and ending on the 11th day of May, 1998.

(2) Paragraph (1) of this bye-law shall not to apply to any locality where the annual close season for salmon and trout ends on or after 11th day of May. 1998.

7. (1) Subject to paragraph (2) of this bye-law and notwithstanding anything contained in any Bye-law fixing the (*qv*) annual close season for salmon and trout in any locality, it is hereby prohibited to take or to fish for, or to attempt to take or to fish for, salmon or trout with a draft net, snap net or other net, or to aid or assist in such taking, fishing or attempting, during the period commencing on the day immediately following the end of the annual close season for salmon and trout and ending on the 11th day of May, 1998.

(2) Paragraph (1) of this bye-law shall not apply to any locality where the annual close season ends on or after 11th May 1998.

8. Notwithstanding anything contained in any Bye-law fixing the annual close season for salmon and trout in any locality, it is hereby prohibited in all localities of the fishery districts, to take or to fish for, or to attempt to take or to fish for, salmon or trout, or to aid or assist in such taking, fishing or attempting –
(a) in the case of drift nets (other than

drift nets in the tidal waters), during the period commencing on the 1st day of August, 1998, and ending on the 31st day of May, 1999,
(b) in the case of drift nets in the tidal waters, draft nets (other than draft nets in the Slaney estuary), or other net, during the period commencing on the 1st day of August, 1998, and ending on the 11th day of May, 1999, and
(c) in the case of draft nets in the Slaney estuary, during the period commencing on the 1st day of September, 1998, and ending on the 11th day of May, 1999.

9. It is hereby prohibited –
(a) to have on board any boat, or
(b) to have in or on any vehicle, or otherwise, with the intention of taking or fishing for, or attempting to take or to fish for, salmon or trout,

a drift net, draft net, snap net or other net during the periods relevant to those nets specified in bye-laws 5, 6, 7 and 8 of this Bye-law.

10. (1) Notwithstanding anything contained in any Bye-law regulating the net to be used in fishing for salmon or trout, it is hereby prohibited to use, or attempt to use, in fishing for salmon or trout –
(a) a drift net in the tidal waters, or
(b) a draft net, snap net, or other net,
made wholly or partly of monofilament or multistrand monofilament.

(2) It is hereby prohibited to have on board any boat, or to have in possession, for the capture of salmon or trout, on any quay on or adjacent to, or on or near any bank of, any waters, a draft net, snap net or other net, mounted or otherwise prepared for use in fishing for salmon or trout, made wholly or partly of monofilament or multistrand monofilament.

(3) It is hereby prohibited to have on board any boat, or to have in possession, for the capture of salmon or trout, on any quay on or adjacent to, or on or near any bank of, the tidal waters, a drift net, mounted or otherwise prepared for use in fishing for salmon or trout, made wholly or partly of monofilament or multistrand monofilament.

11. Where in any proceedings for an offence consisting of a contravention of bye-law 10(1) of this Bye-law, it is proved that the defendant was found using, or attempting to use, in fishing a drift net in the tidal waters, a draft net, snap net or other net made wholly or partly of monofilament or multistrand monofilament, and a sea fisheries protection officer, (*qv*) authorised officer or (*qv*) authorised person states in evidence that he or she had reasonable grounds for believing that the said fishing was for salmon or trout, it shall be presumed until the contrary is proven that said fishing was for salmon or trout, as the case may be."

This bye-law, which is in force for one season only, is a notable attempt to amalgamate all the bye-laws relating to net fishing, annual and weekly close seasons, local net fishing patterns and needs in different localities and waters and reintroduce the ban on the use of monofilament nets.

There are subtle differences between the treatment of monofilament under this bye-law and under the old "restriction on the use or possession of monofilament or multistrand monofilament nets bye-law No. 639 of 1984" but by and large the provisions are the same.

The 1984 bye-law was revoked on January 23, 1997 by bye-law No. 728 of 1997 which declared that monafilament or multistrand monofilament was permitted to be used in fishing for salmon or trout during the legally prescribed fishing season, a situation which only lasted until January 14, 1998 when this 743 of 1998 bye-law was made.

This bye-law is important in that it attempts to create a national standard for the use of nets rather than being dependant on a whole array of local bye-laws.

INDICTMENT

Under section 46(4) of the FA 1980 a person charged under this bye-law can only be prosecuted on indictment if the fishing engine involved is a drift net or the charge relates to the use or possession of a net made wholly or partly of monofilament or multistrand monofilament. *See:* INDICTABLE OFFENCES, INDICTABLE OFFENCES UNDER FA 1980.

SALMON, TROUT, EELS, MOLLUSCAN SHELLFISH, UNSEASONABLE AND UNLAWFULLY CAPTURED, PURCHASE, SALE, POSSESSION

(F(C)A 1959, s.182)

Section 182 of the F(C)A 1959, as amended by substitution by section 21 of the F(A)A 1994, provides:

Offences

"(1) (a) If any person purchases, sells, exposes for sale, keeps for sale or has in his possession or control any (*qv*) unseasonable salmon or trout such person shall be guilty of an offence under this subsection."

Defence

Subsection (1)(b) provides a good defence for a common carrier charged under subsection (1)*(a)* to prove that possession was as a common carrier and not otherwise.

Offences

Subsection (2)(a) provides that if any person purchases, sells, exposes for sale, keeps for sale or has in his possession or control any salmon, trout, eel or molluscan shellfish unlawfully captured, such person shall be guilty of an offence under that subsection.

Defences

Subsection (2)(b) provides that the onus of proving lawful capture in a defence to a charge under (2)(a) lies on the defendant.

Subsection (2)(c) provides that where a common carrier is charged under subsection (2)*(a)* it shall be a good defence for him to prove:

(i) that possession or control by him was as a common carrier and not otherwise, and

(ii) that at the time he accepted the consignment the consignor delivered to him a certificate of lawful capture in a form prescribed by the Minister.

Subsection (2)(d) provides for a defence to a charge under subsection (2) in relation to salmon, that the salmon was lawfully captured at a particular place during a period which was not a close season for salmon at that place by the holder of a valid salmon licence.

Subsection (2)(e) provides the same defence for trout as for salmon in 2(d) supra.

Subsection (2)(f) provides the same defence for eels except the requirements relating to close seasons is omitted as there are none for eels.

Subsection (2)(g) provides a defence to the charge for purchasing or having in possession or control fish specified in the section which are unlawfully captured, of purchase from the holder of a licence under section 159(1) of the F(C)A 1959 in force and purchased at the place specified in the licence. *See:* CERTIFICATE OF FITNESS.

Subsection (5) provides for forfeiture of salmon, trout, eel or molluscan shellfish as a statutory consequence of conviction.

SALMON, WILD SALMON AND SEA TROUT TAGGING SCHEME

(F(A)A 1999, S. 24)

Section 24(1) of the F(A)A 1999 –

"(1) The Minister may, after consultation with the *(qv)* National Salmon Commission, make regulations to provide for a scheme for the management, development and conservation of stocks of wild salmon and sea trout and in particular to provide for the gathering of information by the tagging of such fish."

Subsection (2) provides, without prejudice to the generality of subsection (1), that the regulations may provide for any or all of the following:

The manner, type and colour of the tags to be affixed, the information to be contained on the tags, the issue and distribution of tags and log books to persons fishing, matters relating to the sale, display, import, export and transshipment of wild salmon, sea trout or farmed salmon, log books to be kept by persons fishing, records to be kept by dealers, registers to be kept by providers of tags or log books, inspections by authorised officers of tags, log books, registers and records, furnishing of information on the scheme as is to be provided by the Central Board or regional boards to the Minister.

Subsection (3) provides that the powers conferred by subsection (1) are in addition to and not in substitution for the powers conferred by section 9 of the Fisheries (Consolidation) Act, 1959.

OFFENCES UNDER THE REGULATIONS

Section 24(5) and (6) of the F(A)A 1999 –

Offences

"(5) A person who obstructs or interferes or fails to comply with a requirement of an authorised officer in exercise of any power conferred on the officer under this section or refuses to give up his or her name and address when required under this section shall be guilty of an offence and shall be liable on summary conviction to a fine not exceeding £1,500.00.

(6) Regulations under this section may provide –
 (a) that a person who contravenes or fails to comply with any regulation or provision thereof made under this section shall be guilty of an offence, and
 (b) for penalties for such a contravention or failure to comply of, on summary conviction, a fine not exceeding £1,500.00 or imprisonment for a term not exceeding 6 months, or to both."

Subsection (7) provides for the steps which must be taken by the Minister when he proposes to make regulations consisting of publication, making the notice open to public inspection, taking objections and finally making the regulations with or without modifications.

Subsection (8) provides for definitions in the section of *(qv)* "authorised officer" which means
 (a) an officer of the Minister, appointed in writing by the Minister to be an authorised officer for the purposes of this section, or
 (b) any person, whether or not he or she is an officer of a regional board, appointed in writing by a regional board to be an authorised officer for the purposes of the section,

and "sea trout" which means a wild sea trout *Salmo trutta* and "wild salmon" which means wild Atlantic salmon *Salmo salar*.

The Fisheries (Amendment) Act, 1999 (save for section 23) came into force on 20 December 1999 by virtue of the Fisheries (Amendment) Act, 1999 (Commencement) Order, 1999 (S.I. No. 419 of 1999).

SALMONOID
Regulations, 1988
(LG(WP)A 1977)

The European Communities (Quality of Salmonoid Waters) Regulations 1988 (S.I. No. 293 of 1988) gave effect to Council Directive 78/659/EEC of July 18, 1978 on the quality of fresh waters needing protection or improvement in order to support fish life (O.J. L221/1, 14 August 1978).

The First Schedule set out the fresh waters capable of supporting salmon (*Salmon salar*), trout (*Salmo trutta*), char (Salvelinus) and by Article 3(1) they were designated as salmonoid waters for the purposes of the Regulations.

Article 3(2) provides that salmonoid waters shall meet the quality standards specified in the Second Schedule on the basis of and subject to the conditions so specified and Article 3(3) provides that deviation from these standards resulting from floods or other natural disasters shall not be taken into account when determining conformity with the Regulations.

The Schedule at columns 1 specifies the following rivers: Aherlow, Ahirdeen, Blackwater (Munster), Boyne, Bride, Brown Flesk, Corrib (including Lough Corrib), Dargle, Feale, Fergus, Finn, Glashagn, Lee, Leannan, Lurgy, Maggisburn, Maine, Moy, Tributaries of Moy:– Owengarve, Mulaghanoe, Spaddagh, Trimoge, Glore, Yellow, Gwesstion, Manulla, Castlebar, Deel and Corry, Nore, Slaney, Swilly and Vartry.

In all cases the extent of the specification is the main channel but in the case of the Lee it is the main channel from the source to Cork City waterworks at Lee Road and in the case of the Maine the extent is the main channel downstream of the confluence with the River Brown Flesk.

Article 4 provides for the sampling of salmonoid waters in its functional area by local authorities in respect of the parameters specified in the Second Schedule.

Article 5 places a duty on local authorities to ensure compliance with standards. The Minister can grant a departure from the standards in certain circumstances specified in 5(2).

Article 5(1) provides for failure to comply which obliges the local authority to adopt an action programme, comprising appropriate measures, to reduce pollution and to ensure that the standards are complied with.

Article 6 obliges the local authority to keep a

register of the results of sampling carried out under Article 4 (6(1)) which must be kept available for inspection by any person at the offices of the local authority during office hours.

SAMPLES, TAKING
(F(C)A 1959/LG(WP)A 1977/ APA 1987/EPAA 1992/ WLA 1976/WMA 1996/NH 97)

As one of the powers of authorised persons, authorised officers and others. *See:* ENTRY AND SEARCH.

SANITARY AUTHORITY
(LG(WP)A 1977, s.1(1))

"Means a sanitary authority for the purposes of the Local Government (Sanitary Services) Acts, 1878 to 1964."

(EPAA 1992, s.3(1)

Has the same meaning as in section 1(1) of the LG(WP)A 1977.

SCARECROWS, DECOYS BIRD CALLS AND CALLS
(WLA 1976, s.35)

Section 35 of the WLA 1976 provides:

"(1) Notwithstanding anything contained in this Act apart from this section, but subject to section 42, a person shall not -
(a) use as a scarecrow any live wild bird which is tethered, or
(b) use as a decoy for the purpose of hunting any wild bird, a live wild bird which is tethered or secured by braces or other similar appliances or which is confined in a cage or pen or which is blind, maimed or injured, or
(c) use a stuffed or artificial decoy in the form of any bird for the purpose of hunting any protected wild animals other than wild duck and wild geese, or
(d) use an electrical or other instrument or appliance (including recording apparatus) emitting or imitating bird calls or the calls of wild animals for the purpose of hunting a protected wild bird or a protected wild animal which is a mammal.

(2) Subsection (1) of this section shall not apply to the use of a whistle or similar instrument or appliance imitating, or emitting calls similar to, the calls of, plover, wild duck or wild geese which is operated (whether wholly or partly) manually or orally, for the purpose of hunting any of those wild birds.

(3) Notwithstanding the foregoing provisions of this section, the Minister may by order prohibit throughout the State or in any particular area thereof –
(a) the use for hunting wild duck or wild geese of any stuffed or artificial decoy of a particular class or description specified in the order
(b) the use of any orally or manually operated whistle or other instrument or appliance (not being a recording apparatus) which imitates, or emits call similar to, the calls of the wild duck or wild geese or emits recorded such calls.

(4) Notwithstanding the foregoing provisions of this section, a decoy, or an instrument or appliance, including electrical or other recording apparatus emitting or imitating birdcalls (including distress calls), intended for the purpose of repelling, scaring or capturing a protected wild bird, may be used, pursuant to and in accordance with a licence granted in that behalf by the Minister, for scientific research or for another purpose approved of by the Minister.

(5) The Minister may grant to a person a licence to use as a decoy a live wild bird which is of a species specified in the Third Schedule to this Act and which is confined in a cage or pen and every licence granted pursuant to this subsection shall have attached thereto the following conditions, namely –
(a) the bird shall be so used only for hunting birds of the same species, and
(b) the bird while being so used shall be regularly provided by the holder of the licence, or by someone on his behalf, with ample food and water and shall, when caged, only be kept in a cage which is not of sufficient dimensions to enable it to move and exercise freely."

Offences
(6) A person who -
(a) otherwise than pursuant to and in accordance with a licence granted by the

Minister under subsection (4) or (5) of this section does anything prohibited by subsection (1) of this section,

(b) contravenes an order made by the Minister under this section,

shall be guilty of an offence. *See:* SCHEDULES HERETO, WLA 1976 SCHEDULES.

SCHEDULED ACTIVITY
(WMA 1996, s 5(1))

Means any process, development or operation for the time being specified in the First Schedule to the EPAA 1992. *See:* SCHEDULES HERETO, EPAA 1992 SCHEDULES. This definition is alphabetically misplaced in s.5(1)

SEARCH
(F(C)A 1959/LG(WP)A 1977/
APA 1987/EPAA 1992/WLA 1976
WMA 1996/NH 97)

As one of the powers of authorised persons, authorised officers and others. *See:* ENTRY AND SEARCH.

SEASCAPE
(Heritage 1995, s.2(1))

"Means areas and sites of coastal water including estuaries, bays and lagoons of significant scenic, geological, ecological or other scientific interest."

SEAL OF CENTRAL BOARD AND REGIONAL FISHERIES BOARDS
(FA 1980, Second Schedule)

Article 22 of Part I of the Second Schedule of the FA 1980 in relation to the Central Board and **Article 20 of Part II** of the same schedule in relation to the regional fisheries board provide: The seal of the Central Board/regional fisheries board shall be authenticated by the signature of the chairman of the Central Board/regional fisheries board or some other member thereof authorised by the Central Board/regional fisheries board to act in that behalf, and by the signature of an officer of the Central Board /regional fisheries board authorised by the Central Board /regional fisheries board to act in that behalf.

Articles 23 and 21 deal respectively with judicial notice being taken of the seals of the Central Board and any regional fisheries board and a document purporting to be an instrument made by them and to be sealed with their seal, authenticated as provided above, shall be received in evidence and be deemed to be such instrument without proof, unless the contrary is shown.

SEIZURE
(F(C)A 1959/LG(WP)A 1977
APA 1987/EPAA 1992/
WLA 1976/WMA 1996/NH 97)

As one of the powers of authorised persons, authorised officers and others. *See:* ENTRY AND SEARCH.

SERVICE STATION
(WMA 1996, s.5(1))

"Means any installation where fuel is capable of being dispensed to motor vehicle fuel tanks from stationary storage tanks."

SERVICES, PROVISION OF TO THE AGENCY
(EPAA 1992, s.44(1))

Section 44 of the EPAA 1992 provides:

"(1) For the purposes of enabling the Agency to perform its functions on and from the appropriate day, the Minister may, as an interim measure, supply to the Agency any services, including services of staff, required by the Agency and the Agency may avail of such services for which arrangement are made under this section.

(2) A local authority or any other public authority may supply to the Agency any services required by the Agency, including services of staff, for the performance of any of its functions under the Act on such terms and conditions as may be agreed."

SEVERAL FISHERY
(F(C)A 1959, s.3(1))

"Means any fishery lawfully enjoyed as such under any title whatsoever, being a good and valid title at law, exclusively of the public by any person, whether in navigable waters or in waters not navigable, and whether the soil covered by such waters be vested in such person or in any other person."

PROTECTION OF SEVERAL FISHERY

The protection of several fisheries, in the F(C)A 1959 referred to as "Private Fisheries", is dealt with in the F(C)A 1959, Chapter IV of Part XI (sections 178 to 181). *See:* ENTRY, UNAUTHORISED ONTO A SEVERAL FISHERY.

SEWAGE
(LG(WP)A 1977, s.1(1))

"Includes domestic sewage and a combination of domestic sewage and storm water."

(WMA 1996, s.5(1))

Has the same meaning as in the LG(WP)A 1977.

SEWAGE EFFLUENT
(LG(WP)A 1977, s.1(1))

"Means effluent from any works, apparatus, plant or drainage pipe used for the disposal to waters of sewage whether treated or untreated."

(WMA 1996, s.5(1))

Has the same meaning as in the LG(WP)A 1977.

SEWAGE OR OTHER EFFLUENTS
(EPAA 1992, s.59)

Section 59 of the EPAA 1992, which deals with the implementation of Council Directive, 91/271/EEC on urban waste water treatment (O.J. L135 May 30, 1991 p.40), should be read in conjunction with the preceding section 58 on the implementation of Directive 80/778/EEC on the quality of water intended for human consumption (O.J. L229, August 30, 1980, p.11). *See:* DRINKING WATER and section 60 which deals with the Agency's functions in relation to water or sewage treatment. *See:* WATER AND SEWAGE TREATMENT, AGENCY'S FUNCTIONS.

Section 59 of the EPAA 1992 provides:

"(1) The Minister may, for the purposes of (*qv*) environmental protection and, in particular, for the purpose of giving full effect to Council Directive 91/271/EEC, make regulations for the collection, treatment, discharge or disposal of (*qv*) sewage or other effluents to (*qv*) waters from –
(a) any (*qv*) plant or drainage pipe vested in or controlled or used by a (*qv*) sanitary authority for the treatment of drinking water, or
(b) any plant, sewer or drainage pipe vested in or controlled or used by a sanitary authority for the treatment and disposal of sewage and other effluents.

(2) Without prejudice to the generality of subsection (1), regulations may provide for all or any of the following-
(a) the time within which specified systems or classes of systems for the collection and treatment of sewage effluents shall be provided,
(b) the design, construction and maintenance of collection and treatment systems,
(c) standards or other requirements for effluents specified in subsection (1),
(d) criteria for the designation of areas or classes of areas or waters or classes of waters by such person as may be specified and the times within which such designations shall be made or reviewed for the purposes of subsection (3),
(e) monitoring of sewage or other effluents and of waters to which effluents are discharged.
(f) re-use and disposal of effluents.

(3) Standards or other requirements prescribed under subsection (2) may relate to:
(a) all, or specified classes of or specified volumes of, effluents,
(b) effluents in designated areas or classes of areas or specified plant, sewers or drainage pipes, or specified classes of plant, sewers or drainage pipes, or
(c) effluents discharged to designated waters or classes of waters,
and different standards or other requirements may be prescribed in relation to different effluents or classes of effluents, different areas or classes of areas, different waters or classes of waters or different plant, sewers or drainage pipes or classes of plant, sewers or drainage pipes.

(4) In prescribing standards or other requirements under subsection (2) the Minister shall have regard to any criteria specified and published by the Agency under section 60.
(5) The Minister may make regulations providing for the grant of an authorisation to a sanitary authority by the Agency in respect of the discharge of:
(a) all, or specified classes of, or specified volumes of, effluents,

(b) effluents in designated areas or classes of areas or specified plant, sewers or drainage pipes, or specified classes of plant, sewers or drainage pipes, or
(c) effluents discharged to designated waters or classes of waters,

requiring compliance by such sanitary authority with such standards or other requirements as have been specified under subsection 2(c).

(6) Where a standard or other requirement is prescribed under subsection (2), the sanitary authority shall, where necessary, take steps as soon as is practicable, or within such period as may be prescribed for compliance with such standard or other requirement, to ensure that the said effluent complies with the standard or other requirement.

(7) It shall be a good defence to a prosecution for an offence other than under any enactment this Act that the act constituting the alleged offence was in compliance with a standard or other requirement specified under subsection (2)(c) or an authorisation granted under the section.

Subsection (8) of section 59 provides for an amendment to section 26 of the LG(WP)A 1977. *See:* QUALITY STANDARDS.

The Environmental Protection Agency Act, 1992 (Urban Waste Water Treatment) Regulations 1994 (S.I. No. 419 of 1994) which were passed in exercise of powers conferred on the Minister by section 59 of the EPAA 1992 and for the purpose of giving effect to Council Directive 91/71/EEC of May 30, 1991 deal with the provision by sanitary authorities of collecting systems, treatment standards and other requirements for urban waste water treatment plants generally and in sensitive areas described above.

They prescribe requirements in relation to the provision of collecting systems and treatment standards and other requirements for urban waste water treatment plants, generally and in sensitive areas. The Urban Waste Water Treatments Regulations identify the following ten water bodies as sensitive areas: –

River Boyne, Co. Meath, part of, River Camlin, Co. Longford, part of, River Castlebar, Co. Mayo, part of, River Liffey, part of, River Nenagh, Co. Tipperary, part of, River Tullamore, Co. Offaly, part of (all the parts are downstream of sewage treatment works) and Lough Derg on the River Shannon, Lough Leane, Co. Kerry, Lough Oughter, Co. Cavan and Lough Ree on the River Shannon.

In relation to these "sensitive areas" the Regulations provide at Article 6 that the requirements of Articles 4 and 5 of the Directive, as appropriate, shall be met not later than seven years from the date such an area becomes identified as a sensitive area. The regulations were signed on the December 14, 1994.

The regulations also provide for monitoring procedures in relation to treatment plants and make provision for pre-treatment requirements in relation to industrial waste water entering collecting systems and urban waste water treatment plants.

SITES OF COMMUNITY IMPORTANCE
(NH 97, Reg. 2)

"(a) a site which, in the biogeographical region or regions to which it belongs, contributes significantly to the maintenance or restoration at a favourable conservation status of a natural habitat of a type in Annex I to the *(qv)* Habitats Directive or of a species mentioned in Annex II to that Directive and may also contribute significantly to either or both the coherence of *(qv)* NATURA 2000 referred to in Article 3 of the Habitats Directive, and the maintenance of biological diversity within the biogeographic region or regions concerned, and
(b) in the case of animal species ranging over wide areas, sites of Community importance shall correspond to the places within the natural range of such species which present the physical or biological factors essential to their life and reproduction."

SMOKE
(APA 1987, s.7(1))

"Includes soot, ash, grit and any other particle emitted in smoke."

SPECIAL AMENITY AREA ORDER
(LG(P&D)A 1963, ss. 42 and 43)

Section 42 of the LG(P&D)A 1963, as amended by substitution of subsections (1) and (1A) by section 40(a) of the LG(P&D)A 1976, provides:

"(1) Where it appears to the *(qv)* planning authority that by reason of –
(a) its outstanding natural beauty,
(b) its special recreational value, or
(c) a need for nature conservation,

an area should be declared under this section to be an area of special amenity, they may by order do so and the order may state the objective of the planning authority under this section in relation to the preservation or enhancement of the character or special features of the area including objectives for the prevention or limitation of development in the area.

(1A) The Minister may, if he considers it necessary, direct a planning authority to make an order under this section in relation to an area specified in the direction and may, if he thinks fit, require that objectives specified in the direction be included by the planning authority in their order in respect of matters and in a manner so specified and in case the Minister gives a direction under this subsection the planning authority concerned shall comply with the direction and an order made pursuant to a direction under this subsection shall be revoked or varied only with the consent of the Minister.

(2) An order under this section shall come into operation on being confirmed, whether with or without modification, under the next section.

(3) Where the functional area of two planning authorities are contiguous, either authority may, with the consent of the other, make an order under this section in respect of an area in or partly in the functional area of the other.

(4) Any order under this section for the time being in force may be revoked or varied by a subsequent order under this section.

(5) A planning authority shall, from time to time and at least once in every period of five years, review any order made by them under this section and for the time being in force (excepting any order merely revoking a previous order) for the purpose of deciding whether it is desirable to revoke or amend the order.

(6) The making of an order under this section shall be a (*qv*) reserved function."

Section 43 of the LG(P&D)A 1963 deals with the steps which must be taken by a planning authority after they have made a special amenity area order including:

(1) publication which must include a statement of the right of any person to object and that the order requires the confirmation of the Minister and that if objections are not withdrawn a public local inquiry will be held.

(2) The planning authority, when the time for making objections has expired, must submit the order under section 42 to the Minister with their own submissions and any objections made and not withdrawn.

(3) If no objections are made or if they have been withdrawn the Minister may by order confirm the order made under section 42 with or without modification or refuse to confirm it. In any other case he shall hold a public inquiry before confirming or refusing to confirm.

(4) Every order made under section 43 must be laid before both houses of the Oireachtas and becomes law within 21 days if no resolution seeking to annul it has been passed by either House.

(5) Any reference in this Act to a special amenity area order shall be construed as a reference to an order confirmed under this section.

SPECIAL CASES
(EPAA 1992, s.95)

This section goes to the heart of the EPA system in that it gives the Minister the power to require that any process, development or operation not already appearing in the First Schedule shall be licensable under Part IV. It would then become an (*qv*)activity for the purposes of the EPAA 1992 Act.

This would take the particular process out of the lower tier of licensing under the F(C)A 1959, LG(WP)A 1977 or APA 1987. The effect of the Minister's order under the section would be to require the process to apply for and obtain an Integrated Pollution Control (IPC) licence under Part IV of the EPAA 1992 as is required of all processes appearing in the First Schedule to that Act.

Section 95 of the EPAA 1992 provides:

"(1) The Minister may, by order, require that any process, development or operation not specified in the First Schedule shall be licensable by the Agency under this Part in lieu of being the subject of –

(a) a licence under –
  (i) Part III of the Air Pollution Act, 1987,
  (ii) section 4 or 16 of the Local Government (Water Pollution) Act, 1977, or
  (iii) section 171 of the Fisheries (Consolidation) Act, 1959,

  or
(b) a permit under –
  (i) The European Communities (Toxic and Dangerous Waste) Regulations, 1982, or
  (ii) the European Communities (Waste) Regulations, 1979,

  and in such case the provisions of this Act shall apply in relation to the process, development or operation concerned as if it were an (*qv*) activity for so long as the relevant order remains in force.

(2) Without prejudice to the generality of subsection (1), an order can be made –
  (a) because of the location of the process, development or operation, or the quality of the environment in the area in which the process, development or operation will be carried out,
  (b) because, at the time of the enactment of this Act or the most recent amendment of the First Schedule, no such process, development or operation existed in the State, or
  (c) evidence related to any impact on the environment of such process, development or operation which was not available has become available."

Both of the statutory instruments containing the Regulations referred to in paragraph (b) of subsection (1) above have been revoked by section 6 of the WMA 1996. The provisions of the WMA 1996 now cover those matters. As the Agency is the licensing authority in relation to the grant of a waste licence under section 40 of the WMA 1996 there is no adjustment necessary to section 95.

SPECIAL CONTROL AREA AND SPECIAL CONTROL AREA ORDER
(APA 1987, ss.39 to 44)

A local authority may on its own initiative declare a whole or any part of their functional area as a special control area for the purpose of the prevention or limitation of (*qv*) air pollution and the Minister, if he deems it expedient to do so, may direct a local authority so to do.

"Special control area" in the APA 1987, section 7(1), means an area in relation to which a special control area order is in operation.

"Special control area order" in the APA 1987, section 7(1), has the meaning assigned to it by section 39.

Section 39 of the APA 1987 provides:

"(1) Where it appears to a (*qv*) local authority that the whole or any part of their functional area should, in order to prevent or limit air pollution, be declared to be a special control area, they may make an order (in this Act referred to as a "special control area order") under this section.

(2) In deciding whether it is necessary or expedient to make a special control area order in relation to any area, the local authority shall have regard to –
  (a) the incidence and cause of air pollution in the area, and
  (b) any (*qv*) air quality management plan in force in relation to the area, and
  (c) any relevant (*qv*) air quality standard, and
  (d) the availability of the means necessary for compliance with the order, and
  (e) the expense which would be incurred in complying with the order.

(3) A special control area order shall specify -
  (a) the area to which it relates,
  (b) the (*qv*) pollutant with which it is concerned, and
  (c) the measures to be taken and the requirements which shall have effect in the area to which the order relates.

(4) The Minister may, if he considers it expedient so to do in order to prevent or limit air pollution, having regard to the provisions of paragraphs (a), (b), (c), (d) and (e) of subsection (2), direct a local authority to make a special control area in relation to such area and such pollutant as may be specified in the direction and may, if he thinks fit, further direct the order should specify that particular measures shall be taken and that particular requirements shall have effect in such area and the local authority concerned shall comply with any direction of the Minister given under this subsection within such period as may be specified in

the order.

(5) A local authority may, with the consent of any other local authority concerned, make a special control area order in relation to an area which is within the functional area of the other authority."

The Special Control Area (Ballyfermot) Order, 1988 (S.I. No. 282 of 1988), the Special Control Area (Ballyfermot Area A) Order, 1989 (S.I. No. 291 of 1989), the Special Control Area (Ballyfermot Area B) Order, 1989 (S.I. No. 291 of 1989) and the Special Control Area (Ballyfermot Area B) Order (S.I. No. 26) were made under this section.

PROVISIONS OF A SPECIAL CONTROL AREA ORDER

Section 40 of the APA 1987 provides:

"(1) Without prejudice to the provisions of section 39(3), a special control area order may make provision for the following –

(a) prohibit, subject to such exceptions or limitations as may be specified, the emission of a specified pollutant from specified classes or descriptions of premises;

(b) prohibit, subject to such exceptions and limitations as may be specified, the burning other than in an (*qv*) an authorised fireplace of any fuel other than (*qv*) authorised fuel;

(c) prohibit, subject to such an exceptions as may be specified, the burning of straw, waste or any other substance;

(d) make, having regard to all the circumstances, different provisions for different parts of the area to which the order relates and for different premises or classes of premises;

(e) exempt, with or without conditions, such premises or classes of premises as may be specified from all or any of the requirements of the order;

(f) exempt, with or without conditions, such fireplaces or such classes of fireplaces as may be specified from all or any of the requirements of the order;

(g) specify the types or qualities of fuels to be, or not to be, burnt in such fireplaces or classes of fireplaces as may be specified;

(h) specify the conditions subject to which, or the purposes for which, specified fuels or classes of fuels may be burnt in the special control area;

(i) prohibit or limit the carrying on of such operations or processes as may be specified in the special control area or specify the conditions under which such operations or processes may be carried on;

(j) prohibit or restrict the sale or delivery in a special control area of specified fuels or classes of fuels.

(2) The Minister may, by regulations, declare that any particular class of fireplace shall, subject to such conditions as may be specified in the regulations, be an authorised fireplace for the purposes of a special control area order.

(3) The Minister may, by regulations, declare that any particular type of fuel shall be an authorised fuel for the purposes of a special control area order.

Offence

(4) Any person who contravenes any provision of a special control area order which is in operation shall be guilty of an offence.

Defences

(5) In any proceedings relating to the contravention of a special control area order and involving the emission of a pollutant, it shall be a good defence to establish that –

(a) the emission of the pollutant was not caused by the use of a fuel other than an authorised fuel,

(b) the emission of the pollutant was caused by the burning of a fuel other than an authorised fuel in an authorised fireplace in accordance with the conditions (if any) subject to which the fireplace was declared to be an authorised fireplace."

The Air Pollution Act 1987 (Authorised Fireplace) Regulations 1988 (S.I. No. 297 of 1988) and the Air Pollution Act 1987 (Authorised Fuel) Regulations 1988, (S.I. No. 298 of 1988) refer.

CONFIRMATION OF A SPECIAL CONTROL AREA ORDER

Section 41 of the APA 1987:

"(1) As soon as may be after they have made

a special control area order, a local authority shall publish in one or more newspapers circulating in the area to which the order relates a notice –
(a) stating that a special control area order has been made and specifying the area to which the order relates;
(b) naming the place where a copy of the order and any map or plan referred to therein may be inspected free of charge by any interested person;
(c) specifying the times and the period, being not less than one month, during which the order and the map or plan (if any) can be so inspected;
(d) specifying the period, being not less than one month, within which, and the manner in which, any person affected by the order may make objections thereto;
(e) stating that the order will not come into operation until it has been confirmed by the Minister;
(f) stating that if objections are duly made to the order and are not withdrawn, the Minister, before confirming or refusing to confirm the order, will cause an (*qv*) oral hearing to be held at which any person who has, within the period specified in the notice, made an objection to the order will be afforded an opportunity of being heard.

(2) As soon as may be after the period for the making of objections has expired, the local authority concerned shall transmit the special control area order to the Minister for confirmation and, when so transmitting the order, they shall also transmit to the Minister any objections which have, within the specified period, been made and have not been withdrawn.

(3) Where no objections have, within the specified period, been made to the making of the special control area order or all such objections have been withdrawn, the Minister may –
(a) by order confirm the special control area order with or without modifications, or
(b) refuse to confirm the order, or
(c) if he considers it desirable so to do, before confirming, or refusing to confirm, the order, cause an oral hearing to be held in relation to the order.

(4) Where objections have, within the specified period, been made to the making of a special control area order and such objections have not been withdrawn, the Minister shall cause an oral hearing to be held in relation to the order and shall afford each person who duly made an objection to the order the opportunity of being heard.

(5) When he has considered the report (including any recommendations made therein) of the person who held the oral hearing, the Minister may, by order, confirm the special control area order, with or without modifications, or he may refuse to confirm it.

(6) In deciding whether or not to confirm a special control area order, the Minister shall have regard to the provisions of paragraphs (a), (b), (c), (d) and (e) of section 39(2).

(7) Every order made by the Minister under this section confirming a special control area order shall specify a date, being not less than six months after the date of the making of the confirming order, on which the special control area order shall come into operation: provided always that the date so specified in relation to a special control area order which –
(a) revokes a previous special control area order, or
(b) exempts specified areas or specified buildings or classes of buildings from all or any of the requirements of a special control area order,

may be the date of the making of the confirming order or any date subsequent to that date.

(8) Notice of the making of an order confirming a special control area order and of the date on which the special control area order shall come into operation shall be published, given or served by the local authority concerned in such manner as the Minister may direct."

ORAL HEARINGS

Section 42 of the APA 1987 deals with oral hearings in relation to special control area orders. *See:* ORAL HEARINGS (1).

RELAXATION OR SUSPENSION OF SPECIAL CONTROL AREA ORDERS

Section 43 of the APA 1987 provides:
"(1) If, at any time, it appears to the Minister

to be necessary so to do, he may, by order, suspend or relax the operation of a special control area order in relation to the whole or any part of a special control area for such period as may be specified in the order.

(2) Before making an order under subsection (1), the Minister shall, unless because of the urgency of the situation such consultation is not practicable, consult the local authority concerned.

(3) The Minister may by order amend or revoke an order under this section (including this subsection).

(4) A local authority concerned shall publish, in such manner as the Minister may direct, notice of the making of an order under this section."

POWER OF LOCAL AUTHORITY TO REQUIRE ALTERATION TO PREMISES

Section 44 of the APA 1987 deals with the service of notices by a local authority on the (*qv*) occupier of (*qv*) premises within a special control area requiring alteration to the premises. *See:* ALTERATION OF PREMISES AT REQUEST OF LOCAL AUTHORITY.

FINANCIAL ASSISTANCE FOR CERTAIN WORKS

Section 45 of the APA 1987 deals with the provision by the Minister with the consent of the Minister for Finance of financial assistance to an occupier of premises within a special control area to fund compliance with the requirements of a special control area order or a notice under section 44 (above). *See:* FINANCIAL ASSISTANCE FOR CERTAIN WORKS, SPECIAL CONTROL AREA.

SPECIAL PROTECTION AREAS
(WLA 1976/NH 97)

We have already seen, under the heading (*qv*) Birds Directive, how these special protection areas arise, under the European Communities (Conservation of Wild Birds) Regulations 1985 (S.I. No. 291 of 1985) and amending Regulations.

Regulation 34 of the NH 97 Regulations (S.I. 94 of 1997) provides that the provisions of Regulations 4, 5, 7, 13, 14, 15 and 16 shall, where appropriate, apply with any necessary modifications to areas classified pursuant to paragraph 1 and 2 of Article 4 of the Birds Directive.

The intention is that the named regulations which deal with the identification, selection, notification and protection of special area of conservation sites shall apply to the areas designated as SPAs under the Birds Directive.

Most of these regulations are inappropriate for this purpose. Only regulations 13, 14, 15, and 16 which contain some protective measures would appear to be capable of being so applied.

STAKE NETS
(F(C)A 1959, s.3(1))

"Includes a stake weir and any (*qv*) fixed engine of similar construction to a stake net."

Section 105 of the F(C)A 1959 provides that stake nets are not to extend further than from high to low water mark. *See:* FIXED ENGINES, SITES OF.

STANDARDS, QUALITY

See: QUALITY STANDARDS.

STATE OF THE ENVIRONMENT, REPORTS
(EPAA 1992, s.79)

The Agency shall:
(a) within five years after it is established and in every fifth year thereafter, or
(b) within such other periods as may be prescribed,

prepare and publish a report on the quality and condition of the environment in the State.

It was in the Senate debate on this section that Senator Joe O'Toole attempted to have the word "environment" defined for the purposes of the section but he was overruled on the grounds that it would not give sufficient flexibility to the Agency. The definition of "environmental medium" in the EPAA 1992 is probably more suitable as "the environment" is capable of many subjective definitions.

STATE OWNERSHIP OF CERTAIN INLAND WATERS
(WLA 1976, s.57)

Section 57 of the WLA 1976 provides:

"(1) Where the Minster is of the opinion that there is a doubt as to whether or not any lake or other inland waters belong to the State but, in his opinion, it is likely that the lake or other inland waters do so belong, he may, after consultation with the Minister for Agriculture and Fisheries, publish a notice in Iris Oifigiúil and in at least one newspaper circulating in the locality in which the lake or other inland waters are situate requiring either, as may be stated in the notice –

(a) any person who claims to have or to be entitled to enjoy an interest in or over the lake or other inland waters (which shall be specified in the notice) or, in the case of a lake, in or over the lakeshore accretion (if any) from the lake, or

(b) any person who claims to have or to be entitled to enjoy an interest, other than a right of fishing, in or over the lake or other inland waters (which shall be so specified) or in or over such lakeshore accretion,

to furnish to the Minister within a period specified in the notice (being a period of not less than two months from the publication in the Iris Oifigiúil) particulars of the interest together with an abstract (accompanied by copies of all abstracted documents) of his title to the interest or of the grounds on which his claim is based."

Subsection (2) entitles the Minister to pay the person furnishing particulars costs reasonably incurred by him in so doing.

Subsection (3) provides that if there are no responses to the notice within the period specified therein or if the Minister acquires by agreement all of the interests particulars of which have been furnished and the period has expired he may by order declare that the fee simple in the specified lake or other inland waters and lakeshore accretion (if any), or such part thereof as he has acquired, together with interests inferior to the fee simple but not including rights of fishing, belongs to the State.

"(4) A declaration made under this section shall operate as regards the lands to which it relates in accordance with its terms and shall be conclusive evidence of the matters declared and shall not be questioned in any legal proceedings."

Subsections (5) and (6) provide for the payment of compensation to late claimants, who can establish an interest, the amount of which is determined under the Acquisition of Land (Assessment of Compensation) Act, 1919.

"(7) Nothing in the section shall restrict, prejudice or affect the functions of (*qv*) sanitary authorities or the Minister for Local Government under the Local Government (Sanitary Services) Acts, 1878 to 1964, or the Water Supplies Act, 1942."

SPECIAL LOCAL LICENCES
(F(C)A 1959, s.3(1))

"Means a licence granted under section 74 in respect of (*qv*) special tidal waters."

"Special local licence duty" in section 3(1), means the duty payable under section 74 for a special local licence granted in respect of special tidal waters.

SPECIAL TIDAL WATERS,
(F(C)A 1959, s.3(1))

"Means any tidal waters in respect of which an order made under section 7, is for the time being in force."

ORDER DECLARING SPECIAL TIDAL WATERS

Section 7(1) of the F(C)A 1959 provides for the declaring from time to time by the Minister, with the concurrence of the Minister for Finance, that any particular tidal waters shall be special tidal waters for the purposes of the Act.

Subsection (2) provides that the order must specify and define the special tidal waters and shall be final and conclusive evidence as to the boundaries notwithstanding any discrepancies between the extent of the tidal waters as defined and the extent of the tidal waters in which a (*qv*) several fishery was previously enjoyed.

Subsection (3) provides for the revocation or amendment of an order in relation to special tidal waters made under the section by the Minister by order with the concurrence of the Minister for Finance.

Subsection (4) provides that the section applies to special tidal waters of a particular river or estuary in which for not less than 20 years prior to the 1.1.1993 a several fishery was believed to exist and was enjoyed as of right but in respect of which either –

(a) it was, after the 1.1.1933 judicially determined that no several fishery existed in such tidal waters, or

(b) the person who on the 1.1.1933 exercised as of right the said several fishery in such waters does not nor does any other person claim to have or enjoy as of right a several fishery in such tidal waters.

LICENCES FOR FISHING IN SPECIAL TIDAL WATERS

Offence

Section 73 of the F(C)A 1959 creates the offence of any person using in any special tidal waters any kind of fishing engine for the taking of salmon and trout unless that person is the holder of a special local licence.

(Note that the maximum penalty prescribed under this section has been increased. *See:* FINES AND IMPRISONMENT (IMPOSITION OF)).

Section 74(1) of the F(C)A 1959 deals with the issue by the appropriate regional board, on the order of the Minister, of licences to use in special tidal waters any specific kind of (*qv*)fishing engine (of a kind in respect of which no ordinary licences are issuable) for the taking of salmon and no special local licence can be issued otherwise than with the authority of such an order.

Subsections (2), (3), (4) and (5) deal with the fixing by the Minister of the licence duty payable in respect of such a licence which cannot be less than the ordinary licence payable in respect of a similar fishing engine and there is provision for a reduction, with the consent of the Minister for Finance, in the amount of the duty where a person holds both an ordinary licence to fish for salmon with rod and line and a special local licence.

FORM AND EFFECT

Section 75(1) of the F(C)A 1959 provides for the form of the special local licence which must be in such form as the Minister directs, be sealed by the regional board and specify the year for which it is issued.

Subsection (2) provides that a separate special local licence shall be issued for each separate fishing engine.

Subsection (3) specifies that the licence must be expressed and operate to authorise a person to whom such a licence is issued to use in such tidal waters during the year of issue a fishing engine of the particular kind specified therein for the taking of salmon or trout, but subject to the provisions of this Act and any instrument made thereunder.

This whole area of special local licences and special tidal areas appears to relate to areas where certain privileges in relation to fishing for salmon survived the transfer of privately owned fisheries into State control.

Various orders have been made under the title "control of salmon fishing" – where in areas such as Bangor these privileges survive and some of the designated drift and draft net licences are marked with the word "special". Twenty-five of the draft nets in the Bangor area are so marked meaning that 25 special local draft licences are issued for that area. It is unclear whether or not the waters for which they are issued are classified as "special tidal areas". The Special Tidal Waters (Special Local Licences) Order 1983 (S.I. 41 of 1983) refers.

Section 77 of the F(C)A 1959 provides for further ministerial order in regard to the periodic issue of the licences and payment of the duty by installments.

SPECIES
(WLA 1976, s.2(1))

"Includes subspecies and hybrids."

SPORTING RIGHTS
(WLA 1976, s.29(1))

"Does not include fishing rights."

STATUTORY NATURE RESERVES
(WLA 1976)

This is the environmental designation given by environmentalists to those nature reserves which have been formally established, recognised or designated by order under Part II Chapter II of the WLA 1976. *See:* RESERVES AND REFUGES.

STROKEHAUL
(FA 1980, s.2(1))

"Means any weighted instrument or device which may be used, whether with a rod and line or otherwise, to foul-hook fish."

STRUCTURE
(WMA 1996, s. 5(1))

"Means any building, erection, structure, excavation, or other thing, constructed, erected, or made on, in or under land, or any part of a structure so defined and, where the context so admits, includes the land on, in or under which the structure is situated."

SURFACE WATER
(LG(WP)A 1977)

See: WATER, SURFACE WATER.

SURRENDER OF WASTE LICENCE
(WMA 1996)

Section 48 of the WMA 1996 provides:

"(1) A waste licence may be surrendered by its holder, but only if the Agency accepts the surrender.

(2) The holder of a waste licence who desires to surrender it shall make an application for that purpose to the Agency, in such form, giving such information and accompanied by such evidence as may be prescribed and accompanied by such fee as may be prescribed under section 50.

(3) Upon receiving an application for surrender of a waste licence, the Agency –
(a) shall inspect the (*qv*) facility at which the activity to which the licence relates is carried on ('the relevant facility'), and
(b) may require the holder of the licence to furnish to it such further information or evidence as it may specify.

(4) For the purpose of subsection (3), the Agency may, by notice in writing served on the person, require a person who has made an application to it under subsection (2) to carry out, or arrange to have carried out, in such manner as may be specified in the notice, such monitoring, sampling and investigations, in addition to those which may be required under a condition attached to the waste licence concerned, as the Agency considers necessary, and so specifies, and any requirement so made shall be regarded as a condition attaching to that licence.

(5) Where the Agency proposes to accept the surrender of a waste licence, it shall consult with such persons and in accordance with such procedures as may be prescribed.

(6) Having regard to such information or evidence as is furnished to it under paragraph (b) of subsection (3) and to the results of an inspection under paragraph (a) of that subsection and the monitoring, sampling and investigation required to be carried out under subsection (4), the Agency shall assess the condition of the relevant facility, so far as that condition is the result of the use of the facility for the recovery or disposal of waste (whether or not carried on in accordance with the waste licence concerned) and the likely effect on any (*qv*) environmental media of any (*qv*) emissions from the relevant facility that may occur.

(7) If the Agency is satisfied that the condition of the relevant facility is not causing or likely to cause (*qv*) environmental pollution, it shall accept the surrender of the waste licence, but otherwise shall refuse to accept the surrender of the waste licence.

(8) A decision of the Agency under subsection (7) shall be conveyed to –
(a) the applicant concerned,
(b) the local authority in whose functional area the activity, the subject matter of the waste licence, has been carried on, and
(c) any person concerned that it has consulted under subsection (5),

by notice in writing, as soon as may be after the decision is made and where the decision is a decision to accept the surrender of a waste licence, that licence shall cease to have effect upon the service of the said notice.

(9) The making of the application for the surrender of a waste licence under this section or the cesser of the (*qv*) activity to which the waste licence relates, shall in no way affect or diminish such conditions, requirements or obligations applying to or falling on the holder of such licence as are specified in or arise under the licence."

SURVEILLANCE OF CONSERVATION STATUS
(NH 97)

Regulation 7(1) of the NH 97 Regulations requires the Minister and the Minister or the Marine, in respect of the fish species specified in Part II of the First Schedule, to undertake surveillance of the conservation status of the (*qv*) natural habitats and (*qv*) species referred to in Article 2 of the (*qv*) Habitats Directive with particular regard to (*qv*) priority natural habitat types and (*qv*) priority species and the Minister shall have regard to such surveillance in the adaption of the list of (*qv*) candidate sites to be transmitted to the (*qv*) Commission.

Regulation 7(2)(a) provides that for the purposes of the surveillance at paragraph (1) and generally for the purpose of giving effect to the (*qv*) Birds Directive the Ministers may each appoint in writing (*qv*) authorised persons.

See: PROTECTION, TAKING FLORA AND FAUNA IN THE WILD

SUSPENSION OF OPEN SEASONS
(WLA 1976, s.27)

See: OPEN SEASONS, TEMPORARY SUSPENSION OF.

T

TERMINATION OF A PART X LICENCE
(F(C)A 1959, s.161)

Section 161 of the F(C)A 1959, inserted by section 20 of the F(A)A 1994, provides that a Part X licence shall terminate on the death of the holder, on revocation by the Minister or by surrender by the holder. *See:* CERTIFICATE OF FITNESS.

TERRITORIAL SEAS OF THE STATE
(WLA 1976, s.2(1))

"Means the portion of the sea which for the purposes of the Maritime Jurisdiction Act, 1959, is the territorial seas of the State."

The Maritime Jurisdiction Act of 1959 has been amended by the Maritime Jurisdiction (Amendment) Act 1988, section 2 of which defines the territorial seas of the State as that portion of the sea which lies between the baseline and the outer limits of the territorial seas.

Section 4 defines the baseline as the low-water mark:

(a) on the coast of the mainline or of any island, or
(b) on any low tide elevation situated wholly or partly at a distance not exceeding twelve nautical miles from the mainland or an island

Section 3 defines that outer limit of the territorial seas as the line every point of which is at a distance of 12 nautical miles from the nearest point of the baseline.

TIDAL WATERS
(LG(WP)A 1977, s.1(1))

"Includes the sea and any estuary up to high water mark medium tide and any enclosed dock adjoining tidal waters."

TRADE
(LG(WP)A 1977, s.1(1))

"Includes agriculture, aquaculture, horticulture and any scientific research or experiment."

TRADE EFFLUENT
(LG(WP)A 1977, s.1(1))

"Means effluent from any works, apparatus, plant or drainage pipe used for the disposal to waters or to a sewer of any liquid (whether treated or untreated), either with or without particles of matter in suspension therein, which is discharged from premises used for carrying on any trade or industry (including mining), but does not include domestic sewage or storm water."

TRANSFER OF CERTAIN APPEALS TO AN BORD PLEANÁLA
(LG(WP)A 1977, s.21)

Section 21 of the LG(WP)A 1977, amended by substitution by section 16 of the LG(WP)(A)A 1990:

"(1) The Minister may by regulations provide for –
   (a) any procedural matter in relation to appeals under section 8 and 20, and
   (b) such incidental and supplementary matters (including the modification of any provision of the Local Government (Water Pollution) Acts, 1977 and 1990, and the Local Government (Planning and Development) Acts, 1963 to 1983) as appear to the Minister to be necessary or expedient for the purposes of such appeals.

(2) Section 6(2)(d), 19(2)(d) and subsections (1)(a) and (9) of section 28 shall, as respect such appeals as aforesaid, have effect as if the references therein to the Minister were references to An Bord Pleanála."

Part IV of the Local Government (Water Pollution) Regulations 1992 (S.I. No. 271 of 1992) deals extensively with appeals to An Bord Pleanála under section 8 or 20 of the LG(WP)A 1977.

TRANSFER OF FISHERIES BY ORDER
(FA 1980, ss.40, 41 and 42)

The FA 1980 provides at various sections for the transfer of fisheries or fishery rights by order with the consent of the Minister for Finance as follows:

(1) Section 40 by the (*qv*) Commissioners to the Minister or the (*qv*) Central Board,

(2) Section 41 by the Irish Land Commission to the Minister or the Central Board,

(3) Section 42 by the Minister to the Central Board, the fisheries or fishery rights having been acquired by or vested in the Minister under the Forestry Acts.

In each case the order operates to vest without any further or other conveyance, all the estate and interest in every fishery and fishing right and in all lands, way-leaves, water-rights, rights of access or other easements or rights purported to be transferred by such order.

TRANSFER OF FISHERIES, MOY FISHERY
(FA 1980, s.42)

Transfer of Fisheries (Moy Fishery) Order 1994 (S.I. No. 431 of 1994) by virtue of section 42 of the FA 1980 and with the consent of the Minister for Finance on the January 1, 1995, the Moy Fishery was transferred from the Department of the Marine to the Central Board.

This fishery has very recently been taken by the Minister from the Central Board and given to the regional fisheries board within whose functional area it is located.

TRANSFER OF FUNCTIONS
(APA 1987, s.21)

Section 21 of the APA 1987 provides for the Minister providing by regulation that any function conferred on a local authority under the APA shall, in addition to or in lieu of being performed by a local authority, be performed by such other person (including the Minister or other local body) or body of persons as may be specified and in subsection (2) a body established under the Local Government Services (Corporate Bodies) Act, 1971 is suggested as being such a body.

TRANSFER OF FUNCTIONS FROM PUBLIC AUTHORITY TO AGENCY
(EPAA 1992, s.54)

Section 54 of the EPAA 1992 provides for the transfer by the Minister by regulation from any public authority to the Agency of any function relating to (*qv*) environmental protection where the Minister is satisfied that the functions could be more effectively performed by the Agency. The performance by the Agency could be either in addition to or in lieu of performance by the public body. *See:* FUNCTIONS OF THE EPA.

TRANSFER OF FUNCTIONS FROM LOCAL AUTHORITY TO AGENCY
(WMA 1996, s.21)

Section 21 of the WMA 1996 provides:

"(1) The Minister may, following consultation with the (*qv*) Agency, where he or she is satisfied that any function conferred on a local authority by this Act could be more effectively performed by the Agency in lieu of being performed by that authority, by regulations provide that the function shall be performed by the Agency with effect from a date specified in the regulations.

(2) Whenever regulations under subsection (1) are in force in relation to a particular function, a reference in this Act to a local authority shall, where appropriate, be construed as a reference to the Agency and the function to which the regulations relate shall be a function of the Agency.

(3) The Minister may, where he or she is satisfied that any function conferred by a local authority by this Act could, as respects the functional area of the corporation of a borough (other than a county borough), or the council of an urban district, that is situate in the functional area of that local authority, be more effectively performed by the said corporation or council in lieu of being performed by that authority, by regulations provide that the said function shall, with

effect from a date specified in the regulations, be performed, as respects the first-mentioned functional area, by the said corporation or, as the case may be, council."

Subsection (4) provides that as in (2) above a reference to a local authority shall, where appropriate, be construed as a reference to the corporation of the borough or the council of the urban district to which the regulations relate and the function to which the regulations relate shall be a function of the said corporation or council.

Subsection (5) provides for such incidental, supplementary and consequential provisions for regulations made under this section as appear to the Minister to be necessary.

TRANSFER OF PROPERTIES
(FA 1980, s.9)

Section 9 of the FA 1980 provides for the transfer of certain properties of (*qv*)boards of conservators to the (*qv*) Central Board. *See:* CENTRAL BOARD, FUNCTIONS OF.

TRANSFER OF WASTE LICENCES
(WMA 1996, s.47)

Section 47 of the WMA 1996 provides:

"(1) A waste licence may be transferred from the (*qv*) holder to another person in accordance with this section.

(2) Where the holder of a waste licence desires that the licence be transferred to another person (hereinafter in this section referred to as 'the proposed transferee'), the holder of the licence and the proposed transferee shall jointly make an application to the Agency requesting that such a transfer be effected by the Agency.

(3) An application under subsection (2) shall be made in such form and shall include such information as may be prescribed and shall be accompanied by such fee as may be prescribed under section 50 and the waste licence concerned.

(4) The Agency may require the provision of such further information by the holder of the licence or the proposed transferee as it considers appropriate for the purpose of dealing with an application made by them under the section.

(5) If, on consideration of an application under subsection (2), and any relevant information provided in respect thereof, the Agency is satisfied –
  (a) that the proposed transferee would, if he or she were an applicant for the licence, be regarded by it as a fit and proper person to be granted under section 40 a like waste licence to the licence concerned,
  (b) that the proposed transferee has complied with any requirements under section 53, and
  (c) regarding such other matters as may be prescribed,

  it shall effect a transfer of the licence to the proposed transferee in such manner as may be prescribed.

(6) A person to whom a waste licence is transferred under this section shall be deemed to have assumed and accepted all liabilities, requirements and obligations provided for in and arising under the licence, regardless of how and in respect of what period, including a period prior to the transfer of the licence, they may arise."

For section 50 *see*: CHARGES
For section 39 *see*: WASTE(4) RECOVERY AND DISPOSAL OF WASTE
For section 53 *see*: FINANCIAL PROVISIONS REGARDING WASTE RECOVERY AND DISPOSAL.

TRANSFER OF FUNCTIONS IN RELATION TO WASTE LICENCES
(WMA 1996, s.69)

Section 69 of the WMA 1996 provides:

"(1) The Minister may by order transfer the functions of the Agency under this Act to a local authority in so far as those functions relate to waste licences authorising the carrying on within the functional area of that local authority of such activity or activities as is or are specified in the order.

(2) An order under this section may contain such ancillary, subsidiary and incidental provisions as the Minister may determine, including provisions modifying or

adapting any provision of this Act for the purpose of enabling the order to have full effect.

(3) Without prejudice to the generality of subsection (2), an order under this section may specify terms, conditions and restrictions upon and subject to which a function transferred by the order is to be performed by the local authority to which the function is transferred.

(4) If an order under this section is revoked the functions to which it relates shall thereupon become and be vested in the Agency.

(5) The Minister shall cause an order under this section to be published in the Iris Oifigiúil."

TRANSITIONAL PROVISIONS IN RELATION TO ALKALI ETC

(APA 1987, s.57)

Section 57 of the APA 1987 provides:

"(1) The provisions of the Alkali, etc. Works Regulation Act, 1906, in relation to emissions shall, notwithstanding the repeal of that Act by this Act, apply to every relevant work until the licence under this Act is granted in respect of the work.

(2) Notwithstanding the provisions of subsection (1), the provisions of section 9 of the Alkali, etc. Works Regulation Act, 1906, in relation to the registration of works shall not apply to a relevant work.

(3) A local authority in whose functional area a relevant work is situated shall, on and after the commencement of this section, be responsible for ensuring that it is carried on in accordance with the provisions of subsection (1).

(4) In this section "relevant work" means existing *(qv)* industrial plant which is either –
(a) an alkali work within the meaning of the Alkali, etc. Works Regulation, Act 1906, or
(b) a work listed in the First Schedule to that Act."

TRANSPORT

(WMA 1996, s.5(1))

"Includes, in relation to waste, the movement of waste by road, rail, air, sea or inland waterway but does not include the movement of waste from one place to another:
(a) by means of any pipe or similar apparatus which joins those two places, or
(b) on and within the site at which the waste is held for the time being."

TRAPS, SNARES, NETS, PROHIBITION OF

(WLA 1976, s.34)

Section 34 of the WLA 1976 provides:

"(1) Notwithstanding anything contained in this Act apart from this section but subject to section 42, a person shall not –
(a) hunt any (*qv*) wild bird or (*qv*) wild mammal by means of a trap, snare, net, line, hook, arrow, dart, spear or similar device, instrument or missile, or birdlime or any substance of a like nature, or any poisonous, poisoned or stupefying bait, or
(b) affix, place or set –
(i) any trap, snare or net for killing or taking a wild bird or a wild mammal, or
(ii) any line, hook or other device or instrument, calculated or likely to cause death or bodily injury to any wild bird or wild mammal coming in contact with it,
on any tree, pole, cairn or other structure in, or in the vicinity of, any place frequented by wild birds or by wild mammals, or
(c) lay any poisonous or poisoned substance or stupefying bait, being a substance or bait which is calculated to or is likely to injure, or facilitate the capture of, a wild bird or wild mammal, in, or in the vicinity of, any place mentioned in paragraph (b) of this subsection, or on any tree, pole, cairn or other structure in or in the vicinity of such place.

(2) Subsection (1) of this section shall not apply to or render unlawful –
(a) the affixing, placing or setting of a trap, snare or net which for the time being stands approved for the purposes of this section by virtue of regulation under this section,
(b) the taking or killing by means of any such trap, snare or net of any wild bird which is not a protected wild bird or any wild mammal which is not a protected wild animal,
and nothing in said subsection (1) shall make unlawful anything which is duly

done pursuant to a statute (other than this Act) or statutory instrument, which is permitted to be done under such a statute or instrument or which is done pursuant to and in accordance with a licence or other permission granted or issued pursuant to such a statute or instrument or anything caused by or which results from, or is consequent upon or the effect of any other act or thing which is lawfully done."

This latter paragraph of subsection (2) now sounds strangely at odds with the paramountcy of environmental protection emanating from Europe and demonstrated in the protection section of instruments made under the (*qv*) Birds Directive and the NH 97 Regulations.

"(3) Subsection (1) of this section shall not apply to any of the following if done pursuant to and in accordance with a licence granted in that behalf by the Minister –
(a) the capture alive, on land specified in the licence by means of a trap, snare or net of any species of wild bird specified in the licence, for the purpose of propagating or of improving the quality of such species,
(b) the capture alive by means of nets of hares by or on behalf, or at the request of a coursing club affiliated to the Irish Coursing Club,
(c) the capture alive by means of nets or other devices of hawks or falcons for the purpose of lawful (*qv*) falconry within the state,
(d) the capture alive of wild birds or wild mammals, for research or other scientific or educational purposes or for the removal to a new habitat, or to a place specified in the licence.

(4) The Minister may by regulations declare a trap, snare or net which is of a particular type, class or description specified in the regulations –
(a) to be approved for the purposes of this section and may, if he thinks fit, regulate its use as regards wild birds or wild mammals,
(b) to be a trap, snare or net to which subsection (6) of this section applies."

Offences

Subsection (5) provides that contravention of subsection (1) is an offence and subsection (6) provides that the importation, except under licence, or sale in the course of a trade or business of a trap, snare or net which pursuant to subsection (4) is for the time being declared to be a trap, snare or net to which this subsection applies is also an offence.

"(7) A person shall not be convicted under this section and under section 22 or section 23 of this Act and section 8 of the Protection of Animals Act, 1911, in respect of the same act."

Section 8 of the Protection of Animals Act, 1911 was extended by section 7 of the Protection of Animals (Amendment) Act, 1965.

The Wildlife Act 1976 (Approved Traps, Snares and Nets) Regulations 1977 (S.I. No. 307 of 1977), which replace a Spring Traps Order of 1968, provide:

"1. These regulations may be cited as the Wildlife Act, 1976 (Approved Traps, Snares and Nets) Regulations 1977.

2. The following traps, snares and nets are hereby declared to be approved of, for the purposes of section 34 of the Wildlife Act, 1976 (No. 39 of 1976):
(a) (i) A cage or net trap designed to capture alive wild birds or wild mammals, and
(ii) a spring trap which is not a gin trap and which is designed to secure either –
(i) the immediate death, or
(ii) the immediate unconsciousness and subsequent death without intervening consciousness,
of wild birds or wild mammals which it is designed to trap.
(b) a stop snare with a minimum length from noose to stop of 13 inches in case it is intended to snare foxes and 6 1/2 inches in case it is intended to snare rabbits and which complies with the following, namely:
(i) a swivel is incorporated in the snare,
(ii) the snare is designed so that when it is used it will be securely tied to a fixed object,
(iii) the snare is designed so that for the purpose of avoiding catching large animals (for example deer, cattle or horses) by the leg when it is used a jump bar, i.e. a cross-bar

at least two feet above the ground and supported by a pair of forked sticks fixed not less than two feet apart, may also be used,

(c) a net designed to capture alive wild birds or wild mammals.

3. Any trap, snare or net, other than a trap, snare or net described in Regulation 2 of these Regulations, is hereby declared to be a trap, snare or net to which section 34(6) of the Wildlife Act, 1976 applies."

The effect of this Regulation is to make it an offence to import without a licence or sell any trap, snare or net which is not a trap, snare or net described in Regulation 2 (a), (b) or (c) contrary to section 34(6).

See: RINGING OF BIRDS AND TRAPPING OFFENCES.

TREATMENT
(WMA 1996, s.5(1))

"Includes, in relation to waste, any thermal, physical, chemical or biological processes that change the characteristics of waste in order to reduce its volume or hazardous nature or facilitate its handling, disposal or recovery."

TREE PRESERVATION ORDER
(LG(P&D)A, 1963 s.45)

Section 45 of the LG(P&D)A 1963 provides:

"(1) If it appears to the (*qv*) planning authority that it is expedient to do so in the interests of amenity to make provision for the preservation of any tree, group of trees or woodlands, they may for that purpose make an order with respect to any such tree, group of trees or woodlands as may be specified in the order; and in particular, provision may be made by such order –

(a) for prohibiting (subject to any exemptions for which provision may be made by the order) the cutting down, topping, lopping or wilful destruction of trees except with the consent of the planning authority, and for enabling that authority to give their consent subject to conditions;

(b) for applying, in relation to any consent under the order, and to applications therefor, any of the provisions of Part IV of this Act relating to permission to develop land, and to applications for such permission, subject to such adaptations and modifications as may be specified in the order.

(2) Any person who has suffered damage in consequence of any refusal of consent required under an order under this section, or of any grant of any such consent subject to conditions, shall, if he makes a claim on the planning authority within the time and in the manner specified by the order, be entitled to recover from such authority compensation in respect of the damage, but –

(a) where the order declares that, as respects any tree, trees or group of trees not comprised in woodlands, the tree, trees or group of trees is or are of (*qv*) special amenity value or special interest no compensation shall be payable in relation to the tree, trees or group.

(b) where the order declares that, as respects any trees comprised in woodlands, a condition comprising a requirement to replant is an essential condition for attachment in the interests of amenity to any consent given under the order no compensation shall be payable in relation to such a condition attached to any such consent.

(3) Any order under this section may be revoked or varied by a subsequent order under this section.

(4) Where a planning authority makes an order under this section, they shall serve a notice of the making of the order and a copy of the order on every person who is the owner or occupier of any land affected by the order, and any other person then known to them to be entitled to fell any tree, trees, group of trees or wood lands to which the order relates.

(5) Any person on whom a notice and a copy of the order is served under this section may, at any time before the day specified in that behalf in the notice (not being later than one month after such service), appeal to the Minister against the order.

(6) Where an appeal is brought under this section against an order, the Minister may confirm the order with or without modifications or annul the order.

(7) Without prejudice to any other exemption for which provision may be made by an order under this section, no such order shall apply to the cutting down, topping or lopping of trees which are dying or dead or have become dangerous or the cutting down, topping or lopping of any trees in compliance with any obligation imposed by or under any statute or so far as may be necessary for the prevention or abatement of a nuisance.

Offence

(8) If any person contravenes the provisions of an order under this section (other than an order which has been annulled) he shall be guilty of an offence and shall be liable on summary conviction to a fine not exceeding two hundred pounds.

(9) Particulars of an order under this section shall be entered in the register.

(10) Any reference in this Act to a tree preservation order shall be construed as a reference to an order under this section (other than a order which has been annulled)."

TROUT
(F(C)A 1959, s.3(1))

As amended by substitution by section 2(g) of the F(A)(No. 2)A 1987, when used without any qualification includes:

(a) all fish of the brown trout kind,
(b) rainbow trout and char:
  (i) in Part VI,
  (ii) in any other provision, when that provision also applies to salmon and coarse fish,
(c) save in Part IX pollen or freshwater herring, and
(d) any spawn or fry of a trout,

but does not include sea trout.

This is one of the infamous "rod licence" definitions which is no longer strictly relevant. *See:* DUTIES ON ORDINARY FISHING LICENCES.

SEA TROUT

Sea trout comes within the definition of (*qv*) salmon and not trout.

RAINBOW TROUT

By virtue of section 154 of the F(C)A 1959, which deals with Part X licences, certificate of fitness, the word "trout" includes fish commonly called or known as "rainbow trout".

TROUT ROD LICENCES
(Fisheries Acts)

A number of definitions occur in section 3(1) of the F(C)A 1959 of various trout rod licences.

All such licences have been repealed, those appearing in the F(C)A 1959 in Chapter III (sections 79 to 84) by section 22 of the F(A)(No. 2)A 1987 and those sections appearing in the 1987 Act, which established the licence duty for trout and coarse fish, by inference by section 3 of the F(A)A 1991 which abolished that duty. *See:* DUTIES ON ORDINARY FISHING LICENCES.

TRIAL LICENCES
(F(A)A 1997, s.3(1))

"Trial licence" means a licence granted under section 14 to carry out any operation, activity, trials or experiments referred to in section 9(1)".
See: LICENCE (1) AQUACULTURE LICENCE.

TRIAL OF OFFENCES
(F(C)A 1959)

Section 309(1) of the F(C)A 1959, substituted by section 49 of the FA 1980, provides:

"Notwithstanding anything contained in any other enactment, an offence under any provision of the Fisheries Acts, 1959 to 1980, other than a section specified in Table I to section 2 of the Fisheries (Amendment) Act, 1978, may be heard and determined in a summary way by a District Justice upon the complaint, verbal or otherwise, of a member of the Garda Síochána, the (*qv*) Central Board, a (*qv*) regional board, an officer or servant of a (*qv*) board, a (*qv*) private waterkeeper within the meaning of Part XVIII of this Act or any other person."

Subsection (2) deals with sea fisheries, as does section 2 of the F(A)A 1978, an exclusively Sea Fisheries Act, and sea fisheries are not dealt with in this book.

"(3) Where an offence under the repealed enactments or an offence under any provision of this Act has been, or is alleged to have been committed in or upon any waters forming the boundary between two or more Districts established for the purposes of the District Court, then, notwithstanding section 79 of the Courts of Justice Act, 1924 (No. 10 of 1924), proceedings in respect of the offence may be brought, heard and determined before and by a District Justice for the time being assigned to any one of the said Districts and such offence may be alleged and stated in an information or summons to have been committed in the District where it is proposed to bring the proceedings."

A notable exception to the above arises under section 65 of the F(A)A 1997 which provides that notwithstanding section 309 of the F(C)A 1959 a prosecution for a summary offence under that Act can only be prosecuted by the Minister (meaning some designated officer at the suit of the Minister) or at the suit of the DPP.

TRUST, THE INLAND FISHERIES TRUST
(FA 1980)

"The Trust" in the FA 1980 and by virtue of section 1(1) of same, means Iontaobhas Iascaigh Intíre Ioncorportha (The Inland Fisheries Trust).

By section 35 of the FA 1980 the Inland Fisheries Trust was dissolved and its assets, undertakings, and liabilities transferred to the (*qv*) Central Board.

Section 36 of the FA 1980 saves rights to fish paid for by members of the Trust paid for before the dissolution for the remainder of the period covered by their last annual subscription.

U

UNDERSIZED FISH
(Fisheries Acts)

The length of a fish which is deemed to be undersized varies from place to place and from lake to lake. The information regarding such matters can only be ascertained from local bye-laws which involves checking with the local fisheries board.

UNLAWFUL FISHING ENGINE
(F(C) 1959, s.3(1))

"Means a (*qv*) fishing engine which is not a lawful fishing engine."

UNSEASONABLE SALMON OR TROUT

"Means any salmon or trout which is about to spawn, or which has spawned and has not recovered from spawning."

Offence
Section 176(1) of the FA 1959 creates the offence of taking, killing or destroying any unseasonable salmon or trout and under subsection (2) the salmon in respect of which the offence was committed stands forfeited as a statutory consequence of conviction.

(Note that the maximum penalty prescribed under this subsection has been increased. *See:* FINES AND IMPRISONMENT (IMPOSITION OF)).

Subsection (3) provides that it shall be a good defence to prove that the salmon or trout was taken accidentally and was returned without avoidable injury to the water immediately upon being taken.

Offence
Section 177(1) of the FA 1959 creates the offence of exporting or attempting to export unseasonable salmon or trout and under subsection (2) the salmon in respect of which the offence was committed stands forfeited as a statutory consequence of conviction.

(Note that the maximum penalty prescribed under this subsection has been increased. *See:* FINES AND IMPRISONMENT (IMPOSITION OF)).

UNSEASONABLE/ UNLAWFULLY CAPTURED, SALMON OR TROUT, EELS OR MOLLUSCAN SHELLFISH
(F(C)A 1959)

This offence is described in section 182 of the FA 1959, as amended by substitution by section 21 of the F(A)A 1994. *See:* SALMON, TROUT, MOLLUSCAN SHELLFISH, UNSEASONABLE AND UNLAWFULLY CAPTURED, PURCHASE, SALE, POSSESSION.

URBAN WASTE WATER TREATMENT
(EPAA 1992)

See: SEWAGE OR OTHER EFFLUENTS.

USE
(GMO Regulations, 1994, Art. 3(1))

"means the (*qv*) deliberate release of a (*qv*) product which has been (*qv*) placed on the market."
See: GENETICALLY MODIFIED ORGANISMS.

USE, A BOAT OR VEHICLE TO AID COMMISSION OF AN OFFENCE
(FA 1959, s.285A)

See: BOAT, USE A BOAT OR VEHICLE TO AID THE COMMISSION OF AN OFFENCE.

USE A MECHANICALLY-PROPELLED VEHICLE, VESSEL OR AIRCRAFT IN HUNTING
(WLA 1976, s.36)

Section 36 of the WLA 1976:

"(1) Notwithstanding anything contained in this Act apart from this section but subject to section 42, a person shall not hunt or disturb for the purpose of hunting –
(a) any protected wild animal by means of a mechanically-propelled vehicle, vessel or aircraft, whether it is being

so propelled or is stationary,

(b) any protected wild bird by means of such a vehicle, or aircraft while it is being so propelled.

(2) Notwithstanding subsection (1) of this section, a mechanically-propelled vehicle, vessel or aircraft may be used to capture and kill, pursuant to and in accordance with a licence granted in that behalf by the Minister and for such educational, scientific or other purposes as are specified in the licence, protected wild animals or protected wild birds of a species so specified.

(3) Subsection (1) of this section shall not make unlawful anything which section 3(3) of the Whale Fisheries Act, 1937, permits to be done.

Offence

(4) Subject to subsections (2) and (3) of this section, a person who contravenes subsection (1) of this section shall be guilty of an offence."

USER

(GMO Regulations 1994, Art. 3(1))

"Shall mean any legal or natural person responsible for the (*qv*) contained use of a (*qv*) genetically modified organism or a person carrying out a use as defined above, whichever is appropriate."

See: GENETICALLY MODIFIED ORGANISMS.

V

VEGETATION
(WLA 1976)

(1) Burning of, section of the 39 WLA 1976. *See:* BURNING OF VEGETATION.
(2) Destruction of, on uncultivated land. *See:* DESTRUCTION OF VEGETATION.

VEHICLE
(WMA 1996, s.5(1))

"Includes:
(a) part of a vehicle,
(b) an article designed as a vehicle but not capable of functioning as a vehicle,
(c) a skip designed or used for carriage on a vehicle,
(d) a load on a vehicle."

VEHICLE,
USE HUNTING
(WLA 1976, s.36)

See: USE A MECHANICALLY PROPELLED VEHICLE, VESSEL OR AIRCRAFT IN HUNTING.

VEHICLE OR
BOAT, USE
(F(C)A 1959, s.285A)

See: BOAT OR VEHICLE, USE TO AID THE COMMISSION OF AN OFFENCE.

VEHICLE,
ABANDONED
(WMA 1996, s.71)

Section 71 of the WMA 1996 provides:

"(1) A vehicle shall not be abandoned on any land.

Offence
(2) Where there is a contravention of subsection (1) –
(a) the person who placed the vehicle at the place where it was abandoned, and
(b) if there is a registered owner of the vehicle and the person aforesaid is not its registered owner, the registered owner,

shall each be guilty of an offence.

(3) In a prosecution for an offence under subsection (2), it shall be a good defence to prove –
(a) that the act complained of constituted the transfer of control of the vehicle concerned to a person, with his or her consent, at a (*qv*) facility provided by or on behalf of that person for the purpose of the recovery or disposal of vehicles (including a facility referred to in section 38(3)) and that such transfer of control was not effected in contravention of section 32, or
(b) in case the defendant is the registered owner of the vehicle concerned, that the abandonment of the vehicle was not authorised by him or her.

(4) Without prejudice to the provisions of section 55(6) and 56, and notwithstanding the provisions of any regulations made under section 97 (inserted by section 63 of the Road Traffic Act, 1968) of the Road Traffic Act, 1961, a local authority may enter on any land upon which a vehicle has been abandoned and remove the said vehicle; a local authority shall not, other than with the consent of the occupier, enter into a private dwelling under this subsection unless it has given to the occupier of the dwelling not less than 24 hours notice in writing of its intended entry.

(5) Where, in relation to a vehicle removed from land by a local authority under subsection (4) –
(a) the local authority is of the opinion that the condition of the vehicle is such that it is capable of being used as a vehicle or can, by the expenditure of a reasonable amount of money, be rendered capable of being so used, and
(b) the local authority can by, reasonable enquiry, ascertain the name and address of the owner of the vehicle,

the local authority shall store or arrange for the storage of the vehicle and shall serve a notice on the owner informing him or her of the removal and storage and of the address of the place where the vehicle may be claimed or recovered, and such a notice shall require the owner to claim or recover it within 2 weeks of the date of the service of the notice and inform him or her of the consequences specified in subsection (7) of his or her failure to do so.

(6) A vehicle to which subsection (5) applies shall be given to a person claiming the vehicle if, but only if, he or she makes a declaration in such form as may be specified by the local authority concerned or in a form to the like effect, stating that he or she is the owner of the vehicle or is authorised by the owner to claim it, and pays to the local authority the amount of the expenditure reasonably incurred by the local authority in respect of the removal and storage of the vehicle.

(7) Where a vehicle is removed from land by a local authority under subsection (4), and –
  (a) subsection (5) does not apply in respect of the vehicle, or
  (b) the name and address of the owner of the vehicle cannot be ascertained by the local authority by reasonable enquiry, or
  (c) the said owner fails to claim the vehicle and remove it from the place where it is stored within 4 weeks of the date on which a notice under subsection (5) has been served on him or her,

  the vehicle shall become the property of the local authority.

(8) No action shall lie in respect of anything done in good faith and without negligence in the course of the removal or storage of a vehicle under this section.

Offence

(9) A person who makes a declaration under subsection (6) which to his or her knowledge is false or misleading in a material respect shall be guilty of an offence.

(10) For the purposes of this section –
  'abandoned', in relation to a vehicle, includes left in such circumstances or for such period that it is reasonable to assume that the vehicle has been abandoned, and cognate words shall be construed accordingly,
  'local authority' includes the corporation of a borough of any kind and the council of an urban district,
  'registered owner' has the meaning assigned to it by the Road Traffic Act, 1961."

Section 37(3) of the WMA 1996 provides that a local authority shall provide facilities at which vehicles may be discarded. *See:* WASTE (4), WASTE MANAGEMENT FACILITIES.

The Litter Act 1982 (No.11 of 1982) deals extensively with the prevention of litter. Sections 10, 11, 12, 13 and 14 provided for dealing with "abandoned vehicles and scrap" in somewhat the same manner as is now provided by section 71 of the WMA 1996 for "abandoned vehicles". Section 9 in addition required a local authority to provide a place where vehicles and scrap could be abandoned in the same terms as section 37(3) of the WMA 1996. *See:* WASTE (4) REMOVAL AND DISPOSAL OF WASTE.

Now section 6 of the WMA 1966 repeals the enactments mentioned in its column (2) of Part 1 of the Fifth Schedule to the extent specified in column 93) of the said part which includes, inter alia, sections 9, 10, 11, 12 and 13 of the Litter Act 1982.

VESSEL

(LG(WP)A 1977, s.1(1))

"Means a water-borne craft of any type, whether self-propelled or not, and includes an air-cushion craft."

(EPAA 1992, s.3(1))

"Means a waterborne craft of any type, whether self propelled or not, and includes an air cushion craft and any structure in or on water."

VESSEL, REGULATIONS RESTRICTING USE

(LG(WP)A 1977, s.27)

See: REGULATIONS RESTRICTING THE USE OF CERTAIN VESSELS.

VESTED FISHERIES

(F(C)A 1959)

Vested fisheries, which were the subject matter of Chapters II and III of Part XII of the F(C)A 1959, were abolished by the FA 1980 and section 6, First Schedule, of that Act repealed the appropriate sections 184 to 196 of the 1959 Act.

W

WARNING

(F(C)A 1959, s.291)

The offence of giving a signal or warning to persons fishing unlawfully. *See:* PENALTIES (MEANING OFFENCES) UNDER FISHERIES ACTS.

WASTE

(F(C)A 1959, s.3(1))

"Includes all uncultivated or unprofitable lands."

(WMA 1996, s.4(1))

"(1) (a) In this Act "waste" means any substance or object belonging to a category of waste specified in the First Schedule or for the time being included in the *(qv)* European Waste Catalogue which the *(qv)* holder discards or intends or is required to discard, and anything which is discarded or otherwise dealt with as if it were waste shall be presumed to be waste until the contrary is proved.

(b) A reference in this Act to waste shall be construed as including a reference to *(qv)* hazardous waste unless the contrary intention appears."

See: SCHEDULES HERETO, WMA 1996 SCHEDULES.

WASTE COLLECTION PERMIT

(WMA 1996, s.5(1))

"Has the meaning assigned to it by section 34."

See: WMA 1996 (4), WASTE COLLECTION PERMIT

WASTE LICENCE

(WMA 1996, s.5(1))

"Shall be construed in accordance with section 37."

See: WMA 1996 (4) INTERPRETATION.

WASTE COLLECTION PERMIT AND WASTE LICENCE, DISTINGUISH

(WMA 1996)

Prior to the WMA 1996 permits were issued under European Communities (Waste) Regulations 1979 (No. 390 of 1979) and European Communities (Toxic and Dangerous Waste) Regulations 1982 (S.I. No. 33 of 1982).

These instruments were both repealed by section 6(2) of the WMA 1996 but they retain a transitory identity in that holders of such permits are entitled to continue disposal activities if they apply for a waste licence under Part V of the WMA 1996 and comply with the provisions of section 39(3) of the Act.

A waste licence is granted by the Agency under section 40 of the WMA 1996. *See:* LICENCE (6).

A waste collection permit is granted by a local authority under section 34 of the WMA 1996. *See:* WMA 1996(3)WASTE COLLECTION PERMIT.

WASTE, MAMMALIAN ANIMAL WASTE

There are two sets of Regulations dealing with Mammalian animal waste. Both were passed under section 3 of the European Communities Act, 1972 under the aegis of the Department of Agriculture and Food without reference to the WMA 1996 or the Department of the Environment.

Both, however, deal with the disposal of waste.

Because they are, so to speak, unattached they contain within themselves provisions for their own enforcement. *See:* (1)AUTHORISED OFFICERS; (2) ENTRY AND SEARCH.

The European Communities (Mammalian Animal Waste) Regulations 1998 (S.I. No. 2 of 1998) came into operation on January 12, 1998 and gives effect to Commission Decision 97/735/EC of October 21, 1997 concerning certain protection measures with regard to trade in certain types of mammalian animal waste (O.J. L294 of October 28, 1997, p.7).

The phrase "mammalian animal waste" is not defined in these or in the other Regulations dealing with mammalian animal waste which are dealt with below.

Regulation 4 prohibits the import or export of processed mammalian waste or its use for feeding to animals or poultry but excluding the products listed in Article 1 (2) of the Commission Decision 97/735/EC. (Regulation 3) and the export or import to or from another Member State of processed animal protein intended for animal consumption without certain documentation (Regulation 4).

Regulation 5 entitles the Minister to authorise, notwithstanding Regulation 3, the export of processed mammalian animal waste which has not been duly processed where it is destined for incineration or use as fuel or, until March 31, 1998, for further processing.

Regulation 6 restricts the import of processed mammalian animal waste referred to in Regulation 5 from another Member State.

The European Communities (Processing of Mammalian Animal Waste) Regulations 1998 (S.I. No. 62 of 1998) came into operation on the 16th day of March 1998 and give effect to Commission decision 96/449/EC of July 18, 1996 concerning heat treatment for the processing of animal protein with a view to the inactivation of spongiform encephalopathy agents (O.J. L184 of July 24, 1996, p.43) These regulations were amended by the European Communities (Processing of Mammalian Animal Waste) (Amendment) Regulations, 1999 (S.I. No. 200 of 1999) on 5 July 1999.

Regulation 4, subject to the exceptions in Regulation 3, provides that a person shall not process, sell or supply for sale, use for feeding to animals or poultry, import or export processed mammalian animal waste unless it has been processed in accordance with the parameters laid down in the Schedule. *See:* SCHEDULES HERETO, MAMMALIAN ANIMAL WASTE SCHEDULE.

Regulation 5 provides for Ministerial authorisation of processing of mammalian animal waste by methods which do not achieve the parameters set out in the Schedule if the Minister is satisfied that such processing is preceded or followed by a process which does achieve those parameters and for the supply for burial, incineration, burning as fuel or other methods which ensure safe disposal.

Regulation 6 entitles the Minister to authorise or refuse to authorise a processing plant validated in accordance with procedures defined by the Scientific Veterinary Committee subject to conditions and the Minister may amend, alter or revoke a condition but on notice and after affording an opportunity to make representations.

Regulation 7 provides, in respect of plant authorised under Regulation 6, for the maintaining for examination on request by an (*qv*) authorised officer for five years, of records of the residence time, temperature, pressure and particle size of mammalian animal waste processed.

WASTE MANAGEMENT ACT 1996, NON-APPLICATION OF ACT
(WMA 1996, s.3)

Section 3 of the WMA 1996:

"(1) This Act shall not apply to –
- (a) an (*qv*) emission into the atmosphere, other than an emission from a (*qv*) facility for the holding, (*qv*) recovery or (*qv*) disposal of waste,
- (b) (*qv*) sewage and (*qv*) sewage effluent (other than (*qv*) sludge from a facility for the treatment of sewage),
- (c) the dumping of waste at sea,
- (d) a radioactive substance within the meaning of the Radiological Protection Act 1991 (including a radioactive waste product).

(2) 'Dumping' in paragraph (d) of subsection (1) has the meaning assigned to it by the Dumping at Sea Act, 1981."

WASTE MANAGEMENT ACT 1996

The Waste Management Act 1996 (No. 10 of 1996) deals with its main material, the management of waste, under the following general headings:

(1) WASTE MANAGEMENT PLANNING, PART II (sections 22 to 26)
(2) MEASURES TO REDUCE PRODUCTION AND PROMOTE RECOVERY OF WASTE, Part III (sections 27 to 31)
(3) HOLDING, COLLECTION AND MOVEMENT OF WASTE, PART IV (sections 32 to 36)
(4) RECOVERY AND DISPOSAL OF WASTE, PART V (sections 37 to 54) and

(5) GENERAL PROVISIONS REGARDING ENVIRONMENTAL PROTECTION PART

VI (sections 55 to 59).

This book follows the same general headings as the Act –

(1) WASTE MANAGEMENT PLANNING (WMA 1996, ss. 22 to 26)

Part II of the WMA 1996 completes the cycle of management plans begun by section 15 of the LG(WP)A 1977 when the (*qv*) Water Quality Management Plan was introduced. Then came the (*qv*)Air Quality Management Plan which is dealt with in section 46 and Part V of the APA 1987. Taken together they compliment, to an extent, the (*qv*)Development Plan under Part III of the LG(P&D)A 1963.

They are intended to assist in indicating to an enquirer what the likely parameters will be under the headings, water, air and waste in terms of permitted development and discharges and emissions there from in any given area.

They cover the protection of the elements of air and water and the prevention of the disposal of waste in a manner that would endanger human health or harm the environment envisaged by the important definition of (*qv*) environmental pollution contained at section 4(2) of the EPAA 1992.

The Act creates a distinction between a waste management plan and a (*qv*) Hazardous waste management plan.

Section 22(2) of the WMA 1996

Section 22(1) :

"In this section

'relevant period' means the period beginning on the date of making of the waste management plan concerned or, as the case may be, the date on which the last review of the said plan under subsection (4) was completed and ending on the date on which the local authority or authorities concerned expect to complete or, as may be appropriate, to next complete, a review of the plan under that subsection;

'waste management plan' includes, where the context admits, a replacement waste management plan under subsection (4)."

Subsection (2) provides that subject to subsection (3) and section 24, each local authority shall, not later than such date as may be prescribed, make a waste management plan with regard to:

(a) the prevention, minimisation, collection, (*qv*) recovery and (*qv*) disposal of non-hazardous waste within its functional area, and

(b) the matters specified in subsection (8) in relation to hazardous waste so far as they relate to its functional area.

For hazardous waste management plan *See:* HAZARDOUS WASTE MANAGEMENT PLAN.

Subsections (3) and (4) provide for two or more local authorities jointly making a waste management plan and provides for a five-year review by them and the making of any variations or replacing it with a new waste management plan under section 23.

Subsection (5) provides that before it commences the preparation of a waste management plan, or a variation or replacement plan, or a replacement plan in accordance with a requirement of the Minister under section 24, the local authority shall publish a notice of that intention inviting written representations within a specified period, being not less than two months from the date of publication.

"(6) A waste management plan shall, in respect of non-hazardous waste, contain such objectives as seem to the local authority or local authorities concerned to be reasonable and necessary –

(a) to prevent or minimise the production or harmful nature of waste,

(b) to encourage and support the recovery of waste,

(c) to ensure that such waste as cannot be prevented or recovered is disposed of without causing (*qv*) environmental pollution, and

(d) to ensure in the context of waste disposal that regard is had to the need to give effect to the (*qv*) polluter pays principle,

and shall specify such measures or arrangements as are to be taken or entered into by the local authority or local authorities, with a view to securing the objectives of the plan.

(7) Without prejudice to the generality of subsection (6), a waste management plan shall, subject to such regulations as may be made by the Minister for the purposes of this section, include information on or otherwise have regard to –

(a) the policies and objectives, and the priorities respectively assigned to them, of the local authority or authorities concerned in relation to assisting the prevention and minimisation of waste and in relation to the management generally of activities carried on by it or them or other persons as respects the collection, recovery and disposal of waste within its or their functional area or areas;

(b) the measures which –
   (i) will be taken during the relevant period by the local authority or authorities concerned, and
   (ii) in so far as the local authority or authorities concerned can determine, will or may be taken during the relevant period by persons other than such authority or authorities,

   for the purpose of preventing or minimising the production of waste.

(c) the type, quantity and origin of waste which the local authority or authorities concerned expect to arise during the relevant period in its or their functional area or areas for collection, recovery or disposal;

(d) the type and quantity of waste which the local authority or authorities concerned expect to be transported into, or out of, its or their functional area or areas for recovery and disposal during the relevant period;

(e) facilities, plant and equipment which the local authority or authorities concerned expect to be available or, in its or their opinion, will be required to be available for the collection, recovery or disposal of waste in its or their functional area or areas during the relevant period and matters relevant to the selection of sites in respect of (*qv*) facilities aforesaid;

(f) general requirements of a technical or other nature applicable to the collection, recovery and disposal of waste and the (*qv*) aftercare of facilities used for the disposal of waste;

(g) the steps to be taken generally by the local authority or authorities concerned to enforce the provisions of this Act in its or their functional area or areas;

(h) the identification of sites at which waste disposal or recovery activities have been carried on, the assessment of any risk of environmental pollution arising as a result of such activities, measures proposed to be taken, or, where such an assessment has already been made, measures taken, in order to prevent or limit any such environmental pollution, the identification of necessary remedial measures in respect of such sites, and measures proposed to be taken, or, where such measures have already been identified, measures taken, to achieve such remediation, having regard to the cost-effectiveness of available remediation techniques;

(i) any incidental and ancillary matters;

(j) such other matters as may be prescribed."

Subsection (8) provides for the inclusion, but separate from the other information contained in the plan, of information as respects the implementation of measures consequential on or incidental to the (*qv*) hazardous waste management plan or any recommendation made by the Minister under section 26(6). *See:* HAZARDOUS WASTE MANAGEMENT PLAN.

Subsection (9) provides for ministerial regulations on how the plan should be set out or addressed.

Subsection (10) provides that the making, review, variation or replacement of the plan shall be a (*qv*) reserved function.

"(11) In making or reviewing a waste management plan, the local authority or authorities concerned shall have regard to the proper planning and development of its or their functional area or areas and shall, for this purpose, have regard to the provisions of –

(a) the (*qv*) development plan or plans and any (*qv*) special amenity area order made under the Act of 1963,

(b) a (*qv*) water quality management plan made under the Local Government (Water Pollution) Acts, 1977 and 1990, and

(c) an (*qv*) air quality management plan made under the Air Pollution Act, 1987,

for the time being in force in relation to the said area or areas."

Subsection (12) provides that a local authority will take such steps as are appropriate and necessary to achieve the objective of a waste management plan made by it.

Subsection (13) provides that the corporation of a borough (not being a county borough) or an urban council in performing its functions shall have regard to the provisions of a waste management plan made by the county council within whose functional area the corporation or urban council are situate.

The Act of 1963 is the LG(P&D)A 1963.

"(14) Upon the making of a waste management plan by a local authority –
(a) any plan prepared under Article 4(2) of the European Communities (Waste) Regulations, 1979, by that authority, or
(b) any special waste plan within the meaning of the European Communities (Toxic and Dangerous Waste) Regulations, 1982, prepared by that authority,
that is for the time being in force shall cease to have effect."

1997 PLANNING REGULATIONS

The Waste Management (Planning) Regulations 1997 (S.I. No. 137 of 1997) specify certain matters to be addressed in a waste management plan under section 22 and the manner in which they shall be set out.

They also provide that a copy of the proposed plan or a proposed variation of a plan shall be submitted to the following specified persons: The Minister for Arts, Culture, Gaeltacht and the Islands, the Minister for the Marine, Bord Fáilte, Teagasc, a local authority whose functional area adjoins that of the authority making or varying the plan and any District Council in Northern Ireland whose functional area likewise adjoins.

PUBLICATION OF NOTICES AND PROCEDURE ON REVIEW

Section 23(1) of the WMA 1996 provides that a local authority must publish a notice in at least one newspaper circulating in its functional area of a proposal to make, vary, replace, or replace in compliance with a requirement of the Minister under subsection (4), a waste management plan and must submit copies of the proposed plan or variation to the Minister, the Agency and any other persons prescribed.

Subsection (2) provides that a notice under subsection (1) must state:
(a) where, when and for what period a plan may be inspected and the reasonable cost to purchase a copy,
(b) that written representations made within the same period shall be taken into consideration.

Subsection (3) provides that after considering representations within the relevant period the local authority may make, vary or replace the plan (whether as originally proposed or as amended)

Subsection (4) provides:
(a) for the furnishing of a copy on request and payment of a reasonable fee,
(b) that a copy or copy of an extract from the plan certified by an officer of the local authority as a true copy will be prima facie evidence without the necessity of proving the signature of the officer or that he is an officer,
(c) that production of such a copy certified under this subsection will be evidence of such plan.

JOINT WASTE MANAGEMENT PLANS

Section 24 of the WMA 1996 provides that the Minister may, after consultation with the local authorities concerned, require two or more local authorities jointly to make a waste management plan or co-ordinate plans in such manner or vary or replace such plan as the Minister directs and the local authorities shall comply with such requirements.

DUTY OF LOCAL AUTHORITY IN RELATION TO PLANS

Section 25 of the WMA 1996 provides that as soon as may be after the making, varying or replacing of a waste management plan the local authority or local authorities concerned shall transmit a copy to the Minister, the Agency and any other persons prescribed.

HAZARDOUS WASTE MANAGEMENT PLAN

Section 26 of the WMA 1996
See: HAZARDOUS WASTE MANAGEMENT PLAN.

(2) MEASURES TO REDUCE PRODUCTION AND PROMOTE RECOVERY OF WASTE (WMA 1996 ss.27 to 31)

INTERPRETATION

Section 27(1) of the WMA 1996:

"In this Part –

'deposit and refund scheme' means, in relation to any product, substance, component or packaging, a scheme whereby the (*qv*) producer, distributor or retailer, as the case may be, who operates the scheme requires a purchaser of a (*qv*) product or substance to pay to him or her a refundable deposit in relation to the product or substance or any component thereof or packaging therefor, that is to say a deposit of money the amount of which will be repaid by the producer, distributor or retailer, as the case may be, to the purchaser if the purchaser returns to him or her the product, substance, component or packaging, as the case may be;

'distributor" means a person who sells or supplies a product or substance by wholesale and "distribute" shall be construed accordingly;

'(*qv*) environmental audit' has the same meaning as it has in section 74 of the Act of 1992;

'environmental management system' means a system for managing the carrying on of an activity with regard to its effects on the environment;

'life cycle assessment' means, in relation to a product, an assessment of the effects on the environment of the manufacture, distribution, marketing and use of the product and the (*qv*) recovery or, as appropriate, (*qv*) disposal thereof (including the use of energy and raw materials in, and the production of waste from, any of the said activities);

'producer' includes such person as the Minister may specify by regulations to be a producer for the purposes of this Part (and such specification may include the importer or vendor of the product concerned);

'producer responsibility obligation' means a requirement to take steps for the purpose of the prevention, minimisation, limitation or recovery of waste as respects the class or classes of product to which the requirement relates and may include a requirement to achieve specified targets in relation to those matters;

'waste audit' means an evaluation of the manner in which an activity is carried on with a view to identifying opportunities for –

(a) preventing or minimising the production of waste from the activity or the harmfulness of any waste produced from the activity, and
(b) facilitating the recovery of any waste so produced.

(2) A reference in this Part to the implementation and operation of a waste reduction programme shall be construed as a reference to the taking of steps in a systematic manner for the purpose of –

(a) reducing the production of waste from the activity concerned or the harmfulness of any waste produced from the activity, and
(b) recovering any waste so produced,

having regard to the results of a waste audit conducted in relation to the activity."

WASTE PREVENTION AND MINIMISATION

Section 28 of the WMA 1996 provides:

"(1) For the purpose of promoting, supporting or facilitating the prevention or minimisation of waste, any Minister of the Government or a local authority may provide such support and assistance, including the provision of moneys, as he or she or the local authority considers appropriate in relation to research and development projects being carried out, or proposed to be carried out, by any person in respect of the prevention or minimisation of waste, and for the purposes aforesaid may establish programmes and specify criteria and objectives governing the availability and provision of such assistance and support."

Subsection (2) provides that:

(a) a person carrying on an agricultural, commercial or industrial (including manufacturing) activity shall have due regard to the need to prevent or minimise the production of waste from the activity and shall take reasonable steps necessary for such prevention or minimisation (including steps as respects design of any product).
(b) the Minister may by regulations specify such reasonable steps as respects any particular activity as aforesaid and a person carrying on that activity shall take those steps accordingly.

Subsection (3) provides that:

(a) subject to paragraph (c), the Minister may, after consultation with any other Minister concerned, make regulations for the prevention, minimisation or limitation of the production of waste or a specified class or classes defined by reference to the manufacturing or industrial process or other activity giving rise to the waste concerned or such other matters as appropriate.
(b) these regulations may provide for the imposition of *(qv)* producer responsibility obligations.

(c) such Regulations shall only apply to a (*qv*) scheduled activity to the extent the Minister may determine after consultation with the Agency.

Subsection (4) provides that, without prejudice to the generality of subsection (3), regulations under this section may provide for all or any of the following matters:

(a) requiring the conduct of a waste audit and implementation and operation of a waste reduction programme in relation to an activity,
(b) the recording of such information and specified particulars and the furnishing of information to specified persons or the publication of specified information in relation to such waste audit or the implementation and operation of such a waste reduction programme,
(c) in the case of a person carrying out a specified waste audit or operating a specified environmental management system in relation to a particular activity, exempting him or her from the requirements of regulations under paragraphs (a) and (b),
(d) prohibiting the use of a specified mark or symbol except with the consent of a prescribed person,
(e) prescribing a person for the purposes of (e), the procedures to be followed in granting their consent and permitting the withdrawal of that consent in specified circumstances,
(f) without prejudice to paragraph (g), requiring the use of *(qv)* BATNEEC for preventing or limiting the production of waste from an activity,
(g) the specifying of the BATNEEC as aforesaid,
(h) carrying out a life cycle assessment of a particular class or classes of product by a producer,
(i) prohibiting, limiting or controlling in a specified manner and to a specified extent:
   (i) the production or use, in a production, product or otherwise, of any substance, material or thing,
   (ii) the composition, production, importation, distribution, supply, sale, disposal or advertising of any product or substance,
   (iii) the production of any waste,
(j) specifying requirements as regards design, composition or production of packaging and its uses, including:
   (i) restrictions or limitations to protect product or substance concerned,
   (ii) that packaging be capable of being reused,
(k) regulations under paragraph (l) for standards of design, manufacture and construction of products,
(l) enabling specified persons to prescribe standards for the purposes of paragraph (k),
(m) requiring a producer to produce and publish a plan to prevent or minimise waste from any activity and report on the steps taken and result of the plan,
(n) requiring persons the subject of specified requirements under these regulations (excluding paragraph 'm') to produce and publish a plan of the steps taken to comply with that requirement and to report on the steps taken and the results,
(o) conferring additional functions to secure compliance with or facilitate the operation of these regulations on public authorities including the Minister and specified persons,
(p) matters consequential on or incidental to the foregoing.

Subsection (5) provides (a) regulations made under this section, without prejudice to subsection (3) or section 7(2) (*See:* REGULATIONS), may provide generally in respect of a specified class or classes and (b) a target on obligation imposed may be defined by reference to a specified proportion (by weight, volume or otherwise).

Offence

Subsection (6) provides that contravention of a provision of the regulations under this section constitutes an offence.

Subsection (7) provides that in a prosecution for failing to achieve a specified target it shall be a good defence to prove that the accused took all reasonable steps to achieve the said target.

MEASURES RELATED TO RECOVERY OF WASTE

Section 29 of the WMA 1996:

"(1) A reference in this section to the implementation and operation of a source separation programme for waste shall be construed as a reference to the taking of steps in a systematic manner for the purpose of separating specified waste from other waste and the holding of such waste so separated prior to its collection, (*qv*) recovery or (*qv*) disposal.

(2) For the purpose of promoting, supporting or facilitating the recovery of waste, any Minister of the Government or local authority may provide to any person such support or assistance, including financial assistance, as he or she or the local authority considers appropriate, including the provision of moneys in relation to research and development projects being carried out or proposed to be carried out by any person in respect of the recovery of waste, and for the purpose aforesaid may establish programmes and specify criteria and objectives governing the availability and provision of such assistance and support.

(3) (a) The Minister may, after consultation with any Minister of the Government concerned, make regulations in relation to or for the recovery of waste or a specified class or classes of waste, and any such class may be defined by reference to the manufacturing or industrial process or other activity giving rise to the waste concerned or to such other matters as the Minister thinks appropriate.

(b) Regulations under this section may include provisions for the imposition of *(qv)* producer responsibility obligations on producers of products."

Subsection (4) provides, without prejudice to the generality of subsection (3), that regulations under the section may provide for all or any of the following matters:

(a) requiring labelling, marking or packaging in a specified manner so as to identify or specify:

(i) the composition of the product, substance or packaging,

(ii) the hazards of recovery or disposal,

(iii) the potential for recovery,

(iv) other information as specified,

(b) specifying requirements in relation to packaging including prohibition on use of same except in specified circumstances and designing packaging in accordance with prescribed standards to facilitate recovery,

(c) prohibiting, limiting or controlling the importation, distribution, supply or sale in a specified container or other packaging,

(d) requiring products to be designed or packaged so as to facilitate removal of components or dismantling prior to recovery or disposal,

(e) enabling specified persons to prescribe standards,

(f) requiring the operation of a *(qv)* deposit and refund scheme,

(g) specifying the conditions under which a scheme under paragraph (f) will be operated including the amount of the deposit and the targets to be achieved,

(h) requiring the collection or taking back by a producer, distributor or retailer without charge any product or substance, component or packaging made, distributed or sold by that producer, distributor or retailer,

(i) requiring supermarkets, service stations or other sales outlets to provide free facilities for removing packaging and receptacles for deposit at that outlet,

(j) requiring supermarkets, service stations and other sales outlets to charge customers for packaging an amount equal to the cost of same,

(k) requiring purchasers of products or substances to return same or any component or packaging after he or she has no further use for it to the retailer or to deliver it to an (*qv*) authorised waste collector or other specified person or facility,

(l) requiring a producer to use recovered or recoverable material or components or prohibit or limit the use of certain virgin material,

(m) requiring the implementation or operation of a source separation programme for waste,

(n) requiring that waste the subject of a source separation programme be offered free of charge or otherwise for collection,

(o) requiring supermarkets, service stations

and other sales outlets to provide waste collection receptacles for use by the public and arrange for the transfer of waste so collected to a specified waste recovery facility,

(p) requiring that used products or other waste to which regulations under this section apply be recovered in a specified manner,

(q) requiring specified other steps to be taken in relation to waste referred to in paragraph (p) where, for defined reasons, it is not practicable to recover the waste,

(r) requiring a local authority to provide specified financial assistance to persons engaged in the recovery of (*qv*) household waste,

(s) exempting from the requirements of this section either certified shareholders of an approved association formed to carry out waste recovery activities or persons participating in a satisfactory manner in or complying with specified requirements of such a scheme,

(t) (i) the granting by the Minister of approvals for the purpose of paragraph (s) subject to conditions including the following:

(I) financial and administrative arrangements of an association concerned,

(II) the waste recovery activities to be carried on and the manner in which they are to be carried on by the association,

(III) targets to be achieved by the association in recovering waste,

(ii) the alteration of conditions or revocation of an approval in specified circumstances,

(iii) the means for determining satisfactory participation in or compliance with requirements of a scheme referred to in paragraph (s),

(iv) the grant or revocation by an association of a certificate under regulations under paragraph (s) and notification to be given of such action,

(u) requiring the keeping of specified documents, records or other particulars and the furnishing of specified information to specified persons in relation to compliance with specified regulations under the section and enabling a specified person to verify the information,

(v) requiring a producer or distributor to prepare and publish in a specified manner at a specified frequency:

(i) a plan of the steps proposed to be taken to promote, support or facilitate the recovery of products or substances made, distributed or sold or any component or packaging related to same,

(ii) a report of the steps taken in pursuance of the plan and the results of those steps.

(w) requiring of a person subject to any specified requirement of regulations under this section (other than those imposed by paragraph (v)) to prepare and publish a plan similar to that required at paragraph (v), of the steps taken to comply with such requirement and the steps taken and the results of such steps,

(x) conferring on public authorities (including the Minister) and other specified persons specified additional functions for the purposes aforesaid,

(y) requiring local authorities to facilitate, promote or carry out in a specified manner the composting of (*qv*) municipal waste of an organic nature or any other process for the biological transformation of such waste,

(z) matters consequential on or incidental to the foregoing.

Subsections (5), (6) and (7) are identical to the same subsections in section 28 of the WMA 1996.

1997 PACKAGING REGULATIONS

The Waste Management (Packaging) Regulations 1997 (S.I. No. 242 of 1997) passed under sections 7, 19, 27, 28 and 29 of the WMA 1996 came into operation on the July 1, 1997 and provide for:

Part II Producer Responsibility Obligations,
Part III Approved Bodies,
Part IV Local Authority Functions.

They give effect to Articles 6 and 11 of European Parliament and Council Directive 94/62/EC of December 20, 1994 on packaging and packaging waste (O.J. L365/10 December, 31, 1994)

1997 FARM PLASTICS REGULATIONS

The Waste Management (Farm Plastics) Regulations 1997 (S.I. No. 315 of 1997) passed under sections 7, 19, 27, 28 and 29 of the WMA 1996 came into operation on August 1, 1996 and provide for:

Part II Producer Responsibility Obligations,
Part III Approved Bodies,
Part III Provisions relating to Enforcement.

PUBLIC AUTHORITY WASTE MANAGEMENT

Section 30 of the WMA 1996 provides:

"(1)(a) The Minister shall, as soon as may be after the commencement of this section, promulgate a programme with regard to the prevention, minimisation and recovery of waste arising from the performance by (*qv*) public authorities of their functions,

(b) A programme under this section may deal with such class or classes of waste, or apply to such class or classes of public authorities, as the Minister may consider appropriate.

(2) The Minister shall review from time to time as he or she thinks appropriate a programme under subsection (1) and make such revisions thereto as he or she thinks fit.

(3) Without prejudice to the generality of subsection (1) a programme under that subsection may include –
(a) specific objectives in relation to different types of waste,
(b) measures for the co-ordination of steps being taken or proposed to be taken by public authorities in relation to the prevention, minimisation and recovery of waste,
(c) proposals for the regulation pursuant to powers under this Act or any other enactment of activities carried on for the prevention, minimisation and recovery of waste.

(4) For the purpose of a programme under subsection (1), the Minister shall publish guidelines and criteria in relation to the prevention, minimisation and recovery of waste, to which public authorities shall have regard in the performance of their functions, and such guidelines and criteria may include provision for all or any of the following matters –
(a) consideration being given by public authorities to the likely effects on the environment of particular goods or services which they propose to purchase or engage,
(b) objectives with regard to the use by public authorities of materials recovered from waste,
(c) the conduct by public authorities of waste audits and the implementation and operation by them of waste reduction programmes and the publication of the results of such audits and programmes,
(d) the making by public authorities of plans ('public authority waste management plans'), specifying appropriate measures to facilitate, and objectives with regard to, the prevention, minimisation and recovery of waste by them,
(e) the content, publication, implementation and review of public authority waste management plans,
(f) the preparation and publication by public authorities of reports on the implementation by them of their respective public authority waste management plans and their compliance generally with guidelines and criteria published under this subsection."

RECOVERY OF WASTE BY LOCAL AUTHORITIES

Section 31 of the WMA 1996 provides:

"(1) A local authority may –
(a) engage or participate in the recovery of waste, and for that purpose may enter into one or more agreements with any other local authority or any person,
(b) buy or otherwise acquire waste for the purpose of recovering it,
(c) use, sell or otherwise dispose of any material or thing, including energy, recovered from waste,

(2) For the purpose of subsection (1), 'local authority' includes the corporation of a borough of any kind and the council of an urban district."

(3) HOLDING, COLLECTION AND MOVEMENT OF WASTE

(WMA 1996 ss.32 to s.36)

GENERAL DUTY OF A HOLDER OF WASTE

Section 32 of the WMA 1996:

See: HOLDER OF WASTE, GENERAL DUTY OF.

COLLECTION OF WASTE

Section 33 of the WMA 1996:

See: COLLECTION OF WASTE, OBLIGATIONS OF LOCAL AUTHORITY.

WASTE COLLECTION PERMIT

Section 34 of the WMA 1996 provides:

"(1) (a) Subject to paragraph (b), a person other than a local authority shall not, for the purposes of reward, with a view to profit or otherwise in the course of business, collect waste, on or after such date as may be prescribed, save under and in accordance with a permit (in this act referred to as a 'waste collection permit') granted by the local authority in whose functional area the waste is collected.

(b) The Minister may make regulations providing that paragraph (a) shall not apply in respect of the collection of any class or classes of waste where such collection is carried out in compliance with such requirements (which may include a requirement as to the entry of specified particulars concerning the person carrying out the collection in the register maintained by the local authority under section 19) as are specified in the regulations.

Offence

(c) A person who contravenes paragraph (a) or any requirement of regulations under paragraph (b) shall be guilty of an offence.

(2) (a) The Agency may give such guidance or directions to a local authority or local authorities generally in relation to the control to be exercised or the measures to be taken by it or them of, or with regard to, the collection of (*qv*)hazardous waste by persons in its or their functional area or areas or the grant by it or them of waste collection permits in respect of such waste.

(b) A local authority shall have regard to any guidance and comply with any direction given to it under paragraph (a) in performing any of its functions under this section or section 33, as appropriate.

(3) On an application being made to a local authority for the grant of a permit under this section, the authority may decide to grant the permit, subject to, or without, conditions or refuse to grant the permit.

(4) A local authority shall not grant a waste collection permit unless it is satisfied that the activity in question would not, if carried on in accordance with such conditions as may be attached to the permit, cause (*qv*) environmental pollution, and that the grant of the permit is in accordance with any relevant provisions of that authority's (*qv*) waste management plan and the (*qv*) hazardous waste management plan, as the case may be.

(5) (a) Without prejudice to subsections (3), (4) and (6), an application for a waste collection permit may be refused, or a waste collection permit may be revoked, if the applicant, permit holder or any other relevant person has been convicted of an offence under this Act prescribed for the purposes of this subsection, or of an offence under any other enactment, or instrument under an enactment, as may be prescribed.

(b) The reference in paragraph (a) to a relevant person is a reference to a person whom the local authority determines to be relevant for the purposes of considering the application concerned or, as the case may be, of deciding whether to revoke the waste collection permit, having had regard to any criteria that the Minister by regulations provides it is to have regard to in determining such a matter.

(6) A local authority may at any time review, and decide to amend conditions attached to, or revoke, a permit which it has granted under this section."

Subsection (7) deals with conditions attaching to a permit. *See:* CONDITIONS ATTACHING TO LICENCES ON THEIR GRANT OR REVIEW (5)(B).

"(8) (a) A local authority, before making a decision in relation to an application made to it for the grant of a waste collection permit, shall consider any submissions made to it under and in accordance with regulations under subsection (11) in relation to the application.

(b) A local authority shall, if it decides -

(i) to grant, or amend any conditions it has attached to, a waste collection permit, or

(ii) to refuse to grant, or revoke, such a permit,

forthwith notify the applicant therefor or its holder, as the case may be, of the decision and the reasons for the decision.

(9) (a) An applicant for, or the holder of, a waste collection permit may, within one month of the date of a notice under subsection (8), appeal against the decision of the local authority concerned to the judge of the District Court for the District Court district in which the principal office of the local authority is situate.

(b) On the hearing of an appeal under this subsection, the judge of the District Court may make an order giving such directions to the local authority concerned as he or she thinks proper in relation to the grant or revocation of a waste collection permit or the amendment of conditions attached to such a permit.

(10) A contravention of any provision of section 32 or 39, or of any condition of a waste collection permit, by any person employed by or on behalf of, or otherwise carrying out any waste collection activity for, or on behalf of, the holder of the permit, shall be deemed to also be a contravention of the condition or provision, as the case may be, by that holder."

Subsection (11)*(a)* provides that the Minister may make regulations for the purpose of this section and (b) provides that without prejudice to the generality of paragraph (a), regulations under the section may provide for:

(i) forms of the application and forms of the permit,

(ii) information and particulars from the applicant with verification,

(iii) specifying the period within which the application will be dealt with by the local authority,

(iv) matters on which the local authority must be satisfied prior to granting the licence,

(v) requiring a local authority to attach specified conditions to a licence,

(vi) specifying conditions a local authority may attach,

(vii) the amendment and revocation of a permit an the grounds for same,

(viii) making an application for permits and submissions in relation thereto available for inspection by the public within a specified period,

(ix) the publication by a local authority of its decisions in relation to permits,

(x) requiring applicants for permits to defray or contribute to the local authority's costs of investigation in relation to the application.

"(12) The collection of waste shall, in the period before a waste collection permit in relation to such collection is granted or refused, be deemed not to have contravened the provisions of this section if, before the date prescribed under subsection (1)(a), an application has been made for a waste collection permit in respect of such collection and the requirements of regulations under subsection (11) in relation to the application have been complied with by the applicant therefor."

The date prescribed for the purposes of section 34(1) in relation to the collection of waste oils for the purpose of transporting such waste from the premises at which it is held, is the 20th May 1998 by virtue of Article 5 of the Waste Management (Miscellaneous Provisions), Regulations 1998 (S.I. No. 164 of 1998).

"(13) The reference in subsection (1)(a) to a local authority, where it first occurs, shall be construed as including a reference to the corporation of a borough of any kind and the council of an urban district."

1998 MISCELLANEOUS PROVISIONS REGULATIONS – WASTE OILS

The Waste Management (Miscellaneous Provisions) Regulations 1998 (S.I. No. 164 of

1998) passed under sections 7, 11, 15, 18, 22, 32, 34 and 36 of the WMA 1996, came into operation on May 20, 1998. They give effect to Council Directive 75/439/EEC of June 16t, 1975 on the disposal of waste oils as amended by Council Directive 87/101/EEC of December 22, 1986 (O.J. L194/23, July 25, 1975 and O.J. L42/43 of February 12, 1987)

There are a number of seemingly minor but important articles in the regulations namely:

"4. It is hereby prescribed that summary proceedings for an offence under the Act may be brought by any person.

5. Section 32(2) of the Act shall not apply in respect of the transfer of waste to a person who is not prohibited under the Act or the Act of 1992 from undertaking the collection, recovery or disposal of the category of waste in question.

6. (1) It is hereby prescribed that the 20th day of May, 1998 shall be the prescribed day for the purposes of section 34(1) of the Act in relation to the collection of waste oils for the purpose of transporting such waste from the premises at which it is held.

(2) Section 34(1) of the Act shall not apply in relation to the collection of waste oils by a person for the purpose of transporting such waste from the premises at which it is held, where such collection is carried on under and in accordance with a waste collection permit granted to that person by –
   (a) the local authority in whose functional area the principal place of business of the person is situate, or
   (b) in the case of a person whose principal place of business is situated outside the State, Dublin Corporation.

(3) Section 34(1) of the Act shall not apply in relation to the collection of waste oils by a person for the purpose of transporting such waste from the premises at which it is held, where -
   (a) a permit granted to that person under the 1992 Regulations was in force immediately prior to the commencement of these regulations, and the permit would have continued in force save for the revocation of the 1992 regulations by the Act, and
   (b) the collection activity is carried on in accordance with the terms of the permit.

(4) Article 6 of the Waste Management (Movement of Hazardous Waste) Regulations, 1998 shall not apply in respect of the collection of waste oils carried on in accordance with the requirements of this Article."

Article 6(5) defines "waste oils" as any mineral-based lubrication or industrial oils which have become waste, including used combustion engine oils, gearbox oils, mineral lubricating oils, oils for turbines and hydraulic oils.

Article 7 amends the Schedule to the Waste Management (Planning) Regulations 1997 (S.I. No. 137 of 1997). *See:* WMA(1) PLANNING REGULATIONS 1997.

Offence

Article 8 prohibits the furnishing of information which is false or misleading to a material extent in any document used for the purpose of the regulations.

Article 9 (1) and (2) provides for notices served by the local authority seeking defrayment or contribution towards costs and the obligation of the recipient to comply with same without any right of appeal. The Act of 1992 is the EPAA 1992. The Act is the WMA 1996. The 1992 Regulations are the European Communities (Waste Oils) Regulations 1992 (S.I. No. 399 of 1992).

PRESENTATION OF WASTE FOR COLLECTION

Section 35 of the WMA 1996:

"(1) Whenever a local authority considers that, for the purposes of the proper management of waste or the prevention or control of (*qv*) environmental pollution, it is necessary to do so, it may, subject to subsection (5), make bye-laws -
   (a) requiring a holder of (*qv*) household waste to present such waste for collection by a person collecting waste in accordance with this Part,
   (b) requiring a holder of household or commercial waste who presents such waste for collection as aforesaid (whether pursuant to a requirement of bye-laws under paragraph (a) or not) to so present the waste in a manner specified in the bye-laws.

(2) A bye-law under subsection (1) shall be made in accordance with and construed as if it was made under, Part VII of the

Local Government Act, 1994."

Subsection (3) provides that bye-laws under subsection (1) may, without prejudice to the generality of the subsection or of section 37(4) of the Local Government Act 1994, include provisions specifying:

(a) that waste shall only be placed for collection in receptacles of a particular kind and that different waste shall be placed in different receptacles,
(b) the quantity of waste which may or may not be placed in any receptacle,
(c) the waste, or the mixtures of waste, which may or may not be placed in a receptacle,
(d) the measures or precautions to be taken where particular waste, or mixtures thereof, is or are to be placed in a receptacle,
(e) the size, colour, construction or maintenance of receptacles,
(f) the location at which the waste is to be made available for collection,
(g) times during which the waste is to be made available for collection,
(h) any matters consequential on or incidental to, the foregoing.

"(4) A local authority may provide or, where appropriate may, in accordance with section 34, require the holder of a waste collection permit granted by the authority to provide, receptacles in which (*qv*) household or (*qv*) commercial waste (either generally or of a specified nature or type) presented for collection shall be placed for such collection, and the local authority or the said holder, as the case may be, may require such reasonable payment, as it or he or she may determine, in respect of the provision of receptacles from the persons to whom they are provided.

(5) (a) The Minister may, if he or she considers it expedient so to do for the purpose of the prevention or control of (*qv*) environmental pollution, give a direction to a local authority requiring it to take specified steps (including the making of bye-laws under Part VII of the Local Government Act, 1994) to ensure that specified substances, products, materials or classes of waste arising in household or commercial waste are segregated for the purpose of and in the course of collection, and recovered or disposed of in a specified manner.
(b) A local authority concerned shall comply with any direction of the Minister given under this subsection within such period as may be specified in the direction."

REGULATIONS IN RELATION TO MOVEMENT OF WASTE

Section 36 of the WMA 1996:

See: MOVEMENT OF WASTE, REGULATIONS IN RELATION TO.

(4) RECOVERY AND DISPOSAL OF WASTE
(WMA 1996, ss. 37 to 54)

INTERPRETATION (PART V)

Section 37 of the WMA 1996:

"In this Part, unless the context otherwise requires –

'civic waste facility' shall be construed in accordance with section 38(2);

'waste licence' includes a revised waste licence under section 46(2)."

WASTE MANAGEMENT FACILITIES

Section 38 of the WMA 1996:

"(1) A local authority shall provide and operate, or arrange for the provision and operation of, such facilities as may be necessary for the recovery and disposal of household waste arising within its functional area.

(2) A local authority may provide and operate, or may arrange for or facilitate the provision and operation of –
(a) civic waste facilities, that is to say, facilities at which waste may be disposed of by members of the public, and
(b) other facilities for –
(i) the segregation, mixing, baling, storage or treatment of waste prior to its recovery or disposal,
(ii) the recovery of waste, or
(iii) the disposal of waste (other than

household waste),

(3) Without prejudice to the provisions of subsection (2), a local authority, having made an examination of the matter, shall provide, or arrange for the provision of, such facility or facilities as appears or appear to it to be necessary and reasonable at which vehicles may be discarded."

See: VEHICLES, ABANDONED.

Subsection (4) provides for joint arrangements for the recovery and disposal of waste and the joint provision and operation of a relevant facility by agreement between local authorities or local authorities and persons.

Subsection (5) provides that the repeal of any of the enactments in Part I of the First Schedule shall not prejudice the continued operation of facilities in operation at the commencement of this section. *See:* SCHEDULES HERETO, WMA SCHEDULE.

Subsection (6) provides that the Minister may take such measures as he considers appropriate to promote and support the establishment of such facilities for good management and may, with the consent of the Minister for Finance, give financial assistance in respect of that establishment.

Subsection (7) provides that:

(a) where necessary for the effective and orderly disposal of waste, a local authority or the Agency may require a (*qv*) holder or (*qv*) producer of waste other than (*qv*) household waste to dispose or arrange for disposal of that waste in such manner, under such conditions and at such appropriate waste facility as may be specified.

Offence

(b) A person who fails to comply with a requirement under this subsection shall be guilty of an offence.

"(8) The Agency shall classify facilities that exist in the State for the disposal of waste in such manner and having regard to such criteria as may be prescribed.

(9) For the purpose of subsection (2), other than paragraph (b)(iii), and subsection (3), 'local authority' includes, as appropriate, the corporation of a borough of any kind and the council of an urban district.

(10) Section 3(c) of the Derelict Sites Act, 1990, is hereby amended by the addition of 'or under' after 'conferred by'.

(11) (a) A person shall not deposit or discard waste at a facility provided by a local authority under this section otherwise than in accordance with any conditions for the time being standing specified by the local authority as respects the nature, type and quantity of waste that may be so deposited or discarded or the use otherwise of such a facility.

(b) A local authority shall take such steps as are reasonable to bring to the notice of members of the public any conditions for the time being standing specified by it for the purposes of paragraph (a).

Offence

(c) A person who contravenes paragraph (a) shall be guilty of an offence.

(d) subject to paragraph (e), waste deposited or discarded at a facility provided by a local authority under this section shall become the property of the local authority.

(e) Without prejudice to paragraph (c), where a person deposits or discards waste in contravention of paragraph (a) –

(i) the waste shall not become the property of the local authority concerned unless it decides to assume ownership of the waste

(ii) any expenses incurred by the local authority concerned in recovering or disposing, or arranging for the recovery or disposal, of the waste shall be recoverable by it from the person as a simple contract debt in any court of competent jurisdiction."

REQUIREMENTS TO HOLD A WASTE LICENCE

Section 39 of the WMA 1996, which has been substantially amended by Article 4 of the European Communities (Amendment of Waste Management Act 1996) Regulations, 1998 (S.I. No.166 of 1998) by –

(i) the deletion in subsection (3) of "or" where it last appears,

(ii) in subsection (3), the insertion after "1982" of "or the European Communities (Waste Oils)

Regulations, 1992 (S.I. No.399 of 1992),
(iii) The substitution of new subsection (4),
(iv) the substitution for paragraph (c) of subsection (5) of paragraphs (c), (d), (e) and (f).

Section 39, as amended, provides –

"(1) Subject to subsections (4) and (7), a person shall not dispose of or undertake the recovery of (*qv*) waste at a (*qv*) facility, on or after such date as may be prescribed, save under and in accordance with a licence under this Part (in this Act referred to as a 'waste licence') that is in force in relation to the carrying on of the activity concerned at that facility."

Article 4(1) of the Waste Management (Licensing) Regulations 1997 (S.I. No. 133 of 1997) provides that, subject to sub- article (3), the date specified in column (2) of the First Schedule opposite a class of activity identified in column (2) of the Schedule shall be the prescribed date for such activity for the purposes of section 39 (1) of the Act.

Article 4(2) provides that for the purposes of section 39(1) of the WMA 1996, a class of activity identified in column (1) of the First Schedule shall include a related waste operation.

Article 4(3) provides that sub-article (1) shall not apply in respect of an activity at a facility connected with an activity for the time being specified in the First Schedule to the EPAA 1992.

"Related waste operation" by virtue of Article 3(3), means, in relation to an activity the carrying on of which by a person requires a waste licence, any operation involving the holding, recovery or disposal of waste by or on behalf of the said person which is carried on in, on or adjacent to, the facility at which the said activity is carried on.

"(2) For the purpose of subsection (1), different dates may be prescribed in respect of different waste (*qv*) disposal or (*qv*) recovery activities, different classes of facility and different classes of waste.

(3) The recovery or disposal of waste shall, in the period before a waste licence in relation to such recovery or disposal is granted or refused, be deemed not to have contravened the provisions of this Part if, before the date prescribed under subsection (1) in respect of the activity concerned –

(a) an application has been made for a waste licence in respect of that activity and the requirements of regulations under sections 45 and 50 in relation to the application for a waste licence have been complied with by the applicant therefor, and

(b) in the case of a disposal of waste, other than one carried out by a local authority, the corporation of a borough that is not a county borough, or the council of an urban district, it is carried out in accordance with a permit issued under the European Communities (Waste) Regulations, 1979, the European Communities (Toxic and Dangerous Waste) Regulations, 1982 or the European Communities (Waste Oils) Regulations 1992, as appropriate."

(4) The Minister may by regulations provide that subsection (1) shall not apply in respect of the recovery or disposal in a specified manner of a specified class or classes of waste, recovery or disposal if and for so long as the person carrying out the disposal or recovery of the waste, as the case may be, complies with specified conditions in relation to the carrying out of such recovery or disposal.

(5) Without prejudice to the generality of subsection (4), regulations under that subsection may specify conditions in relation to the following matters –

(a) the quantity of waste concerned which may be recovered or disposed of in a particular period,

(b) the use of the (*qv*) best available technology not entailing excessive costs to prevent or eliminate or, where that is not practicable to limit, abate or reduce, an (*qv*) emission from the recovery or disposal activity concerned,

(c) a requirement that the person concerned obtain from a local authority or the Agency a (*qv*) waste permit or such other authorisation or certificate as may be prescribed in respect of the carrying on by him or her of the activity concerned,

(d) the specification of controls to be exercised or measures to be taken by a local authority or the Agency in relation to the carrying on of an activity in respect of which such a permit, authorisation or certificate is required (which controls and measures a local authority or the Agency is hereby empowered to exercise or take, as the case may be),

(e) a requirement regarding the payment to a local authority or the Agency of a fee of a specified amount in respect of an application for such a permit, authorisation or certificate, or of such charges as are necessary to defray or contribute towards the cost of any investigation carried out or caused to be carried out by the local authority or the Agency in relation to such application,
(f) such other matters as the Minister considers are appropriate to ensure that the recovery or disposal activity concerned will not cause (*qv*)environmental pollution.

(6) The Minister may by regulations –
(a) require the (*qv*) producer of a specified class or classes of waste, other than (*qv*) household waste, to –
(i) comply with specified conditions in relation to the treatment or temporary storage by him or her of the waste at premises where it is produced, including the obtaining of the prior written consent of the relevant local authority to such treatment or storage,
(ii) make a plan with respect to the taking of such measures, in the event of an incident occurring that involves the loss or release of the waste, as will prevent or minimise the risk of (*qv*)environmental pollution there from,
(iii) effect and maintain a policy of insurance insuring him or her to a specified extent as respects any liability on his or her part to pay damages or costs on account of injury to person or property arising from the production or holding of the waste,
(b) enables a local authority to attach specified conditions to a consent granted by it pursuant to regulations under paragraph (a)(i) and to revoke such a consent where any of the conditions so attached are not complied with,
(c) specify a maximum period for which the waste may be stored as aforesaid and deem storage beyond that period to be a disposal or recovery, as appropriate, of the waste.

(7) In addition to the exemption from its terms provided for by section 51, subsection (1) shall not apply to –
(a) the recovery or disposal of waste at a (*qv*) facility connected with an activity in respect of which a licence or a revised licence under Part IV of the Act of 1992 is in force, where such recovery or disposal is subject to the said licence or revised licence,
(b) (*qv*) household waste produced and disposed of within the curtilage of the same dwelling,
(c) the deposit of litter in a litter bin,
(d) ...
(e) the transfer of waste to a local authority, the corporation of a borough that is not a county borough, the council of an urban district or any other person for the purpose of its being recovered or disposed of in accordance with this Act or a licence or a revised licence under Part IV of the Act of 1992,
(f) the disposal of animal bye-products within the meaning of the European Communities (Disposal, Processing and Placing on the Market of Animal Bye-Products) Regulations, 1994, and
(g) such other activities as may be prescribed.

(8) The Minister may make regulations amending the First Schedule of the Act of 1992 by the addition thereto, subject to such modifications, if any, as he or she may determine and specifies in the regulations, of any of the activities specified in the Third or the Fourth Schedule.

Offence
(9) A person who contravenes subsection (1) or a provision of the regulations under subsections (4) or (6) shall be guilty of an offence."

The Act of 1992 is the EPAA 1992. Part IV of that Act is Part IV of the EPAA 1992 which refers to an *(qv)* Integrated Pollution Control Licence (IPC licence). The reference for the Regulations quoted at subsection (7)(f) is (S.I. No.257 of 1994).

RECOVERY OF SLUDGES AND AGRICULTURAL WASTE AND 1998 AMENDMENT REGULATIONS

Section 51 of the WMA 1996, as amended in square brackets by Article 2 of the Waste Management (Amendment of Waste Management Act 1996) Regulations, 1998 (S.I. No. 146 of 1998) which gives effect to the provisions of Council Directive 86/278/EEC of June

12, 1986 on the protection of the environment, and in particular of the soil when sewage sludge is used in agriculture (O.J. L 181/6 July 4, 1986), provides:

"(1) The provisions of this section shall apply notwithstanding the provisions of any bye-law made under section 21 of the Local Government (Water Pollution) (Amendment) Act, 1990.

(2) (a) Subject to paragraph (b) a *(qv)* waste licence under section 39 shall not be required for the (*qv*) recovery of –

[(i) residual sludge from –

(A) sewage plants treating domestic or urban waste waters and from other sewage plants treating waste waters of a composition similar to domestic and urban waste waters,

(B) septic tanks and other similar installations for the treatment of sewage, or

(C) sewage plants other than those referred to in (A) and (B)]

(ii) blood of animal or poultry origin,

(iii) faecal matter of animal or poultry origin in the form of manure or slurry, or

(iv) such natural agricultural waste nature as may be prescribed.

(b) The Minister may make regulations amending paragraph (a) by adding or deleting to or from the provision any specified class or classes of waste.

(c) 'Recovery' for the purpose of this section, includes the injection of waste into land for the purpose of benefiting the carrying on of any agricultural or silvicultural activity or an ecological system.

(3) The Minister may make regulations prohibiting or limiting or controlling in a specified manner and to a specified extent, the recovery of any waste to which subsection (2) applies (hereafter in this section referred to a 'relevant waste').

(4) Without prejudice to the generality of subsection (3), regulations under this section may make provision in relation to all or any of the following matters –

(a) a requirement that the recovery of relevant waste shall not be carried out without the prior written consent of the local authority in whose functional area the proposed recovery activity is to take place, and enabling that local authority to attach such conditions to such a consent as it considers appropriate,

(b) the rate at which relevant waste may be spread on or injected into land,

(c) specifying –

(i) limits in respect of the constituent elements of relevant waste or of the concentration of such elements in land on which relevant waste is recovered, and

(ii) maximum annual quantities of the constituent elements of relevant waste which may be recovered on land,

(d) the treatment, sampling and analysis in a specified manner, of relevant waste and the monitoring, sampling and analysis, in a specified manner, on land on which such waste is recovered,

(e) restricting the use of land on or in which relevant waste is recovered,

(f) (i) the keeping by a person of records containing specified particulars as respects –

(I) the production, treatment, recovery, or transfer to another person, of relevant waste,

(II) the monitoring, sampling and analysis of relevant waste or of land on which such waste is recovered,

(ii) the entry in a (*qv*) register required to be established and maintained for the purpose by a local authority of particulars as aforesaid,

(iii) the furnishing of specified information to a local authority or any other specified person in relation to the matters referred to in sub paragraph (i),

(g) the furnishing by a local authority to the Agency of such information regarding waste referred to in subsection (2)(a)(i), in such manner and at such times, as the Agency may require and the preparation and publication by the Agency –

(i) of a report, by a specified date, regarding the recovery and disposal of the said waste,

(ii) of further reports, at specified intervals after the said date, regarding the said recovery and disposal,

(h) the issue of directions or guidance to local authorities with respect to the performance of their functions under regulations under this section,

(i) requiring compliance by specified persons with specified codes of practice concerning the carrying on of any recovery activity in respect of relevant waste,

(j) any matters consequential on, or incidental to, the foregoing.

Offence

(5) A person who contravenes a provision of regulations under this section is guilty of an offence.

(6) For the purpose of this section, other than subsection (4)(a), 'local authority' includes the corporation of a borough of any kind and the council of an urban district."

For section 21 of the LG(WP)(A)A 1990 *See:* AGRICULTURAL ACTIVITIES.

Waste Management (Use of Sludge in Agriculture) Regulations 1998 (S.I. No. 148 of 1998) passed under sections 7 and 51 of the WMA 1996 came into operation on May 20, 1998 and gives effect to Council Directive 86/278/EEC of June 12, 1986 on the protection of the environment, and in particular of the soil, when sewage sludge is used in agriculture (O.J. L 181/6, July 4, 1986)

Article 2(3) gives the following definitions:

"sludge" means:

(i) residual sludge from sewage plants treating domestic or urban waste waters and from other sewage plants treating waste waters of a composition similar to domestic and urban waste waters;

(ii) residual sludge from septic tanks and other similar installations for the treatment of sewage;

(iii) residual sludge from sewage plants other than those referred to in paragraphs (i) and (ii);

"treated sludge" means sludge which has undergone biological, chemical or heat treatment, long-term storage or any other appropriate process so as significantly to reduce its fermentability and the health hazards resulting from its use;

"agriculture" means the growing of all types of commercial food crops, including food crops for stock-rearing purposes;

"supplier" includes a sanitary authority;

"use" means the spreading or applying by any other means of sludge on or in land.

These Regulations can be summarised as follows by reference to its Articles.

3. Provides that sewage sludge shall not be used in agriculture except in accordance with the Regulations. Only treated sludge may be used or untreated sludge only if injected or worked into the land. Residual sludge from septic tanks may be used on grassland provided it is not grazed for 6 months.
4. In using sludge account must be taken of the nutrient needs of plants, the protection of quality of soil, surface water and groundwater and the increased mobility and availability to crops of heavy metals where the pH is less than 6.
5. There are a series of rules regarding the use of treated and untreated sludge depending of the nature of the crops growing, distinguishing for example between fruit, other than fruit trees, or vegetables which are grown in direct contact with the soil and eaten raw and crops which would not be so grown and eaten distinguishing between the periods which must elapse between use of sludge and growing or harvesting. A longer period must elapse where the produce is in direct contact or eaten raw.
6. By references to Parts I and II of the Schedule to the Regulations calculations are made as to the concentration of heavy metals in the land and the values given in the Schedules and the use of sludge on land is prohibited when these values are exceeded.
7. Provision is made for the analysis of the soil in accordance with the methods set out in part V to the Regulations prior to the use of sludge.
8. Provides for the keeping by the local authority of a 'sludge register" for its functional area containing particulars of the quantities, composition, treatment and the identities of the recipients of sludge. A supplier of sludge must provide user with soil analyses and notify the local authority of particulars of supply for the sludge register.

9. Provides exemption from some of the requirements regarding the sludge register for sludge from septic tanks or group treatment plants with a capacity of less than 300kg. BOD per day corresponding to a population equivalent of 5000 persons, designed primarily for treatment of domestic waste water.
10. A local authority shall be responsible for the supervision of the supply and use of sludge in agriculture in their functional area.
11. Provides for recommendations from the Minister from time to time to local authorities in carrying out their duties under the Regulations to which the local authority must have regard.

(5) GENERAL PROVISIONS REGARDING ENVIRONMENTAL PROTECTION
(WMA 1996, ss. 55 to 59)

POWER OF LOCAL AUTHORITIES TO REQUIRE MEASURES TO BE TAKEN IN RELATION TO THE HOLDING, RECOVERY OR DISPOSAL OF WASTE.

Section 55 of the WMA 1996

See: ENFORCEMENT (3) (E).

POWERS OF LOCAL AUTHORITY TO TAKE MEASURES TO PREVENT OR LIMIT ENVIRONMENTAL POLLUTION CAUSED BY WASTE

Section 56 of the WMA 1996

See: ENFORCEMENT (6) (D).

POWERS OF HIGH COURT IN RELATION TO THE HOLDING, RECOVERY OR DISPOSAL OF WASTE.

Section 57 of the WMA 1996

See: ENFORCEMENT (1) (D).

REMEDIES FOR UNAUTHORISED HOLDING, RECOVERY OR DISPOSAL OF WASTE.

Section 58 of the WMA 1996

See: ENFORCEMENT (1) (D).

FUNCTIONS OF LOCAL AUTHORITIES IN REGARD TO WASTE

Section 59 of the WMA 1996

See: FUNCTIONS OF LOCAL AUTHORITIES IN RELATION TO WASTE.

WASTE PERMITS AND CERTIFICATES OF REGISTRATION
(WMA 1996)

Waste Management (Permit) Regulations 1998 (S.I. No. 165 of 1998) made under sections, 7, 15, 18, 19 and 39 of the WMA 1996 came into operation on May 20, 1998, gives effect to:

(a) Council Directive 75/439/EEC, June 16, 1975 on the disposal of waste oils (O.J. L 194/23, July 25, 1975), as amended by Council Directive 87/101/EEC, December 22. 1986 (O.J. L 42/43, February 12, 1987),
(b) Council Directive 75/442/EEC of July 15, 1975 on waste (O.J. L194/39, July 25, 1975), as amended by Council Directive 91/156/EEC of March 18, 1991 (O.J. L78/32, March 26, 1991)
(c) Council Directive 80/68/EEC of December 17, 1979 on the protection of groundwater against pollution caused by certain dangerous substances (O.J. L20/43 January 26, 1980)
(d) Council Directive 91/689/EEC of 12 December 1991 on hazardous waste (O.J. 377/20, December 31, 1991)

Article 4 of the Regulations:

"(1) Section 39(1) of the Act shall not apply in respect of the carrying on by a person of a (*qv*) waste (*qv*) recovery or (*qv*) disposal activity specified in Parts I or II of the First Schedule if and for so long as the person carrying on the activity complies with the conditions specified in sub-article (2).

(2) The conditions specified for the purposes of sub-article (1) are that –
   (a) in the case of an activity of a class specified in Part I of the First Schedule -
      (i) the activity is being carried on in a manner which does not cause, or is not likely to cause, (*qv*) environmental pollution,

(ii) there is in force in relation to the carrying on of the activity a waste permit granted by the local authority in whose functional area the activity is located, and

(iii) the activity is being carried on in accordance with the conditions attached to the aforementioned permit; and

(b) in the case of an activity of a class specified in Part II of the First Schedule –

(i) a certificate of registration has been granted by the Agency under article 21 in relation to the carrying on of the activity at the (*qv*) facility, and

(ii) the activity is being carried on in accordance with the conditions specified in the Second Schedule.

(3) The recovery or disposal of waste at an existing facility shall, in the period before a waste permit or certificate of registration is granted or refused, be deemed to comply with the conditions specified in sub-article (2) if, before the 1st day of October, 1998 –

(a) an application for a waste permit or a certificate of registration, as the case may be, has been made in respect of the activity in accordance with these Regulations and the application has not been withdrawn by the applicant, and

(b) the activity is being carried on in accordance with a permit issued under the European Communities (Waste) Regulations, 1979 (S.I. No. 390 of 1979), the European Communities (Toxic and Dangerous Waste) Regulations, 1982 (S.I. No. 33 of 1992) or the European Communities (Waste Oils) Regulations, 1992 (S.I. No. 399 of 1992) where such permit is in force in relation to the activity.

(4) In this article 'existing facility' means an existing facility within the meaning of the Waste Management (Licensing) Regulations, 1997 (S.I. No. 133 of 1997)."

'Existing facility' in Article 3.(3) of the Waste Management (Licensing) Regulations, 1997 (S.I. No. 133 of 1997) means –

(i) a certified facility, or

(ii) a facility at which the disposal of waste, was, at any time during the period of twelve months ending on the 1st day of May, 1997, carried on and where such disposal was carried on in accordance with a permit (where required) under the European Communities (Waste) Regulations, 1979 (S.I. No. 390 of 1979) or the European Communities (Toxic and Dangerous Waste) Regulations, 1982 (S.I. No. 33 of 1982) other than a facility which involved or was associated with an unauthorised structure or unauthorised use within the meaning of the Local Government (Planning and Development) Act, 1963.

'Certified facility' in Article 3.(3) of the same Regulations means a waste disposal facility the proposed development of which was certified by the Minister for the Environment under Part IV of the Local Government (Planning and Development) Regulations, 1990 (S.I. No. 25 of 1990) or Part IX of the Local Government (Planning and Development) Regulations, 1994 (S.I. No. 86 of 1994).

"5. (1) A local authority may, on application being made to it in that behalf, grant a waste permit in accordance with these Regulations, or refuse to grant such a permit, in relation to the carrying on by the applicant of an activity specified in the First Schedule at a (*qv*)facility located in the functional area of the said local authority.

(2) A local authority shall not grant a waste permit unless it is satisfied that –

(a) the activity concerned, carried on in accordance with such conditions as are attached to the permit, will not cause (*qv*) environmental pollution,

(b) any (*qv*) emissions from the activity concerned will not result in the contravention of any relevant standard, including any (*qv*) standard for an (*qv*)environmental medium, or any relevant (*qv*) emission limit value, prescribed under any enactment, and

(c) the best available technology not entailing excessive cost will be used to prevent or eliminate or, where that is not practicable, to limit, abate or reduce an emission from the activity concerned."

Articles 6 to 15 of the Regulations deal with specific requirements in relation to an application

for a waste permit:
6. notice of application;
7. requests as to notices;
8. further notice;
9. making of application;
10. contents of application;
11. procedure on receipt of application;
12. further application;
13. availability and inspection of documents;
14. submissions;
15. maximum period of determination.

INVESTIGATIONS CONCERNING DISCHARGES TO GROUNDWATER

Article 16 of the Waste Management (Permit) Regulations 1998 (S.I. No. 165 of 1998):

"Where it appears to a local authority that an activity which is the subject of the application to the authority could give rise to –
(a) the indirect discharge into groundwater of a substance for the time being specified in List I of the Annex to Council Directive 80/68/EEC of 17 December 1979 on the protection of groundwater against pollution caused by certain dangerous substances (O.J. No. L 20/43 26 January 1980), or
(b) the direct or indirect discharge into groundwater of a substance for the time being specified in List II of the said Annex,

the authority shall, before it grants a waste permit, carry out or cause to be carried out (by the applicant or otherwise) such investigations as it considers necessary in order to comply with the relevant requirements of Articles 4, 5 and 7 of the aforesaid Directive."

See: DISCHARGES TO AQUIFERS, CONTROL OF.

Article 18 deals with conditions which shall be attached to a waste permit, Article 19 deals with notice and information to be given to the Agency on the granting of a waste permit and Article 20 deals with a notice required to be given to the local authority of significant change in the information given in the application.

REGISTRATION OF CERTAIN ACTIVITIES

Article 21 of the Waste Management (Permit) Regulations 1998 (S.I. No. 165 of 1998): -

"(1)A person shall not carry on an activity of a class specified in Part III of the First Schedule at a (*qv*) facility on or after the 1st day of October, 1998 unless a certificate of registration has been granted in relation to the carrying on of the said activity at that facility.

(2) The Agency or a local authority, as the case may be, shall, on application being made to it in that behalf in accordance with these Regulations, grant a certificate of registration in relation to the carrying on at a facility of an activity specified in Part I or Part II of the First Schedule.

(3) An application for a certificate of registration shall be made –
(a) in the case of an activity carried on by or on behalf of a local authority, to the Agency,
(b) in the case of an activity carried on by a person other than a local authority, to a local authority in whose functional area the relevant facility is located.
(c) An application for a certificate of registration shall contain the information specified in article 10(1) (other than paragraphs (g) or (h)), where appropriate."

Article 24:

"A person shall not compile information which is false or misleading to a material extent or furnish any such information in any notice or other document used for the purposes of these Regulations."

FALSE OR MISLEADING INFORMATION

See: (1)SCHEDULES HERETO, European Communities (WASTE MANAGEMENT ACT, 1996) REGULATIONS, 1998 SCHEDULES; (2)CONDITIONS.

WASTE,
TEMPORARY STORAGE
(WMA 1996, s.5(3))

"In this Act, a reference to the temporary storage of waste shall, without prejudice to any particular provision that may be made pursuant to section 39(6), be construed as reference to the storage of waste for a period not exceeding 6 months."

WATER POLLUTION ADVISORY COUNCIL
(LG(WP)A 1977, s.2)

Provided for the establishment of such a council by the Minister. This was never done and section 30 of the LG(WP)(A)A 1990 repealed section 2 which means that it cannot now ever be done. The Council was intended to have an advisory function, *e.g.*, under section 4(10) of the LG(WP)A 1977 it was one of the bodies with which the Minister was to consult before exempting certain effluents from the licensing process.

WATER QUALITY MANAGEMENT PLAN
(LG(WP)A 1977, s.15)

As amended by substitution as surrounded by square brackets by section 11(a) and (b) of the LG(WP)(A)A 1990 provides:

"(1) A local authority may and, if so directed by the Minister, shall make a water quality management plan for any (*qv*) waters situated in its functional area or which adjoin that area.

(2) A plan under this section shall contain such objectives for the prevention and abatement of pollution of the waters the subject of the plan and such other provisions as appear to the local authority to be necessary.

[(3) Two or more local authorities may jointly make a water quality management plan in relation to waters part of which are in or adjoin the functional area of each local authority.

(3A) A water quality management plan may be revised or replaced by the local authority or local authorities that made it.]

(4) A plan under this section may relate to the sea to such an extent as the Minister, after consultation with the Minister for Fisheries, may approve.

(5) A plan under this section shall not contain any provisions inconsistent with (*qv*) regulations under section 26.

[(6) As soon as is practiceable after the making, revision or replacement of a plan under this section, a copy of the plan as so made or revised or of the replacement plan shall be given by the local authority concerned to the Minister, and the Minister for the Marine and to any local authority, *(qv)* sanitary authority or *(qv)* regional board whose functional area either adjoins the waters to which the plan relates or the performance of whose functions would affect the implementation of the plan.]"

Subsection (7) provides for two or more local authorities making together a joint plan or replacement plan and for revision of a plan by a local authority in such manner, in relation to such matters and at such intervals as the Minister may direct.

Subsection (8) provides that the making, revision or replacement of a plan shall be a (*qv*) reserved function of the local authority concerned.

Subsection (9) provides that any dispute between authorities as to which shall make a plan shall be determined by the Minister.

Subsection (10) provides for the making by the Minister of regulations for the purpose of the section which may include publication of a notice regarding a proposed plan and a statement of where and when the plan may be inspected and providing for the making of representations in relation to the plan.

Subsection (11) provides for the entitlement of persons to make such representations and every such representation must be considered by the local authority which may then, as it thinks fit, make, revise or replace the plan with or without amendment.

Part VI of the Local Government (Water Pollution) Regulations 1978 (S.I. No. 271 of 1992) refers.

See: MANAGEMENT PLANS

WATER, QUALITY STANDARDS
(LG(WP) 1977)

See: QUALITY STANDARDS, WATERS, TRADE AND SEWAGE EFFLUENT.

WATER, QUALITY OF SURFACE WATER
(LG(WP)A 1977)

The European Communities (Quality of

Surface Water Intended for the Abstraction of Drinking Water) Regulations 1989 (S.I. No. 294 of 1989) prescribe quality standards and methods and frequency of analysis of surface fresh water used or intended for use in the abstraction of drinking water and give effect to Council Directives 74/440/EEC, June 16, 1975 (O.J. L194/26, July 25, 1975) and 79/869/EEC October 9, 1979 (O.J. L271/44, October 29, 1979).

Although these Regulations would properly be made under the LG(WP)A 1977 and LG(WP)(A)A 1990 which provide heavy penalties for non-compliance, these regulations were in fact passed under section 3(1) of the European Communities Act 1972 and therefore these regulations cannot create indictable offences. For this reason, regulations under the majority if not all of the statutes dealing with the environment provide only for summary prosecution.

WATERS
(F(C)A 1959, s.3(1))

"Means any river, lake, watercourse, estuary or any part of the sea."

(LG(WP)A 1977, s.2(1))

"includes –
- (a) any (or any part of any) river, stream, lake, canal, reservoir, aquifer, pond, watercourse or other inland waters, whether natural or artificial,
- (b) any tidal waters,
- (c) where the context permits, any beach, river bank and salt marsh or other area which is contiguous to anything mentioned in paragraph (a) or (b), and the channel or bed of anything mentioned in paragraph (a) which is for the time being dry,

but does not include a sewer."

(WMA 1996, s.5(1))

"Has the meaning assigned to it by the LG(WP)A 1977."

WATERKEEPER, A PRIVATE
(F(C)A 1959 ss. 292, 293, 294)

Appointment of a private waterkeeper for the protection of certain fisheries. *See:* AUTHORISED PERSONS, AUTHORISED OFFICERS AND WATERKEEPERS.

WILD BIRD
(WLA 1976, s.2(1))

"Includes the unflown young of a wild bird."

WILD DUCK
(WLA 1976, s.2(1))

"Means wild duck of any species."

WILD MAMMAL
(WLA 1976, s.2(1))

"Includes both aquatic and terrestrial wild mammals and their young."

WILDLIFE
(WLA 1976, s.2(1))

"Means (*qv*) fauna and (*qv*) flora."

WILDLIFE ADVISORY COUNCIL
(WLA 1976, s.13)

The Wildlife Advisory Council was established under section 13 of the WLA 1976 to make recommendations to the *(qv)* Minister as to the Minister's general policy (including administrative policy but excluding any particular administrative matter) in relation to the conservation of *(qv)* wildlife and as to the objectives to be fixed and the programmes to be implemented by the Minister in relation to such conservation. By virtue of section 6 of the Heritage Act, 1995, these functions were taken over by the *(qv)* Heritage Council.
See: COUNCIL, THE, HERITAGE COUNCIL.

WILDLIFE DEALER
(WLA 1976, s.2(1))

"Means any person who carries on the business of (*qv*) wildlife dealing."

WILDLIFE DEALER'S LICENCE
(WLA 1976, s.2(1))

"Has the meaning assigned to it by section 48 of this Act."

Section 48 of the WLA 1976:

"(1) A Justice of the District Court may, on

application being made in that behalf, if he thinks fit, grant a certificate authorising the issue of a licence (in this Act referred to as a wildlife dealer's licence) to the applicant authorising him to carry on business as a wildlife dealer at premises specified both in the certificate and in the licence."

See: Order 89, District Court Rules, 1997 (S.I. No. 93 of 1997)

Subsection (2) provides that the licence remains in force for the period prescribed under section 46(3) which is one year from the date of issue.

Subsection (3) provides that the court which granted the licence may renew it on application from time to time for the same periods prescribed in said section 46(3).

Subsection (4) provides for the issue of the licence by the Minister on application by the person to whom the certificate has been granted and on payment of the appropriate fee.

"(5) The Court in considering an application for the grant of a certificate under this section may have regard to –
(a) the suitability of the applicant, taking into account the purposes of the Act, to hold a wildlife dealer's licence, and
(b) the ability of the applicant to comply with regulations made under section 46(2) of the Act which are for the time being in force."

The Wildlife Act, 1976 (Wildlife Dealing) Regulations, 1977 (S.I. No. 253 of 1977) refers.

Subsection (6) provides that the Minister must be notified of the application to the District Court for the wildlife dealer's certificate by registered post and is entitled to appear and be heard at the hearing.

Subsection (7) provides for amendment of the certificate by the District Court which granted it by inserting in the licence a reference to specified premises (in addition to the premises already contained), by deleting such a reference from the licence or by substituting, in lieu of such a reference, another such reference.

REVOCATION OF WILDLIFE DEALER's LICENCE

Section 49 of the WLA 1976:

(1) Where a person who holds a wildlife dealer's licence is convicted of an offence under section 31 of this Act, or under section 69(2) of this Act because of a contravention of, or of a failure to comply with, regulations made under section 41 or 46 of this Act, the court by which the person is convicted may revoke the licence and such revocation shall be in addition to any other punishment imposed by the court in respect of the offence.

(2) Where a court revokes a wildlife dealer's licence pursuant to this section, the registrar or clerk of the court shall, as soon as may be, send to the Minister a copy of the court's order."

For section 31 *see:* BIRDS PERCHING, for section 69(2) *see:* ATTEMPTS, MISC. OFFENCES UNDER WLA 1976, for section 41 *see:* FALCONRY and for section 46 *see:* WILDLIFE DEALING.

PUBLICATION OF LISTS OF HOLDERS AND REVOCATIONS

Section 50(1) of the WLA 1976 entitles the Minister to publish a list of licence holders and subsection (2) entitles him to publish a list of revocations of licences under section 49.

WILDLIFE DEALING
(WLA 1976)

Part III of the WLA 1976 (sections 45 to 54) deals with the regulation and control of wildlife dealing and the transport, import and export of wildlife.

Section 45 requires some explanation as it has been amended both by the European Communities (Wildlife Act 1976) (Amendment) Regulations 1985 (S.I. No. 397 of 1985) (hereinafter referred to as the "1985 Regulations") and the NH 97 Regulations.

As a result of these amendment, you now have on the statute book two forms of sections 45(1), one as amended by the 1985 Regulations and the other as amended by the NH 97 Regulations.

SALE, PURCHASE AND POSSESSION OF FAUNA RESTRICTED.

Section 45 of the WLA 1976 as amended by Article 3(e) of the 1985 Regulations:

"(1) A person who is not a licensed (*qv*) wildlife dealer shall not sell, keep for sale, purchase for resale or engage in taxidermy in respect of a (*qv*) protected wild bird or a (*qv*) protected wild animal, whether alive or dead."

Section 45 of the WLA 1976 as amended by Regulation 22 of the NH97 Regulations:

"(1) A person who is not a licensed wildlife dealer shall not keep for sale, sell, transport for the purpose of sale or exchange, offer for sale or exchange, purchase for resale or exchange or engage in taxidermy in respect of (*qv*) fauna, at any stage of life, set out in Part I of the First Schedule to the European Communities (Natural Habitats) Regulations, 1997 (S.I. No. 94 of 1997)."

"(2) Subject to subsections (3) and (8) of this section and to sections 22(5), 23(7)(d) and 42 of this Act, a person who is not a licensed wildlife dealer shall not have in his possession a protected wild bird or a protected wild animal, whether alive or dead, or the eggs of a protected wild bird.

(3) Subsection (1) of this section shall not apply to –
   (a) the sale by any person of any live specimen of a protected wild bird or protected wild animal solely for the purposes of propagating, or of improving the quality of, such species,
   (b) the sale by persons of live hares to a coursing club affiliated to the Irish Coursing Club,
   (c) the sale to a licensed wildlife dealer by a person of any protected wild bird or protected wild animal lawfully killed by him,
   (d) the sale by any person, who has obtained the prior permission of the Minister so to do, of any lawfully killed such protected wild bird or protected wild animal.

(4) A person who is the owner, manager or person otherwise in charge of any hotel, guest house, inn, restaurant, public eating house, registered club within the meaning of the Registration of Clubs Acts, 1904 to 1962, or any other premises in which meals are provided for reward, shall not purchase a protected wild bird or a protected wild animal otherwise than from a licensed wildlife dealer, unless such a person is himself such a dealer.

(5) A person mentioned in subsection (4) of this section who is not a licensed wildlife dealer shall keep in such form as the Minister approves a record of all purchases of protected wild birds or protected wild animals made in relation to the premises so mentioned and of which he is the owner or manager or of which he is otherwise in charge, and records kept pursuant of this section shall be kept available for inspection at the said premises by any (*qv*) authorised person on demand at any reasonable time.

(6) An authorised person may inspect and if he thinks fit, take copies of any entry in any record kept pursuant to subsection (5) of this section.

Offence

(7) A person who contravenes subsection (1), (2), (4), (11), ((12) or (13) of this section or who fails to comply with the requirements of subsection (5) of this section shall be guilty of an offence."

(Subsection (7) was inserted by Article 3(e)(ii) of the 1985 Regulations)

"(8) In any proceedings for an offence under this section in which it is alleged that subsection (2) or (13) of this section was contravened, it shall be a defence for the defendant to prove that –
   (a) he either had lawfully acquired the wild bird, wild animal or eggs, as may be appropriate, before the commencement of this section or had acquired it or them from a person who had lawfully acquired it or them,
   (b) in case the alleged offence refers to a protected wild bird or a protected wild animal, he had lawfully killed or captured it or had lawfully acquired it from a person who had lawfully killed or captured it."

(Subsection (8) was inserted by Article 3(e)(iii) of the 1985 Regulations)

"(9) Nothing in this section shall make unlawful the possession consequent upon any other thing which is either –
   (a) done pursuant to and in accordance with a licence or permission granted under the Act, or
   (b) permitted to be done by or under any statute other than the Act,

of a protected wild bird or a protected wild animal or the eggs of a protected wild bird.

(10) References in this section to a protected wild bird or a protected wild animal shall, except in relation to taxidermy, be construed as including references to the flesh of such bird or animal, and in relation to taxidermy the said reference in this section shall be construed as including references to the skin, plumage or other part of such bird or animal."

(Subsections (11), (12) and (13) which follow were inserted by Article (3)(e)(iv) of the 1985 Regulations.)

"(11) A person who is not a licensed wildlife dealer shall not sell, keep for sale, purchase for resale or engage in taxidermy in respect of eggs taken from the wild of a protected wild bird.

(12) A licensed wildlife dealer shall not sell, keep for sale, purchase for resale or engage in taxidermy in respect of eggs taken from the wild of a protected wild bird,

(13) Subject to subsection (8) of this section and to section 22(5) of the Act, a licensed wildlife dealer shall not have in his possession eggs taken from the wild of a protected wild bird."

The 1985 Regulations also provide at Article 3(f) for the deletion of a list of wild birds from the Third Schedule. This is dealt with elsewhere. *See:* PROTECTION, PROTECTED WILD BIRDS.

Sections 22(5) and 23(7)(d) referred to in section 45(2) supra are exemptions from the offence provisions of sections 22 and one offence provision only of section 23. *See:* PROTECTION, PROTECTED WILD BIRDS and PROTECTION, PROTECTED WILD ANIMALS.

REGULATION AND CONTROL OF WILDLIFE DEALING

Section 46(1) of the WLA 1976:

"(1) Where the Minister is satisfied that it is in the interests of the conservation of any species of protected wild bird or protected wild animal so to do, subject to subsection (5) of this section, he may by regulations prohibit, or control in such manner as he considers appropriate and specifies in the regulations, the purchase or sale of that species for such period as may be specified.

(2) The Minister may make regulations regulating or controlling the carrying on by licensed *(qv)* wildlife dealers of the business of wildlife dealing."

Subsection (3) suggests as headings for such regulations:
premises used for licensed wildlife dealing, the form and period of validity of a wildlife dealer's licence and a renewal of such a licence, the species of fauna which may be sold or purchased for resale pursuant to such a licence, the keeping of registers, books, records, invoices and receipts relating to such a business and the production of same when required, such entries as may be prescribed, the prominent display of the licence, the care of protected wild birds or protected wild animals being transported or displayed or exhibited and ancillary or incidental matters.

Subsection (4) provides for inspection and the taking of copies of entries produced pursuant to the section by (*qv*) authorised officers.

Subsection (5) provides that regulations made under the section which relate to a species of fish or aquatic invertebrate animal shall only be made after consultation with the Minister for Agriculture and Fisheries.

Wildlife Act, 1976 (Wildlife Dealing) Regulations 1977 (S.I. No. 253 of 1977) provide for the regulation of wildlife dealing as follows:

4. (1) Refers to the form of a wildlife dealer's licence which is set out in the First Schedule.
   (2) The licence is valid for one year from the date of issue.

5. (1) The licence must be prominently dis played in the premises specified in the licence.
   (2) Where more than one specified premises a copy of be displayed in each.

6. (1) and (2) Makes a distinction between a dealer who specialises in *(qv)* game species or is one of the categories of persons the owner of premises where food is provided with meals for reward who may only deal in "game" species of fauna and any other wildlife dealer who may deal in any species of fauna.
   (3) provides for an exemption from the pro-

visions of 7(1) and 9 of a wildlife dealer providing a taxidermy service.

In 6(1) reference to protected fauna shall be construed as including a reference to the flesh of such fauna and in 6(2) references to protected fauna shall be construed as including references to specimens, whether alive or dead, of such fauna and to the skin, plumage or other part of such fauna.

7. (1) provide that a licensed wildlife dealer shall not sell protected fauna in a public place and shall not sell to or purchase from a person under the age of 12 years.

8. Provides for the conditions in which live specimens of protected fauna must be kept.

9. Provides that the premises of a wildlife dealer must conform with Food Hygiene regulations in force.

10. Provides for the keeping on the premises of a wildlife register in which must be recorded purchases and sale or other disposals of protected fauna and for the particulars required in such register.

11. Provides for the inspection of the register at reasonable times by an *(qv)* authorised person and backup documents for clarification.

"protected fauna" in the regulations is defined as meaning protected wild birds and protected wild animals.

The European Communities (Wild Birds) (Gadwall and Goldeneye) Regulations 1982 (S.I. No. 241 of 1982) prohibited the sale, keeping for sale or offering for sale, whether live or dead, of any bird of the species, namely, Gadwall (*Anas strepera*) and Goldeneye (*Bucephala clangula*) or any recognisable part or derivative of such bird.

PROHIBITION ON WILDLIFE DEALING WITHOUT WILDLIFE DEALER'S LICENCE

Section 47(1) of the WLA 1976 provides that a person shall not carry on business as a wildlife dealer except under and in accordance with a wildlife dealer's licence.

Subsection (2) provides that the section does not apply to a person carrying on business three months before the coming into operation of the section, June 1, 1977, or to a person purchasing such a business or to the personal representatives of a deceased wildlife dealer for a period of 6 months after the death.

Offence
Subsection (3) creates the offence of contravention of subsection (1).

WILDLIFE HABITAT
(Heritage Act 1995, s.2(1))

"Means the ecological environment in which particular organisms and communities thereof thrive."

Schedules

FISHERIES (CONSOLIDATION) ACT 1959

FOURTH SCHEDULE

Scale of Ordinary Licence Duties

Part I – Licence Duties in Respect of Salmon Rod Ordinary Licences

Classes of Salmon Rod Ordinary Licences

Kind of Engine	Salmon Rod (annual) ordinary licences	Salmon Rod (Annual) (district) ordinary licence	Salmon Rod (seven day) ordinary licence	Salmon Rod (twenty-one day) ordinary licence	Salmon Rod (late season) ordinary licence	Salmon Rod (late season) ordinary licence
(1)	(2)	(3)	(4)	(5)	(6)	(7)
Salmon	L.s.d.	L.s.d.	L.s.d.	L.s.d.	L.s.d.	L.s.d.
Rod	200	200	200	1100	1100	100

PART II Other Ordinary Licence Duties

Ref. No.	Kind of Engine	Annual Licence Duty		
(1)	(2)	(3)		
		L.	s.	d.
1.	Stake net or fly net	30	0	0
2.	Bag net	10	0	0
3.	Head weir	6	0	0
4.	Draft net	4	0	0
5.	Drift net	3	0	0
6.	Snap net	2	10	0
7.	Pole net	0	10	0
8.	Loop net			
9.	Box for taking salmon in a fishing weir or a fishing mill dam	10	0	0
10.	Eye, gap or basket for taking eels in or on a fishing weir or a fishing mill dam.	2	0	0
11.	Eel trap as used under licence in No. 171 of Drogheda District and in No. 13 of Ballyshannon District	2	0	0
12.	Long line for eels	2	0	0
13.	Coghill Net for Eels	2	0	0
14.	Fyke nets for Eels	10	0	0

FISHERIES (AMENDMENT) (NO. 2) ACT 1987

SCHEDULE

Amendment of Part I of Fourth Schedule to Principal Act

PART I Licence Duties in Respect of Freshwater rod Ordinary Licences

Classess of Freshwater Rod Ordinary Licences

Kind of Engine	Composite Freshwater angling ordinary licences	Salmon Rod (annual ordinary licences	Salmon Rod (twenty-one day) ordinary licences	Trout Rod (annual) ordinary licences	Trout Rod (twenty-one day) ordinary licences	Coarse Fish (annual licences	Coarse Fish (Twenty-one day) ordinary licences
(1)	(2)	(3)	(4)		(5)	(6)	(7)
Fresh water	Pounds	Pounds	Pounds	Pounds	Pounds	Pounds	
rod	40	25	21	15	10	10	5

FISHERIES (AMENDMENT) ACT 1991

SCHEDULE (Section 18)

Amendment of Part 1 of the Fourth Schedule to Principal Act PART 1

Classes of Salmon Rod Ordinary Licences

Kind of Engine	Salmon Rod (annual) ordinary licences	Salmon Rod (annual) district licences	Salmon Rod (twenty one day) licences	Salmon Rod annual juvenile licences	Salmon (One-day ordinary) licences
(1)	(2)	(3)	(4)	(5)	(6)
			Salmon		
Rod	25 pounds	12 pounds	10 pounds	8 pounds	3 pounds

LOCAL GOVERNMENT (WATER POLLUTION) ACT 1977

LOCAL GOVERNMENT (WATER POLLUTION) REGULATIONS

1992 (S.I. NO. 271 OF 1992)

FIRST SCHEDULE

HARMFUL SUBSTANCES

Individual substances belonging to the following families and groups of substances:

1. Organohalogen compounds and substances which may form such compounds in the aquatic environment.
2. Organophosphorus compounds.
3. Organotin compounds.
4. Substances which possess carcinogenic, mutagenic or teratogenic properties in or via the aquatic environment, including substances in the Second Schedule which possess such properties in or via the aquatic environment.
5. Mercury and its compounds.
6. Cadmium and its compounds.
7. Mineral oils and hydrocarbons.
8. Cyanides.

SECOND SCHEDULE

HARMFUL SUBSTANCES

Individual substances and categories of substances belonging to the following families and groups of substances:-

1. The following metalloids and metals and their compounds:

1. Zinc	11.Tin
2. Copper	12. Barium
3. Nickel	13. Beryllium
4. Chrome	14. Boron
5. Lead	15. Uranium
6. Selenium	16. Vanadium
7. Arsenic	17. Cobalt
8. Antimony	18. Thallium
9. Molybdenum	19. Tellurium
10. Titanium	20. Silver.

2. Biocides and their derivatives other than those in the First Schedule.
3. Substances which have a deleterious effect on the taste and/or odour of water and compounds liable to cause the formation of such substances in water and to render it unfit for human consumption.
4. Toxic or persistent organic compounds of silicon and substances which may cause the formation of such compounds in water, excluding those which are biologically harmless or are rapidly converted in water into harmless substances.
5. Inorganic compounds of phosphorus and elemental phosphorus.
6. Fluorides.
7. Ammonia and nitrites.

AIR POLLUTION ACT 1987
FIRST SCHEDULE
POLLUTANTS TO WHICH ACT APPLIES
(SECTION 7)

1. All smoke, gas, aerosols and dust.
2. Without prejudice to the generality of paragraph (1), this Act shall apply in particular to smoke, gas, aerosols and dust consisting of:
   (a) sulphur dioxide and other sulphur compounds, or
   (b) oxides of nitrogen and other nitrogen compounds, or
   (c) carbon monoxide, or
   (d) organic compounds, or
   (e) heavy metals and their compounds, or
   (f) asbestos fibres, glass fibres or mineral fibres, or
   (g) chlorine and its compounds, or
   (h) fluorine and its compounds.

THIRD SCHEDULE
INDUSTRIAL PROCESSES TO WHICH ACT APPLIES
(SECTION 6)

No. Process

1. The refining of oil other than operations solely manufacturing lubricants from crude oil.
2. The generation of electricity in plants with a nominal heat output exceeding 50 MW, other than hydro and nuclear plants.
3. The raising of steam in plants with a nominal heat output exceeding 50 MW.
4. The roasting and sintering of metal ores in plants with a capacity of more than 1,000 tonnes per year.
5. The production of pig iron and crude steel in integrated plants.
6. The production of ferrous metals in foundries having melting installations with a capacity greater than 5 tonnes.
7. The production and melting of non-ferrous metals in installations having a capacity greater than 1 tonne for heavy metals and 0.5 tonnes for light metals.
8. The production of cement.
9. The production of a compound or alloy of magnesium.
10. The production of lime in a kiln.
11. The production of a compound or alloy of manganese.
12. The production and processing of asbestos.
13. The manufacture of asbestos-based products.
14. The manufacture of glass fibre or mineral fibre.
15. The production of glass (ordinary or special) in plants with a capacity of more than 5,000 tonnes per year.
16. The manufacture of coarse ceramics including refractory bricks, stoneware pipes, facing and floor bricks and roof tiles.
17. The manufacture of olefins, derivatives of olefins, monomers and polymers.
18. The manufacture of organic intermediate products other than those specified at No. 17.
19. The manufacture of basic inorganic chemicals.
20. Any chemical process in which any of the following basic inorganic chemicals are used or evolved, that is to say, ammonia, bromine, carbon disulphide, chlorine, fluorine, hydrofluoric acid, hydrogen chloride, hydrogen cyanide, or hydrogen sulphide.
21. Any chemical process in which mercaptans are used or evolved.
22. The incineration of solid or liquid wastes.
23. The manufacture of paper pulp by chemical methods in plants with a capacity of greater than 25,000 tonnes per year.
24. The manufacture of artificial fertilisers.
25. The extraction of aluminium oxide from an ore and the reaction of aluminium or its alloys with chlorine or its compounds.
26. The production of tar and bitumen and the manufacture of products containing them.
27. The extraction or recovery, by burning or the application of heat, of aluminium, zinc, copper or lead, from any scrap metal or alloy, waste material or residue including scrap or waste cable.
28. The getting, raising, taking, carrying away and processing (including size reduction, grading and heating) of minerals and the storage of mineral wastes.
29. The manufacture of pesticides, pharmaceutical products and their intermediates.
30. The rendering of animal by-products.

ENVIRONMENTAL PROTECTION AGENCY ACT 1992
FIRST SCHEDULE (SECTIONS 3 AND 82)
ACTIVITIES TO WHICH PART IV APPLIES

1. Minerals and Other Materials
   1.1 The extraction, production and processing of raw asbestos.
   1.2 The extraction of aluminium oxide from an ore.
   1.3 The extraction and processing (including

size reduction, grading and heating) of minerals within the meaning of the Minerals Developments Acts, 1940 to 1979, and storage of related mineral waste.

1.4 The extraction of peat in the course of a business which involves an area exceeding 50 hectares.

2. Energy

2.1 The production of energy in combustion plant the rated thermal input of which is equal to or greater than 50MW other than any such plant which makes direct use of the products of combustion in a manufacturing process.

2.2 The burning of any fuel in a boiler or furnace with a nominal heat output exceeding 50MW.

3. Metals

3.1 The initial melting or production of iron or steel.

3.2 The processing of iron and steel in forges, drawing plants and rolling mills where the production area exceeds 500 square metres.

3.3 The production, recovery, processing or use of ferrous metals in foundries having melting installations with a total capacity exceeding 5 tonnes.

3.4 The production, recovery, processing or use of non-ferrous metals, their compounds or other alloys including antimony, arsenic, beryllium, chromium, lead, magnesium, manganese, phosphorous, selenium, cadmium or mercury, by thermal, chemical or electrolytic means in installations with a batch capacity exceeding 0.5 tonnes.

3.5 The reaction of aluminium or its alloys with chlorine or its compounds.

3.6 The roasting, sintering or calcining of metallic ores in plants with a capacity exceeding 1,000 tonnes per year.

3.7 Swaging by explosives where the production area exceeds 100 square metres.

3.8 The pressing, drawing and stamping of large castings where the production area exceeds 500 square metres.

3.9 Boiler making and the manufacture of reservoirs, tanks and other sheet metal containers where the production area exceeds 500 square metres.

4. Mineral Fibres and Glass

4.1 The processing of asbestos and the manufacture and processing of asbestos-based products.

4.2 The manufacture of glass fibre or mineral fibre.

4.3 The production of glass (ordinary and special) in plants with a capacity exceeding 5,000 tonnes per year.

4.4 The product of industrial diamonds.

5. Chemicals

5.1 The manufacture of chemicals in an integrated chemical installation.

5.2 The manufacture of olefins and their derivatives or of monomers and polymers, including styrene and vinyl chloride.

5.3 The manufacture, by way of chemical reaction processes, of organic or organo-metallic chemical products other then those specified at 5.2.

5.4 The manufacture of inorganic chemicals.

5.5 The manufacture of artificial fertilisers.

5.6 The manufacture of pesticides, pharmaceutical or veterinary products and their intermediates.

5.7 The manufacture of paints, varnishes, resins, inks, dyes, pigments or elastomers where the production capacity exceeds 1,000 litres per week.

5.8 The formulation of pesticides.

5.9 The chemical manufacture of glues, bonding agents and adhesives.

5.10 The manufacture of vitamins involving the use of heavy metals.

5.11 The storage, in quantities exceeding the values shown, of any one or more of the following chemicals (other than as part of any other activity).
methyl acrylate (20 tonnes); acrylonitrile (20 tonnes); toluene di-isocyanate (20 tonnes); anhydrous ammonia (100 tonnes); anhydrous hydrogen fluoride (1 tonne).

6. Intensive agriculture

6.1 The rearing of poultry in installations, whether within the same complex or within 100 metres of that complex, where the capacity exceeds 100,000 units and where units have the following equivalents:
1 broiler = 1 unit,

1 layer, turkey or other fowl = 2 units.

6.2 The rearing of pigs in installations, whether within the one complex or within 100 metres of that complex, where the capacity exceeds 1,000 units on gley soils or 3,000 units on other soils and where units have the following equivalents:
1 pig = 1 unit,
1 sow = 10 units.

7. Food and Drink

7.1 The manufacture of vegetable and animal oils and fats where the capacity for processing raw materials exceeds 40 tonnes per day.

7.2 The manufacture of dairy products where the processing capacity exceeds 50 million gallons of milk equivalent per year.

7.3 Commercial brewing and distilling, and malting in installations where the production capacity exceeds 100,000 tonnes per year.

7.4 The slaughter of animals in installations where the daily capacity exceeds 1,500 units and where units have the following equivalents:
1 sheep = in unit,
1 pig = 2 units,
1 head of cattle = 5 units.

7.5 The manufacture of fish-meal and fish-oil.

7.6 The manufacture of sugar.

7.7 The rendering of animal by-products.

8. Wood, Paper, Textiles and Leather

8.1 The manufacture of paper pulp, paper or board (including fibre-board, particle-board and plywood) in installations with a production capacity equal to or exceeding 25,000 tonnes of product per year.

8.2 The manufacture of bleached pulp.

8.3 The treatment or protection of wood, involving the use of preservatives, with capacity exceeding 10 tonnes per day.

8.4 The manufacture of synthetic fibres.

8.5 The dyeing, treatment or finishing (including moth-proofing and fireproofing) of fibres or textiles (including carpet) where the capacity exceeds 1 tonne per day of fibre, yarn or textile material.

8.6 The fell-mongering of hides and tanning of leather in installations where the capacity exceeds 100 skins per day.

9. Fossil Fuels

9.1 The extraction, other than offshore extraction, of petroleum, natural gas, coat or bituminous shale.

9.2 The handling or storage of crude petroleum.

9.3 The refining of petroleum or gas.

9.4 The pyrolysis, carbonisation, gasification, liquefaction, dry distillation, partial oxidation or heat treatment of coal, lignite, oil or bituminous shale, other carbonaceous materials or mixtures of any of these in installations with a processing capacity exceeding 500 tonnes per day.

10. Cement

10.1 The production of cement.

11. Waste

11.1 The incineration of hazardous waste.

11.2 The incineration of hospital waste.

11.3 The incineration of waste other than that mentioned in 11.1 and 11.2 in plants with a capacity exceeding 1 tonne per hour.

11.4 The use of heat to manufacture fuel from waste.

12. Surface Coatings

12.1 Operations involving coating with organo-tin compounds.

12.2 The manufacture or use of coating materials in processes with a capacity to make or use at least 10 tonnes per year of organic solvents, and powder coating manufacture with a capacity to produce at least 50 tonnes per year.

12.3 Electroplating operations.

13. Other Activities

13.1 The testing of engines, turbines or reactors where the floor area exceeds 500 square metres.

13.2 The manufacture of integrated circuits and printed circuit boards.

13.3 The production of lime in a kiln.

13.4 The manufacture of coarse ceramics including refractory bricks, stoneware pipes, facing and floor bricks and roof tiles.

SECOND SCHEDULE - ENACTMENTS IN RESPECT OF WHICH FUNCTIONS MAY BE TRANSFERRED TO THE AGENCY (SECTION 54)

Air Pollution Act 1987 (Emission Limit Value for the Use of Asbestos) Regulations 1990.
Air Pollution Act 1987 (Sulphur Content of Gas Oil) Regulations 1989.
European Communities (Asbestos Waste) Regulations 1990.
European Communities (Control of Water Pollution by Asbestos) Regulations 1990.
European Communities (Lead Content of Petrol) Regulations 1985 to 1988.
European Communities (Toxic and Dangerous Waste) Regulations 1982.
European Communities (Trans-frontier Shipment of Hazardous Waste) Regulations 1988.
European Communities (Waste) Regulations 1984
Local Government (Water Pollution) Act, 1977 (Control of Cadmium) Discharges 1985.
Local Government (Water Pollution) Act, 1977 (Control of Hexachlorocyclohexane and Mercury Discharges) Regulations 1986.

WASTE MANAGEMENT ACT 1996
FIRST SCHEDULE
CATEGORIES OF WASTE
(SECTION 4(1))

1. Production or consumption residues not otherwise specified in this Schedule.
2. Products which have not been manufactured in accordance with the specifications relating to them.
3. Products whose date for appropriate use has expired.
4. Materials spilled, lost or which have undergone any other mishap (including any materials contaminated as a result of any such mishap).
5. Materials contaminated or soiled as a result of planned actions.
6. Unusable parts.
7. Substances which no longer perform satisfactorily.
8. Residues of industrial processes.
9. Residues from pollution abatement processes.
10. Machining or finishing residues.
11. Residues from the extraction and processing of raw materials.
12. Adulterated materials.
13. Any materials, substances or products whose use is prohibited by or under any enactment.
14. Products for which the holder has no further use.
15. Contaminated materials, substances or products resulting from any remedial action taken with respect to land.
16. Any materials, substances or products which are not otherwise specified in the Schedule.

SECOND SCHEDULE
HAZARDOUS WASTE
(SECTION 4(2))
PART I

Categories of Generic Types of Hazardous Waste.

Category I Waste

1. Anatomical substances, hospital or other clinical waste.
2. Pharmaceutical, medicinal or veterinary compounds.
3. Wood preservatives.
4. Biocides or phyto-pharmaceutical substances.
5. Residue from substances employed as solvents.
6. Halogenated organic substances not employed as solvents, excluding inert polymerized materials.
7. Tempering salts containing cyanides.
8. Mineral oils or oily substances (including cutting sludges).
9. Mixtures or emulsions of oil and water or hydrocarbon and water.
10. Substances containing polychlorinated biphenyls or polychlorinated terphenyls (including dielectrics).
11. Tarry materials arising from refining, distillation or any pyrolytic treatment (including still bottoms).
12. Inks, dyes, pigments, paints, lacquers or varnishes.
13. Resins, latex, plasticizers, glues or adhesives.
14. Chemical substances arising from research and development or teaching activities (including laboratory residues) which are not identified or are new and whose effects on humans or the environment are not known.
15. Pyrotechnics or other explosive materials.
16. Photographic chemicals or processing materials.

17. Any material contaminated with any congener of polychlorinated dibenzo-furan.
18. Any material contaminated with any congener of polychlorinated dibenzo-p-dioxin.

Category II Waste:

19. Animal or vegetable soaps, fats or waxes.
20. Non-halogenated organic substances not employed as solvents.
21. Inorganic substances without metals or metal compounds.
22. Ashes or cinders.
23. Soil, sand or clay (including dredging spoils).
24. Non-cyanide tempering salts.
25. Metallic dust or powder.
26. Spent catalyst materials.
27. Liquids or sludges containing metal or metal compounds.
28. Residue (other than the substances mentioned in paragraphs 29, 30 and 33) from pollution control operations (including baghouse dusts).
29. Scrubber sludges.
30. Sludges from water purification plants.
31. Decarbonization residue.
32. Ion-exchange column residue.
33. Sewage sludges, untreated or unsuitable for use in agriculture.
34. Residue from cleaning of tanks or equipment.
35. Contaminated equipment.
36. Contaminated containers (including packaging and gas cylinders).
37. Batteries or other electrical cells.
38. Vegetable oils.
39. Materials resulting from the selective collection of waste from households.
40. Any other waste.

PART II

Constituents of Category II Waste which render it hazardous when it has the properties specified in PART III.

41. Beryllium or beryllium compounds.
42. Vanadium compounds.
43. Chromium (VI) compounds.
44. Cobalt compounds.
45. Nickel compounds.
46. Copper compounds.
47. Zinc compounds.
48. Arsenic or arsenic compounds.
49. Selenium or selenium compounds.
50. Silver compounds.
51. Cadmium or cadmium compounds.
52. Tin compounds.
53. Antimony or antimony compounds.
54. Tellurium or tellurium compounds.
55. Barium compounds, excluding barium sulphate.
56. Mercury or mercury compounds.
57. Thallium or thallium compounds.
58. Lead or lead compounds.
59. Inorganic sulphides.
60. Inorganic fluorine compounds, excluding calcium fluoride.
61. Inorganic cyanides.
62. Any of the following alkaline or alkaline earth metals namely, lithium, sodium, potassium, calcium, magnesium in uncombined form.
63. Acidic solutions or acids in solid form.
64. Basic solutions or basics in solid form.
65. Asbestos (dust or fibres).
66. Phosphorus: phosphorus compounds, excluding mineral phosphates.
67. Metal carbonyls.
68. Peroxides.
69. Chlorates.
70. Perchlorates.
71. Azides.
72. Polychlorinated biphenyls or polychlorinated terphenyls.
73. Pharmaceutical or veterinary compounds.
74. Biocides or phyto-pharmaceutical substances (including pesticides).
75. Infectious substances.
76. Creosotes.
77. Isocyanates or thiocyanates.
78. Organic cyanides (including nitriles).
79. Phenols or phenol compounds.
80. Halogenated solvents.
81. Organic solvents, including halogenated solvents.
82 Organohalogen compounds, excluding inert polymerized materials and other substances referred to in this Part.
83. Aromatic compounds; polycyclic and heterocyclic organic compounds.
84. Aliphatic amines.
85. Aromatic animes.
86. Ethers.
87. Substances of an explosive character, excluding those referred to elsewhere in this Part.
88. Sulphur organic compounds.

89. Any congener of polychlorinated dibenzo-furan.
90. Any congener of polychlorinated dibenzo-p-dioxin.
91. Hydrocarbons and their oxygen, nitrogen or sulphur compounds not otherwise referred to in this Part.

PART III

Properties of waste which render it hazardous.
There is set out in each paragraph of this Part a general term denoting a particular property of waste which renders it hazardous, followed by an explanation of such general term by reference to a description of substances or preparations which possess the particular property.

92. "Explosive": substances or preparations which may explode under the effect of flame or which are more sensitive to shocks or friction than dinitrobenzene.
93. "Oxidizing": substances or preparations which exhibit highly exothermic reactions when in contact with other substances, particularly flammable substances.
94. "Highly flammable":
    (a) liquid substances or preparations having a flash point below 21°C (including extremely flammable liquids), or
    (b) substances or preparations which may become hot and finally catch fire in contact with air at ambient temperature with out any application of energy, or
    (c) solid substances or preparations which may readily catch fire after brief contact with a source of ignition and which continue to burn or be consumed after removal of the source of ignition, or
    (d) gaseous substances or preparations which are flammable in air at normal temperature, or
    (e) substances or preparations which, in contact with water or damp air, evolve highly flammable gases in dangerous quantities.
95. "Flammable": liquid substances or preparations having a flash point of not less than 21°C and not more than 55°C.
96. "Irritant": non-corrosive substances or preparations which, through immediate, prolonged or repeated contact with the skin or mucous membrane, can cause inflammation.
97. "Harmful": substances or preparations which, if they are inhaled or ingested or if they penetrate the skin, may involve limited health risks.
98. "Toxic": substances or preparations (including very toxic substances and preparations) which, if they are inhaled, or ingested, or if they penetrate the skin, may cause serious, acute or chronic health risks or death.
99. "Carcinogenic": substances or preparations which, if they are inhaled or ingested or if they penetrate the skin, may induce cancer or increase its incidence.
100. "Corrosive": substances or preparations which may destroy living tissue on contact.
101. "Infectious": substances containing viable micro-organisms or their toxins which are known or reliably believed to cause disease in humans or other living organisms.
102. "Teratogenic": substances or preparations which, if they are inhaled or ingested or if they penetrate the skin, may induce non--hereditary congenital malformations or increase their incidence.
103. "Mutagenic": substances or preparations which, if they are inhaled or ingested or if they penetrate the skin, may induce hereditary genetic defects or increase their incidence.
104. "Ecotoxic" substances or preparations which present or may present immediate or delayed risks for one or more sectors of the environment.
105. "Residuary hazardous property":
    (a) substances or preparations which release toxic or very toxic gases in contact with water, air or an acid, or
    (b) substances or preparations capable by any means, after being disposed of, of yielding another substance which possesses any property referred to in this or any other paragraph of this Part.

THIRD SCHEDULE
WASTE DISPOSAL ACTIVITIES

(As amended, as indicated by [] below, by Regulation 5 of the EUROPEAN COMMUNITIES (AMENDMENT OF WASTE MANAGEMENT ACT 1996) REGULATIONS 1998 S.I. NO. 166 of 1998)

1. Deposit on, in or under land [(including land fill)].

2. Land treatment, including biodegradation of liquid or sludge discards in soil.
3. Deep injection of the soil, including injection of pumpable discards into wells, salt domes or naturally occurring repositories.
4. Surface impoundment, including placement of liquid or sludge discards into pits, ponds or lagoons.
5. Specially engineered landfill, including placement into lined discrete cells which are capped and isolated from one another and the environment.
6. Biological treatment not referred to elsewhere in this Schedule which results in final compounds or mixtures which are disposed of by means of any activity referred to in [paragraphs 1. to 10. of] this Schedule.
7. Physio-chemical treatment not referred to elsewhere in this Schedule which results in final compounds or mixtures which are disposed of by means of an activity referred to in [paragraphs 1. to 10. of] this Schedule [including evaporation, drying and calcination].
8. Incineration on land or at sea.
9. Permanent storage, including emplacement of containers in a mine.
10. Release of waste into a water body (including a seabed insertion).
11. Blending or mixture prior to submission to any activity referred to in [a preceding paragraph of] this Schedule.
12. Repackaging prior to submission to any activity referred to in [a preceding paragraph of] this Schedule.
13. Storage prior to submission to any activity referred to in [a preceding paragraph of] this Schedule, other than temporary storage, pending collection, on the premises where the waste concerned is produced.

FOURTH SCHEDULE
WASTE RECOVERY ACTIVITIES

(amended, as indicated by [] below, by Regulation 3 of the EUROPEAN COMMUNITIES (AMENDMENT OF WASTE MANAGEMENT ACT 1996) REGULATIONS, 1998 S.I. NO. 166 of 1998)

1. Solvent reclamation or regeneration.
2. Recycling or reclamation of organic substances which are not used as solvents [including composting and other biological transformation processes]
3. Recycling or reclamation of metals and metal compounds.
4. Recycling or reclamation of other inorganic materials.
5. Regeneration of acids or bases.
6. Recovery of components used for pollution abatement.
7. Recovery of components from catalysts.
8. Oil re-fining or other re-uses of oil.
9. Use of any waste principally as a fuel or other means to generate energy.
10. [The treatment of any waste on land] with a consequential benefit for an agricultural activity or ecological system...
11. Use of waste obtained from any activity referred to in a preceding paragraph to this Schedule.
12. Exchange of waste for submission to any activity referred to in a preceding paragraph of this Schedule.
13. Storage of waste intended for submission to any activity referred to in a preceding paragraph to this Schedule, other than temporary storage, pending collection, on the premises where such waste is produced.

EUROPEAN COMMUNITIES (ENVIRONMENTAL IMPACT ASSESSMENT) REGULATIONS 1989 (S.I. NO. 349 of 1989)

(as inserted by EUROPEAN COMMUNITIES (ENVIRONMENTAL IMPACT ASSESSMENT) REGULATIONS 1999 (S.I. NO. 93 of 1999))

FIRST SCHEDULE

DEVELOPMENT FOR THE PURPOSES OF THESE REGULATIONS

ARTICLE 24

PART I

1. A crude oil refinery (excluding undertakings manufacturing only lubricants from crude oil) or an installation for the gasification and liquefaction of 500 tonnes or more of coal or bituminous shale per day.

2. (a) A thermal power station or other combustion installation with a heat output of 300 mw or more.

(b) A nuclear power station or other nuclear reactor including the dismantling or decommissioning of such a power station or reactor (1) (except a research installation for the production and conversion of fissionable and fertile materials, whose maximum power does not exceed 1 kw continuous thermal load).

3. (a) All installations for the reprocessing of irradiated nuclear fuel.
   (b) Installations designed:
   - for the production or enrichment of nuclear fuel,
   - for the processing of irradiated nuclear fuel or high level radioactive waste,
   - for the final disposal of irradiated fuel,
   - solely for the final disposal of radioactive waste,
   - solely for the storage (planned for more than 10 years) of irradiated fuels or radioactive waste in a different site than the production site.

4. (a) Integrated works for the initial smelting of cast iron and steel.
   (b) Installations for the production of non-ferrous crude metals from ore, concentrates or secondary raw materials by metallurgical, chemical or electrolytic processes.

5. An installation for the extraction of asbestos or for the processing and transformation of asbestos or products containing asbestos:
   (a) in case the installation produces asbestos-cement products, where the annual production would exceed 20,000 tonnes of finished products,
   (b) in case the installation produces friction material, where the annual production would exceed 50 tonnes of finished products, or
   (c) in other cases, where the installation would utilise more than 200 tonnes of asbestos per year.

6. Integrated chemical installations, *i.e.* those installations for the manufacture on an industrial scale of substances using chemical conversion processes, in which several units are juxtaposed and are functionally linked to one another and which are:
   (a) for the production of basic organic chemicals,
   (b) for the production of basic inorganic chemicals,
   (c) for the production of phosphorus, nitrogen or potassium based fertilisers (simple or compound fertilisers),
   (d) for the production of basic plant health products and of biocides,
   (e) for the production of basic pharmaceutical products using a chemical or biological process,
   (f) for the production of explosives.

7. A line for long-distance railway traffic, or an airport (2) with a basic runway length of 2,100 metres or more.

8. (a) Inland waterways and ports for inland waterway traffic which permit the passage of vessels of over 1,350 tonnes.
   (b) Trading ports, piers for loading and unloading connected to land and outside ports (excluding ferry piers) which can take vessels of over 1,350 tonnes.

9. Waste disposal installations for the incineration, chemical treatment as defined in Annex 11A to Directive 75/442/EEC (3) under heading D9, or landfill of hazardous waste (*i.e.* waste to which Directive 91/689/EEC (4) applies).

10. Waste disposal installations for the incineration or chemical treatment as defined in Annex 11A to directive 75/442/EEC under heading D9, of non-hazardous waste with a capacity exceeding 100 tonnes per day.

11. Groundwater abstraction or artificial ground water recharge schemes, where the annual volume of water abstracted or recharged is equivalent to or exceeds 10 million cubic metres.

12. (a) Works for the transfer of water resources between river basins, where this transfer aims at preventing possible shortages of water and where the amount of water transferred exceeds 100 million cubic metres/year.
    (b) In all other cases, works for the transfer of water resources between river basins,

where the multi-annual average flow of the basin of abstraction exceeds 2,000 million cubic metres/year and where the amount of water transferred exceeds 5 per cent of this flow.

13. Waste water treatment plants with a capacity exceeding 150,000 population equivalent as defined in Article 2 point (6) of directive 91/271/EEC (5).

14. Extraction of petroleum and natural gas for commercial purposes where the amount extracted exceeds 500 tonnes/day in the case of petroleum and 500,000 m^3/day in the case of gas.

15. Dams and other installations designed for the holding back or permanent storage of water, where a new or additional amount of water held back or stored exceeds 10 million cubic metres.

16. Pipelines for the transport of gas, oil or chemicals with a diameter of more than 800mm and a length of more than 40km.

17. Installations for the intensive rearing of poultry or pigs with more than:
    (a) 85,000 places for broilers, 60,000 places for hens;
    (b) 3,000 places for production pigs (over 30 kg); or
    (c) 900 places for sows.

18. Industrial plants for the
    (a) production of pulp from timber or similar fibrous materials;
    (b) production of paper and board with a production capacity exceeding 200 tonnes per day.

19. Quarries and open-cast mining where the surface of the site exceeds 25 hectares, or peat extraction, where the surface of the site exceeds 150 hectares.

20. Construction of overhead electrical power lines with a voltage of 220 kV or more and a length of more than 15 km.

21. Installation for storage of petroleum, petrochemical, or chemical products with a capacity of 200,000 tonnes or more.

(1) Nuclear power stations and other nuclear reactors cease to be such an installation when all nuclear fuel and other radioactively contaminated elements have been removed permanently from the installation site.

(2) For the purpose of this Directive "airport" means airports which comply with the definition in the 1944 Chicago Convention for setting up the International Civil Aviation Organisation (Annex IV).
(3) O.J. L194, July 25,, 1995, p.39. Directive as amended by Commission Decision 94/3/EC (OJ L 5, January 7, 1994, p.15).
(4) O.J. L337, December 31, 1991, p.20. Directive as last amended by Directive 94/31 EC (O.J. L 168, July 2,1994, p.28).
(5) O.J. L135, June 30, 1991, p.40. Directive as last amended by the 1994 Act of Accession.

PART II

1. Agriculture, Silviculture and Aquaculture
    (a) Projects for the restructuring of rural land holdings, where the area to be restructured would be greater than 100 hectares.
    (b) The use of uncultivated land or semi-natural areas for intensive agricultural purposes, where the area to be used for such purposes would be greater than 100 hectares.
    (c) Water management projects for agriculture, including irrigation and land drainage projects, where the catchment area involved would be greater than 1,000 hectares, or where more than 20 hectares of wetland would be affected.
    (d) (i) Initial afforestation, where the area involved, either on its own or taken together with any adjacent land planted by or on behalf of the applicant within the previous three years, would result in a total area planted exceeding 70 hectares, and for the purposes of this sub paragraph an area, other than an area planted before October 1, 1996, shall be deemed to be adjacent if its nearest point lies within 500 metres of any part of the area involved.
    (ii) Replacement of broadleaf high forest by conifer species, where the area

involved would be greater than 10 hectares.

(iii) Deforestation for the purpose of conversion to another type of land use, where the area to be deforested would be greater than 10 ha of natural woodlands or 70 hectares of conifer forest.

(e) (i) Installations for intensive rearing of poultry not included in Part I of this Schedule which would have more than 40,000 places for poultry.

(ii) Installations for the intensive rearing of pigs not included in Part I of this Schedule which would have more than 2,000 places for production pigs (over 30 kg) in a finishing unit, more than 400 places for sows in a breeding unit or more than 200 places for sows in an integrated unit.

(f) Seawater fish breeding installations with an output which would exceed 100 tonnes per annum; all fish breeding installations consisting of cage rearing in lakes; all fish breeding installations upstream of drinking water intakes; other freshwater fish breeding installations which would exceed 1 million smolts and with less than 1 cubic metre per second per 1 million smolts low flow diluting water.

(g) Reclamation of land from the sea, where the area of reclaimed land would be greater than 10 hectares.

2. Extractive Industry

(a) Peat extraction not included in Part I of this Schedule which would involve a new or extended area of 50 hectares.

(b) Extraction of stone, gravel, sand or clay, where the area of extraction would be greater than 5 hectares.

(c) All extraction of minerals within the meaning of the Minerals Development Acts, 1940 to 1995.

(d) Extraction of stone, gravel, sand or clay by marine dredging (other than maintenance dredging), where the area involved would be greater than 5 hectares or, in the case of fluvial dredging (other than maintenance dredging), where the length of river involved would be greater than 500 metres.

(e) All geothermal drilling and drilling for the storage of nuclear waste material; drilling, other than test drilling for water supplies, where the expected supply would exceed 2 million cubic metres per annum.

(f) All surface industrial installations for the extraction of coal, petroleum (excluding natural gas), ores, or bituminous shale not included in Part I of this Schedule.

(g) All extraction of petroleum (excluding natural gas) not included in Part I of this Schedule.

(h) All on shore extraction of natural gas and offshore extraction of natural gas (where the extraction would take place within 10 kilometres of the shoreline) not included in Part I of this Schedule.

3. Energy Industry

(a) Industrial installations for the production of electricity, steam and hot water not included in Part I of this Schedule with a heat output of 300 mega watts or more.

(b) Industrial installations for carrying gas, steam and hot water with a potential heat output of 300 megawatts or more, or transmission of electrical energy by overhead cables not included in Part I of this Schedule, where the voltage would be 200 kV or more.

(c) Installations for surface storage of natural gas, where the storage capacity would exceed 200 tonnes.

(d) Installations for underground storage of combustible gases, where the storage capacity would exceed 200 tonnes.

(e) Installations for the surface storage of fossil fuels, where the storage capacity would exceed 100,000 tonnes.

(f) Installations for the industrial briquetting of coal and lignite, where the production capacity would exceed 150 tonnes per day.

(g) Installations for the processing and storage of radioactive waste not included in Part I of this Schedule.

(h) Installations for hydroelectric energy production with an output of 20 megawatts or more, or where the new or extended superficial area of water impounded would be 30 hectares or more, or where there would be a 30 per cent change in the maximum, minimum or mean flows in the main river channel.

(i) Installations for the harnessing of wind

power for energy production (wind farms) with more than 5 turbines or having a total output greater than 5 MW.

4. Production and processing of metals
   (a) All installations for the production of pig iron or steel (primary or secondary fusion) including continuous casting.
   (b) Installations for the processing of ferrous metals:
      (i) hot-rolling mills and smitheries with hammers, where the production area would be greater than 500 square metres,
      (ii)application of protective fused metal coats, where the production area would be greater than 100 square metres.
   (c) Ferrous metal foundries with a batch capacity of 5 tonnes or more or where the production area would be greater than 500 metres.
   (d) Installations for the smelting, including the alloyage, of non-ferrous metals, excluding precious metals, including recovered products (refining foundry casting, etc.), where the melting capacity would exceed 0.5 tonnes or where the production area would be greater than 500 square metres.
   (e) Installations for surface treatment of metals and plastic materials using an electrolytic or chemical process, where the production area would be greater than 100 square metres.
   (f) All installations for manufacture and assembly of motor vehicles or manufacture of motor-vehicle engines.
   (g) Shipyards, where the area would be 5 hectares or more, or with capacity for vessels of 10,000 tonnes or more (deadweight).
   (h) All installations for the construction of aircraft with a seating capacity exceeding 10 passengers.
   (i) Manufacture of railway equipment, where the production area would be greater than 100 square metres.
   (j) Swaging by explosives, where the floor area would be greater than 100 square metres.
   (k) All installations for the roasting and sintering of metallic ores.

5. Mineral Industry
   (a) All coke ovens (dry coal distillation).
   (b) All installations for the manufacture of cement.
   (c) All installations for the production of asbestos and the manufacture of asbestos based products not included in Part I of this Schedule.
   (d) Installations for the manufacture of glass, including glass fibre, where the production capacity would exceed 5,000 tonnes per annum.
   (e) All installations for smelting mineral substances including the production of mineral fibres.
   (f) Manufacture of ceramic products by burning, particularly roofing tiles, bricks, refractory bricks, tiles, stoneware or porcelain with a production capacity exceeding 75 tonnes per day, and/or with a kiln capacity exceeding 4 cubic metres and with a setting density per kiln exceeding 300 kg per cubic metre.

6. Chemical Industry (development not included in Part I of this Schedule)
   (a) Installations for treatment of intermediate products and production of chemicals using a chemical or biological process.
   (b) All installations for production of pesticides and pharmaceutical products, paints and varnishes, elastomers and peroxides using a chemical or biological process.
   (c) Storage facilities for petroleum, where the storage capacity would exceed 50,000 tonnes.
   (d) Storage facilities for petrochemical and chemical products, where such facilities are isolated storage to which the provisions of Articles 9, 11 and 13 of Council Directive 96/82/EC apply.

7. Food Industry
   (a) Installations for manufacture of vegetable and animal oils and fats, where the capacity for processing raw materials would exceed 40 tonnes per day.
   (b) Installations for packing and canning of animal and vegetable products, where the capacity for processing raw materials would exceed 100 tonnes per day.
   (c) Installations for manufacture of dairy products, where the processing capacity

would exceed 50 million gallons of milk equivalent per annum.

(d) Installations for commercial brewing and distilling; installations for malting, where the production capacity would exceed 100,000 tonnes per annum.

(e) Installations for confectionery and syrup manufacture, where the production capacity would exceed 100,000 tonnes per annum.

(f) Installations for the slaughter of animals, where the daily capacity would exceed 1,500 units and where units have the following equivalents:
1 sheep = 1 unit
1 pig = 2 units
1 head of cattle = 5 units.

(g) All industrial starch manufacturing installations.

(h) All fish-meal and fish-oil factories.

(i) All sugar factories.

8. Textile, leather, wood and paper industries

(a) All installations for the production of paper and board not included in Part I of this Schedule.

(b) Plants for the pre-treatment (operations such as washing, bleaching, mercerisation or dyeing of fibres or textiles) where the treatment capacity would exceed 10 tonnes per day.

(c) Plants for the tanning of hides and skins, where the treatment capacity would exceed 100 skins per day.

(d) Cellulose-processing and production installations, where the production capacity would exceed 10,000 tonnes per annum.

9. Rubber Industry

Installations for manufacture and treatment of elastomer based products, where the production capacity would exceed 10,000 tonnes per annum.

10. Infrastructure Projects

(a) Industrial estate development projects, where the area would exceed 15 hectares.

(b) (i) Construction of more than 500 dwelling units.

(ii) Construction of car-parks providing more than 400 spaces.

(iii) Construction of shopping centres with a gross floor space exceeding 10,000 square metres (calculated in accordance with article 100(2) of the Local Government (Planning and Development) Regulations 1994 (S.I. No. 86 of 1994)).

(iv) Urban development (other than that referred to in sub-paragraphs (i) to (iii)) which would involve an area greater than 2 hectares in the case of a business district, 10 hectares in the case of other parts of a built-up area, and 20 hectares elsewhere.

(In this paragraph "business district" means a district within a city or town in which the predominant land use is retail or commercial use.)

(c) All construction of railways and intermodal transhipment facilities and of intermodal terminals not included in Part I of this Schedule which would exceed 15 hectares in area.

(d) All airfields not included in Part I of this Schedule with paved runways which would exceed 800 metres in length.

(e) New or extended harbours and port installations, including fishing harbours, not included in Part I of this Schedule, where the area, or additional area, of water enclosed would be 20 hectares or more, or which would involve the reclamation of 5 hectares or more of land, or which would involve the construction of additional quays exceeding 500 metres in length.

(f) (i) Inland waterways construction not included in Part I of this Schedule which would extend over a length exceeding 2km.

(ii) Canalisation and flood relief works, where the immediate contributing sub-catchment of the proposed works (i.e. the difference between the contributing catchments at the upper and lower extent of the works) would exceed 1,000 hectares or where more than 20 hectares of wetland would be affected or where the length of river channel on which works are proposed would be greater than 2km.

(g) Dams and other installations not included in Part I of this Schedule which are designed to hold water or store it on a long term basis, where the new or extended area of water impounded would be 30 hectares or more.

(h) All tramways, elevated and underground railways, suspended lines or similar lines of a particular type, used exclusively or mainly for passenger transport.

(i) (I) Oil pipelines and associated installations not included in Part I of this Schedule, where the length of the new pipeline would exceed 40 km.

(II) Gas pipelines and associated installations not included in Part I of this Schedule, where the design pressure would exceed 16 bar and the length of new pipeline would exceed 40 kilometres.

(j) Installation of overground aqueducts which would have a diameter of 1,000 millimetres or more and a length of 500 metres or more.

(k) Coastal work to combat erosion and maritime works capable of altering the coast through the construction, for example, of dikes, moles, jetties and other sea defence works, where the length of coastline on which works would take place would exceed 1 km, but excluding the maintenance and reconstruction of such works or works required for emergency purposes.

(l) Groundwater abstraction and artificial groundwater recharge schemes not included in Part I of this Schedule where the average annual volume of water would exceed 2 million cubic metres.

(m) Works for the transfer of water resources between river basins not included in Part I of this Schedule where the annual volume of water abstracted or recharged would exceed 2 million cubic metres.

11. Other Projects

(a) All permanent racing and test tracks for motorised vehicles.

(b) Installations for the disposal of waste with an annual intake greater than 25,000 tonnes not included in Part I of this Schedule.

(c) Waste water treatment plants with a capacity greater than 10,000 population equivalent as defined in Article 2 point (6) of Directive 91/271/EEC not included in Part I of this Schedule.

(d) Sludge-deposition sites where the expected annual deposition is 5,000 tonnes of sludge (wet).

(e) Storage of scrap iron, including scrap vehicles where the site area would be greater than 5 hectares.

(f) Test benches for engines, turbines or reactors where the floor area would exceed 500 square metres.

(g) All installations for the manufacture of artificial mineral fibres.

(h) All installations for the manufacture, packing, loading or placing in cartridges of gunpowder and explosives or for the recovery or destruction of explosive substances.

(i) All knackers' yards in built-up areas.

12. Tourism and leisure

(a) Ski-runs, ski-lifts and cable cars where the length would exceed 500 metres and associated developments.

(b) Sea water marinas where the number of berths would exceed 300 and fresh water marinas where the number of berths would exceed 100.

(c) Holiday villages which would consist of more than 100 holiday homes outside built-up areas; hotel complexes outside built-up areas which would have an area of 20 ha or more or an accommodation capacity exceeding 300 bedrooms.

(d) Permanent camp sites and caravan sites where the number of pitches would be greater than 100.

(e) Theme parks occupying an area greater than 5 ha.

13. Changes, extensions, development and testing

(a) Any change or extension of development which would:

(i) Result in the development being of a class listed in Part I or paragraphs 1 to 12 of Part II of this Schedule.

(ii) Result in an increase in size greater than:

– 25%, or
– an amount equal to 50% of the appropriate threshold,

whichever is the greater.

(b) Projects in Part I undertaken exclusively or mainly for the development and testing of new methods or products and not used for more than two years.

(In this paragraph, an increase in size is calculated in terms of the unit of measure of the appropriate threshold.)

SECOND SCHEDULE

INFORMATION TO BE CONTAINED IN AN ENVIRONMENTAL IMPACT STATEMENT

Article 25

1. (a) A description of the proposed development comprising information on the site, design and size of the proposed development.
   (b) A description of the measures envisaged in order to avoid, reduce and, if possible, remedy significant adverse effects.
   (c) The data required to identify and assess the main effects which the development is likely to have on the environment.
   (d) An outline of the main alternatives studied by the developer and an indication of the main reasons for his choice, taking into account the environmental effects.

2. Further information, by way of explanation or amplification of the information referred to in paragraph 1, on the following matters:-
   (a) (i) a description of the physical characteristics of the whole proposed development and the land-use requirements during the construction and operational phases;
   (ii) a description of the main characteristics of the production processes, for instance, nature and quantity of the materials used;
   (iii) an estimate, by type and quantity, of expected residues and emissions (including water, air and soil pollution, noise, vibration, light, heat and radiation) resulting from the operation of the proposed development;
   (b) a description of the aspects of the environment likely to be significantly affected by the proposed development, including in particular:
   - human beings, fauna and flora,
   - soil, water, air, climatic factors and the landscape,
   - material assets, including the architectural and archaeological heritage and the cultural heritage,
   - the inter-relationship between the above factors;
   (c) a description of the likely significant effects (including direct, indirect, secondary, cumulative, short, medium and long-term, permanent and temporary, positive and negative) of the proposed development on the environment resulting from:
   - the existence of the proposed development,
   - the use of natural resources,
   - the emission of pollutants, the creation of nuisances and the elimination of waste,

   and a description of the forecasting methods used to assess the effects on the environment;
   (d) an indication of any difficulties (technical deficiencies or lack of know-how) encountered by the developer in compiling the required information.

THIRD SCHEDULE
CRITERIA SPECIFIED FOR THE PURPOSE OF ARTICLE 27

1. Characteristics of proposed development

The characteristics of proposed development, in particular:
- the size of the proposed development,
- the cumulation with other proposed development,
- the use of natural resources,
- the production of waste,
- pollution and nuisances,
- the risk of accidents having regard to substances or technologies used.

2. Location of proposed development

The environmental sensitivity of geographical areas likely to be affected by proposed development, having regard in particular to:
- the existing land use,
- the relative abundance, quality and regenerative capacity of natural resources in the area,
- the absorption capacity of the natural environment, paying particular attention

to the following areas :
(a) wetlands,
(b) coastal zones,
(c) mountain and forest areas,
(d) nature reserves and parks,
(e) areas classified or protected under legislation, including special protection areas designated pursuant to Directives 79/409/EEC and 92/43/EEC,
(f) areas in which the environmental quality standards laid down in legislation of the EU have already been exceeded,
(g) densely populated areas,
(h) landscapes of historical, cultural or archaeological significance.

3. Characteristics of potential impacts
The potential significant effects of proposed development in relation to criteria set out under paragraphs 1 and 2 above, and having regard in particular to:
- the extent of the impact (geographical area and size of the affected population),
- the transfrontier nature of the impact,
- the magnitude and complexity of the impact,
- the probability of the impact,
- the duration, frequency and reversibility of the impact.

WASTE MANAGEMENT (PERMIT) REGULATIONS 1998 (S.I. No. 165 of 1998)

FIRST SCHEDULE
ACTIVITIES TO BE PERMITTED OR REGISTERED.

PART I
ACTIVITIES SUBJECT TO WASTE PERMIT - ARTICLE 4.

The carrying on by a person (other than a local authority) at a facility (other than a facility located in whole or in part in an area which is not within the functional area of a local authority) of any of the following activities (provided that the activity is not an activity which is carried on in, or adjacent to, a facility at which a licensable activity is being carried on) :
1. The incineration of waste (other than (*qv*) hazardous or hospital waste) at a facility the capacity of which is equal to or less than 1 tonne per hour;
2. The recovery of scrap metal or other metal waste;
3. the dismantling or recovery of vehicles;
4. the recovery of waste which is composed of or contains mercury or its compounds (including electric lamps, light bulbs and florescent tubes);
5. the recovery of waste (other than hazardous waste) at a facility (other than a facility for the composting of waste where the amount of compost and waste held at the facility exceeds 1000 cubic metres at any time);
6. the disposal of waste (other than hazardous waste) at a facility (other than a landfill facility) where the annual intake does not exceed 5,000 tonnes per annum.

PART II - ACTIVITIES BY LOCAL AUTHORITY - ARTICLES 4 AND 21.

The recovery of waste by a local authority other than:
(a) recovery of waste (at) a facility where the annual intake exceeds 5,000 tonnes, or
(b) the composting of waste at a facility where the amount of waste and compost held at the facility at any time exceeds 1,000 tonnes.

PART III
ACTIVITIES SUBJECT TO REGISTRATION - ARTICLE 21

The temporary storage, on the premises where it is produced, of hazardous waste where the quantities being stored at any one time exceeds -
(a) in the case of liquid waste, 25,000 litres, or
(b) in the case of non-liquid waste, 40 cubic metres,
other than such storage carried on in on, or adjacent to, a facility at which a licensable activity is being carried on or a facility connected with a facility in respect of which a licence or a revised licence under Part IV of the Act of 1992 is in force where such storage is subject to the said licence or revised licence.

SECOND SCHEDULE
CONDITIONS IN RESPECT OF REGISTERED ACTIVITIES - ARTICLE 4

(a) The activity concerned shall not cause, or be likely to cause, (*qv*) environmental pollution.

(b) Any (*qv*) emissions from the activity concerned will not result in the contravention of any relevant standard, including any standard for an (*qv*) environmental medium, or any relevant (*qv*) emission limit value, prescribed under any enactment.

WILDLIFE ACT 1976

SCHEDULES

THIRD SCHEDULE

SPECIES OF BIRD EXCLUDED (SUBJECT TO SECTION 22(2)) FROM SECTIONS 19 AND 22

Bullfinch
Carrion Crow
Greater Black-backed Gull
Herring Gull
Hooded (Grey) Crow
House Sparrow
Jackdaw
Jay
Lesser Black-backed Gull
Magpie
Pigeons, including Wood Pigeons, but not including carrier pigeons, racing homing pigeons or doves
Rook
Starling

FOURTH SCHEDULE
FAUNA REFERRED TO IN SECTION 22(6) OR 23(8)

PART I

SPECIES OF PROTECTED WILD BIRDS REFERRED TO IN SECTION 22(6)

Buzzards
Eagles
Falcons
Harriers
Hawks
Kites
Osprey
Owls

PART II

SPECIES OF PROTECTED WILD ANIMALS REFERRED TO IN SECTION 23(8)
Pine Marten
Red Deer
Seals
Whales

FIFTH SCHEDULE
ANIMALS REFERRED TO IN SECTION 23

LAND MAMMALS

Badger
Bat species
Deer species
Hare species
Hedgehog
Otter
Pine Marten
Red Squirrel

MARINE MAMMALS

Dolphin species
Porpoise species
Seal species
Whale species

AMPHIBIANS

Natterjack Toad

EUROPEAN COMMUNITIES (NATURAL HABITATS) REGULATIONS 1997 (S.I. No. 94 of 1997)

FIRST SCHEDULE
FLORA AND FAUNA

PART I

REGULATIONS 22, 23

1. Mammals
   lutra lutra (Otter)
   Cetacean Species
   Bat species

2. Amphibians
   Bufo calamita (Natterjack toad)

PART II

REGULATIONS 7, 24, 25

1. Mammals
   Martes martes (Pine marten)
   Lepus timidus (Irish hare)
   Halichoerus grypus (Grey seal)
   Phoca vitinula (Common seal)

2. Amphibians
   Rana temporaria (Frog)

3. Fish
   Lampetra fluviatilis (Lampern)
   Coregonus autumnalis (Pollan)
   Alosa alosa (Allis shads)
   Alosa fallax (Twaite shad)
   Salmon salar (Salmon) (only in freshwater)

4. Molluscs
   Helix pomatia (Edible snail)
   Margaritifera margaritifera (Freshwater pearl mussel)

5. Crustaceans
   Austropotamopius pallipes (White-clawed crayfish)

6. Lichens
   Cladonia subgenus Cladina (Reindeer moss)

7. Mosses
   Leoucobryum Glaucum
   All Sphagna

8. Ferns and relatives
   Lycopodium spp. (Clubmosses)

SECOND SCHEDULE

PART I

ENACTMENTS REFERRED TO IN REGULATION 31

Regulation 31(7)

Number and Year Short Title

No. 6 of 1965 Air Navigation and Transport Act, 1965.
No. 3 of 1945 Arterial Drainage Act, 1945.
No. 14 of 1996 Dumping at Sea Act, 1996.
No. 15 of 1959 Fisheries (Consolidation) Act, 1959.
No. 1 of 1980 Fisheries Act, 1980.
No. 12 of 1933 Foreshore Act, 1933.
No. 17 of 1992 Foreshore Act, 1992.
No. 30 of 1976 Gas Act, 1976.
No. 9 of 1946 Harbours Act, 1946.
No. 31 of 1940 Minerals Development Act, 1940.
No. 12 of 1979 Minerals Development Act, 1979.
No. 15 of 1995 Minerals Development Act, 1995
No. 7 of 1960 Petroleum and Other Minerals Development Act, 1960.

PART II

ENACTMENTS REFERRED TO IN REGULATION 32

REGULATION 32(7)

Number and Year Short Title

No. 6 of 1987 Air Pollution Act, 1987
No. 7 of 1992 Environmental Protection Agency Act, 1992
No. 21 of 1990 Local Government (Water Pollution) (Amendment) Act, 1990
No. 1 of 1977 Local Government (Water Pollution) (Amendment) Act, 1977

EUROPEAN COMMUNITIES (PROCESSING OF MAMMALIAN ANIMAL WASTE) REGULATIONS 1998 (S.I. No. 62 of 1998)

SCHEDULE

The minimum parameters for the processing of mammalian animal waste, excluding fats, are

MAXIMUM PARTICLE SIZE: 50 mm

TEMPERATURE: > 133 degrees centigrade

TIME: 20 minutes

PRESSURE (ABSOLUTE): 3 bar.

Processing may be carried out in a batch or continuous system.

Annex

WILDLIFE (AMENDMENT) BILL, 1999

AN ACT TO AMEND AND EXTEND THE WILDLIFE ACT, 1976,
AND TO PROVIDE FOR CONNECTED MATTERS
as initiated,
presented by the Minister for Arts, Heritage, Gaeltacht and the Islands, 29 June 1999"

INTRODUCTION

The Wildlife (Amendment) Bill, 1999 (in this article referred to as "the WLAB 1999"), introduced to the Dáil on the 29th June 1999, amends the Wildlife Act, 1976, number 39 of 1976 (in this article referred to as "the Act" or "the Principal Act"). Most of the preamble to the Act is now very old fashioned and has been superseded by subsequent legislation, notably by the abolition of the almost totally moribund Wildlife Advisory Council by the Heritage Act 1995 and the incorporation of its important functions into the Heritage Council. However the bold statement with which the Wildlife Act preamble commences still has a ring to it "An Act for the conservation of wildlife (including game) and for that purpose to protect certain wild creatures and flora." Another part of the preamble declares "to enable reserves and refuges for wildlife to be established." It is with the extension of this concept of reserves and refuges for wildlife into what will now be known as natural heritage areas, an area described in the WLAB 1999 as being worthy of conservation of one or more species, communities, habitats, landforms or geological or geomorphological features, or for its diversity of natural attributes, that the WLAB is primarily concerned and with the extension of the new thinking behind natural heritage areas and the application of that thinking to the existing reserves and refuges under the Act. *See:* RESERVES AND REFUGES

If you leave aside the innovatary sections, which are dealt with immediately hereunder, the WLAB 1999 is mainly concerned with amendments to the Act to bring it into conformity with contemporary EC attitudes to wildlife protection. The approximate ratio of new or innovatory law to amendments is 2 to 7.

One wonders what brings the WLAB out of the cupboard now. It does not of itself remove any of the pressures being brought to bear by the EC on Ireland at the moment which has mainly to do with the implementation of existing legislation e.g.the Habitats Directive
See: HABITATS DIRECTIVE.

This Bill has been gestating for over 15 years and has been urgently required and its passing vociferously urged by environmentalists for at least 10 of those years. It has been in the form presently presented except for very minor adjustments for at least 4 of those years. The concept of natural heritage areas is in existence under the title Areas of Scientific Interest since the 70s after the great Foras Forbartha survey undertaken, inter alia, by David Cabot. The Cites Convention was in 1973.

Why now?

There was a minor crisis in wildlife in 1998 following action taken by the National Association of Regional Game Councils against the Ministers responsible for wildlife and tourism which arose out of a practice which had become common of the issue of firearms certificates, purportedly under section 29 of the Act, to non-Irish nationals without any or any proper inquiry by the Garda Siochána. The State lost this action which spawned a pretty shoddy piece of emergency legislation, the Firearms (Temporary Provisions) Act 1998 which allowed the practice to continue subject to conditions for a limited period of time. The matter must be addressed before the middle of July 2000.
See: FIREARMS, LICENCE TO HUNT WITH.

Arising out this mini emergency if you group together -

(a) the licensing of "commercial shoot operators" under section 36 of the WLAB 1999,
(b) the removal of the words "by individuals" from sections 24 and 25 of the Act by sections 33 and 34 respectively of the WLAB 1999 which would permit innumerable persons to make use of open seasons orders under sections 24 and 25, and
(c) the new wide powers given by section 37

of the WLAB 1999 to the Minister to make regulations under section 28(2A)(c) dealing with restrictions on hunting with firearms certain exempted wild mammals and protected wild birds,

you have a perfect background for regulating for an entirely new and more flexible system of licensing firearms which would be helpful to tourism but inimical to wildlife.

One hopes there were other good reasons which prompted the introduction of the Bill.

INNOVATORY MEASURES

(1) ACQUISITION OF LAND AND RIGHTS, APPOINTMENT OF ARBITRATOR.

Part III, Lands and Waters, Chapter I, sections 10, 11, 12, 13 and 14 of the WLAB 1999 partially replacing sections 55(2), 55(7), 60, 61 and 63 of the Act.

This was necessary to separate connected powers under the old regime when wildlife and forestry were part of the same Ministry of Lands and is dealt with under Objective (g) hereunder. The only sections wholly repealed are sections 60, 61 and 63.

(2) NATURAL HERITAGE AREAS

Part III, Chapter II, sections 29 to 35 of the WLAB 1999.

Although this is entirely new it closely associated with the fundamental wildlife concepts in "Reserves and Refuges", Part II, Chapter II, sections 15 to 18 of the Act.
See: RESERVES AND REFUGES.

(3) ERECTION OF NOTICES ON NATURAL HERITAGE AREAS AND ON RESERVES AND REFUGES.

Section 25 of the WLAB 1999 provides for the erection of notices on natural heritage areas under the WLAB 1999 and Reserves and Refuges under the Act. It is modelled on provisions which first appeared at Regulation 11 of the EC (Natural Habitats) Regulations, 1997 (S.I.No. 94 of 1997).
See: ERECTION OF NOTICES.

(4) EXCLUSION OF CERTAIN ANIMALS FROM THE PROVISIONS OF THE ACT.

Section 32 of the WLAB 1999 permits the Minister to exclude certain species of fish and aquatic invertebrates from the Act and becomes necessary because of the new definition of "wild animal" appearing at section 6(1)(n) of the WLAB 1999.

(5) REGULATION OF COMMERCIAL SHOOT OPERATORS

Section 36 of the WLAB 1999 provides for this entirely new concept in licensing in wildlife legislation.

(6) REGULATION AND CONTROL OF WILDLIFE DEALING, CITES CONVENTION AND CITES REGULATION

Section 54 of the WLAB 1999 substitutes an entirely new section for section 48 of the Act. Section 59 of the WLAB 1999 inserts a new and important section in the Act, section 53A.

There are also amendments to the Act by the Bill under the heading of regulation and control of wildlife dealing as follows:

Section 52 amends section 45, section 53 amends section 46, section 55 amends section 49, section 56 amends section 51 and section 57 amends section 52.

In fact this part of the WLAB 1999, Part V, makes such substantial changes to Part III of the Act, including the formal recognition of the CITES Convention and the implementation of the CITES Regulations, that it would have been as well to repeal the entire of Part III and substitute an entirely new Part. These matters are dealt with under Objective (d) hereunder.
See: WILDLIFE DEALING.

The Fisheries (Amendment) Act 1994 successfully and with some degree of grace grafted entire new Parts by substitution into the Fisheries (Consolidation) Act 1959 where drastic pruning was called for, notably Part X of the 1959 Act.
See: CERTIFICATE OF FITNESS.

(7) INSPECTION OF LAND

Section 67 of the WLAB 1999 replaces section 68 of the Act which is in turn repealed by section 5(c) of the Bill. Section 68 became impossible to operate because of the division between the functions of the Minister in relation to forestry and to wildlife which is explained under Objective (g) hereunder.

OBJECTIVES

The excellent explanatory memorandum to the WLAB 1999 specifies the main objectives of the WLAB to be, to -

(a) provide statutory protection for Natural Heritage Areas (NHAs);

This is dealt with in Part III Chapter II sections 15 to 24.

In Part I section 6(1) the following definitions are also appropriate.
(c) "conservation"
See: CONSERVATION

This definition and that of "natural heritage areas", given infra, are closely allied. See also section 16(6) which sets out the scientific advice to which the Minister must have regard when commencing the procedure for making a natural heritage order.
(h) "geology", which forms part the new "natural heritage area" definition, is defined for the first time in the context of wildlife.
(h) "geomorphology" ditto.
(h) "habitat" which is defined for the first time in the context of wildlife, is closely allied with both "conservation" and "natural heritage area",
(k) "natural heritage area",

"natural heritage order",

"nature reserve"

See: RESERVES AND REFUGES

The definition of "nature reserve" is post hoc the undefined but extensive use of the phrase in the Act, particularly sections 15 and 16. The WLAB 1999 attempts in sections 26 and 27 to bring sections 15 and 16 forward, so to speak, to 1999 so that they are made to resemble the 1999 conservation concept behind natural heritage areas. It is a complicated but not entirely successful device.
"species" is an important definition under any heading. The definition in section 1(2) of the Act, which has been repealed by the substitution of the new definition, read "includes subspecies and hybrids" which was to say the least unhelpful. The new definition is excellent. Interestingly the Oxford Concise Dictionary defines "species" in its biological meaning as "a category in the system of classification of living organisms consisting of similar individuals capable of exchanging genes or interbreeding." or a Allaby's Concise Dictionary of Biology defines "species""(sing. and pl.) Literally, a group of organisms that resemble one another closely"
See: RESERVES AND REFUGES.

It is important to place this new environmental designation in the context of existing areas of conservation. It is the fourth statutory designation coming after establishment orders (section 15), recognition orders (section 16), designation orders (section 17) and management agreements (section 18). It is the seventh designation if you include the orders made under the Birds Directive and under the Habitats Directive.

It is a great disappointment that the legislators did not introduce natural heritage areas to the Act by inserting the entire of sections 15 to 24 as subsections of a composite section 17A which would come between section 17, designation orders, and section 18, management agreements. At a later stage in the Act the important new section dealing with the regulation of the import and export of wildlife and the CITES Convention and Regulations is inserted by section 59 of the WLAB 1999 as section 53A immediately after the sections dealing with import and export of wildlife.

The portion of the proposed new legislation dealing with natural heritage areas to which conservationists have taken the greatest exception is the definition of "works" in section 15 of the WLAB 1999 the use of which in the rest of this Part effectively and unreservedly excludes development by local authorities from the restrictions on works on a site which has been designated a natural heritage area under section 18. The restriction on "works" without the consent of the Minister and the penalties for contravention is the main method of enforcement in Chapter II. The effect of this is that local authorities can develop without reference to a natural heritage order. There are, of course, other restraints on such development by local authorities.

See:(ENVIRONMENTAL IMPACT ASSESSMENT) EUROPEAN COMMUNITIES, REGULATIONS 1989.

This point of view is expressed forcefully in the Autumn 1989 edition of WINGS, the effective and well informed organ of Bird Watch Ireland, by their countryside officer John Murphy.

Although the legislation dealing with Reserves and Refuges under sections 15, 16, 17 and 18 of the Act and Special Protection Areas under the EC (Conservation of Wildbirds) Regulations, 1985 (S.I.No. 291 of 1985) contain no such exclusion for the benefit of local authorities, the legislation dealing with natural habitats, EC (Natural Habitats) Regulations, 1997 (S.I.No. 94 of 1997) does. It does so in exactly the same manner as is provided in the definition of "works" in Part II of the WLAB 1999 to exclude "works" by local authorities. The definition of "operations or activities" at Regulation 2(1) of the 1997 Regulations, which stand in the same position to special areas of conservation under those Regulations as do "works" to natural heritage areas under the WLAB 1999, excludes operations or activities by local authorities. *See:* OPERATIONS OR ACTIVITIES.

(b) improve a number of measures, or introduce new ones to enhance the conservation of wildlife species and their habitats;

This is an overall aspiration and none the worse for that.

For the first time the WLAB 1999 at section 6(1)(n) defines "wild animal". The Act failed to define "wild animal" for the same reason that its definition of "wild bird" is merely an addendum "includes the unflown young of a wild bird" as neither term really require, or did not in 1976 seem to require, definition. A definition of something which is universally understood can only lead to absolute confusion. However, in the context of fishery protection and wildlife protection and the desirability of bringing the two disciplines together it was necessary to have a definition which explained the extent to which fish become flesh, or, rather, the extent to which the protection of wildlife includes or could include the protection of fish. This can now be done selectively under paragraph (b) of the definition by regulation by the Minister under the new section 32 of the WLAB 1999.

One caveat only and that is that these new provisions do not refer to and fail to clarify section 23(2) of the Act.

Section 23(1) protects any animal which is of a species of fauna specified in the Fifth Schedule and that Schedule specifies dolphin species, porpoise species, seal species and whale species as being Marine mammals to which the section applies. They are therefore protected wild animals within the meaning of the section.

Section 23(2) provides that the Minister may with the consent of the Minister for Agriculture and Fisheries - now Marine and Natural Resources - by regulation either include or exclude in such places and for such periods as may be specified an animal of a species of fauna (in the case of inclusion obviously the species specified in the Fifth Schedule being already there are not taken into account) specified in the regulations. Subsection (3) of section 23 provides that the Minister cannot amend such regulations without the consent of the other Minister mentioned.

It appears that this is the same power to regulate in relation to "fish becoming flesh" as it is now proposed to legislate for in part - exclusion but not inclusion - in section 32 of the WLAB 1999.

This heading covers the substantial adjustment by amendment of the "enforcement" sections of the Act, sections 70, 72, 73, 74, 76, 77 and 78 amended by section 65, 66, 68, 69, 70, 71 and 72 respectively of the WLAB 1999 and section 67 which deals with inspection of land and which replaces section 68 of the Act which has been repealed. The redefinition of "conservation" and new definitions of "habitat" and "wild animal" are also important.

Section 9 of the WLAB 1999 which extends the description at section 11 of the Act of the Minister's functions by adding "biological diversity" is disappointing. The amendment merely satisfies some elevated National obligation to recognise the Minister's obligations to the UN convention on biological diversity and places too great an emphasis on this new function, the application of which no-one appears to understand

Section 25 of the WLAB 1999 deals with the erection of notices on lands the subject of wildlife protection orders and sections 26, 27 and 28 amend the sections dealing with reserves and refuges in the Act, sections 15, 16 and 17, to bring them closer to natural heritage areas.

Section 29 extends the protection of flora in

section 21 of the Act in line with contemporary conservation ideas
See: PROTECTION, FLORA.

Section 30 performs a similar service for section 22 of the Act dealing with the enforcement of the protection of wild birds
See: PROTECTION. PROTECTED WILD BIRDS.

Section 31 performs a similar service for section 23 of the Act dealing with the enforcement of the protection of wild animals other than wild birds.
See: PROTECTION, PROTECTED WILD ANIMALS.

(c) enhance a number of existing controls in respect of hunting, which are designed to serve the interests of wildlife conservation.

Section 6(1) of the WLAB 1999 redefines "hunt" by deleting a nonsensical "tail" to the definition in section 2(1) of the Act.
See: HUNT.

Sections 24 and 25 of the Act deal with Open Seasons
See: OPEN SEASONS.
Sections 34 and 35 of the WLAB 1999 amend each respectively by deleting the words "by individuals" which has the effect of leaving the sections open to permitting hordes of people to kill in hunting in accordance with an open seasons order. This is intended to supplement the new powers to regulate "commercial shoot operators" dealt with hereunder which is an entirely new concept under section 36 of the WLAB 1999.

Section 26 of the Act deals with licences to hunt otters and deer and to hunt or course for hares. Section 35 of the Act amends section 26 by repealing subsection (1)(i) which removes from the Minister the right to grant a licence to the master or other person in charge of a pack of otter hounds authorising the hunting of otters by that pack. As the otter is a protected wild animal, being one of the species of fauna appearing in the Fifth Schedule and referred to in Section 23(1) of the Act, it is therefore now fully protected under the Act.

The law relating to firearms, their licensing and use in relation to wildlife is dealt with under the following legislation:

(1) Section 28 Wildlife Act 1976, General restriction as regards hunting or killing with firearms certain exempted wild mammals and certain protected wild birds.
See: HUNTING OR KILLING WITH FIREARMS.

(2) Section 29 Wildlife Act 1976, Licences to hunt with firearms.
See: FIREARMS, LICENCE TO HUNT WITH.

(3) Section 33 Wildlife Act 1976, Restrictions on the use of certain firearms etc.
See: FIREARMS, RESTRICTIONS ON USE OF

(4) The Wildlife Act 1976 (Firearms and Ammunition) Regulations, 1977 (S.I.No. 239 of 1977)
See: FIREARMS AND AMMUNITION REGULATIONS. 1977.

(5) the Firearms (Temporary Provisions) Act, 1998
See: FIREARMS, LICENCE TO HUNT WITH.

Sections 37 and 38 of the WLAB 1999 amend sections 28 and 29, specified supra, of the Act.

Section 28 is the section dealing with a licence to hunt with firearms as distinct from a firearms certificate; or to hunt game as distinct from merely holding a gun.

A firearms certificate under section 29 is issued by the Garda Siochána and that certificate, if endorsed in the terms provided by section 29(8), becomes a firearms licence and licences the holder to hunt and kill

(a) where there is an open seasons order under section 24, a protected wild bird,
(b) where there is an open seasons order under section 25, any hare.

A hare is the only protected wild animal or exempted wild mammal other than deer, which require a special licence, permitted to be hunted and killed by order.
See: (1) PROTECTION, PROTECTED WILD BIRDS (2) PROTECTION, PROTECTED WILD ANIMALS and (3) OPEN SEASONS

Section 37 will so amend section 28 as to make it possible for the Minister to require by regulation that an applicant for a hunting licence must supply satisfactory evidence that he or she is competent to hold such a licence by, inter alia, being able to identify certain species of fauna and have a satisfactory knowledge of the Wildlife Acts 1976 and 1999 and any instruments made thereunder.

The amendments to section 29 by section 38 deal with licence fees and the making of regulations to provide for what is a new concept of "tagging" any bird captured or killed under a licence.

Section 42 of the WLAB 1999 amends section 33 of the Act. Section 33 makes it an offence to use certain kinds of firearms, as distinct from using a firearm to hunt protected wild birds or protected wild animals, contrary to sections 22 and 23 or with firearms hunt, injure, etc. an exempted wild animal or protected wild bird, contrary to section 28.

The amendments are intended to remove any doubt that hunting (as opposed to killing) a wild bird or wild animals while armed with specific kinds of weapons is an offence and to extend the protection to non-mammalian species, meaning to all wild animals.

This section 33 of the Act and sections 34, 35, 36, and 38 deal with offences consisting of controls over hunting of a technical nature designed to serve the best interests of wildlife conservation by the adoption of proper hunting practices. They are amended by sections 42, see supra, 43, 44, 45 and 46 of the WLAB 1996.

For section 42 amending section 33 *See:* FIREARMS, RESTRICTIONS ON THE USE

For section 43 amending section 34 *See:* TRAPS, SNARES, NETS, PROHIBITION OF

For section 44 amending section 35 *See:* SCARECROWS & DECOYS, BIRD CALLS & CALLS

For section 45 amending section 36 *See:* USE A MECHANICALLY-PROPELLED VEHICLE OR AIRCRAFT IN HUNTING

For section 46 amending section 38 *See:* LAMPS, USE OF IN HUNTING.

The sixth of these technical offences which is not amended by the WLAB 1999 is section 37 which deals with restrictions on hunting by night *See:* HUNTING BY NIGHT.

Commercial Shoot Operators, section 36 WLAB 1999.

This is an entirely new concept unrelated to any material in the Act. It is based on the proposition that there are operators already functioning who either own or have access to shooting rights over land and who use this access to provide hunting for others, particularly non-resident hunters, on a commercial basis. These activities are not regulated at the moment and should be regulated. Section 36 provides for those regulations.

"commercial shoot operators" and "gun days" are defined by section 36(12) for the purpose of the section only.

(d) ensure or strengthen compliance with inter national agreements and, in particular, enable the ratification of the Convention on International Trade in Endangered Species and the Agreement on the Conservation of African-Eurasian Migratory Waterbirds Agreement (AEWA).

The CITES Convention and the Regulations made thereunder are both defined in section 6(1)(a) and (b) of the WLAB 1999 by reference, in the case of the Convention, to the date and place of its doing, Washington on the 3rd March 1973, and in the case of the Regulations by reference to the EC Council Regulations 338/97 of 9 December 1996 (O.J. No. L 61, 3 March 1997, page 1) and 939/97 of 26th May 1997 (O.J.No. L 140, 30 May 1997, page 9).

It is intended that the WLAB 1999 will implement both the Convention and the Regulations. It is also intended, according to the explanatory memorandum, that sections 57 and 58, amending sections 52 and 53 of the Act which deal respectively with the import and export of fauna and flora, and section 59, which is a new section, of the WLAB 1999, will "complement terminology contained in both CITES and the EU Habitats Directive". The EC (Natural Habitats) Regulations 1997 (S.I. No. 94 of 1997) are already in place and they supposedly implement, at some length and with great complexity, the Habitats Directive. These Regulations always had the feeling of having been rushed and perhaps the WLAB 1999 is intended to tidy up some loose ends.

See: (1) HABITATS DIRECTIVE, NATURAL HABITAT'S REGULATIONS (2) FAUNA AND FLORA, IMPORT OF (3) FAUNA AND FLORA, EXPORT OF.

Section 59 of the WLAB 1999 is not an amending section as such. It amends the Principal Act merely by insertion, by inserting section 53A which is an entirely new section intended to be complementary to sections 57 and 58 of the Act.

The difficulty in this attempt to graft the CITES Regulations onto the Act is in the enforcement of the Regulations which is provided for in section 59(4)(a) and (b). Subsection (4)(a) provides for series of instances of contraventions of the CITES Regulations which are stated to be offences under the Act although the actual Regulations do not appear in the Act nor are they expressed anywhere to form part of the Act by reference, if such is possible. The section would require a detailed study of the Regulations to make any real sense. There must be some doubt as to the enforceability of this section as presently framed although of course the Regulations themselves are directly applicable and directly enforceable in Member States of the EU.

The proposed amendment of section 52 of the Act, import of fauna and flora, by section 57 of the WLAB 1999 and of section 53 of the Act, export of fauna and flora, by section 58 of the WLAB 1999 appear to create a further problem in that there are already Regulations under sections 52 and 53 in force which are not mentioned in the Bill or the explanatory memorandum. These are the Wildlife, 1976 (Control of Import of Wild Birds) Regulations, 1989 (S.I.No. 296 of 1989) and the Wildlife Act, 1976 (Control of Export of Fauna) Regulations 1979 (S.I.No. 235 of 1979. As these Regulations predate the WLAB 1999 they would also require to be amended to give effect to the new wording of the sections envisaged by sections 57 and 58 or, as is more likely, is repealed.
See: (1) FAUNA AND FLORA, IMPORT OF and (2) FAUNA AND FLORA. EXPORT OF.

Sections 52, 53, 54, 55 and 56 of the WLAB 1999 which amend sections 45, 46, 48, 49 and 51 of the Principal Act also relate to Wildlife Dealing.
See: (1) WILDLIFE DEALING (2) WILDLIFE DEALER'S LICENCE.

Although section 60 of the WLAB 1999 which follows is not strictly referable to the heading being discussed it is worth noting in relation to its provisions, which deal with permitting actions and measures to be taken in relation to wild birds and wild animals in the interests of public health or safety, that there is extensive provision under the EC (Wildlife Act, 1976) (Amendment) Regulations, 1986 (S.I.No. 254 of 1986) for similar remedies for similar problems where damage is caused by protected wild birds or protected wild animals.
See: DAMAGE BY PROTECTED WILD BIRDS AND PROTECTED WILD ANIMALS.

(e) introduce statutory protection for geological and geomorphological sites.

See under Objective (a) supra.

(f) increase substantially monetary fines for contravention of the Wildlife Acts and introduce prison sentences in addition to those fines.

Section 74 of the Act dealt with categories of offences under three subsections

MINOR OFFENCES

Subsection (1) deals with all offences other than those under subsections (2) and (3)

OFFENCES UNDER REGULATIONS OR ON PROTECTED LANDS

Subsection (2) deals –

(a) with offences in contravention of regulations under section 69(2) or 59, and
(b) with offences committed on land to which orders under sections 15 (establishment), 16 (recognition), 17 (designation or where there are agreements under section 18 (management agreements)

SERIOUS OFFENCES

Subsection (3) deals with offences under sections 21(4)(flora), 22(4) (wild birds), 23(5) (wild animals), 44(1) (entry, hunting), 51 (wildlife transport), 52 (wildlife, import) and 53 (wildlife export). This series of offences which are scattered throughout the Act are at the heart of the protection of fauna and flora.

Section 69 amends subsection 74(2) by including offences on land to which a natural heritage order relates (made under section 18 of the WLAB 1999) and by the enlargement of "seri ous offences" under subsection (3) to include all offences committed under Part II of the Act (Wildlife Conservation and Protection, sections 15,16,17 and 18) or under sections 45, 47, 51, 52, 53, 53A or 58(3)(b) (Wildlife Dealing, Import and Export of Fauna and Flora and CITES Regulations).

There is an apparent duplication here. Sections 15 to 18 appear under both subsection (2) and (3). This is probably intentional so that prosecutions for these offences could be brought either summarily under subsection (2) or an indictment could be preferred under subsection (3).

Section 74 was unique in that although it provided for trial on indictment it did not provide for the penalty of imprisonment for conviction for the offence under subsection (3) although it was regarded as being the most serious under the section. This situation changes under the section as amended by section 69 of the WLAB 1996 which provides for a maximum term of imprisonment under each of the three subsections and increased fines as follows:

Category of offence	Present maximum fine £	Proposed maximum fine £	Proposed maximum prison sentence
Subsection (1) first offence	50	500	3 months
Subsection (1) 2nd offence	100	1,000	6 months
Subsection (1) 3rd offence	200	1,500	12 months
Subsections (2) and (3) summary conviction	250	1,500	12 months
Subsections (2) and (3) conviction on indictment.	500	50,000	2 years

See: FINES AND IMPRISONMENT

(g) enable the Minister to act independently of Forestry legislation (e.g. in relation to the acquisition of land by agreement.

History

The Minister given responsibility for Wildlife in 1976 under the Act was the then Minister for Lands among whose functions were land (the Irish Land Commission) Forestry, Agriculture and Wildlife. Later the portfolios of Agriculture and Fisheries were thrown together for a time.

Up to 1995 the successor to the Minister for Lands continued to have responsibility for the Wildlife Act 1976 but these functions were performed almost exclusively by the Commissioners of Public Works in Ireland who are an adjunct of the Department of Finance.

In the light of ongoing problems arising out of the attempted development by the Commissioners of land at Mullaghmore in County Clare as a Heritage Centre and in an attempt to resolve the considerable difficulties which had arisen between the Commissioners and conservationists who were against the erection of any structures at Mullaghmore, the Heritage Act of 1995, No.4 of 1995, was passed and section 24 of that Act provided that the Commissioners would perform their functions in relation to the national heritage which included wildlife subject to the supervision of the Minister for Arts, Heritage, Gaeltacht and the Islands and to such directions as the Minister may give in relation thereto.

See: COMMISSIONERS, COMMISSIONERS OF PUBLIC WORKS IN IRELAND

One of the difficulties faced by every Minister of Arts, Heritage, Gaeltacht and the Islands in implementing the Act, in so far as any attempt was ever made to do so, was the series of problems faced by him or her in dealing with land under the Wildlife Act, 1976. These problems, which should have been legislated for long ago, arose because of the fact that the first Minister placed in charge of the 1976 Act was the Minister for Lands and. as we have seen, that Ministry was responsible for agriculture, forestry, wildlife and the acquisition and distribution of land through the Irish Land Commission.

The functions which created the greatest difficulties were those exercised by the Minister in relation to the combined functions of wildlife and forestry because of certain assumptions which were made in the 1976 Act. The main assumption was that the Minister could acquire lands under the extensive powers conferred by the Forestry Acts, particularly the Acts of 1946 and 1956, which lands could then be used either for forestry or wildlife or, as was more usual, they could be used for both.

This was articulated in a most convoluted manner by section 56 of the Act.
See: MANAGEMENT OF LAND BY MINISTER.

Section 61 of the WLAB 1999 amends section 56 and provides simply for the management of lands acquired by or vested in the Minister of Arts, Heritage, Gaeltacht and the Islands under the Wildlife Acts 1976 and 1999 to be conducted for the purposes of those Acts, that is, for the conservation of wildlife. This would refer to lands already in the Minister's ownership or acquired by or vested in the Minister at a date subsequent to the commencement date of the WLAB 1999.

REPEALS

In order to achieve this disassociation of Wildlife from Forestry it was necessary for section 4 of the WLAB 1999 to repeal –

(a) Part III (sections 12 to 24) and section 60 of the Forestry Act 1946,
(b) The Forestry Act 1956, and
(c) sections 7, 42(7), 60 and 61, subsections (1) to (4) of section 63 and section 68 of the Wildlife Act 1976.

Paragraphs (a) and (b) removed wildlife from forestry and paragraph (c) removes forestry and the Irish Land Commission from wildlife.

Paragraph (c) requires elucidation as follows:

Section 7 dealt with an annual report by the Minister under the Act. It has not been replaced by the WLAB 1999.

Section 42 deals with the Minister's powers to make regulations in relation to damage to crops, livestock etc. by protected wild birds and protected wild animals and subsection (7) merely refers to the fact that the Minister's powers under the section are in addition to and not in substitution for certain powers under the Forestry Act 1946.

Sections 60 and 61 provided for functions of the Minister in relation to the creation of rights of way and the extinguishment of easements and in both sections the Lay Commissioners of the Irish Land Commission on the application of the Minister for Lands had powers to make orders in relation to rights of way and the extinguishment of easements as the Minister had no such powers. The rights of way could only be made where the land to whose advantage the right of way would be created was owned by the Minister partly for the purposes of the Act and partly for the purposes of the Forestry Act 1946.

The Irish Land Commission was dissolved effectively from the 31st March 1999.
See: (1) RIGHTS OF WAY (2) EXTINGUISHMENT OF EASEMENTS (3) LAY COMMISSIONERS.

Section 63 was a section which made certain amendments to the Forestry Act 1946 and section 68 dealt with the powers of authorised officers appointed by the Minister under the Forestry Act 1946 to enter on and inspect land for the purposes of the Wildlife Act 1976 and specifically for the purpose of ascertaining whether there were fauna on the land in need of protection under section 17 of the Act
See: (1) RESERVES AND REFUGES (2) DESIGNATION ORDERS and (3) ENTRY AND SEARCH, WLA 1976 AND NH 97 (C).

REPLACEMENT LEGISLATION UNDER WLAB 1999

The functions of the Minister under the Forestry Acts and of the Lay Commissioners in relation to rights of way and easements have been replaced in a somewhat different manner by Part III Chapter I, sections 10 to 14 of the WLAB (section 12 rights of way and section 13 extinguishment of easements).

The functions of the Minister in relation to entry on land for inspection purposes is now contained at section 67 of the WLAB 1999 which provides that a person authorised under section 72 of the Act in writing by the Minister to be an authorised person may enter on land for survey or any purposes under the Act but the section specifically at subsection (2) relates the exercise of these functions to the inspection of lands for the purposes of checking the attainment of the objectives of recognition orders, section 16 of the Act, ascertaining whether the land forms or are part of, or are in need of protection as a natural heritage area, section 18 of the WLAB 1999, or ascertaining whether any fauna and flora on

the land are in need of protection under section 17 of the Principal Act, establishment order.
See: RESERVES AND REFUGES.

You can already see the difficulties of reference which could have been overcome by incorporating Part III, including section 18 of the WLAB 1999, into Part II Chapter II of the Principal Act. It would also have ironed out a lot of clumsy drafting forced on the legislators by the division of these vital functions between the two Acts.

Members of the Garda Síochána and authorised officers have a right of entry under section 72 of the Act, mentioned supra in relation to the appointment of authorised officers. These persons have wide powers under subsection (2) of section 72, where they have reasonable grounds for suspecting that certain offences under the Act have been committed, of stopping, questioning, producing for inspection certain things and seizing and detaining specimens so produced which they believe may be required to be produced in evidence and under subsection (3)(a) of searching and (b) of opening packages, parcels etc where they suspect fauna or flora are being transported unlawfully.

Section 72(4) allows these persons to enter on land for the purposes of subsection (2) and subsection (3)(a) and (b) only but the power does not extend to permitting entry into buildings on land. Section 73, which allows the issue of search warrants to dwellings, prohibits, under subsection (3), entry under the warrant to a dwelling by an authorised person unless accompanied by a member of the Garda Síochána.
See: ENTRY AND SEARCH, WLA 1976 AND NH 97.

(h) strengthen the protective regime for Special Areas of Conservation (SACs) by ensuring that protection will in all cases apply from time of notification of proposed sites;

Special areas of conservation arise under the EC (Natural Habitats) Regulations 1997 (S.I.No. 94 of 1997) and at one stage in the various stages of its evolution which is described in the regulations it becomes what the Regulations refer to as a "European site".
See: CONSERVATION, SPECIAL AREAS OF.

These European sites are entitled to certain specific protections under the Regulations against what the Regulations describe as "operations or activities.
See: (1) OPERATIONS OR ACTIVITIES (2) PROHIBITION (9) and (10).

Section 76 of the WLAB 1999 seeks to amend the definition of European site appearing at Regulation 2 of the 1997 Regulations by replacing (b) which reads in the definition in the Regulations as "a site of community importance which has been placed on the list referred to in the third paragraph of Article 4(2) of the habitats Directive" by "a site notified in accordance with Regulation 4 of the Regulations."

It is difficult to know which in fact comes first, that is, whether the paragraph (b) in the Regulations gives an earlier point in the evolution of the special area of conservation to be afforded protection than the new paragraph (b) with which section 76 seeks to replace it. The wording of the Directive itself is vague to the point of obscurity.

(i) give specific recognition to the Minister's responsibilities in regard to promoting the conservation of biological diversity, in the context of Ireland's commitment to the UN Convention on Biological Diversity.

This is achieved under section 9 of the WLAB 1999 which amends section 11 of the Act which provides for the functions of the Minister under the Act in relation to wildlife. Section 11(1) had read with stunning and glorious simplicity "It shall be the function of the Minister to secure the conservation of wildlife."

It seems a shame to tack on the words "and to promote the conservation of biological diversity" thereby destroying the clarity and symmetry of the subsection merely to gratify...who?

"biological diversity" and its definition which now appears at the new subsection (5) of section 11 should have been relegated to section 11(2) which indicates specific functions which the Minister may carry out under the Act.

NEW OFFENCES UNDER THE WLAB 1999

(1) restrictions on carrying out certain works

S.19(1) provides for such restrictions -

(a) on lands where there is a subsisting natural heritage area order, or

(b) where the works are liable to destroy or

significantly alter, damage or interfere with the features by reason of which the order designating the lands as a natural heritage area was made.

offence
S. 19(6) A person who contravenes subsection (1) shall be guilty of an offence.

(2) restoration of land in a natural heritage area

S.21(1) permits the Minister, where works have been carried out on land designated as a natural heritage area, to give a direction in writing requiring restoration of the land.

offences
S.21(4)(a) Any person who fails to comply with a direction under subsection (1) shall be guilty of an offence,

(b) any person who by act or omission impedes an authorised officer entering on land for the purpose of carrying out any required works under the section shall be guilty of an offence.

(3) erection of notices

S.25(1) provides for the erection of notices on land where –

(a) an establishment order, a recognition order or a designation order to which sections 15, 16 and 17 of the Act applies exists,
(b) an agreement under section 18 of the Act applies,
(c) a natural heritage area order under section 18 of the WLAB 1999 exists, or
(d) a "fauna sanctuary order" (a creature created by S.25(1)(d)) is in operation.

offences
S.25(2) Any person who impedes an authorised person in carrying out his or her duties under the section or who wilfully or negligently destroys, alters, defaces, disfigures, marks or otherwise interferes with any notice referred to in subsection (1) shall be guilty of an offence.

(4) regulation of commercial shoot operators

S.36 provides for the regulation by permit issued by the Minister of commercial shoot operators who are defined for the purposes of the section as persons who either own shooting rights on land or have the permission of the owner of those shooting rights and who uses those rights or permissions for the purpose of providing hunting on those lands to others for reward.

S.36(9) prohibits a person from holding himself or herself out as a commercial shoot operator unless he or she is in possession of a subsisting permit issued under the section.

offences
S.36(11) A person who –

(a) contravenes subsection (9) of this section, or
(b) fails to comply with any condition or requirement of a permit, or
(c) makes false or misleading statements or declarations, or furnishes a document or information which is false, with a view to obtaining a permit,

shall be guilty of an offence.

(5) hunting restricted on or over foreshore belonging to State or certain land so belonging

S.39 substitutes a new section for section 30 of the Act which does not provide for an offence.

S.30(1)(a) prohibits the hunting of protected wild birds and wild animals on or over foreshore or other land belonging to the State without the Minister's written permission.

offences
S.30(3) Any person who contravenes subsection (1) of this section or fails to comply with a condition under that subsection shall be guilty of an offence.

S.30(3) would be more accurate if it referred to a contravention of subsection (1)(a) as subsection (1)(b) does not contain any prohibition the contravention of which could give rise to an offence.

(6) Amendment of section 52 (import of fauna and flora) of principal Act.

S.57 amends section 52 of the Act, subsection (1) of which provides for the prohibition by regulation of the importation of certain fauna and flora and parts of fauna and flora save under and in accordance with a licence under the section. S.52 does not provide for an offence.

S.57(d) amends S.52 by adding a subsection

(6) which provides (a) that the Minister may, if considered necessary, by regulations prohibit the introduction of any species of wild bird, wild animal or wild flora or any part, product or derivative of such wild bird, wild animal or wild flora which may be detrimental to native species, and (b) that where non-native species of such wild bird, wild animal or wild flora or any part product or derivative thereof have been introduced the Minister shall, to the extent that it is feasible and appropriate, take measures to ensure that such introductions do not pose a potential hazard to native stocks.

offences
S.52(7), as inserted by section 57, provides that any person who

(a) turns loose, wilfully allows or causes to escape any species of wild animal or the spawn of such wild animal or wild bird or the eggs of such wild bird,
(b) transfers any species of wild animal or the spawn of any such wild animal or wild bird or the eggs of such wild bird from any place in the State to any other place in the State for the purpose of establishing it in a wild state in such other place,
(c) plants or otherwise causes to grow in a wild state in any place in the State any species of flora or the flowers, roots, seeds or spores of flora, otherwise than under and in accordance with a licence granted in that behalf by the Minister shall be guilty of an offence.

(7) regulation of trade in wild flora and fauna and CITES Regulations

S.59 amends the Act by inserting a new section, 53A, after section 53.

S.53A introduces the principles of the CITES Convention and the provisions of the two CITES Regulations, 338/97 and 939/97 into the Act.

The section provides two headings for offences -

(A) offences contrary Minister Regulations under S.53A(3)(a)

S.53A(3)(a) provides that the Minister may make regulations to prohibit the holding or possession of any specimen of a species listed in annexes to the CITES Regulations.

offence
S.53A(3)(b) It shall be an offence to hold or possess any such specimen contrary to any regulations made under subsection (3)(a) of this section.

(B) offences contrary to CITES Regulations

offences
S.53A(4)(a) subject to subsection (5), a person who, in contravention of the CITES Regulations

(i) imports, introduces from the sea, exports, re-exports, engages in movement (of?), holds or possesses any specimen of a species listed in annexes to the CITES Regulations without the required valid permits or certificates, or with forged, altered or otherwise fraudulent certificates, or
(ii) purchases, offers to purchase, acquires for commercial purposes, displays to the public for commercial purposes, uses for commercial gain, sells, keeps for sale, offers for sale or transports for sale contrary to Article 8 of the Council Regulation a species listed in Annex A to the CITES Regulations, or
(iii) purchases, offers to purchase, acquires for commercial purposes, displays to the public for commercial purposes, uses for commercial gain, sells, keeps for sale, offers for sale or transport contrary to Article 8 of the Council Regulations a species listed in Annex B to the CITES Regulations imported or acquired contrary to the CITES Regulations, or
(iv) fails to comply with any condition or requirement of a permit or certificate, or
(v) fails to comply with the requirements of paragraph 1, 4 or 5 of Article 9 relating to the holding or transport or movement of live specimens, or
(vi) makes false or misleading statements or declarations with a view to obtaining a permit, or of clearing specimens for import or export, or
(vii) furnishes a document or information which is false with a view to obtaining a permit or certificate. or falsifies or alters any permit or certificate, or uses or furnishes a false or invalid permit or certificate or one altered without authorisation, or
(viii) fails to make an import notification or

makes a false import notification contrary to Article 4 of the Council Regulations, or

(ix) uses any specimen of a species listed in Annex A to the CITES Regulations otherwise than in accordance with the authorisation given at the time of issue of the import permit or subsequently, or

(x) trades in artificially propagated plants contrary to the provisions of Article 7 of the Council Regulations, or

(xi) uses a permit, certificate or import notification for any specimen other than (the specimen?) for which it was issued, or

(xii) fails to disclose rejection of an application for an import, export or re-export permit or certificate in accordance with Article 6 of the Council Regulations, or

(xiii) engages in transit or transhipment of any specimen of a species listed in annexes to the CITES Regulations without the required valid permit or certificate or document or without satisfactory proof of the existence of such permit or certificate or document, as appropriate,

shall be guilty of an offence.

(b) A person who aids or abets the commission of offences specified in subsection 3(a) shall be guilty of an offence.

Subsection (5), quoted in subsection (4)(a), provides that nothing in the section shall make unlawful anything which is duly done under, and in accordance with the terms of, any certificate or general derogation granted pursuant to the CITES Regulations.

The "CITES Regulations" are defined at section 2 of the Act as inserted by section 6(1)(a) of the WLAB 1999.

(8) amendment of section 58 (right to hunt on or over territorial seas of the State vested in the State) of Principal Act

S.62 amends S.58 of the Act, subsection (2) of which prohibits the hunting of fauna without the permission of the Minister over the portion of sea mentioned in subsection (1).

S.58 provides for prosecution for trespass only and does not create an offence.

offence

S.58(3), substituted by S.62(a) of the WLAB 1999, provides that any person who contravenes subsection (2) of the section shall -(a) commit a trespass, and

(b) be guilty of an offence.

WILDLIFE (AMENDMENT) BILL, 1999

ARRANGEMENT OF SECTIONS

PART I

Preliminary and General

PART II

Amendment of Part I of Principal Act and of Functions of Minister

PART III

LAND AND WATERS

Chapter I

Acquisition of Land and Rights

Chapter II

Natural Heritage Areas

15. Interpretation (Chapter II).
16. Intention to designate natural heritage areas.
17. Decision not to make natural heritage order.
18. Natural heritage order.
19. Restriction on carrying out certain works.
20. Prohibition of works on lands in natural heritage areas.
21. Restoration of land in natural heritage area.
22. Compensation.
23. Registration of natural heritage area order as burden on land.
24. Provisions relating to section 12 (obligations in relation to nature reserves and refuges) of Principal Act.

Chapter III

Nature Reserves and Refuges

25. Erection of notices.
26. Amendment of section 15 (nature reserves on lands owned by the Minister or the State) of Principal Act.
27. Amendment of section 16 (nature reserves on land other than land to which section 15 applies) of Principal Act.
28. Amendment of section 17 (refuges for fauna) of Principal Act.

PART IV

WILDLIFE CONSERVATION AND PROTECTION

Chapter I

Protection of Flora, Wild Birds and Wild Animals

29. Amendment of section 21 (protection of flora) of Principal Act.
30. Amendment of section 22 (enforcement of protection of wild birds) of Principal Act.
31. Amendment of section 23 (enforcement of protection of wild animals (other than wild birds)) of Principal Act.
32. Exclusion of certain wild animals.
33. Amendment of section 24 (open seasons for certain protected wild birds) of Principal Act.
34. Amendment of section 25 (open season for certain wild mammals) of Principal Act.
35. Amendment of section 26 (licences to hunt otters or deer and to hunt or course hares) of Principal Act.

Chapter II

Restrictions to protect wildlife

36. Regulation of commercial shoot operators.
37. Amendment of section 28 (general restriction as regards hunting or killing with firearms certain exempted wild mammals and certain protected wild birds) of Principal Act.
38. Amendment of section 29 (licences to hunt with firearms) of Principal Act.
39. Hunting restricted on or over foreshore belonging to State and certain land so belonging.
40. Amendment of section 31 (sale, purchase and possession of certain perching birds prohibited) of Principal Act.
41. Amendment of section 32 (ringing and marking and possession of cannon-nets, etc. restricted) of Principal Act.
42. Amendment of section 33 (restriction on use of certain firearms etc.) of Principal Act.
43. Amendment of section 34 (certain use of traps, snares etc. prohibited) of Principal Act.
44. Amendment of section 35 (certain use of scarecrows, decoys, birdcalls and calls of wild animals restricted) of Principal Act.
45. Amendment of section 36 (use of mechanically-propelled vehicles, vessels and aircraft in hunting prohibited) of Principal Act.
46. Use of lamps, mirrors etc in hunting prohibited.
47. Amendment of section 40 (destruction of vegetation on uncultivated land restricted) of Principal Act.

Chapter III

Miscellaneous

48. Amendment of section 41 (falconry etc.) of Principal Act.
49. Amendment of section 42 (damage by wild birds etc.) of Principal Act.
50. Amendment of section 50 (land drainage schemes) of Principal Act.
51. Amendment of section 44 (unlawful hunting or entry on land and other miscellaneous

PART V
REGULATION AND CONTROL OF WILDLIFE DEALING

PART VI

MISCELLANEOUS

PART VII

MISCELLANEOUS AMENDMENT OF ENACTMENTS